COMPREHENSIVE CURRICULUM
of Basic Skills

GRADE 4

American Education Publishing™
An imprint of Carson-Dellosa Publishing LLC
Greensboro, North Carolina

American Education Publishing™
An imprint of Carson-Dellosa Publishing LLC
P.O. Box 35665
Greensboro, NC 27425 USA

Printed in the USA • All rights reserved.

ISBN 978-1-60996-333-0

1 2 3 4 5 6 7 8 WAL 15 14 13 12 11

030117810

TABLE OF CONTENTS

READING

Short Vowels 6
Long Vowels 9
The k, f, s Sounds 16
Syllables 23
Synonyms, Antonyms 25
Palindromes 30
Homophones 31
Prefixes and Suffixes 34
Classifying 38
Analogies 43
Following Directions 46
Reading for Information 50
Facts and Opinions 57
Context Clues 59
Sequencing 64
Main Idea, Details, Sequencing 68

READING COMPREHENSION

Fairy Tales 84
Fables and Tall Tales 90
Legends 106
Poetry 125
Early Native Americans 134
Animals 143
Oceanography 153
Space Travel 164
Meteorology 171
Your Five Senses 181

ENGLISH

Kinds of Sentences 192
Subjects and Predicates 197
Nouns: Common, Proper, Plural 209
Pronouns 217
Verbs: Tenses, Irregular 218
Adjectives 231
Adverbs 240
Adjectives and Adverbs 245
Conjunctions 249
Grammar 255

WRITING

Capital Letters and Punctuation 268

Grade 4 - Comprehensive Curriculum

TABLE OF CONTENTS

Proofreading 276
Run-On Sentences 280
Combining Sentences 282
Nouns and Pronouns 287
Topic Sentences 291
Story Map 295
Writing Paragraphs 298
Taking Notes 302
Compare and Contrast 307
Outlining 308
Writing a Summary 315
Library and Encyclopedia Skills 320
Using Reference Sources 335
Writing a Report 337
Writing Poetry 342

MATH

Place Value 348
Addition 351
Subtraction 358
Rounding 363
Estimating 366
Skip Counting/Multiples 369
Multiplication 372
Division 381
Averaging 388
Fractions 391
Mixed Numbers 403
Fractions and Decimals 405
Measurement 410
Graphing 435
Ordered Pairs 436
Geometry 438
Number Patterns 443
Common Attributes 444
Probability 445
Abacus 447
Problem Solving 448

APPENDIX

Glossary 451
Answer Key 457
Teaching Suggestions 529
Index 541

READING

Crocodile Tears & other stories

Spelling: Short Vowels

Vowels are the letters **a, e, i, o, u** and sometimes **y**. There are five short vowels: **ă** as in **a**pple, **ĕ** as in **e**gg and br**ea**th, **ĭ** as in s**i**ck, **ŏ** as in t**o**p and **ŭ** as in **u**p.

Directions: Complete the exercises using words from the box.

blend	insist	health	pump	crop
fact	pinch	pond	hatch	plug

1. Write each word under its vowel sound.

ă	**ĕ**	**ĭ**	**ŏ**	**ŭ**
_____	_____	_____	_____	_____
_____	_____	_____	_____	_____

2. Complete these sentences, using a word with the vowel sound given. Use each word from the box only once.

Here's an interesting (**ă**) _____ about your (**ĕ**) _____ .

Henry was very pleased with his corn (**ŏ**) _____ .

The boys enjoyed fishing in the (**ŏ**) _____ .

They (**ĭ**) _____ on watching the egg (**ă**) _____ .

(**ĕ**) _____ in a (**ĭ**) _____ of salt.

The farmer had to (**ŭ**) _____ water from the lake for his cows to drink.

Did you put the (**ŭ**) _____ in the bathtub this time?

Name: _____

Spelling: Short Vowels

Directions: Read the words. After each, write the correct vowel sound. Underline the letter or letters that spell the sound in the word. The first one has been done for you.

Word	Vowel		Word	Vowel
1. str<u>u</u>ck	_U_		9. breath	____
2. scramble	____		10. edge	____
3. strong	____		11. kick	____
4. chill	____		12. stop	____
5. thud	____		13. quiz	____
6. dread	____		14. brush	____
7. plunge	____		15. crash	____
8. mask	____		16. dodge	____

Directions: List four words (nouns and verbs) with short vowel sounds. Then write two sentences using the words.

Example: Ann, can, hand, Pam
Ann can give Pam a hand.

_____

_____

_____

_____

1. _____

_____

2. _____

_____

Name: _____

Spelling: Listening for Vowels

Directions: Circle the word in each row with the same vowel sound as the first word. The first one has been done for you.

blend	twig	brand	(fed)	bleed
fact	first	bad	shell	bead
plug	card	steal	stuff	plan
pinch	kiss	reach	ripe	come
health	dear	bath	top	head
crop	hope	stock	drip	strap

Directions: Write the words from the box that answer the questions.

| blend | insist | health | pump | crop | fact | pinch | fond | hatch | plug |

1. Which two words have the same vowel as the first vowel in **bundle**?

   _____ , _____

2. Which two words have the same vowel as the first vowel in **bottle**?

   _____ , _____

3. Which two words have the same vowel as the first vowel in **wilderness**?

   _____ , _____

4. Which two words have the same vowel as the first vowel in **manner**?

   _____ , _____

5. Which two words have the same vowel as the first vowel in **measure**?

   _____ , _____

Name: _____

Spelling: Long e and a

Long **ē** can be spelled **ea** as in **real** or **ee** as in **deer**. Long **ā** can be spelled **a** as in **apron**, **ai** as in **pail**, **ay** as in **pay** or **a-e** as in **lake**.

Directions: Complete the exercises with words from the box.

deal	clay	grade	weave	stream
pain	tape	sneeze	claim	treat

1. Write each word in the row with the matching vowel sound.

   ā _____ _____ _____ _____ _____

   ē _____ _____ _____ _____ _____

2. Complete each sentence, using a word with the vowel sound given. Use each word from the word box only once.

   Everyone in (**ā**) _____ four ate an ice-cream (**ē**) _____.

   Every time I (**ē**) _____, I feel (**ā**) _____ in my chest.

   When I (**ē**) _____ with yarn, I put a piece of (**ā**) _____ on the loose ends so they won't come undone.

   You (**ā**) _____ you got a good (**ē**) _____ on your new bike, but I still think you paid too much.

   We camped beside a (**ē**) _____.

   We forgot to wrap up our (**ā**) _____ and it dried out.

Name: _____

Spelling: Long e and a

When a vowel is long, it sounds the same as its letter name.

Examples: Long ē as in **treat**, **eel**, **complete**.
Long ā as in **ape**, **trail**, **say**, **apron**.

Directions: Read the words. After each word, write the correct vowel sound. Underline the letter or letters that spell the sound in the word. The first one has been done for you.

Word	Vowel		Word	Vowel
1. sp<u>ee</u>ch	e	9. plate	
2. grain		10. breeze	
3. deal		11. whale	
4. baste		12. clay	
5. teach		13. veal	
6. waiting		14. apron	
7. cleaning		15. raining	
8. crane		16. freezer	

Directions: Choose one long vowel sound. On another sheet of paper, list six words (nouns and verbs) that have that sound. Below, write two sentences using the words.

Example: freeze, teaches, breeze, speech, keep, Eve

Eve teaches speech in the breeze.

_____

_____

Name: _____

Spelling: Vowel Sounds

Directions: Follow the instructions below.

1. Circle the word in each row with the same vowel sound as the first word. The first one has been done for you.

deal	pail	church	(greet)	stove
pain	free	frame	twice	whole
weave	grape	stripe	least	thrill
grade	teach	case	joke	leave
treat	greed	throw	tent	truck

2. Write a word from the box that rhymes with each word below.

| deal | clay | grade | weave | stream | pain | tape | sneeze | claim | treat |

lame _____   shape _____

may _____   feel _____

cream _____   leave _____

laid _____   drain _____

feet _____   trees _____

3. The words below are written the way they are pronounced. Write the word from the box that sounds like:

klā _____   klām _____

wēv _____   trēt _____

dēl _____   grād _____

strēm _____   pān _____

tāp _____   snēz _____

Spelling: Making New Words

Directions: Unscramble these letters to spell the ā and ē words you have been practicing. If you need help with spelling, look at the box on page 9. The first one has been done for you.

ay + lc = _____clay_____   ee + zsne = _____

ea + mtrs = _____   a-e + pt = _____

ea + vew = _____   a-e + drg = _____

ea + rtt = _____   ai + np = _____

ea + ld = _____   ai + mlc = _____

Directions: Circle the spelling mistakes and write the words correctly. The first one has been done for you.

1. We made statues out of cley

2. Do you ever fish in that streem?

3. Jason sneesed really loudly in class.

4. Running gives me a pane in my side.

5. We are tapeing the show for you.

6. She klaims she won, but I came in first.

7. Would you share your treet with me?

8. He is gradeing our papers right now.

9. She is weeving a placemat of ribbons.

10. What is the big deel, anyway?

_____clay_____

_____

_____

_____

_____

_____

_____

_____

_____

Name: _____

Spelling: Long i and o

Long ī can be spelled **i** as in **wild**, **igh** as in **night**, **i-e** as in **wipe** or **y** as in **try**. Long ō can be spelled **o** as in **most**, **oa** as in **toast**, **ow** as in **throw** or **o-e** as in **hope**.

stripe	groan	glow	toast	grind	fry	sight	stove	toads	flight

Directions: Complete the exercises with words from the box.

1. Write each word from the box with its vowel sound.

ī _____

ō _____

2. Complete these sentences, using a word with the given vowel sound. Use each word from the box only once.

We will (ī) _____ potatoes on the (ō) _____.

I thought I heard a low (ō) _____, but when I looked, there was nothing

in (ī) _____.

The airplane for our (ī) _____ had a (ī) _____ painted on its side.

I saw a strange (ō) _____ coming from the toaster while

making (ō) _____.

Do (ō) _____ live in the water like frogs?

We need to (ī) _____ up the nuts before we put them in the cookie dough.

Name: _____

Spelling: Long i and o

Directions: Read the words. After each word, write the correct vowel sound. Underline the letter or letters that spell the sound. The first one has been done for you.

Word	Vowel		Word	Vowel
1. br<u>igh</u>t	i		9. white	_____
2. globe	_____		10. roast	_____
3. plywood	_____		11. light	_____
4. mankind	_____		12. shallow	_____
5. coaching	_____		13. myself	_____
6. prize	_____		14. throne	_____
7. grind	_____		15. cold	_____
8. withhold	_____		16. snow	_____

Directions: Below are words written as they are pronounced. Write the words that sound like:

1. thrōn _____   5. brīt _____

2. skōld _____   6. grīnd _____

3. prīz _____   7. plīwood _____

4. rōst _____   8. mīself _____

Name: _____

Spelling: Long u

Long **ū** can be spelled, **u-e** as in **cube** or **ew** as in **few**. Some sounds are similar in sound to **u** but are not true **u** sounds, such as the **oo** in **tooth**, the **o-e** in **move** and the **ue** in **blue**.

Directions: Complete each sentence using a word from the box. Do not use the same word more than once.

blew
tune
flute
cute
stew
June
glue

1. Yesterday, the wind _____ so hard it knocked down a tree on our street.

2. My favorite instrument is the _____.

3. The little puppy in the window is so _____.

4. I love _____ because it's so warm, and we get out of school.

5. For that project, you will need scissors, construction paper and _____.

6. I recognize that song because it has a familiar _____.

7. My grandmother's beef _____ is the best I've ever tasted.

Grade 4 - Comprehensive Curriculum

Spelling: The k Sound

The **k** sound can be spelled with **k** as in **peek**, **c** as in **cousin**, **ck** as in **sick**, **ch** as in **Chris** and **cc** as in **accuse**. In some words, however, one **c** may be pronounced **k** and the other **s** as in **accident**.

Directions: Answer the questions with words from the box.

Christmas accused	freckles castle	command stomach	cork rake	jacket accident

1. Which two words spell **k** with a **k**?

   _____   _____

2. Which two words spell **k** with **ck**?

   _____   _____

3. Which two words spell **k** with **ch**?

   _____   _____

4. Which five words spell **k** with **c** or **cc**? _____

   _____   _____

   _____   _____

5. Complete these sentences, using a word with **k** spelled as shown. Use each word from the box only once.

   Dad gave Mom a garden (**k**) _____ for (**ch**) _____.

   There are (**ck**) _____ on my face and (**ch**) _____.

   The people (**cc**) _____ her of taking a (**ck**) _____.

   The police took (**c**) _____ after the (**cc**) _____.

   The model of the (**c**) _____ was made out of

   (**c and k**) _____.

Name: _____

Spelling: The k Sound

Directions: Underline the letters that spell **k** in each word. The first one has been done for you.

toothpick
c – k

1. toothpi**ck**

2. arc

3. kitchen

4. acclaim

5. account

6. Christmas

7. make

8. confirm

9. brick

10. stomach

Directions: Under each spelling for **k**, write five words that have the same **k** spellings.

k	ck	c	ch	cc
	sickness			
			chemical	
		candy		
				accumulate
kite				

Directions: See how many words you can write that have the **cc** spelling, with one **c** pronounced **k** and the other pronounced **s**.

_____

_____

_____

Spelling: The f Sound

The **f** sound can be spelled with **f** as in **fun**, **gh** as in **laugh** or **ph** as in **phone**.

Directions: Answer the questions with words from the box.

fuss	paragraph	phone	friendship	freedom
defend	flood	alphabet	rough	laughter

1. Which three words spell **f** with **ph**?

   _____   _____   _____

2. Which two words spell **f** with **gh**?

   _____   _____

3. Which five words spell **f** with an **f**?

   _____   _____   _____

   _____   _____

4. Complete these sentences, using a word with **f** spelled as shown. Use each word from the box only once.

   I don't know why my teacher makes so much (**f**) _____ over writing

   a (**ph**) _____.

   A (**f**) _____ can help you through (**gh**) _____ times.

   The soldiers will (**f**) _____ our (**f**) _____.

   Can you say the (**ph**) _____ backwards?

   When I answered the (**ph**) _____, all I could

   hear was (**gh**) _____.

   If it keeps raining, we'll have a (**f**) _____.

Name: _____

Spelling: The f Sound

Directions: Read the following words. Underline the letters that spell **f** in each word.

1. laughter
2. football
3. cough
4. paragraph
5. enough

6. phantom
7. roof
8. performance
9. toughest
10. telephone

11. before
12. roughness
13. alphabet
14. grief
15. graph

Directions: Under each spelling for the **f** sound, write five words with the same **f** letter or letters. Use words other than those above.

f	gh	ph
_____	_____	_____
_____	_____	_____
_____	_____	_____
_____	_____	_____
_____	_____	_____

Spelling: Unscrambling Letters

Directions: Put the letters in order to spell the **f** words. If you need help with spelling, look on page 18.

feeddn _____   odolf _____

nopeh _____   dspiienfhr _____

gletharu _____   gruho _____

ssfu _____   taalbehp _____

droefem _____   ghaaprpar _____

RT UAH P GBLRT

Directions: Use the correctly spelled words to answer the questions.

1. Which two words each have one syllable and spell **f** with an **f**?

   _____   _____

2. Which word has two syllables and spells **f** with **gh**?_____

3. Which word has one syllable and spells **f** with **ph**?_____

4. Which three words each have two syllables and spell **f** with an **f**?

   _____   _____

5. Which two words each have three syllables and spell **f** with a **ph**?

   _____   _____

6. Which word has one syllable and spells **f** with **gh**?_____

Name: _____

Spelling: The s Sound

The **s** sound can be spelled with **s** as in **super** or **ss** as in **assign**, **c** as in **city**, **ce** as in **fence** or **sc** as in **scene**. In some words, though, **sc** is pronounced **sk**, as in **scare**.

Directions: Answer the questions using words from the box.

exciting	medicine	lettuce	peace	scissors
slice	scientist	sauce	bracelet	distance

1. Which five words spell **s** with just an **s** or **ss**?

   _____   _____   _____

   _____   _____

2. Which two words spell **s** with just a **c**?

   _____   _____

3. Which six words spell **s** with a **ce**?

   _____   _____   _____

   _____   _____   _____

4. Which two words spell **s** with **sc**?

   _____   _____

5. Complete these sentences, using a word with **s** spelled as shown. Use each word from the box only once.

   My (**ce**) _____ fell off my wrist into the tomato

   _____ (**s and ce**).

   My salad was just a (**s and ce**) _____ of (**ce**) _____.

   It was (**c**) _____ to see the lions, even though they were a long

   (**s and ce**) _____ away.

   The (**sc and s**) _____ invented a new (**c**) _____.

   If I lend you my (**sc**) _____ , will you leave me in

   (**ce**) _____?

Name: _____

Spelling: The s Sound

Directions: Read the following words. Underline the letters that spell **s** in each word. In some words, more than one letter will be underlined.

1. impassive
2. placement
3. question
4. conscious
5. excellence
6. assertive
7. scepter
8. scoundrel

9. assortment
10. ignorance
11. precious
12. judicious
13. difference
14. lifeless
15. solvent
16. scope

17. castle
18. scamper
19. sociable
20. muffins
21. scissors
22. insurance
23. scamp
24. science

Ssss. . . .Ssss. . . .Ssss. . . .Ssss!

Directions: Under each spelling for **s**, write five words with the same **s** letters. Use words other than those above.

s or **ss**	**c**	**ce**	**sc**
_____	_____	_____	_____
_____	_____	_____	_____
_____	_____	_____	_____
_____	_____	_____	_____
_____	_____	_____	_____

Name: _____

Spelling: Syllables

A **syllable** is a word—or part of a word—with only one vowel sound. Some words have just one syllable, such as **cat**, **dog** and **house**. Some words have two syllables, such as **in-sist** and **be-fore**. Some words have three syllables, such as **re-mem-ber**; four syllables, such as **un-der-stand-ing**; or more. Often words are easier to spell if you know how many syllables they have.

syl-la-bles

Directions: Write the number of syllables in each word below.

Word	Syllables	Word	Syllables
1. amphibian	_____	11. want	_____
2. liter	_____	12. communication	_____
3. guild	_____	13. pedestrian	_____
4. chili	_____	14. kilo	_____
5. vegetarian	_____	15. autumn	_____
6. comedian	_____	16. dinosaur	_____
7. warm	_____	17. grammar	_____
8. piano	_____	18. dry	_____
9. barbarian	_____	19. solar	_____
10. chef	_____	20. wild	_____

Directions: Next to each number, write words with the same number of syllables.

1 _____ _____ _____ _____

2 _____ _____ _____

3 _____ _____ _____

4 _____ _____ _____

5 _____ _____

Name: _____

Spelling: Syllables

Directions: Write each word from the box next to the number that shows how many syllables it has.

fuss	paragraph	phone	friendship	freedom
defend	flood	alphabet	rough	laughter

One: _____ _____ _____ _____

Two: _____ _____ _____ _____

Three: _____ _____

How many syllables are there in the word **friendship**?

Directions: Circle the two words in each row that have the same number of syllables as the first word.

Example: fact	(clay)	happy	(phone)	command
rough	freckle	pump	accuse	ghost
jacket	flood	laughter	defend	paragraph
accident	paragraph	carpenter	stomach	castle
comfort	agree	friend	friendship	health
fuss	collect	blend	freedom	hatch
alphabet	thankful	Christmas	enemy	unhappy
glowing	midnight	defending	grading	telephone

Name: _____

Vocabulary: Synonyms

A **synonym** is a word that means the same, or nearly the same, as another word.
Example: quick and **fast**

Directions: Draw lines to match the words in Column A with their synonyms in Column B.

Column A	Column B
plain	unusual
career	vocation
rare	disappear
vanish	greedy
beautiful	finish
selfish	simple
complete	lovely

Directions: Choose a word from Column A or Column B to complete each sentence below.

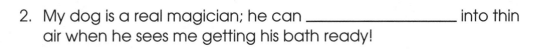

1. Dad was very excited when he discovered the _____ coin for sale on the display counter.

2. My dog is a real magician; he can _____ into thin air when he sees me getting his bath ready!

3. Many of my classmates joined the discussion about _____ choices we had considered.

4. "You will need to _____ your report on ancient Greece before you sign up for computer time," said Mr. Rastetter.

5. Your _____ painting will be on display in the art show.

Name: _____

Vocabulary: Synonyms

| tired | greedy | easy | rough | minute | melted | friend | smart |

Directions: For each sentence, choose a word from the box that is a synonym for the bold word. Write the synonym above the word.

1. Boy, this road is really **bumpy**!

2. The operator said politely, "One **moment**, please."

3. My parents are usually **exhausted** when they get home from work.

4. "Don't be so **selfish**! Can't you share with us?" asked Rob.

5. That puzzle was actually quite **simple**.

6. "Who's your **buddy**?" Dad asked as we walked onto the porch.

7. When it comes to animals, my Uncle Steve is quite **intelligent**.

8. The frozen treat **thawed** while I stood in line for the bus.

Vocabulary: Antonyms

An **antonym** is a word that means the opposite of another word.
Example: difficult and **easy**

Directions: Choose words from the box to complete the crossword puzzle.

friend	vanish	quit	safety	liquids	scatter	help	noisy

ACROSS:

2. Opposite of **gather**

3. Opposite of **enemy**

4. Opposite of **prevent**

6. Opposite of **begin**

7. Opposite of **silent**

DOWN:

1. Opposite of **appear**

2. Opposite of **danger**

5. Opposite of **solids**

Name: _____

Vocabulary: Antonyms

Directions: Each bold word below has an antonym in the box. Use these words to write new sentences. The first one is done for you.

| friend | vanish | quit | safety | liquids | help | scatter | worse |

1. I'll help you **gather** all the papers on the lawn.
   <u>The strong winds will scatter the leaves.</u>

2. The fourth graders were learning about the many **solids** in their classroom.
   _____
   _____

3. "It's time to **begin** our lesson on the continents," said Ms. Haynes.
   _____
   _____

4. "That's strange. The stapler decided to **appear** all of a sudden," said Mr. Jonson.
   _____
   _____

5. The doctor said this new medicine should **prevent** colds.
   _____
   _____

6. "She is our **enemy**, boys, we can't let her in our clubhouse!" cried Paul.
   _____
   _____

7. I'm certain that dark cave is full of **danger**!
   _____
   _____

8. Give me a chance to make the situation **better**.
   _____
   _____

Vocabulary: Synonyms and Antonyms

Directions: Use the words in the box to write a synonym for each word below. Write it next to the S. Next to the A, write an antonym. The first one is done for you.

appear	proud	merry	straight	repair	plain
under	melted	unnecessary	late	new	smooth
embarrassed	gloomy	bent	break	fancy	above
icy	valuable	immediate	old	bumpy	vanish

1. crooked

   S: <u>bent</u>

   A: <u>straight</u>

2. frozen

   S: _____

   A: _____

3. instant

   S: _____

   A: _____

4. damage

   S: _____

   A: _____

5. important

   S: _____

   A: _____

6. ashamed

   S: _____

   A: _____

7. cheerful

   S: _____

   A: _____

8. elegant

   S: _____

   A: _____

9. rough

   S: _____

   A: _____

10. beneath

    S: _____

    A: _____

11. disappear

    S: _____

    A: _____

12. ancient

    S: _____

    A: _____

Palindromes

Can you think forwards and backwards? If so, you should have no problem with palindromes. **Palindromes** are words or sentences that are spelled the same forward or backward.

**Examples: noon, eve, mom, wow
            a man, a plan, a canal, Panama**

Directions: Read the definitions. Write the palindromes on the lines. If you get stuck, work with a partner.

1. Another name for a soft drink _____

2. What you typically call your father _____

3. Short for Nancy _____

4. What one does with one's eyes _____

5. Female sheep _____

6. An instrument used to locate airplanes _____

7. To choke _____

8. Boat used by Eskimos _____

9. Time for lunch _____

10. A paper that shows legal ownership of property _____

Directions: Write as many palindromes as you can. A few have been done for you.

bib, Bob, did, dad _____

_____

_____

Directions: Write a palindrome sentence using these words: I'm, Madam, Adam.

_____

Name: _____

Vocabulary: Homophones

Homophones are two words that sound the same, have different meanings and are usually spelled differently.
Example: write and **right**

Directions: Write the correct homophone in each sentence below.

weight — how heavy something is
wait — to be patient

threw — tossed
through — passing between

steal — to take something that doesn't belong to you
steel — a heavy metal

1. The bands marched _____ the streets lined with many cheering people.

2. _____ for me by the flagpole.

3. One of our strict rules at school is: Never _____ from another person.

4. Could you estimate the _____ of this bowling ball?

5. The bleachers have _____ rods on both ends and in the middle.

6. He walked in the door and _____ his jacket down.

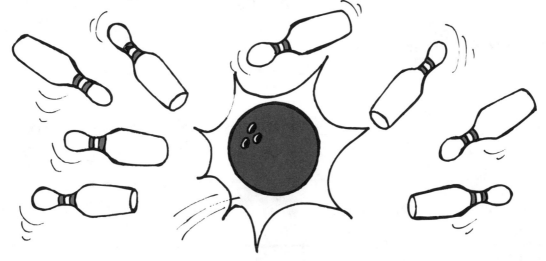

Grade 4 - Comprehensive Curriculum

Vocabulary: Homophones

Directions: Write the correct homophone in each sentence below.

cent — a coin having the value of one penny
scent — odor or aroma

chews — grinds with the teeth
choose — to select

course — the path along which something moves
coarse — rough in texture

heard — received sounds in the ear
herd — a group of animals

1. My uncle Mike always _____

   each bite of his food 20 times!

2. As we walked through her garden, we detected

   the _____ of roses.

3. It was very peaceful sitting on the hillside watching

   the _____ of cattle grazing.

4. Which flavor of ice cream did you _____ ?

5. The friendly clerk let me buy the jacket even though I was one _____ short.

6. You will need _____ sandpaper to make the wood smoother.

Name: _____

Vocabulary: Words That Sound Alike

Directions: Choose the correct word in parentheses to complete each sentence. The first one is done for you.

1. Jimmy was so _____ that he fell asleep. (board, bored)

2. We'll need a _____ and some nails to repair the fence. (board, bored)

3. Do you want _____ after dinner? (desert, dessert)

4. Did the soldier _____ his post. (desert, dessert)

5. The soldier had a _____ pinned to his uniform. (medal, meddle)

6. I told her not to _____ in other people's lives. (medal, meddle)

7. Don't _____ at your present before Christmas! (peak, peek)

8. They climbed to the _____ of the mountain. (peak, peek)

9. Jack had to repair the emergency _____ on his car. (brake, break)

10. Please be careful not to _____ my bicycle. (brake, break)

11. The race _____ was a very difficult one. (coarse, course)

12. We will need some _____ sandpaper to finish the job. (coarse, course)

Grade 4 - Comprehensive Curriculum

Name: _____

Vocabulary: Prefixes

A **prefix** is a syllable at the beginning of a word that changes its meaning.

Directions: Add a prefix to the beginning of each word in the box to make a word with the meaning given in each sentence below. The first one is done for you.

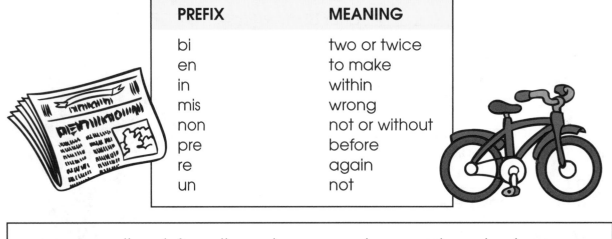

PREFIX	MEANING
bi	two or twice
en	to make
in	within
mis	wrong
non	not or without
pre	before
re	again
un	not

| grown | write | information | large | cycle | usual | school | sense |

1. Jimmy's foot hurt because his toenail was (growing within). __ingrown__

2. If you want to see what is in the background, you will have to (make bigger) the

   photograph. _____

3. I didn't do a very good job on my homework, so I will have to (write it again)

   it. _____

4. The newspaper article about the event has some (wrong facts). _____

5. I hope I get a (vehicle with two wheels) for my birthday. _____

6. The story he told was complete (words without meaning)! _____

7. Did you go to (school that comes before kindergarten) before you went to

   kindergarten? _____

8. The ability to read words upside down is most (not usual). _____

Vocabulary: Prefixes

Directions: Circle the correct word for each sentence.

1. You will need to _____ the directions before you complete this page.

   reset   reread   repair

2. Since she is allergic to milk products she has to

   use _____ products.

   nondairy   nonsense   nonmetallic

3. That certainly was an _____ costume he selected for the Halloween party.

   untied   unusual   unable

4. The directions on the box said to _____ the oven before baking the brownies.

   preheat   preschool   prevent

5. "I'm sorry if I _____ you as to the cost of the trip," explained the travel agent.

   misdialed   misread   misinformed

6. You may use the overhead projector to _____ the picture so the whole class can see it.

   enlarge   enable   endanger

Name: _____

Vocabulary: Suffixes

A **suffix** is a syllable at the end of a word that changes its meaning. In most cases, when adding a suffix that begins with a vowel, drop the final **e** of the root word. For example, **fame** becomes **famous**. Also, change a final **y** in the root word to **i** before adding any suffix except **ing**. For example, **silly** becomes **silliness**.

Directions: Add a suffix to the end of each word in the box to make a word with the meaning given (in parentheses) in each sentence below. The first one is done for you.

SUFFIX	MEANING
ful	full of
ity	quality or degree
ive	have or tend to be
less	without or lacking
able	able to be
ness	state of
ment	act of
or	person that does something
ward	in the direction of

| effect | like | thought | pay | beauty | thank | back | act | happy |

1. Mike was (full of thanks) for a hot meal. _____**thankful**_____

2. I was (without thinking) for forgetting your birthday. _____

3. The mouse trap we put out doesn't seem to be (have an effect). _____

4. In spring, the flower garden is (full of beauty). _____

5. Sally is such a (able to be liked) girl! _____

6. Tim fell over (in the direction of the back) because he wasn't watching where he was going. _____

7. Jill's wedding day was one of great (the state of being happy). _____

8. The (person who performs) was very good in the play. _____

9. I have to make a (act of paying) for the stereo I bought. _____

Name: _____

Vocabulary: Suffixes

Directions: Read the story. Choose the correct word from the box to complete the sentences.

beautiful	colorful	payment
breakable	careful	backward
careless	director	agreement
basement	forward	firmness

Colleen and Marj carried the boxes down to the _____ apartment. "Be

_____ with those," cautioned Colleen's mother. "All the things in that box

are _____ ." As soon as the two girls helped carry all the boxes from the

moving van down the stairs, they would be able to go to school for the play tryouts. That

was the _____ made with Colleen's mother earlier that day.

"It won't do any good to get _____ with your work. Just keep at it

and the job will be done quickly," she spoke with a _____ in her voice.

"It's hard to see where I'm going when I have to walk _____ ," groaned

Marj. "Can we switch places with the next box?"

Colleen agreed to switch places, but they soon discovered that the last two boxes

were lightweight. Each girl had her own box to carry, so each of them got to walk looking

_____ . "These are so light," remarked Marj. "What's in them?"

"These have the _____ , _____ hats I was telling you

about. We can take them to the play tryouts with us," answered Colleen. "I bet we'll impress

the _____ . Even if we don't get parts in the play, I bet our hats will!"

Colleen's mother handed each of the girls a 5-dollar bill. "I really appreciate your help.

Will this be enough?"

"Thanks, Mom. You bet!" Colleen shouted as the girls ran down the sidewalk.

Name: _____

Reading Skills: Classifying

Classifying is placing similar things into categories.

Directions: Classify each group by crossing out the word that does not belong.

1. factory   hotel   lodge   pattern

2. Thursday   September   December   October

3. cottage   hut   carpenter   castle

4. cupboard   orchard   refrigerator   stove

5. Christmas   Thanksgiving   Easter   spring

6. brass   copper   coal   tin

7. stomach   breathe   liver   brain

8. teacher   mother   dentist   office

9. musket   faucet   bathtub   sink

10. basement   attic   kitchen   neighborhood

Reading Skills: Classifying

Directions: Complete each idea by crossing out the word or phrase that does not belong.

1. If the main idea is **things that are green**, I don't need:

     the sun   apples   grass   leaves in summer

2. If the idea is **musical instruments**, I don't need a:

     piano   trombone   beach ball   tuba

3. If the idea is **months of the year**, I don't need:

     Friday   January   July   October

4. If the idea is **colors on the U.S. flag**, I don't need:

     white   blue   black   red

5. If the idea is **types of weather**, I don't need:

     sleet   stormy   roses   sunny

6. If the idea is **fruits**, I don't need:

     kiwi   orange   spinach   banana

7. If the idea is **U.S. presidents**, I don't need:

     Lincoln   Jordan   Washington   Adams

8. If the idea is **flowers**, I don't need:

     oak   daisy   tulip   daffodil

9. If the idea is **sports**, I don't need:

     pears   soccer   wrestling   baseball

Name: _____

Reading Skills: Classifying

Directions: Choose a word or phrase from the box that describes each group below.

color words	vegetables	gems
explorers	metals	vehicles
things that fly	insects

1. _____
   a. hot-air balloons
   b. jets
   c. bi-planes

5. _____
   a. Ponce de Leon
   b. Lewis and Clark
   c. Magellan

2. _____
   a. iron
   b. gold
   c. copper

6. _____
   a. beets
   b. carrots
   c. asparagus

3. _____
   a. ruby
   b. diamond
   c. emerald

7. _____
   a. mosquito
   b. cricket
   c. ant

4. _____
   a. magenta
   b. green
   c. black

8. _____
   a. mini-van
   b. bus
   c. convertible

Name: _____

Reading Skills: Classifying

Directions: Read the title of each TV show. Write the correct number to tell what kind of show it is.

1 — Cooking	3 — Sports	5 — Humor
2 — Nature	4 — Mystery	6 — Famous People

_____ *The Secret of the Lost Locket*

_____ *Learn Tennis With the Pros*

_____ *Birds in the Wild*

_____ *The Life of George Washington*

_____ *Great Recipes From Around the World*

_____ *A Laugh a Minute*

Directions: Read the description of each TV show. Write the number of each show above in the blank.

_____ The years before he became the first president of the United States are examined.

_____ Featured: eagles and owls

_____ Clues lead Detective Logan to a cemetery in his search for the missing necklace.

_____ Famous players give tips on buying a racket.

_____ Six ways to cook chicken

_____ Cartoon characters in short stories

Grade 4 - Comprehensive Curriculum

Name: _____

Reading Skills: Classifying

Directions: Read the story. Find words in the story that belong in the lists below. Write the words under the correct lists.

Meg, Joey and Ryan are talking about what they want to do when they grow up. Meg says, "I want to be a great writer. I'll write lots of books, and articles for newspapers and magazines."

"I want to be a famous athlete," says Joey. "I'll play baseball in the summer and football in the fall."

"Oh, yes," adds Meg. "I want to be a famous tennis star, too. When I'm not busy writing books, I'll play in tournaments all over the world. I'll be the world's champion!"

Ryan says, "That sounds pretty good. But I think I'll be a doctor and a carpenter. I'll build my very own cabin that I can live in during the winter."

"I'm going to live in a lighthouse by the sea," says Joey. "I've always wanted to do that. Then I can go fishing any time I want."

"I suppose I'll live in a castle when I grow up," says Meg. "World champion tennis players make lots of money!"

Jobs

1. _____

2. _____

3. _____

4. _____

Sports

1. _____

2. _____

3. _____

4. _____

Seasons

1. _____

2. _____

3. _____

Houses

1. _____

2. _____

3. _____

Name: _____

Reading Skills: Analogies

An **analogy** indicates how different items go together or are similar in some way.

Examples:
    Petal is to **flower** as **leaf** is to **tree**.
    Book is to **library** as **food** is to **grocery**.

If you study the examples, you will see how the second set of objects is related to the first set. A petal is part of a flower, and a leaf is part of a tree. A book can be found in a library, and food can be found in a grocery store.

Directions: Fill in the blanks to complete the analogies. The first one has been done for you.

1. Cup is to saucer as glass is to _____coaster_____ .

2. Paris is to France as London is to _____ .

3. Clothes are to hangers as _____ are to boxes.

4. California is to _____ as Ohio is to Lake Erie.

5. _____ is to table as blanket is to bed.

6. Pencil is to paper as _____ is to canvas.

7. Cow is to _____ as child is to house.

8. State is to country as _____ is to state.

9. Governor is to state as _____ is to country.

10. _____ is to ocean as sand is to desert.

11. Engine is to car as hard drive is to _____ .

12. Beginning is to _____ as stop is to end.

Directions: Write three analogies of your own.

_____

_____

_____

Grade 4 - Comprehensive Curriculum

Name: _____

Reading Skills: Analogies

Directions: Write a word from the box to complete the following analogies.

fence	club	glove	saw	father
blanket	dish	rug	snow	ten
compass	hat	brake	finger	blue

1. Racket is to tennis as _____ is to golf.

2. Glass is to drink as _____ is to eat.

3. Wheel is to steer as _____ is to stop.

4. Roof is to house as _____ is to floor.

5. Rain is to storm as _____ is to blizzard.

6. Clock is to time as _____ is to directions.

7. Lid is to pan as _____ is to head.

8. Hammer is to pound as _____ is to cut.

9. Mother is to daughter as _____ is to son.

10. Shoe is to foot as _____ is to hand.

11. Five is to ten as _____ is to twenty.

12. Shade is to lamp as _____ is to bed.

13. Toe is to foot as _____ is to hand.

14. Frame is to picture as _____ is to yard.

15. Green is to grass as _____ is to sky.

Name: _____

Review

Directions: Check the three words that belong together. Then draw a line under the sentence that tells how they are alike.

1. ☐ forehead   ☐ jaw   They are all parts of the face.

   ☐ shoulder   ☐ cheek   They are all parts of the arm.

2. ☐ collar   ☐ sleeve   They are all parts of your body.

   ☐ cuff   ☐ heart   They are all parts of a shirt.

3. ☐ camera   ☐ trumpet   They are all used to make music.

   ☐ guitar   ☐ flute   They are all used to take pictures.

Directions: Check the three words that belong together. Then write a sentence to tell how they are alike.

☐ cottage   ☐ princess   ☐ hut   ☐ castle

_____

_____

Directions: Write a word to complete each analogy.

1. Car is to drive as _____ is to fly.

2. Basement is to bottom as attic is to _____ .

3. Calf is to cow as colt is to _____ .

4. Bark is to dog as _____ is to cow.

5. Laugh is to happy as _____ is to sad.

Following Directions: Maps

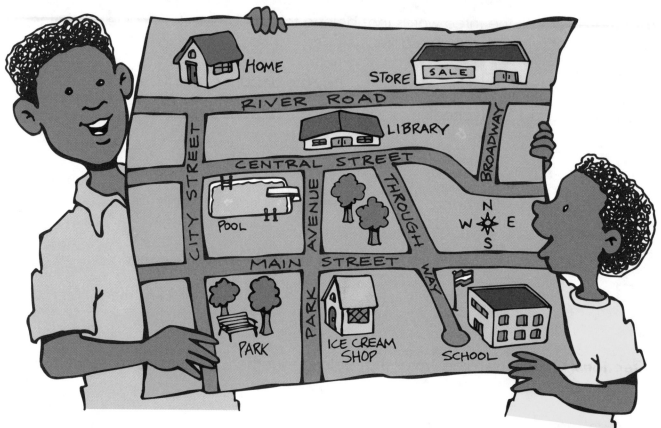

Directions: Follow the directions below to reach a "mystery" location on the map.

1. Begin at home.
2. Drive east on River Road.
3. Turn south on Broadway.
4. Drive to Central Street and turn west.
5. When you get to City Street, turn south.
6. Turn east on Main Street and drive one block to Park Avenue; turn north.
7. At Central Street turn east, then turn southeast on Through Way.
8. Drive to the end of Through Way. Your "mystery" location is to the east.

You are at the _____ .

Can you write an easier way to get back home?

_____

_____

_____

Name: _____

Following Directions: Recipes

Sequencing is putting items or events in logical order.

Directions: Read the recipe. Then number the steps in order for making brownies.

Preheat the oven to 350 degrees. Grease an 8-inch square baking dish.

In a mixing bowl, place two squares (2 ounces) of unsweetened chocolate and 1/3 cup butter. Place the bowl in a pan of hot water and heat it to melt the chocolate and the butter.

When the chocolate is melted, remove the pan from the heat. Add 1 cup sugar and two eggs to the melted chocolate and beat it. Next, stir in 3/4 cup sifted flour, 1/2 teaspoon baking powder and 1/2 teaspoon salt. Finally, mix in 1/2 cup chopped nuts.

Spread the mixture in the greased baking dish. Bake for 30 to 35 minutes. The brownies are done when a toothpick stuck in the center comes out clean. Let the brownies cool. Cut them into squares.

_____ Stick a toothpick in the center of the brownies to make sure they are done.

_____ Mix in chopped nuts.

_____ Melt chocolate and butter in a mixing bowl over a pan of hot water.

_____ Cool brownies and cut into squares.

_____ Beat in sugar and eggs.

_____ Spread mixture in a baking dish.

_____ Stir in flour, baking powder and salt.

_____ Bake for 30 to 35 minutes.

_____ Turn oven to 350 degrees and grease pan.

Grade 4 - Comprehensive Curriculum

Following Directions: Salt Into Pepper

Directions: Read how to do a magic trick that will amaze your friends. Then number the steps in order to do the trick.

Imagine doing this trick for your friends. Pick up a salt shaker that everyone can see is full of salt. Pour some into your hand. Tell your audience that you will change the salt into pepper. Say a few magic words, such as "Fibbiddy, dibbiddy, milkshake and malt. What will be pepper once was salt!" Then open your hand and pour out pepper!

How is it done? First you need a clear salt shaker with a screw-on top. You also need a paper napkin and a small amount of pepper.

Take off the top of the salt shaker. Lay the napkin over the opening and push it down a little to make a small pocket. Fill the pocket with pepper. Put the top back on the salt shaker and tear off the extra napkin. Now you are ready for the trick.

Hold up the salt shaker so your audience can see that it is full of salt. Shake some "salt" into your hand. Close your fist so no one can see that it is really pepper. Say the magic words and open your hand.

_____ Say some magic words.

_____ Find a clear salt shaker with a screw-on top.

_____ Open your hand and pour out the pepper.

_____ Take off the top of the salt shaker.

_____ Show the audience the shaker full of salt.

_____ Place the napkin over the opening of the salt shaker.

_____ Get a paper napkin and some pepper.

_____ Put the pepper in the napkin pocket.

_____ Shake some "salt" into your hand and close your fist.

_____ Put the top back on the salt shaker and tear off the extra napkin.

Name: _____

Following Directions: Recipes

Directions: Follow these steps for making a peanut butter and jelly sandwich.

1. Get a jar of peanut butter, a jar of jelly, two slices of bread and a knife.

2. Open the jar lids.

3. Using the knife, spread peanut butter on one slice of bread.

4. Spread jelly on the other slice of bread.

5. Put the two slices of bread together to make a sandwich.

Directions: Write the steps for a recipe of your own. Be very specific. When you are done, give the recipe to a friend to make. You will know right away if any steps are missing!

Recipe for: _____

1. _____

2. _____

3. _____

4. _____

5. _____

6. _____

Reading Skills: Bus Schedules

Schedules are important to our daily lives. Your parents' jobs, school, even watching television—all are based on schedules. When you travel, you probably follow a schedule, too. Most forms of public transportation, such as subways, buses and trains, run on schedules. These "timetables" tell passengers when they will leave each stop or station.

Directions: Use the following city bus schedule to answer the questions.

No. 2 Cross-Town Bus Schedule

State St. at Park Way	Oak St. at Green Ave.	Fourth St. at Ninth Ave.	Buyall Shopping Center
5:00 a.m.	5:14 a.m.	5:23 a.m.	5:30 a.m.
6:38	6:52	7:01	7:08
7:50	8:05	8:14	8:21
9:04	9:18	9:27	9:34
10:15	10:29	10:38	10:47
12:20 p.m.	12:34 p.m.	12:43 p.m.	12:50 p.m.
1:46	2:00	2:09	2:16
3:30	3:44	3:53	4:00
5:20	5:34	5:43	5:50
6:02	6:16	6:25	6:32

1. The first bus of the day leaves the State St./Park Way stop at 5 a.m. What time does the last bus of the day leave this stop? _____

2. The bus that leaves the Oak St./Green Ave. stop at 8:05 a.m. leaves the Buyall Shopping Center at what time? _____

3. What time does the first afternoon bus leave the Fourth St./Ninth Ave. stop? _____

4. How many buses each day run between the State St./Park Way stop and the Buyall Shopping Center? _____

Name: _____

Reading Skills: Train Schedules

Directions: Below is part of a schedule for trains leaving New York City for cities all around the country. Use the schedule to answer the questions.

Destination	Train Number	Departure Time	Arrival Time
Birmingham	958	9:00 a.m.	12:31 a.m.
Boston	611	7:15 a.m.	4:30 p.m.
Cambridge	398	8:15 a.m.	1:14 p.m.
Cincinnati	242	5:00 a.m.	7:25 p.m.
Detroit	415	1:45 p.m.	4:40 a.m.
Evansville	623	3:00 p.m.	8:28 a.m.

1. What is the number of the train that leaves latest in the day? _____

2. What city is the destination for train number 623? _____

3. What time does the train for Boston leave New York? _____

4. What time does train number 415 arrive in Detroit? _____

5. What is the destination of the train that leaves earliest in the day? _____

Name: _____

Reading Skills: Labels

Directions: You should never take any medicine without your parents' permission, but it is good to know how to read the label of a medicine bottle. Read the label to answer the questions.

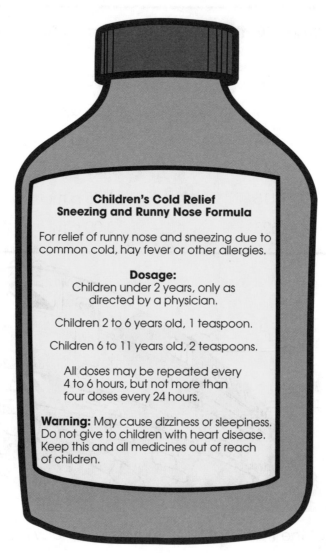

Children's Cold Relief Sneezing and Runny Nose Formula

For relief of runny nose and sneezing due to common cold, hay fever or other allergies.

Dosage:
Children under 2 years, only as directed by a physician.

Children 2 to 6 years old, 1 teaspoon.

Children 6 to 11 years old, 2 teaspoons.

All doses may be repeated every 4 to 6 hours, but not more than four doses every 24 hours.

Warning: May cause dizziness or sleepiness. Do not give to children with heart disease. Keep this and all medicines out of reach of children.

1. How much medicine should a 5 year old take? _____

2. How often can this medicine be taken? _____

3. How do you know how much medicine to give a 1 year old? _____

4. Who should not take this medicine? _____

Name: _____

Reading Skills: Labels

Directions: Use the following medicine bottle label to answer the questions.

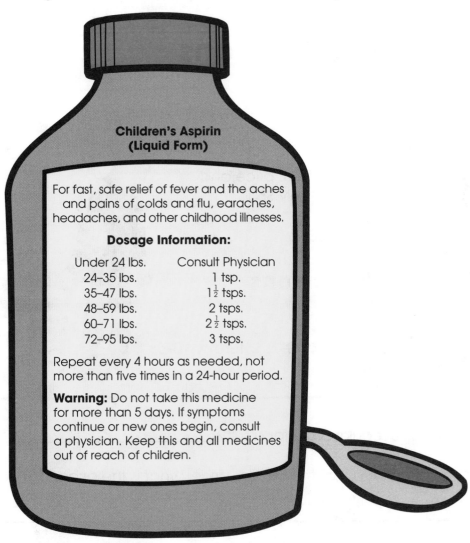

**Children's Aspirin
(Liquid Form)**

For fast, safe relief of fever and the aches
and pains of colds and flu, earaches,
headaches, and other childhood illnesses.

Dosage Information:

Under 24 lbs.	Consult Physician
24–35 lbs.	1 tsp.
35–47 lbs.	$1\frac{1}{2}$ tsps.
48–59 lbs.	2 tsps.
60–71 lbs.	$2\frac{1}{2}$ tsps.
72–95 lbs.	3 tsps.

Repeat every 4 hours as needed, not
more than five times in a 24-hour period.

Warning: Do not take this medicine
for more than 5 days. If symptoms
continue or new ones begin, consult
a physician. Keep this and all medicines
out of reach of children.

1. Circle the correct meaning of **dosage**.
    the kind of medicine
    the amount of medicine to give at one time
    the person who takes the medicine

2. What is the correct dosage for a child weighing 51 pounds? _____

3. Underline the correct meaning of **warning**.
    something that tells you of danger
    the instructions for how much medicine to give
    the person who takes the medicine

Name: _____

Reading Skills: Advertisements

Directions: Use the following newspaper ad to answer the questions.

New-Look Fashions

Final Week!
Spring Suit Sale

Buy one suit at the regular price and get a second one for only $50!

Suits: From $75 to $150

New-Look Fashions

5290 Main Street

Hours: Monday–Friday 10–7; Saturday 10–6; Closed Sunday

1. What is the regular price for a suit? _____

2. If you buy one suit at the regular price, what is the price for a second one?

   _____

3. What day is the store closed? _____

4. What hours is the store open on Wednesday? _____

5. When is the sale? _____

Name: _____

Reading Skills: Advertisements

Directions: Use the following newspaper ad to answer the questions.

House of Plants
Colorful Flowering Trees

Flowering Crab Apple Trees
Sizes up to 10 ft.
Beautiful Colored Spring Flowers
Dark Green Foliage
Red, Pink, White Blossoms

25% OFF

Reg. $29.99 to $149.99
NOW $22.49 to $112.50

House of Plants
6280 River Road

1. How big are the biggest flowering crab apple trees for sale?

   _____

2. What are the regular prices?

   _____

3. What are the sale prices?

   _____

Name: _____

Review

Directions: Use the following "Help Wanted" ads to answer the questions.

Baby-sitter. Caring, responsible person needed to take care of 2 and 4 year old in our home. 25–30 hours per week. Must have own transportation. References required. Call 725-1342 after 7 p.m.

Clerk/Typist. Law firm seeks part-time help. Duties include typing, filing and answering telephone. Monday–Friday, 1–6 p.m. Previous experience preferred. Apply in person. 1392 E. Long St.

Driver for Disabled. Van provided. Includes some evenings and Saturdays. No experience necessary. Call Mike at 769-1533.

Head Nurse. Join in the bloodmobile team at the American Red Cross. Full- and part-time positions available. Great benefits. Apply Monday thru Friday 9–4. 1495 N. State St.

Teachers. For new child-care program. Prefer degree in Early Childhood Development and previous experience. Must be non-smoker. Call 291-5555.

1. For which job would you have to work some evenings and Saturdays?

   _____

2. Which job calls for a person who does not smoke?

   _____

3. For which job would you have to have your own transportation?

   _____

4. For which job must you apply in person?

   _____

5. Which ad offers both part-time and full-time positions?

   _____

Facts and Opinions

Facts are statements or events that have happened and can be proven to be true.

Example: George Washington was the first president of the United States.
This statement is a fact. It can be proven to be true by researching the history of our country.

Opinions are statements that express how someone thinks or feels.

Example: George Washington was the greatest president the United States has ever had.
This statement is an opinion. Many people agree that George Washington was a great president, but not everyone agrees he was the greatest president. In some people's opinion, Abraham Lincoln was our greatest president.

Directions: Read each sentence. Write **F** for fact or **O** for opinion.

_____ 1. There is three feet of snow on the ground.

_____ 2. A lot of snow makes the winter enjoyable.

_____ 3. Chris has a better swing set than Mary.

_____ 4. Both Chris and Mary have swing sets.

_____ 5. California is a state.

_____ 6. California is the best state in the west.

Directions: Write three facts and three opinions.

Facts:

1) _____

2) _____

3) _____

Opinions:

1) _____

2) _____

3) _____

Name: _____

Facts and Opinions

Directions: Write **F** before the facts and **O** before the opinions.

_____ 1. Our school football team has a winning season this year.

_____ 2. Mom's spaghetti is the best in the world!

_____ 3. Autumn is the nicest season of the year.

_____ 4. Mrs. Burns took her class on a field trip last Thursday.

_____ 5. The library always puts 30 books in our classroom book collection.

_____ 6. They should put only books about horses in the collection.

_____ 7. Our new art teacher is very strict.

_____ 8. Everyone should keep take-home papers in a folder so they don't have to look for them when it is time to go home.

_____ 9. The bus to the mall goes right by her house at 7:45 a.m.

_____10. Our new superintendent, Mr. Willeke, is very nice.

Reading Skills: Context Clues

When you read, you may confuse words that look alike. You can tell when you read a word incorrectly because it doesn't make sense. You can tell from the **context** (the other words in the sentence or the sentences before or after) what the word should be. These **context clues** can help you figure out the meaning of a word by relating it to other words in the sentence.

Directions: Circle the correct word for each sentence below. Use the context to help you.

1. We knew we were in trouble as soon as we heard the crash.

   The baseball had gone (through, thought) the picture window!

2. She was not able to answer my question because her (month, mouth) was full of pizza.

3. Asia is the largest continent in the (world, word).

4. I'm not sure I heard the teacher correctly. Did he say what I (through, thought) he said?

5. I was not with them on vacation so I don't know a (think, thing) about what happened.

6. My favorite (month, mouth) of the year is July because I love fireworks and parades!

7. You will do better on your book report if you (think, thing) about what you are going

   to say.

Reading Skills: Context Clues

Directions: Read each sentence carefully and circle the word that makes sense.

1. We didn't (except, expect) you to arrive so early.

2. "I can't hear a (word, world) you are saying. Wait until I turn down the stereo," said Val.

3.   I couldn't sleep last night because of the (noise, nose) from the apartment below us.

4. Did Peggy say (weather, whether) or not we needed our binoculars for the game?

5. He broke his (noise, nose) when he fell off the bicycle.

6. All the students (except, expect) the four in the front row are excused to leave.

7. The teacher said we should have good (whether, weather) for our field trip.

Directions: Choose a word pair from the sentences above to write two sentences of your own.

1. _____

_____

2. _____

_____

Name: _____

Reading Skills: Context Clues

Directions: Use context clues to help you choose the correct word for each sentence below.

designs	studying	collection

Our fourth-grade class will be _____ castles for the next four weeks.

Mrs. Oswalt will be helping with our study. She plans to share her _____

of castle models with the class. We are all looking forward to our morning in the sand at

the school's volleyball court. We all get to try our own _____ to see

how they work.

breath	excited	quietly

Michelle was very _____ the other day when she came into the classroom.

We all noticed that she had trouble sitting _____ in her seat until it was

her turn to share with us. When her turn finally came, she took a deep _____

and told us that her mom was going to have a baby!

responsibility	chooses	messages

Each week, our teacher _____ classroom helpers. They get to be part

of the Job Squad. Some helpers have the _____ of watering the plants.

Everyone's favorite job is when they get to take _____ to the office or to

another teacher's room.

Reading Skills: Context Clues

Directions: Read the story. Match each bold word with its definition below.

Where the northern shores of North America meet the Arctic Ocean, the winters are very long and cold. No plants or crops will grow there. This is the land of the **Eskimo**.

Eskimos have figured out ways to live in the snow and ice. They sometimes live in **igloos**, which are made of snow. It is really very comfortable inside! An oil lamp provides light and warmth.

Often, you will find a big, furry **husky** sleeping in the long tunnel that leads to the igloo. Huskies are very important to Eskimos because they pull their sleds and help with hunting. Eskimos are excellent hunters. Many, many years ago they learned to make **harpoons** and spears to help them hunt their food.

Eskimos get much of their food from the sea, especially fish, seals and whales. Often, an Eskimo will go out in a **kayak** to fish. Only one Eskimo fits inside, and he drives it with a paddle. The waves may turn the kayak upside down, but the Eskimo does not fall out. He is so skillful with a paddle that he quickly is right side up again.

A _____ is a large, strong dog.

An _____ is a member of the race of people who live on the Arctic coasts of North America and in parts of Greenland.

_____ are houses made of packed snow.

A _____ is a one-person canoe made of animal skins.

_____ are spears with a long rope attached. They are used for spearing whales and other large sea animals.

Name: _____

Reading Skills: Context Clues

Directions: In each sentence below, circle the correct meaning for the nonsense word.

1. Be careful when you put that plate back on the shelf—it is **quibbable**.

   flexible   colorful   breakable

2. What is your favorite kind of **tonn**, pears or bananas?

   fruit   salad   purple

3. The **dinlay** outside this morning was very chilly; I needed my sweater.

   tree   vegetable   temperature

4. The whole class enjoyed the **weat**. They wanted to see it again next Friday.

   colorful   plant   video

5. Ashley's mother brought in a **zundy** she made by hand.

   temperature   quilt   plant

6. "Why don't you sit over here, Ronnie? That **sloey** is not very comfortable," said Mr. Gross.

   chair   car   cat

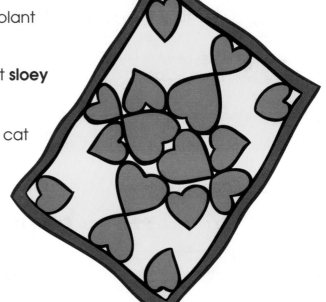

Grade 4 - Comprehensive Curriculum

Name: _____

Reading Skills: Sequencing

Directions: Read each set of events. Then number them in the correct order.

_____ Get dressed for school and hurry downstairs for breakfast.

_____ Roll over, sleepy-eyed, and turn off the alarm clock.

_____ Meet your friends at the corner to walk to school.

_____ The fourth-grade class walked quietly to a safe area away from the building.

_____ The teacher reminded the last student to shut the classroom door.

_____ The loud clanging of the fire alarm startled everyone in the room.

_____ Barb's dad watched from the seat of the tractor as the boys and girls climbed into the wagon.

_____ By the time they returned to the barn, there wasn't much straw left.

_____ As the wagon bumped along the trail, the boys and girls sang songs they learned in music class.

_____ The referee blew his whistle and held up the hand of the winner of the match.

_____ Each wrestler worked hard, trying to outmaneuver his opponent.

_____ The referee said, "Shake hands, boys, and wrestle a fair match."

Reading Skills: Sequencing

Directions: In each group below, one event in the sequence is missing. Write the correct sentence from the box where it belongs.

> • Paul put his bait on the hook and cast out into the pond.
>
> • "Sorry," he said, "but the TV repairman can't get here until Friday."
>
> • Everyone pitched in and helped.
>
> • Corey put the ladder up against the trunk of the tree.

1. "All the housework has to be done before anyone goes to the game," said Mom.

2. _____

3. We all agreed that "many hands make light work."

1. _____

2. It wasn't long until he felt a tug on the line, and we watched the bobber go under.

3. He was the only one to go home with something other than bait!

1. The little girl cried as she stood looking up into the maple tree.

2. Between her tears, she managed to say, "My kitten is up in the tree and can't get down."

3. _____

1. Dad hung up the phone and turned to look at us.

2. _____

3. "This would be a good time to get out those old board games in the hall closet," he said.

Reading Skills: Sequencing

Directions: In each group below, one event in the sequence is missing. Write a sentence that makes sense in the sequence.

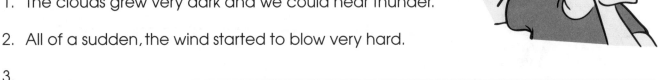

1. The clouds grew very dark and we could hear thunder.

2. All of a sudden, the wind started to blow very hard.

3. _____

1. The volleyball game was very boring at first.

2. _____

3. The home crowd cheered so loudly that I had to cover my ears.

1. _____

2. The boys gathered all the garden tools and put them in the wheelbarrow.

3. "Well, it was hard work, but we got it done, boys!" said Jim.

1. The teacher gave us our homework assignment early in the day.

2. Since the school assembly had to be cancelled, we had an extra study hall.

3. _____

1. Our cat has been acting very strange lately.

2. We heard unusual noises coming from the hall closet.

3. _____

Reading Skills: Sequencing

Directions: Read about how a tadpole becomes a frog. Then number the stages in order below.

Frogs and toads belong to a group of animals called amphibians (am-FIB-ee-ans). This means "living a double life." Frogs and toads live a "double life" because they live part of their lives in water and part on land. They are able to do this because their bodies change as they grow. This series of changes is called metamorphosis (met-a-MORE-fa-sis).

A mother frog lays her eggs in water and then leaves them on their own to grow. The eggs contain cells—the tiny "building blocks" of all living things—that multiply and grow. Soon the cells grow into a swimming tadpole. Tadpoles breathe through gills—small holes in their sides—like fish do. They spend all of their time in the water.

The tadpole changes as it grows. Back legs slowly form. Front legs begin inside the tadpole under the gill holes. They pop out when they are fully developed. At the same time, lungs, which a frog uses to breathe instead of gills, are almost ready to be used.

As the tadpole reaches the last days of its life in the water, its tail seems to disappear. When all of the tadpole's body parts are ready for life on land, it has become a frog.

_____ The front legs pop out. The lungs are ready to use for breathing.

_____ The cells in the egg multiply and grow.

_____ The tadpole has become a frog.

_____ Back legs slowly form.

_____ Soon the cells grow into a swimming tadpole.

_____ Front legs develop inside the tadpole.

_____ The tadpole's tail seems to disappear.

_____ A mother frog lays her eggs in water.

Reading Skills: Main Idea in Sentences

The **main idea** is the most important idea, or main point, in a sentence, paragraph or story.

Directions: Circle the main idea for each sentence.

1. Emily knew she would be late if she watched the end of the TV show.
   a. Emily likes watching TV.
   b. Emily is always running late.
   c. If Emily didn't leave, she would be late.

2. The dog was too strong and pulled Jason across the park on his leash.
   a. The dog is stronger than Jason.
   b. Jason is not very strong.
   c. Jason took the dog for a walk.

3. Jennifer took the book home so she could read it over and over.
   a. Jennifer loves to read.
   b. Jennifer loves the book.
   c. Jennifer is a good reader.

4. Jerome threw the baseball so hard it broke the window.
   a. Jerome throws baseballs very hard.
   b. Jerome was mad at the window.
   c. Jerome can't throw very straight.

5. Lori came home and decided to clean the kitchen for her parents.
   a. Lori is a very nice person.
   b. Lori did a favor for her parents.
   c. Lori likes to cook.

6. It was raining so hard that it was hard to see the road through the windshield.
   a. It always rains hard in April.
   b. The rain blurred our vision.
   c. It's hard to drive in the rain.

Main Idea: Snow Fun

The **main idea** of a story or report is a sentence that summarizes the most important point. If a story or report is only one paragraph in length, then the main idea is usually stated in the first sentence (topic sentence). If it is longer than one paragraph, then the main idea is a general sentence including all the important points of the story or report.

Directions: Read the story about snow fun. Then draw an **X** in the blank for the main idea.

After a big snowfall, my friends and I enjoy playing in the snow. We bundle up in snow clothes at our homes, then meet with sleds at the hill by my house.

One by one, we take turns sledding down the hill to see who will go the farthest and the fastest. Sometimes we have a contest to see whose sled will reach the fence at the foot of the hill first.

When we tire of sledding, we may build a snowman or snowforts. Sometimes we have a friendly snowball fight.

The end of our snow fun comes too quickly, and we head home to warm houses, dry clothes and hot chocolate.

1. What is the main idea?

_____ Playing in the snow with friends is an enjoyable activity.

_____ Sledding in the snow is fast and fun.

If you selected the first option, you are correct. The paragraphs discuss the enjoyable things friends do on a snowy day.

The second option is not correct because the entire story is not about sledding. Only the second paragraph discusses sledding. The other paragraphs discuss the additional ways friends have fun in the snow.

2. Write a paragraph about what you like to do on snowy days. Remember to make the first sentence your main idea.

_____

_____

_____

_____

Reading Skills: Main Idea in Paragraphs

Directions: Read each paragraph below. Then circle the sentence that tells the main idea.

It looked as if our class field day would have to be cancelled due to the weather. We tried not to show our disappointment, but Mr. Wade knew that it was hard to keep our minds on the math lesson. We noticed that even he had been sneaking glances out the window. All morning the classroom had been buzzing with plans. Each team met to plan team strategies for winning the events. Then, it happened! Clouds began to cover the sky, and soon the thunder and lightning confirmed what we were afraid of—field day was cancelled. Mr. Wade explained that we could still keep our same teams. We could put all of our plans into motion, but we would have to get busy and come up with some inside games and competitions. I guess the day would not be a total disaster!

a. Many storms occur in the late afternoon.

b. Our class field day had to be cancelled due to the weather.

c. Each team came up with its own strategies.

Allison and Emma had to work quietly and quickly to get Mom's birthday cake baked before she got home from work. Each of the girls had certain jobs to do—Allison set the oven temperature and got the cake pans prepared, while Emma got out all the ingredients. As they stirred and mixed, the two girls talked about the surprise party Dad had planned for Mom. Even Dad didn't know that the girls were baking this special cake. The cake was delicious. "It shows you what teamwork can do!" said the girls in unison.

a. Dad worked with the girls to bake the cake.

b. Mom's favorite frosting is chocolate cream.

c. Allison and Emma baked a birthday cake for Mom.

Main Idea: Busy Beavers

Directions: Read about busy beavers. Then answer the questions.

Has anyone ever told you that you are as busy as a beaver? If they have, then they mean that you are very busy. Beavers swim easily in streams, picking up rocks and sticks to build their dams. They gnaw at trees with their big front teeth to cut them down. Then they use parts of the trees to build their houses.

Beavers are clever builders. They know exactly what they need to build their beaver dams. They use mud from the stream to make their dams stay together. They use their tails to pat down the mud.

Beavers put a snug room at the top of their dams for their babies. They store their food underwater. Beavers eat the bark from the trees that they cut down!

1. What is the main idea of the first paragraph? _____

_____

2. What is the main idea of the second paragraph? _____

_____

3. What is the main idea of the third paragraph? _____

_____

_____

4. What do beavers use for their dams? _____

5. What parts of their bodies do beavers use to build their homes? _____

_____

_____

Name: _____

Main Idea: Bats

Directions: Read about bats. Then answer the questions.

Bats are unusual animals. Even though they fly, they are not birds. A bat's body is covered with fur. Its wings are made of skin. Bats do not have any feathers.

Bats are the only mammals that fly. A mammal is an animal that has hair and feeds its babies with its own milk. Humans are mammals, too. Mother bats have one or two babies each spring. Baby bats hang onto their mothers until they learn to fly by themselves.

Bats can be many different colors. Most are brown, but some are black, orange, gray or even green.

Even though many people do not like bats, bats don't usually bother people. Only vampire bats, which live in hot jungles, are very dangerous. Bats in the United States help people. Every year they eat billions and billions of harmful insects! Some bats also eat fruit or pollen from flowers.

1. What is the main idea?

   _____ Bats are mammals.

   _____ Bats are unusual animals.

   _____ Some people are afraid of bats.

2. What covers a bat's body? _____

3. How do bats in the United States help people? _____

_____

Directions: Read the clues. Find the answers in the story.

Across:
   2. Vampire bats live in hot _____.
   4. What do bats eat?
   5. Most bats are what color?

Down:
   1. Bats are not ____.
   3. What are bats' wings made of?

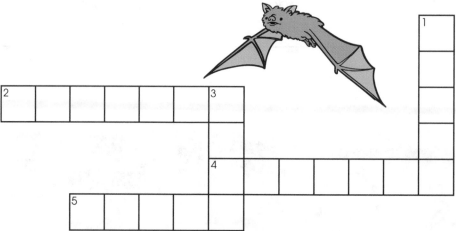

Name: _____

Recognizing Details

The main idea of a paragraph or story is supported by **details**. Details tell the who, what, when, where, why and how of a story or report. Recognizing details can help you remember what you have read.

Directions: Reread "Snow Fun." Then write two detail sentences that support the main idea.

_____
_____
_____
_____

_____

Directions: Reread the article on beavers. Then write two detail sentences that support the main idea.

_____
_____
_____
_____

_____

Directions: Reread the article on bats. Then write two detail sentences that support the main idea.

_____
_____
_____
_____

_____

Grade 4 - Comprehensive Curriculum

Name: _____

Recognizing Details: Blind Bats

Directions: Read about bats. Then answer the questions.

Bats sleep all day because they cannot see well in the bright sunlight. They hang upside down in dark places such as barns, caves or hollow trees. As soon as darkness begins to fall, bats wake up. They fly around easily and quickly at night.

Bats make sounds that help them fly, since they cannot see well. People cannot hear these sounds. When bats make sounds, the sounds hit objects in front of them and bounce back at them. Bats can tell if something is in their way because there is an echo. Some people say this is like a radar system!

There are many different kinds of bats. Some bats fly all night, while others fly only in the evening or the early morning.

Most bats eat mosquitoes and moths, but there are some bats that will catch fish swimming in water and eat them. Still other kinds of bats eat birds or mice. Bats that live in very hot areas eat only some parts of flowers.

Bats that live in cold areas of the country sometimes sleep all winter. That means they hibernate. Other bats that live in cold areas fly to warmer places for the winter. We call this migration.

1. Who cannot hear the sounds bats make? _____

2. Why do bats sleep all day? _____

3. When do bats eat? _____

4. Where do bats that eat only parts of flowers live? _____

5. Why do bats make sounds? _____

6. What does **hibernate** mean? _____

7. What is the main idea of this selection? _____

_____

8. Do you think a bat would make a good pet? Why or why not? _____

_____

_____

Name: _____

Reading Skills: Class Field Trip

Directions: Read this story about a class field trip. Pay careful attention to the details. As you read, think about the beginning, middle and end of the story.

Megan was very excited on her way to school. This was the day her fourth-grade class was going on its field trip to the town historical museum. As she looked out the bus window, she noticed that the bus was stopping at her friend Emily's house. She watched as Emily and her little sister climbed aboard the bus.

"I see you remembered your sack lunch," said Megan as her friend plopped down into the seat next to her.

"Remember? How could I forget?" said Emily breathlessly. "That's all we've talked about in class for the last two days."

The girls knew everyone was looking forward to the trip. Some children in the class were looking forward to the trip because they usually didn't get to ride a bus to school. Others in the class had been enjoying the study of their town's history and learning about what early life had been like for their ancestors. The girls laughed as they remembered what their classmate Paul had said, "I can't wait for the field trip—a day out of school!"

Soon they were at school and joined the rest of the fourth graders in homeroom. Obviously, by the chatter around them, their classmates were just as excited as they were.

Grade 4 - Comprehensive Curriculum

Reading Skills: Class Field Trip

"Take your seats, class," said Miss Haynes. "No one gets on the bus for the trip until we take care of some business first. After I check attendance and all of you have your name tags, we can think about getting lined up. While I check attendance, Ms. Diehl and Mrs. Denes will collect your lunch sacks and put them in the cooler. Make sure your names are on your lunch sacks, please!"

All heads turned and looked at the back of the room as Paul let out a loud moan. "Oh, no! I left my lunch at home on the table by the door!"

Miss Haynes said, "Fortunately, the cafeteria will be able to put together a sack lunch for you." She wrote a note to the kitchen staff to explain the problem and sent a much happier Paul on his way down the hall. "Hurry, Paul, we load the bus for our trip in 10 minutes."

"Don't worry, Miss Haynes, I'll be there in time!" replied Paul as he hurried out the door.

True to his word, Paul returned, sack lunch in hand, with plenty of time to spare. Business was soon taken care of and the children and adults were on the bus, heading for their exciting day at the museum.

Name: _____

Reading Skills: Sequencing

Directions: Reread the story, if necessary. Then choose an important event from the beginning, middle and end of the story, and write it below.

Beginning: _____

_____

Middle: _____

_____

End: _____

_____

Directions: Number these story events in the order in which they happened.

_____ Paul moaned, "Oh, no! I left my lunch on the table at home!"

_____ Megan watched as the bus stopped at Emily's house to pick up Emily and her little sister.

_____ Miss Haynes sent Paul to the cafeteria with a note explaining the problem.

_____ The teacher said they had some business to take care of before they could leave on the trip.

_____ Paul quickly returned with a sack lunch packed by the cafeteria helpers.

_____ Megan told Emily, "I see you remembered your sack lunch."

_____ The fourth graders finally loaded onto the bus for the field trip.

Grade 4 - Comprehensive Curriculum

Reading Skills: Recalling Details

Directions: Answer the questions below about "Class Field Trip."

1. Who were the two adult helpers that would be going on the trip with Miss Haynes'
   class? _____

2. The students in Miss Haynes' class were excited about the field trip for different reasons.
   What were the three different reasons mentioned in the story?

   a. _____

   b. _____

   c. _____

3. What business did Miss Haynes need to take care of before the class could leave on
   its trip? _____

Directions: Write the letter of the definition beside the word it defines. If you need help,
use a dictionary or check the context of the story.

a. sat down, not very gently
b. easy to understand; without doubt
c. family members that lived in the past,
   such as grandparents
d. in a favorable way

_____ ancestors

_____ fortunately

_____ plopped

_____ obviously

Name: _____

Reading Skills: Jonny's Story

Directions: Read the following true story about a little boy. Pay careful attention to the details. As you read, think about the beginning, middle and end of the story.

Jonny got out of bed. It hurt for him to walk. He could hear his mother calling for him so he limped over to the top of the stairs.

"Jonny, hurry up. I have to get to work," his mom called from the kitchen. When 3 1/2-year-old Jonny didn't hurry down the stairs, his mother went to the door and called again. As she looked up, she noticed that he was moving very slowly. "I guess you will have to eat your breakfast at the sitter's house since we are running so late."

"Mom, my leg hurts," Jonny said. His mother bent down to take a look. Jonny's left ankle was slightly red and swollen.

"I'm sure it does hurt," his mother said as she lifted him up and sat him on the counter to get a closer look. "It feels warm, too. I should call the doctor and try to get an appointment for you today."

It was hard to leave him at the sitter's, but Jonny's mom knew she could call as soon as the doctor's office opened. She left him at the sitter's with an extra big hug and asked the sitter to call if Jonny got any worse.

The appointment was scheduled for later that afternoon. Jonny's mom picked him up from the sitter's and found that Jonny had slept most of the day. He also had a fever. "I'm glad you have an appointment for him at the doctor's," said the sitter.

Reading Skills: Jonny's Story

Jonny's mom sat in the busy waiting room as one patient after another was called in to see the doctor. The whole time she sat there, she held him. He slept the whole time. Usually he was a very busy little boy, so his mom knew he must not be feeling well.

"With his high fever and that swollen ankle, he must have picked up an infection," said the doctor. "This prescription for an antibiotic should have him feeling much better and running around in no time!"

It was quite the opposite, Jonny's family soon discovered. The next morning, Jonny's mom stayed home from work because he was worse, not better. By late afternoon, his fever rose to 105 degrees! "Better bring him into the emergency room," said the doctor.

Jonny was admitted to the hospital and had test after test. Many doctors, some of them specialists, were called in, but no one had an answer. One doctor did have a guess. The pediatrician wondered aloud, "Do you suppose it could be JRA (juvenile rheumatoid arthritis)?"

More tests were done at another hospital, and the pediatrician's diagnosis was confirmed—Jonny did have JRA. This "little boy" is now 29 years old and still has rheumatoid arthritis. He has had many operations and has to take medicine every day for the pain, but he is able to lead a happy, normal life.

Reading Skills: Sequencing

Directions: Reread the story, if necessary. Then choose an important event from the beginning, middle and end of the story, and write it below.

Beginning: _____

_____

_____

Middle: _____

_____

_____

End: _____

_____

_____

_____

_____

Directions: Number these story events in the order in which they happened.

_____ Jonny's mom called the doctor to get an appointment since Jonny's ankle was red and swollen.

_____ Jonny limped to the top of the stairs.

_____ The pediatrician thought Jonny might have JRA.

_____ The sitter told Jonny's mom that he had slept most of the day.

_____ The doctor gave them a prescription for an antibiotic.

_____ Jonny is now 29 years old.

_____ Jonny told his mom, "My leg hurts."

Reading Skills: Recalling Details

Directions: Answer the questions below about "Jonny's Story."

1. How old was Jonny when his ankle began to bother him? _____

2. Why did Jonny's mom stay home from work the second day? _____

   _____

3. What do the letters JRA stand for? _____

4. When Jonny and his mom were waiting to see the doctor, how did Jonny's mom know

   he must not be feeling well? _____

5. Where did Jonny's mom take him when she picked him up at the sitter's house?

   _____

Directions: Write the letter of the definition beside the word it defines. If you need help, use a dictionary or check the context of the story.

a. strong medicine used to treat infections
b. found to be true
c. doctor that specializes in child care
d. not yet an adult
e. did not walk correctly

_____ pediatrician

_____ antibiotic

_____ confirmed

_____ limped

_____ juvenile

Name: _____

Comprehension: "The Frog Prince"

Directions: Review the story "The Frog Prince." Then answer the questions.

1. What does the Princess lose in the lake? _____

2. How does she get it back? _____

_____

_____

3. How does the frog turn back into a prince? _____

_____

4. What phrases are used to begin and end this story? _____

_____ .

5. Are these words used frequently to begin and end fairy tales? _____

There is more than one version of most fairy tales. In another version of this story, the Princess has to kiss the frog in order for him to change back into a prince.

Directions: Write your answers.

6. What do you think would happen in a story where the Princess kisses the frog, but he remains a frog?

_____

_____

7. What kinds of problems would a princess have with a bossy frog in the castle? Brainstorm ideas and write them here.

_____

_____

8. Rewrite the ending to "The Frog Prince" so that the frog remains a frog and does not turn into a handsome prince. Continue your story on another sheet of paper.

_____

Name: _____

Review

Directions: Think of fairy tales you know from books or videos, like "Cinderella," "Snow White," "Sleeping Beauty," "Rapunzel" and "Beauty and the Beast." Then answer the questions.

1. What are some common elements in all fairy tales? _____

_____

2. How do fairy tales usually begin? _____

_____

3. How do fairy tales usually end? _____

_____

Directions: Locate and read several different versions of the same fairy tale. For example, "Cinderella," "Princess Furball," "Cinderlad" and "Yah Shen." Then answer the questions.

4. How are the stories alike? _____

_____

_____

_____

5. How are they different? _____

_____

_____

_____

6. Which story is best developed by the author? _____

7. Which story did you like best? Why? _____

_____

_____

Name: _____

Review

Most of us have read many fairy tales and have seen them in movies. Fairy tales have a certain style and format they usually follow.

Directions: Use another sheet of paper to write another fairy tale. Use the following questions to help you brainstorm ideas.

1. What is the name of the kingdom? _____

2. What is the size of the kingdom, its climate, trees, plants, animals, etc.? _____

_____

_____

3. What kind of magic happens there? _____

_____

4. Who are the characters?

    Good guys   Bad guys

    _____   _____

    _____   _____

5. What does each character look like? _____

_____

6. What kind of spell is cast on a particular character and why? _____

_____

_____

_____

7. What happens to the good characters and the bad characters in the end?

_____

_____

Main Idea: "The Hare and the Tortoise"

The story of "The Hare and the Tortoise" is called a **fable.** Fables are usually short stories. As you read this story and the other fables on the next few pages, look for two characteristics the fables have in common.

Directions: Read the fable "The Hare and the Tortoise." Then answer the questions.

One day the hare and the tortoise were talking. Or rather, the hare was bragging and the tortoise was listening.

"I am faster than the wind," bragged the hare. "I feel sorry for you because you are so slow! Why, you are the slowest fellow I have ever seen."

"Do you think so?" asked the tortoise with a smile. "I will race you to that big tree across the field."

Slowly, he lifted a leg. Slowly, he pointed toward the tree.

"Ha!" scoffed the hare. "You must be kidding! You will most certainly be the loser! But, if you insist, we will race."

The tortoise nodded politely. "I'll be off," he said. Slowly and steadily, the tortoise moved across the field.

The hare stood back and laughed. "How sad that he should compete with me!" he said. His chest puffed up with pride. "I will take a little nap while the poor old tortoise lumbers along. When I wake up, he will still be only halfway across the field."

The tortoise kept on, slow and steady, across the field. Some time later, the hare awoke. He discovered that while he slept, the tortoise had won the race.

1. What is the main idea? (Check one.)

_____ Tortoises are faster than hares.

_____ Hares need more sleep than tortoises.

_____ Slow and steady wins the race.

2. The hare brags that he is faster than what? (Check one.)

_____ a bullet

_____ a greyhound

_____ the wind

3. Who is modest, the tortoise or the hare? _____

Cause and Effect: "The Hare and the Tortoise"

Another important skill in reading is recognizing cause and effect. The **cause** is the reason something happens. The **effect** is what happens or the situation that results from the cause. In the story, the hare falling asleep is a cause. It causes the hare to lose the race. Losing the race is the effect.

Directions: Identify the underlined words or phrases by writing **cause** or **effect** in the blanks.

1. <u>The hare and tortoise had a race</u> because the hare bragged about being faster.   _____

2. The tortoise won the race <u>because he continued on, slowly, but steadily.</u>   _____

Directions: Review the fable "The Hare and the Tortoise." Then answer the questions.

1. Who are the two main characters? _____

2. Where does the story take place? _____

3. What lessons can be learned from this story? _____

_____

4. The lesson that is learned at the end of a fable has a special name. What is that special name?

_____

5. Why did the tortoise want to race the hare? _____

_____

6. How do you think the hare felt at the end of the story? _____

_____

7. How do you think the tortoise felt at the end of the story? _____

_____

_____

_____

Sequencing: "The Fox and the Crow"

Directions: Read the fable "The Fox and the Crow." Then number the events in order.

Once upon a time, a crow found a piece of cheese on the ground. "Aha!" he said to himself. "This dropped from a workman's sandwich. It will make a fine lunch for me."

The crow picked up the cheese in his beak. He flew to a tree to eat it. Just as he began to chew it, a fox trotted by.

"Hello, crow!" he said slyly, for he wanted the cheese. The fox knew if the crow answered, the cheese would fall from its mouth. Then the fox would have cheese for lunch!

The crow just nodded.

"It's a wonderful day, isn't it?" asked the fox.

The crow nodded again and held onto the cheese.

"You are the most beautiful bird I have ever seen," added the fox.

The crow spread his feathers. Everyone likes a compliment. Still, the crow held firmly to the cheese.

"There is something I have heard," said the fox, "and I wonder if it is true. I heard that you sing more sweetly than any of the other birds."

The crow was eager to show off his talents. He opened his beak to sing. The cheese dropped to the ground.

"I said you were beautiful," said the fox as he ran away with the cheese. "I did not say you were smart!"

_____ The crow drops the cheese.

_____ The crow flies to a tree with the cheese.

_____ The fox tells the crow he is beautiful.

_____ The fox runs off with the cheese.

_____ A workman loses the cheese from his sandwich.

_____ The fox comes along.

_____ The fox tells the crow he has heard that crows sing beautifully.

_____ The crow picks up the cheese.

Predicting: "The Fox and the Crow"

Directions: Review the fable "The Fox and the Crow." Then answer the questions.

1. With what words does the story begin? _____

2. What other type of story often begins with these same words? _____

3. Although it is not stated, where do you think the story takes place?

_____

4. How does the fox get what he wants from the crow? _____

_____

_____

5. How is the crow in this story like the hare in the last fable? _____

_____

_____

Predicting is telling or guessing what you think might happen in a story or situation based on what you already know.

Directions: Write predictions to answer these questions.

6. Based on what you read, what do you think the crow will do the next time he finds a piece of cheese?

_____

_____

7. What do you think the fox will do the next time he wants to trick the crow? _____

_____

_____

_____

Following Directions: "The Boy Who Cried Wolf"

Directions: Read the fable "The Boy Who Cried Wolf." Then complete the puzzle.

Once there was a shepherd boy who tended his sheep alone. Sheep are gentle animals. They are easy to take care of. The boy grew bored.

"I can't stand another minute alone with these sheep," he said crossly. He knew only one thing would bring people quickly to him. If he cried, "Wolf!" the men in the village would run up the mountain. They would come to help save the sheep from the wolf.

"Wolf!" he yelled loudly, and he blew on his horn.

Quick as a wink, a dozen men came running. When they realized it was a joke, they were very angry. The boy promised never to do it again. But a week later, he grew bored and cried, "Wolf!" again. Again, the men ran to him. This time they were very, very angry.

Soon afterwards, a wolf really came. The boy was scared. "Wolf!" he cried. "Wolf! Wolf! Wolf!"

He blew his horn, but no one came, and the wolf ate all his sheep.

Across:

2. This is where the boy tends sheep.

4. When no one came, the wolf _____ all the sheep.

5. Sheep are _____ and easy to take care of.

Down:

1. The people who come are from here.

2. At first, when the boy cries, "Wolf!" the _____ come running.

3. When a wolf really comes, this is how the boy feels.

Cause and Effect: "The Boy Who Cried Wolf"

Directions: Identify the underlined words as a cause or an effect.

1. <u>The boy cries wolf</u> because he is bored. _____

2. <u>The boy blows his horn</u> and the men come running. _____

3. No one comes, and <u>the wolf eats all the sheep</u>. _____

Directions: Answer the questions.

4. What lesson can be learned from this story? _____

_____

_____

_____

5. How is this story like the two other fables you read? _____

_____

_____

_____

6. Is the boy in the story more like the fox or the hare? How so? _____

_____

_____

_____

_____

_____

Comprehension:
"The City Mouse and the Country Mouse"

Directions: Read the fable "The City Mouse and the Country Mouse." Then answer the questions.

Once there were two mice, a city mouse and a country mouse. They were cousins. The country mouse was always begging his cousin to visit him. Finally, the city mouse agreed.

When he arrived, the city mouse was not very polite. "How do you stand it here?" he asked, wrinkling his nose. "All you have to eat is corn and barley. All you have to wear is old, tattered work clothes. And all you have to listen to are the other animals. Why don't you come and visit me? Then you will see what it's like to really live!"

The country mouse liked corn and barley. He liked the sounds of the other animals. And he liked his old work clothes fine. Secretly, he thought his cousin was silly to wear fancy clothes. Still, the city sounded exciting. Why not give it a try?

Since he had no clothes to pack, the country mouse was ready in no time. His cousin told him stories about the city as they traveled. The buildings were so high! The food was so good! The girl mice were so beautiful!

The home of the city mouse was nice. He lived in a hole in the wall in an old castle. "It is only a hole in the wall," said the city mouse, "but it is a very nice wall, indeed!"

That night, the mice crept out of the wall. Everyone had eaten, but the maid had not cleaned up. The table was still loaded with good food. The mice ate and ate. The country mouse was not used to rich food. He began to feel sick to his stomach.

Just then, they heard loud barking. Two huge dogs ran into the room. They nearly bit off the country mouse's tail! He barely made it to the hole in the wall in time. That did it!

"Thank you for showing me the city," said the country mouse, "but it is too exciting for me. I am going home where it is peaceful. I can't wait to settle my stomach with some corn and barley."

1. What are three things the city mouse says are wrong with the country? _____

_____

2. Why doesn't it take the country mouse long to get ready to leave with the city mouse?

_____

3. Why does the country mouse secretly think his cousin is silly? _____

_____

Sequencing:
"The City Mouse and the Country Mouse"

Directions: Review the fable "The City Mouse and the Country Mouse." Use the Venn diagram to compare and contrast the lifestyles of the city mouse and the country mouse.

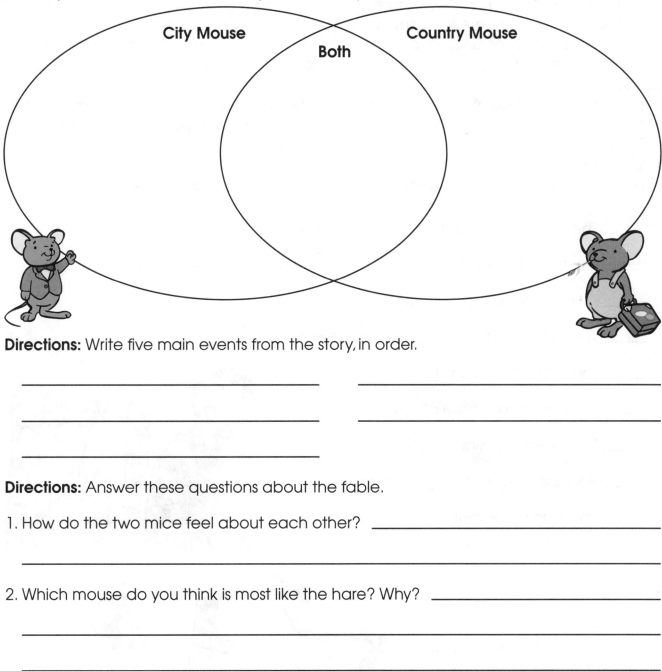

City Mouse   Both   Country Mouse

Directions: Write five main events from the story, in order.

_____   _____

_____   _____

_____

Directions: Answer these questions about the fable.

1. How do the two mice feel about each other? _____

_____

2. Which mouse do you think is most like the hare? Why? _____

_____

_____

Sequencing: "The Man and the Snake"

Directions: Read the fable "The Man and the Snake." Then number the events in order.

Once, a kind man saw a snake in the road. It was winter and the poor snake was nearly frozen. The man began to walk away, but he could not.

"The snake is one of Earth's creatures, too," he said. He picked up the snake and put it in a sack. "I will take it home to warm up by my fire. Then I will set it free."

The man stopped for lunch at a village inn. He put his coat and his sack on a bench by the fireplace. He planned to sit nearby, but the inn was crowded, so he had to sit across the room.

He soon forgot about the snake. As he was eating his soup, he heard screams. Warmed by the fire, the snake had crawled from the bag. It hissed at the people near the fire.

The man jumped up and ran to the fireplace. "Is this how you repay the kindness of others?" he shouted.

He grabbed a stick used for stirring the fire and chased the snake out of the inn.

_____ The man puts his bag down by the fireplace.

_____ The man chases the snake.

_____ A kind man rescues the snake.

_____ The snake warms up and crawls out of the bag.

_____ The man plans to take the snake home.

_____ The man eats a bowl of soup.

_____ The snake hisses at people.

_____ A snake is nearly frozen in the road.

_____ The man grabs a stick from the fireplace.

Name: _____

Sequencing: "The Wind and the Sun"

Directions: Read the fable "The Wind and the Sun." Then number the events in order.

One day, North Wind and Sun began to argue about who was stronger.
"I am stronger," declared North Wind.
"No," said Sun. "I am much stronger than you."
They argued for three days and three nights.
Finally, Sun said, "I know how we can settle the argument. See that traveler walking down the road? Whoever can make him take off his cloak first is the stronger. Do you agree?"
North Wind agreed. He wanted to try first. He blew and blew. The traveler shivered and pulled his cloak tightly around his body. North Wind sent a blast of wind so strong it almost pulled the cloak off the traveler, but the traveler only held tighter to his cloak.
Then it was Sun's turn. When Sun sent gentle, warm sunbeams, the traveler loosened his cloak. Then Sun sent his warmest beams to the traveler. After a short time, the traveler became so warm he threw off his cloak and ran to the shade of the nearest tree.

_____ Sun sent warm beams to the traveler.

_____ Sun and North Wind argued.

_____ The traveler threw off his cloak and ran to the shade.

_____ The traveler pulled his cloak tightly around his body.

_____ North Wind blew cold air on the traveler.

Directions: Answer the questions. (Check one.)

What is the moral of this fable?

_____ Sun is stronger than North Wind.

_____ North Wind is cold.

_____ A kind and gentle manner works better than force.

_____ Travelers should hold on to their cloaks when the wind blows.

_____ Stay out of arguments between Sun and North Wind.

Who do you think is stronger, North Wind or Sun? Why? _____

_____

Review

At the beginning of the section on fables, you were asked to discover two elements common to the fables.

Directions: Review the fables you read. Then answer the questions.

1. What are the two elements common to fables? _____

_____

_____

2. Each fable has a "moral" or lesson to be learned. What is the moral of each of the fables?

   "The Hare and the Tortoise" _____

   "The Fox and the Crow" _____

   "The Boy Who Cried Wolf" _____

   "The City Mouse and the Country Mouse" _____

   "The Man and the Snake" _____

3. How do the titles of the fables give clues to what or who the fables were about?

_____

_____

4. For each fable, write the character you think is the good character and the one you think is the bad character.

	"Good character"	"Bad character"
"The Hare and the Tortoise"	_____	_____
"The Fox and the Crow"	_____	_____
"The Wind and the Sun"	_____	_____
"The City Mouse and the Country Mouse"	_____	_____
"The Man and the Snake"	_____	_____

Fable Writing Organizer

Fables are short stories with animals as the main characters. Each story teaches a lesson.

Directions: Select one of the following pairs of animals as characters to use for a fable of your own.

A pig and an ox	An ant and a frog	A cat and a monkey
A fly and a butterfly	A spider and a bear	A goose and a deer
A snail and a lion	A horse and a dog	A T-Rex and a shark

Directions: Fill in the outline below with words and phrases to organize a fable of your own.

Animal pair _____

Type of conflict between the animals _____

_____

_____

How the conflict is settled _____

_____

_____

_____

Moral of the story _____

_____

Directions: Write your fable. Give your fable a title. Illustrate it if you like.

_____

_____

_____

_____

_____

_____

Grade 4 - Comprehensive Curriculum

Name: _Angel 4/20/12_

Reading Comprehension: Paul Bunyan

There is a certain kind of fable called a "tall tale." In these stories, each storyteller tries to "top" the other. The stories get more and more unbelievable. A popular hero of American tall tales is Paul Bunyan—a giant of a man. Here are some of the stories that have been told about him.

Even as a baby, Paul was very big. One night, he rolled over in his sleep and knocked down a mile of trees. Of course, Paul's father wanted to find some way to keep Paul from getting hurt in his sleep and to keep him from knocking down all the forests. So he cut down some tall trees and made a boat for Paul to use as a cradle. He tied a long rope to the boat and let it drift out a little way into the sea to rock Paul to sleep.

One night, Paul had trouble sleeping. He kept turning over in his bed. Each time he turned, the cradle rocked. And each time the cradle rocked, it sent up waves as big as buildings. The waves got bigger and bigger until the people on the land were afraid they would all be drowned. They told Paul's parents that Paul was a danger to the whole state! So Paul and his parents had to move away.

After that, Paul didn't get into much trouble when he was growing up. His father taught him some very important lessons, such as, "If there are any towns or farms in your way, be sure to step around them!"

Directions: Answer these questions about Paul Bunyan.

1. What kind of fable is the story of Paul Bunyan? _American tall tale_

2. What did Paul's father make for Paul to use as a cradle? _A boat_

3. What happened when Paul rolled over in his cradle? _it made a_
huge wave

4. What did Paul's father tell Paul to do to towns and farms that were in his way?
~~mmmmmmmmmmm~~ Step around
them

Name: _Angel_ _45/20/12_

Reading Comprehension: Paul Bunyan

When Paul Bunyan grew up, he was taller than other men—by about 50 feet or so! Because of his size, he could do almost anything. One of the things he did best was to cut down trees and turn them into lumber. With only four strokes of his axe, he could cut off all the branches and bark. After he turned all the trees for miles into these tall square posts, he tied a long rope to an axe head. Then he yelled, "T-I-M-B-E-R-R-R!" and swung the rope around in a huge circle. With every swing, 100 trees fell to the ground.

One cold winter day, Paul found a huge blue ox stuck in the snow. It was nearly frozen. Although it was only a baby, even Paul could hardly lift it. Paul took the ox home and cared for it. He named it Babe, and they became best friends. Babe was a big help to Paul when he was cutting down trees.

When Babe was full grown, it was hard to tell how big he was. There were no scales big enough to weigh him. Paul once measured the distance between Babe's eyes. It was the length of 42 axe handles!

Once Paul and Babe were working with other men to cut lumber. The job was very hard because the road was so long and winding. It was said that the road was so crooked that men starting home for camp would meet themselves coming back! Well, Paul hitched Babe to the end of that crooked road. Babe pulled and pulled. He pulled so hard that his eyes nearly turned pink. There was a loud snap. The first curve came out of the road and Babe pulled harder. Finally the whole road started to move. Babe pulled it completely straight!

Directions: Answer these questions about Paul Bunyan and Babe.

1. What was Paul Bunyan particularly good at doing? _Cutting down trees._

2. What did Paul find in the snow? _a ox._

3. How big was the distance between Babe's eyes? _42 ax handles._

4. What did Babe do to the crooked road? _Maded it Move._

Reading Comprehension: Mermaids

One of the most popular fantasy characters is the mermaid. Many different countries have stories about these lovely creatures, which are half woman and half fish. In these fables, the mermaid is always beautiful—except perhaps for her greenish skin and webbed fingers!

There are some stories about mermen, too. They are said to have fine torsos with big, strong muscles in their chests and arms. But they have the most ugly faces—eyes like a pig, red noses, green teeth and seaweed hair!

A famous fable told in Ireland tells about a mermaid who was said to have been seen nearly 1,400 years ago. The story says that she could be heard singing beneath the waters for many years. One day, some men rowed out and caught her with a net. They were surprised to learn that she had once been a little human girl. Her family had died in a flood. But she survived beneath the waves and gradually changed into a mermaid.

Directions: Answer these questions about the story.

1. Which definition is correct for **fantasy**?

   ☐ from the imagination and not real   ☐ real   ☐ living in the sea

2. Which definition is correct for **fable**?

   ☐ a true story   ☐ a made-up story   ☐ a story about fish

3. Which definition is correct for **torso**?

   ☐ the head   ☐ the upper body but not the head   ☐ the lower body

4. Which definition is correct for **survived**?

   ☐ swam   ☐ died   ☐ continued to live

Name: _____

Review: Venn Diagram

Directions: A **Venn diagram** is used to chart information that shows similarities and differences between two things. The Venn diagram below compares a mermaid (see page 104) and Paul Bunyan (see pages 102 and 103).

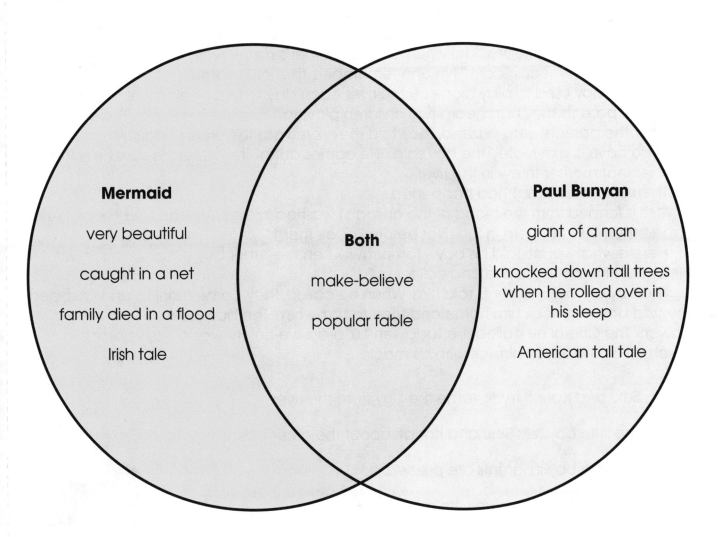

Mermaid

very beautiful

caught in a net

family died in a flood

Irish tale

Both

make-believe

popular fable

Paul Bunyan

giant of a man

knocked down tall trees when he rolled over in his sleep

American tall tale

Grade 4 - Comprehensive Curriculum

Name: _____

Sequencing: Kanati's Son

A **legend** is a story or group of stories handed down through generations. Legends are usually about an actual person.

Directions: Read about Kanati's son. Then number the events in order.

This legend is told by a tribe called the Cherokee (chair-oh-key).

Long ago, soon after the world was made, a hunter and his wife lived on a big mountain with their son. The father's name was Kanati (kah-na-tee), which means "lucky hunter." The mother's name was Selu (see-loo), which means "corn." No one remembers the son's name.

The little boy used to play alone by the river each day. One day, elders of the tribe told the boy's parents they had heard two children playing. Since their boy was the only child around, the parents were puzzled. They told their son what the elders had said.

"I do have a playmate," the boy said. "He comes out of the water. He says he is the brother that mother threw in the river."

Then Selu knew what had happened.

"He is formed from the blood of the animals I washed in the river," she told Kanati. "After you kill them, I wash them in the river before I cook them."

Here is what Kanati told his boy: "Tomorrow when the other boy comes, wrestle with him. Hold him to the ground and call for us."

The boy did as his parents told him. When he called, they came running and grabbed the wild boy. They took him home and tried to tame him. The boy grew up with magic powers. The Cherokee called this "adawehi" (ad-da-we-hi). He was always getting into mischief! But he saved himself with his magic.

_____ Selu and Kanati try to tame the boy from the river.

_____ The little boy tells Selu and Kanati about the other boy.

_____ The little boy's parents are puzzled.

_____ The new boy grows up with magic powers.

_____ The elders tell Selu and Kanati they heard two children playing.

_____ The little boy wrestles his new playmate to the ground.

Recognizing Details:
"Why Bear Has a Short Tail"

Some stories try to explain the reasons why certain things occur in nature.

Directions: Read the legend "Why Bear Has a Short Tail." Then answer the questions.

Long ago, Bear had a long tail like Fox. One winter day, Bear met Fox coming out of the woods. Fox was carrying a long string of fish. He had stolen the fish, but that is not what he told Bear.

"Where did you get those fish?" asked Bear, rubbing his paws together. Bear loved fish. It was his favorite food.

"I was out fishing and caught them," replied Fox.

Bear did not know how to fish. He had only tasted fish that others gave him. He was eager to learn to catch his own.

"Please Fox, will you tell me how to fish?" asked Bear.

So, the mean old Fox said to Bear, "Cut a hole in the ice and stick your tail in the hole. It will get cold, but soon the fish will begin to bite. When you can stand it no longer, pull your tail out. It will be covered with fish!"

"Will it hurt?" asked Bear, patting his tail.

"It will hurt some," admitted Fox. "But the longer you leave your tail in the water, the more fish you will catch."

Bear did as Fox told him. He loved fish, so he left his tail in the icy water a very, very long time. The ice froze around Bear's tail. When he pulled free, his tail remained stuck in the ice. That is why bears today have short tails.

1. How does Fox get his string of fish? _____

2. What does he tell Bear to do? _____

_____

3. Why does Bear do as Fox told him? _____

_____

4. How many fish does Bear catch? _____

5. What happens when Bear tries to pull his tail out? _____

_____

Recognizing Details:
"Why Bear Has a Short Tail"

Directions: Review the legend "Why Bear Has a Short Tail." Then answer the questions.

1. When Bear asks Fox where he got his fish, is Fox truthful in his response? Why or why not?

_____

_____

2. Why does Bear want to know how to fish? _____

_____

3. In reality, are bears able to catch their own fish? How? _____

_____

4. Is Bear very smart to believe Fox? Why or why not? _____

_____

5. How would you have told Bear to catch his own fish? _____

_____

6. What is one word you would use to describe Fox? _____

Explain your answer. _____

_____

7. What is one word you would use to describe Bear? _____

Explain your answer. _____

_____

8. Is this story realistic? _____

9. Could it have really happened? Explain your answer. _____

_____

Predicting: "How the Donkey Got Long Ears"

Directions: Write your predictions to answer these questions.

1. How do you think animals got their names? _____

_____

2. Why would it be confusing if animals did not have names? _____

_____

Directions: Read the legend "How the Donkey Got Long Ears." Then answer the questions.

In the beginning when the world was young, animals had no names. It was very confusing! A woman would say, "Tell the thingamajig to bring in the paper." The man would say, "What thingamajig?" She was talking about the dog, of course, but the man didn't know that.

Together, they decided to name the animals on their farm. First, they named their pet thingamajig Dog. They named the pink thingamajig that oinked Pig. They named the red thingamajig that crowed Rooster. They named the white thingamajig that laid eggs Hen. They named the little yellow thingamajigs that cheeped Chicks. They named the big brown thingamajig they rode Horse.

Then they came to another thingamajig. It looked like Horse, but was smaller. It would be confusing to call the smaller thingamajig Horse, they decided.

"Let's name it Donkey," said the woman. So they did.

Soon all the animals knew their names. All but Donkey, that is. Donkey kept forgetting.

"What kind of a thingamajig am I again?" he would ask the man.

"You are Donkey!" the man would answer. Each time Donkey forgot, the man tugged on Donkey's ears to help him remember.

Soon, however, Donkey would forget his name again.

"Uh, what's my name?" he would ask the woman.

She would answer, "Donkey! Donkey! Donkey!" and pull his ears each time. She was a clever woman but not very patient.

At first, the man and woman did not notice that Donkey's ears grew longer each time they were pulled. Donkey was patient but not very clever. It took him a long time to learn his name. By the time he remembered his name was Donkey, his ears were much longer than Horse's ears. That is why donkeys have long ears.

3. What words could you use to describe Donkey? _____

Explain your choice. _____

Comprehension:
"How the Donkey Got Long Ears"

Directions: Review the legend "How the Donkey Got Long Ears." Then answer the questions.

1. What do the man and woman call the animals before they have names?

   _____

2. Why do they decide to name the animals? _____

   _____

3. What is the first animal they name? _____

4. Besides being impatient, what else is the woman? _____

5. What did the people do each time they reminded Donkey of his name? _____

   _____

6. Which thingamajigs are yellow? _____

7. Which thingamajig is pink? _____

8. What is the thingamajig they ride? _____

9. Why don't they call the donkey Horse? _____

Directions: Imagine that you are the one who gets to name the animals. Write names for these new "animals."

10. A thingamajig with yellow spots that swims _____

11. A thingamajig with large ears, a short tail and six legs _____

12. A thingamajig with purple wings that flies and sings sweet melodies

   _____

13. A thingamajig that gives chocolate milk _____

   _____

Name: _____

Following Directions: Puzzling Out the Animals

Directions: Review the legend "How the Donkey Got Long Ears." Then work the puzzle.

Across:

3. Is the woman patient?
4. This thingamajig cheeps.
5. This thingamajig lays eggs.
6. Is the woman clever?
7. This thingamajig is pink.

Down:

1. This animal can't remember its name.
2. This is what the animals are called before they have names.
5. People ride this brown animal.

Grade 4 - Comprehensive Curriculum

Comprehension: "Why Owls Have Big Eyes"

Directions: Read the Native American legend "Why Owls Have Big Eyes." Then answer the questions.

Creator made all the animals, one by one. He made each one the way they wanted to look. Owl interrupted when Creator was making Rabbit.

"Whooo, whooo," he said. "Make me now. I want a long neck like Swan, red feathers like Cardinal and a sharp beak like Eagle. Make me the most beautiful bird in the world."

"Quiet!" shouted Creator. "I am making Rabbit. Turn around and wait your turn."

Creator made Rabbit's long ears and long back legs. Before he could make Rabbit's long front legs, Owl interrupted again.

"Whooo, whooo," Owl said. "Make me now. Make me the most beautiful bird in the world."

"Close your eyes. No one may watch me work," said Creator. "Wait your turn. Do not interrupt again."

Owl would not wait. He was very rude. "I will watch if I want to," he said.

"All right then," said Creator. "I will make you now."

He pushed Owl's head until it was close to his body. He shook Owl until his eyes grew big with fright. He pulled on Owl's ears so they stuck out on both sides. Then he covered Owl's feathers with mud.

"There," he said. "That's what you get for not waiting your turn. You have big ears to listen so you can hear when you are told what to do. You have big eyes, but you can't watch me with them. I work only in the day and you will be awake only at night. Your feathers will forever be the color of mud, not red like Cardinal's."

When he heard Creator's words, Owl flew away. Creator turned to finish Rabbit, but Rabbit had run away before Creator could finish his front legs or give him sharp claws to defend himself. To this day, rabbits have short front legs, are afraid of owls and cannot defend themselves. And that's why owls have short necks, big eyes, brownish feathers and ears that stick out.

1. According to this legend, who made all the animals?_____

2. Why did Rabbit run away before Creator finished making him?

_____

3. Why didn't Creator make Owl beautiful? _____

_____

4. Why are rabbits afraid of owls? _____

Review

Rudyard Kipling wrote many legends explaining such things as why bears have short tails, how the camel got his hump and why a leopard has spots. He wrote his stories in a book called *Just So Stories for Little Children*. You can find a copy of Kipling's book at the library or a bookstore.

Directions: Think about how animals look and behave. Using your wildest imagination, write a short explanation for the following situations.

1. Why the pig has a short tail _____

_____

2. How the elephant got his big ears _____

_____

3. Why birds fly _____

_____

4. Why rabbits are timid _____

_____

5. How the giraffe got a long neck _____

_____

6. How the mouse got his tail _____

_____

Directions: Illustrate one of your stories as a three- or four-panel cartoon.

Comprehension: "Why Cats and Dogs Fight"

Directions: Read the legend "Why Cats and Dogs Fight." Then answer the questions.

Long ago, Cat and Dog were friends. They played together. They ate together. They even slept near one another.

Yes, Cat and Dog got along very well! The reason was simple. All the other animals had to work for humans. But because Cat was so clean, it did not have to work. And because Dog was so loyal, it did not have to work either. Cat and Dog were the only animals who had time to play. They enjoyed themselves very much.

Everything was too good to be true! Cat and Dog wanted to make sure their lives stayed easy. They asked the old man and woman who owned them to sign a paper saying they would never have to work. That way, they would have proof that they could spend their lives at play.

The old man and woman signed the paper. Then Dog buried it in the ground with his bones. After their masters died, the other animals grew more and more jealous.

"The people aren't here any more to protect them. Why should they get off so easy?" Ox asked Cow.

"You're right," said Cow. "Let's find that paper and destroy it. Then there will be no proof that Cat and Dog can play. They will have to work like we do."

Ox and Cow looked everywhere, but they could not find the paper. Finally, they asked Rat to help. Rat sniffed and sniffed. At last, he smelled the paper. He pulled it from the ground and gave it to Ox. Ox ground it under his hoof and destroyed it. Then Dog had to go to work as a hunter. Cat had to catch mice. Cat never forgave Dog for burying the paper in a spot Rat could find. To this day, that's why cats and dogs fight.

1. Why didn't Cat have to work? _____

2. Why didn't Dog have to work? _____

3. What animals talk about finding the paper? _____

4. Who destroys the paper? _____

5. Who finds the paper? _____

Comprehension: "Why Cats and Dogs Fight"

Directions: Review the legend "Why Cats and Dogs Fight." Then answer the questions.

1. What do Cat and Dog do to make sure their life stays easy? _____

_____

_____

2. Does their plan work? _____

3. Why not? _____

4. When does the easy time stop for the cat and dog? _____

5. Cat gets mad at Dog for burying the paper in a place where Rat can easily find it. Do you think Dog also gets mad at Cat? Explain your answer.

_____

_____

6. What other animal pair could you compare to Cat and Dog? _____

7. Why did you select this animal pair? _____

8. Does the quarreling of Dog and Cat with the other animals remind you of your own quarrels with your brothers or sisters? Explain.

_____

_____

_____

9. What if Rat never found the paper? Rewrite the end of the story, beginning with these words: "And to this day, that's why cats and dogs . . ."

_____

_____

_____

Name: _____

Main Idea: "The Sly Fox"

Directions: Read the legend "The Sly Fox." Then answer the questions.

One evening, Fox met Wolf in the forest. Wolf was in a terrible mood. He felt hungry, too. So he said to Fox, "Don't move! I'm going to eat you this minute."

As he spoke, Wolf backed Fox up against a tree. Fox realized she couldn't run away. "I will have to use my wits instead of my legs," she thought to herself.

Aloud to Wolf, Fox said calmly, "I would have made a good dinner for you last year. But I've had three little babies since then. I spend all my time looking for food to feed them."

Before she could go on, Wolf interrupted. "I don't care how many children you have! I'm going to eat you right now." Wolf began closing in on Fox.

"Stop!" shouted Fox. "Look how skinny I am. I ran off all my fat looking for food for my children. But I know where you can find something that's good and fat!" Wolf backed off to listen.

"There's a well near here. In the bottom of it is a big fat piece of cheese. I don't like cheese, so it's of no use to me. Come, I'll show you."

Wolf trotted off after Fox, making sure she could not run away.

"See," said Fox when they got to the well.

Inside was what looked like a round yellow piece of cheese. It was really the moon's reflection, but Wolf didn't know this. Wolf leaned over the well, wondering how to get the cheese. Fox jumped up quickly and pushed Wolf in.

"I am a sly, old thing," Fox chuckled as she trotted home to her children. And to this day, that's why foxes are sly.

1. What is the main idea of this legend? (Check one.)

_____ Fox is cornered but uses her wits to outsmart Wolf and save her own life.

_____ Wolf is in a terrible mood and wants to eat Fox.

_____ Wolf thinks the moon was made of cheese.

2. Why did Fox say she will not make a good meal for Wolf? _____

_____

_____

3. What happens to Wolf at the end? _____

_____

Recognizing Details: "The Sly Fox"

Directions: Review the legend "The Sly Fox." Then answer the questions.

1. What are three events in the story that show Wolf's bad mood? _____

_____

_____

_____

2. What does Fox say she will have to use to get away from Wolf? _____

3. Where does Fox tell Wolf he can find a nice fat meal? _____

_____

4. How does Fox finally rid herself of Wolf? _____

5. What does Fox say as she trots home? _____

6. Have you ever been in a situation where you used words to solve a problem instead of fighting with someone? Write about it.

_____

_____

_____

7. In addition to teaching why foxes are sly, what other lesson does this story teach?

_____

_____

_____

_____

_____

Name: _____

Comprehension: "King of the Beasts"

Directions: Read the legend "King of the Beasts." Then answer the questions.

Once, a shy little rabbit was sleeping under a palm tree. Suddenly, a coconut fell and startled the rabbit awake. The rabbit began to twitch and worry.

"What was that awful noise?" he said. He looked around but didn't see the coconut. "The Earth must be breaking apart. Oh dear, oh dear, oh dear."

The little rabbit began running in circles. Soon a monkey joined him.

"Why are you running?" the monkey asked, trotting along beside the rabbit.

"The Earth is breaking apart, and I'm trying to escape," panted the little rabbit.

They were joined by a deer, a fox and an elephant. When they heard the Earth was breaking up, they all followed the rabbit. Soon a huge herd of animals was running in a circle.

"What's going on?" roared the lion to the elephant when he saw the herd.

"The Earth is breaking up!" shouted the elephant. "We are trying to escape."

The lion looked around. Except for all the dust, everything looked fine.

"Who said the Earth is breaking up?" he roared back to the elephant.

"The fox told me!" the elephant replied.

The lion asked the fox, and the fox said the deer told him. The deer said the monkey had told him. Finally, the lion traced the story to the rabbit.

"Show me the place!" the lion demanded.

The rabbit led the lion back to the palm tree. Right away, the lion saw the coconut on the ground.

"Silly rabbit!" he roared. "What you heard was a coconut falling. Go and tell the other animals they are safe."

The rabbit rushed to tell the other animals. They stopped running.

"The lion is smart!" said the monkey. "Let's name him 'King of the Beasts.' " So they did.

1. What kind of tree is the rabbit sleeping under? _____

2. Why does he think the Earth is breaking up? _____

_____

_____

3. Which animal is the first to join the rabbit? _____

4. What does the lion call the rabbit? _____

5. Who suggests naming the lion "King of the Beasts"? _____

Comprehension: "King of the Beasts"

Directions: Review the legend "King of the Beasts." Then answer the questions.

1. How does the lion become "King of the Beasts"? _____

_____

2. Instead of panicking about the Earth breaking apart, what should the rabbit have done?

_____

_____

_____

3. Instead of following the rabbit around in a circle, what should the monkey, deer and fox have done?

_____

_____

_____

4. Do you think naming the lion "King of the Beasts" was a good idea? Why or why not?

_____

_____

_____

5. What does this story teach you about peer pressure? Explain.

_____

_____

_____

_____

Grade 4 - Comprehensive Curriculum

Recognizing Details: "Lazy Sheep"

Directions: Read the poem about the lazy sheep. Then answer the questions.

"Lazy sheep, please tell me why

In the grassy field you lie?

You eat and sleep away your day

While people work and sweat for pay!"

"Boy, do not talk to me so mean!"

Replied the sheep, so white he gleamed.

"I'm busy growing wool that's new

To spin into some clothes for you!"

The boy looked sad, his face got red.

"I'm sorry for the things I said!"

1. Why does the boy accuse the sheep of being lazy? _____

_____

2. What is the sheep actually doing? _____

_____

3. Where does the boy see the sheep? _____

_____

4. Why does the boy look sad? _____

_____

5. How does the boy apologize? _____

_____

Name: _____

Main Idea: "The Mouse"

Directions: Read the story "The Mouse." Then answer the questions.

One day when the cat and mouse were playing, the cat bit off the mouse's tail.
"Ouch!" cried the mouse. "Give me back my tail this instant!"

"I'll give your tail back when you go to the cow and bring me some milk!" replied the cat.

She held the mouse's tail high so the mouse could not reach it.

Right away, the mouse went to ask the cow for milk.

"I'll give you milk if you go to the farmer and get me some hay," said the cow.

When the mouse asked the farmer for hay, he said: "I'll give you hay if you go to the butcher and get me some meat."

The mouse wanted her tail back, so she went to the butcher. "I'll give you meat if you go to the baker and bring me some bread," said the butcher.

The mouse went to the baker, who said, "I'll give you bread. But if you get into my grain, I'll cut off your head!" The mouse quickly promised never to get into the baker's grain.

Then the baker gave the mouse bread. The mouse gave the bread to the butcher and the butcher gave the mouse meat. The mouse gave the meat to the farmer and the farmer gave the mouse hay. The mouse gave the hay to the cow and the cow gave the mouse milk. The mouse gave the cat milk and—finally!—the mouse got her tail back!

1. The main idea is: (Check one.)

_____ To get what you want, you must be persistent.

_____ A mouse's tail is worth a lot of work to a mouse.

_____ Everybody is greedy, especially the baker.

2. What does the mouse promise the baker never to get into?_____

Directions: Fill in the blanks to show the steps the mouse follows to get her tail back.

3. She gets bread from the baker and gives it to _____ .

4. She gets meat from the butcher and gives it to _____ .

5. She gets hay from the farmer and gives it to _____ .

6. She gets milk from the cow and gives it to _____ .

7. That's when she _____

Sequencing: "The Mouse"

Directions: Review the story of "The Mouse." Then answer the questions.

1. Why do you think the cat does not simply give the tail back to the mouse when he asks for it?

   _____

   _____

   _____

2. Have you ever done anything similar to a brother, sister or friend when they asked for something? Explain.

   _____

   _____

   _____

   _____

Directions: List the things the mouse has to do to get his tail back.

First _____

   _____

Second _____

   _____

Third _____

   _____

Fourth _____

   _____

Fifth _____

   _____

Animal Legend Organizer

Directions: Follow the instructions to write a legend of your own.

1. Select one of the following titles for your legend. Circle the one you plan to use.

How the Tiger Got Stripes   How the Elephant Got a Tusk

How the Giraffe Got a Long Neck   How the Kangaroo Got Her Pouch

How the Gazelle Got Twisty Horns   Why the Pig Has a Short Tail

How the Elephant Got Big Ears   Why Birds Fly

Why Rabbits Are Timid   How the Giraffe Got a Long Neck

How the Mouse Got a Long Tail   Why Fish Swim

2. Briefly explain the type of conflict that will be in your legend. _____

_____

_____

3. Write words and phrases to show events you plan to include in your legend. _____

_____

_____

4. Summarize how you plan to settle the conflict or solve the problem. _____

_____

_____

Directions: Write your legend. Give it a title. Illustrate it if you like.

_____

_____

_____

_____

_____

_____

Review

Directions: Review the fables and legends you read. Then write your answers.

1. Explain how "The Mouse" and "The Sly Fox" are similar stories. _____

_____

_____

_____

2. Explain how "King of the Beasts" and "The Sheep" are different. _____

_____

_____

_____

3. Compare and contrast the rabbit to the mouse. _____

_____

_____

_____

4. Compare and contrast one animal legend with one animal fable. _____

_____

_____

_____

5. Read one of Kipling's *Just So Stories*. Write your reaction to the story. _____

_____

_____

Sequencing: "Mr. Nobody"

Directions: After reading the poem "Mr. Nobody," number in order the things people blame him for.

I know a funny little man
As quiet as a mouse,
Who does the mischief that is done
In everybody's house!
No one ever sees his face.
And yet we all agree
That every plate we break was cracked
By Mr. Nobody.

It's he who always tears out books,
Who leaves the door ajar,
He pulls the buttons from our shirts,
And scatters pins afar;
That squeaking door will always squeak,
The reason is, you see,
We leave the oiling to be done
By Mr. Nobody.

The finger marks upon the wall
By none of us are made;
We never leave the blinds unclosed,
To let the carpet fade.
The bowl of soup we do not spill,
It's not our fault, you see
These mishaps—every one is caused
By Mr. Nobody.

_____ Putting finger marks on walls   _____ Scattering pins

_____ Leaving the door ajar   _____ Breaking plates

_____ Spilling soup   _____ Pulling buttons off shirts

_____ Tearing out books   _____ Squeaking doors

_____ Leaving the blinds open

Comprehension: "The Chickens"

Directions: Read the poem "The Chickens." Then answer the questions.

Said the first little chicken
With a queer little squirm,
"I wish I could find
A fat little worm!"

Said the next little chicken
With an odd little shrug.
"I wish I could find
A fat little bug!"

Said the third little chicken
With a small sigh of grief,
"I wish I could find
A green little leaf!"

Said the fourth little chicken
With a faint little moan,
"I wish I could find
A small gravel stone!"

"See here!" said the mother
From the green garden patch,
"If you want any breakfast,
Just come here and scratch!"

1. What does the second little chicken want? _____

2. Which meal are all the chickens wishing for? _____

3. Where is the mother hen? _____

4. Which of the following do the chickens not want?

    _____ leaf   _____ corn   _____ worm   _____ bug   _____ stone

5. What does the mother hen tell her chicks to do if they want breakfast?

    _____

Following Directions: "I'm Glad"

Directions: Read the poem "I'm Glad." Then work the puzzle.

I'm glad the sky is painted blue
And the Earth is painted green,
With such a lot of nice fresh air
All sandwiched in between.

Across:

3. The sky is painted this color.

4. How what we breathe is placed between the Earth and sky

6. This is what we breathe, and it's between the Earth and sky.

Down:

1. The color of the Earth in the poem

2. How the speaker feels

4. Painted blue

5. Painted green

Name: _____

Comprehension: "Over the Hills and Far Away"

Directions: Read "Over the Hills and Far Away." Then answer the questions.

Tom, Tom the piper's son,
Learned to play when he was one,
But the only tune that he could play
Was "Over the Hills and Far Away."

Now Tom with his pipe made such a noise
That he pleased the girls and he pleased the boys,
And they all danced when they heard him play
"Over the Hills and Far Away."

Tom played his pipe with such great skill,
Even pigs and dogs could not keep still.
The dogs would wag their tails and dance,
The pigs would oink and grunt and prance.

Yes, Tom could play, his music soared—
But soon the pigs and dogs got bored.
The children, too, thought it was wrong,
For Tom to play just one dull song.

1. How old is Tom when he learns to play? _____

2. What tune does Tom play? _____

_____

3. What do the dogs do when Tom plays? _____

_____

4. Why does everyone get tired of Tom's music? _____

_____

5. What do the pigs do when Tom plays? _____

_____

6. What instrument does Tom play? _____

Sequencing: "The Spider and the Fly"

Directions: Read the poem "The Spider and the Fly." Then number the events in order.

"Won't you come into my parlor?" said the spider to the fly.
"It's the nicest little parlor that you will ever spy.
The way into my parlor is up a winding stair.
I have so many pretty things to show you inside there."

The little fly said, "No! No! No! To do so is not sane.
For those who travel up your stair do not come down again."

The spider turned himself around and went back in his den—
He knew for sure the silly fly would visit him again.
The spider wove a tiny web, for he was very sly
He was making preparations to trap the silly fly.

Then out his door the spider came and merrily did sing,
"Oh, fly, oh lovely, lovely fly with pearl and silver wings."

Alas! How quickly did the fly come buzzing back to hear
The spider's words of flattery, which drew the fly quite near.

The fly was trapped within the web, the spider's winding stair,
Then the spider jumped upon him, and ate the fly right there!

_____ The spider sings a song about how beautiful the fly is.

_____ The spider jumps on the fly.

_____ The spider invites the fly into his parlor.

_____ The spider spins a tiny new web to catch the fly.

_____ The fly becomes caught in the spider's web.

_____ The fly says he knows it's dangerous to go into the spider's parlor.

_____ The spider eats the fly.

_____ The fly comes near the web to hear the song.

Comprehension: "Grasshopper Green"

Directions: Read the poem "Grasshopper Green." Then answer the questions.

Grasshopper Green is a comical guy,
He lives on the best of fare.
Bright little trousers, jacket and cap,
These are his summer wear.

Out in the meadow he loves to go,
Playing away in the sun.
It's hopperty, skipperty, high and low,
Summer's the time for fun.

Grasshopper Green has a cute little house,
He stays near it every day.
It's under the hedge where he is safe,
Out of the gardener's way.

Gladly he's calling the children to play
Out in the beautiful sun
It's hopperty, skipperty, high and low,
Summer's the time for fun.

1. What does **comical** mean in this poem?_____

2. What are three things Grasshopper Green wears in the summer?

_____

3. Where does he love to go and play?_____

4. Whom does Grasshopper Green call to play? _____

5. What is summer the time for?_____

6. Use a dictionary. What does **fare** mean in this poem? _____

7. You won't find the words **hopperty** and **skipperty** in a dictionary. Based on the poem, write your own definitions of these words.

_____

_____

Main Idea: "Little Robin Redbreast"

Directions: Read the poem "Little Robin Redbreast." Then answer the questions.

Little Robin Redbreast
Sat up in a tree,
Up went the kitty cat
Down went he.

Down came the kitty cat—
Away Robin ran,
Said little Robin Redbreast,
"Catch me if you can."

Then Little Robin Redbreast
Hopped upon a wall,
Kitty cat jumped after him,
And almost had a fall.

Little Robin chirped and sang,
And what did kitty say?
Kitty cat said, "Meow!" quite loud,
And Robin flew away.

1. What is the main idea? (Check one.)

_____ The robin is smarter than the cat and a lot faster, too.

_____ When people see a robin, it means spring is near.

_____ The robin is scared away.

2. What nearly happens when the cat jumps on the wall?

_____

3. Where is the robin when the cat first goes after him? _____

4. Where does the robin go after the cat climbs the tree? _____

5. What does the robin say to the cat? _____

Sequencing: "Hickory, Dickory, Dock"

Directions: Read the poem "Hickory, Dickory, Dock." Then answer the questions.

Hickory, dickory, dock,
The mouse ran up the clock.
The clock struck one,
And down he run,
Hickory, dickory, dock.

Dickory, dickory, dare,
The pig flew in the air.
The man in brown
Soon brought him down,
Dickory, dickory, dare.

Hickory
Dickory
Dock

1. What is the main idea? (Check one.)

_____ Mice and pigs can cause a lot of problems
to clocks and men in brown suits.

_____ There is no main idea. This poem is just for fun.

_____ Beware of mice in your clocks and flying pigs.

2. Why do you think the mouse runs down the clock? _____

_____

Directions: Number these events in order.

_____ The clock strikes one.

_____ The mouse runs back down the clock.

_____ The mouse runs up the clock.

_____ The man in brown brings the pig down.

_____ The pig flies in the air.

Review

Directions: Review the poems you read. Then answer the questions.

1. How is the spider in the poem "The Spider and the Fly" like the fox in the fable "The Fox and the Crow"?

_____

_____

_____

2. Which of the poems that you read did you like the best? _____

   Why? _____

   _____

   _____

3. Which of the poems that you read did you like the least? _____

   Why? _____

   _____

   _____

   _____

One way to remember what you read is to make a comic strip of the story or poem. Think about the poem "Mr. Nobody." Imagine what "Mr. Nobody" would look like.

Directions: Follow the sequence of events in the "Mr. Nobody" poem to make a cartoon of the poem in the boxes below

Name: _____

Following Directions: Early Native Americans

Directions: Read about the early Native Americans. Then work the puzzle.

There were about 300 Native American tribes in North America when the first white settlers came to New England in the 1500s. These Native Americans loved and respected the earth. They hunted buffalo on the plains. They fished in the clear rivers. They planted corn and beans on the rich land. They gathered roots and herbs. Before the white settlers drove them out, the Native Americans were masters of the land and all its riches.

The Native Americans grew crops, hunted for food, made clothing and built their homes from what they found on the land in the area where they lived. That is why each tribe of Native Americans was different. Some Native Americans lived in special tents called tepees. Some lived in adobe pueblos. Some lived in simple huts called hogans.

Across:

2. Native American homes made of adobe
3. Native Americans hunted this animal.
4. Tents some Native Americans lived in

Down:

1. Huts some Native Americans lived in
4. There were this many hundred tribes of Native Americans when settlers came.
5. All the tribes loved the _____.

Comprehension: The Pueblo People

Directions: Read about the Pueblo people. Then answer the questions.

Long ago, Native Americans occupied all the land that is now Arizona, New Mexico, Utah and parts of California and Colorado. Twenty-five different tribes lived in this southwestern area. Several of the tribes lived in villages called pueblos. The Hopi (hope-ee) Indians lived in pueblos. So did the Zuñi (zoo-nee) and the Laguna (lah-goon-nah). These and other tribes who lived in villages were called the "Pueblo people."

When it was time for the Pueblo people to plant crops, everyone helped. The men kept the weeds pulled. Native Americans prayed for rain to make their crops grow. As part of their worship, they also had special dances called rain dances. When it was time for harvest, the women helped.

The land was bountiful to the Pueblo people. They grew many different crops. They planted beans, squash and 19 different kinds of corn. They gathered wild nuts and berries. They hunted for deer and rabbits. They also traded with other tribes for things they could not grow or hunt.

The Pueblo people lived in unusual houses. Their homes were made of adobe brick. Adobe is a type of mud. They shaped the mud into bricks, dried them, then built with them. Many adobe homes exist today in the Southwest.

The adobe homes of long ago had no doors. The Pueblo people entered through a type of trapdoor at the top. The homes were three or four stories high. The ground floor had no windows and was used for storage. These adobe homes were clustered around a central plaza. Each village had several clusters of homes. Villages also had two or three clubhouses where people could gather for celebrations. Each village also had places for worship.

1. What were the five states where the Pueblo people lived? _____

_____

2. What were three crops the Pueblo people grew? _____

_____

3. The early pueblo houses had no

☐ yards. ☐ windows. ☐ doors.

Recognizing Details: The Pueblo People

"At the edge of the world
It grows light.
The trees stand shining."
(Pueblo poem)

Directions: Read more about the Pueblo people. Then answer the questions.

The Pueblo people were peaceful. They loved nature, and they seldom fought in wars. When they did fight, it was to protect their people or their land. Their dances, too, were gentle. The Pueblo people danced to ask the gods to bring rain or sunshine. Sometimes they asked the gods to help the women have children.

Some Native Americans wore masks when they danced. The masks were called kachinas (ka-chee-nas). They represented the faces of dead ancestors. (Ancestors are all the family members who have lived and died before.)

The Pueblo people were talented at crafts. The men of many tribes made beautiful jewelry. The women made pottery and painted it with beautiful colors. They traded some of the things they made with people from other tribes.

Both boys and girls needed their parents' permission to marry. After they married, they were given a room next to the bride's mother. If the marriage did not work out, sometimes the groom moved back home again.

1. Among the Pueblo people, who made jewelry? _____

2. Who made pottery? _____

3. What did some of the Pueblo people wear when they danced? _____

_____

4. Why did the Pueblo people dance for the gods? _____

_____

5. Where did newly married couples live? _____

_____

6. Why would a man move back home after marriage? _____

_____

Recognizing Details: The Pueblo People

Directions: Review what you learned about the Pueblo people. Then answer the questions.

1. How many different tribes lived in the Southwestern part of the United States? _____

2. The article specifically names three of the Pueblo tribes. Where could you find the names of the other Pueblo tribes?

_____

_____

3. How did the Pueblo people build their adobe homes? _____

_____

4. How did the location and climate affect their lifestyle? _____

_____

_____

_____

5. How were the jobs of the men and women of a Pueblo tribe alike? _____

_____

_____

6. How were their jobs different? _____

_____

7. How do the responsibilities of the Pueblo men and women discussed differ from those of men and women today?

_____

_____

_____

_____

Name: _____

Comprehension: A California Tribe

Directions: Read about the Yuma. Then answer the questions.

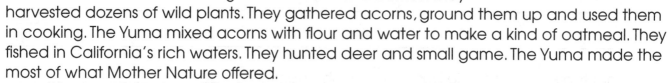

California was home to many Native Americans. The weather was warm, and food was plentiful. California was an ideal place to live.

One California tribe that made good use of the land was the Yuma. The Yuma farmed and gathered roots and berries. They harvested dozens of wild plants. They gathered acorns, ground them up and used them in cooking. The Yuma mixed acorns with flour and water to make a kind of oatmeal. They fished in California's rich waters. They hunted deer and small game. The Yuma made the most of what Mother Nature offered.

The Yuma lived in huts. The roofs were made of dirt. The walls were made of grass. Some Yuma lived together in big round buildings made with poles and woven grasses. As many as 50 people lived in these large homes.

Like other tribes, the Yuma made crafts. Their woven baskets were especially beautiful. The women also wove cradles, hats, bowls and other useful items for the tribe.

When it was time to marry, a boy's parents chose a 15-year-old girl for him. The girl was a Yuma, too, but from another village. Except for the chief, each man took only one wife.

When a Yuma died, a big ceremony was held. The Yumas had great respect for death. After someone died, his or her name was never spoken again.

1. What were two reasons why California was an ideal place to live?

_____

_____

2. What did the Yuma use acorns for? _____

_____

3. What was a beautiful craft made by the Yuma? _____

4. How old was a Yuma bride? _____

5. What types of homes did the Yuma live in? _____

6. How did the Yuma feel about death? _____

_____

Recognizing Details: The Yuma

Directions: Review what you read about the Yuma. Write the answers.

1. How did the Yuma make good use of the land?

_____

_____

2. How were the Yuma like the Pueblo people? _____

_____

_____

3. How were they different? _____

_____

_____

4. Why did the Yuma have homes different than those of the Pueblo tribes?

_____

_____

5. When it was time for a young Yuma man to marry, his parents selected a fifteen-year-old bride for him from another tribe. Do you think this is a good idea? Why or why not?

_____

_____

6. Why do you suppose the Yuma never spoke a person's name after he/she died?

_____

_____

7. Do you think this would be an easy thing to do? Explain your answer. _____

_____

Name: _____

Following Directions: Sailor Native Americans

Directions: Read about the Sailor Native Americans of Puget Sound. Then work the puzzle.

Three tribes lived on Puget (pew-jit) Sound in Washington state. They made their living from the sea. People later called them the "Sailor" Indians.

These Native Americans fished for salmon. They trapped the salmon in large baskets. Sometimes they used large nets. The sea was filled with fish. Their nets rarely came up empty.

The Sailor Native Americans also gathered roots and berries. They hunted deer, black bear and ducks.

Their homes were amazing! They built big wooden buildings without nails. They did not use saws to cut the wood. The walls and roofs were tied together. Each building had different homes inside. As many as 50 families lived in each big building.

Across:

1. The three tribes on Puget Sound were called the "_____" Native Americans.

2. The _____ and roofs of their buildings were tied together.

4. Because their buildings were tied together, they did not need ____.

Down:

1. Type of fish the "Sailor" Native Americans caught

3. As many as _____ families could live in their big buildings.

5. The buildings were put together without using _____ to cut the wood.

Following Directions: Sailor Native Americans

Directions: Review what you read about the Sailor Native Americans. Write your answers.

1. How were the housing arrangements of the Puget Sound Native Americans similar to those of the Yuma?

   _____

2. How was the diet of the Sailor Native Americans like those of the Yuma and Pueblo?

   _____

3. How was it different? _____

   _____

4. The Sailor Native Americans made a living from the sea, and their nets were rarely empty. What type of transportation do you think these Native Americans used to get their nets to the sea?

   _____

5. Where could you find more information on this group of Native Americans to check your answer?

   _____

6. Verify your answer. Were you correct? _____

7. Who do you think performed the many tasks in the Sailor village? Write men, women, boys and/or girls for your answers.

   Built homes? _____   Made fishing baskets? _____

   Fished? _____   Gathered roots and berries? _____

   Hunted game? _____   Made fishing nets? _____

8. The homes of the Sailor Native Americans could be compared to what type of modern dwelling?

   _____

Grade 4 - Comprehensive Curriculum

Review

Review what you read about Native Americans. Then answer the questions.

1. Of the tribes discussed, which one would you most like to have been a member of? Explain your answer.

_____

_____

2. Why did each of the tribes have a different lifestyle? _____

_____

_____

3. How did their location influence how each of the tribes functioned? _____

_____

_____

Directions: Select two of the Native American tribes you read about. Compare and contrast their homes, clothing and lifestyle in the Venn diagram. Write words and phrases that were unique to one group or the other in the correct parts of the circle. Write words and phrases that are common to both groups in the section where the circles intersect.

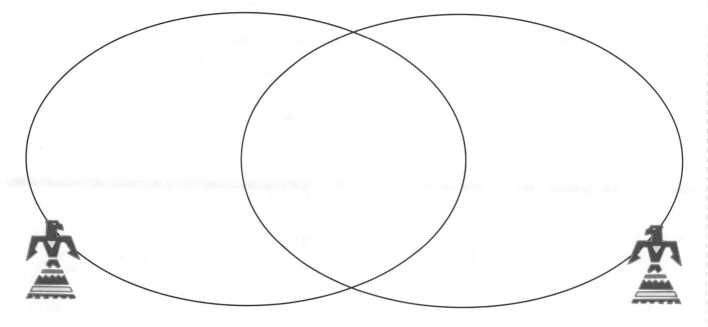

Name: _____

Reading Comprehension: Hummingbirds

Hummingbirds are very small birds. This tiny bird is quite an acrobat. Only a few birds, such as kingfishers and sunbirds, can hover, which means to stay in one place in the air. But no other bird can match the flying skills of the hummingbird. The hummingbird can hover, fly backward and fly upside down!

Hummingbirds got their name because their wings move very quickly when they fly. This causes a humming sound. Their wings move so fast that you can't see them at all. This takes a lot of energy. These little birds must have food about every 20 minutes to have enough strength to fly. Their favorite foods are insects and nectar. Nectar is the sweet water deep inside a flower. Hummingbirds use their long, thin bills to drink from flowers. When a hummingbird sips nectar, it hovers in front of a flower. It never touches the flower with its wings or feet.

Besides being the best at flying, the hummingbird is also one of the prettiest birds. Of all the birds in the world, the hummingbird's colors are among the brightest. Some are bright green with red and white markings. Some are purple. One kind of hummingbird can change its color from reddish-brown to purple to red!

The hummingbird's nest is special, too. It looks like a tiny cup. The inside of the nest is very soft. This is because one of the things the mother bird uses to build the nest is the silk from a spider's web.

Directions: Answer these questions about hummingbirds.

1. How did hummingbirds get their name? _____

_____

2. What does **hover** mean? _____

3. How often do hummingbirds need to eat? _____

4. Name two things that hummingbirds eat. _____

5. What is one of the things a mother hummingbird uses to build her nest?

_____

Name: _____

Reading Comprehension: Bats

Bats are the only mammals that can fly. They have wings made of thin skin stretched between long fingers. Bats can fly amazing distances. Some small bats have been known to fly more than 25 miles in one night.

Most bats eat insects or fruit. But some eat only fish, others only blood and still others the nectar and pollen of flowers that bloom at night. Bats are active only at night. They sleep during the day in caves or other dark places. At rest, they always hang with their heads down.

You may have heard the expression "blind as a bat." But bats are not blind. They don't, however, use their eyes to guide their flight or to find the insects they eat. A bat makes a high-pitched squeak, then waits for the echo to return to it. This echo tells it how far away an object is. This is often called the bat's sonar system. Using this system, a bat can fly through a dark cave without bumping into anything. Hundreds of bats can fly about in the dark without ever running into each other. They do not get confused by the squeaks of the other bats. They always recognize their own echoes.

Directions: Answer these questions about bats.

1. Bats are the only mammals that
    ☐ eat insects.   ☐ fly.   ☐ live in caves.

2. Most bats eat
    ☐ plants.   ☐ other animals.   ☐ fruits and insects.

3. Bats always sleep
    ☐ with their heads down.   ☐ lying down.   ☐ during the night.

4. Bats are blind.   True   False

5. Bats use a built-in sonar system to guide them.   True   False

6. Bats are confused by the squeaks of other bats.   True   False

Review: Venn Diagram

Directions: Make a Venn diagram comparing hummingbirds (see page 143) and bats (see page 144). Refer to the sample diagram on page 105 to help you. Write at least three characteristics for each section of the diagram.

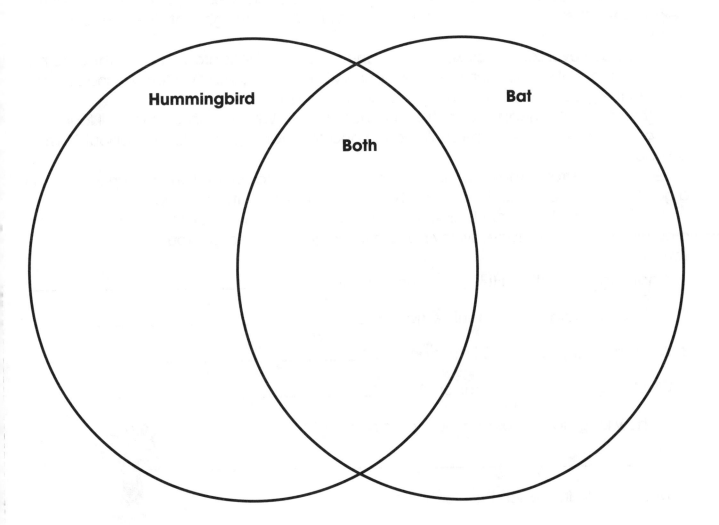

Hummingbird

Both

Bat

Name: _____

Recognizing Details: Giraffes

Directions: Read about giraffes. Then answer the questions.

Giraffes are tall, beautiful, graceful animals that live in Africa. When they are grown, male giraffes are about 18 feet tall. Adult females are about 14 feet tall.

Giraffes are not fat animals, but because they are so big, they weigh a lot. The average male weighs 2,800 pounds. Females weigh about 400 pounds less. Giraffes reach their full height when they are four years old. They continue to gain weight until they are about eight years old.

If you have ever seen giraffes, you know their necks and legs are very long. They are not awkward, though! Giraffes can move very quickly. They like to jump over fences and streams. They do this gracefully. They do not trip over their long legs.

If they are frightened, they can run 35 miles an hour. When giraffes gallop, all four feet are sometimes off the ground! Usually, young and old giraffes pace along at about 10 miles an hour.

Giraffes are strong. They can use their back legs as weapons. A lion can run faster than a giraffe, but a giraffe can kill a lion with one quick kick from its back legs.

Giraffes do not look scary. Their long eyelashes make them look gentle. They usually have a curious look on their faces. Many people think they are cute. Do you?

1. What is the weight of a full-grown male giraffe? _____

2. What is the weight of an adult female? _____

3. When does a giraffe run 35 miles an hour? _____

4. What do giraffes use as weapons? _____

5. For how long do giraffes continue to gain weight?

_____

6. When do giraffes reach their full height?

_____

7. Use a dictionary. What does **gallop** mean?

_____

_____

Name: _____

Comprehension: More About Giraffes

Directions: Read more about giraffes. Then answer the questions.

Most people don't notice, but giraffes have different patterns of spots. Certain species of giraffes have small spots. Other species have large spots. Some species have spots that are very regular. You can tell where one spot ends and another begins. Other species have spots that are kind of blotchy. This means the spots are not set off from each other as clearly. There are many other kinds of spot patterns. The pattern of a giraffe's spots is called "markings." No two giraffes have exactly the same markings.

There is one very rare type of giraffe. It is totally black! Have you ever seen one? This kind of giraffe is called a melanistic (mell-an-iss-tick) giraffe. The name comes from the word "melanin," which is the substance in cells that gives them color. Giraffes' spots help them blend in with their surroundings. A black giraffe would not blend in well with tree trunks and leaves. Maybe that is why they are so rare.

Being able to blend with surroundings helps animals survive. If a lion can't see a giraffe, he certainly can't eat it. This is called "protective coloration." The animal's color helps protect it.

Another protection giraffes have is their keen eyesight. Their large eyes are on the sides of their heads. Giraffes see anything that moves. They can see another animal a mile away! It is very hard to sneak up on a giraffe. Those who try usually get a quick kick with a powerful back leg.

1. What are markings? _____

2. How far away can a giraffe see another animal? _____

3. Where are a giraffe's eyes? _____

4. What is protective coloration? _____

5. What color is the very rare type of giraffe? _____

6. How do giraffes protect themselves? _____

7. How many kinds of spot patterns do giraffes have? ☐ two ☐ four ☐ many

8. Use a dictionary. What does **species** mean? _____

_____

_____

Grade 4 - Comprehensive Curriculum

Name: _____

Following Directions: Puzzling Out Giraffes

Directions: Review what you read about giraffes. Read more about giraffes below. Then work the puzzle.

Have you noticed that giraffes have a curious look? That is because they are always paying attention. Their lives depend upon it! Giraffes cannot save themselves from a lion if they don't see it. Giraffes look around a lot. Even when they are chewing their food, they are checking to see if danger is near.

By nature, giraffes are gentle. They do not attack unless they are in danger. A giraffe will lower its head when it is angry. It will open its nostrils and its mouth. Then watch out!

Across:

2. How a giraffe feels when it lowers its head and opens its nose and mouth

4. Giraffes look this way because they are always paying attention.

6. By nature, giraffes are _____.

7. The continent where giraffes live

9. Another name for a black giraffe is

_____.

Down:

1. The patterns of a giraffe's spots

3. An animal's ability to blend with surroundings is called protective _____.

5. _____ means a certain kind of animal.

8. Giraffes' eyes are so keen they can see another animal a mile _____.

10. Are giraffes often mean?

Recognizing Details: Giraffes

Directions: Review what you learned about giraffes. Then answer the questions.

1. How are a giraffe's spots helpful? _____

_____

2. Is it easy to sneak up on a giraffe? Why not? _____

_____

3. What makes a giraffe look so gentle? _____

_____

4. How do you know when a giraffe is angry? _____

_____

5. Do you think a giraffe in a zoo is as observant as a giraffe in the wilds of Africa? Why or why not?

_____

_____

6. Do you think giraffes have any other enemies besides lions? _____

What animals might they be? _____

_____

7. Why do you suppose giraffes grow so large? _____

_____

8. Use a dictionary. What does **habitat** mean? Describe the giraffe's natural habitat.

_____

_____

Comprehension: Wild Horses

Directions: Read about wild horses. Then answer the questions.

Have you ever heard of a car called a Mustang? It is named after a type of wild horse.

In the 1600s, the Spanish explorers who came to North America brought horses with them. Some of these horses escaped onto the prairies and plains. With no one to feed them or ride them, they became wild. Their numbers quickly grew, and they roamed in herds. They ran free and ate grass on the prairie.

Later, when the West was settled, people needed horses. They captured wild ones. This was not easy to do. Wild horses could run very fast. They did not want to be captured!

Some men made their living by capturing wild horses, taming them and selling them. These men were called "mustangers." Can you guess why?

After cars were invented, people did not need as many horses. Not as many mustangers were needed to catch them. More and more wild horses roamed the western prairies. In 1925, about a million mustangs were running loose.

The government was worried that the herds would eat too much grass. Ranchers who owned big herds of cattle complained that their animals didn't have enough to eat because the mustangs ate all the grass. Permission was given to ranchers and others to kill many of the horses. Thousands were killed and sold to companies that made them into pet food.

Now, wild horses live in only 12 states. The largest herds are in California, New Mexico, Oregon, Wyoming and Nevada. Most people who live in these states never see wild horses. The herds live away from people in the distant plains and mountains. They are safer there.

1. What is one type of wild horse called? _____

2. What were men called who captured wild horses? _____

3. About how many wild horses were running free in the U.S. in 1925? _____

4. The wild mustangs were killed and turned into ☐ cars. ☐ pet food. ☐ lunch meat.

5. The largest herds of wild horses are now in

☐ Oregon. ☐ Ohio. ☐ New Mexico. ☐ Wyoming.

☐ California. ☐ Nevada. ☐ Kansas. ☐ Arkansas.

Name: _____

Main Idea: More About Wild Horses

Directions: Read more about wild horses. Then answer the questions.

Have you noticed that in any large group, one person seems to be the leader? This is true for wild horses, too. The leader of a band of wild horses is a stallion. Stallions are adult male horses.

The stallion's job is important. He watches out for danger. If a bear or other animal comes close, he lets out a warning cry. This helps keep the other horses safe. Sometimes they all run away together. Other times, the stallion protects the other horses. He shows his teeth. He rears up on his back legs. Often, he scares the other animal away. Then the horses can safely continue eating grass.

Much of the grass on the prairies is gone now. Wild horses must move around a lot to find new grass. They spend about half their time eating and looking for food. If they cannot find prairie grass, wild horses will eat tree bark. They will eat flowers. If they can't find these either, wild horses will eat anything that grows!

Wild horses also need plenty of water. It is often hot in the places where they roam. At least twice a day, they find streams and take long, long drinks. Like people, wild horses lose water when they sweat. They run and sweat a lot in hot weather. To survive, they need as much water as they can get.

Wild horses also use water another way. When they find deep water, they wade into it. It feels good! It cools their skin.

1. What is the main idea? (Check one.)

_____ Wild horses need plenty of water.

_____ Wild horses move in bands protected by a stallion.

_____ Wild horses eat grass.

2. What are two reasons why wild horses need water? _____

_____

3. Why do wild horses move around so much? _____

4. What do wild horses most like to eat? _____

5. What do wild horses spend half their time doing? _____

_____

Recognizing Details: Wild Horses

Directions: Review what you read about wild horses. Then answer the questions.

1. How did horses come to North America and become wild? _____

_____

2. Why is it so difficult to capture, tame and train wild horses? _____

_____

3. Do you think it was right of the government to allow the killing of wild horses? _____

   Explain your answer. _____

_____

4. Do you think the remaining wild horses should be protected? _____

   Explain your answer. _____

_____

5. What is the role of the lead stallion in a wild horse herd? _____

_____

6. What are some things wild horses have in common with giraffes? _____

_____

_____

_____

7. What do you think will happen to wild horses as the prairie lands continue to disappear as a result of developments for homes and businesses?

_____

_____

_____

Reading Comprehension: Oceans

If you looked at Earth from up in space, you would see a planet that is mostly blue. This is because more than two-thirds of Earth is covered with water. You already know that this is what makes our planet different from the others, and what makes life on Earth possible. Most of this water is in the four great oceans: Pacific, Atlantic, Indian and Arctic. The Pacific is by far the largest and the deepest. It is more than twice as big as the Atlantic, the second largest ocean.

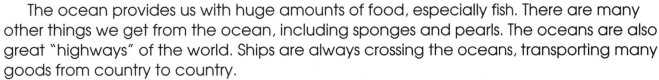

The water in the ocean is salty. This is because rivers are always pouring water into the oceans. Some of this water picks up salt from the rocks it flows over. It is not enough salt to make the rivers taste salty. But the salt in the oceans has been building up over millions of years. The oceans get more and more salty every century.

The ocean provides us with huge amounts of food, especially fish. There are many other things we get from the ocean, including sponges and pearls. The oceans are also great "highways" of the world. Ships are always crossing the oceans, transporting many goods from country to country.

The science of studying the ocean is called oceanography. Today, oceanographers have special equipment to help them learn about the oceans and seas. Electronic instruments can be sent deep below the surface to make measurements. The newest equipment uses sonar or echo-sounding systems that bounce sound waves off the sea bed and use the echoes to make pictures of the ocean floor.

Directions: Answer these questions about the oceans.

1. How much of the Earth is covered by water? _____

2. Which is the largest and deepest ocean? _____

3. What is the science of studying the ocean? _____

4. What new equipment do oceanographers use? _____

Reading Comprehension: Whales

The biggest animal in the world is the whale. The blue whale is the largest animal that ever lived. It is even bigger than the great dinosaurs of long ago. Whales are close cousins to dolphins and porpoises, but these animals are fewer than 13 feet in length.

Whales spend their entire lives in water, usually in the ocean. Because of this, many people think that whales are fish. They are not. They are mammals. There are four things that prove that whales are mammals instead of fish: 1) Whales breathe with lungs instead of gills. A whale must come to the surface to breathe. It blows the old air from its lungs out of a hole in the top of its head. 2) They are warm-blooded. 3) They have hair—though not very much! 4) Baby whales are born alive and get milk from their mothers.

Because whales often live in cold water, they have a thick layer of fat under their skin to protect them. This fat is called blubber. For many centuries, people have hunted the whale for its blubber.

Whales are very sociable animals and "talk" with each other by making different noises, including clicks, whistles, squeaks, thumps and low moans. Because sound waves travel well in water, the "song" of some whales can be heard more than 100 miles away.

Directions: Answer these questions about whales.

1. Which whale is the biggest animal that has ever lived? _____

2. List four things proving that whales are mammals and not fish.

    a. _____

    b. _____

    c. _____

    d. _____

3. What are two "cousins" to the whale? _____

4. What is the thick layer of fat under a whale's skin called? _____

Name: _____

Reading Comprehension:
Dolphins and Porpoises

Dolphins and porpoises are members of the whale family. In fact, they are the most common whales. If they have pointed or "beaked" faces, they are dolphins. If they have short faces, they are porpoises. Sometimes large groups of more than 1,000 dolphins can be seen.

Dolphins and porpoises swim in a special way called "porpoising." They swim through the surface waters, diving down and then leaping up—sometimes into the air. As their heads come out of the water, they breathe in air. Dolphins are acrobatic swimmers, often spinning in the air as they leap.

Humans have always had a special relationship with dolphins. Stories dating back to the ancient Greeks talk about dolphins as friendly, helpful creatures. There have been reports over the years of people in trouble on the seas who have been rescued and helped by dolphins.

Directions: Answer these questions about dolphins and porpoises.

1. The small members of the whale family with the pointed faces are _____ .

2. Those members of the whale family with short faces are _____ .

3. What do you call the special way dolphins and porpoises swim? _____ .

4. Do dolphins breathe with lungs or gills? _____

5. How did ancient Greeks describe dolphins? _____

6. Where have dolphins been reported to help people? _____

Name: _____

Reading Comprehension: Sharks

Sharks are known as the hunters of the sea. They are fish who eat other fish and even other sharks. Most people are frightened of sharks, but only a few of the more than 300 types of sharks are dangerous to people. Sharks vary in size and shape. The whale shark can be up to 60 feet long, but it is harmless. Some kinds of dogfish sharks are only a few inches long!

Sharks usually live in warm water, although they can be found anywhere in the ocean. Because of their shape, they are great swimmers.

Sharks are different from most other fish in a few ways. One important way is that they don't have any bones. Instead, their bodies have tough material called cartilage. Another way sharks are different is that their mouths are on the underside of the head. Most sharks have several rows of very sharp teeth. They never stop growing teeth. If a tooth wears out or is lost, a new one grows in its place.

Sharks spend most of their time eating and looking for food. They are excellent hunters. They can smell the smallest amount of blood from a long way off. Some kinds of sharks swim in packs, but the larger sharks hunt alone. Sharks usually approach their prey carefully, especially if it is big. Unless they are very hungry, they will swim around in a circle for some time before attacking. Experienced divers know how to swim with sharks and feed them. They can tell by the way a shark comes up to them if they should be afraid.

Directions: Answer these questions about sharks.

1. Sharks are the hunters of the sea.   True   False

2. There are thousands of kinds of sharks.   True   False

3. All sharks are dangerous to humans.   True   False

4. Sharks actually have very few teeth.   True   False

5. Sharks spend most of their time eating and looking for food.   True   False

Name: _____

Reading Comprehension: Jacques Cousteau

Jacques Cousteau was one of the most famous undersea explorers in history. He revolutionized this study with his inventions. His inventions include the aqua-lung and the diving saucer.

Jacques-Yves Cousteau was born in France in 1910. His family traveled a lot when he was a boy. They often visited the Atlantic Ocean. Even then, he was developing what would become a lifelong love for the sea.

Because of all the moving his family did, Cousteau was a poor student in school. He was often in trouble. But there were some areas in which he did very well. He was a wonderful swimmer, and he loved to invent things. Even as a teenager, he invented things that amazed grown-ups. He also learned a lot about other languages. By the time he started college, he was one of the best students in school. Because of his good grades, he was able to go to the French Naval Academy.

During World War II, Cousteau served as an officer in the French Navy. Most of his life became centered around the sea. He dreamed of owning his own ship. Finally, in 1950, he bought the *Calypso* (ca-LIP-so) and turned it into a research ship. Cousteau and his sailors explored the oceans. They searched shipwrecks and made underwater movies. He eventually won three Academy Awards for his undersea films. He also wrote many books about sea life. He worked very hard to teach people about the sea and how to take care of it.

Directions: Complete these statements about Jacques Cousteau.

1. Jacques Cousteau was born in _____.

2. As a boy, Cousteau liked to swim and to _____.

3. Cousteau's ship was called _____.

4. Cousteau's undersea films won him _____.

Reading Comprehension: Deep-Sea Diving

One part of the world is still largely unexplored. It is the deep sea. Over the years, many people have explored the sea. But the first deep-sea divers wanted to find sunken treasure. They weren't really interested in studying the creatures or life there. Only recently have they begun to learn some of the mysteries of the sea.

It's not easy to explore the deep sea. A diver must have a way of breathing under water. He must be able to protect himself from the terrific pressure. The pressure of air is about 15 pounds on every square inch. But the pressure of water is about 1,300 pounds on every square inch!

The first diving suits were made of rubber. They had a helmet of brass with windows in it. The shoes were made of lead and weighed 20 pounds each! These suits let divers go down a few hundred feet, but they were no good for exploring very deep waters. With a metal diving suit, a diver could go down 700 feet. Metal suits were first used in the 1930s.

In 1937, a diver named William Beebe wanted to explore deeper than anyone had ever gone before. He was not interested in finding treasure. He wanted to study deep-sea creatures and plants. He invented a hollow metal ball called the bathysphere. It weighed more than 5,000 pounds, but in it Beebe went down 3,028 feet. He saw many things that had never been seen by humans before.

Directions: Answer these questions about early deep-sea diving.

1. What were the first deep-sea divers interested in? _____

2. What are two problems that must be overcome in deep-sea diving?

   a. _____

   b. _____

3. How deep could a diver go wearing a metal suit? _____

4. Who was the deep-sea explorer who invented the bathysphere?

   _____

Comprehension: Sea Lions

Directions: Read about sea lions. Then answer the questions.

Sea lions are friendly-looking animals. Their round faces and whiskers remind people of the faces of small dogs. The almond shape of their eyes gives them a look of intelligence. Whether it is true or not, sea lions often look as though they are thinking.

Sea lions behave like playful children. They push each other off rocks. They slide into the water. Sometimes they body surf! Like people, they often ride the crest of waves. They let the waves carry them near the shore. Then they swim back out to ride more waves.

Although sea lions do not have real toys, they like to play with seaweed. They toss it in the air. They catch it in their mouths. Yuck! They must not mind the taste!

If you have been to a marine park, you may have watched sea lions. Sea lions can be taught many tricks. They can balance balls on their noses. They can jump through hoops. Their trainers give them fish to reward them for doing tricks. Sea lions look very pleased with themselves when they perform. They love fish, and they grow to love applause.

1. What are three ways sea lions play? _____

_____

_____

_____

2. Why do sea lions look intelligent? _____

_____

3. What tricks can sea lions be taught to do? _____

_____

4. As a reward, trainers give sea lions

☐ fish.   ☐ hugs.   ☐ applause.

Recognizing Details: More About Sea Lions

Directions: Read more about sea lions. Then answer the questions.

Sea lions love water! That is a good thing, because they spend most of their lives in it. Usually, the water is very cold. People cannot stay in cold water very long. The coldness slows down a person's heartbeat. It can actually make a person's heart stop beating.

Sea lions do not feel the cold. Their bodies are covered with a special layer of fat called blubber. The blubber is like a thick coat. It keeps the sea lion's body heat in. It keeps the bone-chilling cold out.

Like people, sea lions are mammals. They have warm blood. They breathe air. Baby sea lions are born on land. The mother sea lions produce milk for their babies. Like human babies, sea lions snuggle up with their mothers when they nurse. The mother knows just what her baby smells like. This is how she tells which baby is hers. She will only nurse her own baby.

Baby sea lions are called pups. Female sea lions are called cows. Male sea lions are called bulls. When pups are a few days old, their mothers leave them for a while each day. They go into the ocean to hunt fish. The pups don't seem to mind. They gather together in small groups called pods. The pods are like a nursery school! But no teacher is in charge. As many as 200 pups may spend the day together playing, swimming and sleeping.

1. What are male, female and baby sea lions called? _____

_____

2. How do sea lions stay warm in cold water? _____

_____

3. When do cows begin to leave their pups? _____

4. Where do the cows go? _____

5. What are small groups of pups called? _____

6. How can a cow tell which pup is hers? _____

_____

Name: _____

Main Idea: Pupping Time

Directions: Read about sea lion "pupping time." Then answer the questions.

When sea lion cows gather on the beach to give birth, it is called "pupping time." Pupping time is never a surprise. It always occurs in June. Thousands of sea lions may gather in one spot for pupping time. It is sort of like one big birthday party.

The cow stays with her pup for about a week after birth. During that time, she never leaves her baby. If she must go somewhere, she drags her pup along. She grabs the loose skin around her pup's neck with her teeth. To humans, it doesn't look comfortable, but it doesn't hurt the pup.

One place the mother must go is to the water. Because of her blubber, she gets hot on land. To cool off, she takes a dip in the ocean. When she comes out, she sniffs her pup to make sure she's got the right baby. Then she drags him back again to a spot she has staked out. After a week of being dragged around, do you think the pup is ready to play?

1. Why do thousands of sea lions gather together at a certain time? _____

_____

2. Why isn't pupping time ever a surprise? _____

_____

3. How does a cow take her pup along when she goes for a cool dip?

First, grab _____.

Then, _____.

After the swim, sniff _____.

4. What is the main idea?(Check one.)

_____ Thousands of cows gather at pupping time to give birth and afterwards stay with their pups for a week.

_____ Thousands of sea lions take cools dips and usually drag their pups along.

_____ Pups are born in June.

Comprehension: Sea Lions

Directions: Review what you read about sea lions. Then answer the questions.

1. What makes sea lions so friendly looking? _____

_____

2. How are people like sea lions? _____

_____

_____

3. Pretend you are a pup in a pod. What would your day be like? What would you do? What would you play?

_____

_____

_____

_____

4. Why do sea lions go into the water so much?_____

_____

5. How do you think sea lions protect themselves?_____

_____

6. What is the sea lion's habitat like? _____

_____

_____

_____

_____

_____

Review

Directions: Follow the instructions. Write your answers.

1. Create a wild animal alphabet and illustrate it on drawing paper.

   Example: A — ALLIGATOR

   B — BEAR

   C — CROCODILE

2. Select one of the wild animals you read about. Make a diorama of its habitat. A **diorama** is a three-dimensional model of a scene.

3. Compare the giraffe, wild horse and sea lion. List the ways the three animals are alike and the ways they are different.

	Giraffe	Wild Horses	Seal Lions
Alike	_____	_____	_____
Different	_____	_____	_____

4. What physical characteristics of the three animals help them survive. Which do you think is the best and why?

   _____

   _____

   _____

5. How do these animal stories differ from the animal legends and fables you read?

   _____

   _____

   _____

   _____

Recognizing Details: Orbiting Earth

Directions: Read about orbiting Earth. Then answer the questions.

John Glenn was the first American to circle Earth. When someone circles a planet, it is called "orbiting."

On February 20, 1962, John Glenn first went into space and started his trip around Earth. The name of his spaceship was *Friendship 7*.

Other American astronauts had already been into space. They knew what it was like to have no gravity. Their work helped John Glenn when he took his flight into space. John Glenn went around Earth all by himself. He was the only astronaut on board *Friendship 7*!

John Glenn was not the first person to orbit Earth, though. The year before Glenn orbited Earth, a Russian man did it. Yuri Gagarin was the first person to travel around Earth.

1. Who was the first American to orbit Earth? _____

2. What does **orbit** mean? _____

3. When did John Glenn orbit Earth? _____

4. What was the name of John Glenn's spaceship? _____

5. Who orbited Earth before John Glenn? _____

6. How long after the Russian orbited Earth did John Glenn make his journey? _____

7. People who are the first to do something that has never been done before are called "pioneers." What could you do so that you would be considered to be a "pioneer"? Explain your choice.

_____

_____

_____

_____

Main Idea: Chimpanzees Went First

Directions: Read about chimpanzees in space. Then answer the questions.

Chimpanzees went into space before astronauts! In the 1950s, scientists decided to try sending chimps into space because they are much like humans, except they are stronger.

The first two chimps to ride in a rocket were named Pat and Mike. Their ride was in 1953. Ham was the first chimpanzee to go into space. That was in 1961.

Before John Glenn orbited Earth, a chimpanzee had already done it. The chimp, named Enos, had circled Earth twice!

1. What is the main idea?

_____ Chimpanzees are better astronauts than people.

_____ Chimpanzees went into space before humans did.

_____ Only chimpanzees with names could become astronauts.

2. Who were the first chimpanzees to ride in a rocket? _____

3. Which chimpanzee orbited Earth before John Glenn? _____

4. How many times did he circle Earth? _____

Directions: Circle the names of the four chimpanzees mentioned in the story.

```
L  M  P  P  A  T  A
O  I  S  A  R  A  H
U  K  T  I  M  E  A
I  E  W  D  A  N  N
E  H  A  M  T  O  K
D  O  N  M  A  S  R
```

Space Pioneer

Neil Armstrong is one of the great pioneers of space. On July 20, 1969, Armstrong was commander of *Apollo 11*, the first manned American spacecraft to land on the Moon. He was the first person to walk on the Moon.

Armstrong was born in Ohio in 1930. He took his first airplane ride when he was 6 years old. As he grew older, he did jobs to earn money to learn to fly. On his 16th birthday, he received his student pilot's license.

Armstrong served as a Navy fighter pilot during the Korean War. He received three medals. Later, he was a test pilot. He was known as one of the best pilots in the world. He was also an engineer. He contributed much to the development of new methods of flying. In 1962, he was into an astronaut training program.

Armstrong had much experience when he was named to command the historic flight to the Moon. It took four days to fly to the Moon. As he climbed down the ladder to be the first person to step onto the Moon, he said these now famous words: "That's one small step for man, one giant leap for mankind."

Directions: Answer these questions about Neil Armstrong.

1. What did Neil Armstrong do before any other person in the world?

   _____

2. How old was Neil Armstrong when he got his student pilot's license?

   _____

3. What did Armstrong do during the Korean War?

   _____

4. On what date did a person first walk on the Moon?

   _____

Recognizing Details:
Sally Ride, First Woman in Space

Directions: Read about Sally Ride. Then answer the questions.

Sally Ride was the first American woman in space. She was only 31 years old when she went into space in 1982. Besides being the first American woman, she was also the youngest person ever to go into space!

Many people wanted to be astronauts. When Sally Ride was chosen, there were 8,000 people who wanted to be in the class. Only 35 were selected. Six of those people were women.

Sally Ride rode in the spaceship *Challenger*. She was called a mission specialist. Like any astronaut, Sally Ride had to study for several years before she went into space. She spent 6 days on her journey. She has even written a book for children about her adventure! It is called *To Space and Back*.

1. What was significant about Sally Ride's journey into space? _____

_____

2. How old was Sally ride when she went into space? _____

3. What was the name of her spaceship? _____

4. What was her title on the trip into space? _____

5. How long did Sally Ride's journey last? _____

6. What was the name of the book she wrote? _____

7. Why do you think many people want to be astronauts? _____

_____

_____

_____

_____

Main Idea: Floating in Space

Directions: Read about life in space. Then answer the questions.

Life in space is very different from life on Earth. There is no gravity in space. Gravity is what holds us to the ground. In space, everything floats around.

Astronauts wear suction cups on their shoes to hold them to the floor of their spaceships. At night, they do not crawl into bed like you do. Instead, they climb into sleeping bags that hang on the wall and then they zip themselves in.

If an astronaut is thirsty, he or she cannot simply pour a glass of water. The water would form little balls that would float around the spaceship! Instead, water has to be squirted into the astronauts' mouths from bottles or containers.

When astronauts are in space, they do a lot of floating around outside their spaceship. Astronauts always have special jobs to do in space. One astronaut is the pilot of the spaceship. The other astronauts do experiments, make repairs and gather information about their trip.

1. What is the main idea?

   _____ Life in space is much different than it is on Earth.

   _____ Without gravity, people on Earth would float around.

   _____ Gravity makes life on Earth much different than life in space.

2. What does gravity do? _____

   _____

3. How do astronauts sleep? _____

   _____

4. What do astronauts do in space? _____

   _____

5. How do astronauts drink water? _____

6. Would you like to be an astronaut? Why or why not? _____

   _____

Name: _____

Review

Directions: Read about early ideas for space travel. Then answer the questions.

People have dreamed about going into space for thousands of years. There are legends that tell about inventors who wanted to get birds to fly to the Moon. In 1864, a French author named Jules Verne wrote a book called *From the Earth to the Moon*. In the book, he wrote about men being shot into space from a huge cannon.

Jules Verne made up that story. Other writers also made up stories about going to the Moon. During the 1920s, several scientists wrote about sending rockets into space. They decided that liquid fuel was needed. Since then, space exploration has come a long way!

A Russian named Yuri A. Gagarin was the first person in space. An American, Alan B. Shepard, Jr., went into space next. Both men did experiments that later helped other astronauts in their trips to outer space!

1. What is the main idea?

   _____ People have thought about going into space since 1920.

   _____ People have thought about going into space for many years.

   _____ People like Jules Verne had many ideas about how to get to the Moon.

2. Who wrote a book called *From the Earth to the Moon*? _____

3. What did he write about? _____

_____

4. When was that book written? _____

5. In what country did Jules Verne live? _____

6. What did scientists in the 1920s think we needed to go to space? _____

7. How did Yuri Gagarin and Alan Shepard help future astronauts? _____

_____

Reading Comprehension: Telescopes

A telescope is an instrument that makes distant objects, such as the stars and planets, seem closer and bigger. This allows us to get a better look at them and scientists to learn more about them. In 1990, a very special telescope was launched into the sky aboard the space shuttle *Discovery*. The Hubble Space Telescope (HST), which is named for the man who invented it, cost almost 2 billion dollars to make.

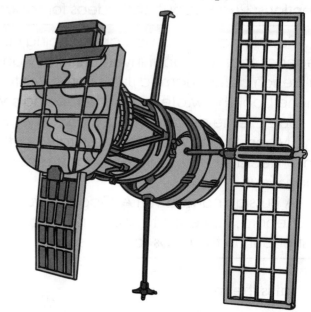

HST is a powerful eye in the sky that may help answer questions scientists have asked for a long time: How did the universe begin? How will it end? Is there other life in the universe?

Scientists need big telescopes to explore the universe. On Earth, there are two big problems that keep scientists from clearly seeing the heavens. The lights from the cities are so bright that they wash out the lights from the stars. A bigger problem is the blanket of air that covers Earth. It blurs the view. The HST will overcome these problems. In space there are no clouds and no bright city lights.

The HST is a huge telescope. It is 43 feet long and 14 feet across. It weighs 24,250 pounds. It is very powerful, too. Scientists say that if you put a dime on the top of the Washington Monument in Washington, D.C., you would be able to clearly read the date on it from New York City using the HST. That is 175 miles away!

Directions: Answer these questions about a special telescope.

1. What is a telescope? _____

_____

2. What is the name of the giant telescope that was launched into space in 1990?

_____

3. What are two problems for scientists trying to look at the stars and planets from Earth?

_____

4. How much does the HST weigh? _____

Comprehension: Clouds

Directions: Read about clouds. Then answer the questions.

Have you ever wondered where clouds come from? Clouds are made from billions and billions of tiny water droplets in the air. The water droplets form into clouds when warm, moist air rises and is cooled.

Have you ever seen your breath when you were outside on a very cold day? Your breath is warm and moist. When it hits the cold air, it is cooled. A kind of small cloud is formed by your breath!

Clouds come in many sizes and shapes. On some days, clouds blanket the whole sky. Other times, clouds look like wispy puffs of smoke. There are other types of clouds as well.

Weather experts have named clouds. Big, fluffy clouds that look flat on the bottom are called **cumulus** clouds. **Stratocumulus** is the name for rounded clouds that are packed very close together. You can still see patches of sky, but stratocumulus clouds are thicker than cumulus ones.

If you spot **cumulonimbus** clouds, go inside. These clouds are wide at the bottom and have thin tops. The tops of these clouds are filled with ice crystals. On hot summer days, you may even have seen cumulonimbus clouds growing. They seem to boil and grow as though they are coming from a big pot. A violent thunderstorm usually occurs after you see these clouds. Often, there is hail.

Cumulus, stratocumulus and cumulonimbus are only three of many types of clouds. If you listen closely, you will hear television weather forecasters talk about these and other clouds. Why? Because clouds are good indicators of weather.

1. How are clouds formed? _____

_____

2. How can you make your own cloud? _____

_____

3. What should you do when you spot cumulonimbus clouds?

_____

4. What often happens after you see cumulonimbus clouds? _____

_____

5. What kind of big fluffy clouds look flat on the bottom? _____

Recognizing Details: Clouds

Directions: Review what you learned about clouds. Then answer the questions.

1. How are clouds a good indicator of the weather? _____

_____

2. When you take something out of the freezer on a warm day, why do you think it looks like steam is rising from the object? _____

_____

3. What does this have to do with clouds? _____

_____

Directions: Use cotton balls to make models of the three types of clouds.

Following Directions: Rain

Directions: Read about rain. Then work the puzzle.

Rain develops from water vapor, dust and temperature inside clouds. From this combination, water droplets form and grow. When the droplets become too heavy for the cloud, they fall as rain. Weather experts say that when it storms, the raindrops are about 0.02 inches (0.5 millimeters) in size.

Sometimes the air below the rain cloud is very dry. The dry air dries out the wetness of the raindrop and turns it back into water vapor before it hits the ground. This is what happens in the summer when it looks as though it will rain but doesn't. The rain begins to fall, but it dries up before it falls all the way to the ground.

Across:

2. These form from water vapor, dust and the temperature inside clouds.

4. Falls when the water droplets become too heavy for the clouds.

5. Season when the air under the cloud sometimes dries the rain before it hits the ground.

Down:

1. When water droplets inside clouds get this way, rain falls.

2. Combines with water vapor and the temperature inside clouds

3. Raindrops measure about 0.02 inches (0.5 mm) when it _____.

Comprehension: Thunderstorms

Directions: Read about thunderstorms. Then answer the questions.

Thunderstorms can be scary! The sky darkens. The air feels heavy. Then the thunder begins. Sometimes the thunder sounds like a low rumble. Other times thunder is very loud. Loud thunder can be heard 15 miles away.

Thunderstorms begin inside big cumulonimbus clouds. Remember, cumulonimbus are the summer clouds that seem to boil and grow. It is as though there is a big pot under the clouds.

Thunder is heard after lightning flashes across the sky. The noise of thunder happens when lightning heats the air as it cuts through it. Some people call this quick, sharp sound a thunderclap. Sometimes thunder sounds "rumbly." This rumble is the thunder's sound wave bouncing off hills and mountains.

Weather experts say there is an easy way to figure out how far away a storm is. First, look at your watch. Count the number of seconds between the flash of lightning and the sound of thunder. To find how far away the storm is, divide the number of seconds by five. This will give the number of miles the storm is from you.

How far away is the storm if you count 20 seconds between the flash of lightning and the sound of thunder? Twenty divided by five is four miles. What if you count only five seconds? One mile! Get inside quickly. The air is charged with electricity. You could be struck by lightning. It is not safe to be outside in a thunderstorm.

1. Where do thunderstorms begin? _____

2. When is thunder heard? _____

3. What causes thunder to sound rumbly? _____

_____

4. To find out how far away a storm is, count the seconds between the thunder and lightning and divide by what number?

_____

5. If you count 40 seconds between the lightning and thunder, how far away is the storm?

_____

6. What comes first, thunder or lightning? _____

Recognizing Details: Lightning Safety

Directions: Read about safety rules for lightning. Then answer the questions.

During a storm, lightning can be very dangerous. If you are outside when a thunderstorm begins, look for shelter in a building. If you are in the woods, look for a cave. If you are in an open field, lie down in a hole. If there is no hole, lie flat on the ground.

Standing in an open field, your body is like a lightning rod. Never look for shelter under a tree during a thunderstorm. Lightning is even more likely to strike there! You and the tree are two lightning rods standing together.

Water is also a good conductor of electricity. You must never go into the water when a storm is brewing. The air becomes charged. The charge attracts lightning. The lightning has to go somewhere, and it may go into the water. That is why lifeguards order everyone out of the pool even before a storm comes.

If a thunderstorm comes up when you are boating, get to shore fast. Do not hold fishing rods or other metal objects. They attract lightning.

A car is a good, safe place to be in a thunderstorm. The rubber tires "ground" the car's metal body and remove its charge. This means the electricity cannot go through the car. Lightning does not strike cars. You are safe inside a car.

1. What should you do if you are in a field when a thunderstorm begins? _____

   _____

2. What is your body like if you are outside during a thunderstorm?

   _____

3. Why do lifeguards order people from the pool before a thunderstorm?

   _____

4. Where is a good place to be during a thunderstorm? _____

   _____

5. Besides the human body, name two things that attract lightning. _____

   _____

Review

Directions: Review what you learned about rain, thunder and lightning. Then answer the questions.

1. How are thunderstorms different from rain showers? _____

_____

_____

2. Do you think thunderstorms are scary? Explain. _____

_____

3. What is thunder? _____

_____

4. Why do you think some thunder is louder or softer than other thunder? _____

_____

5. Why shouldn't you be outside in a storm? _____

_____

6. Name ways you can seek shelter during a storm if you are:

outside: _____

in the woods: _____

in a field: _____

in a field with no hole: _____

7. What makes a car a safe place during a storm? _____

_____

8. Would you have thought this to be true? Why or why not? _____

_____

Name: _____

Comprehension: Hurricanes

Directions: Read about hurricanes. Then answer the questions.

Have you ever been in a hurricane? If you are lucky, you have not. Hurricanes are deadly! Thunderstorms are scary and can cause damage, but hurricanes are the most destructive storms on Earth.

There are three "ingredients" in a hurricane. They are turbulent oceans, fierce winds and lashing rains. Hurricane winds can blow as fast as 180 miles (290 kilometers) an hour. They can pull up trees, buildings, cars and people. Hurricanes can destroy anything in their paths.

There are other names for hurricanes. In some parts of the world, they are called cyclones. The people who live on the islands in the Pacific Ocean call them typhoons. In Australia, some people use a funny name to describe these terrible storms. They call them "willy-willies."

Although hurricanes can occur in most parts of the world, they all start in the same place. The place hurricanes are "born" is over the ocean near the equator.

Here is how a hurricane is born. At the equator, the sun is very, very hot. The scorching sun beats down on the ocean water. It heats the water and the air above the water. The heated air begins to spiral upward in tiny, hot circles. When the heated air combines with moist air, it is drawn farther up toward the sky.

The spiral of heated air and moist air begins to twist. As it twists, it grows. As it grows, it spins faster and faster in a counterclockwise direction. (This means in the opposite direction from the way a clock's hands move.) Huge rain clouds form at the top of the spiral as the air at the top is cooled. The combination of rain, hot air and spiraling winds creates a hurricane.

1. What are other names for hurricanes? _____

_____

2. Where do all hurricanes begin? _____

_____

3. What direction does a hurricane's spiral move?

_____

4. What three "ingredients" are needed to produce a hurricane? _____

_____

Recognizing Details: Hurricanes

Directions: Review what you learned about hurricanes. Then answer the questions.

1. What is the most destructive type of storm on Earth? _____

2. What makes them so destructive? _____

_____

_____

3. What makes hurricanes scarier than thunderstorms? _____

_____

4. How do hurricanes form? _____

_____

_____

5. What parts of the United States are most likely to be struck by a hurricane?

_____

_____

6. Many people enjoy living or vacationing in beach areas. Do you think they would feel the same way if they were on the coast when a hurricane happened? Explain.

_____

_____

_____

7. What does counterclockwise mean? _____

_____

_____

Main Idea: Tornadoes

Directions: Read about tornadoes. Then answer the questions.

Another type of dangerous weather condition is a tornado. While hurricanes form over water, tornadoes form over land. Tornadoes are more likely to form in some locations than in others. The areas where tornadoes frequently form are called "tornado belts." In the United States, a major tornado belt is the basin of land between Missouri and Mississippi.

Tornadoes are formed when masses of hot air meet masses of cold air. When these air masses slam together, bad thunderstorms begin. People in tornado belts are fearful when a severe storm threatens. They know a tornado may occur if the warm, moist air rushes upward and begins to spiral.

The tornado forms a funnel cloud. The funnel is narrow at the base and broad at the top. The tornado's funnel cloud can move very fast. The winds around the funnel can move 300 miles an hour. The winds inside the funnel are fast, too. The tornado acts like a giant vacuum cleaner. It sucks up everything in its path. People, animals, cars and houses are all in danger when a tornado strikes.

It is difficult to stay out of a tornado's path. The way it moves is unpredictable. It may move straight or in a zig-zag pattern. The winds of the tornado make a screaming noise like a huge train rushing by. People who have lived through a tornado usually say it was the most frightening experience of their lives.

1. What is the main idea? (Check one.)

    _____ Tornadoes form over land and hurricanes form over water.

    _____ Tornados sound like a rushing train.

    _____ Tornadoes, which form over land under certain weather conditions, are dangerous and frightening.

2. How fast can the winds around the funnel cloud move? _____

_____

3. Why is it hard to stay out of the path of a tornado? _____

_____

4. What household appliance can a tornado be compared to? _____

_____

Recognizing Details: Tornadoes

Directions: Review what you learned about tornadoes. Then answer the questions.

1. How do tornadoes form? _____

_____

2. What shape is a tornado? _____

3. What makes a tornado so dangerous? _____

_____

4. Which type of storm do you think is more dangerous, a tornado or a hurricane? Why?

_____

5. What types of weather conditions are not dangerous? _____

_____

6. What types of winter storms are also dangerous? Why? _____

_____

Directions: Compare and contrast tornadoes and hurricanes in the Venn diagram.

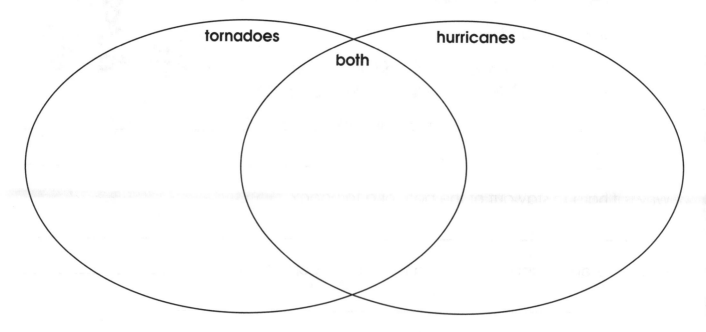

Name: _____

Reading Comprehension: Your Five Senses

Your senses are very important to you. You depend on them every day. They tell you where you are and what is going on around you. Your senses are sight, hearing, touch, smell and taste.

Try to imagine for a minute that you were suddenly unable to use your senses. Imagine, for instance, that you are in a cave and your only source of light is a candle. Without warning, a gust of wind blows out the flame.

Your senses are always at work. Your eyes let you read this book. Your nose brings the scent of dinner cooking. Your tongue helps you taste dinner later. Your hand feels the softness as you stroke a puppy. Your ears tell you that a storm is approaching.

Your senses also help keep you from harm. They warn you if you touch something that will burn you. They keep you from looking at a light that is too bright, and they tell you if a car is coming up behind you. Each of your senses collects information and sends it as a message to your brain. The brain is like the control center for your body. It sorts out the messages sent by your senses and acts on them.

Directions: Answer these questions about the five senses.

1. Circle the main idea:

   Your senses keep you from harm.

   Your senses are important to you in many ways.

2. Name the five senses.

   a. _____

   b. _____

   c. _____

   d. _____

   e. _____

3. Which part of your body acts as the "control center"?

   _____

Reading Comprehension: Touch

Unlike the other senses, which are located only in your head, your sense of touch is all over your body. Throughout your life, you receive an endless flow of information about the world and yourself from your sense of touch. It tells you if something is hot or cold, hard or soft. It sends messages of pain, such as a headache or sore throat, if there is a problem.

There are thousands of tiny sensors all over your body. They are all linked together. These sensors are also linked to your spinal cord and your brain to make up your central nervous system. Through this system, the various parts of your body can send messages to your brain. It is then the brain's job to decide what it is you are actually feeling. All this happens in just a split second.

Not all parts of your body have the same amount of feeling. Areas that have the most nerves, or sensors, have the greatest amount of feeling. For instance, the tips of your fingers have more feeling than parts of your arm.

Some sensors get used to the feeling of an object after a period of time. When you first put your shirt on in the morning, you can feel its pressure on your skin. However, some of the sensors stop responding during the day.

One feeling you cannot get used to is the feeling of pain. Pain is an important message, because it tells your brain that something harmful is happening to you. Your brain reacts by doing something right away to protect you.

Directions: Answer these questions about the sense of touch.

1. Circle the main idea:

   The sense of touch is all over your body.

   You cannot get used to the sense of pain.

2. The nerves, spinal cord and brain are linked together to make the _____

   _____ .

3. One feeling you can never get used to is _____ .

4. All parts of your body have the same amount of feeling.   True   False

5. It is the brain's job to receive messages from the sensors
   on your body and decide what you are actually feeling.   True   False

Reading Comprehension: Smell

Your nose is your sense organ for smelling. Smells are mixed into the air around you. They enter your nose when you breathe.

In the upper part of your nose, there are special smell sensors. They pick up smells and send messages to your brain. The brain then decides what it is you are smelling.

Smelling can be a pleasant sense. Sometimes smells can remind you of a person or place. For instance, have you ever smelled a particular scent and then suddenly thought about your grandmother's house? Smell also can make you feel hungry. In fact, your sense of smell is linked very closely to your sense of taste. Without your sense of smell, you would not taste food as strongly.

Smelling also can be quite unpleasant. But this, too, is important. By smelling food you can tell if it is spoiled and not fit to eat. Your sense of smell also can sometimes warn you of danger, such as a fire.

The sense of smell tires out more quickly than your other senses. This is why you get used to some everyday smells and no longer notice them after a while.

Directions: Answer these questions about the sense of smell.

1. Smells are mixed in _____ .

2. The sense of smell is linked closely to the sense of _____ .

3. Give an example of why smelling bad smells can be important to you.

_____

_____

Reading Comprehension: Taste

The senses of taste and smell work very closely together. If you can't smell your food, it is difficult to recognize the taste. You may have noticed this when you've had a bad cold with a stuffed-up nose.

Tasting is the work of your tongue. All over your tongue are tiny taste sensors called taste buds. If you look at your tongue in a mirror, you can see small groups of taste buds. They are what give your tongue its rough appearance. Each taste bud has a small opening in it. Tiny pieces of food and drink enter this opening. There taste sensors gather information about the taste and send messages to your brain. Your brain decides what the taste is.

Taste buds located in different areas of your tongue recognize different tastes. There are only four tastes your tongue can recognize: sweet, sour, bitter and salty. All other flavors are a mixture of taste and smell.

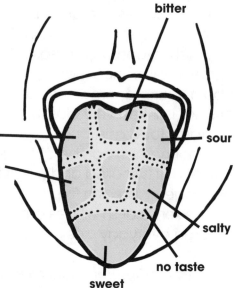

Directions: Answer these questions about the sense of taste.

1. It is difficult to taste your food if you can't _____ .

2. The tiny taste sensors on your tongue are called _____ .

3. The four tastes that your tongue can recognize are _____

   _____ .

4. All other flavors are a mixture of _____ .

Reading Comprehension: Sight

You can see this page because of light. Without light, there would be no sight. In a dark room, you might see only a few large shapes. If it is pitch black, you can't see anything at all.

Light reflects or bounces off things and then travels to your eyes. The light enters your eye through the pupil. The pupil is the black circle in the middle of your eye. It gets bigger in low light to let in as much light as possible. In bright light, it shrinks so that too much light doesn't get in.

Light enters through the pupil and then passes through the lens. The lens bends the light so that it falls on the back of your eye on the retina. The retina has millions of tiny cells that are very sensitive to light. When an image is formed in the eye, it is upside down. This image is sent to your brain. The brain receives the message and turns the picture right side up again.

Some people are far-sighted. This means they can clearly see things that are far away, but things close by may be blurred. People who are near-sighted can clearly see things better if they are close by. Glasses or contact lenses can help correct these problems.

Some people can see only a little bit or perhaps not at all. This is called being blind. Blind people rely on their sense of touch to learn more about the world. They can even use their sense of touch to read. Some blind people read with a special printing system called Braille. The system is named for the man who invented it. Braille has small raised dots instead of letters on a page.

Directions: Answer these questions about the sense of sight.

1. Without _____ , there would be no sight.

2. **Reflect** means _____ .

3. The part of the eye that controls the amount of light entering your eye by getting

   bigger and smaller is called the _____ .

4. To correct near-sightedness or far-sightedness, you can wear _____

   _____ .

5. What is the name of the special printing system for blind people? _____

Reading Comprehension: Hearing

Every sound you hear is made by the movement of air. These movements, called vibrations, spread out in waves. Your outer ear collects these "sound waves" and sends them down a tube to the inner ear. The vibrations hit the eardrum, a flap of skin stretched across the inner end of the tube. As the eardrum vibrates, a tiny bone called the hammer moves back and forth. This helps the vibrations move to three small bones and then to the cochlea, where they are changed to nerve impulses. The impulses travel to the brain where they are recognized as sounds.

Some people have trouble hearing or cannot hear at all. This is called being deaf. Some deaf people can understand what you are saying by watching how your lips move. They use their eyes as their ears. Sometimes a hearing aid can help improve hearing. It is like a tiny radio that fits into the ear. Sounds enter the hearing aid and are made much louder.

Deaf people also have difficulty learning to speak because they cannot hear how to say words. Many deaf people "talk" by making pictures with their hands. This kind of talking is called sign language. Every letter of the alphabet has a sign. These signs are shown above.

Directions: Answer these questions about the sense of hearing.

1. Sound is made by movements of the air called _____ .

2. The flap of skin stretched over the inner end of the tube inside your ear is called

   the _____ .

3. People who cannot hear are said to be _____ .

4. The language of making pictures with your hands is called _____ .

5. Read this word in sign language.

   It says _____ .

Name: _____

Reading Comprehension: The Five Senses

Directions: Before each sentence, write the sense—hearing, sight, smell, taste or touch—that is being used. The first one is done for you.

___hearing___   1. The rooster crows outside my window early each morning.

_____   2. After playing in the snow, our fingers and toes were freezing.

_____   3. I could hear sirens in the distance.

_____   4. I think this tree is taller than that one.

_____   5. The delicious salad was filled with fresh, juicy fruits.

_____   6. The odor of the bread baking in the oven was wonderful.

_____   7. There was a rainbow in the sky today.

_____   8. The kitten was soft and fluffy.

_____   9. Her perfume filled the air when she walked by.

_____   10. An airplane wrote a message in the sky.

_____   11. The chocolate cake was yummy.

_____   12. The steamboat whistle frightened the baby.

_____   13. The sour lemon made my lips pucker.

_____   14. Her gum-popping got on my nerves.

Reading Comprehension: The Five Senses

Directions: Each word in the word box makes you think of hearing, sight, smell, taste or touch. Write each word under the sense that is used. One is done for you.

music	rainbow	talking	hot	sour
honking	moldy	butterfly	green	book
crying	~~silky~~	sweet	smoky	bitter
salty	skunk	cold	smooth	stinky

Touch

_____silky_____

_____

_____

_____

Sight

_____

_____

_____

_____

Taste

_____

_____

_____

_____

Smell

_____

_____

_____

Hearing

_____

_____

_____

Reading Comprehension: Helen Keller

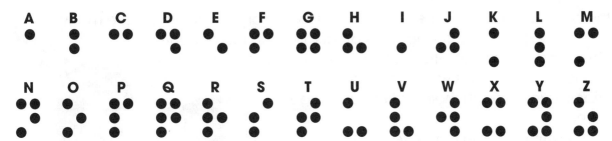

The story of Helen Keller has given courage and hope to many people. Helen had many problems, but she used her life to do great things.

When Helen Keller was a child, she often behaved in a wild way. She was very bright and strong, but she could not tell people what she was thinking or feeling. And she didn't know how others thought or felt. Helen was blind and deaf.

Helen was born with normal hearing and sight, but this changed when she was 1 year old. She had a serious illness with a very high fever. After that, Helen was never able to see or hear again.

As a child, Helen was angry and lonely. But when she was 6 years old, her parents got a teacher for her. They brought a young woman named Anne Sullivan to stay at their house and help Helen. After much hard work, Helen began to learn sign language. Anne taught Helen many important things, such as how to behave like other children. Because Helen was so smart, she learned things very quickly. She learned how to read Braille. By the time she was 8 years old, she was becoming very famous. People were amazed at what she could do.

Helen continued to learn. She even learned how to speak. When she was 20 years old, she went to college. Helen did so well in college that a magazine paid her to write the story of her life. After college, she earned money by writing and giving speeches. She traveled all around the world. She worked to get special schools and libraries for the blind and deaf. She wrote many books, including one about her teacher, Anne Sullivan.

Here is how "Helen" is written in Braille:

Directions: Answer these questions about Helen Keller.

1. What caused Helen to be blind and deaf? _____

   _____

2. What happy thing happened when Helen was 6 years old? _____

   _____

3. What was her teacher's name? _____

Review

In this book, you have learned new ways to write and "talk." There are many other ways to express your thoughts to others. Here is another one.

For hundreds of years, Native Americans used their own system of sign language. These signs were understood by all tribes, even though their spoken languages were different.

The Plains tribes helped to develop and spread sign language. The Plains tribes liked to wander. They never camped in any one place for long. They used sign language so they could talk with other Native Americans wherever they went.

The first white adventurers and trappers in America also learned Native American sign language. They wanted to understand and be understood by the Native Americans.

Many Native Americans today still use this ancient form of talking. It is no longer necessary, but it is an important link to their past.

Directions: Answer these questions about sign language.

1. Circle the main idea:

    Native Americans used a kind of sign language.

    There are many ways to express your thoughts to others.

2. Every tribe had its own sign language.   True   False

3. The Plains tribes did not use sign language.   True   False

4. Many Native Americans today still use this sign language.   True   False

5. Sign language is still necessary among Native Americans.   True   False

ENGLISH

highest

higher

high

Name: _____

Writing: Sentences

A **sentence** is a group of words that expresses a complete thought.

Directions: Write **S** by each group of words that is a sentence and **NS** by those that are not a complete sentence.

Examples:

<u>NS</u> A pinch of salt in the soup.

<u>S</u> Grandmother was fond of her flower garden.

_____ 1. Tigers blend in with their surroundings.

_____ 2. Our crop of vegetables for this summer.

_____ 3. Don't forget to put the plug in the sink.

_____ 4. Usually older people in good health.

_____ 5. Fond of lying in the sun for hours.

_____ 6. Will ducks hatch a swan egg?

_____ 7. I hope he won't insist on coming with us.

_____ 8. Regular exercise will pump up your muscles.

_____ 9. A fact printed in all the newspapers.

_____10. Did you pinch the baby?

_____11. Plug the hole with your finger.

_____12. A new teacher today in health class.

_____13. I insist on giving you some of my candy.

_____14. A blend of peanut butter and honey.

_____15. As many facts as possible in your report.

Name: _____

Kinds of Sentences: Statements and Questions

A **statement** tells some kind of information. It is followed by a period (.).

Examples: It is a rainy day. We are going to the beach next summer.

A **question** asks for a specific piece of information. It is followed by a question mark (?).

Examples: What is the weather like today? When are you going to the beach?

Directions: Write whether each sentence is a statement or question. The first one has been done for you.

1. Jamie went for a walk at the zoo. _____statement_____
2. The leaves turn bright colors in the fall. _____
3. When does the Easter Bunny arrive? _____
4. Madeleine went to the new art school. _____
5. Is school over at 3:30? _____
6. Grandma and Grandpa are moving. _____
7. Anthony went home. _____
8. Did Mary go to Amy's house? _____
9. Who went to work late? _____
10. Ms. McDaniel is a good teacher. _____

Directions: Write two statements and two questions below.

Statements:

_____

_____

Questions:

_____

_____

Name: _____

Kinds of Sentences: Commands and Exclamations

A **command** tells someone to do something. It is followed by a period (.).

Examples: Get your math book. Do your homework.

An **exclamation** shows strong feeling or excitement. It is followed by an exclamation mark (!).

Examples: Watch out for that car! Oh, no! There's a snake!

Directions: Write whether each sentence is a command or exclamation. The first one has been done for you.

1. Please clean your room. _____ command _____

2. Wow! Those fireworks are beautiful! _____

3. Come to dinner now. _____

4. Color the sky and water blue. _____

5. Trim the paper carefully. _____

6. Hurry, here comes the bus! _____

7. Isn't that a lovely picture! _____

8. Time to stop playing and clean up. _____

9. Brush your teeth before bedtime. _____

10. Wash your hands before you eat! _____

Directions: Write two commands and two exclamations below.

Commands:

_____

_____

Exclamations:

_____

_____

Writing: Four Kinds of Sentences

Directions: Write **S** for statement, **Q** for question, **C** for command or **E** for exclamation. End each sentence with a period, question mark or exclamation mark.

Example: __E__ You better watch out!

_____ 1. My little brother insists on coming with us

_____ 2. Tell him movies are bad for his health

_____ 3. He says he's fond of movies

_____ 4. Does he know there are monsters in this movie

_____ 5. He says he needs facts for his science report

_____ 6. He's writing about something that hatched from an old egg

_____ 7. Couldn't he just go to the library

_____ 8. Could we dress him like us so he'll blend in

_____ 9. Are you kidding

_____ 10. Would he sit by himself at the movie

_____ 11. That would be too dangerous

_____ 12. Mom said she'd give us money for candy if we took him with us

_____ 13. Why didn't you say that earlier

_____ 14. Get your brother and let's go

Name: _____

Writing: Four Kinds of Sentences

Directions: For each pair of words, write two kinds of sentences (any combination of question, command, statement or exclamation). Use one or both words in each sentence. Name each kind of sentence you wrote.

Example: pump   crop

Question: <u>What kind of crops did you plant?</u>

Command: <u>Pump the water as fast as you can.</u>

1. pinch   health

_____ : _____

_____ : _____

2. fond   fact

_____ : _____

_____ : _____

3. insist   hatch

_____ : _____

_____ : _____

exclamation   command   statement   question

Sentences: Subjects

The **subject** of a sentence tells you who or what the sentence is about. A subject is either a common noun, a proper noun or a pronoun.

Examples: Sue went to the store.

Sue is the subject of the sentence.

The tired boys and girls walked home slowly.

The tired boys and girls is the subject of the sentence.

Directions: Underline the subject of each sentence. The first one has been done for you.

1. <u>The birthday cake</u> was pink and white.
2. Anthony celebrated his fourth birthday.
3. The tower of building blocks fell over.
4. On Saturday, our family will go to a movie.
5. The busy editor was writing sentences.
6. Seven children painted pictures.
7. Two happy dolphins played cheerfully on the surf.
8. A sand crab buried itself in the dunes.
9. Blue waves ran peacefully ashore.
10. Sleepily, she went to bed.

Directions: Write a subject for each sentence.

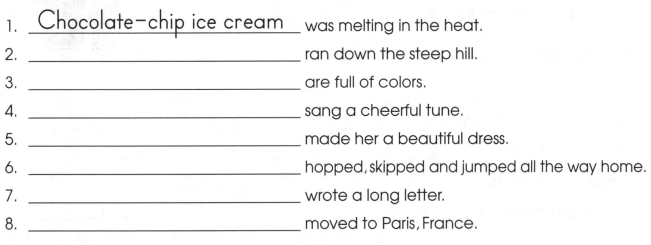

1. __Chocolate-chip ice cream__ was melting in the heat.
2. _____ ran down the steep hill.
3. _____ are full of colors.
4. _____ sang a cheerful tune.
5. _____ made her a beautiful dress.
6. _____ hopped, skipped and jumped all the way home.
7. _____ wrote a long letter.
8. _____ moved to Paris, France.

Sentences: Predicates

The **predicate** of a sentence tells what the subject is doing. The predicate contains the action, linking and/or helping verb.

Examples: Sue went to the store.

Went to the store is the predicate.

The tired boys and girls walked home slowly.

Walked home slowly is the predicate.

Hint: When identifying the predicate, look for the verb. The verb is usually the first word of the predicate.

Directions: Underline the predicate in each sentence with two lines. The first one has been done for you.

1. The choir <u>sang joyfully</u>.
2. Their song had both high and low notes.
3. Sal played the piano while they sang.
4. This Sunday the orchestra will have a concert in the park.
5. John is working hard on his homework.
6. He will write a report on electricity.
7. The report will tell about Ben Franklin's kite experiment.
8. Jackie, Mary and Amy played on the swings.
9. They also climbed the rope ladder.
10. Before the girls went home, they slid down the slide.

Directions: Write a predicate for each sentence.

1. Sam and Libby _____.
2. At school, the children _____.
3. The football team _____.
4. Seven silly serpents _____.
5. At the zoo, the animals _____.

Changing the Predicate

Directions: Circle the predicate in each sentence. Change the predicate to make a new sentence. The words you add must make sense with the rest of the sentence. The first one has been done for you.

1. Twelve students (signed up for the student council elections.)

   Twelve students were absent from my class today!

2. Our whole family went to the science museum last week.

   _____

   _____

3. The funny story made us laugh.

   _____

   _____

4. The brightly colored kites drifted lazily across the sky.

   _____

   _____

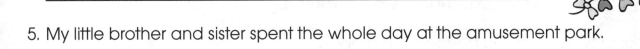

5. My little brother and sister spent the whole day at the amusement park.

   _____

   _____

6. The tiny sparrow made a tapping sound at my window.

   _____

   _____

Subjects and Predicates

The **subject** tells who or what the sentence is about. The **predicate** tells what the subject does, did, is doing or will do. A complete sentence must have a subject and a predicate.

Examples:

Subject	Predicate
Sharon	writes to her grandmother every week.
The horse	ran around the track quickly.
My mom's car	is bright green.
Denise	will be here after lunch.

Directions: Circle the subject of each sentence. Underline the predicate.

1. My sister is a very happy person.

2. I wish we had more holidays in the year.

3. Laura is one of the nicest girls in our class.

4. John is fun to have as a friend.

5. The rain nearly ruined our picnic!

6. My birthday present was exactly what I wanted.

7. Your bicycle is parked beside my skateboard.

8. The printer will need to be filled with paper before you use it.

9. Six dogs chased my cat home yesterday!

10. Anthony likes to read anything he can get his hands on.

11. Twelve students signed up for the dance committee.

12. Your teacher seems to be a reasonable person.

Name: _____

Subjects and Predicates

Directions: Write subjects to complete the following sentences.

1. _____ went to school last Wednesday.

2. _____ did not understand the joke.

3. _____ barked so loudly that no one could sleep a wink.

4. _____ felt unhappy when the ball game was rained out.

5. _____ wonder what happened at the end of the book.

6. _____ jumped for joy when she won the contest.

Directions: Write predicates to complete the following sentences.

7. Everyone _____.

8. Dogs _____.

9. I _____.

10. Justin _____.

11. Jokes _____.

12. Twelve people _____.

Name: _____

Subjects and Predicates

A **sentence** is a group of words that expresses a complete thought. It must have at least one subject and one verb.

Examples:

Sentence: John felt tired and went to bed early.

Not a sentence: Went to bed early.

Directions: Write **S** if the group of words is a complete sentence. Write **NS** if the group of words is not a sentence.

_____ 1. Which one of you?

_____ 2. We're happy for the family.

_____ 3. We enjoyed the program very much.

_____ 4. Felt left out and lonely afterwards.

_____ 5. Everyone said it was the best party ever!

_____ 6. No one knows better than I what the problem is.

_____ 7. Seventeen of us!

_____ 8. Quickly before they.

_____ 9. Squirrels are lively animals.

_____ 10. Not many people believe it really happened.

_____ 11. Certainly, we enjoyed ourselves.

_____ 12. Tuned her out.

Name: _____

Subjects and Predicates

Directions: On the previous page, some of the groups of words are not sentences. Rewrite them to make complete sentences.

1. _____

   _____

2. _____

   _____

3. _____

   _____

4. _____

   _____

5. _____

   _____

Grade 4 - Comprehensive Curriculum

Name: _____

Compound Subjects

A **compound subject** is a subject with two parts joined by the word **and** or another conjunction. Compound subjects share the same predicate.

Example:

Her shoes were covered with mud. Her ankles were covered with mud, too.

Compound subject: Her shoes and ankles were covered with mud.

The predicate in both sentences is **were covered with mud**.

Directions: Combine each pair of sentences into one sentence with a compound subject.

1. Bill sneezed. Kassie sneezed.

_____

2. Kristin made cookies. Joey made cookies.

_____

3. Fruit flies are insects. Ladybugs are insects.

_____

4. The girls are planning a dance. The boys are planning a dance.

_____

5. Our dog ran after the ducks. Our cat ran after the ducks.

_____

6. Joshua got lost in the parking lot. Daniel got lost in the parking lot.

_____

Compound Subjects

If sentences do not share the same predicate, they cannot be combined to write a sentence with a compound subject.

Example: Mary laughed at the story.
Tanya laughed at the television show.

Directions: Combine the pairs of sentences that share the same predicate. Write new sentences with compound subjects.

1. Pete loves swimming. Jake loves swimming.

_____

2. A bee stung Elizabeth. A hornet stung Elizabeth.

_____

3. Sharon is smiling. Susan is frowning.

_____

4. The boys have great suntans. The girls have great suntans.

_____

5. Six squirrels chased the kitten. Ten dogs chased the kitten.

_____

6. The trees were covered with insects. The roads were covered with ice.

_____

Name: _____

Compound Predicates

A **compound predicate** is a predicate with two parts joined by the word **and** or another conjunction. Compound predicates share the same subject.

Example: The baby grabbed the ball. The baby threw the ball.

Compound predicate: The baby grabbed the ball and threw it. The subject in both sentences is **the baby**.

Directions: Combine each pair of sentences into one sentence to make a compound predicate.

1. Leah jumped on her bike. Leah rode around the block.

_____

2. Father rolled out the pie crust. Father put the pie crust in the pan.

_____

3. Anthony slipped on the snow. Anthony nearly fell down.

_____

4. My friend lives in a green house. My friend rides a red bicycle.

_____

5. I opened the magazine. I began to read it quietly.

_____

6. My father bought a new plaid shirt. My father wore his new red tie.

_____

Name: _____

Compound Predicates

Directions: Combine the pairs of sentences that share the same subject. Write new sentences with compound predicates.

1. Jenny picked a bouquet of flowers. Jenny put the flowers in a vase.

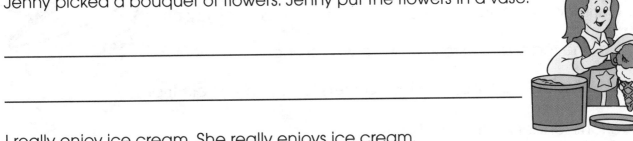

_____

_____

2. I really enjoy ice cream. She really enjoys ice cream.

_____

_____

3. Everyone had a great time at the pep rally. Then everyone went out for a pizza.

_____

_____

4. Cassandra built a model airplane.
   She painted the airplane bright yellow.

_____

_____

5. Her brother was really a hard person to get to know. Her sister was very shy, too.

_____

_____

Review

Directions: Circle the subjects.

1. Everyone felt the day had been a great success.

2. Christina and Andrea were both happy to take the day off.

3. No one really understood why he was crying.

4. Mr. Winston, Ms. Fuller and Ms. Landers took us on a field trip.

Directions: Underline the predicates.

5. Who can tell what will happen tomorrow?

6. Mark was a carpenter by trade and a talented painter, too.

7. The animals yelped and whined in their cages.

8. Airplane rides made her feel sick to her stomach.

Directions: Combine the sentences to make one sentence with a compound subject.

9. Elizabeth ate everything in sight. George ate everything in sight.

_____

10. Wishing something will happen won't make it so. Dreaming something will happen won't make it so.

_____

Directions: Combine the sentences to make one sentence with a compound predicate.

11. I jumped for joy. I hugged all my friends.

_____

12. She ran around the track before the race. She warmed up before the race.

_____

Name: _____

Writing: Nouns

A **noun** names a person, place or thing.

Examples: Persons — boy, girl, Mom, Dad
Places — park, pool, house, office
Things — bike, swing, desk, book

Directions: Read the following sentences.
Underline the nouns. The first one has been done for you.

1. The girl went to school.

2. Grandma and Grandpa will visit us soon.

3. The bike is in the garage.

4. Dad went to his office.

5. Mom is at her desk in the den.

6. John's house is near the park.

7. Her brothers are at school.

8. We took the books to the library.

Directions: Read the following words. Underline the nouns. Then categorize the nouns on another sheet of paper into groups of people, places and things.

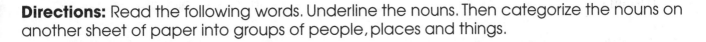

tree	Mrs. Smith	Dad	cards	Grandma	skip	sell
house	car	truck	Mom	office	grass	sign
boy	run	Sam	stove	greet	grade	school
girl	camp	jump	weave	free	driver	room
salesperson	sad	teach	treat	stripe	paint	Jane
clay	man	leave	happy	play	desk	tape
watch	lives	painter	brother	rain	window	hop

Grade 4 - Comprehensive Curriculum

Name: _____

Nouns

Directions: Write nouns that name persons.

1. Could you please give this report to my _____ ?

2. The _____ works many long hours to plant crops.

3. I had to help my little _____ when he wrecked his bike yesterday.

Directions: Write nouns that name places.

4. I always keep my library books on top of the _____ so I can find them.

5. We enjoyed watching the kites flying high in the _____ .

6. Dad built a nice fire in the _____ to keep us warm.

Directions: Write nouns that name things.

7. The little _____ purred softly as I held it.

8. Wouldn't you think a _____ would get tired of carrying its house around all day?

9. The _____ scurried into its hole with the piece of cheese.

10. I can tell by the writing that this _____ is mine.

11. Look at the _____ I made in art.

12. His _____ blew away because of the strong wind.

Name: _____

Writing: Common and Proper Nouns

Common nouns name general people, places and things.

Examples: boy, girl, cat, dog, park, city, building

Proper nouns name specific persons, places and things.

Examples: John, Mary, Fluffy, Rover, Central Park, Chicago, Empire State Building

Proper nouns begin with capital letters.

Directions: Read the following nouns. On the blanks, indicate whether the nouns are common or proper. The first two have been done for you.

1. New York City   _proper_   9. Dr. DiCarlo   _____

2. house   _common_   10. man   _____

3. car   _____   11. Rock River   _____

4. Ohio   _____   12. building   _____

5. river   _____   13. lawyer   _____

6. Rocky Mountains   _____   14. Grand Canyon   _____

7. Mrs. Jones   _____   15. city   _____

8. nurse   _____   16. state   _____

On another sheet of paper, write proper nouns for the above common nouns.

Directions: Read the following sentences. Underline the common nouns. Circle the proper nouns.

1. Mary's birthday is Friday, October 7.

2. She likes having her birthday in a fall month.

3. Her friends will meet her at the Video Arcade for a party.

4. Ms. McCarthy and Mr. Landry will help with the birthday party games.

5. Mary's friends will play video games all afternoon.

6. Amy and John will bring refreshments and games to the party.

     Grade 4 - Comprehensive Curriculum

Proper Nouns: Capitalization

Proper nouns always begin with a capital letter.

Examples:

    Monday

    Texas

    Karen

    Mr. Logan

    Hamburger Avenue

    Rover

Directions: Cross out the lower-case letters at the beginning of the proper nouns. Write capital letters above them. The first one has been done for you

1. My teddy bear's name is ~~c~~ocoa. _C

2. ms. bernhard does an excellent job at crestview elementary school.

3. emily, elizabeth and megan live on main street.

4. I am sure our teacher said the book report is due on monday.

5. I believe you can find lake street if you turn left at the next light.

6. Will your family be able join our family for dinner at burger barn?

7. The weather forecasters think the storm will hit the coast of louisiana friday afternoon.

8. My family went to washington, d.c. this summer.

9. Remember, we don't have school on tuesday because of the teachers' meeting.

10. Who do you think will win the game, the cougars or the arrows?

Name: _____

Spelling: Plurals

Nouns come in two forms: singular and plural. When a noun is **singular**, it means there is only one person, place or thing.

Examples: car, swing, box, truck, slide, bus

When a noun is **plural**, it means there is more than one person, place or thing.

Examples: two cars, four trucks, three swings, five slides, six boxes, three buses

Usually an **s** is added to most nouns to make them plural. However, if the noun ends in **s**, **x**, **ch** or **sh**, then **es** is added to make it plural.

Directions: Write the singular or plural form of each word.

Singular	Plural	Singular	Plural
1. car	_____	9. _____	tricks
2. bush	_____	10. mess	_____
3. wish	_____	11. box	_____
4. _____	foxes	12. dish	_____
5. _____	rules	13. _____	boats
6. stitch	_____	14. path	_____
7. _____	switches	15. _____	arms
8. barn	_____	16. _____	sticks

Directions: Rewrite the following sentences and change the bold nouns from singular to plural or from plural to singular. The first one has been done for you.

1. She took a **book** to school.
   She took books to school. _____

2. Tommy made **wishes** at his birthday party.

   _____

3. The **fox** ran away from the hunters.

   _____

4. The **houses** were painted white.

   _____

Name: _____

Spelling: Plurals

When a word ends with a consonant before **y**, to make it plural, drop the **y** and add **ies**.

Examples:

party	parties
cherry	cherries
daisy	daisies

However, if the word ends with a vowel before **y**, just add **s**.

Examples:

boy	boys
toy	toys
monkey	monkeys

Directions: Write the singular or plural form of each word.

	Singular	Plural		Singular	Plural
1.	fly	_____	7.	_____	decoys
2.	_____	boys	8.	candy	_____
3.	_____	joys	9.	toy	_____
4.	spy	_____	10.	_____	cries
5.	_____	keys	11.	monkey	_____
6.	_____	dries	12.	daisy	_____

Directions: Write six sentences of your own using any of the plurals above.

_____

_____

_____

_____

_____

_____

Name: _____

Spelling: Plurals

Some words in the English language do not follow any of the plural rules discussed earlier. These words may not change at all from singular to plural, or they may completely change spellings.

No Change	Examples:	Complete Change	Examples:
Singular	**Plural**	**Singular**	**Plural**
deer	deer	goose	geese
pants	pants	ox	oxen
scissors	scissors	man	men
moose	moose	child	children
sheep	sheep	leaf	leaves

Directions: Write the singular or plural form of each word. Use a dictionary to help if necessary.

	Singular	Plural		Singular	Plural
1.	moose	_____	6.	leaf	_____
2.	woman	_____	7.	_____	sheep
3.	_____	deer	8.	scissors	_____
4.	_____	children	9.	tooth	_____
5.	_____	hooves	10.	wharf	_____

Directions: Write four sentences of your own using two singular and two plural words from above.

_____

_____

_____

_____

Name: _____

Review

Review these rules for making singular words plural.

For most words, simply add **s**.

Examples: one book — two books   one house — four houses

For words ending with **s**, **ss**, **sh**, **ch** and **x**, add **es**.

Examples: one class — two classes   one church — three churches
one box — four boxes   one crash — five crashes

For words ending with a consonant before **y**, drop the **y** and add **ies**.

Examples: one daisy — three daisies   one cherry — two cherries

For words ending with a vowel before **y**, just add **s**.

Examples: one key — eight keys   one monkey — four monkeys

Directions: Write the singular or plural form of each word.

Singular	Plural	Singular	Plural
1. mattress	_____	10. _____	candies
2. _____	bushes	11. try	_____
3. sandwich	_____	12. _____	turkeys
4. fry	_____	13. copy	_____
5. _____	crosses	14. _____	factories
6. marsh	_____	15. _____	foxes
7. _____	supplies	16. ax	_____
8. donkey	_____	17. berry	_____
9. _____	stoves	18. day	_____

Pronouns

A **pronoun** is a word that takes the place of a noun in a sentence.

Examples:

I, my, mine, me

we, our, ours, us

you, your, yours

he, his, him

she, her, hers

it, its

they, their, theirs, them

Directions: Underline the pronouns in each sentence.

1. Bring them to us as soon as you are finished.

2. She has been my best friend for many years.

3. They should be here soon.

4. We enjoyed our trip to the Mustard Museum.

5. Would you be able to help us with the project on Saturday?

6. Our homeroom teacher will not be here tomorrow.

7. My uncle said that he will be leaving soon for Australia.

8. Hurry! Could you please open the door for him?

9. She dropped her gloves when she got off the bus.

10. I can't figure out who the mystery writer is today.

Writing: Verbs

Verbs are the action words in a sentence. There are three kinds of verbs: action verbs, linking verbs and helping verbs.

An **action verb** tells the action of a sentence.

Examples: run, hop, skip, sleep, jump, talk, snore
Michael **ran** to the store. **Ran** is the action verb.

A **linking verb** joins the subject and predicate of a sentence.

Examples: am, is, are, was, were
Michael **was** at the store. **Was** is the linking verb.

A **helping verb** is used with an action verb to "help" the action of the sentence.

Examples: am, is, are, was, were
Matthew **was** helping Michael. **Was** helps the action verb **helping**.

Directions: Read the following sentences. Underline the verbs. Above each, write **A** for action verb, **L** for linking verb and **H** for helping verb. The first one has been done for you.

1. Amy <u>jumps</u> rope.
　　　　A

2. Paul was jumping rope, too.

3. They were working on their homework.

4. The math problem requires a lot of thinking.

5. Addition problems are fun to do.

6. The baby sleeps in the afternoon.

7. Grandma is napping also.

8. Sam is going to bed.

9. John paints a lovely picture of the sea.

10. The colors in the picture are soft and pale.

Name: _____

Writing: Verb Tense

Not only do verbs tell the action of a sentence but they also tell when the action takes place. This is called the **verb tense**. There are three verb tenses: past, present and future tense.

Present-tense verbs tell what is happening now.

Example: Jane **spells** words with long vowel sounds.

Past-tense verbs tell about action that has already happened. Past-tense verbs are usually formed by adding **ed** to the verb.

Example: stay — stayed
John **stayed** home yesterday.

Past-tense verbs can also be made by adding helping verbs **was** or **were** before the verb and adding **ing** to the verb.

Example: talk — was talking
Sally **was talking** to her mom.

Future-tense verbs tell what will happen in the future. Future-tense verbs are made by putting the word **will** before the verb.

Example: paint — will paint
Susie and Sherry **will paint** the house.

Directions: Read the following verbs. Write whether the verb tense is past, present or future.

Verb	Tense		Verb	Tense
1. watches	present		8. writes	_____
2. wanted	_____		9. vaulted	_____
3. will eat	_____		10. were sleeping	_____
4. was squawking	_____		11. will sing	_____
5. yawns	_____		12. is speaking	_____
6. crawled	_____		13. will cook	_____
7. will hunt	_____		14. likes	_____

Grade 4 - Comprehensive Curriculum

Name: _____

Verbs: Present, Past and Future Tense

Directions: Read the following sentences. Write **PRES** if the sentence is in present tense. Write **PAST** if the sentence is in past tense. Write **FUT** if the sentence is in future tense. The first one has been done for you.

FUT   1. I will be thrilled to accept the award.

_____ 2. Will you go with me to the dentist?

_____ 3. I thought he looked familiar!

_____ 4. They ate every single slice of pizza.

_____ 5. I run myself ragged sometimes.

_____ 6. Do you think this project is worthwhile?

_____ 7. No one has been able to repair the broken plate.

_____ 8. Thoughtful gifts are always appreciated.

_____ 9. I liked the way he sang!

_____ 10. With a voice like that, he will go a long way.

_____ 11. It's my fondest hope that they visit soon.

_____ 12. I wanted that coat very much.

_____ 13. She'll be happy to take your place.

_____ 14. Everyone thinks the test is easy.

_____ 15. Collecting stamps is her favorite hobby.

Writing: Using ing Verbs

Remember, use **is** and **are** when describing something happening right now. Use **was** and **were** when describing something that already happened.

Directions: Use the verb in bold to complete each sentence. Add **ing** to the verb and use **is**, **are**, **was** or **were**.

Examples:

When it started to rain, we _were raking_
the leaves.   **rake**

When the soldiers marched up that hill,

Captain Stevens _was commanding_ them.
          command

1. Now, the police _____ them of stealing the money.
          accuse

2. Look! The eggs _____.
          hatch

3. A minute ago, the sky _____.
          glow

4. My dad says he _____ us to ice cream!
          treat

5. She _____ the whole time we were at the mall.
          sneeze

6. While we were playing outside at recess, he _____
   our tests.   **grade**

7. I hear something. Who _____?
          groan

8. As I watched, the workers _____ the wood into
   little chips.   **grind**

Writing: Present-Tense Verbs

Directions: Write two sentences for each verb below. Tell about something that is happening now and write the verb as both simple present tense and present tense with a helping verb.

Example: run

Mia runs to the store.   Mia is running to the store.

1. hatch

_____

_____

2. check

_____

_____

3. spell

_____

_____

4. blend

_____

_____

5. lick

_____

_____

6. cry

_____

_____

7. write

_____

_____

8. dream

_____

_____

Writing: Verb Tense

Directions: Read the following sentences. Underline the verbs. Above each verb, write whether it is past, present or future tense.

           past

1. The crowd <u>was booing</u> the referee.

2. Sally will compete on the balance beam.

3. Matt marches with the band.

4. Nick is marching, too.

5. The geese swooped down to the pond.

6. Dad will fly home tomorrow.

7. They were looking for a new book.

8. Presently, they are going to the garden.

9. The children will pick the ripe vegetables.

10. Grandmother canned the green beans.

Directions: Write six sentences of your own using the correct verb tense.

Past tense:

_____

_____

Present tense:

_____

_____

Future tense:

_____

_____

Adding "ed" to Make Verbs Past Tense

To make many verbs past tense, add **ed**.

Examples:

      cook + ed = cooked   wish + ed = wished   play + ed = played

When a verb ends in a **silent e**, drop the **e** and add **ed**.

Examples:

      hope + ed = hoped   hate + ed = hated

When a verb ends in **y** after a consonant, change the **y** to **i** and add **ed**.

Examples:

      hurry + ed = hurried   marry + ed = married

When a verb ends in a single consonant after a single short vowel, double the final consonant before adding **ed**.

Examples:

      stop + ed = stopped   hop + ed = hopped

Directions: Write the past tense of the verb correctly. The first one has been done for you.

1. call   _____called_____
2. copy   _____
3. frown   _____
4. smile   _____
5. live   _____
6. talk   _____
7. name   _____
8. list   _____
9. spy   _____
10. phone   _____

11. reply   _____
12. top   _____
13. clean   _____
14. scream   _____
15. clap   _____
16. mop   _____
17. soap   _____
18. choke   _____
19. scurry   _____
20. drop   _____

Writing: Past-Tense Verbs

To write about something that already happened, you can add **ed** to the verb.

Example: Yesterday, we **talked**.

You can also use **was** and **were** and add **ing** to the verb.

Example: Yesterday, we **were talking**.

When a verb ends with **e**, you usually drop the **e** before adding **ing**.

Examples: grade — was grading   weave — were weaving
tape — was taping   sneeze — were sneezing

Directions: Write two sentences for each verb below. Tell about something that has already happened and write the verb both ways. (Watch the spelling of the verbs that end with **e**.)

Example: stream

The rain streamed down the window.
The rain was streaming down the window.

1. grade

_____

_____

2. tape

_____

_____

3. weave

_____

_____

4. sneeze

_____

_____

Irregular Verbs: Past Tense

Irregular verbs change completely in the past tense. Unlike regular verbs, past-tense forms of irregular verbs are not formed by adding **ed**.

Example: The past tense of **go** is **went**.

Other verbs change some letters to form the past tense.
Example: The past tense of **break** is **broke**.

A **helping verb** helps to tell about the past. **Has**, **have** and **had** are helping verbs used with action verbs to show the action occurred in the past. The past-tense form of the irregular verb sometimes changes when a helping verb is added.

Present Tense Irregular Verb	Past Tense Irregular Verb	Past Tense Irregular Verb With Helper
go	went	have/has/had gone
see	saw	have/has/had seen
do	did	have/has/had done
bring	brought	have/has/had brought
sing	sang	have/has/had sung
drive	drove	have/has/had driven
swim	swam	have/has/had swum
sleep	slept	have/has/had slept

Directions: Choose four words from the chart. Write one sentence using the past-tense form of the verb without a helping verb. Write another sentence using the past-tense form with a helping verb.

1. _____

    _____

2. _____

    _____

3. _____

    _____

4. _____

    _____

The Irregular Verb "Be"

Be is an irregular verb. The present-tense forms of **be** are **be**, **am**, **is** and **are**. The past-tense forms of **be** are **was** and **were**.

Directions: Write the correct form of **be** in the blanks. The first one has been done for you.

1. I _____ am _____ so happy for you!

2. Jared _____ unfriendly yesterday.

3. English can _____ a lot of fun to learn.

4. They _____ among the nicest people I know.

5. They _____ late yesterday.

6. She promises she _____ going to arrive on time.

7. I _____ nervous right now about the test.

8. If you _____ satisfied now, so am I.

9. He _____ as nice to me last week as I had hoped.

10. He can _____ very gracious.

11. Would you _____ offended if I moved your desk?

12. He _____ watching at the window for me yesterday.

Verbs: "Was" and "Were"

Singular	Plural
I was	we were
you were	you were
he, she, it was	they were

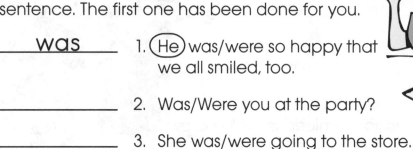

I was over there when it happened

You were?

Directions: Write the correct form of the verb in the blanks. Circle the subject of each sentence. The first one has been done for you.

__was__   1. (He) was/were so happy that we all smiled, too.

_____ 2. Was/Were you at the party?

_____ 3. She was/were going to the store.

_____ 4. He was/were always forgetting his hat.

_____ 5. Was/Were she there?

_____ 6. Was/Were you sure of your answers?

_____ 7. She was/were glad to help.

_____ 8. They was/were excited.

_____ 9. Exactly what was/were you planning to do?

_____ 10. It was/were wet outside.

_____ 11. They was/were scared by the noise.

_____ 12. Was/Were they expected before noon?

_____ 13. It was/were too early to get up!

_____ 14. She was/were always early.

_____ 15. You were/was the first person I asked.

Verbs: "Went" and "Gone"

The word **went** is used without a helping verb.

Examples:

Correct: Susan **went** to the store.

Incorrect: Susan **has went** to the store.

Gone is used with a helping verb.

Examples:

Correct: Susan **has gone** to the store.

Incorrect: Susan **gone** to the store.

Directions: Write **C** in the blank if the verb is used correctly. Draw an **X** in the blank if the verb is not used correctly.

_____C_____ 1. She has gone to my school since last year.

_____ 2. Has he been gone a long time?

_____ 3. He has went to the same class all year.

_____ 4. I have went to that doctor since I was born.

_____ 5. She is long gone!

_____ 6. Who among us has not gone to get a drink yet?

_____ 7. The class has gone on three field trips this year.

_____ 8. The class went on three field trips this year.

_____ 9. Who has not went to the board with the right answer?

_____ 10. We have not went on our vacation yet.

_____ 11. Who is went for the pizza?

_____ 12. The train has been gone for 2 hours.

_____ 13. The family had gone to the movies.

_____ 14. Have you went to visit the new bookstore?

_____ 15. He has gone on and on about how smart you are!

Review

Directions: Write **PRES** for present tense, **PAST** for past tense or **FUT** for future tense.

_____ 1. She will help him study.

_____ 2. She helped him study.

_____ 3. She helps him study.

_____ 4. She promised to help him study.

Directions: Write the past-tense form of these verbs.

5. cry _____

6. sigh _____

7. hurry _____

8. pop _____

Direction: Write the past tense of these irregular verbs with helpers.

9. (go) have   _____

10. (sleep) have _____

11. (sing) have   _____

12. (see) have   _____

Directions: Write the correct form of **be**.

13. They_____ my closest neighbors.

14. I _____very happy for you today.

15. He _____ there on time yesterday.

16. She _____ still the nicest girl I know.

Directions: Circle the correct verb.

17. He went/gone to my locker.

18. I went/gone to the beach many times.

19. Have you went/gone to this show before?

20. We went/gone all the way to the top!

Adding "er" and "est" to Adjectives

Directions: Circle the correct adjective for each sentence. The first one has been done for you.

1. Of all the students in the gym, her voice was (louder, (loudest).

2. "I can tell you are (busier, busiest) than I am," he said to the librarian.

3. If you and Carl stand back to back, I can see which one is (taller, tallest).

4. She is the (kinder, kindest) teacher in the whole building.

5. Wow! That is the (bigger, biggest) pumpkin I have ever seen!

6. I believe your flashlight is (brighter, brightest) than mine.

7. "This is the (cleaner, cleanest) your room has been in a long time," Mother said.

8. The leaves on that plant are (prettier, prettiest) than the ones on this plant.

Grade 4 - Comprehensive Curriculum

Adjectives Preceded by "More"

Most adjectives of two or more syllables are preceded by the word **more** as a way to show comparison between two things.

Examples:

Correct: intelligent, more intelligent

Incorrect: intelligenter

Correct: famous, more famous

Incorrect: famouser

Directions: Write **more** before the adjectives that fit the rule. Draw an **X** in the blanks of the adjectives that do not fit the rule. To test yourself, say the words aloud using **more** and adding **er** to hear which way sounds correct. The first two have been done for you.

_____X_____ 1. cheap   _____ 11. awful

__more__ 2. beautiful   _____ 12. delicious

_____ 3. quick   _____ 13. embarrassing

_____ 4. terrible   _____ 14. nice

_____ 5. difficult   _____ 15. often

_____ 6. interesting   _____ 16. hard

_____ 7. polite   _____ 17. valuable

_____ 8. cute   _____ 18. close

_____ 9. dark   _____ 19. fast

_____ 10. sad   _____ 20. important

Name: _____

Adjectives Using "er" or "More"

Directions: Add the word or words needed in each sentence. The first one has been done for you.

1. I thought the book was <u>**more interesting**</u> than the movie. (interesting)

2. Do you want to carry this box? It is _____ than the one you have now. (light)

3. I noticed you are moving _____ this morning. Does your ankle still bother you? (slow)

4. Thomas Edison is probably _____ for his invention of the electric light bulb than of the phonograph. (famous)

5. She stuck out her lower lip and whined, "Your ice-cream cone is _____ than mine!" (big)

6. Mom said my room was _____ than it has been in a long time. (clean)

Adjectives Preceded by "Most"

Most adjectives of two or more syllables are preceded by the word **most** as a way to show comparison between more than two things.

Examples:

Correct:	intelligent, most intelligent
Incorrect:	intelligentest
Correct:	famous, most famous
Incorrect:	famousest

Directions: Read the following groups of sentences. In the last sentence for each group, write the adjective preceded by **most**. The first one has been done for you.

1. My uncle is intelligent.
   My aunt is more intelligent.
   My cousin is the _____ most intelligent _____.

2. I am thankful.
   My brother is more thankful.
   My parents are the _____.

3. Your sister is polite.
   Your brother is more polite.
   You are the _____.

4. The blouse was expensive.
   The sweater was more expensive.
   The coat was the _____.

5. The class was fortunate.
   The teacher was more fortunate.
   The principal was the _____.

6. The cookies were delicious.
   The cake was even more delicious.
   The brownies were the _____.

7. That painting is elaborate.
   The sculpture is more elaborate.
   The finger painting is the _____.

Name: _____

Adjectives Using "est" or "Most"

Directions: Add the word or words needed to complete each sentence. The first one has been done for you.

1. The star over there is the ____**brightest**____ of all! (bright)

2. "I believe this is the _____ time I have ever had," said Mackenzie. (delightful)

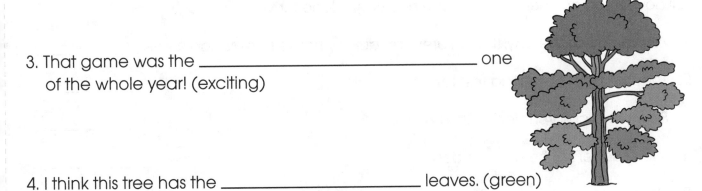

3. That game was the _____ one of the whole year! (exciting)

4. I think this tree has the _____ leaves. (green)

5. We will need the _____ knife you have to cut the face for the jack-o-lantern. (sharp)

6. Everyone agreed that your chocolate chip cookies

   were the _____ of all. (delicious)

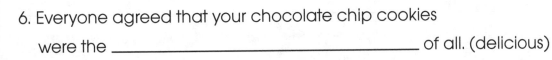

Grade 4 - Comprehensive Curriculum

Writing: Adverbs

Like adjectives, **adverbs** are describing words. They describe verbs. Adverbs tell how, when or where action takes place.

Examples:

How	When	Where
slowly	yesterday	here
gracefully	today	there
swiftly	tomorrow	everywhere
quickly	soon	

Hint: To identify an adverb, locate the verb, then ask yourself if there are any words that tell how, when or where action takes place.

Directions: Read the following sentences. Underline the adverbs, then write whether they tell how, when or where. The first one has been done for you.

1. At the end of the day, the children ran <u>quickly</u> home from school.   _____how_____

2. They will have a spelling test tomorrow.   _____

3. Slowly, the children filed to their seats.   _____

4. The teacher sat here at her desk.   _____

5. She will pass the tests back later.   _____

6. The students received their grades happily.   _____

Directions: Write four sentences of your own using any of the adverbs above.

_____

_____

_____

_____

Name: _____

Adverbs

Adverbs are words that tell when, where or how.

Adverbs of time tell when.

Example:

The train left yesterday.

Yesterday is an adverb of time. It tells when the train left.

Adverbs of place tell where.

Example:

The girl walked away.

Away is an adverb of place. It tells where the girl walked.

Adverbs of manner tell how.

Example:

The boy walked quickly.

Quickly is an adverb of manner. It tells how the boy walked.

Directions: Write the adverb for each sentence in the first blank. In the second blank, write whether it is an adverb of time, place or manner. The first one has been done for you.

1. The family ate downstairs. _____downstairs_____ _____place_____

2. The relatives laughed loudly. _____ _____

3. We will finish tomorrow. _____ _____

4. The snowstorm will stop soon. _____ _____

5. She sings beautifully! _____ _____

6. The baby slept soundly. _____ _____

7. The elevator stopped suddenly. _____ _____

8. Does the plane leave today? _____ _____

9. The phone call came yesterday. _____ _____

10. She ran outside. _____ _____

Grade 4 - Comprehensive Curriculum

Adverbs of Time

Directions: Choose a word or group of words from the box to complete each sentence. Make sure the adverb you choose makes sense with the rest of the sentence.

in 2 weeks	last winter
next week	at the end of the day
soon	right now
2 days ago	tonight

1. We had a surprise birthday party for him _____ .

2. Our science projects are due _____ .

3. My best friend will be moving _____ .

4. Justin and Ronnie need our help _____ !

5. We will find out who the winners are _____ .

6. Can you take me to ball practice _____ ?

7. She said we will be getting a letter _____ .

8. Diane made the quilt _____ .

Name: _____

Adverbs of Place

Directions: Choose one word from the box to complete each sentence. Make sure the adverb you choose makes sense with the rest of the sentence.

inside	upstairs	below	everywhere
home	somewhere	outside	there

1. Each child took a new library book _____ .

2. We looked _____ for his jacket.

3. We will have recess _____ because it is raining.

4. From the top of the mountain we could see the village far
   _____ .

5. My sister and I share a bedroom _____ .

6. The teacher warned the children, "You must play with the ball
   _____ ."

7. Mother said, "I know that recipe is _____
   in this file box!"

8. You can put the chair _____ .

Adverbs of Manner

Directions: Choose a word from the box to complete each sentence. Make sure the adverb you choose makes sense with the rest of the sentence. One word will be used twice.

quickly	carefully	loudly	easily	carelessly	slowly

1. The scouts crossed the old bridge _____ .

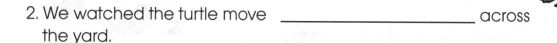

2. We watched the turtle move _____ across the yard.

3. Everyone completed the math test _____ .

4. The quarterback scampered _____ down the sideline.

5. The mother _____ cleaned the child's sore knee.

6. The fire was caused by someone _____ tossing a match.

7. The alarm rang _____ while we were eating.

Adjectives and Adverbs

Directions: Write **ADJ** on the line if the bold word is an adjective. Write **ADV** if the bold word is an adverb. The first one has been done for you.

_____ADV_____ 1. That road leads **nowhere**.

_____ 2. The squirrel was **nearby**.

_____ 3. Her **delicious** cookies were all eaten.

_____ 4. Everyone rushed **indoors**.

_____ 5. He **quickly** zipped his jacket.

_____ 6. She hummed a **popular** tune.

_____ 7. Her **sunny** smile warmed my heart.

_____ 8. I hung your coat **there**.

_____ 9. Bring that **here** this minute!

_____ 10. We all walked **back** to school.

_____ 11. The **skinniest** boy ate the most food!

_____ 12. She acts like a **famous** person.

_____ 13. The **silliest** jokes always make me laugh.

_____ 14. She must have parked her car **somewhere**!

_____ 15. Did you take the test **today**?

Name: _____

Adjectives and Adverbs

Directions: Read this story. Underline the adjectives. Circle the adverbs. Write the words in the correct column at the end of the story.

Surprise!

Emily and Elizabeth tiptoed quietly through the dark hallway. Even though none of the lights were lit, they knew the presents were there. Every year the two sisters had gone to Mom and Dad's bedroom to wake them on Christmas morning. This year would be different, they decided.

Last night after supper, they had secretly plotted to look early in the morning before Mom and Dad were awake. The girls knew that Emily's red-and-green stocking and Elizabeth's striped stocking hung by the brick fireplace. They knew the beautiful tree was in the corner by the rocking chair.

"Won't Mom and Dad be surprised to awaken on their own?" asked Elizabeth quietly.

Emily whispered, "Click the overhead lights so we can see better."

"You don't have to whisper," said a voice.

There sat Mom and Dad as the Christmas-tree lights suddenly shone.

Dad said, "I guess the surprise is on you two!"

Adverbs	Adjectives
_____	_____
_____	_____
_____	_____
_____	_____
_____	_____
_____	_____
_____	_____

Review

Directions: Write the correct words to complete the sentences. Use the words on the presents at the bottom of the page.

1. The suffix _____ and the word _____ are used when comparing two things.

2. One example of an adverb of time is _____ .

3. When an adjective ends with_____ , you change the y to i before adding er or est.

4. An _____ is a word that tells when, where or how.

5. An example of an adverb of place is _____ .

6. The suffix _____ and the word _____ are used when comparing more than two things.

7. An _____ is a word that describes a noun.

8. An example of an adverb of manner is _____ .

adjective est softly adverb er y most there more tomorrow

Name: _____

Review

Directions: For the bold word in each sentence, write **N** for noun, **V** for verb, **ADJ** for adjective or **ADV** for adverb.

_____ 1. She is the **tallest** one outside.

_____ 2. **She** is the tallest one outside.

_____ 3. She **is** the tallest one outside.

_____ 4. She is the tallest one **outside**.

Directions: For the bold word in each sentence, write **P** for adverb of place, **T** for adverb of time or **M** for adverb of manner.

_____ 5. Your shoes are **downstairs**.

_____ 6. His response was **speedy**.

_____ 7. **Here** is my homework.

_____ 8. The present will be mailed **tomorrow**.

Directions: Add **er** and **est** or **more** and **most** to the words below to show comparison.

9. fat _____   _____

10. grateful _____   _____

11. serious _____   _____

12. easy _____   _____

Directions: For the bold word in each sentence, write **ADV** for adverb or **ADJ** for adjective.

_____ 13. **Grumpy** people are not pleasant.

_____ 14. Put the package **there**, please.

_____ 15. **Upstairs** is where I sleep.

_____ 16. **Warm** blankets feel toasty on cold nights.

Writing: Using Conjunctions

Conjunctions are joining words that can be used to combine sentences. Words such as **and**, **but**, **or**, **when** and **after** are conjunctions.

Examples:
Sally went to the mall. She went to the movies.
Sally went to the mall, and she went to the movies.

We can have our vacation at home. We can vacation at the beach.
We can have our vacation at home, or we can vacation at the beach.

Mary fell on the playground. She did not hurt herself.
Mary fell on the playground, but she did not hurt herself.

Note: The conjunctions **after** or **when** are usually placed at the beginning of the sentence.

Example: Marge went to the store. She went to the gas station.
After Marge went to the store, she went to the gas station.

Directions: Combine the following sentences using a conjunction.

1. Peter fell down the steps. He broke his foot. (and)

   _____

2. I visited New York. I would like to see Chicago. (but)

   _____

3. Amy can edit books. She can write stories. (or)

   _____

4. He played in the barn. John started to sneeze. (when)

   _____

5. The team won the playoffs. They went to the championships. (after)

   _____

Directions: Write three sentences of your own using the conjunctions **and**, **but**, **or**, **when** or **after**.

_____

_____

_____

_____

"And," "But," "Or"

Directions: Write **and**, **but** or **or** to complete the sentences.

1. I thought we might try that new hamburger place, _____ Mom wants to eat at the Spaghetti Shop.

2. We could stay home, _____ would you rather go to the game?

3. She went right home after school, _____ he stopped at the store.

4. Mother held the piece of paneling, _____ Father nailed it in place.

5. She babysat last weekend, _____ her big sister went with her.

6. She likes raisins in her oatmeal, _____ I would rather have mine with brown sugar.

7. She was planning on coming over tomorrow, _____ I asked her if she could wait until the weekend.

8. Tomato soup with crackers sounds good to me, _____ would you rather have vegetable beef soup?

"Because" and "So"

Directions: Write **because** or **so** to complete the sentences.

1. She cleaned the paint brushes _____ they would be ready in the morning.

2. Father called home complaining of a sore throat _____ Mom stopped by the pharmacy.

3. His bus will be running late _____ it has a flat tire.

4. We all worked together _____ we could get the job done sooner.

5. We took a variety of sandwiches on the picnic _____ we knew not everyone liked cheese and olives with mayonnaise.

6. All the school children were sent home _____ the electricity went off at school.

7. My brother wants us to meet his girlfriend _____ she will be coming to dinner with us on Friday.

8. He forgot to take his umbrella along this morning _____ now his clothes are very wet.

Name: _____

"When" and "After"

Directions: Write **when** or **after** to complete the sentences.

1. I knew we were in trouble _____ I heard the thunder in the distance.

2. We carried the baskets of cherries to the car _____ we were finished picking them.

3. Mother took off her apron _____ I reminded her that our dinner guests would be here any minute.

4. I wondered if we would have school tomorrow _____ I noticed the snow begin to fall.

5. The boys and girls all clapped _____ the magician pulled the colored scarves out of his sleeve.

6. I was startled _____ the phone rang so late last night.

7. You will need to get the film developed _____ you have taken all the pictures.

8. The children began to run _____ the snake started to move!

Conjunctions

Directions: Choose the best conjunction from the box to combine the pairs of sentences. Then rewrite the sentences.

and	but	or	because	when	after	so

1. I like Leah. I like Ben.

_____

2. Should I eat the orange? Should I eat the apple?

_____

3. You will get a reward. You turned in the lost item.

_____

4. I really mean what I say! You had better listen!

_____

5. I like you. You're nice, friendly, helpful and kind.

_____

6. You can have dessert. You ate all your peas.

_____

7. I like your shirt better. You should decide for yourself.

_____

8. We walked out of the building. We heard the fire alarm.

_____

9. I like to sing folk songs. I like to play the guitar.

_____

Grade 4 - Comprehensive Curriculum

Writing: Using Conjunctions

Directions: Combine each pair of sentences using the conjunctions **or**, **and**, **but**, **after** or **when**. You may need to change the word order in the sentences.

Example:

My stomach hurts.   I still want to go to the movies.

My stomach hurts, but I still want to go to the movies.

1. He accused me of peeking.   I felt very angry.

   _____

2. The accident was over.   I started shaking.

   _____

3. Is that a freckle?   Is that dirt?

   _____

4. I forgot my jacket.   I had to go back and get it.

   _____

5. I like Christmas.   I don't like waiting for it.

   _____

6. Would you like to live in a castle?   Would you like to live on a houseboat?

   _____

7. The general gave the command.   The army marched.

   _____

8. The trees dropped all their leaves.   We raked them up.

   _____

"Good" and "Well"

Use the word **good** to describe a noun. Good is an adjective.

Example: She is a **good** teacher.

Use the word **well** to tell or ask how something is done or to describe someone's health. Well is an adverb. It describes a verb.

Example: She is not feeling **well**.

Directions: Write **good** or **well** in the blanks to complete the sentences correctly. The first one has been done for you.

**good** 1. Our team could use a good/well captain.

_____ 2. The puny kitten doesn't look good/well.

_____ 3. He did his job so good/well that everyone praised him.

_____ 4. Whining isn't a good/well habit.

_____ 5. I might just as good/well do it myself.

_____ 6. She was one of the most well-/good- liked girls at school.

_____ 7. I did the book report as good/well as I could.

_____ 8. The television works very good/well.

_____ 9. You did a good/well job repairing the TV!

_____ 10. Thanks for a job good/well done!

_____ 11. You did a good/well job fixing the computer.

_____ 12. You had better treat your friends good/well.

_____ 13. Can your grandmother hear good/well?

_____ 14. Your brother will be well/good soon.

"Your" and "You're"

The word **your** shows possession.

Examples:

    Is that **your** book?

    I visited **your** class.

The word **you're** is a contraction for **you are**. A **contraction** is two words joined together as one. An apostrophe shows where letters have been left out.

Examples:

    You're doing well on that painting.

    If **you're** going to pass the test, you should study.

Directions: Write **your** or **you're** in the blanks to complete the sentences correctly. The first one has been done for you.

    You're   1. Your/You're the best friend I have!

    _____   2. Your/You're going to drop that!

    _____   3. Your/You're brother came to see me.

    _____   4. Is that your/you're cat?

    _____   5. If your/you're going, you'd better hurry!

    _____   6. Why are your/you're fingers so red?

    _____   7. It's none of your/you're business!

    _____   8. Your/You're bike's front tire is low.

    _____   9. Your/You're kidding!

    _____ 10. Have it your/you're way.

    _____ 11. I thought your/you're report was great!

    _____ 12. He thinks your/you're wonderful!

    _____ 13. What is your/you're first choice?

    _____ 14. What's your/you're opinion?

    _____ 15. If your/you're going, so am I!

    _____ 16. Your/You're welcome.

Name: _____

"Good" and "Well"; "Your" and "You're"

Directions: Choose the correct word for each sentence: **good**, **well**, **your** or **you're**.

1. Are you sure you can see _____ enough to read with the lighting you have?

2. _____ going to need a paint smock when you go to art class tomorrow afternoon.

3. I can see _____ having some trouble. Can I help with that?

4. The music department needs to buy a speaker system that has _____ quality sound.

5. The principal asked, "Where is _____ hall pass?"

6. You must do the job _____ if you expect to keep it.

7. The traffic policeman said, "May I please see _____ driver's license?"

8. The story you wrote for English class was done quite _____ .

9. That radio station you listen to is a _____ one.

10. Let us know if _____ unable to attend the meeting on Saturday.

"Its" and "It's"

The word **its** shows ownership.

Examples:

> **Its** leaves have all turned red.
> **Its** paw was injured.

The word **it's** is a contraction for **it is**.

Examples:

> **It's** better to be early than late.
> **It's** not fair!

Directions: Write **its** or **it's** to complete the sentences correctly. The first one has been done for you.

___It's___ 1. Its/It's never too late for ice cream!

_____ 2. Its/It's eyes are already open.

_____ 3. Its/It's your turn to wash the dishes!

_____ 4. Its/It's cage was left open.

_____ 5. Its/It's engine was beyond repair.

_____ 6. Its/It's teeth were long and pointed.

_____ 7. Did you see its/it's hind legs?

_____ 8. Why do you think its/it's mine?

_____ 9. Do you think its/it's the right color?

_____ 10. Don't pet its/it's fur too hard!

_____ 11. Its/It's from my Uncle Harry.

_____ 12. Can you tell its/it's a surprise?

_____ 13. Is its/it's stall always this clean?

_____ 14. Its/It's not time to eat yet.

_____ 15. She says its/it's working now.

"Can" and "May"

The word **can** means am able to or to be able to.

Examples:

>   I **can** do that for you.
>   **Can** you do that for me?

The word **may** means be allowed to or permitted to. May is used to ask or give permission. **May** can also mean **might** or **perhaps**.

Examples:

>   **May** I be excused?
>   You **may** sit here.

Directions: Write **can** or **may** in the blanks to complete the sentences correctly. The first one has been done for you.

May   1. Can/May I help you?

_____ 2. He's smart. He can/may do it himself.

_____ 3. When can/may I have my dessert?

_____ 4. I can/may tell you exactly what she said.

_____ 5. He can/may speak French fluently.

_____ 6. You can/may use my pencil.

_____ 7. I can/may be allowed to attend the concert.

_____ 8. It's bright. I can/may see you!

_____ 9. Can/May my friend stay for dinner?

_____ 10. You can/may leave when your report is finished.

_____ 11. I can/may see your point!

_____ 12. She can/may dance well.

_____ 13. Can/May you hear the dog barking?

_____ 14. Can/May you help me button this sweater?

_____ 15. Mother, can/may I go to the movies?

"Its" and "It's"; "Can" and "May"

Directions: Choose the correct word for each sentence: **its**, **it's**, **can** or **may**.

1. "It looks as though your arms are full, Diane. _____ I help you with some of those things?" asked Michele.

2. The squirrel _____ climb up the tree quickly with his mouth full of acorns.

3. She has had her school jacket so long that it is beginning to lose _____ color.

4. How many laps around the track _____ you do?

5. Sometimes you can tell what a story is going to be about by looking at _____ title.

6. Our house _____ need to be painted again in two or three years.

7. Mother asked, "Jon, _____ you open the door for your father?"

8. _____ going to be a while until your birthday, but do you know what you want?

9. I can feel it in the air; _____ going to snow soon.

10. If I'm careful with it, _____ I borrow your CD player?

"Sit" and "Set"

The word **sit** means to rest.

Examples:

> Please **sit** here!
>
> Will you **sit** by me?

The word **set** means to put or place something.

Examples:

> **Set** your purse there.
>
> **Set** the dishes on the table.

Directions: Write **sit** or **set** to complete the sentences correctly. The first one has been done for you.

_____sit_____ 1. Would you please sit/set down here?

_____ 2. You can sit/set the groceries there.

_____ 3. She sit/set her suitcase in the closet.

_____ 4. He sit/set his watch for half past three.

_____ 5. She's a person who can't sit/set still.

_____ 6. Sit/set the baby on the couch beside me.

_____ 7. Where did you sit/set your new shoes?

_____ 8. They decided to sit/set together during the movie.

_____ 9. Let me sit/set you straight on that!

_____ 10. Instead of swimming, he decided to sit/set in the water.

_____ 11. He sit/set the greasy pan in the sink.

_____ 12. She sit/set the file folder on her desk.

_____ 13. Don't ever sit/set on the refrigerator!

_____ 14. She sit/set the candles on the cake.

"They're," "Their," "There"

The word **they're** is a contraction for **they are**.

Examples:

> **They're** our very best friends!
>
> Ask them if **they're** coming over tomorrow.

The word **their** shows ownership.

Examples:

> **Their** dog is friendly.
>
> It's **their** bicycle.

The word **there** shows place or direction.

Examples:

> Look over **there**.
>
> **There** it is.

Directions: Write **they're**, **their** or **there** to complete the sentences correctly. The first one has been done for you.

There ___ 1. They're/Their/There is the sweater I want!

_____ 2. Do you believe they're/their/there stories?

_____ 3. Be they're/their/there by one o'clock.

_____ 4. Were you they're/their/there last night?

_____ 5. I know they're/their/there going to attend.

_____ 6. Have you met they're/their/there mother?

_____ 7. I can go they're/their/there with you.

_____ 8. Do you like they're/their/there new car?

_____ 9. They're/Their/There friendly to everyone.

_____ 10. Did she say they're/their/there ready to go?

_____ 11. She said she'd walk by they're/their/there house.

_____ 12. Is anyone they're/their/there?

_____ 13. I put it right over they're/their/there!

Name: _____

"Sit" and "Set"; "They're," "There," "Their"

Directions: Choose the correct word for each sentence: **sit**, **set**, **they're**, **there** or **their**.

1. _____ your pencil on your desk when you finish working.

2. When we choose our seats on the bus will you _____ with me?

3. _____ is my library book! I wondered where I had left it!

4. My little brother and his friend said _____ not going to the ball game with us.

5. Before the test, the teacher wants the students to sharpen _____ pencils.

6. She blew the whistle and shouted, "Everyone _____ down on the floor!"

7. All the books for the fourth graders belong over _____ on the top shelf.

8. The little kittens are beginning to open _____ eyes.

9. I'm going to _____ the dishes on the table.

10. _____ going to be fine by themselves for a few minutes.

Grade 4 - Comprehensive Curriculum

Name: _____

"This" and "These"

The word **this** is an adjective that refers to things that are near. **This** always describes a singular noun. Singular means one.

Example:

I'll buy **this** coat.

(Coat is singular.)

The word **these** is also an adjective that refers to things that are near. **These** always describes a plural noun. A plural refers to more than one thing.

Example:

I will buy **these** flowers.

(Flowers is a plural noun.)

Directions: Write **this** or **these** to complete the sentences correctly. The first one has been done for you.

____these____ 1. I will take this/these cookies with me.

_____ 2. Do you want this/these seeds?

_____ 3. Did you try this/these nuts?

_____ 4. Do it this/these way!

_____ 5. What do you know about this/these situation?

_____ 6. Did you open this/these doors?

_____ 7. Did you open this/these window?

_____ 8. What is the meaning of this/these letters?

_____ 9. Will you carry this/these books for me?

_____ 10. This/These pans are hot!

_____ 11. Do you think this/these light is too bright?

_____ 12. Are this/these boots yours?

_____ 13. Do you like this/these rainy weather?

Name: _____

Review

Directions: Complete the sentences by writing the correct words in the blanks.

_____ 1. You have a good/well attitude.

_____ 2. The teacher was not feeling good/well.

_____ 3. She sang extremely good/well.

_____ 4. Everyone said Josh was a good/well boy.

_____ 5. Your/You're going to be sorry for that!

_____ 6. Tell her your/you're serious.

_____ 7. Your/You're report was wonderful!

_____ 8. Your/You're the best person for the job.

_____ 9. Do you think its/it's going to have babies?

_____ 10. Its/It's back paw had a thorn in it.

_____ 11. Its/It's fun to make new friends.

_____ 12. Is its/it's mother always nearby?

_____ 13. How can/may I help you?

_____ 14. You can/may come in now.

_____ 15. Can/May you lift this for me?

_____ 16. She can/may sing soprano.

_____ 17. I'll wait for you to sit/set down first.

_____ 18. We sit/set our dirty boots outside.

_____ 19. It's they're/their/there turn to choose.

_____ 20. They're/Their/There is your answer!

_____ 21. They say they're/their/there coming.

_____ 22. I must have this/these one!

_____ 23. I saw this/these gloves at the store.

_____ 24. He said this/these were his.

Review

Directions: Write the correct answers in the blanks using the words in the box.

good	well	your	you're	its
it's	can	may	sit	set
they're	there	their	this	these

1. _____ is an adjective that refers to a particular thing.

2. Use _____ to tell or ask how something is done or to describe someone's health.

3. _____ is a contraction for it is.

4. _____ describes a plural noun and refers to particular things.

5. _____ means to rest.

6. _____ means am able to or to be able to.

7. _____ is a contraction for they are.

8. _____ , _____ and _____ show ownership or possession.

9. Use _____ to ask politely to be permitted to do something.

10. _____ is a contraction for you are.

11. _____ means to place or put.

12. _____ describes a noun.

13. Use _____ to show direction or placement.

Name: _____

Capital Letters and Periods

The first letter of a person's first, last and middle name is always capitalized.

Example: Elizabeth Jane Marks is my best friend.

The first letter of a person's title is always capitalized.
If the title is abbreviated, the title is followed by a period.

Examples: Her mother is **Dr**. Susan Jones Marks.
Ms. Jessica Joseph was a visitor.

Directions: Write **C** if the sentence is punctuated and capitalized correctly. Draw an **X** if the sentence is not punctuated and capitalized correctly. The first one has been done for you.

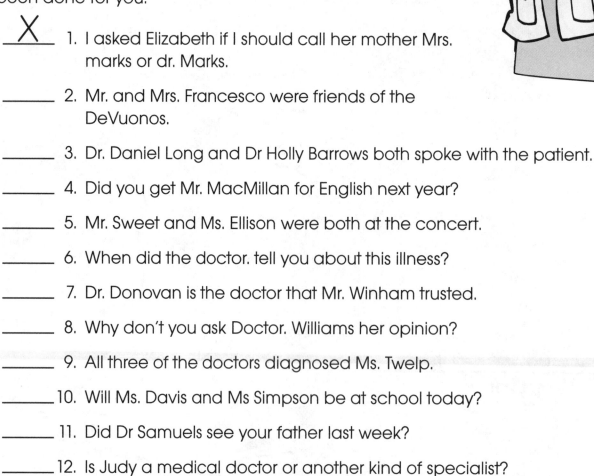

____X____ 1. I asked Elizabeth if I should call her mother Mrs. marks or dr. Marks.

_____ 2. Mr. and Mrs. Francesco were friends of the DeVuonos.

_____ 3. Dr. Daniel Long and Dr Holly Barrows both spoke with the patient.

_____ 4. Did you get Mr. MacMillan for English next year?

_____ 5. Mr. Sweet and Ms. Ellison were both at the concert.

_____ 6. When did the doctor. tell you about this illness?

_____ 7. Dr. Donovan is the doctor that Mr. Winham trusted.

_____ 8. Why don't you ask Doctor. Williams her opinion?

_____ 9. All three of the doctors diagnosed Ms. Twelp.

_____ 10. Will Ms. Davis and Ms Simpson be at school today?

_____ 11. Did Dr Samuels see your father last week?

_____ 12. Is Judy a medical doctor or another kind of specialist?

_____ 13. We are pleased to introduce Ms King and Mr. Graham.

Name: _____

Punctuation: Commas

Use a comma to separate the number of the day of a month and the year. Do not use a comma to separate the month and year if no day is given.

Examples:

> June 14, 1999
>
> June 1999

Use a comma after **yes** or **no** when it is the first word in a sentence.

Examples:

> Yes, I will do it right now.
>
> No, I don't want any.

Directions: Write **C** if the sentence is punctuated correctly. Draw an **X** if the sentence is not punctuated correctly. The first one has been done for you.

___C___ 1. No, I don't plan to attend.

_____ 2. I told them, oh yes, I would go.

_____ 3. Her birthday is March 13, 1995.

_____ 4. He was born in May, 1997.

_____ 5. Yes, of course I like you!

_____ 6. No I will not be there.

_____ 7. They left for vacation on February, 14.

_____ 8. No, today is Monday.

_____ 9. The program was first shown on August 12, 1991.

_____10. In September, 2007 how old will you be?

_____ 11. He turned 12 years old on November, 13.

_____12. I said no, I will not come no matter what!

_____13. Yes, she is a friend of mine.

_____14. His birthday is June 12, 1992, and mine is June 12, 1993.

_____15. No I would not like more dessert.

Punctuation: Commas

Use a comma to separate words in a series. A comma is used after each word in a series but is not needed before the last word. Both ways are correct. In your own writing, be consistent about which style you use.

Examples:

We ate apples, oranges, and pears.
We ate apples, oranges and pears.

Always use a comma between the name of a city and a state.

Example:

She lives in Fresno, California.
He lives in Wilmington, Delaware.

Directions: Write **C** if the sentence is punctuated correctly. Draw an **X** if the sentence is not punctuated correctly. The first one has been done for you.

___X___ 1. She ordered shoes, dresses and shirts to be sent to her home in Oakland California.

_____ 2. No one knew her pets' names were Fido, Spot and Tiger.

_____ 3. He likes green beans lima beans, and corn on the cob.

_____ 4. Typing paper, pens and pencils are all needed for school.

_____ 5. Send your letters to her in College Park, Maryland.

_____ 6. Orlando Florida is the home of Disney World.

_____ 7. Mickey, Minnie, Goofy and Daisy are all favorites of mine.

_____ 8. Send your letter to her in Reno, Nevada.

_____ 9. Before he lived in New York, City he lived in San Diego, California.

_____ 10. She mailed postcards, and letters to him in Lexington, Kentucky.

_____ 11. Teacups, saucers, napkins, and silverware were piled high.

_____ 12. Can someone give me a ride to Indianapolis, Indiana?

_____ 13. He took a train a car, then a boat to visit his old friend.

_____ 14. Why can't I go to Disney World to see Mickey, and Minnie?

Book Titles

All words in the title of a book are underlined. Underlined words also mean italics.

Examples:

<u>The Hunt for Red October</u> was a best-seller!
(*The Hunt for Red October*)

Have you read <u>Lost in Space</u>? (*Lost in Space*)

Directions: Underline the book titles in these sentences. The first one has been done for you.

1. <u>The Dinosaur Poster Book</u> is for eight year olds.

2. Have you read Lion Dancer by Kate Waters?

3. Baby Dinosaurs and Giant Dinosaurs were both written by Peter Dodson.

4. Have you heard of the book That's What Friends Are For by Carol Adorjan?

5. J.B. Stamper wrote a book called The Totally Terrific Valentine Party Book.

6. The teacher read Almost Ten and a Half aloud to our class.

7. Marrying Off Mom is about a girl who tries to get her widowed mother to start dating.

8. The Snow and The Fire are the second and third books by author Caroline Cooney.

9. The title sounds silly, but Goofbang Value Daze really is the name of a book!

10. A book about space exploration is The Day We Walked on the Moon by George Sullivan.

11. Alice and the Birthday Giant tells about a giant who came to a girl's birthday party.

12. A book about a girl who is sad about her father's death is called Rachel and the Upside Down Heart by Eileen Douglas.

13. Two books about baseball are Baseball Bloopers and Oddball Baseball.

14. Katharine Ross wrote Teenage Mutant Ninja Turtles: The Movie Storybook.

Name: _____

Book Titles

Capitalize the first and last word of book titles. Capitalize all other words of book titles except short prepositions, such as **of**, **at** and **in**; conjunctions, such as **and**, **or** and **but**; and articles, such as **a**, **an** and **the**.

Examples:

Have you read <u>War and Peace</u>?

Pippi Longstocking in Moscow is her favorite book.

Directions: Underline the book titles. Circle the words that should be capitalized. The first one has been done for you.

1. (murder) in the (blue room) by Elliot Roosevelt

2. growing up in a divided society by Sandra Burnham

3. the corn king and the spring queen by Naomi Mitchison

4. new kids on the block by Grace Catalano

5. best friends don't tell lies by Linda Barr

6. turn your kid into a computer genius by Carole Gerber

7. 50 simple things you can do to save the earth by Earth Works Press

8. garfield goes to waist by Jim Davis

9. the hunt for red october by Tom Clancy

10. fall into darkness by Christopher Pike

11. oh the places you'll go! by Dr. Seuss

12. amy the dancing bear by Carly Simon

13. the great waldo search by Martin Handford

14. the time and space of uncle albert by Russel Stannard

15. true stories about abraham lincoln by Ruth Gross

Name: _____

Punctuation: Quotation Marks

Use quotation marks (" ") before and after the exact words of a speaker.

Examples:

I asked Aunt Martha, "How do you feel?"

"I feel awful," Aunt Martha replied.

Do not put quotation marks around words that report what the speaker said.

Examples:

Aunt Martha said she felt awful.

I asked Aunt Martha how she felt.

Directions: Write **C** if the sentence is punctuated correctly. Draw an **X** if the sentence is not punctuated correctly. The first one has been done for you.

___C___ 1. "I want it right now!" she demanded angrily.

_____ 2 "Do you want it now? I asked."

_____ 3. She said "she felt better" now.

_____ 4. Her exact words were, "I feel much better now!"

_____ 5. "I am so thrilled to be here!" he shouted.

_____ 6. "Yes, I will attend," she replied.

_____ 7. Elizabeth said "she was unhappy."

_____ 8. "I'm unhappy," Elizabeth reported.

_____ 9. "Did you know her mother?" I asked.

_____ 10. I asked "whether you knew her mother."

_____ 11. I wondered, "What will dessert be?"

_____ 12. "Which will it be, salt or pepper?" the waiter asked.

_____ 13. "No, I don't know the answer!" he snapped.

_____ 14. He said "yes he'd take her on the trip.

_____ 15. Be patient, he said. "it will soon be over."

Name: _____

Punctuation: Quotation Marks

Use quotation marks around the titles of songs and poems.

Examples:

Have you heard "Still Cruising" by the Beach Boys?

"Ode To a Nightingale" is a famous poem.

Directions: Write **C** if the sentence is punctuated correctly. Draw an **X** if the sentence is not punctuated correctly. The first one has been done for you.

__C__ 1. Do you know "My Bonnie Lies Over the Ocean"?

_____ 2. We sang The Stars and Stripes Forever" at school.

_____ 3. Her favorite song is "The Eensy Weensy Spider."

_____ 4. Turn the music up when "A Hard Day's "Night comes on!

_____ 5. "Yesterday" was one of Paul McCartney's most famous songs.

_____ 6. "Mary Had a Little Lamb" is a very silly poem!

_____ 7. A song everyone knows is "Happy Birthday."

_____ 8. "Swing Low, Sweet Chariot" was first sung by slaves.

_____ 9. Do you know the words to Home on "the Range"?

_____10. "Hiawatha" is a poem many older people had to memorize.

_____11. "Happy Days Are Here Again! is an upbeat tune.

_____12. Frankie Valli and the Four Seasons sang "Sherry."

_____13. The words to "Rain, Rain" Go Away are easy to learn.

_____14. A slow song I know is called "Summertime."

_____15. Little children like to hear "The Night Before Christmas."

Review

Directions: The following sentences have errors in punctuation, capitalization or both. The number in parentheses **( )** at the end of each sentence tells you how many errors it contains. Correct the errors by rewriting each sentence.

1. I saw mr. Johnson reading War And Peace to his class. (3)

_____

2. Do you like to sing "Take me Out to The Ballgame"? (2)

_____

3. He recited Hiawatha to Miss. Simpson's class. (2)

_____

4. Bananas, and oranges are among Dr smith's favorite fruits. (3)

_____

5. "Daisy, daisy is a song about a bicycle built for two. (2)

_____

6. Good Morning, Granny Rose is about a woman and her dog. (1)

_____

7. Garfield goes to waist is a very funny book! (3)

_____

8. Peanut butter, jelly, and bread are Miss. Lee's favorite treats. (1)

_____

Proofreading

Proofreading means searching for and correcting errors by carefully reading and rereading what has been written. Use the proofreading marks below when correcting your writing or someone else's.

To insert a word or a punctuation mark that has been left out, use this mark: ∧. It is called a caret.

Example: We∧to the dance together.
       went

To show that a letter should be capitalized, put three lines under it.

Example: Mrs. jones drove us to school.

To show that a capital letter should be small or lowercase, draw a diagonal line through it.

Example: Mrs. Jones Drove us to school.

To show that a word is spelled incorrectly, draw a horizontal line through it and write the correct spelling above it.

Example: The wolros is an amazing animal.
       walrus

Directions: Proofread the two paragraphs using the proofreading marks you lear The author's last name, Towne, is spelled correctly.

The Modern ark

My book report is on the modern ark by Cecilia Fitzsimmons. The book tells abut 80 of worlds endangered animals. The book also an arc and animals inside for kids put together.

Their House

there house is a Great book! The arthur's name is Mary Towne. they're house tells about a girl name Molly. Molly's Family bys an old house from some people named warren. Then there big problems begin!

Name: _____

Proofreading

Directions: Proofread the sentences. Write **C** if the sentence has no errors. Draw an **X** if the sentence contains missing words or other errors. The first one has been done for you.

__C__ 1. The new Ship Wreck Museum in Key West is exciting!

_____ 2. Another thing I liked was the litehouse.

_____ 3. Do you remember Hemingway's address in Key West?

_____ 4. The Key West semetery is on 21 acres of ground.

_____ 5. Ponce de eon discovered Key West.

_____ 6. The cemetery in Key West is on Francis Street.

_____ 7. My favorete tombstone was the sailor's.

_____ 8. His wife wrote the words on it. Remember?

_____ 9. The words said, "at least I know where to find him now!"

_____ 10. That sailor must have been away at sea all the time.

_____ 11. The troley ride around Key West is very interesting.

_____ 12. Do you why it is called Key West?

_____ 13. Can you imagine a lighthouse in the middle of your town?

_____ 14. It's interesting to no that Key West is our southernmost city.

_____ 15. Besides Harry Truman and Hemingway, did other famous people live there?

Name: _____

Proofreading

Directions: Proofread the paragraphs, using the proofreading marks you learned. There are seven capitalization errors, three missing words and eleven errors in spelling or word usage.

Key West

key West has been tropical paradise ever since Ponce de Leon first saw the set of islands called the keys in 1513. Two famus streets in Key West are named duval and whitehead. You will find the city semetery on Francis Street. The tombstones are funny!

The message on one is, "I told you I was sick!" On sailor's tombston is this mesage his widow: "At lease I no where to find him now."

The cemetery is on 21 akres in the midle of town. The most famous home in key west is that of the authur, Ernest Hemingway. Heminway's home was at 907 whitehead Street. He lived their for 30 years.

Name: _____

Proofreading

Directions: Read more about Key West. Proofread and correct the errors. There are eight errors in capitalization, seven misspelled words and three missing words.

More About Key West

a good way to lern more about key West is to ride the trolley. Key West has a great troley system. The trolley will take on a tour of the salt ponds. You can also three red brick forts. The troley tour goes by a 110-foot high lighthouse. It is rite in the middle of the city. Key west is the only city with a Lighthouse in the midle of it! It is also the southernmost city in the United States.

If you have time, the new Ship Wreck Museum. Key west was also the hom of former president Harry truman. During his presidency, Trueman spent many vacations on key west.

Grade 4 - Comprehensive Curriculum

Run-On Sentences

A **run-on sentence** occurs when two or more sentences are joined together without punctuation.

Examples:

Run-on sentence: I lost my way once did you?
Two sentences with correct punctuation: I lost my way once. Did you?
Run-on sentence: I found the recipe it was not hard to follow.
Two sentences with correct punctuation: I found the recipe. It was not hard to follow.

Directions: Rewrite the run-on sentences correctly with periods, exclamation points and question marks. The first one has been done for you.

1. Did you take my umbrella I can't find it anywhere!

Did you take my umbrella? I can't find it anywhere!

2. How can you stand that noise I can't!

_____

3. The cookies are gone I see only crumbs.

_____

4. The dogs were barking they were hungry.

_____

5. She is quite ill please call a doctor immediately!

_____

6. The clouds came up we knew the storm would hit soon.

_____

7. You weren't home he stopped by this morning.

_____

Name: _____

Writing: Punctuation

Directions: In the paragraphs below, use periods, question marks or exclamation marks to show where one sentence ends and the next begins. Circle the first letter of each new sentence to show the capital.

Example: my sister accused me of not helping her rake the leaves. that's silly! i helped at least a hundred times.

1. I always tie on my fishing line when it moves up and down, I know a fish is there after waiting a minute or two, I pull up the fish it's fun

2. I tried putting lemon juice on my freckles to make them go away did you ever do that it didn't work my skin just got sticky now, I'm slowly getting used to my freckles

3. once, I had an accident on my bike I was on my way home from school what do you think happened my wheel slipped in the loose dirt at the side of the road my bike slid into the road

4. one night, I dreamed I lived in a castle in my dream, I was the king or maybe the queen everyone listened to my commands then Mom woke me up for school I tried commanding her to let me sleep it didn't work

5. what's your favorite holiday Christmas is mine for months before Christmas, I save my money, so I can give a present to everyone in my family last year, I gave my big sister earrings they cost me five dollars

6. my dad does exercises every night to make his stomach flat he says he doesn't want to grow old I think it's too late don't tell him I said that

Name: _____

Writing: Putting Ideas Together

Directions: Make each pair of sentences into one sentence. (You may have to change the verbs for some sentences—from **is** to **are**, for example.)

Example: Our house was flooded. Our car was flooded.

Our house and car were flooded.

1. Kenny sees a glow.   Carrie sees a glow.

_____

2. Our new stove came today.   Our new refrigerator came today.

_____

3. The pond is full of toads.   The field is full of toads.

_____

4. Stripes are on the flag.   Stars are on the flag.

_____

5. The ducks took flight.   The geese took flight.

_____

6. Joe reads stories.   Dana reads stories.

_____

7. French fries will make you fat.   Milkshakes will make you fat.

_____

8. Justine heard someone groan.   Kevin heard someone groan.

_____

Name: _____

Writing: Putting Ideas Together

Directions: Write each pair of sentences as one sentence.

Example: Jim will deal the cards one at a time. Jim will give four cards to everyone.

Jim will deal the cards one at a time and give four cards to everyone.

1. Amy won the contest.   Amy claimed the prize.

   _____

2. We need to find the scissors.   We need to buy some tape.

   _____

3. The stream runs through the woods.   The stream empties into the East River.

   _____

   _____

4. Katie tripped on the steps.   Katie has a pain in her left foot.

   _____

   _____

5. Grandpa took me to the store.   Grandpa bought me a treat.

   _____

6. Charity ran 2 miles.   She walked 1 mile to cool down afterwards.

   _____

   _____

Name: _____

Writing: Using Fewer Words

Writing can be more interesting when fewer words are used. Combining sentences is easy when the subjects are the same. Notice how the comma is used.

Example: Sally woke up. Sally ate breakfast. Sally brushed her teeth.

Sally woke up, ate breakfast and brushed her teeth.

Combining sentences with more than one subject is a little more complicated. Notice how commas are used to "set off" information.

Examples: Jane went to the store. Jane is Sally's sister.

Jane went to the store with Sally, her sister.

Eddie likes to play with cars. Eddie is my younger brother.

Eddie, my younger brother, likes to play with cars.

Directions: Write each pair of sentences as one sentence.

1. Jerry played soccer after school. He played with his best friend, Tom.

   _____

2. Spot likes to chase cats. Spot is my dog.

   _____

3. Lori and Janice both love ice cream. Janice is Lori's cousin.

   _____

4. Jayna is my cousin. Jayna helped me move into my new apartment.

   _____

5. Romeo is a big tomcat. Romeo loves to hunt mice.

   _____

Name: _____

Combining Sentences

Some simple sentences can be easily combined into one sentence.

Examples:

Simple sentences: The bird sang. The bird was tiny. The bird was in the tree.
Combined sentence: The tiny bird sang in the tree.

Directions: Combine each set of simple sentences into one sentence. The first one has been done for you.

1. The big girls laughed. They were friendly. They helped the little girls.

<u>The big, friendly girls laughed as they helped the little girls.</u>

2. The dog was hungry. The dog whimpered. The dog looked at its bowl.

_____

3. Be quiet now. I want you to listen. You listen to my joke!

_____

4. I lost my pencil. My pencil was stubby. I lost it on the bus.

_____

5. I see my mother. My mother is walking. My mother is walking down the street.

_____

6. Do you like ice cream? Do you like hot dogs? Do you like mustard?

_____

7. Tell me you'll do it! Tell me you will! Tell me right now!

_____

Combining Sentences in Paragraph Form

A **paragraph** is a group of sentences that share the same idea.

Directions: Rewrite the paragraph by combining the simple sentences into larger sentences.

Jason awoke early. He threw off his covers. He ran to his window. He looked outside. He saw snow. It was white and fluffy. Jason thought of something. He thought of his sled. His sled was in the garage. He quickly ate breakfast. He dressed warmly. He got his sled. He went outside. He went to play in the snow.

_____

_____

_____

_____

_____

_____

_____

_____

_____

_____

_____

Name: _____

Nouns and Pronouns

To make a story or report more interesting, pronouns can be substituted for "overused" nouns.

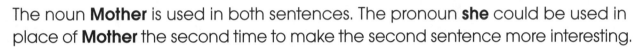

Example:

Mother made the beds. Then Mother started the laundry.

The noun **Mother** is used in both sentences. The pronoun **she** could be used in place of **Mother** the second time to make the second sentence more interesting.

Directions: Cross out nouns when they appear a second and/or third time. Write a pronoun that could be used instead. The first one has been done for you.

we 1. My friends and I like to go ice skating in the winter. ~~My friends and I~~ usually fall down a lot, but ~~my friends and~~ I have fun!

_____ 2. All the children in the fourth-grade class next to us must have been having a party. All the children were very loud. All the children were happy it was Friday.

_____ 3. I try to help my father with work around the house on the weekends. My father works many hours during the week and would not be able to get everything done.

_____ 4. Can I share my birthday treat with the secretary and the principal? The secretary and the principal could probably use a snack right now!

_____ 5. I know Mr. Jones needs a copy of this history report. Please take it to Mr. Jones when you finish.

Nouns and Pronouns

Directions: Cross out nouns when they appear a second and/or third time. Write a pronoun that could be used instead.

_____ 1. The merry-go-round is one of my favorite rides at the county fair. I ride the merry-go-round so many times that I sometimes get sick.

_____ 2. My parents and I are planning a 2-week vacation next year. My parents and I will be driving across the country to see the Grand Canyon. My parents and I hope to have a great time.

_____ 3. The new art teacher brought many ideas from the city school where the art teacher worked before.

_____ 4. Green beans, corn and potatoes are my favorite vegetables. I could eat green beans, corn and potatoes for every meal. I especially like green beans, corn and potatoes in stew.

_____ 5. I think I left my pen in the library when I was looking up reference materials earlier today. Did you find my pen when you cleaned?

_____ 6. My grandmother makes very good apple pie. My grandmother said I could learn how to make one the next time we visit.

_____ 7. My brothers and I could take care of your pets while you are away if you show my brothers and me what you want done.

Name: _____

Pronoun Referents

A **pronoun referent** is the noun or nouns a pronoun refers to.

Example:

Green beans, corn and potatoes are my favorite vegetables. I could eat them for every meal.

The pronoun **them** refers to the nouns green beans, corn and potatoes.

Directions: Find the pronoun in each sentence, and write it in the blank below. Underline the word or words the pronoun refers to. The first one has been done for you.

1. The fruit trees look so beautiful in the spring when they are covered with blossoms.

   _____they_____

2. Tori is a high school cheerleader. She spends many hours at practice.

   _____

3. The football must have been slippery because of the rain. The quarterback could not hold on to it.

   _____

4. Aunt Donna needs a babysitter for her three year old tonight.

   _____

5. The art projects are on the table. Could you please put them on the top shelf along the wall?

   _____

Name: _____

Pronoun Referents

Directions: Find the pronoun in each sentence, and write it in the blank below. Underline the word or words the pronoun refers to.

1. Did Aaron see the movie *Titanic*? Jay thought it was a very good movie.

   _____

2. Maysie can help you with the spelling words now, Tasha.

   _____

3. The new tennis coach said to call him after 6:00 tonight.

   _____

4. Jim, John and Jason called to say they would be later than planned.

   _____

5. Mrs. Burns enjoyed the cake her class had for the surprise party.

   _____

6. The children are waiting outside. Ask Josh to take the pinwheels out to them.

   _____

7. Mrs. Taylor said to go on ahead because she will be late.

   _____

8. The whole team must sit on the bus until the driver gives us permission to get off.

   _____

9. Dad said the umbrella did a poor job of keeping the rain off him.

   _____

10. The umbrella was blowing around too much. That's probably why it didn't do a good job.

    _____

Writing: Topic Sentences

A **paragraph** is a group of sentences that tells about one main idea. A **topic sentence** tells the main idea of a paragraph.

Many topic sentences come first in the paragraph. The topic sentence in the paragraph below is underlined. Do you see how it tells the reader what the whole paragraph is about?

   <u>Friendships can make you happy or make you sad</u>. You feel happy to do things and go places with your friends. You get to know each other so well that you can almost read each others' minds. But friendships can be sad when your friend moves away—or decides to be best friends with someone else.

Directions: Underline the topic sentence in the paragraph below.

   <u>We have two rules about using the phone at our house</u>. Our whole family agreed on them. The first rule is not to talk longer than 10 minutes. The second rule is to take good messages if you answer the phone for someone else.

Directions: After you read the paragraph below, write a topic sentence for it.

<u>You can earn money by doing things for people.</u>

   For one thing, you could ask your neighbors if they need any help. They might be willing to pay you for walking their dog or mowing their grass or weeding their garden. Maybe your older brothers or sisters would pay you to do some of their chores. You also could ask your parents if there's an extra job you could do around the house to make money.

Directions: Write a topic sentence for a paragraph on each of these subjects.

Homework: <u>You have to do your homework every night.</u>

Television: <u>People should not wath to Much Television</u>

Writing: Supporting Sentences

Supporting sentences provide details about the topic sentence of a paragraph.

Directions: In the paragraph below, underline the topic sentence. Then cross out the supporting sentence that does not belong in the paragraph.

One spring it started to rain and didn't stop for 2 weeks. All the rivers flooded. Some people living near the rivers had to leave their homes. Farmers couldn't plant their crops because the fields were so wet. Plants need water to grow. The sky was dark and gloomy all the time.

Directions: Write three supporting sentences to go with each topic sentence below. Make sure each supporting sentence stays on the same subject as the topic sentence.

Not everyone should have a pet.

A lot of people are afraic to dogs and cats.
Pets are expsins. because you have to buy them and ta
Some pets are Mean they bite.

I like to go on field trips with my class.

field trips are fun to go on.
When we go on feild trips we alwas ride the bus.
Alot of field trips are fun.

I've been thinking about what I want to be when I get older.

I really want to be a teacher.
I really want to be a Doctor
I really want to be a Sergan

Writing:
Topic Sentences and Supporting Details

Directions: For each topic below, write a topic sentence and four supporting details.

Example:

Playing with friends: (topic sentence) Playing with my friends can be lots of fun.

(details)

1. We like to ride our bikes together.

2. We play fun games like "dress up" and "animal hospital."

3. Sometimes, we swing on the swings or slide down the slides on our swingsets.

4. We like to pretend we are having tea with our stuffed animals.

Recess at school: _____

_____

_____

_____

_____

Summer vacation: _____

_____

_____

_____

_____

Brothers or sisters: _____

_____

_____

_____

_____

Writing:
Topic Sentences and Supporting Details

Directions: Select a topic from page 293. Arrange the topic sentence and detail sentences in paragraph form.

Example: Playing With Friends

    Playing with my friends can be lots of fun. We play fun games like "animal hospita"l and "dress up." We like to pretend we are having tea with our stuffed animals. Sometimes, we swing on the swings or slide down the slides on our swingsets. We also like to ride our bikes together.

Note: Notice how the first line of the paragraph is indented. Also note how the order of the sentences changed to make the paragraph easier to read.

Directions: Choose a topic. Write a five-sentence paragraph about it. Don't forget the topic sentence, supporting details and to indent your paragraph. Make sure the detail sentences stick to the topic.

_____

_____

_____

_____

_____

_____

Writing: Story Map

A **story map** helps to organize your thoughts in a logical sequence before you begin to write a story or report.

Directions: Use the following story map to arrange your thoughts for the police report on page 296.

Characters:

Setting: (time, place)

Problem: (what needs to be fixed or solved)

Goal: (what characters want to accomplish)

Action: (events, reasons)

Outcome: (results of action)

Review

Directions: Write a police report about an event in which someone your age was a hero or heroine. Follow these steps:

1. Write all your ideas in any order on another sheet of paper. What happened? Who saw it? Who or what do you think caused it? Why were the police called?

2. Choose the ideas you want to use and organize them with the story map on page 295.

3. Now, write in complete sentences to tell what happened. Combine some short sentences using **and, but, or, after** or **when**. Make sure all your sentences end with a period or question mark.

4. Read your sentences aloud. Did you leave out any important facts? Will your "commanding officer" know what happened?

5. Make any necessary changes and write your report below.

6. Read your report to someone.

OFFICIAL POLICE REPORT

Reporting officer: _____

Date of accident: _____ Time of accident: _____

_____

_____

_____

_____

_____

_____

_____

_____

Name: _____

Review

Directions: On another sheet of paper, write three paragraphs that tell a story about the picture below. Tell who lives in the house, what happened and why it happened. Begin each paragraph with a topic sentence that tells the main idea. Read your paragraphs aloud, make any necessary changes and copy them below.

Who lives there:

_____

_____

_____

What happened:

_____

_____

_____

Why it happened:

_____

_____

_____

Writing: Paragraphs

Each paragraph should have one main idea. If you have a lot of ideas, you need to write several paragraphs.

Directions: Read the ideas below and number them:
1. If the idea tells about Jill herself.
2. If the idea tells what she did.
3. If the idea tells why she did it.

_____ found a bird caught in a kite string

_____ plays outside a lot

_____ in grade four at Center School

_____ knew the bird was wild

_____ untangled the bird

_____ likes pets

_____ wouldn't want to live in a cage

_____ gave the bird its freedom

Now, use the ideas to write three paragraphs. Use your own paper if necessary. Write paragraph 1 about Jill. Write paragraph 2 about what she did. Write paragraph 3 about why she did it.

_____

_____

_____

_____

_____

_____

_____

_____

Name: _____

Writing: Paragraphs

When you have many good ideas about a subject, you need to organize your writing into more than one paragraph. It is easy to organize your thoughts about a topic if you use a "cluster of ideas" chart.

Example:

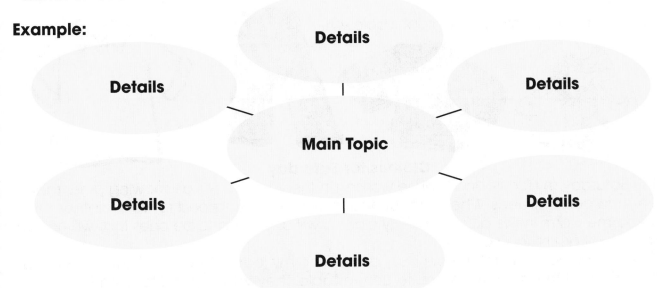

The main topic of your story is stated in the middle circle. Details about the main topic are listed in the outer circles.

Study the following "cluster of ideas" and note how the thoughts are organized in paragraph form on the following page.

1. **Introduction:** working in yard, autumn—cool weather

2. **Pants:** blue jeans, old, cotton, good for yard work, comfortable

3. **Shirt:** yellow, short-sleeved, matches slacks and sweater, not too hot

4. **Sweater:** red with yellow and blue designs, white buttons, warmth for cold day, cotton, long sleeves

5. **Shoes:** white sneakers, comfortable, good for walking and standing

6. **Closing:** busy, but ready

Clothes for Saturday

Writing: Paragraphs

Once your ideas are "clustered," go back and decide which ideas should be the first, second, third, and so on. These numbers will be the order of the paragraph in the finished story.

Directions: Read the story paragraphs below.

Clothes for Saturday

This Saturday, my family and I will be working in the yard. We will be mowing grass, raking leaves and pulling weeds. When I get up that day, I know I will need to wear clothes that will keep me warm in the autumn air. My clothes will also need to be ones that will not be ruined if they get muddy or dirty.

The best choice of pants for our busy day will be my jeans. They are nicely faded and well worn, which means they are quite comfortable. They will be good for yard work since mud and grass stains wash out of them easily.

My shirt will be my yellow golf shirt. It will match the blue of my jeans. Also, its short sleeves will be fine if the weather is warm.

For warmth on Saturday, if the day is cool, will be my yellow and red sweater. It is made from cotton and has long sleeves and high buttons to keep out frosty air.

Yard work means lots of walking, so I will need comfortable shoes. The best choice will be my white sneakers. They aren't too tight or too loose and keep my feet strong.

Saturday will be a busy day, but I'll be ready!

When "Clothes for Saturday" was written, the author added both an introductory and concluding paragraph. This helps the reader with the flow of the story.

Directions: Now, it's your turn. Select a topic from the list below or choose one of your own. Complete the "cluster of ideas" chart on page 301 and write a brief story. (You may or may not use all the clusters.)

Topics:

chores	holidays	all about me	sports
homework	family	pets	vacation

Name: _____

Writing: Cluster of Ideas

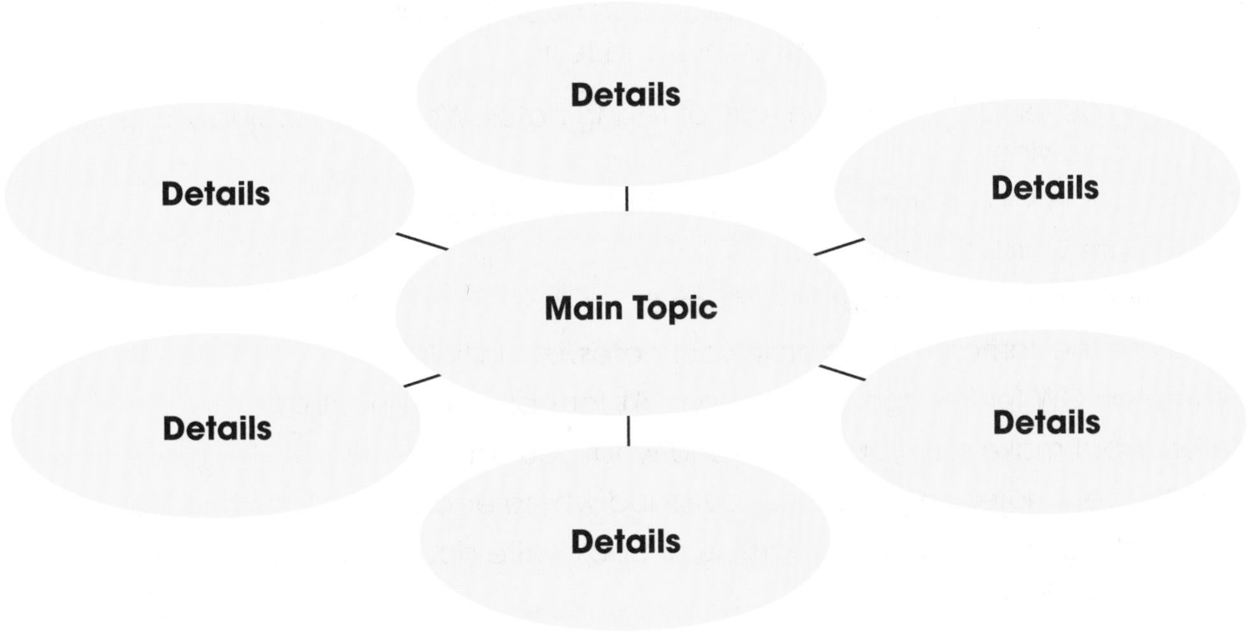

Details

Details

Details

Main Topic

Details

Details

Details

_____

_____

_____

_____

_____

_____

_____

_____

_____

_____

_____

_____

Taking Notes

Taking notes effectively can help you in many ways with schoolwork. It will help you better understand and remember what you read and hear. It will also help you keep track of important facts needed for reports, essays and tests.

Each person develops his/her own way of taking notes. While developing your style, keep in mind the following:

► Write notes in short phrases instead of whole sentences.

► Abbreviate words to save time.

　　Examples: pres for president or **&** for and

► If you use the same name often in your notes, use initials.

　　Examples: GW for George Washington　**AL** for Abraham Lincoln.

► Be brief, but make sure you understand what you write.

► Number your notes, so you can understand where each note starts and stops.

► When taking notes from a long article or book, write down one or two important points per paragraph or chapter.

Directions: Reread the article "Floating in Space" on page 168. As you read the first three paragraphs, fill in the note-taking format below with your notes.

Title of Article or Story _____

Important Points

Paragraph 1 _____

_____

_____

Paragraph 2 _____

_____

_____

Paragraph 3 _____

_____

_____

Name: _____

Taking Notes

Directions: Use this guide for taking notes on the articles in the next two pages. Set up your own paper in a similar way, or make several photocopies, for note-taking on future pages.

Penguins Are Unusual Birds
(Title)

Paragraph or
Chapter numbers

Important Points

1 _____

_____

2 _____

_____

3 _____

_____

_____

From Grapes to Raisins
(Title)

Paragraph or
Chapter numbers

Important Points

1 _____

_____

2 _____

_____

3 _____

_____

_____

Taking Notes: Penguins Are Unusual Birds

Directions: Use a sheet of paper to cover up the story about penguins. Then read the questions.

1. Why are penguins unusual?

2. Do penguins swim?

3. Where do penguins live?

4. Do penguins lay eggs like other birds?

Directions: Read about penguins. While reading, make notes on the note-taking sheet on the previous page.

Penguins may be the most unusual birds. They cannot fly, but they can swim very fast through ice-cold water. They can dive deep into the water, and they can jump high out of it. Sometimes they make their nests out of rocks instead of twigs and grass. Some penguins live in very cold parts of the world. Others live in warmer climates. All penguins live south of the equator.

Unlike other birds, penguins lay only one egg at a time. Right after a mother penguin lays her egg, she waddles back to the ocean. The father penguin holds the egg on his feet, covering it with part of his stomach to keep it warm. When the egg is ready to hatch, the mother penguin returns. Then the father penguin takes a turn looking for food.

When a penguin swims, its white belly and dark back help it hide from enemies. From under the water, predators cannot see it. From on top of the water, large birds cannot see it either. This is how the penguin stays safe!

Directions: Use your notes to complete these sentences.

1. Penguins cannot fly, but _____ .

2. Penguins can dive deep and _____ .

3. Penguins lay only _____ .

4. Father penguins keep the egg _____ .

5. Mother penguins return when the egg _____ .

Name: _____

Taking Notes: From Grapes to Raisins

Directions: Use a piece of paper to cover up the story about how grapes become raisins. Then read the questions.

1. How do grapes become raisins?

2. What happens after the grapes become raisins?

3. Why are raisins brown?

4. In what countries do grapes grow?

Directions: Read about how grapes become raisins. While reading, make notes on the note-taking sheet on page 303.

> Grapes grow well in places that have lots of sun. In the United States, California is a big producer of grapes and raisins. When grapes are plump and round, they can be picked from their vines to be made into raisins. After the grapes are picked, they are put on big wooden or paper trays. They sit in the sun for many days.
>
> Slowly, the grapes begin to dry and turn into wrinkled raisins. The sun causes them to change colors. Grapes turn brown as they become raisins. Machines take off the stems. Then the raisins are washed. After being dried again, they are put into boxes.
>
> Some places use machines to make raisins dry faster. The grapes are put into ovens that have hot air blowing around inside. These ovens make the grapes shrivel and dry.
>
> Raisins are made in many countries that grow grapes. Besides the United States, countries such as Greece, Turkey, Iran, Spain and Australia produce a lot of raisins.

Directions: Use your notes to answer the four questions at the top of the page. Write your answers on the lines below.

1. _____

_____

2. _____

_____

3. _____

4. _____

Name: _____

Taking Notes: Graham Crackers

Directions: Use a piece of paper to cover up the story about Graham crackers. Then read the questions.

1. Where did Graham crackers come from?

2. Who invented Graham crackers?

3. What are Graham crackers made of?

4. Why were Graham crackers made?

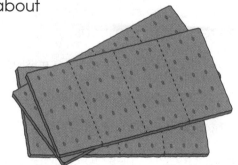

Directions: Read about Graham crackers. While reading, make notes on another sheet of paper.

> Graham crackers were invented around 1830. A minister named Sylvester Graham wanted people to eat healthier foods. He did not think that people should eat meat or white bread. He wanted people to eat more fruits and vegetables and wheat breads that were brown instead of white.
>
> Graham crackers were named after Sylvester Graham. He liked them because they were made of whole-wheat flour. There are many other kinds of crackers, but not all of them are as good for you as Graham crackers. Graham crackers are still considered a healthy snack!

Directions: Use your notes to answer the four questions at the top of the page. Write your answers on the lines below.

1. _____

_____

2. _____

_____

3. _____

_____

4. _____

_____

Name: _____

Compare and Contrast

To **compare** means to look for ways two items are alike. To **contrast** means to look for ways two items are different.

Directions: Use the Venn diagram to compare and contrast penguins (page 304) with most birds you see where you live.

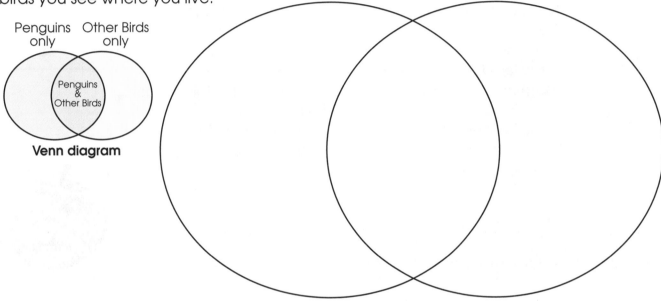

Penguins only   Other Birds only

Penguins & Other Birds

Venn diagram

To write a comparison paragraph, begin with a topic sentence which states your main idea. Write sentences that provide supporting details. End your paragraph with a conclusion sentence. A conclusion sentence often restates the topic sentence.

Directions: Use the information from your Venn diagram to write a short comparison paragraph.

_____

_____

_____

_____

_____

_____

_____

Name: _____

Outlining

Outlines are plans that help you organize your thoughts. If you are writing an essay, an outline helps you decide what to write. An outline should look similar to this:

I. First main idea
   A. A smaller idea
      1. An example
      2. An example
II. Second main idea
   A. A smaller idea
   B. Another smaller idea
III. Third main idea
   A. A smaller idea
   B. Another smaller idea
      1. An example

I. Planting a garden
   A. Choosing seeds
      1. Tomatoes
      2. Lettuce
II. Taking care of the garden
   A. Pulling the weeds
   B. Watering the garden
III. Harvesting
   A. Are they ripe?
   B. How to pick them
      1. Pick only the tomato off the vine

Directions: Use the outline for planting a garden to answer the questions.

1. What are the three main ideas?

   1) _____

   2) _____

   3) _____

2. What are the two smaller ideas listed under "Taking care of the garden"?

   1) _____

   2) _____

3. What are the smaller ideas listed under "Harvesting"?

   1) _____

   2) _____

4. What is listed under the smaller idea "How to pick them"?

   _____

Outlining: Building a Tree House

Directions: Study the sample outline for building a house. Then use words and phrases from the box to fill in the missing parts of the outline on how to build a tree house.

I. Find land
    A. On a hill
    B. By a lake
    C. In the city
II. Gather materials
    A. Buy wood
    B. Buy nails
    C. Buy tools
        1. Hammer
        2. Screwdriver
        3. Drill
        4. Saw
III. Build the house
    A. Who will use the tools?
    B. Who will carry the wood?

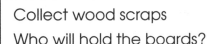

> Collect wood scraps
> Who will hold the boards?
> Who will use the hammer?
> Gather tools
> Can we climb it easily?
> Saw
> How will we get things off the ground?

I. Find a tree
    A. Is it sturdy?

    B. _____

II. Gather supplies

    A. _____

    B. _____

        1. Hammer and nails

        2. _____

III. Build the tree house

    A. _____

    B. _____

    C. _____

Outlining: Finishing the Tree House

Directions: Use words and phrases from the box to fill in the missing parts of the outline of what to do once your tree house is built.

Sisters and brothers	When can they visit?
Parents	Spray paint
Tables	Choose a kind of paint
Chairs	Who can visit?

I. Painting the tree house

   A. Choose a color of paint

   B. _____

      1. Cans of paint

      2. _____

II. Putting furniture in the tree house

   A. _____

   B. _____

III. Making a visitors' policy

   A. _____

      1. Friends

      2. _____

      3. _____

   B. _____

Name: _____

Outlining: The *Mayflower*'s Voyage

Directions: Read about the *Mayflower*. Then complete the outline for an essay.

The *Mayflower* left England in 1620. It carried 101 passengers. Some of those passengers were called Pilgrims. Pilgrims were people who had wandered from country to country looking for a place to make their home.

It took 66 days to cross the Atlantic Ocean. The ship was crowded. There were some accidents on board. The *Mayflower* landed at the tip of Cape Cod in Massachusetts. Several men searched the area to find the best place to start a colony. They finally settled on Plymouth.

The Pilgrims lived on the *Mayflower* through the winter. The *Mayflower* returned to England in April 1621. None of the Pilgrims went back with it.

I. The *Mayflower* leaves England

    A. _____

    B. _____

II. The journey

    A. _____

    B. _____

    C. _____

III. Landing in America

    A. _____

    B. _____

Outlining: The First Thanksgiving

Directions: Read about the first Thanksgiving. Then complete the outline.

> The Pilgrims arrived at Plymouth Rock just as winter set in. Many people died that winter from cold and hunger. The following spring, the Pilgrims started planting vegetable gardens. A Native American named Squanto helped them. They planted peas, wheat, beans, corn and pumpkins.
>
> When fall came, the Pilgrims were so glad to have enough food that they invited the Native Americans to share their first Thanksgiving. In addition to food from their garden, they also shared wild geese that they had killed and other food like sweet potatoes and fresh berries.

I. The first winter

    A. _____

    B. _____

II. Spring

    A. _____

    B. _____

III. Fall

    A. _____

    B. _____

        1. _____

        2. _____

        3. _____

Name: _____

Using an Outline to Write an Essay

Outlines help you organize information and notes into a manageable form. Outlines also help you prepare to write reports and essays by keeping your thoughts in a logical order or sequence. Once you have a good outline, converting it to paragraph form is easy.

To convert an outline to an essay, add your own words to expand the words and phrases in the outline into sentence form. Information from the first main topic becomes the first paragraph.

    I. Painting the tree house
       A. Choose a color of paint
       B. Choose a kind of paint
          1. Cans of paint
          2. Spray paint

Information from the second and third main topics become the second and third paragraphs of the essay.

    II. Putting furniture in the tree house
       A. Tables
       B. Chairs
   III. Making a visitors' policy
       A. Who can visit?
          1. Friends
          2. Sisters and brothers
          3. Parents
       B. When can they visit?

To write an essay, remember to indent each paragraph, begin each paragraph with a topic sentence and include supporting details.

Directions: Read the beginning of the essay. Then finish it on another sheet of paper using your own words and information from the outline.

Finishing Touches

    Finishing a tree house takes a lot of thought and planning. First, it needs to be painted. The paint will help protect the wood from rain and snow. The best kind of paint for finishing the wood would be in cans. It would brush on easily, smoothly and quickly. Green would be a great color for the tree house because it would blend in with the green leaves of the trees.

Name: _____

Using an Outline to Write a Book Review

Directions: Prepare to write a book review by organizing your thoughts in the outline form provided.

Sample	Your Book Review
I. Book information	I. _____
A. Title	A. _____
B. Author	B. _____
C. Illustrator	C. _____
D. Publisher and publishing date	D. _____
II. Fun facts of book	II. _____
A. Setting	A. _____
B. Characters	B. _____
C. Plot	C. _____
III. Good points	III. _____
A. What I liked best about book	A. _____
1. Why?	1. _____
IV. Not so good points	IV. _____
A. What I didn't like about book	A. _____
1. Why?	1. _____
V. Should others read book?	V. _____
A. Why or why not?	A. _____

Directions: Write a book review essay on another sheet of paper, using notes from your outline.

Name: _____

Summarizing: Writing an Autobiography

When you **summarize** an article, book or speech, you are simply writing a shorter article that contains only the main points. This shorter article of main points is called a **summary**.

To prepare for writing a summary of your life, you would begin with an outline. Since a summary is a brief account of main points, you will not be able to include every detail of your life. Your summary should include only basic facts.

I. Yourself
   A. Name
   B. Age and grade in school
      1. Subjects you like in school
      2. Subjects you do not like in school
   C. Looks
      1. Eye color
      2. Hair color
      3. Other features
II. Your family
   A. Parents
   B. Brothers/sisters
   C. Pets
III. Hobbies and interests
   A. Sports
   B. Clubs

Directions: Follow the format above to write an outline about your life. Feel free to add more main ideas, smaller ideas or examples.

_____

_____

_____

_____

_____

_____

_____

_____

Name: _____

Summarizing: Writing an Autobiography

A summary of your life would include when you were born, who your parents are, other members of your family, your age and your grade in school. Details like your favorite joke, today's weather or how much homework you had yesterday would not be included in a summary.

Directions: Use the information from your outline to write a summary of your life.

_____

_____

_____

_____

_____

_____

_____

_____

_____

_____

_____

_____

_____

_____

_____

_____

_____

_____

Name: _____

Summarizing: The North Pole

Directions: Read about the North Pole. Then use the main points of the article to write a paragraph summarizing conditions at the North Pole.

At the North Pole, the sun does not shine for half of the year. It stays dark outside for six months, but for the other six months of the year, the sun does not set. It is light through the night.

The North Pole is as far north as you can go. If you traveled north to the North Pole and kept going, you would start going south. You could call the North Pole the top of the Earth.

The average temperature at the North Pole is –9 degrees Fahrenheit. That is not any colder than many places in the United States get in the winter. In fact, some places get much colder than that, but at the North Pole, it stays very cold for a very long time.

The cold winds that blow off the Arctic Ocean make the North Pole a very cold place most of the time. In the summer when the sun is shining all day and all night, the temperature can rise to 38 degrees Fahrenheit in places that are sheltered from the wind. But that is still very cold.

The Arctic Ocean is at the North Pole. The area surrounding the North Pole is called the Arctic Region. Some of Canada, Alaska, Greenland, Russia and Scandinavia are in the Arctic Region. These places get very cold in the long, dark winters, too!

The main points of this article are:

1. At the North Pole, the sun is never out in the winter. It is always out in the summer.
2. The North Pole is very cold all year.
3. Winds from the Arctic Ocean make the North Pole stay very cold. The Arctic Ocean surrounds the North Pole.
4. There is some land in the Arctic Region.

_____

_____

_____

_____

_____

_____

Summarizing: Settler Children

Directions: Read about settler children. Then complete the list of main points at the end of the article.

In the 1700s and 1800s, many children from other countries came with their parents to America. In the beginning, they had no time to go to school. They had to help their families work in the fields, care for the animals and clean the house. They also helped care for their younger brothers and sisters.

Sometimes settler children helped build houses and schools. Usually, these early school buildings were just one room. There was only one teacher for all the children. Settler children were very happy when they could attend school.

Because settler children worked so much, they had little time to play. There were not many things settler children could do just for fun. One pastime was gardening. Weeding their gardens taught them how to be orderly. Children sometimes made gifts out of the things they grew.

The settlers also encouraged their children to sing. Each one was expected to play at least one musical instrument. Parents wanted their children to walk, ride horses, visit friends and relatives and read nonfiction books.

Most settler children did not have many toys. The toys they owned were made by their parents and grandparents. They were usually made of cloth or carved from wood. The children made up games with string, like "cat's cradle." They also made things out of wood, such as seesaws. Settler children did not have all the toys we have today, but they managed to have fun anyway!

The main points of this article are:

1. Settler children worked hard.

2. Settler children had many jobs.

3. _____

4. _____

5. _____

Directions: Use the main points to write a summary of this article on a separate sheet of paper.

Name: _____

Summarizing: On Your Own

Directions: Read a story or a short book from your library. Write the title and author, then list the main points.

Title: _____

Author: _____

The main points are:

1. _____

2. _____

3. _____

4. _____

5. _____

Directions: Use the format you learned to outline this story or book.

_____

_____

_____

_____

_____

_____

_____

_____

_____

Directions: Use the main points you listed and your outline to write a summary of this book or story on another sheet of paper.

Library Skills: Using the Library Catalog

Every book in a library is listed in the library's catalog. Videos, CD's, and other materials may also be included. Some library catalogs are drawers filled with file cards; some are computerized. Here is an example of a card from a card catalog:

970.2	
G84a	Indians
	Gridley, Marion E.
	American Indian Women
	Hawthorn Books, Inc., 1974

The catalog helps you find books and other materials. Library catalogs list items by titles, authors and subjects. All three of these listings are in alphabetical order.

To find a book titled *Great Explorer: Christopher Columbus*, you would look under G in the card catalog. To find other books about Columbus, you would look under C. If you knew the name of an author who had written a book about Columbus, you could look in the card catalog under the author's last name.

Many libraries use computer catalogs instead of card catalogs. The computer catalog is also organized by titles, authors and subjects. To find a book, type in the title, subject or author's name.

Directions: Answer the questions about using a library catalog.

1. To find the book *American Indian Women*, would you look under the author, title or subject? _____

2. To find a book about the Cherokee people, would you look under the author, title or subject? _____

3. To find a book called *Animals of Long Ago,* would you look under the author, title or subject? _____

4. Marion E. Gridley has written books about Native Americans. To find one of her books, would you look under the author, title or subject? _____

5. To find books about the Moon, would you look under the author, title or subject? _____

6. To find the book *Easy Microwave Cooking for Kids,* would you look under the author, title or subject? _____

7. Diana Reische has written a book about the Pilgrims. Would you look under the author, title or subject to find it? _____

Name: _____

Library Skills: Using the Library Catalog

Authors are alphabetized by their last names first. In a library catalog, Blume, Judy would come before Voirst, Judith. Books are alphabetized by title. If a title begins with **The**, **A** or **An**, ignore it, and use the second word of the title.

Directions: Look at the list of authors, subjects and titles. Write **A** for author, **S** for subject or **T** for title in the blanks. Then write each on the card where it belongs in alphabetical order. Some have been done for you.

_**A**_ Gallant, Roy A.

_____ Native Americans

_**T**_ *Animals of Long Ago*

_**S**_ gardens

_____ *The White House*

_____ Sandak, Cass R.

_____ *The Pony Express*

_____ Herbst, Judith

_____ Pilgrims

_____ *The Hobbit*

_**A**_ Dicerto, Joseph J.

_____ planets

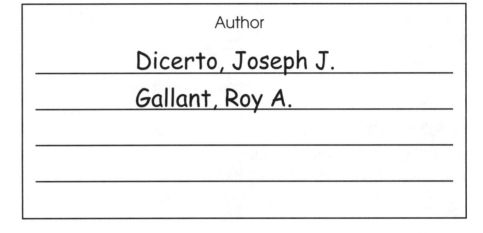

Author

____ Dicerto, Joseph J. ____

____ Gallant, Roy A. ____

_____

_____

Title

____ *Animals of Long Ago* ____

_____

_____

_____

Subject

____ gardens ____

_____

_____

_____

Library Skills: Call Numbers

The **call number** of a book tells where it can be found among nonfiction books.

Information is presented differently on the title, subject and author card for the same book. A computer listing for this book would look quite similar.

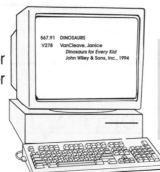

567.91   DINOSAURS
V278   VanCleave, Janice
         Dinosaurs for Every Kid
         John Wiley & Sons, Inc., 1994

Author card

567.91   VanCleave, Janice
V278   Dinosaurs for Every Kid
         John Wiley & Sons, Inc., 1994

Subject card

567.91   DINOSAURS
V278   VanCleave, Janice
         Dinosaurs for Every Kid
         John Wiley & Sons, Inc., 1994

Title card

567.91   Dinosaurs for Every Kid
V278   VanCleave, Janice
         John Wiley & Sons, Inc., 1994

Directions: Answer the questions about what is shown on these cards.

1. What is written at the top of the subject card?

_____

2. What is written at the top of the title card?

_____

3. What is written at the top of the author card?

_____

4. Why do libraries have three different kinds of listings for the same book?

_____

5. What is the number listed at the top left of each card? _____

6. What other information is on the cards? _____

_____

Library Skills: The Dewey Decimal System

Using a library catalog helps you find the books you want. All nonfiction books—except biographies and autobiographies—are filed according to their call number. **Nonfiction books** are books based on facts. **Biographies** are true books that tell about people's lives. **Autobiographies** are books that people write about their own lives.

The call numbers are part of the **Dewey Decimal System**. Each listing in a library catalog will include a book's call number.

Example:
918.8   Bringle, Mary
B85e   Eskimos
        F. Watts, 1973

All libraries using the **Dewey Decimal System** follow the same system for filing books. The system divides all nonfiction books into 10 main groups, each represented by numbers.

0–099	General works (libraries, computers, etc.)
100–199	Philosophy
200–299	Religion
300–399	Social Sciences
400–499	Language
500–599	Pure Science (math, astronomy, chemistry, etc.)
600–699	Applied Science (medicine, engineering, etc.)
700–799	Arts and Recreation
800–899	Literature
900–999	History

Each book is given a specific call number. A book about ghosts could be 133.1.

This is where some subjects fall in the Dewey Decimal System.

Pets	630	Maps	910	Cathedrals	236	Dinosaurs	560
Baseball	796	Monsters	791	Trees	580	Presidents	920
Butterflies	595	Mummies	390	Space	620	Cooking	640

Directions: Write the Dewey Decimal number for the following books.

_____ *Animals of Long Ago*   _____ *Our American Presidents*

_____ *City Leaves, City Trees*   _____ *Mummies Made in Egypt*

_____ *Easy Microwave Cooking for Kids*   _____ *Real-Life Monsters*

_____ *To Space and Back*   _____ *Great Churches in Europe*

_____ *Amazing Baseball Teams*   _____ *The Children's Atlas*

Name: _____

Library Skills: The Dewey Decimal System

All libraries that use the Dewey Decimal System follow the same order. All books between 500 and 599 are related to science. All books between 900 and 999 are history.

Each library divides its system even further. For example, one library may have kites at 796.15, while another library may have kites at 791.13.

Directions: Look at the number on each book. Then use the Dewey Decimal System directory at the bottom of the page to find out what the book is about. Write the subject on the line.

560   915.2   391   612   599

Fossils

793.8   796.41   923.1   636.9   581

Dewey Decimal System directory:

390–399 Costumes	590–599 Big Foot	790–795 Magic	920–929 Presidents
560–569 Fossils	610–619 Human Body	796–799 Gymnastics	
580–589 Plants	630–639 Pets	910–919 Japan	

Library Skills

Some books in a library are not filed by the Dewey Decimal System. Those books include biographies, autobiographies and fiction. Biographies and autobiographies may be filed together in the 920s or be assigned a call number by subject.

Fiction books are stories that someone has made up. They are filed in alphabetical order by the author's last name in the fiction section of the library.

Directions: For each title, write **B** if it is a biography, **A** if it is an autobiography or **F** if it is fiction. Then circle the titles that would not be filed by the Dewey Decimal System.

_____ *Tales of a Fourth Grade Nothing*

_____ *The Real Tom Thumb*

_____ *Ramona the Pest*

_____ *Bill Peet: An Autobiography*

_____ *Abraham Lincoln*

_____ *Charlotte's Web*

_____ *The King and I*

_____ *My Life With Chimpanzees*

_____ *Sara Plain and Tall*

_____ *Michael Jordan, Basketball's Soaring Star*

_____ *The First Book of Presidents*

_____ *The Helen Keller Story*

Name: _____

Putting Library Skills to Use

You can improve your library skills by using them at your local library.

Directions: While at the library, follow the instructions and answer the questions.

1. Use the library catalog to find a book about dinosaurs. What is its title? _____

_____

2. What is the call number for that book? _____

3. Who is the author of that book? _____

4. Go to the shelf and look for the book. Did you find it? _____

5. Use the library catalog to find the author of the book, *Mummies Made in Egypt*. Who wrote it?

_____

6. Use the library catalog to find other books by that author. What are the names of four other books by that author?

_____

_____

_____

_____

7. Use the library catalog to find a book written by Judy Blume with the word "fudge" in the title. What is its title?

_____

8. What is the library's most recent book by Ezra Jack Keats?_____

_____

Review

Directions: Write **A** for author, **S** for subject or **T** for title to show how you would look for each item in the library catalog.

1. _____ dinosaurs

2. _____ Russia

3. _____ Scarry, Richard

4. _____ Christopher, Matt

5. _____ Milne, A.A.

6. _____ *The Arctic and the Antarctic*

7. _____ *The Figure in the Shadows*

8. _____ Eskimos

Directions: Write **T** for true or **F** for false in the blanks.

9. _____ A biography is a story that someone writes about himself or herself.

10. _____ A fiction book is based on facts.

11. _____ A fiction book is a story someone made up.

12. _____ Nonfiction books use facts.

13. _____ An autobiography is a story that someone writes about himself or herself.

14. _____ A biography is the story of someone's life.

Directions: Identify the parts of this library catalog listing.

15. _____ 560

16. _____ DINOSAURS

17. _____ Shapp, Martha and Charles

18. _____ *Animals of Long Ago*

19. _____ Franklin Watts

20. _____ 1968

Name: _____

Encyclopedia Skills

Encyclopedias are sets of books that provide information about different subjects. If you want to know when cars were first made or who invented the phonograph, you could find the information in an encyclopedia.

Encyclopedias come in sets of books and on computer CD's. They contain many facts, illustrations, maps, graphs and tables. Encyclopedias are **reference books** found in the reference section of the library.

Each subject listed in an encyclopedia is called an **entry**. Entries are organized alphabetically.

Some good encyclopedias for students are *World Book Encyclopedia, Compton's Encyclopedia* and *Children's Britannica*.

Specialty encyclopedias, like the *McGraw-Hill Encyclopedia of Science and Technology*, contain information on one particular subject.

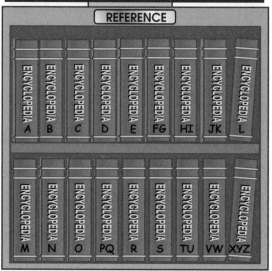

Directions: Number these encyclopedia entries in alphabetical order. The first one has been done for you.

_____	deep-sea diving	_____	Little League
_____	deer	_____	Little Rock
_____	Florida	_____	metric system
_____	natural fiber	_____	United Nations
_____	Death Valley	_____	poison oak
_____	flour	__1__	Air Force
_____	Gretzky, Wayne	_____	Carter, Jimmy

Encyclopedia Skills: Using the Index

The **index** of an encyclopedia contains an alphabetical listing of all entries. To find information about a subject, decide on the best word to describe the subject. If you want to know about ducks, look up the word "duck" in the index. If you're really interested in learning about mallard ducks, then look under "mallard ducks." The index shows the page number and volume where the information is located.

Look at the index entry below about Neil Armstrong. Most index entries also tell you when a person lived and died and give a short description of the person.

> ARMSTRONG, NEIL   United States astronaut, b. 1930
>   Commander of *Gemini 8*, 1966; first man to walk on the Moon, July 1969
>   References in
>   Astronaut: illus. 2:56
>   Space travel 17:214

Neil Armstrong is listed under "Astronaut" and "Space travel." You can find information about him in both articles. The first entry shows there is an illustration (illus.) of Neil Armstrong in volume 2 on page 56 (2:56).

If Neil Armstrong were listed in a separate article in the encyclopedia, the index would look something like this:

> main article Armstrong, Neil
> 2:48

Directions: Answer these questions about using an encyclopedia index.

1. According to the index listing for Neil Armstrong, when was he born? _____

2. According to the index listing, who was Neil Armstrong? _____

_____

3. When did he walk on the Moon? _____

4. What are the titles of the two articles containing information about Neil Armstrong?

_____   _____

5. Where would you find the article on Space travel?

    Volume number _____ , page number _____ .

Name: _____

Encyclopedia Skills

Directions: Answer each question about using the encyclopedia.

1. To find information about Tyrannosaurus Rex, where would you look first?

   _____

2. If there is no listing in the index for Tyrannosaurus,
   what other subject(s) could you look under? _____

   _____

3. To find information about President George Bush,
   under which index entry would you look? _____

4. If there is no separate entry for George Bush, where else could you look?

   _____

5. Why should you use the encyclopedia index first? _____

   _____

6. If the encyclopedia says that Tyrannosaurus is in 17:97, what does that mean?

   _____

7. If the encyclopedia says "references in," does
   that refer you to a main article about the subject? _____

8. Is there always only one place to find a subject in the encyclopedia? Why or why not?

   _____

   _____

9. Will an encyclopedia index tell you when a person was born?_____

10. To find information about the *Discovery* space shuttle, where would you look?

    _____

    _____

Name: _____

Encyclopedia Skills

Each book in a set of encyclopedias has a volume number and lists the range of subjects included. Volume 10 shown below includes all articles that would fall alphabetically between insect and leaf. Note that Volume 30 in this set is the Index.

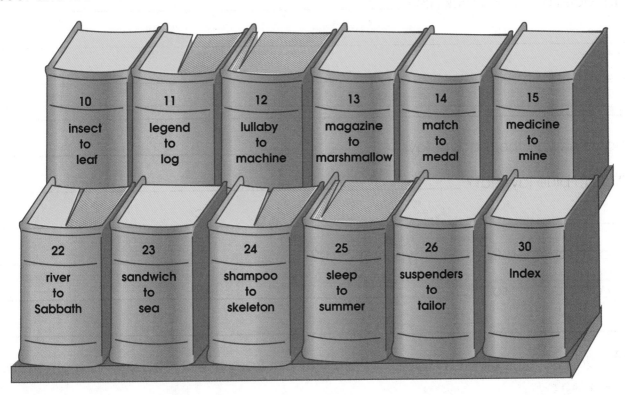

Directions: Answer the questions.

_____ 1. In which volume would you look to find an article on lungs?

_____ 2. Which volume would contain an article on ladybugs?

_____ 3. In which volume would an article on Saturn be found?

_____ 4. Which volume would contain an article on swimming?

_____ 5. In which volume would you check for an article on John D. Rockefeller?

_____ 6. An article on soccer would be in which volume?

_____ 7. Which volume would contain an article on magic?

_____ 8. In which volume would you look to find an article on melons?

Name: _____

Putting Encyclopedia Skills to Use

Directions: Read the questions below about blue jays. Use the index to find **blue jay** in the encyclopedia. Read the article about blue jays and take notes. Then answer the questions.

1. What does a blue jay look like? _____

_____

_____

_____

2. What are two other kinds of jays? _____

3. What do blue jays eat? _____

_____

4. Are blue jays friendly to other types of birds? _____

5. How do blue jays sound? _____

_____

6. What do you think blue jays do if they want to eat from a bird feeder where other birds are eating?

_____

_____

7. Are all jays blue? _____

8. Can blue jays be tamed? _____

9. How would you tame a blue jay? _____

_____

_____

_____

3

BAY
TO
BUS

Name: _____

Putting Encyclopedia Skills to Use

Directions: Read the questions about comets. Use the index to find **comet** in the encyclopedia. Read the article about comets and take notes. Then answer the questions.

1. What did the Greeks call comets? _____

2. What does "comet" mean in Greek? _____

3. Were comets recently discovered? _____

_____

4. What do you have to use sometimes to see comets? _____

5. Can you ever see comets with your eyes only? _____

6. Name the comet that came close to Earth in 1986. _____

7. Who discovered that comet? _____

8. Name the comet that came close to Earth in 1997. _____

9. Who discovered that comet? _____

10. What did Sir Isaac Newton discover about comets? _____

_____

11. Are comets lighter or heavier than moons? _____

12. Did your encyclopedia refer you to other articles
    that include more information related to comets? _____

13. To what other articles does your encyclopedia refer? _____

_____

_____

_____

_____

_____

Review

Directions: Write **T** for true or **F** for false.

1. _____ Every subject you look up in an encyclopedia will have a whole article written about it.

2. _____ You should always use the index to find a subject in the encyclopedia.

3. _____ An index may refer you to more than one article about a subject.

4. _____ Entries in an encyclopedia are in order according to when they happened.

5. _____ The index will give you some information about your subject.

Directions: Write the answers.

6. Name two subjects you could look under in an index to find **Jupiter** in an encyclopedia.

   1) _____

   2) _____

7. Name two possible entries for **George Washington** in an encyclopedia.

   1) _____

   2) _____

8. Which entry would include information about ants, flies, bees and gnats?

_____

Directions: Number these encyclopedia entries in alphabetical order.

_____ Bush, George   _____ meteor

_____ planets   _____ Brazil

_____ bush   _____ William I

_____ whole wheat flour   _____ Lincoln, Abraham

_____ Bell, Alexander Graham   _____ Japan

Name: _____

Using Reference Sources: Out of This World

The history of the American space program is a very fascinating topic. The articles presented earlier in this book (pages 164–170) provided many interesting facts about some of the astronauts, what their jobs were and what space travel was like.

Besides books and encyclopedias, magazine articles and the Internet are other good reference sources you can use to learn more about a topic.

Directions: Neil Armstrong was the first man to walk on the Moon in July 1969. Use reference sources to answer these questions.

1. What two other astronauts were with him? _____

_____

2. What was the name of the Apollo mission that went to the Moon? _____

3. What was the exact date of the first Moon landing? _____

4. Why was the U.S. racing Russia to the Moon? _____

_____

Directions: John Glenn first orbited Earth in 1962. Use reference sources to answer these questions.

5. How old was he then? _____

6. When did John Glenn return to space? _____

7. How old was he on this second trip? _____

8. Why did he return to space? _____

_____

Directions: Compare and contrast Glenn's two trips.

9. _____

_____

_____

Name: _____

Using Reference Sources: Out of This World

Directions: Use reference sources to answer these questions.

1. What caused the "Space Race" in the 1950s? _____

_____

_____

_____

2. In testing rockets, why were chimps used instead of other animals? _____

_____

_____

3. What is the astronaut training program like? _____

_____

_____

4. Why do you think the training is so difficult? _____

_____

_____

Directions: Use what you learned to answer these questions.

5. Do you think being an astronaut is a career for you? Explain. _____

_____

_____

6. What do you think life would be like on a space station or in a space colony?

_____

_____

For fun, look up information on "Space Camp" at one of NASA's training centers in Alabama.

Putting It All Together

You have learned many new skills. Now it's time to use those skills to write a report about a planet.

Directions: Choose a planet in our solar system other than Earth. Then answer the following questions about the report you will write.

1. What planet will you write about? _____

2. Decide on questions you want to answer about your planet. What are they?

_____

_____

_____

_____

_____

3. Where will you find information about the planet? _____

_____

_____

4. What should you do while you read about the planet?

_____

_____

5. After you have taken notes about your planet, what should you do next?

_____

_____

_____

_____

Name: _____

Putting It All Together

It's time to begin your research. You can use reference books as well as information from the Internet.

Directions: Fill in the information below to help you continue preparing to write a report about a planet.

1. Begin gathering information about your planet by looking for books with the planet's name in the title. What other subjects could you look under that might include information about your planet?

   _____

   _____

2. Use the library catalog to find the names of four books that contain information about your planet. List their titles, authors and call numbers.

   TITLE   AUTHOR   CALL NUMBER

   1) _____

   2) _____

   3) _____

   4) _____

3. Name at least two sources that you will use for your report.

   1) _____

   2) _____

4. Read the books and take notes. Your notes should cover the main points. Use separate sheets of paper to write your notes.

Name: _____

Putting It All Together

Now it's time to move on and gather information from encyclopedias for your report. There are many good encyclopedias available on CD's.

Directions: Fill in the information below to help you continue preparing to write a report about a planet.

1. When you use an encyclopedia to get information, what should you do first?

_____

_____

2. Where does the index say to look for information about your planet? _____

_____

_____

3. Read the article or articles. Then write notes about your planet. _____

_____

_____

_____

_____

_____

_____

_____

_____

_____

_____

_____

Putting It All Together

Once you have gathered information and made notes, it's time to make an outline of your report.

Directions: Complete the outline using the information you found in books, encyclopedias and other sources.

I. The location of the planet

    A. _____

        1. _____

        2. _____

    B. _____

II. What does the planet look like?

    A. _____

    B. _____

III. What is the surface of the planet like?

    A. _____

    B. _____

    C. _____

IV. Could we live there? Why or why not?

    A. _____

    B. _____

    C. _____

Now, you are ready to write!

Name: _____

Putting It All Together

Directions: Use your outline and notes to write a report about your planet. Use your own paper to finish this writing project. Add illustrations to make your report more interesting.

_____

_____

_____

_____

_____

_____

_____

_____

_____

_____

_____

_____

_____

_____

_____

_____

_____

_____

_____

Name: _____

Writing Haiku

Haiku is a form of unrhymed Japanese poetry. A haiku poem has only three lines. Each line has a specific number of syllables.

Haiku poems usually describe a season or something in nature. Sometimes haiku are written about feelings.

The Haiku pattern:
Line 1 — 5 syllables
Line 2 — 7 syllables
Line 3 — 5 syllables

Example haiku:
Winter snow slides from
The eave. Drops—plop—on my head,
As I walk under.
— *D.S. Underwood*

When writing haiku you do not count words per line. Count only the number of syllables.

Directions: To prepare for writing your poem, think of words about a snowy day. Write them on the lines. After each word, write the number of syllables in the word.

frosty   (2)   white (1)   snowflakes   (2)

_____   _____   _____

_____   _____   _____

_____   _____   _____

When writing any type of poetry, it is a good idea to start on scrap paper so you can write, erase, cross out and rewrite.

Directions: Write a haiku poem about a snowy day on scrap paper. When you are satisfied with your poem, rewrite it below. At the end of each line, write the number of syllables in the line.

_____   _____

_____   _____

_____   _____

Directions: Select one of the topics in the box. Prewrite your poem on scrap paper. Write it on good paper when you are satisfied with it.

rainy day	summer	spring	fall
a sparrow	joy	sadness	friendship

Name: _____

Tankas

Haiku poems are given to friends as gifts. A **tanka** is a poem written in response to haiku. If a person receives a haiku, he or she is supposed to send a tanka in reply! A tanka is much like a haiku but has two more lines.

The tanka pattern:
Line 1 — 5 syllables
Line 2 — 7 syllables
Line 3 — 5 syllables
Line 4 — 7 syllables
Line 5 — 7 syllables

Example tanka:
The snow on your head
It did plop—slop and slide down
Your neck to your socks.
The winter wind blew, gave you
A chill, now you sneeze—Ah choo!
— *D.S. Underwood*

Remember to count syllables per line.

Directions: Write a tanka in response to one of the two haiku poems you wrote. Prewrite on scrap paper. When you are satisfied with your tanka, rewrite it below. At the end of each line, write the number of syllables in the line.

_____   _____

_____   _____

_____   _____

_____   _____

_____   _____

Directions: Trade your haiku with a partner. Write a tanka in response to your partner's haiku.

_____

_____

_____

_____

_____

Name: _____

Cinquains

Another form of unrhymed poetry that can express many ideas in only a few words is the **cinquain**. A cinquain is a simple five-line verse.

In a cinquain, the number of syllables does not matter. What is important is the number of words in each line and the specific type of words used.

Cinquain pattern:
Line 1 — A noun
Line 2 — 2 adjectives describing the noun in line 1
Line 3 — 3 ing verbs describing the noun in line 1
Line 4 — A 4-word phrase
Line 5 — A noun that is a synonym for the word in line 1

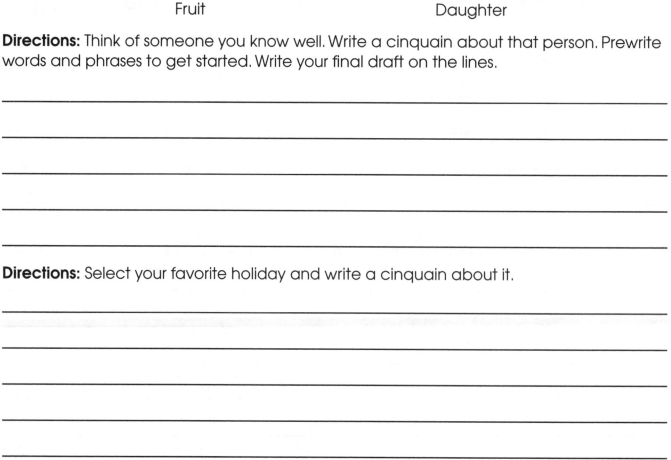

Example cinquains:

Apple
Shiny, smooth
Crunching, munching, slurping
Healthy snack to eat
Fruit

Mary
Young, active
Trying, discovering, learning
Anxious to grow up
Daughter

Directions: Think of someone you know well. Write a cinquain about that person. Prewrite words and phrases to get started. Write your final draft on the lines.

_____

_____

_____

_____

_____

Directions: Select your favorite holiday and write a cinquain about it.

_____

_____

_____

_____

_____

Shape Poems

A **shape poem** or **pattern poem** uses its shape or pattern of words to tell what the poem is about.

Example:

To make a shape or pattern poem, lightly sketch the shape you wish to describe. Then use words to fill up the shape or go around the outline.

Directions: Write a shape poem for the heart and the house shown below.

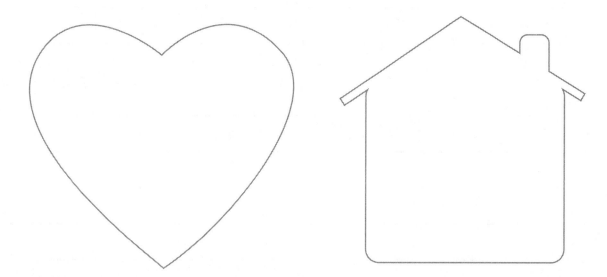

Directions: On another sheet of paper, create a pattern poem in the shape of your choice.

Limericks

A **limerick** is a short, silly poem. Limericks are five lines long and follow a specific pattern.

Limerick pattern:
Lines 1, 2 and 5 rhyme and have 8, 9 or 10 syllables per line.
Lines 3 and 4 rhyme and have 5, 6 or 7 syllables per line.

Example limerick:
There once was a lion at the zoo
Who in his mane got sticky goo.
The situation looked grim,
So they gave him a trim
And turned his one mane into two.

Directions: Write two limericks. Prewrite on scrap paper.
Write your final drafts below. Add a short title to your limericks.

_____

_____

_____

_____

_____

_____

_____

_____

_____

_____

_____

MATH

Place Value

Place value is the value of a digit, or numeral, shown by where it is in the number. For example, in 1,234, 1 has the place value of thousands, 2 is hundreds, 3 is tens and 4 is ones.

Directions: Write the numbers in the correct boxes to find how far the car has traveled.

one thousand

six hundreds

eight ones

nine ten thousands

four tens

two millions

five hundred thousands

milions	hundred thousands	ten thousands	thousands	hundreds	tens	ones

How many miles has the car traveled?_____

Directions: In the number . . .

2,386 _____ is in the ones place.

4,957 _____ is in the hundreds place.

102,432 _____ is in the ten thousands place.

489,753 _____ is in the thousands place.

1,743,998 _____ is in the millions place.

9,301,671 _____ is in the hundred thousands place.

7,521,834 _____ is in the tens place.

Name: _____

Place Value: Standard Form

For this activity, you will need a number spinner or number cube.

Directions: Roll the cube or spin the spinner the same number of times as there are spaces in each place value box. The first number rolled or spun goes in the ones place, the second number in the tens place, and so on.

Example:

thousands	hundreds	tens	ones
4	5	6	7

Standard Form

4,567

_____

	hundreds	tens	ones

_____

thousands	hundreds	tens	ones

_____

ten thousands	thousands	hundreds	tens	ones

_____

hundred thousands	ten thousands	thousands	hundreds	tens	ones

_____

millions	hundred thousands	ten thousands	thousands	hundreds	tens	ones

_____

Directions: Write the number words for the numerals above.

_____

_____

_____

_____

_____

Name: _____

Place Value:
Expanded Notation and Standard Form

Directions: Use the number cube or spinner to create numbers for the place value boxes below. Then write the number in expanded notation and standard form.

Example:

thousands	hundreds	tens	ones
8	6	2	4

Standard Form ___8,624___

Expanded Notation ___8,000 + 600 + 20 + 4___

thousands	hundreds	tens	ones

Standard Form _____

Expanded Notation _____

ten thousands	thousands	hundreds	tens	ones

Standard Form _____

Expanded Notation _____

hundred thousands	ten thousands	thousands	hundreds	tens	ones

Standard Form _____

Expanded Notation _____

Directions: Write the value of the 4 in each number below.

742,521 _____

456 _____

1,234,567 _____

65,504 _____

937,641 _____

Name: _____

Add 'Em Up!

Addition is "putting together" or adding two or more numbers to find the sum.

Directions: Add the following problems as quickly and as accurately as you can.

$$\begin{array}{r} 3 \\ +2 \\ \hline \end{array} \qquad \begin{array}{r} 6 \\ +4 \\ \hline \end{array} \qquad \begin{array}{r} 5 \\ +4 \\ \hline \end{array} \qquad \begin{array}{r} 2 \\ +9 \\ \hline \end{array}$$

$$\begin{array}{r} 6 \\ +2 \\ \hline \end{array} \qquad \begin{array}{r} 4 \\ +1 \\ \hline \end{array} \qquad \begin{array}{r} 9 \\ +6 \\ \hline \end{array} \qquad \begin{array}{r} 7 \\ +6 \\ \hline \end{array} \qquad \begin{array}{r} 8 \\ +7 \\ \hline \end{array} \qquad \begin{array}{r} 8 \\ +9 \\ \hline \end{array}$$

$$\begin{array}{r} 9 \\ +4 \\ \hline \end{array} \qquad \begin{array}{r} 1 \\ +8 \\ \hline \end{array} \qquad \begin{array}{r} 4 \\ +7 \\ \hline \end{array} \qquad \begin{array}{r} 7 \\ +9 \\ \hline \end{array} \qquad \begin{array}{r} 5 \\ +6 \\ \hline \end{array} \qquad \begin{array}{r} 5 \\ +3 \\ \hline \end{array}$$

$$\begin{array}{r} 6 \\ +6 \\ \hline \end{array} \qquad \begin{array}{r} 8 \\ +8 \\ \hline \end{array} \qquad \begin{array}{r} 7 \\ +7 \\ \hline \end{array} \qquad \begin{array}{r} 4 \\ +4 \\ \hline \end{array}$$

$$\begin{array}{r} 2 \\ +8 \\ \hline \end{array} \qquad \begin{array}{r} 5 \\ +2 \\ \hline \end{array} \qquad \begin{array}{r} 3 \\ +6 \\ \hline \end{array} \qquad \begin{array}{r} 5 \\ +8 \\ \hline \end{array}$$

How quickly did you complete this page? _____

Grade 4 - Comprehensive Curriculum

Name: _____

Going in Circles

Directions: Where the circles meet, write the sum of the numbers from the circles on the right and left and above and below. The first row shows you what to do.

7 (16) 9 (21) 12 (20) 8

4   6   5   1

0   3   2   10

11   15   20   12

13   16   14   17

Addition Games

Directions: Play the following addition games to practice your math facts.

1. ROLL 'EM!

For one or more players.

Materials: 2 number cubes or dice or 2 number spinners per player

How to play: Each player rolls his/her number cubes (dice) or spins his/her spinners at the same time. As quickly as possible, he/she adds the two numbers rolled or spun. Whoever is first to add the numbers correctly wins the round.

Variation: Subtract the numbers.

2. FLASH 'EM!

For one or more players.

Materials: addition/subtraction flash cards

How to play: An adult shows the flash cards one at a time to each player, who solves the addition problem. Place correctly answered cards in one stack and incorrectly answered cards in another. Which stack is larger? Try again. This time try to answer all the cards correctly.

Variations: Set a time limit for play. How many flash cards can be correctly answered in 5, 4 or 3 minutes?

Name: _____

Magic Squares

Directions: Some of the number squares below are "magic" and some are not. Squares that add up to the same number horizontally, vertically and diagonally are "magic." Add the numbers horizontally and vertically in each square to discover which ones are "magic."

Example:

4	9	2
3	5	7
8	1	6

15
15
15

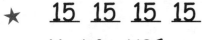

15 15 15 15

Magic? **yes**

1.

7	2	1
3	4	8
5	9	6

___
___
___

___ ___ ___ ___

Magic? _____

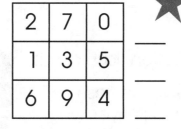

2.

6	11	4
5	7	9
10	3	8

___
___
___

Magic? _____

3.

3	8	1
2	4	6
7	0	5

___

Magic? _____

4.

2	7	0
1	3	5
6	9	4

Magic? _____

5.

5	10	3
4	6	8
9	2	7

___

Magic? _____

6.

7	12	5
6	8	10
11	4	9

___

___ ___ ___

Magic? _____

7.

1	2	3
4	5	6
7	8	9

___

Magic? _____

8.

6	7	4
1	5	9
8	3	2

___

Magic? _____

Challenge: Can you discover a pattern for number placement in the magic squares? Try to make a magic square of your own.

Name: _____

Adding Larger Numbers

When adding two-, three- and four-digit numbers, add the ones first, then tens, hundreds, thousands, and so on.

Examples:

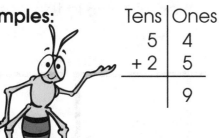

Tens	Ones
5	4
+ 2	5
	9

Tens	Ones
5	4
+ 2	5
7	9

Directions: Add the following numbers.

81	67	34	730
+23	+22	+82	+265

76	1,803	523	267
+73	+1,104	+476	+ 12

		4,254	111
		+ 545	+ 82

		164	727
		+425	+ 51

Grade 4 - Comprehensive Curriculum

Addition: Regrouping

Regrouping uses 10 ones to form one 10, 10 tens to form one hundred, one 10 and 5 ones to form 15, and so on.

Directions: Add using regrouping. Color in all the boxes with a 5 in the answer to help the dog find its way home.

63 + 22	5,268 4,910 + 1,683	248 + 463	291 + 543	2,934 + 112
1,736 + 5,367	2,946 + 7,384	3,245 1,239 + 981	738 + 692	896 + 728	594 + 738
2,603 + 5,004	4,507 + 289	1,483 + 6,753	1,258 + 6,301	27 469 + 6,002	4,637 + 7,531
782 + 65	485 + 276	3,421 + 8,064		
48 93 + 26	90 263 + 864	362 453 + 800		

Name: _____

Leafy Addition

Directions: Add, then color according to the code.

Code:

green — 79   orange — 35   red — 78

yellow — 87   purple — 56   brown — 94

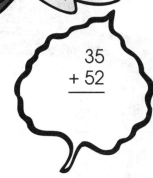

57
+ 21

34
+ 22

23
+ 12

35
+ 52

15
+ 41

62
+ 32

20
+ 74

34
+ 44

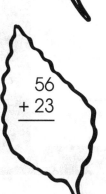
56
+ 23

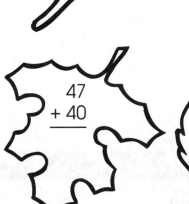
47
+ 40

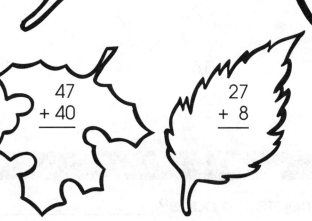
27
+ 8

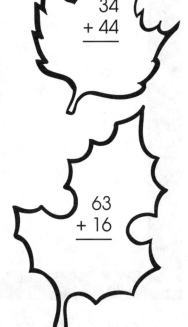
63
+ 16

Grade 4 - Comprehensive Curriculum

Name: _____

Subtraction

Subtraction is "taking away" or subtracting one number from another.

Directions: Complete the following problems as quickly and as accurately as you can.

18 − 9	13 − 6	12 − 5	17 − 8	16 − 8
12 − 5	10 − 4	5 − 3	14 − 6	15 − 9
9 − 5	8 − 3	6 − 2	5 − 4	10 − 7
11 − 4	12 − 8	16 − 9	11 − 8	10 −10

How quickly did you complete this page? _____

Name: _____

Subtracting Larger Numbers

When you subtract larger numbers, subtract the ones first, then the tens, hundreds, thousands, and so on.

Example:

Tens	Ones
9	4
− 2	1
	3

Tens	Ones
9	4
− 2	1
7	3

Directions: Solve these subtraction problems.

```
   29          99         359
 − 26        − 58        −  55
```

```
  735         849        7,678
− 734       − 726      − 4,321
```

```
  865          55        9,876
− 731        − 25      − 1,234
```

Subtraction: Regrouping

Directions: Subtract using regrouping.

Examples:

	$\overset{1\,\,1}{\cancel{2}\cancel{3}}$		$\overset{1\,\,13}{\cancel{2}\cancel{4}3}$
23		243	
− 18	− 18	− 96	− 96
	5		147

81	76	94	156	341	726
− 53	− 49	− 38	− 77	− 83	− 29

568	806	743	903	647	254
− 173	− 738	− 550	− 336	− 289	− 69

730	961	573	604	265	372
− 518	− 846	− 76	− 55	− 19	− 59

111	358	147
− 82	− 99	− 49

180	325	873
− 106	− 68	− 35

Name: _____

Addition and Subtraction

Directions: Add or subtract, using regrouping when needed.

```
   32        183        456
   68        246        398        643
 + 43       + 89      + 597      - 377
 ____       ____      _____      _____
```

```
 1,563      3,586      8,711      9,361
 -  941    + 4,218    - 4,937    - 7,452
 _____    _____    _____    _____
```

```
             293                    849
 5,734       431        743         250
+ 6,298     + 93       - 529       + 82
_____     ____       _____       ____
```

```
 1,227
 2,431      9,117
+ 5,792    - 3,828
_____    _____
```

68 + 93 + 146 = _____   73 + 246 + 1,579 = _____

43 + 745 − 29 = _____   128 + 403 + 2,571 = _____

156 + 627 + 541 = _____   97 + 51 + 37 + 79 = _____

Tom walks 389 steps from his house to the video store. It is 149 steps to Elm Street. It is 52 steps from Maple Street to the video store. How many steps is it from Elm Street to Maple Street? _____

Name: _____

Addition and Subtraction

Directions: Add or subtract, using regrouping when needed.

38	1,269		629	
43	2,453	5,792	491	4,697
+ 21	+ 8,219	− 4,814	+ 308	− 2,988

	68	197		
5,280	27	436	7,321	456
− 3,147	+ 42	+ 213	− 2,789	+ 974

	492			
3,932	863	9,873	4,978	6,235
+ 4,681	+ 57	+ 5,483	+ 2,131	+ 2,986

Sue stocked her pond with 263 bass and 187 trout. 97 fish swam away in a flood. How many fish are left?

_____

Rounding: Tens

Rounding a number means expressing it to the nearest ten, hundred, thousand, and so on. Knowing how to round numbers makes estimating sums, differences and products easier. When rounding to the nearest ten, the key number is in the ones place. If the ones digit is 5 or larger, round up to the next highest ten. If the ones digit is 4 or less, round down to the nearest ten.

Examples:

- Round 81 to the nearest ten.
- 1 is the key digit.
- If it is less than 5, round down.
- Answer: <u>80</u>

- Round 246 to the nearest ten.
- 6 is the key digit.
- If it is more than 5, round up.
- Answer: <u>250</u>

Directions:
Round these numbers to the nearest ten.

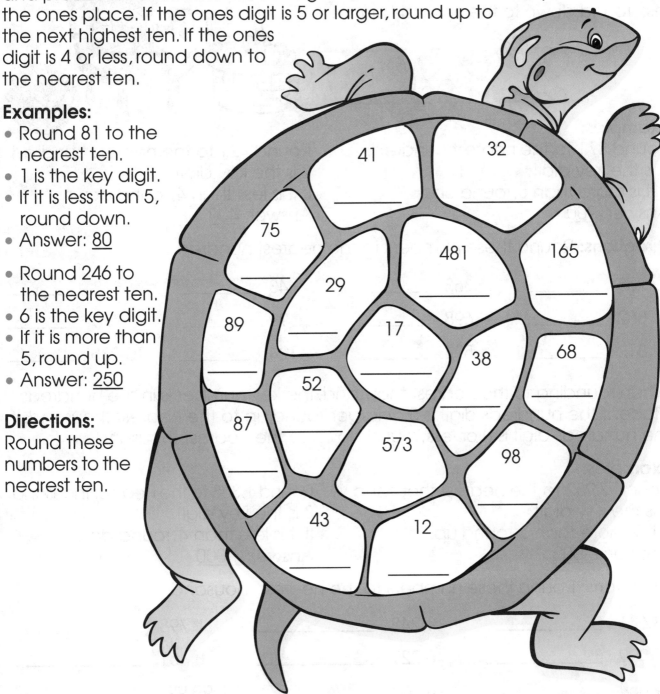

Grade 4 - Comprehensive Curriculum

Rounding: Hundreds and Thousands

When rounding to the nearest hundred, the key number is in the tens place. If the tens digit is 5 or larger, round up to nearest hundred. If the tens digit is 4 or less, round down to the nearest hundred.

Examples:

Round 871 to the nearest hundred.
7 is the key digit.
If it is more than 5, round up.
Answer: <u>900</u>

Round 421 to the nearest hundred.
2 is the key digit.
If it is less than 4, round down.
Answer: <u>400</u>

Directions: Round these numbers to the nearest hundred.

255 _____	368 _____	443 _____	578 _____
562 _____	698 _____	99 _____	775 _____
812 _____	592 _____	124 _____	10,235 _____

When rounding to the nearest thousand, the key number is in the hundreds place. If the hundreds digit is 5 or larger, round up to the nearest thousand. If the hundreds digit is 4 or less, round down to the nearest thousand.

Examples:

Round 7,932 to the nearest thousand.
9 is the key digit.
If it is more than 5, round up.
Answer: <u>8,000</u>

Round 1,368 to the nearest thousand.
3 is the key digit.
If it is less than 4, round down.
Answer: <u>1,000</u>

Directions: Round these numbers to the nearest thousand.

8,631 _____	1,248 _____	798 _____
999 _____	6,229 _____	8,461 _____
9,654 _____	4,963 _____	99,923 _____

Rounding

Directions: Round these numbers to the nearest ten.

18 _____ 33 _____ 82 _____ 56 _____

24 _____ 49 _____ 91 _____ 67 _____

Directions: Round these numbers to the nearest hundred.

243 _____ 689 _____ 263 _____ 162 _____

389 _____ 720 _____ 351 _____ 490 _____

463 _____ 846 _____ 928 _____ 733 _____

Directions: Round these numbers to the nearest thousand.

2,638 _____ 3,940 _____ 8,653 _____

6,238 _____ 1,429 _____ 5,061 _____

7,289 _____ 2,742 _____ 9,460 _____

3,109 _____ 4,697 _____ 8,302 _____

Directions: Round these numbers to the nearest ten thousand.

11,368 _____ 38,421 _____

75,302 _____ 67,932 _____

14,569 _____ 49,926 _____

93,694 _____ 81,648 _____

26,784 _____ 87,065 _____

57,843 _____ 29,399 _____

Grade 4 - Comprehensive Curriculum

Name: _____

Estimating

Estimating is used for certain mathematical calculations. For example, to figure the cost of several items, round their prices to the nearest dollar, then add up the approximate cost. A store clerk, on the other hand, needs to know the exact prices in order to charge the correct amount. To estimate to the nearest hundred, round up numbers over 50. **Example:** 251 is rounded up to 300. Round down numbers less than 50. **Example:** 128 is rounded down to 100.

Directions: In the following situations, write whether an exact or estimated answer should be used.

Example:
You make a deposit in your bank account. Do you want an estimated total or an exact total?   _____Exact_____

1. Your family just ate dinner at a restaurant. Your parents are trying to calculate the tip for your server. Should they estimate by rounding or use exact numbers?

   _____

2. You are at the store buying candy, and you want to know if you have enough money to pay for it. Should you estimate or use exact numbers?

   _____

3. Some friends are planning a trip from New York City to Washington, D.C. They need to know about how far they will travel in miles. Should they estimate or use exact numbers?

   _____

4. You plan a trip to the zoo. Beforehand, you call the zoo for the price of admission. Should the person at the zoo tell you an estimated or exact price?

   _____

5. The teacher is grading your papers. Should your scores be exact or estimated?

   _____

Name: _____

Estimating

To **estimate** means to give an approximate, rather than an exact, answer. To find an estimated sum or difference, round the numbers of the problem, then add or subtract. If the number has 5 ones or more, round up to the nearest ten. If the number has 4 ones or less, round down to the nearest ten.

Directions: Round the numbers to the nearest ten, hundred or thousand. Then add or subtract.

Examples:

Ten				Hundred		Thousand	
74 → 70	64 → 60			352 → 400		7,681 → 8,000	
+ 39 → + 40	− 25 → − 30			− 164 → − 200		+ 4,321 → + 4,000	
110	30			200		12,000	

Round these numbers to the nearest ten.

$$18 \rightarrow \qquad 49 \rightarrow \qquad 67 \rightarrow$$
$$+ 24 \rightarrow \qquad - 33 \rightarrow \qquad - 56 \rightarrow$$

Round these numbers to the nearest hundred.

$$255 \rightarrow \qquad 526 \rightarrow \qquad 102 \rightarrow$$
$$- 99 \rightarrow \qquad + 145 \rightarrow \qquad - 75 \rightarrow$$

Round these numbers to the nearest thousand.

$$8,361 \rightarrow \qquad 9,926 \rightarrow$$
$$+ 889 \rightarrow \qquad + 3,645 \rightarrow$$

Name: _____

Estimating

Directions: Round the numbers to the nearest hundred. Then solve the problems.

Example:

Jack and Alex were playing a computer game. Jack scored 428 points. Alex scored 132. About how many more points did Jack score than Alex?

Round Jack's 428 points down to the nearest hundred, 400.

Round Alex's 132 points down to 100. Subtract.

$$
\begin{array}{r}
400 \\
- 100 \\
\hline
\textbf{estimate} \quad 300
\end{array}
$$

$\begin{array}{r} 258 \rightarrow \\ + 117 \rightarrow \\ \hline 375 \end{array}$ $\begin{array}{r} 300 \\ +100 \\ \hline 400 \end{array}$	$\begin{array}{r} 493 \rightarrow \\ +114 \rightarrow \\ \hline \end{array}$	$\begin{array}{r} 837 \rightarrow \\ -252 \rightarrow \\ \hline \end{array}$
$\begin{array}{r} 928 \rightarrow \\ -437 \rightarrow \\ \hline \end{array}$	$\begin{array}{r} 700 \rightarrow \\ -491 \rightarrow \\ \hline \end{array}$	$\begin{array}{r} 319 \rightarrow \\ +630 \rightarrow \\ \hline \end{array}$
$\begin{array}{r} 332 \rightarrow \\ +567 \rightarrow \\ \hline \end{array}$	$\begin{array}{r} 493 \rightarrow \\ -162 \rightarrow \\ \hline \end{array}$	$\begin{array}{r} 1,356 \rightarrow \\ +2,941 \rightarrow \\ \hline \end{array}$

Name: _____

Skip Counting

Skip counting is a quick way to count by skipping numbers. For example, when you skip count by 2's, you count 2, 4, 6, 8, and so on. You can skip count by many different numbers such as 2's, 4's, 5's, 10's and 100's.

The illustration below shows skip counting by 2's to 14.

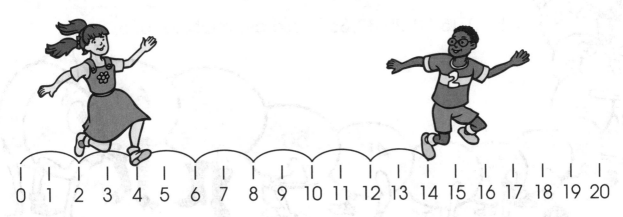

Directions: Use the number line to help you skip count by 2's from 0 to 20.

0, _____, _____, _____, 8, _____, _____, 14, _____, _____, _____

Directions: Skip count by 3's by filling in the rocks across the pond.

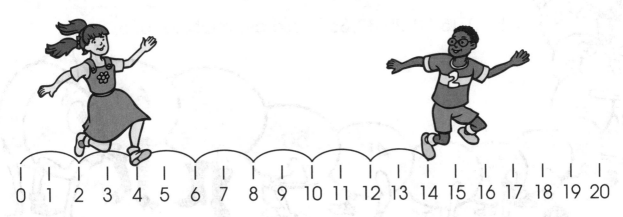

Grade 4 - Comprehensive Curriculum

Multiples

A **multiple** is the product of a specific number and any other number. For example, the multiples of 2 are 2 (2 x 1), 4 (2 x 2), 6, 8, 10, 12, and so on.

Directions: Write the missing multiples.

Example: Count by 5's.

5, 10, 15, 20, 25, 30, 35. These are multiples of 5.

Name: _____

Review

Directions: Add or subtract using regrouping.

```
   67                      732
   93        5,029         801      2,467      8,453
 + 48      - 3,068       +  18    + 3,184    - 6,087
 ____      _____       _____    _____    _____
```

```
  5,792      7,489        463      3,567      6,342
- 3,889    + 5,938      - 209    - 2,394    +  959
_____    _____      _____    _____    _____
```

Directions: Write the numbers in the boxes. In the blanks, write the numbers in standard form.

millions	hundred thousands	ten thousands	thousands	hundreds	tens	ones

_____

eight millions, four hundred thousands, zero ten thousands, zero thousands, nine hundreds, five tens, two ones

hundred thousands	ten thousands	thousands	hundreds	tens	ones

_____

five hundred thousands, three ten thousands, five thousands, zero hundreds, four tens, one one

Directions: Write the missing multiples in the blanks.

6, 12, 18, _____, 30, _____   3, _____, _____, 12, 15

4, _____, 12, 16, _____, 24   _____, 10, 15, _____, _____

Multiplication

Multiplication is a short way to find the sum of adding the same number a certain amount of times, such as 7 x 4 = 28 instead of 7 + 7 + 7 + 7 = 28.

Directions: Multiply as quickly and as accurately as you can.

4 x 7	7 x 6	0 x 8	7 x 2	9 x 5	1 x 5	6 x 4

8 x 3	7 x 1	4 x 2	9 x 6	8 x 5	6 x 7	9 x 8

3 x 5	7 x 8	3 x 9	5 x 6	9 x 9	7 x 5	9 x 4

3 x 6	2 x 8	8 x 6	7 x 7

0 x 7	3 x 3	5 x 9

How quickly did you complete this page? _____

Fact Factory

Factors are the numbers multiplied together in a multiplication problem. The **product** is the answer.

Directions: Write the missing factors or products.

X	5
1	5
5	
4	20
6	
3	
2	10
7	
9	45

X	9
8	72
3	
4	
9	
6	54
7	
2	
1	9

X	7
2	14
5	
	42
8	
7	
4	
	21
0	

X	3
7	
4	
6	
1	
3	
2	
5	
8	

X	1
1	
12	
10	
3	3
5	
7	
6	
4	

X	8
9	
8	
4	
5	
6	
7	
3	
2	

X	2
	24
	2
	22
	4
	20
	6
	18
	8

X	4
2	
4	
6	
8	
	4
	12
	20
	28

X	6
7	
6	
5	
4	
3	
2	
1	
0	

X	10
	20
3	
	40
5	
	60
7	
	80
9	

X	11
4	
7	
9	
10	
3	
5	
6	
8	

X	12
1	
2	24
3	
4	48
5	
6	
7	
8	

Grade 4 - Comprehensive Curriculum

Multiplication: Tens, Hundreds, Thousands

When multiplying a number by 10, the answer is the number with a 0. It is like counting by tens.

Examples:

10 x 1 –– 10	10 x 2 –– 20	10 x 3 –– 30	10 x 4 –– 40	10 x 5 –– 50	10 x 6 –– 60

When multiplying a number by 100, the answer is the number with two 0's. When multiplying by 1,000, the answer is the number with three 0's.

Examples:

100 x 1 –––– 100	100 x 2 –––– 200	100 x 3 –––– 300	1,000 x 1 –––––– 1,000	1,000 x 2 –––––– 2,000	1,000 x 3 –––––– 3,000
4 x 2 –– 8	400 x 2 –––– 800	8 x 3 –– 24	800 x 3 –––– 2,400	7 x 5 –– 35	700 x 5 –––– 3,500

Directions: Multiply.

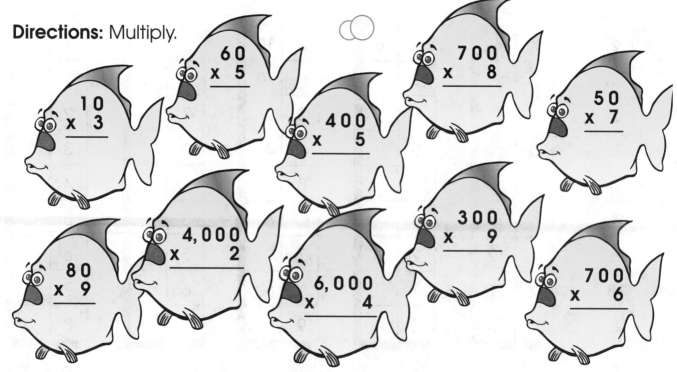

$$\begin{array}{r} 10 \\ \times\ \ 3 \\ \hline \end{array}$$

$$\begin{array}{r} 60 \\ \times\ 5 \\ \hline \end{array}$$

$$\begin{array}{r} 700 \\ \times\ \ \ 8 \\ \hline \end{array}$$

$$\begin{array}{r} 400 \\ \times\ \ \ \ 5 \\ \hline \end{array}$$

$$\begin{array}{r} 50 \\ \times\ 7 \\ \hline \end{array}$$

$$\begin{array}{r} 80 \\ \times\ 9 \\ \hline \end{array}$$

$$\begin{array}{r} 4,000 \\ \times\ \ \ \ \ \ 2 \\ \hline \end{array}$$

$$\begin{array}{r} 6,000 \\ \times\ \ \ \ \ \ 4 \\ \hline \end{array}$$

$$\begin{array}{r} 300 \\ \times\ \ \ 9 \\ \hline \end{array}$$

$$\begin{array}{r} 700 \\ \times\ \ \ 6 \\ \hline \end{array}$$

Name: _____

Multiplication:
One-Digit Numbers Times Two-Digit Numbers

Follow the steps for multiplying a one-digit number by a two-digit number using regrouping.

Example: **Step 1:** Multiply the ones.
Regroup.

$$\begin{array}{r} \overset{2}{5}4 \\ \times\ 7 \\ \hline 8 \end{array}$$

Step 2: Multiply the tens.
Add two tens.

$$\begin{array}{r} \overset{2}{5}4 \\ \times\ 7 \\ \hline 378 \end{array}$$

Directions: Multiply.

$$\begin{array}{r} 27 \\ \times\ 3 \\ \hline \end{array} \qquad \begin{array}{r} 63 \\ \times\ 4 \\ \hline \end{array} \qquad \begin{array}{r} 52 \\ \times\ 5 \\ \hline \end{array} \qquad \begin{array}{r} 91 \\ \times\ 9 \\ \hline \end{array} \qquad \begin{array}{r} 45 \\ \times\ 7 \\ \hline \end{array} \qquad \begin{array}{r} 75 \\ \times\ 2 \\ \hline \end{array}$$

$$\begin{array}{r} 64 \\ \times\ 5 \\ \hline \end{array} \qquad \begin{array}{r} 76 \\ \times\ 3 \\ \hline \end{array} \qquad \begin{array}{r} 93 \\ \times\ 6 \\ \hline \end{array} \qquad \begin{array}{r} 87 \\ \times\ 4 \\ \hline \end{array} \qquad \begin{array}{r} 66 \\ \times\ 7 \\ \hline \end{array} \qquad \begin{array}{r} 38 \\ \times\ 2 \\ \hline \end{array}$$

$$\begin{array}{r} 47 \\ \times\ 8 \\ \hline \end{array} \qquad \begin{array}{r} 64 \\ \times\ 9 \\ \hline \end{array} \qquad \begin{array}{r} 51 \\ \times\ 8 \\ \hline \end{array} \qquad \begin{array}{r} 99 \\ \times\ 3 \\ \hline \end{array}$$

$$\begin{array}{r} 13 \\ \times\ 7 \\ \hline \end{array} \qquad \begin{array}{r} 32 \\ \times\ 4 \\ \hline \end{array} \qquad \begin{array}{r} 25 \\ \times\ 8 \\ \hline \end{array} \qquad \begin{array}{r} 15 \\ \times\ 7 \\ \hline \end{array}$$

The chickens on the Smith farm produce 48 dozen eggs each day. How many dozen eggs do they produce in 7 days?

_____

Name: _____

Multiplication:
Two-Digit Numbers Times Two-Digit Numbers

Follow the steps for multiplying a two-digit number by a two-digit number using regrouping.

Example:

Step 1: Multiply the ones. Regroup.

```
            2
  6 3      6 3
x 6 8    x  6 8
         ─────
           5 0 4
```

Step 2: Multiply the tens. Regroup. Add.

```
     1
   6 3         6 3
 x 6 8       x 6 8
 ─────       ─────
 3,7 8 0       5 0 4
           + 3,7 8 0
           ─────────
             4,2 8 4
```

Directions: Multiply.

```
  1 2        2 7        6 5        1 9        9 9        3 5
x 5 5      x 1 5      x 2 7      x 3 9      x 1 3      x 1 4
```

```
  4 3        3 8        5 3        4 7        5 7        4 8
x 2 6      x 1 7      x 8 6      x 7 2      x 6 2      x 3 3
```

```
  2 7        9 3        6 4        5 3
x 5 4      x 4 5      x 1 6      x 2 3
```

The Jones farm has 24 cows that each produce 52 quarts of milk a day. How many quarts are produced each day altogether? _____

Multiplication:
Two-Digit Numbers Times Three-Digit Numbers

Follow the steps for multiplying a two-digit number by a three-digit number using regrouping.

Example: **Step 1:** Multiply the ones. Regroup.

$$
\begin{array}{r} 287 \\ \times\ 43 \\ \hline \end{array}
\qquad
\begin{array}{r} {}^{2\ 2} \\ 287 \\ \times\ \ 43 \\ \hline 861 \end{array}
$$

Step 2: Multiply the tens. Regroup. Add.

$$
\begin{array}{r} 287 \\ \times\ 43 \\ \hline 11{,}480 \end{array}
\qquad
\begin{array}{r} 287 \\ \times\ 43 \\ \hline 861 \\ +\ 11{,}480 \\ \hline 12{,}341 \end{array}
$$

Directions: Multiply.

$$
\begin{array}{r} 261 \\ \times\ 36 \\ \hline \end{array}
\qquad
\begin{array}{r} 434 \\ \times\ 48 \\ \hline \end{array}
\qquad
\begin{array}{r} 357 \\ \times\ 75 \\ \hline \end{array}
$$

$$
\begin{array}{r} 231 \\ \times\ 46 \\ \hline \end{array}
\qquad
\begin{array}{r} 754 \\ \times\ 65 \\ \hline \end{array}
\qquad
\begin{array}{r} 614 \\ \times\ 59 \\ \hline \end{array}
$$

$$
\begin{array}{r} 549 \\ \times\ 89 \\ \hline \end{array}
\qquad
\begin{array}{r} 372 \\ \times\ 94 \\ \hline \end{array}
\qquad
\begin{array}{r} 458 \\ \times\ 85 \\ \hline \end{array}
\qquad
\begin{array}{r} 368 \\ \times\ 98 \\ \hline \end{array}
$$

At the Douglas berry farm, workers pick 378 baskets of peaches each day. Each basket holds 65 peaches. How many peaches are picked each day? _____

Name: _____

Multiplication: Two-Digit Numbers Times Two- and Three-Digit Numbers

Directions: Multiply.

25 x 72	70 x 66	844 x 24	124 x 15
45 x 41	76 x 78	74 x 69	261 x 88
48 x 36	263 x 57	37 x 64	52 x 43
321 x 78	544 x 58	797 x 24	998 x 37
249 x 33	24 x 19	48 x 20	817 x 59

Multiplication:
Three-Digit Numbers Times Three-Digit Numbers

Directions: Multiply. Regroup when needed.

Example:

```
    563
  x 248
  ------
   4,504
  22,520
+112,600
--------
 139,624
```

Hint: When multiplying by the tens, start writing the number in the tens place. When multiplying by the hundreds, start in the hundreds place.

```
   842          932          759          531
 x 167        x 272        x 468        x 556
```

```
   383          523          229          738
 x 476        x 349        x 189        x 513
```

James grows pumpkins on his farm. He has 362 rows of pumpkins. There are 593 pumpkins in each row. How many pumpkins does James grow? _____

Name: _____

Multiplication Drill

Directions: Multiply.

134 x 22	48 x 66	876 x 13	432 x 64

68 x 11	5,478 x 8	248 x 61	6,897 x 6

82 x 4	6,798 x 5	79 x 86	694 x 38

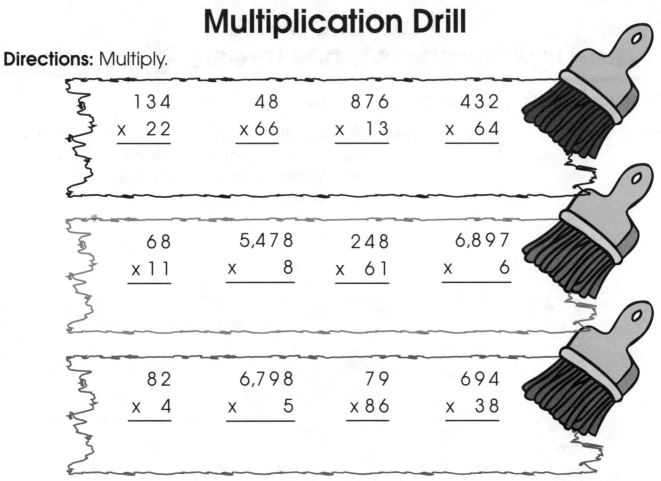

Directions: Color the picture by matching each number with its paintbrush.

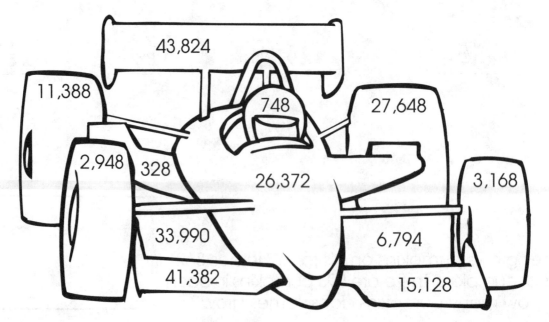

Name: _____

Division

Division is a way to find out how many times one number is contained in another number. For example, $28 \div 7 = 4$ means that there are 4 groups of 7 in 28.

Division problems can be written two ways: $36 \div 6 = 6$ or $6\overline{)36}$

These are the parts of a division problem: dividend ⟶ $36 \div 6 = 6$ ⟵ quotient
divisor

Directions: Divide.

divisor ⟶ $6\overline{)36}$ ⟵ dividend, quotient ⟵

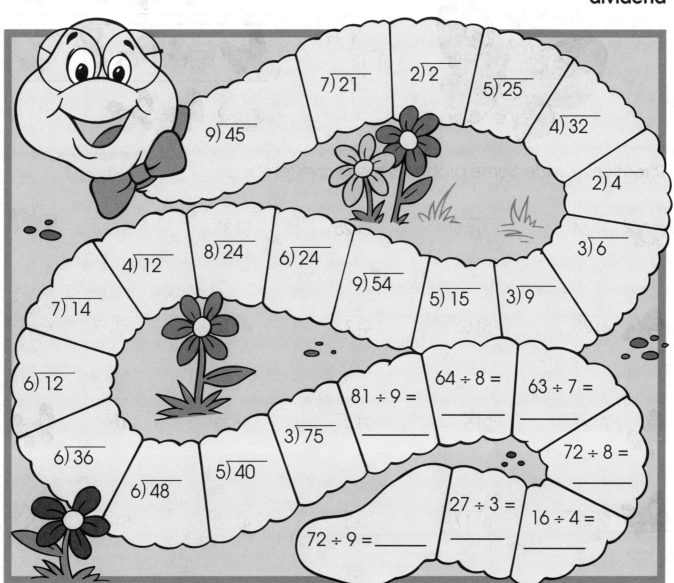

$7\overline{)21}$ $2\overline{)2}$ $5\overline{)25}$

$9\overline{)45}$ $4\overline{)32}$

$2\overline{)4}$

$8\overline{)24}$ $6\overline{)24}$ $3\overline{)6}$

$4\overline{)12}$ $9\overline{)54}$

$7\overline{)14}$ $5\overline{)15}$ $3\overline{)9}$

$6\overline{)12}$

$64 \div 8 =$ _____ $63 \div 7 =$ _____

$81 \div 9 =$ _____

$6\overline{)36}$ $3\overline{)75}$ $72 \div 8 =$ _____

$5\overline{)40}$

$6\overline{)48}$ $27 \div 3 =$ _____ $16 \div 4 =$ _____

$72 \div 9 =$ _____

Grade 4 - Comprehensive Curriculum

Name: _____

Division With Remainders

Sometimes groups of objects or numbers cannot be divided into equal groups. The **remainder** is the number left over in the quotient of a division problem. The remainder must be smaller than the divisor.

Example:

Divide 18 butterflies into groups of 5.
You have 3 equal groups,
with 3 butterflies left over.

$18 \div 5 = 3 \text{ R}3$

or

$$\begin{array}{r} 3 \text{ R}3 \\ 5\overline{)18} \\ -15 \\ \hline 3 \end{array}$$

Directions: Divide. Some problems may have remainders.

 $9\overline{)84}$ $7\overline{)65}$ $8\overline{)25}$ $5\overline{)35}$ $5\overline{)34}$

 $4\overline{)25}$ $6\overline{)56}$ $4\overline{)7}$ $4\overline{)16}$ $8\overline{)37}$

 $7\overline{)27}$ $2\overline{)5}$ $2\overline{)4}$ $8\overline{)73}$ $4\overline{)9}$

 $9\overline{)46}$ $5\overline{)17}$ $2\overline{)3}$ $4\overline{)13}$ $5\overline{)25}$

Name: _____

Division: Larger Numbers

Follow the steps for dividing larger numbers.

Example:

$3\overline{)66}$

Step 1: Divide the tens first.

$$\begin{array}{r} 2 \\ 3\overline{)6\,6} \\ -6 \\ \hline 0\,6 \end{array}$$

Step 2: Divide the ones next.

$$\begin{array}{r} 2\,2 \\ 3\overline{)6\,6} \\ -6 \\ \hline 0\,6 \\ -6 \\ \hline 0 \end{array}$$

Directions: Divide.

$4\overline{)8\,4}$ $2\overline{)9\,0}$ $2\overline{)6\,4}$ $2\overline{)5\,0}$ $3\overline{)4\,5}$

$3\overline{)7\,5}$ $3\overline{)3\,6}$ $4\overline{)9\,2}$ $2\overline{)7\,6}$ $5\overline{)6\,5}$

In some larger numbers, the divisor goes into the first two digits of the dividend.

Example:

$9\overline{)7\,2\,9}$

$$\begin{array}{r} 8 \\ 9\overline{)7\,2\,9} \\ -7\,2 \\ \hline 0\,9 \end{array}$$

$$\begin{array}{r} 8\,1 \\ 9\overline{)7\,2\,9} \\ -7\,2 \\ \hline 0\,9 \\ -9 \\ \hline 0 \end{array}$$

Directions: Divide.

$7\overline{)6\,3\,0}$ $5\overline{)1\,2\,5}$ $6\overline{)4\,8\,6}$ $5\overline{)1\,0\,0}$ $6\overline{)5\,4\,0}$

Grade 4 - Comprehensive Curriculum

Name: _____

Division

Directions: Divide.

7)860   6)611   8)279   4)338   6)979

3)792   5)463   6)940   4)647   3)814

7)758   5)356   4)276   8)328   9)306

4)579   8)932   3)102   2)821   6)489

The music store has 491 CD's. The store sells 8 CD's a day. How many days will it take to sell all of the CD's?

_____

Division: Checking the Answers

To check a division problem, multiply the quotient by the divisor. Add the remainder. The answer will be the dividend.

Example:

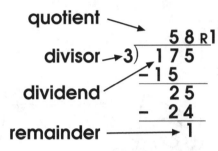

quotient ⟶ 58 R1
divisor ⟶ 3) 175
         − 15
dividend ⟶ 25
         − 24
remainder ⟶ 1

```
    58 ← quotient
  x  3 ← divisor
  ─────
   174
  +  1 ← remainder
  ─────
   175 ← dividend
```

Directions: Divide each problem, then draw a line from the division problem to the correct checking problem.

33	53	97	135	113	119
x 7	x 7	x 7	x 7	x 7	x 7
	+ 2	+ 3	+ 1	+ 1	+ 1

7)682   7)231   7)373   7)792   7)834   7)946

The toy factory puts 7 robot dogs in each box. The factory has 256 robot dogs. How many boxes will they need?

_____

Division: Checking the Answers

Directions: Divide, then check your answers.

Example:

```
    1 8 2 R1
4) 7 2 9
  - 4
    3 2
  - 3 2
      9
    - 8
      1
```

Check:

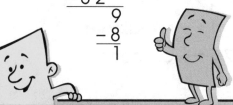

```
    1 8 2
  x     4
    7 2 8
  +     1
    7 2 9
```

Divide	Check	Divide	Check
35)468	☐ x 35	77)819	☐ x 77
29)568	☐ x 29	53)2,795	☐ x 53

The bookstore puts 53 books on a shelf. How many shelves will it need for 1,590 books? _____

Name: _____

Division: Two-Digit Divisors

Directions: Divide. Then check each answer on another sheet of paper by multiplying it by the divisor and adding the remainder.

Example:

```
        2
  12)256
   -24
     1
```

```
        21 R4
  12)256
   -24
     16
    -12
      4
```

Check:

```
      21
    x 12
      42
     210
     252
   +   4
     256
```

27)880   81)913   65)790   42)674   67)823

72)977   54)743   45)863   24)432   18)372

28)175   49)538   77)936   37)603   63)835

The Allen farm has 882 chickens. The chickens are kept in 21 coops. How many chickens are there in each coop? _____

Averaging

An **average** is found by adding two or more quantities and dividing by the number of quantities.

🔵 **Example:**
Step 1: Find the sum of the numbers.
$24 + 36 + 30 = 90$
Step 2: Divide by the number of quantities.
$90 \div 3 = 30$
The average is 30.

Directions: Find the average of each group of numbers. Draw a line from each problem to the correct average.

$12 + 14 + 29 + 1 =$	410
$4 + 10 + 25 =$	83
$33 + 17 + 14 + 20 + 16 =$	40
$782 + 276 + 172 =$	15
$81 + 82 + 91 + 78 =$	13
$21 + 34 + 44 =$	33
$14 + 24 + 10 + 31 + 5 + 6 =$	14
$278 + 246 =$	20
$48 + 32 + 18 + 62 =$	262

A baseball player had 3 hits in game one, 2 hits in game two and 4 hits in game three. How many hits did she average over the three games? _____

Name: _____

Averaging

Directions: Find the averages.

Ted went bowling. He had scores of 112, 124 and 100. What was his average?

_____

Sue ran 3 races. Her times were 9 seconds, 10 seconds and 8 seconds. What was her average?

_____

The baseball team played 6 games. They had 12 hits, 6 hits, 18 hits, 36 hits, 11 hits and 7 hits. What is the average number of hits in a game?

_____

In 3 games of football, Chris gained 156, 268 and 176 yards running. How many yards did he average in a game?

_____

Jane scored 18, 15, 26 and 21 points in 4 basketball games. How many points did she average?

_____

Review

Directions: Divide.

$3\overline{)268}$ $15\overline{)165}$ $27\overline{)489}$ $48\overline{)695}$

$79\overline{)937}$ $49\overline{)683}$ $91\overline{)848}$ $73\overline{)592}$ $59\overline{)473}$

$23\overline{)1,268}$ $67\overline{)2,543}$ $81\overline{)3,608}$ $37\overline{)8,432}$ $97\overline{)4,528}$

Directions: Find the averages.

22, 38 _____   105, 263, 331 _____

48, 100, 62 _____   248, 325, 250, 69 _____

17, 18, 36, 28, 6 _____   87, 91, 55, 48, 119 _____

Fractions

A **fraction** is a number that names part of a whole, such as $\frac{1}{2}$ or $\frac{1}{3}$.

A fraction is made up of two numbers—the **numerator** (top number) and the **denominator** (bottom number). The larger the denominator, the smaller each of the equal parts: $\frac{1}{16}$ is smaller than $\frac{1}{2}$.

Directions: Study the fractions below.

1 whole.

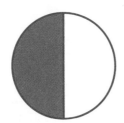

2 equal parts or halves

One-half of the circle is shaded. $\frac{1}{2}$

3 equal parts or thirds

One-third of the circle is shaded. $\frac{1}{3}$

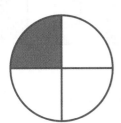

4 equal parts or fourths

One-fourth of the circle is shaded. $\frac{1}{4}$

5 equal parts or fifths

One-fifth of the circle is shaded. $\frac{1}{5}$

6 equal parts or sixths

One-sixth of the circle is shaded. $\frac{1}{6}$

8 equal parts or eighths

One-eighth of the circle is shaded. $\frac{1}{8}$

10 equal parts or tenths

One-tenth of the circle is shaded. $\frac{1}{10}$

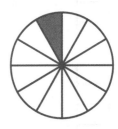

12 equal parts or twelfths

One-twelfth of the circle is shaded. $\frac{1}{12}$

Name: _____

Fractions

Directions: Name the fraction that is shaded.

Examples:

3 of 4 equal parts are shaded.

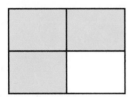

12 of 16 equal parts are shaded.

$$\frac{3}{4}$$

$$\frac{12}{16}$$

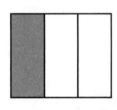

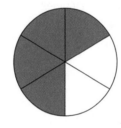

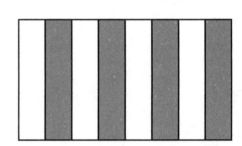

_____

_____

_____

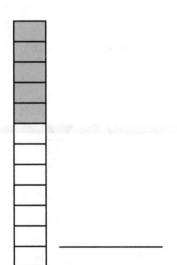

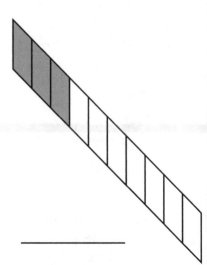

_____

_____

_____

Name: _____

Fraction Pieces

Directions: Cut apart the fraction pieces below. Use them to help you work with fractions. Store the fraction sets in separate plastic bags.

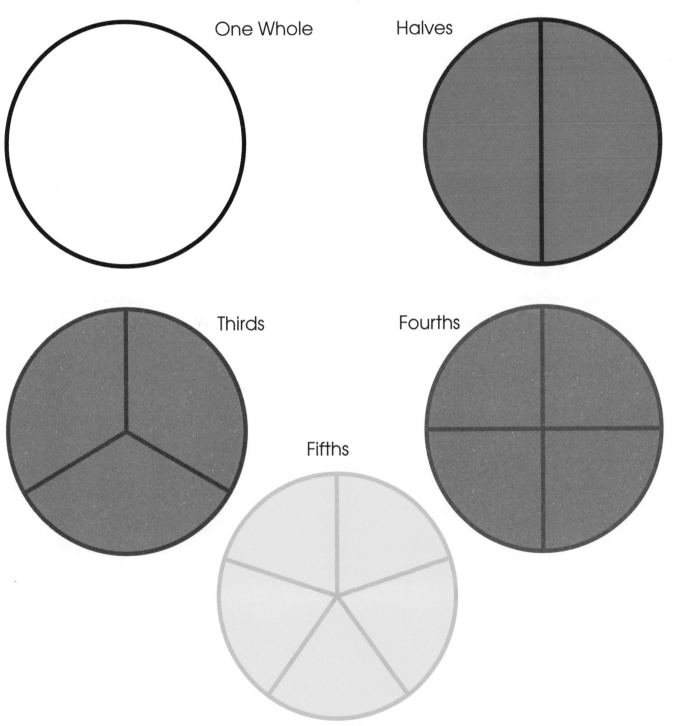

One Whole

Halves

Thirds

Fourths

Fifths

Page is blank for cutting exercise on previous page.

Name: _____

Fraction Pieces

Directions: Cut apart the fraction pieces below. Use them to help you work with fractions. Store the fraction sets in separate plastic bags.

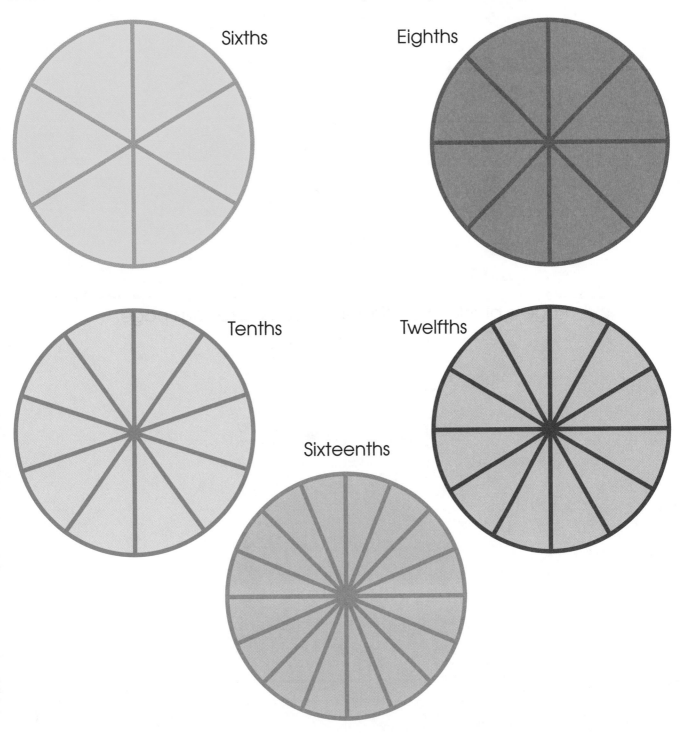

Sixths

Eighths

Tenths

Twelfths

Sixteenths

Page is blank for cutting exercise on previous page.

Name: _____

Fractions: Addition

When adding fractions with the same denominator, the denominator stays the same. Add only the numerators.

Example: numerator
denominator $\frac{1}{8} + \frac{2}{8} = \frac{3}{8}$

Directions: Add the fractions on the flowers. Begin in the center of each flower and add each petal. The first one is done for you.

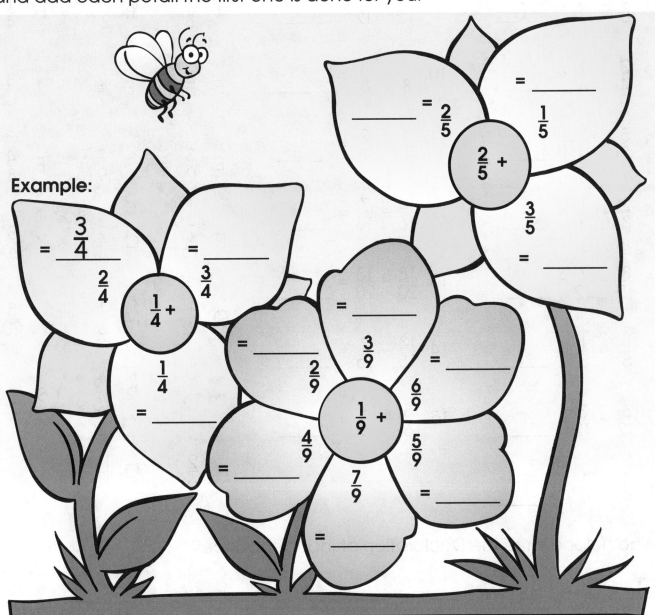

Grade 4 - Comprehensive Curriculum

Name: _____

Fractions: Subtraction

When subtracting fractions with the same denominator, the denominator stays the same. Subtract only the numerators.

Directions: Solve the problems, working from left to right. As you find each answer, copy the letter from the key into the numbered blanks. The answer is the name of a famous American. The first one is done for you.

1. $\frac{3}{8} - \frac{2}{8} = \underline{\frac{1}{8}}$

2. $\frac{2}{4} - \frac{1}{4} = \underline{\quad}$

3. $\frac{5}{9} - \frac{3}{9} = \underline{\quad}$

4. $\frac{2}{3} - \frac{1}{3} = \underline{\quad}$

5. $\frac{8}{12} - \frac{7}{12} = \underline{\quad}$

6. $\frac{4}{5} - \frac{1}{5} = \underline{\quad}$

7. $\frac{6}{12} - \frac{3}{12} = \underline{\quad}$

8. $\frac{4}{9} - \frac{1}{9} = \underline{\quad}$

9. $\frac{11}{12} - \frac{7}{12} = \underline{\quad}$

10. $\frac{7}{8} - \frac{3}{8} = \underline{\quad}$

11. $\frac{4}{7} - \frac{2}{7} = \underline{\quad}$

12. $\frac{14}{16} - \frac{7}{16} = \underline{\quad}$

13. $\frac{18}{20} - \frac{13}{20} = \underline{\quad}$

14. $\frac{13}{15} - \frac{2}{15} = \underline{\quad}$

15. $\frac{5}{6} - \frac{3}{6} = \underline{\quad}$

T $\frac{1}{8}$	P $\frac{5}{24}$	H $\frac{1}{4}$
F $\frac{4}{12}$	E $\frac{2}{7}$	J $\frac{3}{12}$
E $\frac{3}{9}$	O $\frac{2}{9}$	F $\frac{4}{8}$
R $\frac{7}{16}$	O $\frac{2}{8}$	Y $\frac{8}{20}$
Q $\frac{1}{32}$	M $\frac{1}{3}$	S $\frac{5}{20}$
A $\frac{1}{12}$	R $\frac{12}{15}$	S $\frac{3}{5}$
N $\frac{2}{6}$	O $\frac{11}{15}$	

Who helped write the Declaration of Independence?

$\underset{1}{\overset{T}{\underline{\quad}}}$ $\underset{2}{\underline{\quad}}$ $\underset{3}{\underline{\quad}}$ $\underset{4}{\underline{\quad}}$ $\underset{5}{\underline{\quad}}$ $\underset{6}{\underline{\quad}}$ $\underset{7}{\underline{\quad}}$ $\underset{8}{\underline{\quad}}$ $\underset{9}{\underline{\quad}}$ $\underset{10}{\underline{\quad}}$ $\underset{11}{\underline{\quad}}$ $\underset{12}{\underline{\quad}}$ $\underset{13}{\underline{\quad}}$ $\underset{14}{\underline{\quad}}$ $\underset{15}{\underline{\quad}}$

Equivalent Fractions

Equivalent fractions are two different fractions that represent the same number. **Example:**

 $\frac{1}{2} = \frac{3}{6}$

Directions: Complete these equivalent fractions. Use your fraction pieces from pages 393 and 395.

$\frac{1}{3} = \frac{}{6}$ $\frac{1}{2} = \frac{}{4}$ $\frac{3}{4} = \frac{}{8}$ $\frac{1}{3} = \frac{}{9}$

Directions: Circle the figures that show a fraction equivalent to figure a. Write the fraction for the shaded area under each figure.

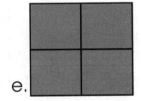
a. _____

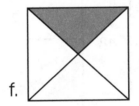
b. _____

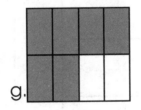
c. _____

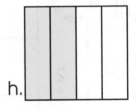
d. _____

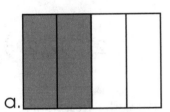
e. _____

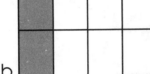
f. _____

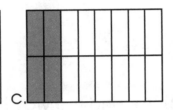
g. _____

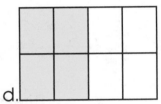
h. _____

To find an equivalent fraction, multiply both parts of the fraction by the same number.

Example: $\frac{2}{3} \times \frac{3}{3} = \frac{6}{9}$

Directions: Find an equivalent fraction.

$\frac{1}{4} = \frac{}{8}$ $\frac{3}{4} = \frac{}{16}$ $\frac{4}{5} = \frac{8}{}$ $\frac{3}{8} = \frac{}{24}$

Grade 4 - Comprehensive Curriculum

Reducing Fractions

Reducing a fraction means to find the greatest common factor and divide.

Example: $\frac{5}{15}$ factors of 5: 1, 5
factors of 15: 1, 3, 5, 15

5 is the greatest common factor. Divide both the numerator and denominator by 5.

$5 \div 5 = 1$
$15 \div 5 = 3$

$$\frac{5 \div 5}{15 \div 5} = \frac{1}{3}$$

Directions: Reduce each fraction. Circle the correct answer.

$\frac{2}{4} = \frac{1}{2}, \frac{1}{6}, \frac{1}{8}$ $\frac{3}{9} = \frac{1}{6}, \frac{1}{3}, \frac{3}{6}$ $\frac{5}{10} = \frac{1}{5}, \frac{1}{2}, \frac{5}{6}$ $\frac{4}{12} = \frac{1}{4}, \frac{1}{3}, \frac{2}{3}$ $\frac{10}{15} = \frac{2}{3}, \frac{2}{5}, \frac{2}{7}$

$\frac{12}{14} = \frac{1}{8}, \frac{6}{7}, \frac{3}{5}$ $\frac{3}{24} = \frac{2}{12}, \frac{3}{6}, \frac{1}{8}$ $\frac{1}{11} = \frac{1}{11}, \frac{2}{5}, \frac{3}{4}$ $\frac{11}{22} = \frac{1}{12}, \frac{1}{2}, \frac{2}{5}$

Directions: Find the way home. Color the boxes with fractions equivalent to $\frac{1}{8}$ and $\frac{1}{3}$.

$\frac{4}{9}$	$\frac{2}{6}$	$\frac{4}{5}$ / $\frac{5}{6}$ / $\frac{2}{16}$	$\frac{7}{32}$	$\frac{10}{33}$	$\frac{6}{48}$	$\frac{3}{24}$ / $\frac{2}{8}$	$\frac{5}{15}$	$\frac{3}{5}$	
$\frac{5}{12}$	$\frac{5}{8}$ / $\frac{4}{16}$	$\frac{9}{27}$	$\frac{6}{18}$		$\frac{1}{4}$	$\frac{2}{12}$	$\frac{8}{24}$	$\frac{1}{2}$ / $\frac{4}{32}$
$\frac{3}{7}$	$\frac{2}{21}$	$\frac{3}{5}$						

Fractions: Mixed Numbers

A **mixed number** is a number written as a whole number and a fraction, such as $6\frac{5}{8}$.

To change a fraction into a mixed number, divide the denominator (bottom number) into the numerator (top number). Write the remainder over the denominator.

Example:

$$\frac{14}{6} = 2\frac{2}{6} \qquad 6\overline{)\begin{array}{l} 2 \ \text{R}2 \\ 14 \\ \underline{12} \\ 2 \end{array}}$$

To change a mixed number into a fraction, multiply the denominator by the whole number, add the numerator and write it on top of the denominator.

Example:

$$3\frac{1}{7} = \frac{22}{7} \qquad (7 \times 3) + 1 = \frac{22}{7}$$

Directions: Write each fraction as a mixed number. Write each mixed number as a fraction.

$\frac{21}{6} =$ _____ $\frac{24}{5} =$ _____ $\frac{10}{3} =$ _____ $\frac{21}{4} =$ _____

$\frac{11}{6} =$ _____ $\frac{13}{4} =$ _____ $\frac{12}{5} =$ _____ $\frac{10}{9} =$ _____

$4\frac{3}{8} = \frac{\square}{8}$ $2\frac{1}{3} = \frac{\square}{3}$ $4\frac{3}{5} = \frac{\square}{5}$ $3\frac{4}{6} = \frac{\square}{6}$

$7\frac{1}{4} = \frac{\square}{4}$ $2\frac{3}{5} = \frac{\square}{5}$ $7\frac{1}{2} = \frac{\square}{2}$ $6\frac{5}{7} = \frac{\square}{7}$

$\frac{11}{8} =$ _____ $\frac{21}{4} =$ _____ $\frac{33}{5} =$ _____ $\frac{13}{6} =$ _____

$\frac{23}{7} =$ _____ $8\frac{1}{3} =$ _____ $9\frac{3}{7} =$ _____ $\frac{32}{24} =$ _____

Fractions: Adding Mixed Numbers

When adding mixed numbers, add the fractions first, then the whole numbers.

Examples:

$$9\frac{1}{3}$$
$$+3\frac{1}{3}$$
$$\overline{12\frac{2}{3}}$$

$$2\frac{3}{6}$$
$$+1\frac{1}{6}$$
$$\overline{3\frac{4}{6}}$$

Directions: Add the number in the center to the number in each surrounding section.

Name: _____

Fractions: Subtracting Mixed Numbers

When subtracting mixed numbers, subtract the fractions first, then the whole numbers.

Directions: Subtract the mixed numbers. The first one is done for you.

$$7\frac{3}{8} - 4\frac{2}{8} = 3\frac{1}{8}$$

$$4\frac{5}{6} - 3\frac{1}{6}$$

$$4\frac{1}{2} - 3$$

$$7\frac{5}{8} - 6\frac{3}{8}$$

$$6\frac{6}{8} - 1\frac{1}{8}$$

$$5\frac{3}{4} - 1\frac{1}{4}$$

$$5\frac{2}{3} - 3\frac{1}{3}$$

$$4\frac{8}{10} - 3\frac{3}{10}$$

$$9\frac{8}{9} - 4\frac{3}{9}$$

$$7\frac{2}{3} - 6\frac{1}{3}$$

$$7\frac{2}{3} - 5$$

$$9\frac{8}{10} - 6\frac{3}{10}$$

$$4\frac{7}{9} - 2$$

$$6\frac{7}{8} - 5\frac{3}{8}$$

$$6\frac{3}{4} - 3\frac{1}{4}$$

$$5\frac{6}{7} - 3\frac{1}{7}$$

$$7\frac{6}{7} - 2\frac{4}{7}$$

Sally needs $1\frac{3}{8}$ yards of cloth to make a dress. She has $4\frac{5}{8}$ yards. How much cloth will be left over? _____

Grade 4 - Comprehensive Curriculum

Review

Directions: Add or subtract the fractions and mixed numbers. Reduce, if possible.

$$4\tfrac{7}{8}$$
$$-2\tfrac{5}{8}$$

$$8\tfrac{3}{9}$$
$$+2\tfrac{5}{9}$$

$$3\tfrac{1}{8}$$
$$+1\tfrac{3}{8}$$

$$4\tfrac{5}{6}$$
$$-3\tfrac{1}{6}$$

$$7\tfrac{5}{11}$$
$$+3\tfrac{3}{11}$$

$\dfrac{4}{12} + \dfrac{3}{12} =$ _____

$\dfrac{3}{5} + \dfrac{1}{5} =$ _____

$\dfrac{3}{8} - \dfrac{1}{8} =$ _____

$\dfrac{3}{9} + \dfrac{1}{9} =$ _____

$\dfrac{3}{4} - \dfrac{2}{4} =$ _____

Directions:
Reduce the fractions.

$\dfrac{4}{6} =$ _____

$\dfrac{7}{21} =$ _____

$\dfrac{9}{12} =$ _____

$\dfrac{2}{4} =$ _____

$\dfrac{6}{24} =$ _____

$\dfrac{8}{32} =$ _____

Directions: Change the mixed numbers to fractions and the fractions to mixed numbers.

$3\tfrac{1}{3} = \dfrac{\boxed{}}{3}$

$\dfrac{14}{4} =$ _____

$\dfrac{26}{6} =$ _____

$3\tfrac{7}{12} = \dfrac{\boxed{}}{12}$

$\dfrac{22}{7} =$ _____

Fractions to Decimals

When a figure is divided into 10 equal parts, the parts are called tenths. Tenths can be written two ways—as a fraction or a decimal. A **decimal** is a number with one or more places to the right of a decimal point, such as 6.5 or 2.25. A **decimal point** is the dot between the ones place and the tenths place.

Examples:

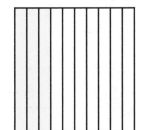

ones	tenths
0 .	3

$\frac{3}{10}$ or 0.3 of the square is shaded.

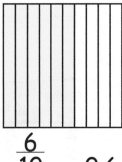

Directions: Write the decimal and fraction for the shaded parts of the following figures. The first one is done for you.

$\frac{6}{10}$ 0.6

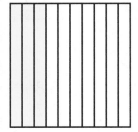
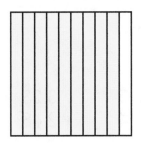
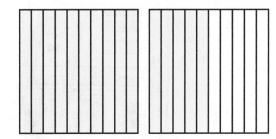

_____   _____   _____   _____

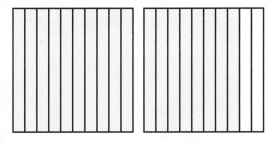
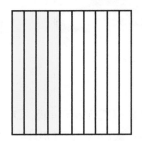
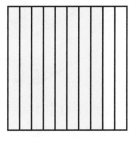

_____   _____   _____   _____

Decimals

Directions: Add or subtract. Remember to include the decimal point in your answers.

Example:

$1\frac{3}{10} = 1.3$

$1\frac{6}{10} = 1.6$

$$\begin{array}{r} 1.3 \\ + 1.6 \\ \hline 2.9 \end{array}$$

8.1 + 1.7	4.1 + 6.2	0.5 + 1.6	7.6 − 6.5	7.2 − 2.6	1.2 + 5.0	8.7 − 3.9	6.8 − 3.7

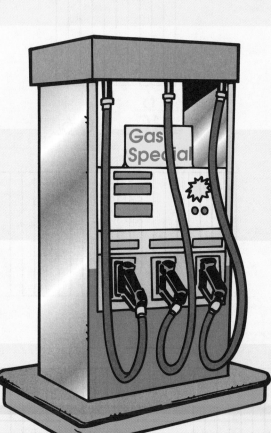

7.8 − 6.8	16.5 − 7.3	6.4 + 5.3	10.0 + 3.5
0.42 + 0.35	0.98 − 0.87	0.78 − 0.13	0.83 + 0.12
0.95 − 0.14	3.23 + 2.48	4.68 − 2.65	5.86 − 2.73
6.98 + 1.40	3.27 + 1.82	4.65 − 1.32	5.97 + 2.77

Mr. Martin went on a car trip with his family. Mr. Martin purchased gas 3 times. He bought 6.7 gallons, 7.3 gallons, then 5.8 gallons of gas. How much gas did he purchase in all? _____

Decimals: Hundredths

The next smallest decimal unit after a tenth is called a hundredth. One hundredth is one unit of a figure divided into 100 units. Written as a decimal, it is one digit to the right of the tenths place.

Example:

One square divided into hundredths, 34 hundredths are shaded. Write: 0.34.

ones	tenths	hundredths
0 .	3	4

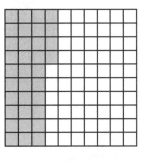

0.34

Directions: Write the decimal for the shaded parts of the following figures.

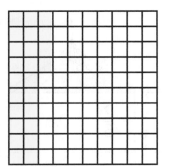 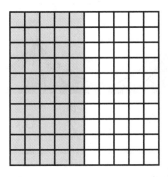 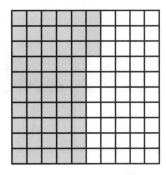 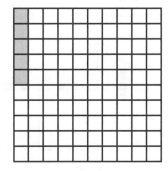

_____   _____   _____   _____

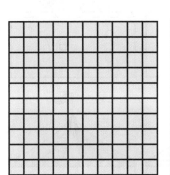    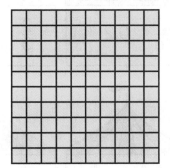 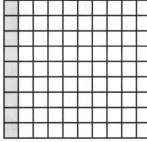

_____   _____

Name: _____

Fractions and Decimals

Directions: Compare the fraction to the decimal in each box. Circle the larger number.

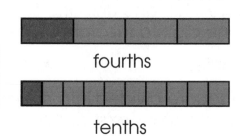

fourths

tenths

Example:

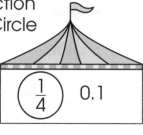

$\left(\dfrac{1}{4}\right)$ 0.1

$\dfrac{2}{4}$ 0.2

$\dfrac{3}{4}$ 0.3

$\dfrac{1}{2}$ 0.6

$\dfrac{1}{4}$ 0.4

$\dfrac{1}{3}$ 0.1

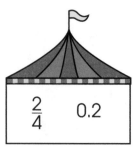 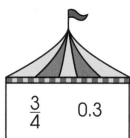  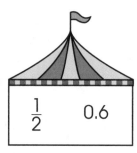 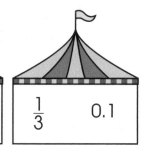

$\dfrac{1}{4}$ 0.7

$\dfrac{2}{4}$ 0.8

$\dfrac{3}{4}$ 0.9

$\dfrac{5}{6}$ 0.5

$\dfrac{2}{5}$ 0.6

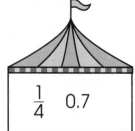 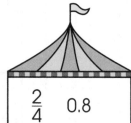 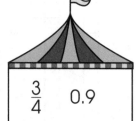 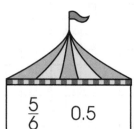 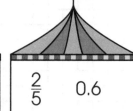

$\dfrac{3}{12}$ 0.9

$\dfrac{1}{6}$ 0.2

$\dfrac{2}{3}$ 0.8

$\dfrac{1}{5}$ 0.3

$\dfrac{2}{5}$ 0.7

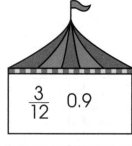 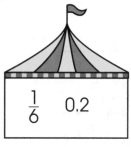 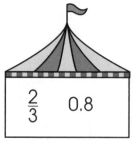 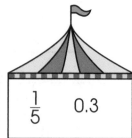 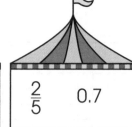

$\dfrac{3}{10}$ 0.5

$\dfrac{1}{9}$ 0.4

$\dfrac{4}{5}$ 0.7

$\dfrac{1}{3}$ 0.7

$\dfrac{6}{12}$ 0.1

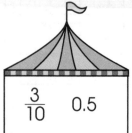  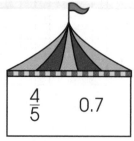  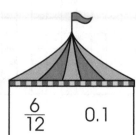

Name: _____

Adding and Subtracting Decimals

Directions: Add or subtract the problems. Then fill in the circle next to the correct answer.

Example:

$$2.4 + 1.7$$
○ 2.5
○ 3.1
● 4.1

$$2.8 + 3.4$$
○ 5.2
○ 7.4
○ 6.2

$$5.7 - 3.8$$
○ 1.9
○ 2.5
○ 2.9

$$7.6 + 8.9$$
○ 15.9
○ 16.5
○ 17.3

$$16.3 + 9.8$$
○ 25.11
○ 26.1
○ 26.01

$$28.6 + 43.9$$
○ 73.6
○ 72.5
○ 71.9

$$43.9 + 56.5$$
○ 100.4
○ 107.4
○ 101.4

$$12.87 - 3.45$$
○ 16.32
○ 10.31
○ 9.42

$$47.56 - 33.95$$
○ 13.61
○ 80.41
○ 14.61

$$93.6 - 79.8$$
○ 14.8
○ 15.3
○ 13.8

$$11.57 + 10.64$$
○ 22.21
○ 1.93
○ 21.12

$$27.83 - 14.94$$
○ 14.09
○ 12.89
○ 11.97

$$106.935 - 95.824$$
○ 111.1
○ 111.11
○ 11.111

Math Rules

The high-speed train traveled 87.90 miles on day one, 127.86 miles on day two and 113.41 miles on day three. How many miles did it travel in all? _____

Grade 4 - Comprehensive Curriculum

Measurement: Inches

An **inch** is a unit of length in the standard system equal to $\frac{1}{12}$ of a foot. A ruler is used to measure inches.

This illustration shows a ruler measuring a 4-inch pencil, which can be written as 4" or 4 in.

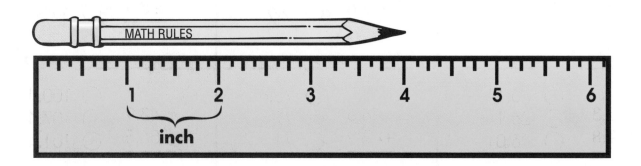

Directions: Use a ruler to measure each object to the nearest inch.

1. The length of your foot   _____

2. The width of your hand   _____

3. The length of this page   _____

4. The width of this page   _____

5. The length of a large paper clip _____

6. The length of your toothbrush   _____

7. The length of a comb   _____

8. The height of a juice glass   _____

9. The length of your shoe   _____

10. The length of a fork   _____

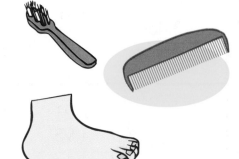

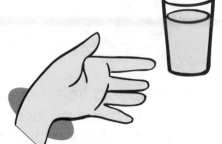

Measurement: Inches

Directions: Use a ruler to measure the width of each foot to the nearest inch.

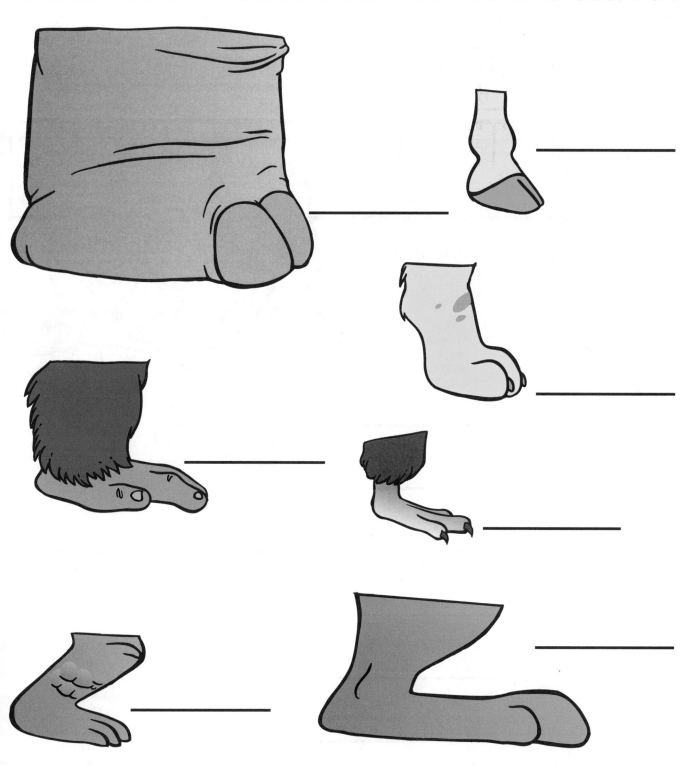

Measurement: Fractions of an Inch

An inch is divided into smaller units, or fractions of an inch.

Example: This stick of gum is $2\frac{3}{4}$ inches long.

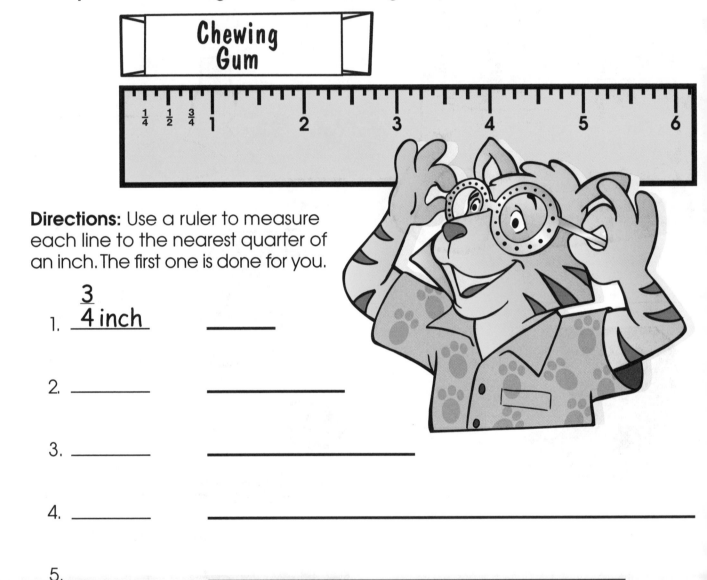

Directions: Use a ruler to measure each line to the nearest quarter of an inch. The first one is done for you.

1. $\frac{3}{4}$ inch _____

2. _____ _____

3. _____ _____

4. _____ _____

5. _____ _____

6. _____ _____

7. _____ _____

Name: _____

Measurement: Fractions of an Inch

Directions: Use a ruler to measure to the nearest quarter of an inch.

How far did the grasshopper jump?

_____ + _____ + _____ + _____ = _____

What is the total length of the paintbrushes?

_____ + _____ + _____ + _____ + _____ = _____

Grade 4 - Comprehensive Curriculum

Measurement: Foot, Yard, Mile

Directions: Choose the measure of distance you would use for each object.

1 foot = 12 inches
1 yard = 3 feet
1 mile = 1,760 yards or 5,280 feet

inches _____

_____

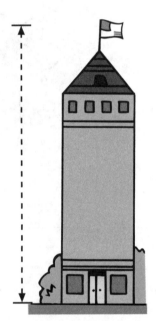

_____

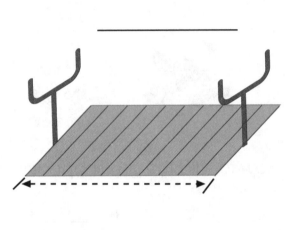

_____

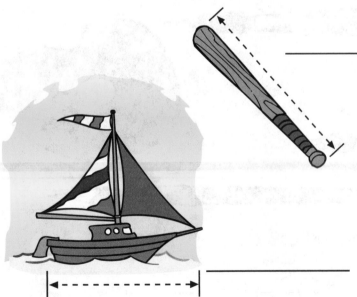

_____

_____

Metric Measurement:
Centimeter, Meter, Kilometer

In the metric system, there are three units of linear measurement: centimeter (cm), meter (m) and kilometer (km).

Centimeters (cm) are used to measure the lengths of small to medium-sized objects. **Meters (m)** measure the lengths of longer objects, such as the width of a swimming pool or height of a tree (100 cm = 1 meter). **Kilometers (km)** measure long distances, such as the distance from Cleveland to Cincinnati or the width of the Atlantic Ocean (1,000 m = 1 km).

Directions: Write whether you would use cm, m or km to measure each object.

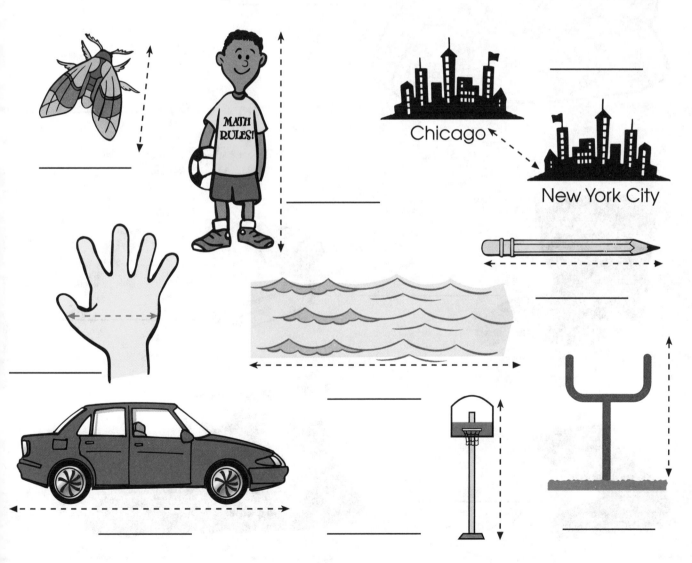

Chicago

New York City

Grade 4 - Comprehensive Curriculum

Name: _____

Metric Measurement: Centimeter

Directions: Use a centimeter ruler to measure the width of each foot to the nearest centimeter.

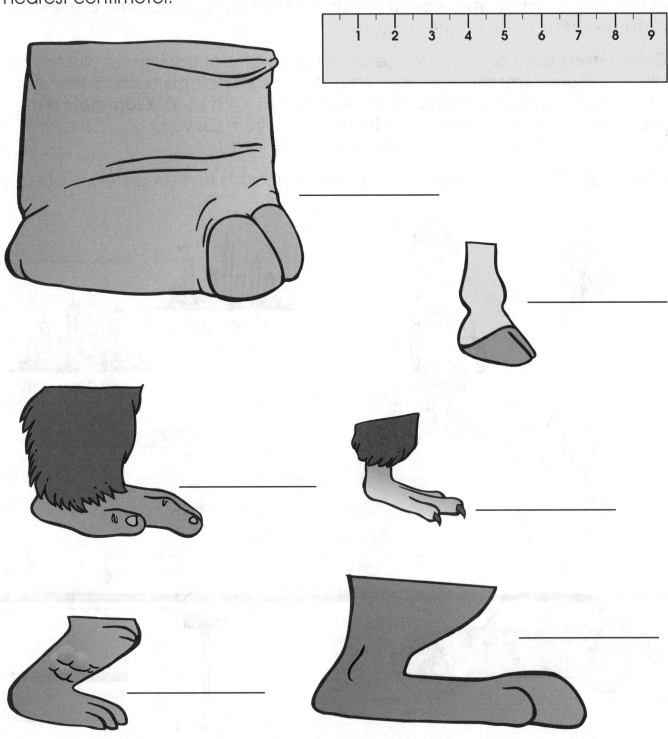

Metric Measurement: Meter and Kilometer

A meter is a little longer than a yard—39.37 inches (a yard is 36 inches).
A kilometer is equal to about $\frac{5}{8}$ of a mile.

Directions: Choose the measure of distance you would use for the following.

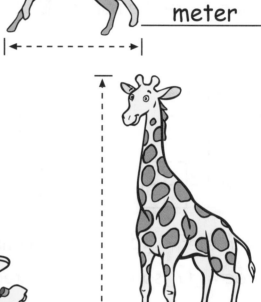

_____ meter _____

_____

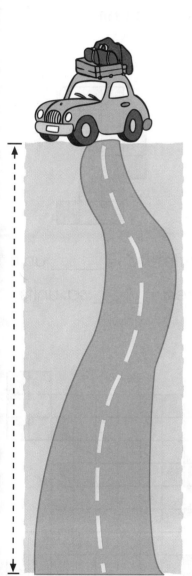

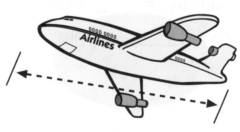

_____

_____

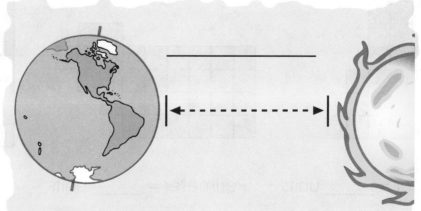

_____

_____

Name: _____

Measurement: Perimeter and Area

Perimeter is the distance around a figure. It is found by adding the lengths of the sides. **Area** is the number of square units needed to cover a region. The area is found by adding the number of square units. A unit can be any unit of measure. Most often, inches, feet or yards are used.

Directions: Find the perimeter and area for each figure. The first one is done for you.

☐ = 1 square unit

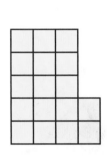

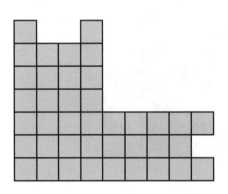

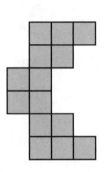

Perimeter = __18__ units

Area = __17__ sq. units

Perimeter = _____ units

Area = _____ sq. units

Perimeter = _____ units

Area = _____ sq. units

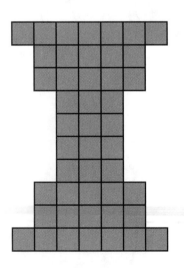

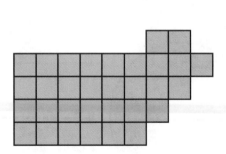

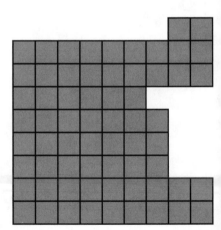

Perimeter = _____ units

Area = _____ sq. units

Perimeter = _____ units

Area = _____ sq. units

Perimeter = _____ units

Area = _____ sq. units

Name: _____

Measurement: Perimeter

Perimeter is calculated by adding the lengths of the sides of a figure.

Examples:

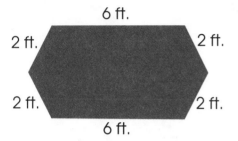

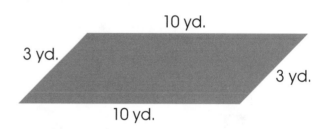

2 + 2 + 2 + 2 + 6 + 6 = 20
The perimeter of this
hexagon is 20 ft.

10 + 10 + 3 + 3 = 26
The perimeter of this
parallelogram is 26 yd.

Directions: Find the perimeter of the following figures.

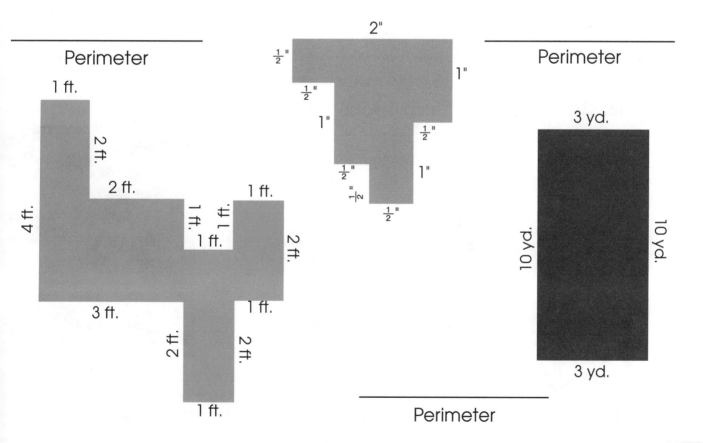

_____
Perimeter

Perimeter

_____
Perimeter

Measurement: Perimeter and Area

Area is also calculated by multiplying the length times the width of a square or rectangular figure. Use the formula: A = l x w.

Directions: Calculate the perimeter of each figure.

2 ft.
2 ft.
2 ft.
2 ft.
2 ft.
2 ft.

_____

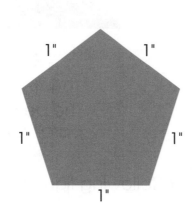

1"
1"
1"
1"
1"

_____

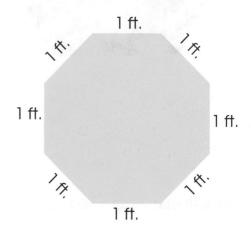

1 ft.
1 ft.
1 ft.
1 ft.
1 ft.
1 ft.
1 ft.
1 ft.

_____

Directions: Calculate the area of each figure.

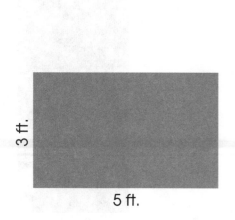

3 ft.
5 ft.

_____

4 yd.
1 yd.

_____

24 ft.
20 ft.

_____

Name: _____

Measurement: Volume

Volume is the number of cubic units that fit inside a figure.

Directions: Find the volume of each figure. The first one is done for you.

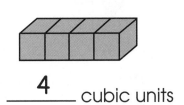

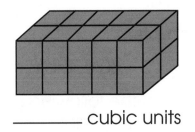

__4__ cubic units

_____ cubic units

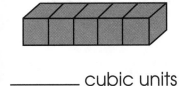

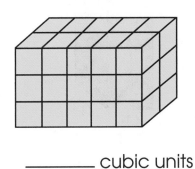

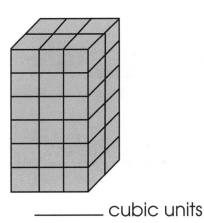

_____ cubic units

_____ cubic units

_____ cubic units

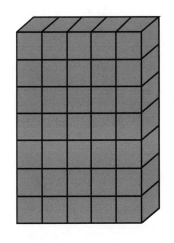

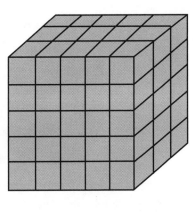

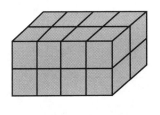

_____ cubic units

_____ cubic units

_____ cubic units

Grade 4 - Comprehensive Curriculum

Measurement: Volume

The volume of a figure can also be calculated by multiplying the length times the width times the height.
Use the formula: V= l x w x h.

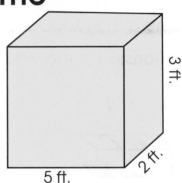

Example:

3 x 5 x 2 = 30 cubic feet

Directions: Find the volume of the following figures. Label your answers in cubic feet, inches or yards. The first one is done for you.

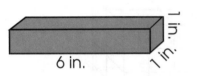

6 cubic inches

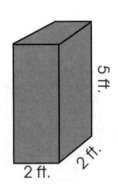

_____

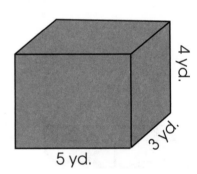

_____

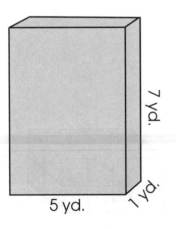

_____

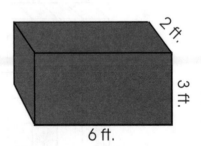

_____

Metric Measurement: Perimeter

Directions: Calculate the perimeter of each figure.

Example:

$4 + 5 + 4 + 1 + 2 + 3 + 2 = 21$ meters

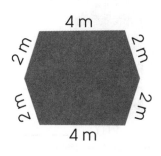
5 m
4 m
4 m
1 m
2 m
2 m
3 m

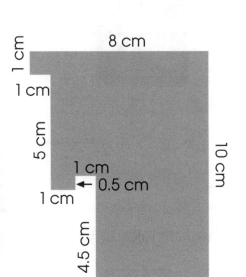
1 cm
1 cm
8 cm
5 cm
1 cm
1 cm
0.5 cm
4.5 cm
10 cm
5 cm

_____

4 m
2 m
2 m
2 m
2 m
4 m

_____

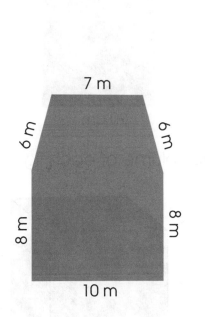
7 m
6 m
6 m
8 m
8 m
10 m

_____

6.5 cm
6.5 cm
5.5 cm
5.5 cm
2.5 cm

_____

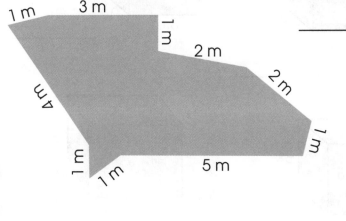
1 m
3 m
1 m
2 m
2 m
4 m
1 m
1 m
1 m
5 m

_____

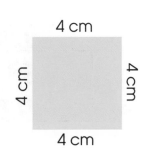
4 cm
4 cm
4 cm
4 cm

_____

Name: _____

Metric Measurement: Area and Volume

Directions: Calculate the area of each figure. Use the formula: A = l x w.

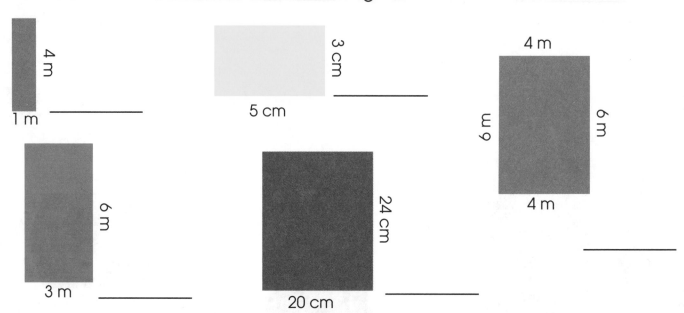

Directions: Calculate the volume of each figure. Use the formula: V = l x w x h.

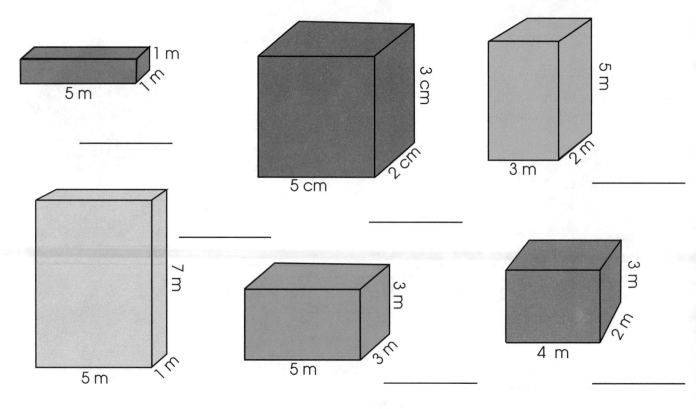

Measurement: Ounce, Pound, Ton

The **ounce**, **pound** and **ton** are units in the standard system for measuring weight.

Directions: Choose the measure of weight you would use for each object.

16 ounces = 1 pound
2,000 pounds = 1 ton

ounce   **pound**   **ton**

Example:  ___ounces___

 _____

 _____

 _____

 _____

 _____

 _____

 _____

Metric Measurement: Gram and Kilogram

Grams and **kilograms** are measurements of weight in the metric system. A gram (g) weighs about $\frac{1}{28}$ of an ounce. A grape or paper clip weighs about one gram. There are 1,000 grams in a kilogram. A kilogram (kg) weighs about 2.2 pounds. A brick weighs about 1 kilogram.

Directions: Choose grams or kilograms to measure the following.

Example: grams

_____

_____

_____

_____

_____

_____

_____

_____

_____

_____

Measurement: Liquid

The **cup**, **pint**, **quart** and **gallon** are units in the standard system for measuring liquids.

Directions: Gather the following materials: 2 dish tubs, one filled with water, sand or rice; measuring cups; pint container; quart container; gallon container. Then answer the questions and complete the chart.

1. Use the cup measure to pour water, sand or rice into the pint container. How many cups did it take?

   _____ cups = 1 pint

2. Use the cup measure to find out how many cups are in a quart and a gallon.

   _____ cups = 1 quart

   _____ cups = 1 gallon

3. Use the pint container to pour water, sand or rice into the quart container. How many pints are in a quart?

   _____ pints = 1 quart

4. How many pints does it take to fill a gallon?

   _____ pints = 1 gallon

5. Use the quart measure to find out how many quarts are in a gallon.

   _____ quarts = 1 gallon

Measurement Chart

_____ cups = 1 pint   _____ pints = 1 quart

_____ cups = 1 quart   _____ pints = 1 gallon

_____ cups = 1 gallon   _____ quarts = 1 gallon

Measurement: Cup, Pint, Quart, Gallon

Directions: Circle the number of objects to the right that equal the objects on the left. The first one is done for you.

2 cups = 1 pint
2 pints = 1 quart
4 quarts = 1 gallon

= 1 cup   = 1 pint   = 1 quart   = 1 gallon

Metric Measurement: Milliliter and Liter

Liters and **milliliters** are measurements of liquid in the metric system. A milliliter (mL) equals 0.001 liter or 0.03 fluid ounces. A drop of water equals about 1 milliliter. Liters (L) measure large amounts of liquid. There are 1,000 milliliters in a liter. One liter measures 1.06 quarts. Soft drinks are often sold in 2-liter bottles.

Directions: Choose milliliters or liters to measure these liquids.

Example: <u>milliliters</u>

_____

_____

_____

_____

_____

_____

Metric Measurement: Weight and Liquid

Directions: Choose grams (g) or kilograms (kg) to weigh the following objects. The first one is done for you.

rhinoceros ___**kg**___   person _____

dime _____   airplane _____

bucket of wet sand _____   spider _____

eyeglasses _____   pair of scissors _____

toy train engine _____   horse _____

Directions: Choose milliliters (mL) or liters (L) to measure the liquids in the following containers. The first one is done for you.

swimming pool ___**L**___   baby bottle _____

small juice glass _____   teapot _____

gasoline tank _____   outdoor fountain _____

test tube _____   ink pen _____

washing machine _____   Lake Erie _____

Temperature: Fahrenheit

28°F

Fahrenheit is used to measure temperature in the standard system. °**F** stands for degrees Fahrenheit.

72°F

Directions: Use the thermometer to answer these questions.

At what temperature does water boil?

_____

At what temperature does water freeze?

_____

What is normal body temperature?

_____

Is a 100°F day warm, hot or cold?

_____

Is a 0°F day warm, hot or cold?

_____

Which temperature best describes room temperature?
58°F   70°F   80°F

_____

Which temperature best describes a cold winter day?
22°F   38°F   32°F

_____

water
boils
210° F ➔

body
temperature
98.6° F ➔

water
freezes
32° F ➔

°F

220
210
200
190
180
170
160
150
140
130
120
110
100
90
80
70
60
50
40
30
20
10
0
-10
-20

Temperature: Celsius

Celsius is used to measure temperature in the metric system. °**C** stands for degrees Celsius.

0°C

30°C

Directions: Use the thermometer to answer these questions.

At what temperature does water boil? _____

At what temperature does water freeze? _____

What is normal body temperature? _____

Is it a hot or cold day when the temperature is 30°C? _____

Is it a hot or cold day when the temperature is 5°C? _____

Which temperature best describes a hot summer day?
5°C 40°C 20°C _____

Which temperature best describes an icy winter day?
0°C 15°C 10°C _____

°C

water boils 100°C → 100

90

80

70

60

body temperature 37°C → 50

40

30

20

water freezes 0°C → 10

0

Review

Directions: Find the perimeter and area of each figure.

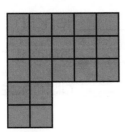

$\square$ = 1 square unit

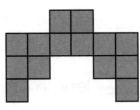

Perimeter = _____ units

Area = _____ sq. units

Perimeter = _____ units

Area = _____ sq. units

Directions: How much does it equal?

= _____ pints

= _____ quarts

Directions: Write whether you would use ounce, pound or ton to weigh the following.

_____

_____

_____

Directions: Write whether you would use an inch, foot, yard or mile to measure the following.

_____

_____

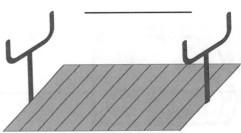

_____

Name: _____

Review

Directions: Choose centimeters, meters or kilometers to measure the following.

_____ height of a tree

_____ distance around Earth

_____ length of your yard

_____ length of a shoe

_____ height of a building

_____ distance a plane flies

Directions: Choose grams or kilograms to measure the following.

 _____

 _____

 _____

 _____

Directions: Choose liters or milliliters to measure the following.

 _____

 _____

 _____

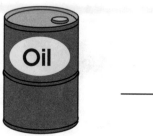 _____

Graphing

A **graph** is a drawing that shows information about changes in numbers.

Directions: Answer the questions by reading the graphs.

Bar Graph

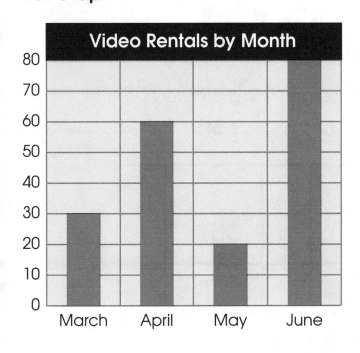

How many videos did the store rent in June?

_____

In which month did the store rent the fewest videos?

_____

How many videos did the store rent for all 4 months?

_____

Line Graph

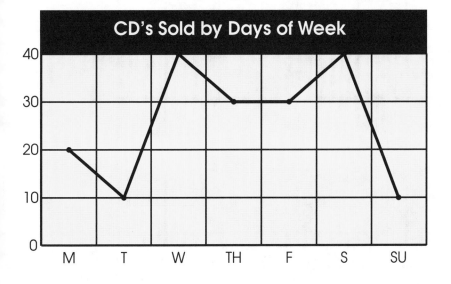

On which days did the store sell the fewest CD's?

_____

How many CD's did the store sell in 1 week?

_____

Name: _____

Ordered Pairs

An **ordered pair** is a pair of numbers used to locate a point.

Example: (8, 3)

Step 1: Count across to line 8 on the graph.
Step 2: Count up to line 3 on the graph.
Step 3: Draw a dot to mark the spot.

Directions: Map the following spots on the grid using ordered pairs.

(4, 7)   (9, 10)   (2, 1)   (5, 6)   (2, 2)   (1, 5)   (7, 4)   (3, 8)

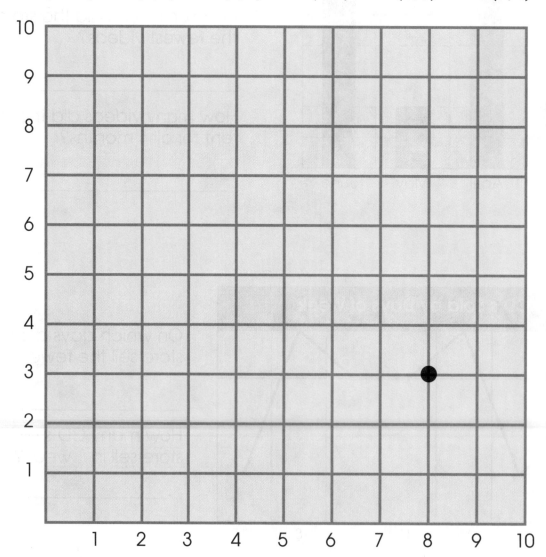

Graphing: Finding Ordered Pairs

Graphs or grids are sometimes used to find the location of objects.

Example: The ice-cream cone is located at point (5, 6) on the graph. To find the ice cream's location, follow the line to the bottom of the grid to get the first number — 5. Then go back to the ice cream and follow the grid line to the left for the second number — 6.

Directions: Write the ordered pair for the following objects. The first one is done for you.

book __(4, 8)__   bike _____   suitcase _____   house _____

globe _____   cup _____   triangle _____   airplane _____

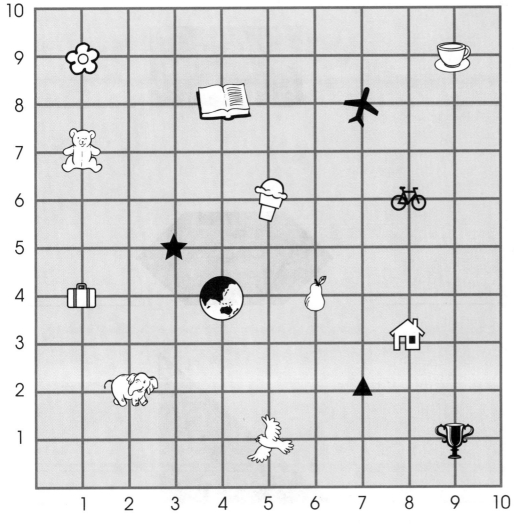

Directions: Identify the objects located at the following points. The first one is done for you.

(9, 1) __trophy__

(3, 5) _____

(2, 2) _____

(6, 4) _____

(1, 9) _____

(5, 1) _____

(1, 7) _____

Geometry: Polygons

A **polygon** is a closed figure with three or more sides.

Examples:

triangle
3 sides

square
4 equal
sides

rectangle
4 sides

pentagon
5 sides

hexagon
6 sides

octagon
8 sides

Directions: Identify the polygons.

   _____

   _____

   _____

   _____

   _____

   _____

Geometry: Line, Ray, Segment

A **line segment** has two end points.

Write: $\overline{AB}$

A **line** has no end points and goes on in both directions.

Write: $\overleftrightarrow{CD}$

A **ray** is part of a line and goes on in one direction. It has one end point.

Write: $\overrightarrow{EF}$

Directions: Identify each of the following as a line, line segment or ray.

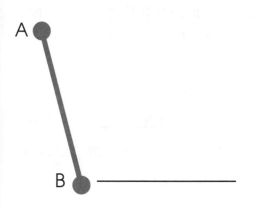
_____

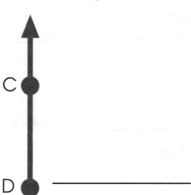
_____

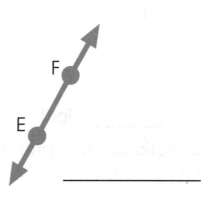
_____

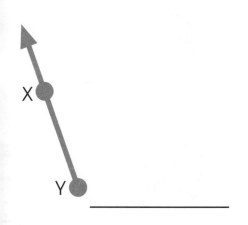
_____

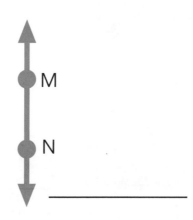
_____

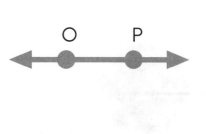
_____

Name: _____

Geometry: Angles

The point at which two line segments meet is called an **angle**. There are three types of angles — right, acute and obtuse.

A **right angle** is formed when the two lines meet at 90°.

An **acute angle** is formed when the two lines meet at less than 90°.

An **obtuse angle** is formed when the two lines meet at greater than 90°.

Angles can be measured with a protractor or index card. With a protractor, align the bottom edge of the angle with the bottom of the protractor, with the angle point at the circle of the protractor. Note the direction of the other ray and the number of degrees of the angle.

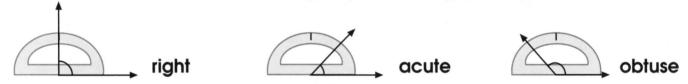

right   acute   obtuse

Place the corner of an index card in the corner of the angle. If the edges line up with the card, it is a right angle. If not, the angle is acute or obtuse.

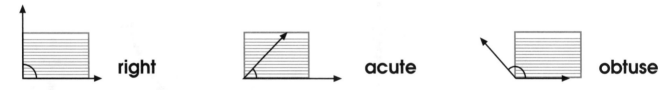

right   acute   obtuse

Directions: Use a protractor or index card to identify the following angles as right, obtuse or acute.

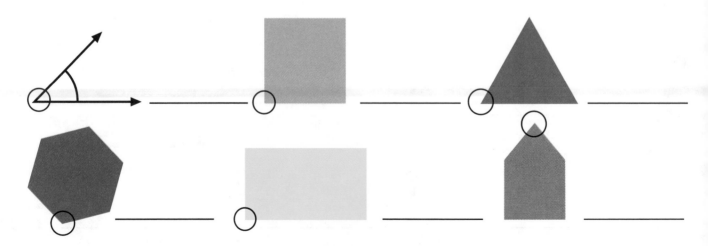

Geometry: Circles

A **circle** is a round figure. It is named by its center. A **radius** is a line segment from the center of a circle to any point on the circle. A **diameter** is a line segment with both end points on the circle. The diameter always passes through the center of the circle.

Directions: Name the radius, diameter and circle.

Example:

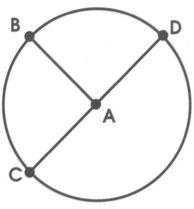

Circle ___A___

Radius ___AB___

Diameter ___DC___

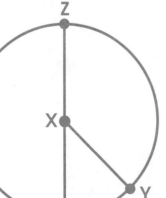

Circle _____

Radius _____

Diameter _____

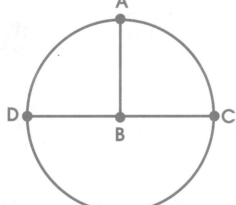

Circle _____

Radius _____

Diameter _____

Review

Directions: Complete the line graph using the information in the box.

Team	Games Played
Red	10
Blue	20
Green	15
Yellow	25

Directions: Draw a line from the figure to its name.

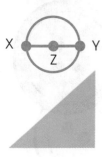

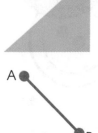

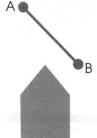

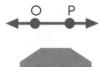

line

square

segment

diameter

octagon

triangle

pentagon

Number Patterns

Figuring out the secret to a number pattern or code can send you into "thinking overtime."

Directions: Discover the pattern for each set of numbers. Then write the missing numbers.

a) 20, 21, 19, 20, 18, 19, 17, _____ , 16, 17, 15, _____ , _____ , _____ , _____ , _____ .

b) 1, 6, 16, 31, 51, _____ , _____ , 141, _____ , 226.

c) 3, 5, 9, 15, _____ , _____ , 45, _____ , 75.

d) 55, 52, 50, 49, 46, _____ , _____ , _____ , _____ , _____ , 34.

e) 1, 3, 6, 10, 15, 21, _____ , _____ , _____ , 55, 66, 78.

f) 10, 16, 13, 19, 16, _____ , 19, _____ , _____ , 28, _____ .

g) 3, 4, 7, 12, _____ , _____ , 39, _____ , 67, _____ .

h) 100, 90, 95, 85, 90, 80, 85, _____ , _____ , _____ , 75.

Directions: Make up a number pattern of your own. Have a parent, brother or sister figure it out!

_____ , _____ , _____ , _____ , _____ , _____ , _____ , _____ , _____ , _____ .

Directions: Follow the instructions to solve the number puzzler.

Use only these numbers: 2, 4, 5, 7, 8, 11, 13, 14, 16.

Each number may only be used once.

Write even numbers in the squares.

Write odd numbers in the circles.

Each row must add up to 26.

Hint: Work the puzzle in pencil, so you can erase and retry numbers if needed.

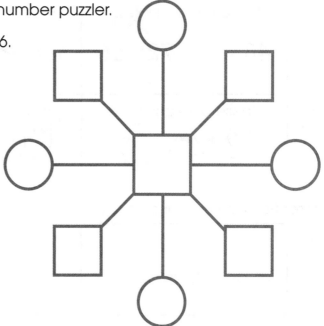

Finding Common Attributes

The things that items have in common are called **common attributes**.

Example:

These are Pee-Wees.	These are not Pee-Wees.	Circle the Pee-Wees.
A E I O U	B C M W Z	S (O) T (U) R (E)

When you look at the Pee-Wees, you see what they have in common. They are all vowels. That is their common attribute. The items in the middle box are not Pee-Wees because they are all consonants. In the last box, only the vowels are circled.

Directions: Find the common attributes of the Wobbles, Whimzees, Dwibbles and Zanies. Circle the correct answers.

1.

These are Wobbles.	These are not Wobbles.	Circle the Wobbles.

2.

These are Whimzees.	These are not Whimzees.	Circle the Whimzees.

3.

These are Dwibbles.	These are not Dwibbles.	Circle the Dwibbles.
48 32 72 56	28 54 36 12	16 18 4 24 40

4.

These are Zanies.	These are not Zanies.	Circle the Zanies.

Directions: Write your own attribute puzzle in the boxes.

Probability

One thinking skill to get your brain in gear is figuring probability. **Probability** is the likelihood or chance that something will happen. Probability is expressed and written as a ratio.

The probability of tossing heads or tails on a coin is one in two (1:2).

The probability of rolling any number on a die is one in six (1:6).

The probability of getting a red on this spinner is two in four (2:4).

The probability of drawing an ace from a deck of cards is four in fifty-two (4:52).

Directions: Write the probability ratios to answer these questions.

1. There are 26 letters in the alphabet. What is the probability of drawing any letter from a set of alphabet cards? _____

2. Five of the 26 alphabet letters are vowels. What is the probability of drawing a vowel from the alphabet cards? _____

3. Matt takes 10 shots at the basketball hoop. Six of his shots are baskets. What is the probability of Matt's next shot being a basket? _____

4. A box contains 10 marbles: 2 white, 3 green, 1 red, 2 orange and 2 blue. What is the probability of pulling a green marble from the box? _____

   A red marble? _____

5. What is the probability of pulling a marble that is not blue? _____

Name: _____

Probability

Directions: Write the probability ratios to answer these questions.

1. Using the spinner shown, what is the probability of spinning a 4? _____

2. Using the spinner show, what is the chance of not spinning a 2? _____

3. Using the spinner shown, what is the probability of spinning a 6, 7 or 3? _____

4. What is the probability of getting heads or tails when you toss a coin? _____

Directions: Toss a coin 20 times and record the outcome of each toss. Then answer the questions.   _____ Heads _____ Tails

5. What was the ratio of heads to tails in the 20 tosses? _____

6. Was the outcome of getting heads or tails in the 20 tosses the same as the probability ratio? _____

7. Why or why not? _____

The probability ratio of getting any number on a cube of dice is 1:6.

Directions: Toss a die 36 times and record how many times it lands on each number. Then answer the questions.

_____ one   _____ two   _____ three   _____ four   _____ five   _____ six

8. What was the ratio for each number on the die?

_____ one   _____ two   _____ three   _____ four   _____ five   _____ six

9. Did any of the numbers have a ratio close to the actual probability ratio? _____

10. What do the outcomes of flipping a coin and tossing a die tell you about the probability of an event happening?

_____

Computing

Many people use computers on a daily basis at home, work or school. Computers help us to complete many tasks quickly and efficiently.

The Chinese used a computing device more than 4,000 years ago. It was called an abacus. An **abacus** is a wooden frame with four rows of beads representing ones, tens, hundreds and thousands.

The beads on the bottom half of the abacus are worth one unit. The beads on the top half of the unit are worth five units.

The bottom beads are pushed up to the middle bar of the abacus. The top beads are pushed down to the middle bar of the abacus.

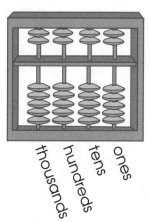

thousands hundreds tens ones

Directions: Determine the number shown on each abacus and write it on the blank. The first one has been done for you.

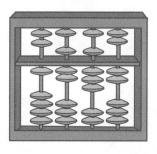

1. __6,047__

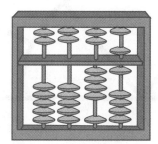

2. _____

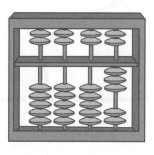

3. _____

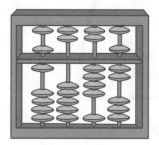

4. _____

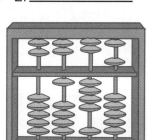

5. _____

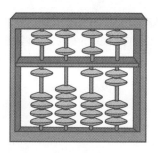

6. _____

Problem Solving: A Garden Puzzle

Grace is planting a garden. The garden will be a semi-circle in shape and have two rows. The first row will have three sections and the back row will have six sections. Grace needs to decide how many plants she can put in each section of her garden.

She wants the total number of plants in the back row to be double the total number of plants in front.

Directions: Help Grace finish her garden plan by using the numbers 1, 2, 3, 4, 5, 6, 7, 8 and 9. Each number may only be used once. Three numbers have been written in place for you.

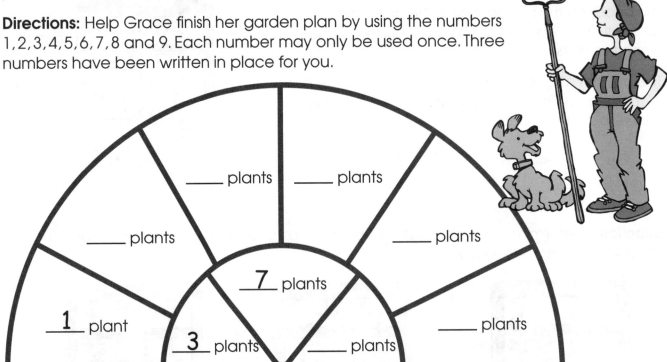

Directions: Arrange the digits 1 through 9 in the circles on the triangle so the numbers on each of the sides add up to 17.

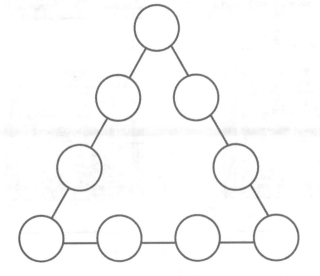

Name: _____

Problem Solving: Sorting Information

When you have two sets of items, they can be grouped in pairs (with one item from each set) in many ways.

Example:

While shopping, Sally bought three pairs of shorts and three blouses. How many different outfits can she make from these items?

To solve, you could draw a picture or make a list:

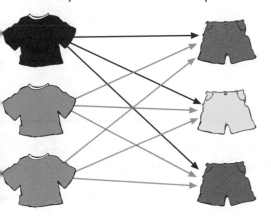

Black shirt — Blue shorts
Black shirt — Yellow shorts
Black shirt — Purple shorts
Red shirt — Blue shorts
Red shirt — Yellow shorts
Red shirt — Purple shorts
Green shirt — Blue shorts
Green shirt — Yellow shorts
Green shirt — Purple shorts

There are nine possible combinations.
3 (shirts) x 3 (shorts) = 9 (outfits)

Directions: Either draw a picture or make a list to solve the problem. Then write the answer.

Sally's mom gave her $37.00 for shopping and lunch. She gave Sally 11 bills—some are ones, some are fives and some are tens.

How many ones, fives and tens does Sally have?

_____ ones _____ fives _____ tens

Problem Solving: Sorting Information

Directions: Solve these problems the same way you did on the last page. Then write the answers.

1. Jodie stopped at the Food Court for lunch. She can have a hamburger or hot dog to eat and a soda, milk or lemonade to drink. Make a list or draw a picture to show all possible combinations.

How many lunch possibilities does she have? _____

2. Jodie saw Maria and Dawn sitting on a bench in the Food Court. Jodie can't decide where to sit. Make a list or draw a picture to show all possible combinations of the three girls on the bench.

How many different ways can the three girls sit on the bench? _____

3. After shopping, Jodie can participate in any two of these activities: swimming, crafts, soccer and tennis. Make a list or draw a picture to show all possible combinations of activities Jodie could select.

How many different choices does Jodie have? _____

Abacus: A frame with sliding beads for doing math.

Acute Angle: An angle formed when two lines meet at less than 90°.

Addition: "Putting together" or adding two or more numbers to find the sum.

Adjective: A word that describes a noun. Examples: fuzzy sweater, green car, nice boy.

Adverb: A word that tells when, where or how. Example: The train will leave early.

Analogy: A way of comparing things to show how they are similar. Example: Nose is to smell as tongue is to taste.

Angle: The point at which two line segments meet.

Antonym: A word that means the opposite of another word. Example: in and out.

Area: The number of square units needed to cover a region.

Autobiography: A book someone writes about his/her own life.

Average: The result of adding two or more quantities and dividing by the number of quantities.

Biography: A book written about the life of someone by another person.

Call Number: The number assigned to all nonfiction books in a library.

Celsius: A metric system measurement of temperature. °C stands for degrees Celsius.

Centimeter: A metric system measurement of length. There are 2.54 centimeters in an inch.

Cinquain: A form of poetry with five lines consisting of one noun, two adjectives, three verbs, a four-word phrase and a noun, respectively.

Circle: A round figure in which each point on the outside of the figure is equidistant from the center of the figure.

Classifying: Placing similar things into categories.

Command: A sentence that orders someone to do something. It ends with a period or exclamation mark.

Compound Predicate: A predicate with two parts joined by the word "and" or another conjunction.

Compound Subject: A subject with two parts joined by the word "and" or another conjunction.

Comprehension: Understanding what is seen, heard or read.

Conjunction: A word that joins sentences or combines ideas. "And," "but," "or," "because," "when," "after" and "so" are conjunctions.

Context: The other words in the sentence or sentences before or after a word.

Context Clues: A way to figure out the meaning of a word by relating it to other words in the sentence.

Contraction: Two words joined together as one. An apostrophe shows where some letters have been left out. Example: cannot—can't.

Cup: A unit of volume in the standard system equal to 8 ounces.

Decimal: A number with one or more places to the right of a decimal point, such as 6.5 or 2.25.

Decimal Point: The dot between the ones place and the tenths place in a decimal

Denominator: The number below the fraction bar in a fraction.

Details: The who, what, when, where, why and how of what is read.

Dewey Decimal System: A system used to file books in libraries by assigning call numbers to them and dividing them into ten main groups.

Diameter: A line segment that passes through the center of a circle and has both end points on the circle.

Difference: The answer in a subtraction problem.

Digits: The symbols used to write numbers: 0, 1, 2, 3, 4, 5, 6, 7, 8, 9.

Dividend: The larger number being divided by the smaller number, or divisor, in a division problem. Example: $28 \div 7 = 4$; 28 is the dividend.

Division: A way to find how many times a number is contained in another number Example: $28 \div 7 = 4$ means that there are 4 groups of 7 in 28.

Encyclopedia: A set of books or CD's that gives information about different subjects in alphabetical order.

Equivalent Fractions: Two different fractions that represent the same number, such as $\frac{1}{2}$ and $\frac{2}{4}$.

Estimate: To give an approximate, rather than an exact, answer.

Exclamation: A sentence that shows strong feeling. It ends with an exclamation mark (!).

Fact: A statement that can be proven true.

Factors: The numbers multiplied together in a multiplication problem.

Fahrenheit: A standard system measurement of temperature. °F stands for degree Fahrenheit.

Fiction: A book that contains made-up stories.

Following Directions: Doing what the directions say to do.

Foot (ft.): A unit of measure in the standard system equal to 12 inches.

Fraction: A number that names part of a whole, such as $\frac{1}{2}$ or $\frac{2}{3}$.

Future-Tense Verb: A verb form that tells what is going to happen. Examples: I will be happy. She will run fast.

Gallon: A unit of liquid measure in the standard system equal to 4 quarts.

Gram (g): A metric measurement of weight. One gram equals 0.001 kilogram, or $\frac{1}{28}$ of an ounce.

Graph: A drawing that shows information about changes in numbers.

Haiku: A form of Japanese poetry with three lines of five, seven and five syllables, respectively.

Hexagon: A polygon with six sides.

Homophones: Two words that sound the same, but have different meanings and are usually spelled differently. Example: write and right.

Inch (in.): A unit of length in the standard system equal to $\frac{1}{12}$ of a foot.

Index: The section in the back of a nonfiction book or a separate volume of an encyclopedia that indicates the page number and/or volume number where information on a specific topic is located.

Kilogram (kg): A metric system measurement of weight. One kilogram equals 1,000 grams or 2.2 pounds.

Kilometer (km): A metric system measurement of length. One kilometer equals 1,000 meters or 0.62 miles.

Library Catalog: An alphabetical listing of books and other items in a library which lists items by author, title and subject and also shows their call numbers. A library catalog may be on index cards or on a computer.

Limerick: A short, silly poem with five lines, in which lines one, two and five rhyme, and lines three and four rhyme.

Line: A line with no end points that goes on in both directions.

Line Segment: A line with two end points.

Liter (L): A metric system measurement of liquid. One liter equals 1,000 milliliters or 1.06 quarts.

Main Idea: The most important idea, or main points, of a sentence, paragraph or story.

Meter (m): A metric system measurement of length. One meter equals 39.37 inches

Mile (mi.): A unit of length in the standard system equal to 1,760 yards or 5,280 feet.

Milliliter (mL): A metric system measurement of liquid. One milliliter equals 0.001 liter or 0.03 fluid ounce.

Mixed Number: A number written as a whole number and a fraction, such as $6\frac{5}{8}$.

Multiple: The product of a specific number and any other number.
Example: The multiples of 2 are 2 (2 x 1), 4 (2 x 2), 6, 8, 10, 12, and so on.

Multiplication: A short way to find the sum of adding the same number a certain amount of times, such as 7 x 4 = 28 instead of 7 + 7 + 7 + 7 = 28.

Nonfiction: A book that contains facts and information.

Noun: A word that names a person, place or thing. Examples: boy, town, radish.

Numerator: The number above the fraction bar in a fraction.

Obtuse Angle: An angle formed when two lines meet at greater than 90°.

Octagon: A polygon with eight sides.

Opinion: A statement that tells how someone feels or what he/she thinks about something or someone.

Ordered Pair: A pair of numbers used to locate a point.

Ounce (oz.): A unit of measure in the standard system for weight. One ounce equals $\frac{1}{16}$ of a pound.

Outline: A written plan that helps organize the writer's thoughts in preparation for writing a report.

Palindrome: A word or sentence that is spelled the same forward and backward. Examples: noon, dad, pop, radar.

Paragraph: A group of sentences that share the same idea.

Past-Tense Verb: A verb form that tells what has already happened.
Example: I was happy.

Pentagon: A polygon with five sides.

Perimeter: The distance around a figure, found by adding the length of the sides.

Pint (pt.): A unit of liquid measure in the standard system equal to 2 cups.

Place Value: The value of a digit or numeral shown by where it is in a number.

Plural: A word that refers to more than one thing.

Polygon: A closed figure with three or more sides.

Pound (lb.): A unit of measure in the standard system for weight. One pound equals 16 ounces.

Predicate: The part of the sentence that tells what the subject does, did, is doing or will do. Example: I am happy.

Prefix: A syllable at the beginning of a word that changes its meaning.

Present-Tense Verb: A verb form that tells what is happening now.

Probability: The likelihood that something will happen, usually expressed as a ratio. Examples: 1:2, 6:48.

Product: The answer in a multiplication problem.

Pronoun: A word that takes the place of a noun. Examples: I, me, my, he, she, it, we, us, their, them.

Pronoun Referent: The noun or nouns that a pronoun refers to.

Proofreading: Searching for and correcting errors by carefully reading and rereading what has been written.

Proper Noun: Name of specific persons, places or things. Examples: Abe Lincoln, Empire State Building, Magna Carta.

Quart (qt.): A unit of liquid measure in the standard system equal to 4 cups or 2 pints.

Question: A sentence that asks something. It ends with a question mark (?).

Quotient: The answer in a division problem.

Radius: A line segment from the center of a circle to any point on the circle. It is equal to half the length of the diameter.

Ray: A part of a line that goes on in one direction. It has one end point.

Recognizing Details: Being able to pick out and remember who, what, when, where, why and how of what is read.

Rectangle: A figure with four 90° angles and four sides. The sides opposite one another are the same length.

Reduce: To divide by the greatest common factor in a fraction.

Regroup: To use 10 ones to form one 10, 10 tens to form one hundred, one 10 and 5 ones to form 15, and so on.

Remainder: The number left over in the quotient of a division problem.

Request: A sentence that asks someone to do something. It ends with a period or question mark.

Right Angle: An angle formed when two lines meet at 90°.

Rounding: Expressing a number to the nearest ten, hundred, thousand, and so on. Examples: Round 18 to 20; round 11 to 10.

Run-On Sentence: A run-on sentence occurs when two or more sentences are joined together without punctuation.

Sentence: A group of words that expresses a complete thought. It must have at least one subject and one verb.

Sequencing: Putting things or events in order.

Singular: A word that refers to only one thing.

Skip Counting: A quick way to count by skipping numbers.

Square: A figure with four 90° angles and four sides of equal length.

Statement: A sentence that tells something. It ends with a period (.).

Subject: The part of the sentence that tells who or what the sentence is about.

Subtraction: "Taking away" or subtracting one number from another.

Suffix: A syllable at the end of a word that changes its meaning.

Sum: The answer in an addition problem.

Summarizing: Writing a short report that gives the main points of a story or article.

Syllable: Part of a word. Each syllable has one vowel sound.

Synonym: A word that means the same, or nearly the same, as another word. Example: brave and courageous.

Taking Notes: Writing important information from a story, book, article or lecture that can be used later in writing a report or taking a test.

Tanka: A Japanese poem written in response to a haiku. It has five lines of five, seven, five, seven and seven syllables, respectively.

Temperature: A unit of measurement that shows how hot or cold something is.

Ton: A unit of measure in the standard system for weight. One ton is 2,000 pounds.

Triangle: A closed figure with three angles and three sides.

Verb: A word that tells what something does or that something exists. Example: Pete ran down the street.

Venn Diagram: A diagram used to chart information that shows similarities and differences between two things.

Volume: The number of cubic units that fit inside a figure.

Yard (yd.): A unit of distance in the standard system. There are 3 feet in a yard.

Page 6

Spelling: Short Vowels

Vowels are the letters **a, e, i, o, u** and sometimes **y**. There are five short vowels: **ă** as in **a**pple, **ĕ** as in **e**gg and br**ea**th, **ĭ** as in s**i**ck, **ŏ** as in t**o**p and **ŭ** as in **u**p.

Directions: Complete the exercises using words from the box.

blend	insist	health	pump	crop
fact	pinch	pond	hatch	plug

1. Write each word under its vowel sound.

ă	ĕ	ĭ	ŏ	ŭ
fact	blend	insist	pond	pump
hatch	health	pinch	crop	plug

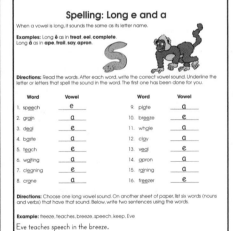

↑UP

2. Complete these sentences, using a word with the vowel sound given. Use each word from the box only once.

Here's an interesting (ă) __fact__ about your (ĕ) __health__.

Henry was very pleased with his corn (ŏ) __crop__.

The boys enjoyed fishing in the (ŏ) __pond__.

They (ĭ) __insist__ on watching the egg (ă) __hatch__.

(ĕ) __Blend__ in a (ĭ) __pinch__ of salt.

The farmer had to (ŭ) __pump__ water from the lake for his cows to drink.

Did you put the (ŭ) __plug__ in the bathtub this time?

Page 7

Spelling: Short Vowels

Directions: Read the words. After each, write the correct vowel sound. Underline the letter or letters that spell the sound in the word. The first one has been done for you.

	Word	Vowel			Word	Vowel
1.	str<u>u</u>ck	u		9.	br<u>ea</u>th	e
2.	scr<u>a</u>mble	a		10.	<u>e</u>dge	e
3.	str<u>o</u>ng	o		11.	k<u>i</u>ck	i
4.	ch<u>i</u>ll	i		12.	st<u>o</u>p	o
5.	th<u>u</u>d	u		13.	qu<u>i</u>z	i
6.	dr<u>ea</u>d	e		14.	br<u>u</u>sh	u
7.	pl<u>u</u>nge	u		15.	cr<u>a</u>sh	a
8.	m<u>a</u>sk	a		16.	d<u>o</u>dge	o

Directions: List four words (nouns and verbs) with short vowel sounds. Then write two sentences using the words.

Example: Ann, can, hand, Pam
Ann can give Pam a hand.

__Answers will vary.__

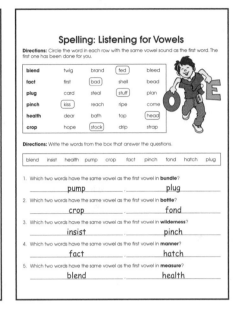

1. __Sentences will vary.__

2. _____

Page 8

Spelling: Listening for Vowels

Directions: Circle the word in each row with the same vowel sound as the first word. The first one has been done for you.

blend	twig	brand	(fed)	bleed
fact	first	(bad)	shell	bead
plug	card	steal	(stuff)	plan
pinch	(kiss)	reach	ripe	come
health	dear	bath	top	(head)
crop	hope	(stock)	drip	strap

Directions: Write the words from the box that answer the questions.

blend	insist	health	pump	crop	fact	pinch	fond	hatch	plug

1. Which two words have the same vowel as the first vowel in **bundle**?
__pump__ , __plug__

2. Which two words have the same vowel as the first vowel in **bottle**?
__crop__ , __fond__

3. Which two words have the same vowel as the first vowel in **wilderness**?
__insist__ , __pinch__

4. Which two words have the same vowel as the first vowel in **manner**?
__fact__ , __hatch__

5. Which two words have the same vowel as the first vowel in **measure**?
__blend__ , __health__

Page 9

Spelling: Long e and a

Long **ē** can be spelled **ea** as in **real** or **ee** as in **deer**. Long **ā** can be spelled **a** as in **apron**, **ai** as in **pail**, **ay** as in **pay** or **a-e** as in **lake**.

stream s-t-r-e-a-m stream

Directions: Complete the exercises with words from the box.

deal	clay	grade	weave	stream
pain	tape	sneeze	claim	treat

1. Write each word in the row with the matching vowel sound.

ā __pain__ __clay__ __tape__ __grade__ __claim__
ē __deal__ __sneeze__ __weave__ __stream__ __treat__

2. Complete each sentence, using a word with the vowel sound given. Use each word from the word box only once.

Everyone in (ā) __grade__ four ate an ice-cream (ē) __treat__.

Every time I (ē) __sneeze__, I feel (ā) __pain__ in my chest.

When I (ē) __weave__ with yarn, I put a piece of (ā) __tape__ on the loose ends so they won't come undone.

You (ā) __claim__ you got a good (ē) __deal__ on your new bike, but I still think you paid too much.

We camped beside a (ē) __stream__.

We forgot to wrap up our (ā) __clay__ and it dried out.

Page 10

Spelling: Long e and a

When a vowel is long, it sounds the same as its letter name.

Examples: Long **ē** as in **treat, eel, complete**.
Long **ā** as in **ape, trail, say, apron**.

Directions: Read the words. After each word, write the correct vowel sound. Underline the letter or letters that spell the sound in the word. The first one has been done for you.

	Word	Vowel			Word	Vowel
1.	sp<u>ee</u>ch	e		9.	pl<u>a</u>te	a
2.	gr<u>ai</u>n	a		10.	br<u>ee</u>ze	e
3.	d<u>ea</u>l	e		11.	wh<u>a</u>le	a
4.	b<u>a</u>ste	a		12.	cl<u>a</u>y	a
5.	t<u>ea</u>ch	e		13.	v<u>ea</u>l	e
6.	w<u>ai</u>ting	a		14.	<u>a</u>pron	a
7.	cl<u>ea</u>ning	e		15.	r<u>ai</u>ning	a
8.	cr<u>a</u>ne	a		16.	fr<u>ee</u>zer	e

Directions: Choose one long vowel sound. On another sheet of paper, list six words (nouns and verbs) that have that sound. Below, write two sentences using the words.

Example: freeze, teaches, breeze, speech, keep, Eve

Eve teaches speech in the breeze.

__Sentences will vary.__

Page 11

Spelling: Vowel Sounds

Directions: Follow the instructions below.

1. Circle the word in each row with the same vowel sound as the first word. The first one has been done for you.

deal	pail	church	(greet)	stove
pain	free	(frame)	twice	whole
weave	grape	stripe	(least)	thrill
grade	teach	(case)	joke	leave
treat	(greed)	throw	tent	truck

2. Write a word from the box that rhymes with each word below.

deal	clay	grade	weave	stream	pain	tape	sneeze	claim	treat

lame __claim__ shape __tape__
may __clay__ feel __deal__
cream __stream__ leave __weave__
laid __grade__ drain __pain__
feet __treat__ trees __sneeze__

3. The words below are written the way they are pronounced. Write the word from the box that sounds like:

klā __clay__ klām __claim__
wēv __weave__ trēt __treat__
dēl __deal__ grād __grade__
strēm __stream__ pān __pain__
tāp __tape__ snēz __sneeze__

Page 12

Spelling: Making New Words

Directions: Unscramble these letters to spell the **ā** and **ē** words you have been practicing. If you need help with spelling, look at the box on page 9. The first one has been done for you.

ay + lc = __clay__		ee + zsne = __sneeze__
ea + mtrs = __stream__		a-e + pt = __tape__
ea + vew = __weave__		a-e + drg = __grade__
ea + rtt = __treat__		ai + np = __pain__
ea + ld = __lead__		ai + mlc = __claim__

Directions: Circle the spelling mistakes and write the words correctly. The first one has been done for you.

1. We made statues out of (clay)   __clay__
2. Do you ever fish in that (streem)?   __stream__
3. Jason (sneesed) really loudly in class.   __sneezed__
4. Running gives me a (pane) in my side.   __pain__
5. We are (tapeing) the show for you.   __taping__
6. She (klaims) she won, but I came in first.   __claims__
7. Would you share your (treet) with me?   __treat__
8. He is (gradeing) our papers right now.   __grading__
9. She is (weeving) a placemat of ribbons.   __weaving__
10. What is the big (deel) anyway?   __deal__

Page 13

Spelling: Long i and o

Long **ī** can be spelled **i** as in **wild**, **igh** as in **night**, **i-e** as in **wipe** or **y** as in **try**. Long **ō** can be spelled **o** as in **most**, **oa** as in **toast**, **ow** as in **throw** or **o-e** as in **hope**.

| stripe | groan | glow | toast | grind | fry | sight | stove | toads | flight |

Directions: Complete the exercises with words from the box.

1. Write each word from the box with its vowel sound.

ī   stripe, grind, fry, sight, flight
ō   groan, glow, toast, stove, toads

2. Complete these sentences, using a word with the given vowel sound. Use each word from the box only once.

We will (ī) __fry__ potatoes on the (ō) __stove__

I thought I heard a low (ō) __groan__, but when I looked, there was nothing in (ī) __sight__

The airplane for our (ī) __flight__ had a (ī) __stripe__ painted on its side.

I saw a strange (ō) __glow__ coming from the toaster while making (ō) __toast__

Do (ō) __toads__ live in the water like frogs?

We need to (ī) __grind__ up the nuts before we put them in the cookie dough.

Page 14

Spelling: Long i and o

Directions: Read the words. After each word, write the correct vowel sound. Underline the letter or letters that spell the sound. The first one has been done for you.

bright

	Word	Vowel		Word	Vowel
1.	bright	i	9.	white	i
2.	globe	o	10.	roast	o
3.	plywood	i	11.	light	i
4.	mankind	i	12.	shallow	o
5.	coaching	o	13.	myself	i
6.	prize	i	14.	throne	o
7.	grind	i	15.	cold	o
8.	withhold	o	16.	snow	o

Directions: Below are words written as they are pronounced. Write the words that sound like:

1. thrōn __throne__   5. brīt __bright__
2. skōld __scold__   6. grīnd __grind__
3. prīz __prize__   7. plī wood __plywood__
4. rōst __roast__   8. mīself __myself__

Page 15

Spelling: Long u

Long **ū** can be spelled, **u-e** as in **cube** or **ew** as in **few**. Some sounds are similar in sound to **u** but are not true **u** sounds, such as the **oo** in **tooth**, the **o-e** in **move** and the **ue** in **blue**.

Directions: Complete each sentence using a word from the box. Do not use the same word more than once.

| blew |
| tune |
| flute |
| cute |
| stew |
| June |
| glue |

1. Yesterday, the wind __blew__ so hard it knocked down a tree on our street.
2. My favorite instrument is the __flute__.
3. The little puppy in the window is so __cute__.
4. I love __June__ because it's so warm, and we get out of school.
5. For that project, you will need scissors, construction paper and __glue__
6. I recognize that song because it has a familiar __tune__
7. My grandmother's beef __stew__ is the best I've ever tasted.

Page 16

Spelling: The k Sound

The **k** sound can be spelled with **k** as in **peek**, **c** as in **cousin**, **ck** as in **sick**, **ch** as in **Chris** and **cc** as in **accuse**. In some words, however, one **c** may be pronounced **k** and the other **s** as in **accident**.

Directions: Answer the questions with words from the box.

| Christmas | freckles | command | cork | jacket |
| accused | castle | stomach | rake | accident |

1. Which two words spell **k** with a **k**?
   __cork__   __rake__
2. Which two words spell **k** with **ck**?
   __freckles__   __jacket__
3. Which two words spell **k** with **ch**?
   __Christmas__   __stomach__
4. Which five words spell **k** with **c** or **cc**?
   __accused__   __cork__
   __command__   __castle__
   __accident__

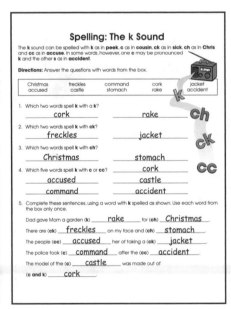

5. Complete these sentences, using a word with **k** spelled as shown. Use each word from the box only once.

Dad gave Mom a garden (k) __rake__ for (ch) __Christmas__

There are (ck) __freckles__ on my face and (ch) __stomach__

The people (cc) __accused__ her of taking a (ck) __jacket__

The police took (c) __command__ after the (cc) __accident__

The model of the (c) __castle__ was made out of

(c and k) __cork__

Page 17

Spelling: The k Sound

Directions: Underline the letters that spell **k** in each word. The first one has been done for you.

1. toothpick
2. arc
3. kitchen
4. acclaim
5. account
6. Christmas
7. make
8. confirm
9. brick
10. stomach

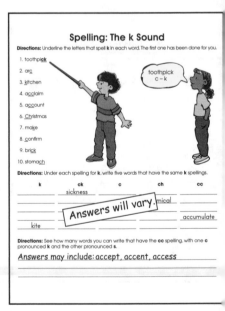

toothpick
c – k

Directions: Under each spelling for **k**, write five words that have the same **k** spellings.

k	ck	c	ch	cc
	sickness			
			...mical	
kite				accumulate

Answers will vary.

Directions: See how many words you can write that have the **cc** spelling, with one **c** pronounced **k** and the other pronounced **s**.

__Answers may include: accept, accent, access__

Page 18

Spelling: The f Sound

The f sound can be spelled with **f** as in **fun**, **gh** as in **laugh** or **ph** as in **phone**.

Directions: Answer the questions with words from the box.

fuss	paragraph	phone	friendship	freedom
defend	flood	alphabet	rough	laughter

Which three words spell **f** with **ph**?

paragraph   phone   alphabet

Which two words spell **f** with **gh**?

rough   laughter

Which five words spell **f** with an **f**?

fuss   defend   flood

friendship   freedom

Complete these sentences, using a word with **f** spelled as shown. Use each word from the box only once.

I don't know why my teacher makes so much (f) __fuss__ over writing a (ph) __paragraph__ .

A (f) __friendship__ can help you through (gh) __rough__ times.

The soldiers will (f) __defend__ our (f) __freedom__ .

Can you say the (ph) __alphabet__ backwards?

When I answered the (ph) __phone__ , all I could hear was (gh) __laughter__ .

If it keeps raining, we'll have a (f) __flood__ .

Page 19

Spelling: The f Sound

Directions: Read the following words. Underline the letters that spell **f** in each word.

1. lau<u>gh</u>ter
2. <u>f</u>ootball
3. cou<u>gh</u>
4. <u>p</u>aragraph
5. enou<u>gh</u>
6. <u>ph</u>antom
7. roo<u>f</u>
8. per<u>f</u>ormance
9. tou<u>gh</u>est
10. tele<u>ph</u>one
11. be<u>f</u>ore
12. rou<u>gh</u>ness
13. al<u>ph</u>abet
14. grie<u>f</u>
15. gra<u>ph</u>

Directions: Under each spelling for the **f** sound, write five words with the same **f** letter or letters. Use words other than those above.

f	gh	ph

Answers will vary.

Page 20

Spelling: Unscrambling Letters

Directions: Put the letters in order to spell the **f** words. If you need help with spelling, look on page 18.

feeddn	__defend__	odolf	__flood__
nopeh	__phone__	dspllenthr	__friendship__
gletharu	__laughter__	gruho	__rough__
ssfu	__fuss__	taalbehp	__alphabet__
droefem	__freedom__	ghaaprpar	__paragraph__

RT UAH P GBLRT

Directions: Use the correctly spelled words to answer the questions.

1. Which two words each have one syllable and spell **f** with an **f**?

__fuss__   __flood__

2. Which word has two syllables and spells **f** with **gh**?   __laughter__

3. Which word has one syllable and spells **f** with **ph**?   __phone__

4. Which three words each have two syllables and spell **f** with an **f**?

__defend__   __freedom__   __friendship__

5. Which two words each have three syllables and spell **f** with a **ph**?

__alphabet__   __paragraph__

6. Which word has one syllable and spells **f** with **gh**?   __rough__

Page 21

Spelling: The s Sound

The **s** sound can be spelled with **s** as in **super** or **ss** as in **assign**, **c** as in **city**, **ce** as in **fence** or **sc** as in **scene**. In some words, though, **sc** is pronounced **sk**, as in **scare**.

Directions: Answer the questions using words from the box.

exciting	medicine	lettuce	peace	scissors
slice	scientist	sauce	bracelet	distance

1. Which five words spell **s** with an **s** or **ss**?

__slice__   __sauce__   __distance__

__scissors__   __scientist__

2. Which two words spell **s** with just a **c**?

__exciting__   __medicine__

3. Which six words spell **s** with a **ce**?

__slice__   __sauce__   __bracelet__

__lettuce__   __peace__   __distance__

4. Which two words spell **s** with **sc**?

__scientist__   __scissors__

5. Complete these sentences, using a word with **s** spelled as shown. Use each word from the box only once.

My (ce) __bracelet__ fell off my wrist into the tomato __sauce__ (s and ce).

My salad was just a (s and ce) __slice__ of (ce) __lettuce__ .

It was (c) __exciting__ to see the lions, even though they were a long (s and ce) __distance__ away.

The (sc and s) __scientist__ invented a new (c) __medicine__ .

If I lend you my (sc) __scissors__ , will you leave me in (ce) __peace__ ?

Page 22

Spelling: The s Sound

Directions: Read the following words. Underline the letters that spell **s** in each word. In some words, more than one letter will be underlined.

1. impa<u>ss</u>ive
2. pla<u>c</u>ement
3. que<u>s</u>tion
4. con<u>sc</u>ious
5. ex<u>c</u>ellence
6. a<u>ss</u>ertive
7. <u>sc</u>epter
8. <u>sc</u>oundrel
9. a<u>ss</u>ortment
10. ignoran<u>ce</u>
11. pre<u>c</u>ious
12. judi<u>c</u>ious
13. differen<u>ce</u>
14. life<u>s</u>e<u>ss</u>
15. <u>s</u>olvent
16. <u>s</u>cope
17. ca<u>s</u>tle
18. <u>s</u>camper
19. <u>s</u>ociable
20. muffin<u>s</u>
21. <u>s</u>cissors
22. in<u>s</u>urance
23. <u>s</u>camp
24. <u>s</u>cience

Directions: Under each spelling for **s**, write five words with the same **s** letters. Use words other than those above.

s or ss	c	ce	sc

Answers will vary.

Page 23

Spelling: Syllables

A **syllable** is a word—or part of a word—with only one vowel sound. Some words have just one syllable, such as **cat**, **dog** and **house**. Some words have two syllables, such as **in-sist** and **be-fore**. Some words have three syllables, such as **re-mem-ber**; four syllables, such as **un-der-stand-ing**; or more. Often words are easier to spell if you know how many syllables they have.

Syl-la-bles

Directions: Write the number of syllables in each word below.

	Word	Syllables		Word	Syllables
1.	amphibian	4	11.	want	1
2.	liter	2	12.	communication	5
3.	guild	1	13.	pedestrian	4
4.	chill	1	14.	kilo	2
5.	vegetarian	5	15.	autumn	2
6.	comedian	4	16.	dinosaur	3
7.	warm	1	17.	grammar	2
8.	piano	3	18.	dry	1
9.	barbarian	4	19.	solar	2
10.	chef	1	20.	wild	1

Directions: Next to each number, write words with the same number of syllables.

1
2
3
4
5

Answers will vary.

Page 24

Spelling: Syllables

Directions: Write each word from the box next to the number that shows how many syllables it has.

| fuss | paragraph | phone | friendship | freedom |
| defend | flood | alphabet | rough | laughter |

One: __fuss__ __flood__ __phone__ __rough__

Two: __defend__ __friendship__ __freedom__ __laughter__

Three: __paragraph__ __alphabet__

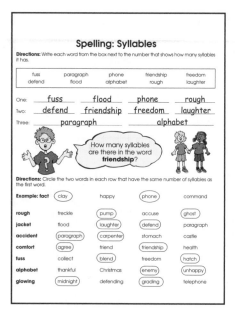

How many syllables are there in the word **friendship**?

Directions: Circle the two words in each row that have the same number of syllables as the first word.

Example: fact (clay) happy (phone) command

rough	freckle	(pump)	accuse	(ghost)
jacket	flood	(laughter)	(defend)	paragraph
accident	(paragraph)	(carpenter)	stomach	castle
comfort	(agree)	friend	(friendship)	health
fuss	collect	(blend)	freedom	(hatch)
alphabet	thankful	Christmas	(enemy)	(unhappy)
glowing	(midnight)	defending	(grading)	telephone

Page 25

Vocabulary: Synonyms

A **synonym** is a word that means the same, or nearly the same, as another word.
Example: quick and fast

Directions: Draw lines to match the words in Column A with their synonyms in Column B.

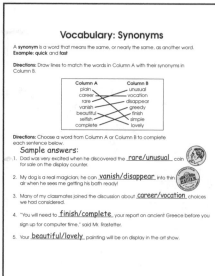

Column A	Column B
plain	unusual
career	vocation
rare	disappear
vanish	greedy
beautiful	finish
selfish	simple
complete	lovely

Directions: Choose a word from Column A or Column B to complete each sentence below.

Sample answers:

1. Dad was very excited when he discovered the __rare/unusual__ coin for sale on the display counter.

2. My dog is a real magician; he can __vanish/disappear__ into thin air when he sees me getting his bath ready!

3. Many of my classmates joined the discussion about __career/vocation__ choices we had considered.

4. "You will need to __finish/complete__ your report on ancient Greece before you sign up for computer time," said Mr. Rastetter.

5. Your __beautiful/lovely__ painting will be on display in the art show.

Page 26

Vocabulary: Synonyms

| tired | greedy | easy | rough | minute | melted | friend | smart |

Directions: For each sentence, choose a word from the box that is a synonym for the bold word. Write the synonym above the word.

1. Boy, this road is really **bumpy**! — __rough__

2. The operator said politely, "One **moment**, please." — __minute__

3. My parents are usually **exhausted** when they get home from work. — __tired__

4. "Don't be so **selfish**! Can't you share with us?" asked Rob. — __greedy__

5. That puzzle was actually quite **simple**. — __easy__

6. "Who's your **buddy**?" Dad asked as we walked onto the porch. — __friend__

7. When it comes to animals, my Uncle Steve is quite **intelligent**. — __smart__

8. The frozen treat **thawed** while I stood in line for the bus. — __melted__

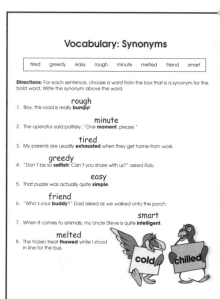

cold chilled

Page 27

Vocabulary: Antonyms

An **antonym** is a word that means the opposite of another word.
Example: difficult and easy

Directions: Choose words from the box to complete the crossword puzzle.

| friend | vanish | quit | safety | liquids | scatter | help | noisy |

ACROSS:
2. Opposite of **gather**
3. Opposite of **enemy**
4. Opposite of **prevent**
6. Opposite of **begin**
7. Opposite of **silent**

DOWN:
1. Opposite of **appear**
2. Opposite of **danger**
5. Opposite of **solids**

Crossword solution: SCATTER, FRIEND, HELP, QUIT, NOISY, VANISH, SAFETY, LIQUIDS

Page 28

Vocabulary: Antonyms

Directions: Each bold word below has an antonym in the box. Use these words to write new sentences. The first one is done for you.

| friend | vanish | quit | safety | liquids | help | scatter | worse |

1. I'll help you **gather** all the papers on the lawn.
   The strong winds will scatter the leaves.

2. The fourth graders were learning about the many **solids** in their classroom.
   Answer should include "liquids."

3. "It's time to **begin** our lesson on the continents," said Ms. Haynes.
   Answer should include "quit."

4. "That's strange. The stapler decided to **appear** all of a sudden," said Mr. Jonson.
   Answer should include "vanish."

5. The doctor said this new medicine should **prevent** colds.
   Answer should include "help."

6. "She is our **enemy**, boys, we can't let her in our clubhouse!" cried Paul.
   Answer should include "friend."

7. I'm certain that dark cave is full of **danger**!
   Answer should include "safety."

8. Give me a chance to make the situation **better**.
   Answer should include "worse."

Page 29

Vocabulary: Synonyms and Antonyms

Directions: Use the words in the box to write a synonym for each word below. Write it next to the S. Next to the A, write an antonym. The first one is done for you.

appear	proud	merry	straight	repair	plain
under	melted	unnecessary	late	new	smooth
embarrassed	gloomy	bent	break	old	bumpy
icy	valuable	immediate			vanish

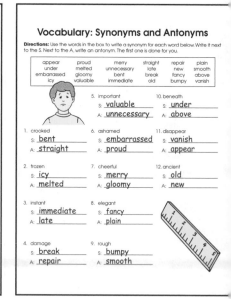

1. crooked
   S: __bent__
   A: __straight__

2. frozen
   S: __icy__
   A: __melted__

3. instant
   S: __immediate__
   A: __late__

4. damage
   S: __break__
   A: __repair__

5. important
   S: __valuable__
   A: __unnecessary__

6. ashamed
   S: __embarrassed__
   A: __proud__

7. cheerful
   S: __merry__
   A: __gloomy__

8. elegant
   S: __fancy__
   A: __plain__

9. rough
   S: __bumpy__
   A: __smooth__

10. beneath
    S: __under__
    A: __above__

11. disappear
    S: __vanish__
    A: __appear__

12. ancient
    S: __old__
    A: __new__

Page 30

Palindromes

Can you think forwards and backwards? If so, you should have no problem with palindromes. **Palindromes** are words or sentences that are spelled the same forward or backward.

Examples: noon, eve, mom, wow
a man, a plan, a canal, Panama

Directions: Read the definitions. Write the palindromes on the lines. If you get stuck, work with a partner.

1. Another name for a soft drink — pop
2. What you typically call your father — dad (or pop)
3. Short for Nancy — Nan
4. What one does with one's eyes — sees
5. Female sheep — ewe
6. An instrument used to locate airplanes — radar
7. To choke — gag
8. Boat used by Eskimos — kayak
9. Time for lunch — noon
10. A paper that shows legal ownership of property — deed

Directions: Write as many palindromes as you can. A few have been done for you.

bib, Bob, did, dad Answers may include: dud, mom, ma'am, mum, pip, pep, pup, sis, peep

Directions: Write a palindrome sentence using these words: I'm, Madam, Adam.
Sentences will vary.

Page 31

Vocabulary: Homophones

Homophones are two words that sound the same, have different meanings and are usually spelled differently.
Example: write and right

Directions: Write the correct homophone in each sentence below.

weight — how heavy something is
wait — to be patient

threw — tossed
through — passing between

steal — to take something that doesn't belong to you
steel — a heavy metal

1. The bands marched __through__ the streets lined with many cheering people.
2. __Wait__ for me by the flagpole.
3. One of our strict rules at school is: Never __steal__ from another person.
4. Could you estimate the __weight__ of this bowling ball?
5. The bleachers have __steel__ rods on both ends and in the middle.
6. He walked in the door and __threw__ his jacket down.

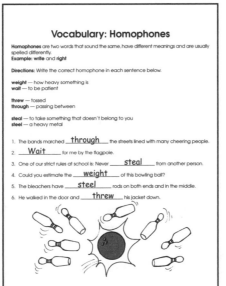

Page 32

Vocabulary: Homophones

Directions: Write the correct homophone in each sentence below.

cent — a coin having the value of one penny
scent — odor or aroma

chews — grinds with the teeth
choose — to select

course — the path along which something moves
coarse — rough in texture

heard — received sounds in the ear
herd — a group of animals

1. My uncle Mike always __chews__ each bite of his food 20 times!
2. As we walked through her garden, we detected the __scent__ of roses.
3. It was very peaceful sitting on the hillside watching the __herd__ of cattle grazing.
4. Which flavor of ice cream did you __choose__ ?
5. The friendly clerk let me buy the jacket even though I was one __cent__ short.
6. You will need __coarse__ sandpaper to make the wood smoother.

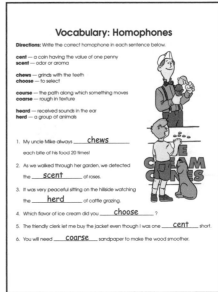

Page 33

Vocabulary: Words That Sound Alike

Directions: Choose the correct word in parentheses to complete each sentence. The first one is done for you.

1. Jimmy was so __bored__ that he fell asleep. (board, bored)
2. We'll need a __board__ and some nails to repair the fence. (board, bored)
3. Do you want __dessert__ after dinner? (desert, dessert)
4. Did the soldier __desert__ his post. (desert, dessert)
5. The soldier had a __medal__ pinned to his uniform. (medal, meddle)
6. I told her not to __meddle__ in other people's lives. (medal, meddle)
7. Don't __peek__ at your present before Christmas! (peak, peek)
8. They climbed to the __peak__ of the mountain. (peak, peek)
9. Jack had to repair the emergency __brake__ on his car. (brake, break)
10. Please be careful not to __break__ my bicycle. (brake, break)
11. The race __course__ was a very difficult one. (coarse, course)
12. We will need some __coarse__ sandpaper to finish the job. (coarse, course)

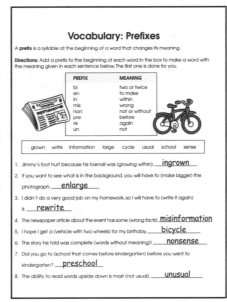

Page 34

Vocabulary: Prefixes

A **prefix** is a syllable at the beginning of a word that changes its meaning.

Directions: Add a prefix to the beginning of each word in the box to make a word with the meaning given in each sentence below. The first one is done for you.

PREFIX	MEANING
bi	two or twice
en	to make
in	within
mis	wrong
non	not or without
pre	before
re	again
un	not

grown write information large cycle usual school sense

1. Jimmy's foot hurt because his toenail was (growing within). __ingrown__
2. If you want to see what is in the background, you will have to (make bigger) the photograph. __enlarge__
3. I didn't do a very good job on my homework, so I will have to (write it again) it. __rewrite__
4. The newspaper article about the event has some (wrong facts). __misinformation__
5. I hope I get a (vehicle with two wheels) for my birthday. __bicycle__
6. The story he told was complete (words without meaning)! __nonsense__
7. Did you go to (school that comes before kindergarten) before you went to kindergarten? __preschool__
8. The ability to read words upside down is most (not usual). __unusual__

Page 35

Vocabulary: Prefixes

Directions: Circle the correct word for each sentence.

1. You will need to _____ the directions before you complete this page.
   reset   (reread)   repair
2. Since she is allergic to milk products she has to use _____ products.
   (nondairy)   nonsense   nonmetallic
3. That certainly was an _____ costume he selected for the Halloween party.
   untied   (unusual)   unable
4. The directions on the box said to _____ the oven before baking the brownies.
   (preheat)   preschool   prevent
5. "I'm sorry if I _____ you as to the cost of the trip," explained the travel agent.
   misdialed   misread   (misinformed)
6. You may use the overhead projector to _____ the picture so the whole class can see it.
   (enlarge)   enable   endanger

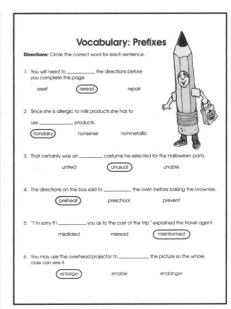

Page 36

Vocabulary: Suffixes

A **suffix** is a syllable at the end of a word that changes its meaning. In most cases, when adding a suffix that begins with a vowel, drop the final **e** of the root word. For example, **fame** becomes **famous**. Also, change a final **y** in the root word to **i** before adding any suffix except **ing**. For example, **silly** becomes **silliness**.

Directions: Add a suffix to the end of each word in the box to make a word with the meaning given (in parentheses) in each sentence below. The first one is done for you.

SUFFIX	MEANING
ful	full of
ity	quality or degree
ive	have or tend to be
less	without or lacking
able	able to be
ness	state of
ment	act of
or	person that does something
ward	in the direction of

| effect | like | thought | pay | beauty | thank | back | act | happy |

1. Mike was (full of thanks) for a hot meal. __thankful__
2. I was (without thinking) for forgetting your birthday. __thoughtless__
3. The mouse trap we put out doesn't seem to be (have an effect). __effective__
4. In spring, the flower garden is (full of beauty). __beautiful__
5. Sally is such a (able to be liked) girl! __likable__
6. Tim fell over (in the direction of the back) because he wasn't watching where he was going. __backward__
7. Jill's wedding day was one of great (the state of being happy). __happiness__
8. The (person who performs) was very good in the play. __actor__
9. I have to make a (act of paying) for the stereo I bought. __payment__

Page 37

Vocabulary: Suffixes

Directions: Read the story. Choose the correct word from the box to complete the sentences.

beautiful	colorful	payment
breakable	careful	backward
careless	director	agreement
basement	forward	firmness

Colleen and Marj carried the boxes down to the __basement__ apartment. "Be __careful__ with those," cautioned Colleen's mother. "All the things in that box are __breakable__." As soon as the two girls helped carry all the boxes from the moving van down the stairs, they would be able to go to school for the play tryouts. That was the __agreement__ made with Colleen's mother earlier that day.

"It won't do any good to get __careless__ with your work. Just keep at it and the job will be done quickly," she spoke with a __firmness__ in her voice.

"It's hard to see where I'm going when I have to walk __backward__," groaned Marj. "Can we switch places with the next box?"

Colleen agreed to switch places, but they soon discovered that the last two boxes were lightweight. Each girl had her own box to carry, so each of them got to walk looking __forward__. "These are so light," remarked Marj. "What's in them?"

"These have the __beautiful__, __colorful__ hats I was telling you about. We can take them to the play tryouts with us," beamed Colleen. "I bet we'll impress the __director__. Even if we don't get parts in the play, I bet our hats will!"

Colleen's mother handed each of the girls a 5-dollar bill. "I really appreciate your help. Will this be enough?"

"Thanks, Mom. You bet!" Colleen shouted as the girls ran down the sidewalk.

Page 38

Reading Skills: Classifying

Classifying is placing similar things into categories.

Directions: Classify each group by crossing out the word that does not belong.

1. factory   hotel   lodge   ~~pattern~~
2. ~~Thursday~~   September   December   October
3. cottage   hut   ~~carpenter~~   castle
4. cupboard   ~~orchard~~   refrigerator   stove
5. Christmas   Thanksgiving   Easter   ~~spring~~
6. brass   copper   ~~silk~~   tin
7. stomach   ~~breathe~~   liver   brain
8. teacher   mother   dentist   ~~cake~~
9. ~~market~~   faucet   bathtub   sink
10. basement   attic   kitchen   ~~neighborhood~~

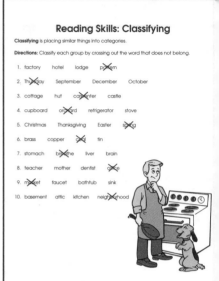

Page 39

Reading Skills: Classifying

Directions: Complete each idea by crossing out the word or phrase that does not belong.

1. If the main idea is **things that are green**, I don't need:
   ~~the sun~~   apples   grass   leaves in summer
2. If the idea is **musical instruments**, I don't need a:
   piano   trombone   ~~beach ball~~   tuba
3. If the idea is **months of the year**, I don't need:
   ~~Friday~~   January   July   October
4. If the idea is **colors on the U.S. flag**, I don't need:
   white   blue   ~~black~~   red
5. If the idea is **types of weather**, I don't need:
   sleet   stormy   ~~rose~~   sunny
6. If the idea is **fruits**, I don't need:
   kiwi   orange   ~~spinach~~   banana
7. If the idea is **U.S. presidents**, I don't need:
   Lincoln   ~~Jordan~~   Washington   Adams
8. If the idea is **flowers**, I don't need:
   ~~tree~~   daisy   tulip   daffodil
9. If the idea is **sports**, I don't need:
   ~~papers~~   soccer   wrestling   baseball

Page 40

Reading Skills: Classifying

Directions: Choose a word or phrase from the box that describes each group below.

color words	vegetables	gems
explorers	metals	vehicles
things that fly	insects	

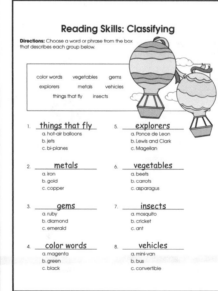

1. __things that fly__
   a. hot-air balloons
   b. jets
   c. bi-planes

2. __metals__
   a. iron
   b. gold
   c. copper

3. __gems__
   a. ruby
   b. diamond
   c. emerald

4. __color words__
   a. magenta
   b. green
   c. black

5. __explorers__
   a. Ponce de Leon
   b. Lewis and Clark
   c. Magellan

6. __vegetables__
   a. beets
   b. carrots
   c. asparagus

7. __insects__
   a. mosquito
   b. cricket
   c. ant

8. __vehicles__
   a. mini-van
   b. bus
   c. convertible

Page 41

Reading Skills: Classifying

Directions: Read the title of each TV show. Write the correct number to tell what kind of show it is.

1 — Cooking	3 — Sports	5 — Humor
2 — Nature	4 — Mystery	6 — Famous People

__4__ The Secret of the Lost Locket
__3__ Learn Tennis With the Pros
__2__ Birds in the Wild
__6__ The Life of George Washington
__1__ Great Recipes From Around the World
__5__ A Laugh a Minute

Directions: Read the description of each TV show. Write the number of each show above in the blank.

__6__ The years before he became the first president of the United States are examined.
__2__ Featured: eagles and owls
__4__ Clues lead Detective Logan to a cemetery in his search for the missing necklace.
__3__ Famous players give tips on buying a racket.
__1__ Six ways to cook chicken
__5__ Cartoon characters in short stories

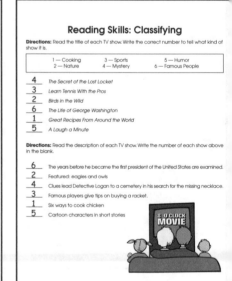

Page 42

Reading Skills: Classifying

Directions: Read the story. Find words in the story that belong in the lists below. Write the words under the correct lists.

Meg, Joey and Ryan are talking about what they want to do when they grow up. Meg says, "I want to be a great writer. I'll write lots of books, and articles for newspapers and magazines."

"I want to be a famous athlete," says Joey. "I'll play baseball in the summer and football in the fall."

"Oh, yes," adds Meg. "I want to be a famous tennis star, too. When I'm not busy writing books, I'll play in tournaments all over the world. I'll be the world's champion!"

Ryan says, "That sounds pretty good. But I think I'll be a doctor and a carpenter. I'll build my very own cabin that I can live in during the winter."

"I'm going to live in a lighthouse by the sea," says Joey. "I've always wanted to do that. Then I can go fishing any time I want."

"I suppose I'll live in a castle when I grow up," says Meg. "World champion tennis players make lots of money!"

Jobs
1. writer
2. athlete
3. doctor
4. carpenter

Sports
1. football
2. baseball
3. tennis
4. fishing

Seasons
1. summer
2. fall
3. winter

Houses
1. cabin
2. lighthouse
3. castle

Page 43

Reading Skills: Analogies

An **analogy** indicates how different items go together or are similar in some way.

Examples:
Petal is to **flower** as **leaf** is to **tree**.
Book is to **library** as **food** is to **grocery**.

If you study the examples, you will see how the second set of objects is related to the first set. A petal is part of a flower, and a leaf is part of a tree. A book can be found in a library, and food can be found in a grocery store.

Directions: Fill in the blanks to complete the analogies. The first one has been done for you.

1. Cup is to saucer as glass is to **coaster**.
2. Paris is to France as London is to **England**.
3. Clothes are to hangers as **shoes** are to boxes.
4. California is to **Pacific Ocean** as Ohio is to Lake Erie.
5. **Tablecloth** is to table as blanket is to bed.
6. Pencil is to paper as **paintbrush** is to canvas.
7. Cow is to **barn** as child is to house.
8. State is to country as **county** is to state.
9. Governor is to state as **president** is to country.
10. **Water** is to ocean as sand is to desert.
11. Engine is to car as hard drive is to **computer**.
12. Beginning is to **start** as stop is to end.

Directions: Write three analogies of your own.

Answers will vary.

Page 44

Reading Skills: Analogies

Directions: Write a word from the box to complete the following analogies.

fence	club	glove	saw	father
blanket	dish	rug	snow	ten
compass	hat	brake	finger	blue

1. Racket is to tennis as **club** is to golf.
2. Glass is to drink as **dish** is to eat.
3. Wheel is to steer as **brake** is to stop.
4. Root is to house as **rug** is to floor.
5. Rain is to storm as **snow** is to blizzard.
6. Clock is to time as **compass** is to directions.
7. Lid is to pan as **hat** is to head.
8. Hammer is to pound as **saw** is to cut.
9. Mother is to daughter as **father** is to son.
10. Shoe is to foot as **glove** is to hand.
11. Five is to ten as **ten** is to twenty.
12. Shade is to lamp as **blanket** is to bed.
13. Toe is to foot as **finger** is to hand.
14. Frame is to picture as **fence** is to yard.
15. Green is to grass as **blue** is to sky.

Page 45

Review

Directions: Check the three words that belong together. Then draw a line under the sentence that tells how they are alike.

1. ☑ forehead ☑ jaw They are all parts of the face.
   ☐ shoulder ☑ cheek They are all parts of the arm.

2. ☑ collar ☑ sleeve They are all parts of your body.
   ☑ cuff ☐ heart They are all parts of a shirt.

3. ☐ camera ☑ trumpet They are all used to make music.
   ☑ guitar ☑ flute They are all used to take pictures.

Directions: Check the three words that belong together. Then write a sentence to tell how they are alike.

☑ cottage ☐ princess ☑ hut ☑ castle

They are all places to live.

Directions: Write a word to complete each analogy.

1. Car is to drive as **plane** is to fly.
2. Basement is to bottom as attic is to **top**.
3. Calf is to cow as colt is to **horse**.
4. Bark is to dog as **moo** is to cow.
5. Laugh is to happy as **cry** is to sad.

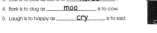

Page 46

Following Directions: Maps

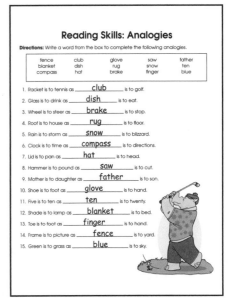

Directions: Follow the directions below to reach a "mystery" location on the map.
1. Begin at home.
2. Drive east on River Road.
3. Turn south on Broadway.
4. Drive to Central Street and turn west.
5. When you get to City Street, turn south.
6. Turn east on Main Street and drive one block to Park Avenue; turn north.
7. At Central Street turn east, then turn southeast on Through Way.
8. Drive to the end of Through Way. Your "mystery" location is to the east.

You are at the **school**.

Can you write an easier way to get back home?

Answers will vary.

Page 47

Following Directions: Recipes

Sequencing is putting items or events in logical order.

Directions: Read the recipe. Then number the steps in order for making brownies.

Preheat the oven to 350 degrees. Grease an 8-inch square baking dish.

In a mixing bowl, place two squares (2 ounces) of unsweetened chocolate and 1/3 cup butter. Place the bowl in a pan of hot water and heat it to melt the chocolate and the butter.

When the chocolate is melted, remove the pan from the heat. Add 1 cup sugar and two eggs to the melted chocolate and beat it. Next, stir in 3/4 cup sifted flour, 1/2 teaspoon baking powder and 1/2 teaspoon salt. Finally, mix in 1/2 cup chopped nuts.

Spread the mixture in the greased baking dish. Bake for 30 to 35 minutes. The brownies are done when a toothpick stuck in the center comes out clean. Let the brownies cool. Cut them into squares.

8 Stick a toothpick in the center of the brownies to make sure they are done.
5 Mix in chopped nuts.
2 Melt chocolate and butter in a mixing bowl over a pan of hot water.
9 Cool brownies and cut into squares.
3 Beat in sugar and eggs.
6 Spread mixture in a baking dish.
4 Stir in flour, baking powder and salt.
7 Bake for 30 to 35 minutes.
1 Turn oven to 350 degrees and grease pan.

Page 48

Following Directions: Salt Into Pepper

Directions: Read how to do a magic trick that will amaze your friends. Then number the steps in order to do the trick.

Imagine doing this trick for your friends. Pick up a salt shaker that everyone can see is full of salt. Pour some into your hand. Tell your audience that you will change the salt into pepper. Say a few magic words, such as "Fibbiddy, dibbiddy, milkshake and malt. What will be pepper once was salt!" Then open your hand and pour out pepper!

How is it done? First you need a clear salt shaker with a screw-on top. You also need a paper napkin and a small amount of pepper.

Take off the top of the salt shaker. Lay the napkin over the opening and push it down a little to make a small pocket. Fill the pocket with pepper. Put the top back on the salt shaker and tear off the extra napkin.

Hold up the salt shaker so your audience can see that it is full of salt. Shake some "salt" into your hand. Close your fist so no one can see that it is really pepper. Say the magic words and open your hand.

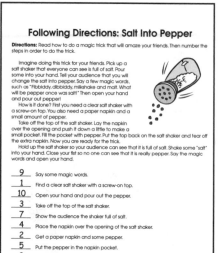

- **9** Say some magic words.
- **1** Find a clear salt shaker with a screw-on top.
- **10** Open your hand and pour out the pepper.
- **3** Take off the top of the salt shaker.
- **7** Show the audience the shaker full of salt.
- **4** Place the napkin over the opening of the salt shaker.
- **2** Get a paper napkin and some pepper.
- **5** Put the pepper in the napkin pocket.
- **8** Shake some "salt" into your hand and close your fist.
- **6** Put the top back on the salt shaker and tear off the extra napkin.

Page 49

Following Directions: Recipes

Directions: Follow these steps for making a peanut butter and jelly sandwich.

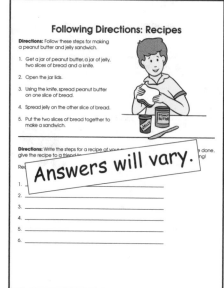

1. Get a jar of peanut butter, a jar of jelly, two slices of bread and a knife.
2. Open the jar lids.
3. Using the knife, spread peanut butter on one slice of bread.
4. Spread jelly on the other slice of bread.
5. Put the two slices of bread together to make a sandwich.

Directions: Write the steps for a recipe of your ~~one~~ ... e done, give the recipe to a friend ...

Answers will vary.

1. _____
2. _____
3. _____
4. _____
5. _____
6. _____

Page 50

Reading Skills: Bus Schedules

Schedules are important to our daily lives. Your parents' jobs, school, even watching television—all are based on schedules. When you travel, you probably follow a schedule, too. Most forms of public transportation, such as subways, buses and trains, run on schedules. These "timetables" tell passengers when they will leave each stop or station.

Directions: Use the following city bus schedule to answer the questions.

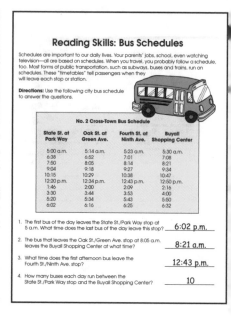

No. 2 Cross-Town Bus Schedule

State St. at Park Way	Oak St. at Green Ave.	Fourth St. at Ninth Ave.	Buyall Shopping Center
5:00 a.m.	5:14 a.m.	5:23 a.m.	5:30 a.m.
6:38	6:52	7:01	7:08
7:50	8:05	8:14	8:21
9:04	9:18	9:27	9:34
10:15	10:29	10:38	10:47
12:20 p.m.	12:34 p.m.	12:43 p.m.	12:50 p.m.
1:46	2:00	2:09	2:16
3:30	3:44	3:53	4:00
5:20	5:34	5:43	5:50
6:02	6:16	6:25	6:32

1. The first bus of the day leaves the State St./Park Way stop at 5 a.m. What time does the last bus of the day leave this stop? **6:02 p.m.**

2. The bus that leaves the Oak St./Green Ave. stop at 8:05 a.m. leaves the Buyall Shopping Center at what time? **8:21 a.m.**

3. What time does the first afternoon bus leave the Fourth St./Ninth Ave. stop? **12:43 p.m.**

4. How many buses each day run between the State St./Park Way stop and the Buyall Shopping Center? **10**

Page 51

Reading Skills: Train Schedules

Directions: Below is part of a schedule for trains leaving New York City for cities all around the country. Use the schedule to answer the questions.

Destination	Train Number	Departure Time	Arrival Time
Birmingham	958	9:00 a.m.	12:31 a.m.
Boston	611	7:15 a.m.	4:30 p.m.
Cambridge	398	8:15 a.m.	1:14 p.m.
Cincinnati	242	5:00 p.m.	7:25 p.m.
Detroit	415	1:45 p.m.	4:40 p.m.
Evansville	623	3:00 p.m.	8:28 p.m.

1. What is the number of the train that leaves latest in the day? **623**
2. What city is the destination for train number 623? **Evansville**
3. What time does the train for Boston leave New York? **7:15 a.m.**
4. What time does train number 415 arrive in Detroit? **4:40 a.m.**
5. What is the destination of the train that leaves earliest in the day? **Cincinnati**

Page 52

Reading Skills: Labels

Directions: You should never take any medicine without your parents' permission, but it is good to know how to read the label of a medicine bottle. Read the label to answer the questions.

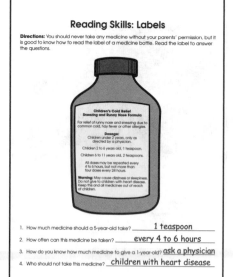

1. How much medicine should a 5-year-old take? **1 teaspoon**
2. How often can this medicine be taken? **every 4 to 6 hours**
3. How do you know how much medicine to give a 1-year-old? **ask a physician**
4. Who should not take this medicine? **children with heart disease**

Page 53

Reading Skills: Labels

Directions: Use the following medicine bottle label to answer the questions.

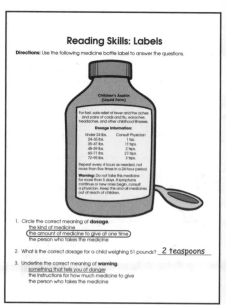

1. Circle the correct meaning of **dosage**.
   the kind of medicine
   (the amount of medicine to give at one time)
   the person who takes the medicine

2. What is the correct dosage for a child weighing 51 pounds? **2 teaspoons**

3. Underline the correct meaning of **warning**.
   something that tells you of danger
   the instructions for how much medicine to give
   the person who takes the medicine

Page 54

Reading Skills: Advertisements

Directions: Use the following newspaper ad to answer the questions.

New-Look Fashions

Final Week!
Spring Suit Sale

Buy one suit at the regular price and get a second one for only $50!

Suits: From $75 to $150

New-Look Fashions
5290 Main Street

Hours: Monday–Friday 10–7; Saturday 10–6; Closed Sunday

1. What is the regular price for a suit? **$75 to $150**
2. If you buy one suit at the regular price, what is the price for a second one? **$50**
3. What day is the store closed? **Sunday**
4. What hours is the store open on Wednesday? **between 10 a.m. and 7 p.m.**
5. When is the sale? **this week**

Page 55

Reading Skills: Advertisements

Directions: Use the following newspaper ad to answer the questions.

House of Plants
Colorful Flowering Trees

Flowering Crab Apple Trees
Sizes up to 10 ft.
Beautiful Colored Spring Flowers
Dark Green Foliage
Red, Pink, White Blossoms

25% OFF

Reg. $29.99 to $149.99
NOW $22.49 to $112.50

House of Plants
6280 River Road

1. How big are the biggest flowering crab apple trees for sale? **Up to 10 feet**
2. What are the regular prices? **$29.99 to $149.99**
3. What are the sale prices? **$22.49 to $112.50**

Page 56

Review

Directions: Use the following "Help Wanted" ads to answer the questions.

Baby-sitter. Caring, responsible person needed to take care of 2 and 4 year old in our home. 25–30 hours per week. Must have own transportation. References required. Call 725-1342 after 7 p.m.

Clerk/Typist. Law firm seeks part-time help. Duties include typing, filing and answering telephone. Monday–Friday, 1–6 p.m. Previous experience preferred. Apply in person. 1392 E. Long St.

Driver for Disabled. Van provided. Includes some evenings and Saturdays. No experience necessary. Call Mike at 769-1533.

Head Nurse. Join in the bloodmobile team at the American Red Cross. Full- and part-time positions available. Great benefits. Apply Monday thru Friday 9–4. 1495 N. State St.

Teachers. For new child-care program. Prefer degree in Early Childhood Development and previous experience. Must be non-smoker. Call 291-5555.

1. For which job would you have to work some evenings and Saturdays? **Driver for Disabled**
2. Which job calls for a person who does not smoke? **Teacher**
3. For which job would you have to have your own transportation? **Baby-sitter**
4. For which job must you apply in person? **Clerk/Typist**
5. Which ad offers both part-time and full-time positions? **Head Nurse**

Page 57

Facts and Opinions

Facts are statements or events that have happened and can be proven to be true.

Example: George Washington was the first president of the United States. This statement is a fact. It can be proven to be true by researching the history of our country.

Opinions are statements that express how someone thinks or feels.

Example: George Washington was the greatest president the United States has ever had. This statement is an opinion. Many people agree that George Washington was a great president, but not everyone agrees he was the greatest president. In some people's opinion, Abraham Lincoln was our greatest president.

Directions: Read each sentence. Write **F** for fact or **O** for opinion.

F 1. There is three feet of snow on the ground.
O 2. A lot of snow makes the winter enjoyable.
O 3. Chris has a better swing set than Mary.
F 4. Both Chris and Mary have swing sets.
F 5. California is a state.
O 6. California is the best state in the west.

Directions: Write three facts and three opinions.

Facts:
1) _____
2) _____
3) _____

Opinions:
1) _____
2) _____
3) _____

Answers will vary.

Page 58

Facts and Opinions

Directions: Write **F** before the facts and **O** before the opinions.

F 1. Our school football team has a winning season this year.
O 2. Mom's spaghetti is the best in the world!
O 3. Autumn is the nicest season of the year.
F 4. Mrs. Burns took her class on a field trip last Thursday.
F 5. The library always puts 30 books in our classroom book collection.
O 6. They should put only books about horses in the collection.
O 7. Our new art teacher is very strict.
O 8. Everyone should keep take-home papers in a folder so they don't have to look for them when it is time to go home.
F 9. The bus to the mall goes right by her house at 7:45 a.m.
O 10. Our new superintendent, Mr. Willeke, is very nice.

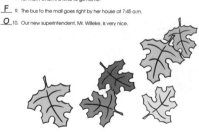

Page 59

Reading Skills: Context Clues

When you read, you may confuse words that look alike. You can tell when you read a word incorrectly because it doesn't make sense. You can tell from the **context** (the other words in the sentence or the sentences before or after) what the word should be. These **context clues** can help you figure out the meaning of a word by relating it to other words in the sentence.

Directions: Circle the correct word for each sentence below. Use the context to help you.

1. We knew we were in trouble as soon as we heard the crash.
   The baseball had gone (**through**/thought) the picture window!
2. She was not able to answer my question because her (month/**mouth**) was full of pizza.
3. Asia is the largest continent in the (**world**/word).
4. I'm not sure I heard the teacher correctly. Did he say what I (through/**thought**) he said?
5. I was not with them on vacation so I don't know a (think/**thing**) about what happened.
6. My favorite (**month**/mouth) of the year is July because I love fireworks and parades!
7. You will do better on your book report if you (**think**/thing) about what you are going to say.

Page 60

Reading Skills: Context Clues

Directions: Read each sentence carefully and circle the word that makes sense.

1. We didn't (except / **expect**) you to arrive so early.
2. "I can't hear a (**word** / world) you are saying. Wait until I turn down the stereo," said Val.
3. I couldn't sleep last night because of the (**noise** / nose) from the apartment below us.
4. Did Peggy say (weather / **whether**) or not we needed our binoculars for the game?
5. He broke his (noise / **nose**) when he fell off the bicycle.
6. All the students (**except** / expect) the four in the front row are excused to leave.
7. The teacher said we should have good (whether / **weather**) for our field trip.

Context **Clues**

Directions: Choose a word pair from the sentence... ...e two sentences of your own.

1. _____
2. _____

Answers will vary.

Page 61

Reading Skills: Context Clues

Directions: Use context clues to help you choose the correct word for each sentence below.

designs	studying	collection

Our fourth-grade class will be __studying__ castles for the next four weeks. Mrs. Oswalt is helping with our study. She plans to share her __collection__ of castle models with the class. We are all looking forward to our morning in the sand at the school's volleyball court. We all get to try our own __designs__ to see how they work.

breath	excited	quietly

Michelle was very __excited__ the other day when she came into the classroom. We all noticed that she had trouble sitting __quietly__ in her seat until it was her turn to share with us. When her turn finally came, she took a deep __breath__ and told us that her mom was going to have a baby!

responsibility	chooses	messages

Each week, our teacher __chooses__ classroom helpers. They get to be part of the Job Squad. Some helpers have the __responsibility__ of watering the plants. Everyone's favorite job is when they get to take __messages__ to the office or to another teacher's room.

Page 62

Reading Skills: Context Clues

Directions: Read the story. Match each bold word with its definition below.

Where the northern shores of North America meet the Arctic Ocean, the winters are very long and cold. No plants or crops will grow there. This is the land of the **Eskimo**.

Eskimos have figured out ways to live in the snow and ice. They sometimes live in **igloos**, which are made of snow. It is really very comfortable inside! An oil lamp provides light and warmth.

Often, you will find a big, furry **husky** sleeping in the long tunnel that leads to the igloo. Huskies are very important to Eskimos because they pull their sleds and help with hunting. Eskimos are excellent hunters. Many, many years ago they learned to make **harpoons** and spears to help them hunt their food.

Eskimos get much of their food from the sea, especially fish, seals and whales. Often, an Eskimo will go out in a **kayak** to fish. Only one Eskimo fits inside, and he drives it with a paddle. The waves may turn the kayak upside down, but the Eskimo does not fall out. He is so skillful with a paddle that he quickly is right side up again.

A __husky__ is a large, strong dog.

An __Eskimo__ is a member of the race of people who live on the Arctic coasts of North America and in parts of Greenland.

__Igloos__ are houses made of packed snow.

A __kayak__ is a one-person canoe made of animal skins.

__Harpoons__ are spears with a long rope attached. They are used for spearing whales and other large sea animals.

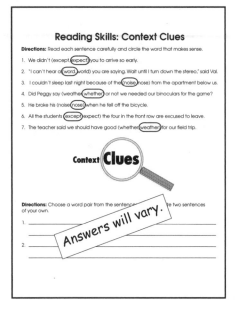

Page 63

Reading Skills: Context Clues

Directions: In each sentence below, circle the correct meaning for the nonsense word.

1. Be careful when you put that plate back on the shelf—it is **quibbable**.
   flexible   colorful   (**breakable**)

2. What is your favorite kind of **tonn**, pears or bananas?
   (**fruit**)   salad   purple

3. The **dinlay** outside this morning was very chilly; I needed my sweater.
   tree   vegetable   (**temperature**)

4. The whole class enjoyed the **weat**. They wanted to see it again next Friday.
   colorful   plant   (**video**)

5. Ashley's mother brought in a **zundy** she made by hand.
   temperature   (**quilt**)   plant

6. "Why don't you sit over here, Ronnie? That **sloey** is not very comfortable," said Mr. Gross.
   (**chair**)   car   cat

Page 64

Reading Skills: Sequencing

Directions: Read each set of events. Then number them in the correct order.

2 Get dressed for school and hurry downstairs for breakfast.
1 Roll over, sleepy-eyed, and turn off the alarm clock.
3 Meet your friends at the corner to walk to school.

3 The fourth-grade class walked quietly to a safe area away from the building.
2 The teacher reminded the last student to shut the classroom door.
1 The loud clanging of the fire alarm startled everyone in the room.

1 Barb's dad watched from the seat of the tractor as the boys and girls climbed into the wagon.
3 By the time they returned to the barn, there wasn't much straw left.
2 As the wagon bumped along the trail, the boys and girls sang songs they learned in music class.

3 The referee blew his whistle and held up the hand of the winner of the match.
2 Each wrestler worked hard, trying to outmaneuver his opponent.
1 The referee said, "Shake hands, boys, and wrestle a fair match."

Page 65

Reading Skills: Sequencing

Directions: In each group below, one event in the sequence is missing. Write the correct sentence from the box where it belongs.

- Paul put his bait on the hook and cast out into the pond.
- "Sorry," he said, "but the TV repairman can't get here until Friday."
- Everyone pitched in and helped.
- Corey put the ladder up against the trunk of the tree.

1. "All the housework has to be done before anyone goes to the game," said Mom.
2. __Everyone pitched in and helped.__
3. We all agreed that "many hands make light work."

1. __Paul put his bait on the hook and cast out into the pond.__
2. It wasn't long until he felt a tug on the line, and we watched the bobber go under.
3. He was the only one to go home with something other than bait!

1. The little girl cried as she stood looking up into the maple tree.
2. Between her tears, she managed to say, "My kitten is up in the tree and can't get down."
3. __Corey put the ladder up against the trunk of the tree.__

1. Dad hung up the phone and turned to look at us.
2. __"Sorry," he said, "but the TV repairman can't get here until Friday."__
3. "This would be a good time to get out those old board games in the hall closet," he said.

Page 66

Reading Skills: Sequencing

Directions: In each group below, one event in the sequence is missing. Write a sentence that makes sense in the sequence.

1. The clouds grew very dark and we could hear thunder.
2. All of a sudden, the wind started to blow very hard.
3. _____

1. The volleyball game was very boring at first.
2. _____
3. The b_____

Answers will vary.

1. _____
2. The boys gathered all the garden tools and put them in the wheelbarrow.
3. "Well, it was hard work, but we got it done, boys!" said Jim.

1. The teacher gave us our homework assignment early in the day.
2. Since the school assembly had to be cancelled, we had an extra study hall.
3. _____

1. Our cat has been acting very strange lately.
2. We heard unusual noises coming from the hall closet.
3. _____

Page 67

Reading Skills: Sequencing

Directions: Read about how a tadpole becomes a frog. Then number the stages in order below.

Frogs and toads belong to a group of animals called amphibians (am-FIB-ee-ans). This means "living a double life." Frogs and toads live a "double life" because they live part of their lives in water and part on land. They are able to do this because their bodies change as they grow. This series of changes is called metamorphosis (met-a-MORE-fa-sis).

A mother frog lays her eggs in water and then leaves them on their own to grow. The eggs contain cells—the tiny "building blocks" of all living things—that multiply and grow. Soon the cells grow into a swimming tadpole. Tadpoles breathe through gills—small holes in their sides—like fish do. They spend all of their time in the water.

The tadpole changes as it grows. Back legs slowly form. Front legs begin inside the tadpole under the gill holes. They pop out when they are fully developed. At the same time, lungs, which a frog uses to breathe instead of gills, are almost ready to be used.

As the tadpole reaches the last days of its life in the water, its tail seems to disappear. When all of the tadpole's body parts are ready for life on land, it has become a frog.

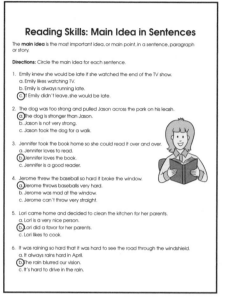

6	The front legs pop out. The lungs are ready to use for breathing.
2	The cells in the egg multiply and grow.
8	The tadpole has become a frog.
4	Back legs slowly form.
3	Soon the cells grow into a swimming tadpole.
5	Front legs develop inside the tadpole.
7	The tadpole's tail seems to disappear.
1	A mother frog lays her eggs in water.

Page 68

Reading Skills: Main Idea in Sentences

The **main idea** is the most important idea, or main point, in a sentence, paragraph or story.

Directions: Circle the main idea for each sentence.

1. Emily knew she would be late if she watched the end of the TV show.
   a. Emily likes watching TV.
   b. Emily is always running late.
   c. *If Emily didn't leave, she would be late.*

2. The dog was too strong and pulled Jason across the park on his leash.
   a. *The dog is stronger than Jason.*
   b. Jason is not very strong.
   c. Jason took the dog for a walk.

3. Jennifer took the book home so she could read it over and over.
   a. Jennifer loves to read.
   b. *Jennifer loves the book.*
   c. Jennifer is a good reader.

4. Jerome threw the baseball so hard it broke the window.
   a. *Jerome throws baseballs very hard.*
   b. Jerome was mad at the window.
   c. Jerome can't throw very straight.

5. Lori came home and decided to clean the kitchen for her parents.
   a. Lori is a very nice person.
   b. *Lori did a favor for her parents.*
   c. Lori likes to cook.

6. It was raining so hard that it was hard to see the road through the windshield.
   a. It always rains hard in April.
   b. *The rain blurred our vision.*
   c. It's hard to drive in the rain.

Page 69

Main Idea: Snow Fun

The **main idea** of a story or report is a sentence that summarizes the most important point. If a story or report is only one paragraph in length, then the main idea is usually stated in the first sentence (topic sentence). If it is longer than one paragraph, then the main idea is a general sentence including all the important points of the story or report.

Directions: Read the story about snow fun. Then draw an **X** in the blank for the main idea.

After a big snowfall, my friends and I enjoy playing in the snow. We bundle up in snow clothes at our homes, then meet with sleds at the hill by my house.

One by one, we take turns sledding down the hill to see who will go the farthest and the fastest. Sometimes we have a contest to see whose sled will reach the fence at the foot of the hill first.

When we tire of sledding, we may build a snowman or snowforts. Sometimes we have a friendly snowball fight.

The end of our snow fun comes too quickly, and we head home to warm houses, dry clothes and hot chocolate.

1. What is the main idea?
   ✓ Playing in the snow with friends is an enjoyable activity.
   ___ Sledding in the snow is fast and fun.

If you selected the first option, you are correct. The paragraphs discuss the enjoyable things friends do on a snowy day.

The second option is not correct because the entire story is not about sledding. Only the second paragraph discusses sledding. The other paragraphs discuss the additional ways friends have fun in the snow.

2. Write a paragraph about what you like to do on snowy days. Remember to make the first sentence your main idea.

_____**Paragraphs will vary.**_____

Page 70

Reading Skills: Main Idea in Paragraphs

Directions: Read each paragraph below. Then circle the sentence that tells the main idea.

It looked as if our class field day would have to be cancelled due to the weather. We tried not to show our disappointment, but Mr. Wade knew that it was hard to keep our minds on the math lesson. We noticed that even he had been sneaking glances out the window. All morning the classroom had been buzzing with plans. Each team met to plan team strategies for winning the events. Then, it happened! Clouds began to cover the sky, and soon the thunder and lightning confirmed what we were afraid of—field day was cancelled. Mr. Wade explained that we could still keep our same teams. We could put all of our plans into motion, but we would have to get busy and come up with some inside games and competitions. I guess the day would not be a total disaster!

a. Many storms occur in the late afternoon.

b. *Our class field day had to be cancelled due to the weather.*

c. Each team came up with its own strategies.

Allison and Emma had to work quietly and quickly to get Mom's birthday cake baked before she got home from work. Each of the girls had certain jobs to do—Allison set the oven temperature and got the cake pans prepared, while Emma got out all the ingredients. As they stirred and mixed, the two girls talked about the surprise party Dad had planned for Mom. Even Dad didn't know that the girls were baking this special cake. The cake was delicious. "It shows you what teamwork can do!" said the girls in unison.

a. Dad worked with the girls to bake the cake.

b. Mom's favorite frosting is chocolate cream.

c. *Allison and Emma baked a birthday cake for Mom.*

Page 71

Main Idea: Busy Beavers

Directions: Read about busy beavers. Then answer the questions.

Has anyone ever told you that you are as busy as a beaver? If they have, then they mean that you are very busy. Beavers swim easily in streams, picking up rocks and sticks to build their dams. They gnaw at trees with their big front teeth to cut them down. Then they use parts of the trees to build their houses.

Beavers are clever builders. They know exactly what they need to build their beaver dams. They use mud from the stream to make their dams stay together. They use their tails to pat down the mud.

Beavers put a snug room at the top of their dams for their babies. They store their food underwater. Beavers eat the bark from the trees that they cut down!

1. What is the main idea of the first paragraph? _**Beavers are very busy.**_

2. What is the main idea of the second paragraph? _**Beavers are clever builders.**_

3. What is the main idea of the third paragraph? _**Beavers' homes provide a snug place for their babies and a place to store food.**_

4. What do beavers use for their dams? _**sticks, rocks, trees and mud**_

5. What parts of their bodies do beavers use to build their homes? _**They use their teeth to cut down trees and their tails to pat down mud.**_

Page 72

Main Idea: Bats

Directions: Read about bats. Then answer the questions.

Bats are unusual animals. Even though they fly, they are not birds. A bat's body is covered with fur. Its wings are made of skin. Bats do not have any feathers.

Bats are the only mammals that fly. A mammal is an animal that has hair and feeds its babies with its own milk. Humans are mammals, too. Mother bats have one or two babies each spring. Baby bats hang onto their mothers until they learn to fly by themselves.

Bats can be many different colors. Most are brown, but some are black, orange, gray or even green.

Even though many people do not like bats, bats don't usually bother people. Only vampire bats, which live in hot jungles, are very dangerous. Bats in the United States help people. Every year they eat billions and billions of harmful insects! Some bats also eat fruit or pollen from flowers.

1. What is the main idea?
   ___ Bats are mammals.
   ✓ Bats are unusual animals.
   ___ Some people are afraid of bats.

2. What covers a bat's body? __fur__

3. How do bats in the United States help people? __They eat billions of__ __harmful insects.__

Directions: Read the clues. Find the answers in the story.

Across:
2. Vampire bats live in hot ____.
4. What do bats eat?
5. Most bats are what color?

Down:
1. Bats are not ____.
3. What are bats' wings made of?

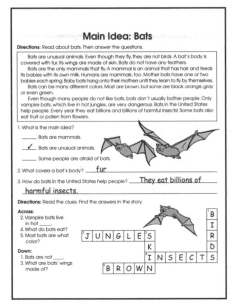

J U N G L E S
I N S E C T S
B R O W N
B I R D S K I N

Page 73

Recognizing Details

The main idea of a paragraph or story is supported by **details**. Details tell the who, what, when, where, why and how of a story or report. Recognizing details can help you remember what you have read.

Directions: Reread "Snow Fun." Then write two detail sentences that support the main idea.

Directions: Reread the article on beavers. Then write two detail sentences that support the main idea.

Directions: Reread the ... write two detail sentences that support the main idea.

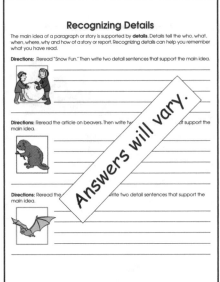

Answers will vary.

Page 74

Recognizing Details: Blind Bats

Directions: Read about bats. Then answer the questions.

Bats sleep all day because they cannot see well in the bright sunlight. They hang upside down in dark places such as barns, caves or hollow trees. As soon as darkness begins to fall, bats wake up. They fly around easily and quickly at night.

Bats make sounds that help them fly, since they cannot see well. People cannot hear these sounds. When bats make sounds, the sounds hit objects in front of them and bounce back at them. Bats can tell if something is in their way because there is an echo. Some people say this is like a radar system!

There are many different kinds of bats. Some bats fly all night, while others fly only in the evening or the early morning.

Most bats eat mosquitoes and moths, but there are some bats that will catch fish swimming in water and eat them. Still other kinds of bats eat birds or mice. Bats that live in very hot areas eat only some parts of flowers.

Bats that live in cold areas of the country sometimes sleep all winter. That means they hibernate. Other bats that live in cold areas fly to warmer places for the winter. We call this migration.

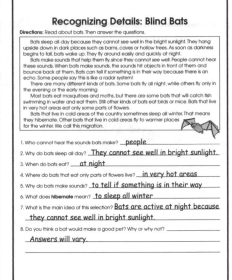

1. Who cannot hear the sounds bats make? __people__

2. Why do bats sleep all day? __They cannot see well in bright sunlight.__

3. When do bats eat? __at night__

4. Where do bats that eat only parts of flowers live? __in very hot areas__

5. Why do bats make sounds? __to tell if something is in their way__

6. What does **hibernate** mean? __to sleep all winter__

7. What is the main idea of this selection? __Bats are active at night because__ __they cannot see well in bright sunlight.__

8. Do you think a bat would make a good pet? Why or why not? ____ __Answers will vary.__

Page 77

Reading Skills: Sequencing

Directions: Reread the story, if necessary. Then choose an important event from the beginning, middle and end of the story, and write it below.

Beginning: ____

Middle: ____

End: ____

Answers will vary.

Directions: Number these story events in the order in which they happened.

__4__ Paul moaned, "Oh, no! I left my lunch on the table at home!"

__1__ Megan watched as the bus stopped at Emily's house to pick up Emily and her little sister.

__5__ Miss Haynes sent Paul to the cafeteria with a note explaining the problem.

__3__ The teacher said they had some business to take care of before they could leave on the trip.

__6__ Paul quickly returned with a sack lunch packed by the cafeteria helpers.

__2__ Megan told Emily, "I see you remembered your sack lunch."

__7__ The fourth graders finally loaded onto the bus for the field trip.

Page 78

Reading Skills: Recalling Details

Directions: Answer the questions below about "Class Field Trip."

1. Who were the two adult helpers that would be going on the trip with Miss Haynes' class? __Ms. Diehl and Mrs. Denes__

2. The students in Miss Haynes' class were excited about the field trip for different reasons. What were the three different reasons mentioned in the story?
   a. __They got to ride the bus.__
   b. __They enjoyed learning about their town's history.__
   c. __They got a day out of school.__

3. What business did Miss Haynes need to take care of before the class could leave on its trip? __Check attendance and pass out name tags.__

Directions: Write the letter of the definition beside the word it defines. If you need help, use a dictionary or check the context of the story.

a. sat down, not very gently
b. easy to understand; without doubt
c. family members that lived in the past, such as grandparents
d. in a favorable way

__C__ ancestors
__D__ fortunately
__A__ plopped
__B__ obviously

Page 81

Reading Skills: Sequencing

Directions: Reread the story, if necessary. Then choose an important event from the beginning, middle and end of the story, and write it below.

Beginning: ____

Middle: ____

End: ____

Answers will vary.

Directions: Number these story events in the order in which they happened.

__3__ Jonny's mom called the doctor to get an appointment since Jonny's ankle was red and swollen.

__1__ Jonny limped to the top of the stairs.

__6__ The pediatrician thought Jonny might have JRA.

__4__ The sitter told Jonny's mom that he had slept most of the day.

__5__ The doctor gave them a prescription for an antibiotic.

__7__ Jonny is now 29 years old.

__2__ Jonny told his mom, "My leg hurts."

Page 82

Reading Skills: Recalling Details

Directions: Answer the questions below about "Jonny's Story."

1. How old was Jonny when his ankle began to bother him? __3 1/2 years__

2. Why did Jonny's mom stay home from work the second day? __Because Jonny was feeling worse.__

3. What do the letters JRA stand for? __juvenile rheumatoid arthritis__

4. When Jonny and his mom were waiting to see the doctor, how did Jonny's mom know he must not be feeling well? __Because he slept the whole time.__

5. Where did Jonny's mom take him when she picked him up at the sitter's house? __to the doctor's office.__

Directions: Write the letter of the definition beside the word it defines. If you need help, use a dictionary or check the context of the story.

a. strong medicine used to treat infections
b. found to be true
c. doctor that specializes in child care
d. not yet an adult
e. did not walk correctly

__C__ pediatrician
__A__ antibiotic
__B__ confirmed
__E__ limped
__D__ juvenile

Page 84

Comprehension: "The Princess and the Pea"

Fairy tales are short stories written for children involving magical characters.

Directions: Read the story. Then answer the questions.

Once there was a prince who wanted to get married. The catch was, he had to marry a *real* princess. The Prince knew that real princesses were few and far between. When they heard he was looking for a bride, many young women came to the palace. All claimed to be real princesses.

"Hmmm," thought the Prince. "I must think of a way to sort out the real princesses from the fake ones. I will ask the Queen for advice."

Luckily, since he was a prince, the Queen was also his mother. So of course she had her son's best interests at heart. "A real princess is very delicate," said the Queen. "She must sleep on a mattress as soft as a cloud. If there is even a small lump, she will not be able to sleep."

"Why not?" asked the Prince. He was a nice man but not as smart as his mother.

"Because she is so delicate!" said the Queen impatiently. "Let's figure out a way to test her. Better still, let me figure out a test. You go down and pick a girl to try out my plan."

The Prince went down to the lobby of the castle. A very pretty but humble-looking girl caught his eye. He brought her back to his mother, who welcomed her.

"Please be our guest at the castle tonight," said the Queen. "Tomorrow we will talk with you about whether you are a real princess."

The pretty but humble girl was shown to her room. In it was a pile of five mattresses, all fluffy and clean. "A princess is delicate," said the Queen. "Sweet dreams!"

The girl climbed to the top of the pile and laid down, but she could not sleep. She tossed and turned and was quite cross that morning.

"I found this under the fourth mattress when I got up this morning," she said. She handed a small green pea to the Queen. "No wonder I couldn't sleep!"

The Queen clapped her hands. The Prince looked confused. "A real princess is delicate. If this pea I put under the mattress kept you awake, you are definitely a princess."

"Of course I am," said the Princess. "Now may I please take a nap?"

1. Why does the Prince worry about finding a bride? __His bride must be a real princess and real princesses are hard to find.__

2. According to the Queen, how can the Prince tell who is a real princess? __A real princess is very delicate.__

3. Who hides something under the girl's mattress? __the Queen__

Page 85

Comprehension: "The Princess and the Pea"

Directions: Review the story "The Princess and the Pea." Then answer the questions.

1. Why does the Prince need a test to see who is a real princess? __Many young women wanted to marry him, but the Prince could only marry a "real" princess.__

2. Why does the Princess have trouble sleeping? __There was a pea under her mattress.__

3. In this story, the Queen puts a small pea under a pile of mattresses to see if the girl is delicate. What else could be done to test a princess for delicacy?

The story does not tell whether or not the Prince and live happily ever after, only that the Pr

Directions: Write a new ending to the

4. What do you think happens aft

Answers will vary.

Page 86

Comprehension: "The Frog Prince"

Directions: Read the story "The Frog Prince." Then answer the questions.

Once upon a time, there lived a beautiful princess who liked to play alone in the woods. One day, as she was playing with her golden ball, it rolled into a lake. The water was so deep she could not see the ball. The Princess was very sad. She cried out, "I would give anything to have my golden ball back!"

Suddenly, a large ugly frog popped out of the water. "Anything?" he croaked. The Princess looked at him with distaste. "Yes," she said, "I would give anything."

"I will get your golden ball," said the frog. "In return, you must take me back to the castle. You must let me live with you and eat from your golden plate."

"Whatever you want," said the Princess. She thought the frog was very ugly, but she wanted her golden ball.

The frog dove down and brought the ball to the Princess. She put the frog in her pocket and took him home. "He is ugly," the Princess said. "But a promise is a promise. And a princess always keeps her word."

The Princess changed her clothes and forgot all about the frog. That evening, she heard a tapping at her door. She ran to the door to open it and a handsome prince stepped in. "Who are you?" asked the Princess, already half in love.

"I am the prince you rescued at the lake," said the handsome Prince. "I was turned into a frog one hundred years ago today by a wicked lady. Because they always keep their promises, only a beautiful princess could break the spell. You are a little forgetful, but you did keep your word!"

Can you guess what happened next? Of course, they were married and lived happily ever after.

1. What does the frog ask the Princess to promise? __to take him back to the castle, let him live with her and eat from her golden plate.__

2. Where does the Princess put the frog when she leaves the lake? __in her pocket__

3. Why could only a princess break the spell? __Because they always keep their promises.__

Page 87

Comprehension: "The Frog Prince"

Directions: Review the story "The Frog Prince." Then answer the questions.

1. What does the Princess lose in the lake? __a golden ball__

2. How does she get it back? __A frog dove to the bottom of the lake and got it for her in return for a promise from the Princess.__

3. How does the frog turn back into a prince? __The spell is broken when the Princess keeps her word.__

4. What phrases are used to begin and end this story? __"once upon a time" and "happily ever after"__

5. Are these words used frequently to begin and end fairy tales? __yes__

There is more than one version of most fairy tales. In another version of this story, the Princess has to kiss the frog in order for him to change back into a prince.

Directions: Write your answers.

6. What do you think would happen in a story Princess kisses the frog, but he remains a

7. What kinds of problems with a bossy frog in the castle? Brainstorm ideas and write the

8. Rewrite the Frog Prince" so that the frog remains a frog and does not tur into a handso ce. Continue your story on another sheet of paper.

Answers will vary.

Page 88

Review

Directions: Think of fairy tales you know from books or videos, like "Cinderella," "Snow White," "Sleeping Beauty," "Rapunzel" and "Beauty and the Beast." Then answer the questions.

1. What are some common elements in all fairy tales? __Answers may include: a hero or heroine, a villain, a problem, a happy ending__

2. How do fairy tales usually begin? __"Once upon a time"__

3. How do fairy tales usually end? __with a happy ending__

Directions: Locate and read several different versions of the same fairy tale. For example, "Cinderella," "Princess Furball," "Cinderlad" and "Yah Shen." Then ans r the questions.

4. How are the stories alike? _____

5. How are they different? _____

6. Which s y the author? _____

7. Which st est? Why? _____

Answers will vary.

Page 89

Review

Most of us have read many fairy tales and have seen them in movies. Fairy tales have a certain style and format they usually follow.

Directions: Use another sheet of paper to write another fairy tale. Use the following questions to help you brainstorm ideas.

1. What is the name of the kingdom?

2. What is the size of the kingdom, its climate, trees, plants, animals, etc.?

3. What kind of magic happens there?

4. Who are the characters?
   Good guys _____ Bad guys

5. What does each char_____

6. What kind of _____ cular character and why?

7. What happens to the good characters and the bad characters in the end?

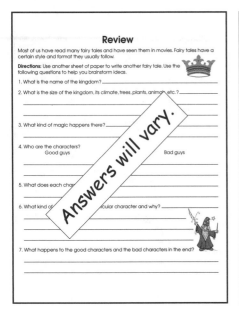

Answers will vary.

Page 90

Main Idea: "The Hare and the Tortoise"

The story of "The Hare and the Tortoise" is called a **fable.** Fables are usually short stories. As you read this story and the other fables on the next few pages, look for two characteristics the fables have in common.

Directions: Read the fable "The Hare and the Tortoise." Then answer the questions.

One day the hare and the tortoise were talking. Or rather, the hare was bragging and the tortoise was listening.

"I am faster than the wind," bragged the hare. "I feel sorry for you because you are so slow! Why, you are the slowest fellow I have ever seen."

"Do you think so?" asked the tortoise with a smile. "I will race you to that big tree across the field."

Slowly, he lifted a leg. Slowly, he pointed toward the tree.

"Ha!" scoffed the hare. "You must be kidding! You will most certainly be the loser! But, if you insist, we will race."

The tortoise nodded politely. "I'll be off," he said. Slowly and steadily, the tortoise moved across the field.

The hare stood back and laughed. "How sad that he should compete with me!" he said. His chest puffed up with pride. "I will take a little nap while the poor old tortoise lumbers along. When I wake up, he will still be only halfway across the field."

The tortoise kept on, slow and steady, across the field. Some time later, the hare awoke. He discovered that while he slept, the tortoise had won the race.

1. What is the main idea? (Check one.)

   _____ Tortoises are faster than hares.

   _____ Hares need more sleep than tortoises.

   ✓ Slow and steady wins the race.

2. The hare brags that he is faster than what? (Check one.)

   _____ a bullet

   _____ a greyhound

   ✓ the wind

3. Who is modest, the tortoise or the hare? _____ the tortoise

Page 91

Cause and Effect: "The Hare and the Tortoise"

Another important skill in reading is recognizing cause and effect. The **cause** is the reason something happens. The **effect** is what happens or the situation that results from the cause. In the story, the hare falling asleep is a cause. It causes the hare to lose the race. Losing the race is the effect.

Directions: Identify the underlined words or phrases by writing **cause** or **effect** in the blanks.

1. The hare and tortoise had a race because the hare bragged about being faster. _____ effect

2. The tortoise won the race because he continued on, slowly but steadily. _____ cause

Directions: Review the fable "The Hare and the Tortoise." Then answer the questions.

1. Who are the two main characters? _____ hare and tortoise

2. Where does the story take place? _____ in a field with trees

3. What lessons can be learned from this story? _____ slow and steady wins the race, people shouldn't brag

4. The lesson that is learned at the end of a fable has a special name. What is that special name? _____ moral

5. Why did the tortoise want to race the hare? _____ to prove that he could beat the hare

6. How do you think the hare felt at the end of the story?

7. How do you think the tortoise felt at the e_____

Answers will vary.

Page 92

Sequencing: "The Fox and the Crow"

Directions: Read the fable "The Fox and the Crow." Then number the events in order.

Once upon a time, a crow found a piece of cheese on the ground. "Aha!" he said to himself. "This dropped from a workman's sandwich. It will make a fine lunch for me."

The crow picked up the cheese in his beak. He flew to a tree to eat it. Just as he began to chew it, a fox trotted by.

"Hello, crow!" he said slyly, for he wanted the cheese. The fox knew if the crow answered, the cheese would fall from its mouth. Then the fox would have cheese for lunch!

The crow just nodded.

"It's a wonderful day, isn't it?" asked the fox.

The crow nodded again and held onto the cheese.

"You are the most beautiful bird I have ever seen," added the fox.

The crow spread his feathers. Everyone likes a compliment. Still, the crow held firmly to the cheese.

"There is something I have heard," said the fox, "and I wonder if it is true. I heard that you sing more sweetly than any of the other birds."

The crow was eager to show off his talents. He opened his beak to sing. The cheese dropped to the ground.

"I said you were beautiful," said the fox as he ran away with the cheese. "I did not say you were smart!"

   _7_ The crow drops the cheese.

   _3_ The crow flies to a tree with the cheese.

   _5_ The fox tells the crow he is beautiful.

   _8_ The fox runs off with the cheese.

   _1_ A workman loses the cheese from his sandwich.

   _4_ The fox comes along.

   _6_ The fox tells the crow he has heard that crows sing beautifully.

   _2_ The crow picks up the cheese.

Page 93

Predicting: "The Fox and the Crow"

Directions: Review the fable "The Fox and the Crow." Then answer the questions.

1. With what words does the story begin? _____ "Once upon a time"

2. What other type of story often begins with these same words? _____ fairy tales

3. Although it is not stated, where do you think the story takes place? _____ in a woods or forest

4. How does the fox get what he wants from the crow? _____ The fox appealed to the crow's vanity by saying he heard that crows sing beautifully.

5. How is the crow in this story like the hare in the last fable? _____ They are both proud, and when they bragged and tried to show off, they lost.

Predicting is telling or guessing what you think might happen in a story or situation based on what you already know.

Directions: Write predictions to answer these questions.

6. Based on what you read, what do you think the crow will do the next time he finds a piece of cheese?

7. What do you think the fox w_____ wants to trick the crow? _____

Answers will vary.

Page 94

Following Directions: "The Boy Who Cried Wolf"

Directions: Read the fable "The Boy Who Cried Wolf." Then complete the puzzle.

Once there was a shepherd boy who tended his sheep alone. Sheep are gentle animals. They are easy to take care of. The boy grew bored.

"I can't stand another minute alone with these sheep," he said crossly. He knew only one thing would bring people quickly to him. If he cried, "Wolf!" the men in the village would run up the mountain. They would come to help save the sheep from the wolf.

"Wolf!" he yelled loudly, and he blew on his horn.

Quick as a wink, a dozen men came running. When they realized it was a joke, they were very angry. The boy promised never to do it again. But a week later, he grew bored and cried, "Wolf!" again. Again, the men ran to him. This time they were very, very angry. Soon afterwards, a wolf really came. The boy was scared. "Wolf!" he cried. "Wolf! Wolf! Wolf!"

He blew his horn, but no one came, and the wolf ate all his sheep.

Crossword puzzle answers:
- M O U N T A I N
- V I L L A G E
- S C A R E D
- A T E
- G E N T L E
- M E N

Across:
2. This is where the boy tends sheep.
4. When no one came, the wolf _____ all the sheep.
5. Sheep are _____ and easy to take care of.

Down:
1. The people who come are from here.
2. At first, when the boy cries, "Wolf!" the _____ come running.
3. When a wolf really comes, this is how the boy feels.

Page 95

Cause and Effect: "The Boy Who Cried Wolf"

Directions: Identify the underlined words as a cause or an effect.

1. The boy cries wolf because he is bored. _____effect_____
2. The boy blows his horn and the men come running. _____effect_____
3. No one comes, and the wolf eats all the sheep. _____effect_____

Directions: Answer the questions.

4. What lesson can be learned from this story? **Sample answer:**
   Always tell the truth.

5. How is this story like the two other fables you read?

6. Is the boy in the story more like the fox

Answers will vary.

Page 96

Comprehension: "The City Mouse and the Country Mouse"

Directions: Read the fable "The City Mouse and the Country Mouse." Then answer the questions.

Once there were two mice, a city mouse and a country mouse. They were cousins. The country mouse was always begging his cousin to visit him. Finally, the city mouse agreed.

When he arrived, the city mouse was not very polite. "How do you stand it here?" he asked, wrinkling his nose. "All you have to eat is corn and barley. All you have to wear is old, tattered work clothes. And all you have to listen to are the other animals. Why don't you come and visit me? Then you will see what it's like to really live!"

The country mouse liked corn and barley. He liked the sounds of the other animals. And he liked his old work clothes fine. Secretly, he thought his cousin was silly to wear fancy clothes. Still, the city sounded exciting. Why not give it a try?

Since he had no clothes to pack, the country mouse was ready in no time. His cousin told him stories about the city as they traveled. The buildings were so high! The food was so good! The girl mice were so beautiful!

The home of the city mouse was nice. He lived in a hole in the wall in an old castle. "It is only a hole in the wall," said the city mouse, "but it is a very nice wall, indeed!"

That night, the mice crept out of the wall. Everyone had eaten, but the maid had not cleaned up. The table was still loaded with good food. The mice ate and ate. The country mouse was not used to rich food. He began to feel sick to his stomach.

Just then, they heard loud barking. Two huge dogs ran into the room. They nearly bit off the country mouse's tail! He barely made it to the hole in the wall in time. That did it!

"Thank you for showing me the city," said the country mouse, "but it is too exciting for me. I am going home where it is peaceful. I can't wait to settle my stomach with some corn and barley."

1. What are three things the city mouse says are wrong with the country? _____
   no good food, old clothes to wear, animal noises

2. Why doesn't it take the country mouse long to get ready to leave with the city mouse?
   He has no clothes to pack.

3. Why does the country mouse secretly think his cousin is silly? **because he wears**
   fancy clothes

Page 97

Sequencing: "The City Mouse and the Country Mouse"

Directions: Review the fable "The City Mouse and the Country Mouse." Use the Venn diagram to compare and contrast the lifestyles of the city mouse and the country mouse.

City Mouse — Both — Country Mouse

Answers will vary.

Directions: Write five _____ the story, in order.

Directions: Answer these questions about the fable.

1. How do the two mice feel about each other? **They do not understand**
   each other's way of life.

2. Which mouse do you think is most like the hare? Why? _____Answers will vary._____

Page 98

Sequencing: "The Man and the Snake"

Directions: Read the fable "The Man and the Snake." Then number the events in order.

Once, a kind man saw a snake in the road. It was winter and the poor snake was nearly frozen. The man began to walk away, but he could not.

"The snake is one of Earth's creatures, too," he said. He picked up the snake and put it in a sack. "I will take it home to warm up by my fire. Then I will set it free."

The man stopped for lunch at a village inn. He put his coat and his sack on a bench by the fireplace. He planned to sit nearby, but the inn was crowded, so he had to sit across the room.

He soon forgot about the snake. As he was eating his soup, he heard screams. Warmed by the fire, the snake had crawled from the bag. It hissed at the people near the fire.

The man jumped up and ran to the fireplace. "Is this how you repay the kindness of others?" he shouted.

He grabbed a stick used for stirring the fire and chased the snake out of the inn.

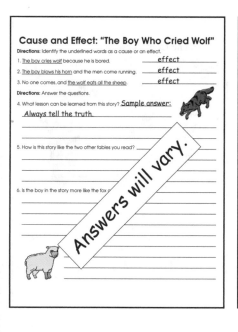

_4_ The man puts his bag down by the fireplace.
_9_ The man chases the snake.
_2_ A kind man rescues the snake.
_6_ The snake warms up and crawls out of the bag.
_3_ The man plans to take the snake home.
_5_ The man eats a bowl of soup.
_7_ The snake hisses at people.
_1_ A snake is nearly frozen in a road.
_8_ The man grabs a stick from the fireplace.

Page 99

Sequencing: "The Wind and the Sun"

Directions: Read the fable "The Wind and the Sun." Then number the events in order.

One day, North Wind and Sun began to argue about who was stronger.

"I am stronger," declared North Wind.

"No," said Sun. "I am much stronger than you."

They argued for three days and three nights.

Finally, Sun said, "I know how we can settle the argument. See that traveler walking down the road? Whoever can make him take off his cloak first is the stronger. Do you agree?"

North Wind agreed. He wanted to try first. He blew and blew. The traveler shivered and pulled his cloak tightly around his body. North Wind sent a blast of wind so strong it almost pulled the cloak off the traveler, but the traveler only held tighter to his cloak.

Then it was Sun's turn. When Sun sent gentle, warm sunbeams, the traveler loosened his cloak. Then Sun sent his warmest beams to the traveler. After a short time, the traveler became so warm he threw off his cloak and ran to the shade of the nearest tree.

_4_ Sun sent warm beams to the traveler.
_1_ Sun and North Wind argued.
_5_ The traveler threw off his cloak and ran to the shade.
_3_ The traveler pulled his cloak tightly around his body.
_2_ North Wind blew cold air on the traveler.

Directions: Answer the questions. (Check one.)

What is the moral of this fable?

_____ Sun is stronger than North Wind.
_____ North Wind is cold.
_✓_ A kind and gentle manner works better than force.
_____ Travelers should hold on to their cloaks when the wind blows.
_____ Stay out of arguments between Sun and North Wind.

Who do you think is stronger, North Wind or Sun? Why? _____Answers will vary._____

Page 100

Review

At the beginning of the section on fables, you were asked to discover two elements common to the fables.

Directions: Review the fables you read. Then answer the questions.

1. What are the two elements common to fables? **Main characters are often**
   animals that talk and act like people. Stories teach a
   lesson.

2. Each fable has a "moral" or lesson to be learned. What is the moral of each of the fables?

   "The Hare and the Tortoise" _____
   "The Fox and the Crow" _____
   "The Boy Who Cried Wolf" _____
   "The City Mouse and the Country _____
   "The Man and the Snake" _____

   Answers will vary.

3. How do the titles of the fables give clues to what or who the fables were about?
   The titles name the main characters.

4. For each fable, write the character you think is the good character and the one you think is the bad character.

	"Good character"	"Bad character"
"The Hare and the Tortoise"		
"The Fox and the Crow"		
"The Wind and the Sun"		
"The City Mouse and the Country Mouse"		
"The Man and the Snake"		

   Answers will vary.

Page 101

Fable Writing Organizer

Fables are short stories with animals as the main characters. Each story teaches a lesson.

Directions: Select one of the following pairs of animals as characters to use for a fable of your own.

A pig and an ox   An ant and a frog   A cat and a monkey
A fly and a butterfly   A spider and a bear   A goose and a deer
A snail and a lion   A horse and a dog   A T-Rex and a shark

Directions: Fill in the outline below with words and phrases to organize a fable of your own.

Animal pair

Type of conflict between the animals

How the conflict is settled

Moral of the story

Directions: Write *Answers will vary.* a title. Illustrate it if you like.

Page 102

Reading Comprehension: Paul Bunyan

There is a certain kind of fable called a "tall tale." In these stories, each storyteller tries to "top" the other. The stories get more and more unbelievable. A popular hero of American tall tales is Paul Bunyan—a giant of a man. Here are some of the stories that have been told about him.

Even as a baby, Paul was very big. One night, he rolled over in his sleep and knocked down a mile of trees. Of course, Paul's father wanted to find some way to keep Paul from getting hurt in his sleep and to keep him from knocking down all the forests. So he cut down some tall trees and made a boat for Paul to use as a cradle. He tied a long rope to the boat and let it drift out a little way into the sea to rock Paul to sleep.

One night, Paul had trouble sleeping. He kept turning over in his bed. Each time he turned, the cradle rocked. And each time the cradle rocked, it sent up waves as big as buildings. The waves got bigger and bigger until the people on the land were afraid they would all be drowned. They told Paul's parents that Paul was a danger to the whole state! So Paul and his parents had to move away.

After that, Paul didn't get into much trouble when he was growing up. His father taught him some very important lessons, such as, "If there are any towns or farms in your way, be sure to step around them!"

Directions: Answer these questions about Paul Bunyan.

1. What kind of fable is the story of Paul Bunyan? _____ tall tale
2. What did Paul's father make for Paul to use as a cradle? _____ boat
3. What happened when Paul rolled over in his cradle? _____ He made waves as big as buildings.
4. What did Paul's father tell Paul to do to towns and farms that were in his way?
   Step around them!

Page 103

Reading Comprehension: Paul Bunyan

When Paul Bunyan grew up, he was taller than other men—by about 50 feet or so! Because of his size, he could do almost anything. One of the things he did best was to cut down trees and turn them into lumber. With only four strokes of his axe, he could cut off all the branches and bark. After he turned all the trees for miles into these tall square posts, he tied a long rope to an axe head. Then he yelled, "T-I-M-B-E-R-R-R!" and swung the rope around in a huge circle. With every swing, 100 trees fell to the ground.

One cold winter day, Paul found a huge blue ox stuck in the snow. It was nearly frozen. Although it was only a baby, even Paul could hardly lift it. Paul took the ox home and cared for it. He named it Babe, and they became best friends. Babe was a big help to Paul when he was cutting down trees.

When Babe was full grown, it was hard to tell how big he was. There were no scales big enough to weigh him. Paul once measured the distance between Babe's eyes. It was the length of 42 axe handles!

Once Paul and Babe were working with other men to cut lumber. The job was very hard because the road was so long and winding. It was said that the road was so crooked that men starting home for camp would meet themselves coming back! Well, Paul hitched Babe to the end of that crooked road. Babe pulled and pulled. He pulled so hard that his eyes nearly turned pink. There was a loud snap. The first curve came out of the road and Babe pulled harder. Finally the whole road started to move. Babe pulled it completely straight!

Directions: Answer these questions about Paul Bunyan and Babe.

1. What was Paul Bunyan particularly good at doing? _____ Cutting down trees
2. What did Paul find in the snow? _____ a huge blue ox
3. How big was the distance between Babe's eyes? _____ 42 axe handles
4. What did Babe do to the crooked road? _____ He pulled it completely straight.

Page 104

Reading Comprehension: Mermaids

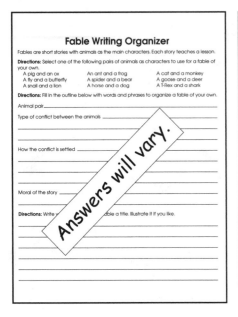

One of the most popular fantasy characters is the mermaid. Many different countries have stories about these lovely creatures. In these fables, the mermaid is always beautiful—except perhaps for her greenish skin and webbed fingers!

There are some stories about mermen, too. They are said to have fine torsos with big, strong muscles in their chests and arms. But they have the most ugly faces—eyes like a pig, red noses, green teeth and seaweed hair!

A famous fable told in Ireland tells about a mermaid who was said to have been seen nearly 1,400 years ago. The story says that she could be heard singing beneath the waters for many years. One day, some men rowed out and caught her with a net. They were surprised to learn that she had once been a little human girl. Her family had died in a flood. But she survived beneath the waves and gradually changed into a mermaid.

Directions: Answer these questions about the story.

1. Which definition is correct for **fantasy**?
   ☒ from the imagination and not real   ☐ real   ☐ living in the sea
2. Which definition is correct for **fable**?
   ☐ a true story   ☒ a made-up story   ☐ a story about fish
3. Which definition is correct for **torso**?
   ☐ the head   ☒ the upper body but not the head   ☐ the lower body
4. Which definition is correct for **survived**?
   ☐ swam   ☐ died   ☒ continued to live

Page 106

Sequencing: Kanati's Son

A **legend** is a story or group of stories handed down through generations. Legends are usually about an actual person.

Directions: Read about Kanati's son. Then number the events in order.

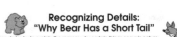

This legend is told by a tribe called the Cherokee (chair-oh-key). Long ago, soon after the world was made, a hunter and his wife lived on a big mountain with their son. The father's name was Kanati (kah-na-tee), which means "lucky hunter." The mother's name was Selu (see-loo), which means "corn." No one remembers the son's name.

The little boy used to play alone by the river each day. One day, elders of the tribe told the boy's parents they'd heard two children playing. Since their son was the only child around, the parents were puzzled. They told their son what the elders had said.

"I do have a playmate," the boy said. "He comes out of the water. He says he is the brother that mother threw in the river."

Then Selu knew what had happened.

"He is formed from the blood of the animals I washed in the river," she told Kanati. "After you kill them, I wash them in the river before I cook them."

Here is what Kanati told his boy: "Tomorrow when the other boy comes, wrestle with him. Hold him to the ground and call for us."

The boy did as his parents told him. When he called, they came running and grabbed the wild boy. They took him home and tried to tame him. The boy grew up with magic powers. The Cherokee called this "adawehi" (ad-da-we-hi). He was always getting into mischief! But he saved himself with his magic.

5 _____ Selu and Kanati try to tame the boy from the river.
3 _____ The little boy tells Selu and Kanati about the other boy.
2 _____ The little boy's parents are puzzled.
6 _____ The new boy grows up with magic powers.
1 _____ The elders tell Selu and Kanati they heard two children playing.
4 _____ The little boy wrestles his new playmate to the ground.

Page 107

Recognizing Details: "Why Bear Has a Short Tail"

Some stories try to explain the reasons why certain things occur in nature.

Directions: Read the legend "Why Bear Has a Short Tail." Then answer the questions.

Long ago, Bear had a long tail like Fox. One winter day, Bear met Fox coming out of the woods. Fox was carrying a long string of fish. He had stolen the fish, but that is not what he told Bear.

"Where did you get those fish?" asked Bear, rubbing his paws together. Bear loved fish. It was his favorite food.

"I was out fishing and caught them," replied Fox.

Bear did not know how to fish. He had only tasted fish that others gave him. He was eager to learn to catch his own.

"Please Fox, will you tell me how to fish?" asked Bear.

So, the mean old Fox said to Bear, "Cut a hole in the ice and stick your tail in the hole. It will get cold, but soon the fish will begin to bite. When you can stand it no longer, pull your tail out. It will be covered with fish!"

"Will it hurt?" asked Bear, patting his tail.

"It will hurt some," admitted Fox. "But the longer you leave your tail in the water, the more fish you will catch."

Bear did as his instructions told him. He loved fish, so he left his tail in the icy water a very, very long time. The ice froze around Bear's tail. When he pulled free, his tail remained stuck in the ice. That is why bears today have short tails.

1. How does Fox get his string of fish? _____ He stole it.
2. What does he tell Bear to do? _____ to put his tail in a hole in the ice to catch fish
3. Why does Bear do as Fox told him? _____ He loves to eat fish but doesn't know how to catch them.
4. How many fish does Bear catch? _____ none
5. What happens when Bear tries to pull his tail out? _____ His tail remains stuck in the ice.

Page 108

Recognizing Details: "Why Bear Has a Short Tail"

Directions: Review the legend "Why Bear Has a Short Tail." Then answer the questions.

1. When Bear asks Fox where he got his fish, is Fox truthful in his response? Why or why not?
   No. Fox lies to trick Bear.

2. Why does Bear want to know how to fish? He loves to eat fish. It is his favorite food.

3. In reality, are bears able to catch their own fish? How? Yes, with their paws.

4. Is Bear very smart to believe Fox? Why or why not? No. Bear should have known Fox was sly and tricky.

5. How would you have told Bear to catch his own fish? Answers will vary.

6. What is one word you would use to describe Fox? sly, tricky, crafty
   Explain your answer. Answers will vary.

7. What is one word you would use to describe Bear? silly, trusting
   Explain your answer. Answers will vary.

8. Is this story realistic? No.

9. Could it have really happened? Explain your answer. Answers will vary.

Page 109

Predicting: "How the Donkey Got Long Ears"

Directions: Write your predictions to answer these questions.

1. How do you think animals got their names?

2. Why would it be confusing if anima...

Answers will vary.

Directions: Read the legend "How the Donkey Got Long Ears." Then answer the questions.

In the beginning when the world was young, animals had no names. It was very confusing! A woman would say, "Tell the thingamajig to bring in the paper." The man would say, "What thingamajig?" She was talking about the dog, of course, but the man didn't know that.

Together, they decided to name the animals on their farm. First, they named their pet thingamajig Dog. They named the pink thingamajig that oinked Pig. They named the red thingamajig that crowed Rooster. They named the white thingamajig that laid eggs Hen. They named the little yellow thingamajigs that cheeped Chicks. They named the big brown thingamajig they rode Horse.

Then they came to another thingamajig. It looked like Horse, but was smaller. It would be confusing to call the smaller thingamajig Horse, they decided.

"Let's name it Donkey," said the woman. So they did.

Soon all the animals knew their names. All but Donkey, that is. Donkey kept forgetting. "What kind of a thingamajig am I again?" he would ask the man.

"You are Donkey," the man would answer. Each time Donkey forgot, the man tugged on Donkey's ears to help him remember.

Soon, however, Donkey would forget his name again.

"Uh, what's my name?" he would ask the woman.

She would answer, "Donkey! Donkey! Donkey!" and pull his ears each time. She was a clever woman but not very patient.

At first, the man and woman did not notice that Donkey's ears grew longer each time they were pulled. Donkey was patient but not very clever. It took him a long time to learn his name. By the time he remembered his name was Donkey, his ears were much longer than Horse's ears. That is why donkeys have long ears.

3. What words could you use to describe Donkey? forgetful, patient
   Explain your choice. Answers will vary.

Page 110

Comprehension: "How the Donkey Got Long Ears"

Directions: Review the legend "How the Donkey Got Long Ears." Then answer the questions.

1. What do the man and woman call the animals before they have names?
   thingamajigs

2. Why do they decide to name the animals? because it was too confusing when they didn't have names

3. What is the first animal they name? Dog

4. Besides being impatient, what else is the woman? clever

5. What did the people do each time they reminded Donkey of his name?
   They tugged on his ears.

6. Which thingamajigs are yellow? Chicks

7. Which thingamajig is pink? Pig

8. What is the thingamajig they ride? Horse

9. Why don't they call the donkey Horse? Donkey is smaller.

Directions: Imagine that you are the one who gets to name the animals. Write names for these new "animals."

10. A thingamajig with yellow spots that swims

11. A thingamajig with large ears, a short tail and...

12. A thingamajig with purple...

13. A thingamajig...

Answers will vary.

Page 111

Following Directions: Puzzling Out the Animals

Directions: Review the legend "How the Donkey Got Long Ears." Then work the puzzle.

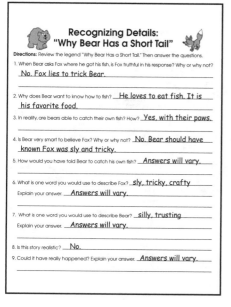

Across:
3. Is the woman patient?
4. This thingamajig cheeps.
5. This thingamajig lays eggs.
6. Is the woman clever?
7. This thingamajig is pink.

Down:
1. This animal can't remember its name.
2. This is what the animals are called before they have names.
5. People ride this brown animal.

(Crossword answers: DONKEY, THINGAMAJIGS, CHICK, YES, HEN, HORSE, PIGS)

Page 112

Comprehension: "Why Owls Have Big Eyes"

Directions: Read the Native American legend "Why Owls Have Big Eyes." Then answer the questions.

Creator made all the animals, one by one. He made each one the way they wanted to look. Owl interrupted when Creator was making Rabbit.

"Whooo, whooo," he said. "Make me now. I want a long neck like Swan, red feathers like Cardinal and a sharp beak like Eagle. Make me the most beautiful bird in the world."

"Quiet!" shouted Creator. "I am making Rabbit. Turn around and wait your turn."

Creator made Rabbit's long ears and long back legs. Before he could make Rabbit's long front legs, Owl interrupted again.

"Whooo, whooo," Owl said. "Make me now. Make me the most beautiful bird in the world."

"Close your eyes. No one may watch me work," said Creator. "Wait your turn. Do not interrupt again."

Owl would not wait. He was very rude. "I will watch if I want to," he said.

"All right then," said Creator. "I will make you now."

He pushed Owl's head until it was close to his body. He shook Owl until his eyes grew big with fright. He pulled on Owl's ears so they stuck out on both sides. Then he covered Owl's feathers with mud.

"There," he said. "That's what you get for not waiting your turn. You have big ears to listen so you can hear when you are told what to do. You have big eyes, but you can't watch me with them. I work only in the day and you will be awake only at night. Your feathers will forever be the color of mud, not red like Cardinal's."

When he heard Creator's words, Owl flew away. Creator turned to finish Rabbit, but Rabbit had run away before Creator could finish his front legs or give him sharp claws to defend himself. To this day, rabbits have short front legs, are afraid of owls and cannot defend themselves. And that's why owls have short necks, big eyes, brownish feathers and ears that stick out.

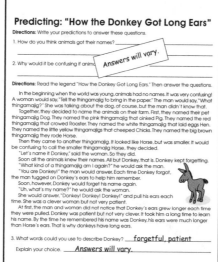

1. According to this legend, who made all the animals? Creator

2. Why did Rabbit run away before Creator finished making him?
   He was afraid.

3. Why didn't Creator make Owl beautiful? because Owl would not wait his turn

4. Why are rabbits afraid of owls? Owls hunt rabbits.

Page 113

Review

Rudyard Kipling wrote many legends explaining such things as why bears have short tails, how the camel got his hump and why a leopard has spots. He wrote his stories in a book called *Just So Stories for Little Children.* You can find a copy of Kipling's book at the library or a bookstore.

Directions: Think about how animals look and behave. Using your wildest imagination, write a short explanation for the following situations.

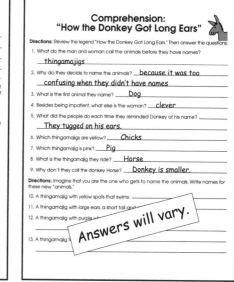

1. Why the pig has a short tail

2. How the elephant got his big ears

3. Why birds fly

4. Why rabbits are timid

5. How the giraffe got a l...

6. How the mou...

Answers will vary.

Directions: Illustrate on... our stories as a three- or four-panel cartoon.

Page 114

Comprehension: "Why Cats and Dogs Fight"

Directions: Read the legend "Why Cats and Dogs Fight." Then answer the questions.

Long ago, Cat and Dog were friends. They played together. They ate together. They even slept near one another.

Yes, Cat and Dog got along very well! The reason was simple. All the other animals had to work for humans. But because Cat was so clean, it did not have to work. And because Dog was so loyal, it did not have to work either. Cat and Dog were the only animals who had time to play. They enjoyed themselves very much.

Everything was too good to be true! Cat and Dog wanted to make sure their lives stayed easy. They asked the old man and woman who owned them to sign a paper saying they would never have to work. That way, they would have proof that they could spend their lives at play.

The old man and woman signed the paper. Then Dog buried it in the ground with his bones. After their masters died, the other animals grew more and more jealous.

"The people aren't here any more to protect them. Why should they get off so easy?" Ox asked Cow.

"You're right," said Cow. "Let's find that paper and destroy it. Then there will be no proof that Cat and Dog can play. They will have to work like we do."

Ox and Cow looked everywhere, but they could not find the paper. Finally, they asked Rat to help. Rat sniffed and sniffed. At last, he smelled the paper. He pulled it from the ground and gave it to Ox. Ox ground it under his hoof and destroyed it. Then Dog had to go to work as a hunter. Cat had to catch mice. Cat never forgave Dog for burying the paper in a spot Rat could find. To this day, that's why cats and dogs fight.

1. Why didn't Cat have to work? __Cat was so clean.__
2. Why didn't Dog have to work? __Dog was so loyal.__
3. What animals talk about finding the paper? __Ox and Cow__
4. Who destroys the paper? __Ox__
5. Who finds the paper? __Rat__

Page 115

Comprehension: "Why Cats and Dogs Fight"

Directions: Review the legend "Why Cats and Dogs Fight." Then answer the questions.

1. What do Cat and Dog do to make sure their life stays easy? __They make their owners sign a paper saying they would never have to work.__

2. Does their plan work? __No.__

3. Why not? __The other animals were jealous.__

4. When does the easy time stop for the cat c __when Ox destroys the paper__

5. Cat gets mad at Dog for burying the paper in a place where Rat can easily find it. Do you think Dog also gets mad at Cat? Explain your answ

6. What other animal pair could you compo

7. Why did you select this animal pair?

8. Does the quarreling of Dog and   als remind you of your own quarrels with your brothers or

9. What if Ra   er? Rewrite the end of the story, beginning with these words: why cats and dogs . . ."

Answers will vary.

Page 116

Main Idea: "The Sly Fox"

Directions: Read the legend "The Sly Fox." Then answer the questions.

One evening, Fox met Wolf in the forest. Wolf was in a terrible mood. He felt hungry, too. So he said to Fox, "Don't move! I'm going to eat you this minute."

As he spoke, Wolf backed Fox up against a tree. Fox realized she couldn't run away.

"I will have to use my wits instead of my legs," she thought to herself.

Aloud to Wolf, Fox said calmly, "I would have made a good dinner for you last year. But I've had three little babies since then. I spend all my time looking for food to feed them."

Before she could go on, Wolf interrupted. "I don't care how many children you have! I'm going to eat you right now." Wolf began closing in on Fox.

"Stop!" shouted Fox. "Look how skinny I am. I ran off all my fat looking for food for my children. But I know where you can find something that's good and fat!" Wolf backed off to listen.

"There's a well near here. In the bottom of it is a big fat piece of cheese. I don't like cheese, so it's of no use to me. Come, I'll show you."

Wolf trotted off after Fox, making sure she could not run away.

"See," said Fox when they got to the well.

Inside was what looked like a round yellow piece of cheese. It was really the moon's reflection, but Wolf didn't know this. Wolf leaned over the well, wondering how to get the cheese. Fox jumped up quickly and pushed Wolf in.

"I am a sly, old thing," Fox chuckled as she trotted home to her children. And to this day, that's why foxes are sly.

1. What is the main idea of this legend? (Check one.)

   __✓__ Fox is cornered but uses her wits to outsmart Wolf and save her own life.

   _____ Wolf is in a terrible mood and wants to eat Fox.

   _____ Wolf thinks the moon was made of cheese.

2. Why did Fox say she will not make a good meal for Wolf? __She was too thin because she spent all her time searching for food for her babies.__

3. What happens to Wolf at the end? __Fox pushes Wolf into the well.__

Page 117

Recognizing Details: "The Sly Fox"

Directions: Review the legend "The Sly Fox." Then answer the questions.

1. What are three events in the story that show Wolf's bad mood? _____
   __Answers will vary.__

2. What does Fox say she will have to use to get away from Wolf? __her wits__
3. Where does Fox tell Wolf he can find a nice fat meal? __at the bottom of the well__
4. How does Fox finally rid herself of Wolf? __She pushes him into the well.__
5. What does Fox say as she trots home? __"I am a sly old thing."__
6. Have you ever been in a situation where you used words to solve a problem instead of fighting with someone? Write about it.

7. In addition to teaching why foxes are sly, who   this story teach?

Answers will vary.

Page 118

Comprehension: "King of the Beasts"

Directions: Read the legend "King of the Beasts." Then answer the questions.

Once, a shy little rabbit was sleeping under a palm tree. Suddenly, a coconut fell and startled the rabbit awake. The rabbit began to twitch and worry.

"What was that awful noise?" he said. He looked around but didn't see the coconut. "The Earth must be breaking apart. Oh dear, oh dear, oh dear."

The little rabbit began running in circles. Soon a monkey joined him.

"Why are you running?" the monkey asked, trotting along beside the rabbit.

"The Earth is breaking apart, and I'm trying to escape," panted the little rabbit.

They were joined by a deer, a fox and an elephant. When they heard the Earth was breaking up, they all followed the rabbit. Soon a huge herd of animals was running in a circle.

"What's going on?" roared the lion to the elephant when he saw the herd.

"The Earth is breaking up!" shouted the elephant. "We are trying to escape."

The lion looked around. Except for all the dust, everything looked fine.

"Who said the Earth is breaking up?" he roared back to the elephant.

"The fox told me!" the elephant replied.

The lion asked the fox, and the fox said the deer told him. The deer said the monkey had told him. Finally, the lion traced the story to the rabbit.

"Show me the place!" the lion demanded.

The rabbit led the lion back to the palm tree. Right away, the lion saw the coconut on the ground.

"Silly rabbit!" he roared. "What you heard was a coconut falling. Go and tell the other animals they are safe."

The rabbit rushed to tell the other animals. They stopped running.

"The lion is smart!" said the monkey. "Let's name him 'King of the Beasts.'" So they did.

1. What kind of tree is the rabbit sleeping under? __a palm tree__
2. Why does he think the Earth is breaking up? __A coconut fell and startled him awake.__
3. Which animal is the first to join the rabbit? __monkey__
4. What does the lion call the rabbit? __"silly rabbit"__
5. Who suggests naming the lion "King of the Beasts"? __monkey__

Page 119

Comprehension: "King of the Beasts"

Directions: Review the legend "King of the Beasts." Then answer the questions.

1. How does the lion become "King of the Beasts"? __He discovers that the Earth is not breaking apart.__

2. Instead of panicking about the Earth breaking apart, what should the rabbit have done? __He could have looked to see what made the loud noise.__

3. Instead of following the rabbit around in a circle, what should the monkey, deer and fox have done?

4. Do you think naming the lion "King of the B   dea? Why or why not?

5. What does this story te   ressure? Explain.

Answers will vary.

Page 120

Recognizing Details: "Lazy Sheep"

Directions: Read the poem about the lazy sheep. Then answer the questions.

"Lazy sheep, please tell me why
In the grassy field you lie?
You eat and sleep away your day
While people work and sweat for pay!"
"Boy, do not talk to me so mean!"
Replied the sheep, so white he gleamed.
"I'm busy growing wool that's new
To spin into some clothes for you!"
The boy looked sad, his face got red.
"I'm sorry for the things I said!"

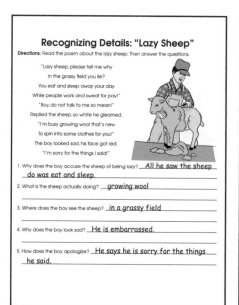

1. Why does the boy accuse the sheep of being lazy? _All he saw the sheep do was eat and sleep._

2. What is the sheep actually doing? _growing wool_

3. Where does the boy see the sheep? _in a grassy field_

4. Why does the boy look sad? _He is embarrassed._

5. How does the boy apologize? _He says he is sorry for the things he said._

Page 121

Main Idea: "The Mouse"

Directions: Read the story "The Mouse." Then answer the questions.

One day when the cat and mouse were playing, the cat bit off the mouse's tail.
"Ouch!" cried the mouse. "Give me back my tail this instant!"
"I'll give your tail back when you go to the cow and bring me some milk!" replied the cat.
She held the mouse's tail high so mouse could not reach it.
Right away, the mouse ran to ask the cow for milk.
"I'll give you milk if you go to the farmer and get me some hay," said the cow.
When the mouse asked the farmer for hay, he said: "I'll give you hay if you go to the butcher and get me some meat."
The mouse went to the baker, who said, "I'll give you meat if you go to the baker and bring me some bread," said the butcher.
The mouse went to the baker, who said, "I'll give you bread. But if you get into my grain, I'll cut off your head!" The mouse quickly promised never to get into the baker's grain.
Then the baker gave the mouse bread. The mouse gave the bread to the butcher and the butcher gave the mouse meat. The mouse gave the meat to the farmer and the farmer gave the mouse hay. The mouse gave the hay to the cow and the cow gave the mouse milk. The mouse gave the cat milk and—finally!—the mouse got her tail back!

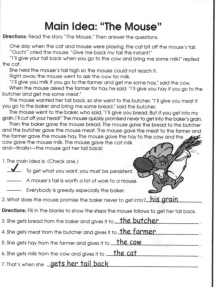

1. The main idea is: (Check one.)
   ✓ To get what you want, you must be persistent.
   ___ A mouse's tail is worth a lot of work to a mouse.
   ___ Everybody is greedy, especially the baker.

2. What does the mouse promise the baker never to get into? _his grain_

Directions: Fill in the blanks to show the steps the mouse follows to get her tail back.

3. She gets bread from the baker and gives it to _the butcher_.

4. She gets meat from the butcher and gives it to _the farmer_.

5. She gets hay from the farmer and gives it to _the cow_.

6. She gets milk from the cow and gives it to _the cat_.

7. That's when she _gets her tail back_.

Page 122

Sequencing: "The Mouse"

Directions: Review the story of "The Mouse." Then answer the questions.

1. Why do you think the cat does not simply give the tail back to the mouse when he asks for it?

Answers will vary.

2. Have you ever done anything ... or friend when they asked for something? Explain.

Answers will vary.

Directions: List the things the mouse has to do to get his tail back.

First _Get bread from the baker for the butcher, after promising not to get into the grain._

Second _Get meat from the butcher for the farmer._

Third _Get hay from the farmer for the cow._

Fourth _Get milk from the cow for the cat._

Fifth _Give the milk to the cat._

Page 123

Animal Legend Organizer

Directions: Follow the instructions to write a legend of your own.

1. Select one of the following titles for your legend. Circle the one you plan to use.
   How the Tiger Got Stripes
   How the Giraffe Got a Long Neck
   How the Gazelle Got Twisty Horns
   How the Elephant Got Big Ears
   Why Rabbits Are Timid
   How the Mouse Got a Long Tail
   How the Elephant Got a Tusk
   How the Kangaroo Got Her Pouch
   Why the Pig Has a Short Tail
   Why Birds Fly
   How the Giraffe Got a Long Neck
   Why Fish Swim

2. Briefly explain the type of conflict that will be in your legend.

3. Write words and phrases to show events you plan ... legend.

4. Summarize how you plan to settle ... the problem.

Directions: Write your ... illustrate it if you like.

Answers will vary.

Page 124

Review

Directions: Review the fables and legends you read. Then write your answers.

1. Explain how "The Mouse" and "The Sly Fox" are similar stories.

2. Explain how "King of the Beasts" and "The Sheep" are ...

3. Compare and contrast the rabbit ...

4. Compare and c... d with one animal fable.

5. Rea... ust So Stories. Write your reaction to the story.

Answers will vary.

Page 125

Sequencing: "Mr. Nobody"

Directions: After reading the poem "Mr. Nobody," number in order the things people blame him for.

I know a funny little man
As quiet as a mouse,
Who does the mischief that is done
In everybody's house!
No one ever sees his face.
And yet we all agree
That every plate we break was cracked
By Mr. Nobody.

It's he who always tears out books,
Who leaves the door ajar,
He pulls the buttons from our shirts,
And scatters pins afar;
That squeaking door will always squeak,
The reason is, you see,
We leave the oiling to be done
By Mr. Nobody.

The finger marks upon the wall
By none of us are made;
We never leave the blinds unclosed,
To let the carpet fade.
The bowl of soup we do not spill,
It's not our fault, you see
These mishaps—every one is caused
By Mr. Nobody.

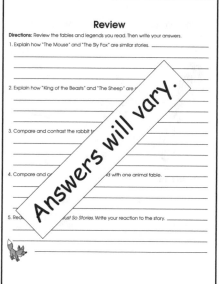

_7_ Putting finger marks on walls
_3_ Leaving the door ajar
_9_ Spilling soup
_2_ Tearing out books
_8_ Leaving the blinds open
_5_ Scattering pins
_1_ Breaking plates
_4_ Pulling buttons off shirts
_6_ Squeaking doors

Page 126

Comprehension: "The Chickens"

Directions: Read the poem "The Chickens." Then answer the questions.

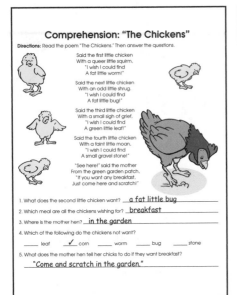

Said the first little chicken
With a queer little squirm,
"I wish I could find
A fat little worm!"

Said the next little chicken
With an odd little shrug,
"I wish I could find
A fat little bug!"

Said the third little chicken
With a small sigh of grief,
"I wish I could find
A green little leaf!"

Said the fourth little chicken
With a faint little moan,
"I wish I could find
A small gravel stone!"

"See here!" said the mother
From the green garden patch,
"If you want any breakfast,
Just come here and scratch!"

1. What does the second little chicken want? __a fat little bug__
2. Which meal are all the chickens wishing for? __breakfast__
3. Where is the mother hen? __in the garden__
4. Which of the following do the chickens not want?

_____ leaf   __✓__ corn   _____ worm   _____ bug   _____ stone

5. What does the mother hen tell her chicks to do if they want breakfast?
__"Come and scratch in the garden."__

Page 127

Following Directions: "I'm Glad"

Directions: Read the poem "I'm Glad." Then work the puzzle.

I'm glad the sky is painted blue
And the Earth is painted green,
With such a lot of nice fresh air
All sandwiched in between.

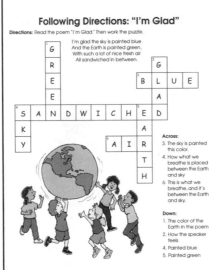

Crossword answers: GREENSKY, BLUE, EARTH, SANDWICHED, AIR

Across:
3. The sky is painted this color.
4. How what we breathe is placed between the Earth and sky
5. This is what we breathe, and it's between the Earth and sky.

Down:
1. The color of the Earth in the poem
2. How the speaker feels
4. Painted blue
5. Painted green

Page 128

Comprehension: "Over the Hills and Far Away"

Directions: Read "Over the Hills and Far Away." Then answer the questions.

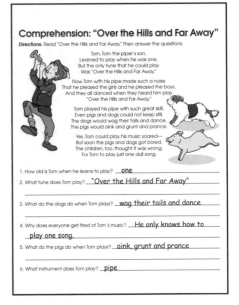

Tom, Tom, the piper's son,
Learned to play when he was one,
But the only tune that he could play
Was "Over the Hills and Far Away."

Now Tom with his pipe made such a noise
That he pleased the girls and he pleased the boys,
And they all danced when they heard him play
"Over the Hills and Far Away."

Tom played his pipe with such great skill,
Even pigs and dogs could not keep still.
The dogs would wag their tails and dance,
The pigs would oink and grunt and prance.

Yes, Tom could play, his music soared—
But soon the pigs and dogs got bored.
The children, too, thought it was wrong,
For Tom to play just one dull song.

1. How old is Tom when he learns to play? __one__
2. What tune does Tom play? __"Over the Hills and Far Away"__
3. What do the dogs do when Tom plays? __wag their tails and dance__
4. Why does everyone get tired of Tom's music? __He only knows how to play one song.__
5. What do the pigs do when Tom plays? __oink, grunt and prance__
6. What instrument does Tom play? __pipe__

Page 129

Sequencing: "The Spider and the Fly"

Directions: Read the poem "The Spider and the Fly." Then number the events in order.

"Won't you come into my parlor?" said the spider to the fly.
"It's the nicest little parlor that you will ever see.
The way into my parlor is up a winding stair.
I have so many pretty things to show you inside there."

The little fly said, "No! No! No! To do so is not sane.
For those who travel up your stair do not come down again."

The spider turned himself around and went back in his den—
He knew for sure the silly fly would visit him again.
The spider wove a tiny web, for he was very sly
He was making preparations to trap the silly fly.

Then out his door the spider came and merrily did sing,
"Oh, fly, oh lovely, lovely fly with pearl and silver wings."

Alas! How quickly did the fly come buzzing back to hear
The spider's words of flattery, which drew the fly quite near.

The fly was trapped within the web, the spider's winding stair,
Then the spider jumped upon him, and ate the fly right there!

__4__ The spider sings a song about how beautiful the fly is.

__7__ The spider jumps on the fly.

__1__ The spider invites the fly into his parlor.

__3__ The spider spins a tiny new web to catch the fly.

__6__ The fly becomes caught in the spider's web.

__2__ The fly says he knows it's dangerous to go into the spider's parlor.

__8__ The spider eats the fly.

__5__ The fly comes near the web to hear the song.

Page 130

Comprehension: "Grasshopper Green"

Directions: Read the poem "Grasshopper Green." Then answer the questions.

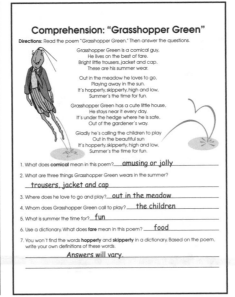

Grasshopper Green is a comical guy,
He lives on the best of fare.
Bright little trousers, jacket and cap,
These are his summer wear.

Out in the meadow he loves to go.
Playing away in the sun.
It's hopperty, skipperty, high and low,
Summer's the time for fun.

Grasshopper Green has a cute little house,
He stays near it every day.
It's under the hedge where he is safe,
Out of the gardener's way.

Gladly he's calling the children to play
Out in the beautiful sun
It's hopperty, skipperty, high and low,
Summer's the time for fun.

1. What does **comical** mean in this poem? __amusing or jolly__
2. What are three things Grasshopper Green wears in the summer? __trousers, jacket and cap__
3. Where does he love to go and play? __out in the meadow__
4. Whom does Grasshopper Green call to play? __the children__
5. What is summer the time for? __fun__
6. Use a dictionary. What does **fare** mean in this poem? __food__
7. You won't find the words **hopperty** and **skipperty** in a dictionary. Based on the poem, write your own definitions of these words. __Answers will vary.__

Page 131

Main Idea: "Little Robin Redbreast"

Directions: Read the poem "Little Robin Redbreast." Then answer the questions.

Little Robin Redbreast
Sat up in a tree.
Up went the kitty cat
Down went he.

Down came the kitty cat—
Away Robin ran,
Said little Robin Redbreast,
"Catch me if you can."

Then Little Robin Redbreast
Hopped upon a wall.
Kitty cat jumped after him,
And almost had a fall.

Little Robin chirped and sang,
And what did kitty say?
Kitty cat said, "Meow!" quite loud,
And Robin flew away.

1. What is the main idea? (Check one.)

__✓__ The robin is smarter than the cat and a lot faster, too.

_____ When people see a robin, it means spring is near.

_____ The robin is scared away.

2. What nearly happens when the cat jumps on the wall? __He almost falls off.__
3. Where is the robin when the cat first goes after him? __up in a tree__
4. Where does the robin go after the cat climbs the tree? __down__
5. What does the robin say to the cat? __"Catch me if you can."__

Page 132

Sequencing: "Hickory, Dickory, Dock"

Directions: Read the poem "Hickory, Dickory, Dock." Then answer the questions.

Hickory, dickory, dock,
The mouse ran up the clock.
The clock struck one,
And down he run,
Hickory, dickory, dock.

Dickory, dickory, dare,
The pig flew in the air.
The man in brown
Soon brought him down,
Dickory, dickory, dare.

Hickory Dickory Dock

1. What is the main idea? (Check one.)

____ Mice and pigs can cause a lot of problems to clocks and men in brown suits.

__✓__ There is no main idea. This poem is just for fun.

____ Beware of mice in your clocks and flying pigs.

2. Why do you think the mouse runs down the clock? __Answers will vary.__

Directions: Number these events in order.

__2__ The clock strikes one.

__3__ The mouse runs back down the clock.

__1__ The mouse runs up the clock.

__5__ The man in brown brings the pig down.

__4__ The pig flies in the air.

Page 133

Review

Directions: Review the poems you read. Then answer the questions.

1. How is the spider in the poem "The Spider and the Fly" like the fox in the fable "The Fox and the Crow"?

__Answers may include: Both the spider and the fox use__
__flattery to trick someone.__

2. Which of the poems that you read did you like the best? _____

Why? _____

_____

3. Which of the poems that you _____

Why? _____

Answers will vary.

One way to remember what you read is to make a comic strip of the story or poem. Think about the poem "Mr. Nobody." Imagine what "Mr. Nobody" would look like.

Directions: Follow the sequence of events in the "Mr. Nobody" poem to make a cartoon of the poem in the boxes below

Cartoons will vary.

Page 134

Following Directions: Early Native Americans

Directions: Read about the early Native Americans. Then work the puzzle.

There were about 300 Native American tribes in North America when the first white settlers came to New England in the 1500s. These Native Americans loved and respected the earth. They hunted buffalo on the plains. They fished in the clear rivers. They planted corn and beans on the rich land. They gathered roots and herbs. Before the white settlers drove them out, the Native Americans were masters of the land and all its riches.

The Native Americans grew crops, hunted for food, made clothing and built their homes from what they found on the land in the area where they lived. That is why each tribe of Native Americans was different. Some Native Americans lived in special tents called tepees. Some lived in adobe pueblos. Some lived in simple huts called hogans.

Crossword puzzle:
- Across: 2. PUEBLOS
- 3. BUFFALO
- 4. TEPEES
- Down (H, O, G, A, N for HOGAN); (H, A, R, T, H for HEARTH); (T, H, R, E, E)

Across:
2. Native American homes made of adobe
3. Native Americans hunted this animal.
4. Tents some Native Americans lived in

Down:
1. Huts some Native Americans lived in
4. There were this many hundred tribes of Native Americans when settlers came.
5. All the tribes loved the _____.

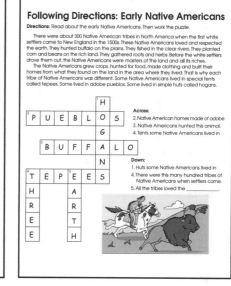

Page 135

Comprehension: The Pueblo People

Directions: Read about the Pueblo people. Then answer the questions.

Long ago, Native Americans occupied all the land that is now Arizona, New Mexico, Utah and parts of California and Colorado. Twenty-five different tribes lived in this southwestern area. Several of the tribes lived in villages called pueblos. The Hopi (hope-ee) Indians lived in pueblos. So did the Zuñi (zoo-nee) and the Laguna (lah-goon-nah). These and other tribes who lived in villages were called the "Pueblo people."

When it was time for the Pueblo people to plant crops, everyone helped. The men kept the weeds pulled. Native Americans prayed for rain to make their crops grow. As part of their worship, they also had special dances called rain dances. When it was time for harvest, the women helped.

The land was bountiful to the Pueblo people. They grew many different crops. They planted beans, squash and 19 different kinds of corn. They gathered wild nuts and berries. They hunted for deer and rabbits. They also traded with other tribes for things they could not grow or hunt.

The Pueblo people lived in unusual houses. Their homes were made of adobe brick. Adobe is a type of mud. They shaped the mud into bricks, dried them, then built with them. Many adobe homes exist today in the Southwest.

The adobe homes of long ago had no doors. The Pueblo people entered through a type of trapdoor at the top. The homes were three or four stories high. The ground floor had no windows and was used for storage. These adobe homes were clustered around a central plaza. Each village had several clusters of homes. Villages also had two or three clubhouses where people could gather for celebrations. Each village also had places for worship.

1. What were the five states where the Pueblo people lived? __Arizona, Utah__ __New Mexico, California, Colorado__

2. What were three crops the Pueblo people grew? __beans, squash, corn__

3. The early pueblo houses had no

☐ yards. ☐ windows. ☑ doors.

Page 136

Recognizing Details: The Pueblo People

"At the edge of the world
It grows light.
The trees stand shining."
(Pueblo poem)

Directions: Read more about the Pueblo people. Then answer the questions.

The Pueblo people were peaceful. They loved nature, and they seldom fought in wars. When they did fight, it was to protect their people or their land. Their dances, too, were gentle. The Pueblo people danced to ask the gods to bring rain or sunshine. Sometimes they asked the gods to help the women have children.

Some Native Americans wore masks when they danced. The masks were called kachinas (ka-chee-nas). They represented the faces of dead ancestors. (Ancestors are all the family members who have lived and died before.)

The Pueblo people were talented at crafts. The men of many tribes made beautiful jewelry. The women made pottery and painted it with beautiful colors. They traded some of the things they made with people from other tribes.

Both boys and girls needed their parents' permission to marry. After they married, they were given a room next to the bride's mother. If the marriage did not work out, sometimes the groom moved back home again.

1. Among the Pueblo people, who made jewelry? __the men__

2. Who made pottery? __the women__

3. What did some of the Pueblo people wear when they danced? __masks called kachinas__

4. Why did the Pueblo people dance for the gods? __to ask the gods for rain or sunshine or help with childbirth__

5. Where did newly married couples live? __in a room next to the bride's mother__

6. Why would a man move back home after marriage? __He would move out if the marriage did not work out.__

Page 137

Recognizing Details: The Pueblo People

Directions: Review what you learned about the Pueblo people. Then answer the questions.

1. How many different tribes lived in the Southwestern part of the United States? __25__

2. The article specifically names three of the Pueblo tribes. Where could you find the names of the other Pueblo tribes?
__reference sources like encyclopedias or the Internet__

3. How did the Pueblo people build their adobe homes? __They shaped mud into bricks, dried them, then built with them.__

4. How did the location and climate affect their lifestyle? __Location and climate affected what they wore, what crops they grew, the animals they hunted and materials used for building homes.__

5. How were the jobs of the men and women of a Pueblo tribe alike? __Both helped care for crops.__

6. How were their jobs different? __Men made jewelry. Women made pottery.__

7. How do the responsibilities of the Pueblo men and women discussed differ from those of men and women today?
__Answers will vary.__

Page 138

Comprehension: A California Tribe

Directions: Read about the Yuma. Then answer the questions.

California was home to many Native Americans. The weather was warm, and food was plentiful. California was an ideal place to live.

One California tribe that made good use of the land was the Yuma. The Yuma farmed and gathered roots and berries. They harvested dozens of wild plants. They gathered acorns, ground them up and used them in cooking. The Yuma mixed acorns with flour and water to make a kind of oatmeal. They fished in California's rich waters. They hunted deer and small game. The Yuma made the most of what Mother Nature offered.

The Yuma lived in huts. The roofs were made of dirt. The walls were made of grass. Some Yuma lived together in big round buildings made with poles and woven grasses. As many as 50 people lived in these large homes.

Like other tribes, the Yuma made crafts. Their woven baskets were especially beautiful. The women also wove cradles, hats, bows and other useful items for the tribe.

When it was time to marry, a boy's parents chose a 15-year-old girl for him. The girl was a Yuma, too, but from another village. Except for the chief, each man took only one wife.

When a Yuma died, a big ceremony was held. The Yumas had great respect for death. After someone died, his or her name was never spoken again.

1. What were two reasons why California was an ideal place to live?
   <u>The weather was warm and food was plentiful.</u>

2. What did the Yuma use acorns for? <u>They ground them up and used</u>
   <u>them for cooking.</u>

3. What was a beautiful craft made by the Yuma? <u>woven baskets</u>

4. How old was a Yuma bride? <u>15</u>

5. What types of homes did the Yuma live in? <u>dirt and grass huts</u>

6. How did the Yuma feel about death? <u>They had great respect for</u>
   <u>death.</u>

Page 139

Recognizing Details: The Yuma

Directions: Review what you read about the Yuma. Write the answers.

1. How did the Yuma make good use of the land?
   <u>They farmed and gathered roots, acorns and berries.</u>
   <u>They fished and hunted.</u>

2. How were the Yuma like the Pueblo people? <u>Both hunted deer and</u>
   <u>small game, farmed, gathered berries and made crafts.</u>

3. How were they different? <u>The Yuma fished, made baskets and</u>
   <u>lived in huts. The Pueblos made pottery and jewelry and</u>
   <u>lived in adobe homes.</u>

4. Why did the Yuma have homes different than those of the Pueblo tribes?
   <u>Answers should indicate differences in natural materials</u>
   <u>available due to different climates.</u>

5. When it was time for a young Yuma man to marry, his parents selected a fifteen-year-old bride for him from another tribe. Do you think this is a good idea? Why or why not?

6. Why do you suppose the Yuma never spoke a person's name after he/she died?
   Answers will vary.

7. Do you think this was an easy thing to do? Explain your answer.

Page 140

Following Directions: Sailor Native Americans

Directions: Read about the Sailor Native Americans of Puget Sound. Then work the puzzle.

Three tribes lived on Puget (pew-jit) Sound in Washington state. They made their living from the sea. People later called them the "Sailor" Indians.

These Native Americans fished for salmon. They trapped the salmon in large baskets. Sometimes they used large nets. The sea was filled with fish. Their nets rarely came up empty. The Sailor Native Americans also gathered roots and berries. They hunted deer, black bear and ducks.

Their homes were amazing! They built big wooden buildings without nails. They did not use saws to cut the wood. The walls and roofs were tied together. Each building had different homes inside. As many as 50 families lived in each big building.

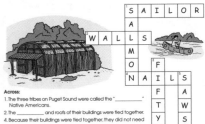

Across:
1. The three tribes on Puget Sound were called the "_____" Native Americans.
2. The _____ and roofs of their buildings were tied together.
4. Because their buildings were tied together, they did not need _____.

Down:
1. Type of fish the "Sailor" Native Americans caught
3. As many as _____ families could live in their big buildings.
5. The buildings were put together without using _____ to cut the wood.

Page 141

Following Directions: Sailor Native Americans

Directions: Review what you read about the Sailor Native Americans. Write your answers.

1. How were the housing arrangements of the Puget Sound Native Americans similar to those of the Yuma?
   <u>Many families lived together in large buildings.</u>

2. How was the diet of the Sailor Native Americans like those of the Yuma and Pueblo?
   <u>All three hunted and gathered berries.</u>

3. How was it different? <u>Yumas and Pueblos grew their own crops.</u>

4. The Sailor Native Americans made a living from the sea, and their nets were rarely empty. What type of transportation do you think these Native Americans used to get their nets to the sea?
   <u>canoes, boats or rafts</u>

5. Where could you find more information on this group of Native Americans to check your answer?
   <u>reference sources like encyclopedias and the Internet</u>

6. Verify your answer. Were you correct? <u>Answers will vary.</u>

7. Who do you think performed the many tasks in the Sailor village? Write men, women, boys and/or girls for your answers.
   Built homes? _____
   Fished? _____ and berries? _____
   Hunted game? _____ Made fishing nets? _____
   Answers will vary.

8. The homes of the Sailor Native Americans could be compared to what type of modern dwelling?
   <u>apartment buildings or condos</u>

Page 142

Review

Review what you read about Native Americans. Then answer the questions.

1. Of the tribes discussed, which one would you most like to have been a member of? Explain your answer.
   <u>Answers will vary.</u>

2. Why did each of the tribes have a different lifestyle? <u>because of their</u>
   <u>location, different climates and resources were available.</u>

3. How did their location influence how each of the tribes functioned? <u>Food, plants,</u>
   <u>animals, fish, climate and building materials all influenced</u>
   <u>the people and how they lived.</u>

Directions: Select two of the Native American tribes you read about. Compare and contrast their homes, clothing and lifestyle in the Venn diagram. Write words and phrases that are unique to one group or the other in the correct parts of the circle. Write words and phrases that are common to both groups in the section where the circles intersect.

Answers will vary.

Page 143

Reading Comprehension: Hummingbirds

Hummingbirds are very small birds. This tiny bird is quite an acrobat. Only a few birds, such as kingfishers and sunbirds, can hover, which means to stay in one place in the air. But no other bird can match the flying skills of the hummingbird. The hummingbird can hover, fly backward and fly upside down!

Hummingbirds got their name because their wings move very quickly when they fly. Their wings move so fast that you can't see them at all. This takes a lot of energy. These little birds must have food about every 20 minutes to have enough strength to fly. Their favorite foods are insects and nectar. Nectar is the sweet water deep inside a flower. Hummingbirds use their long, thin bills to drink from flowers. When a hummingbird sips nectar, it hovers in front of a flower. It never touches the flower with its wings or feet.

Besides being the best at flying, the hummingbird is also one of the prettiest birds. Of all the birds in the world, the hummingbird's colors are among the brightest. Some are bright green with red and white markings. Some are purple. One kind of hummingbird can change its color from reddish-brown to purple to red!

The hummingbird's nest is special, too. It looks like a tiny cup. The inside of the nest is very soft. This is because one of the things the mother bird uses to build the nest is the silk from a spider's web.

Directions: Answer these questions about hummingbirds.

1. How did hummingbirds get their name? <u>Because their wings move</u>
   <u>very quickly when they fly, and it causes a humming sound.</u>

2. What does *hover* mean? <u>to hang in the air</u>

3. How often do hummingbirds need to eat? <u>every 20 minutes</u>

4. Name two things that hummingbirds eat. <u>insects and nectar</u>

5. What is one of the things a mother hummingbird uses to build her nest?
   <u>silk from a spider's web</u>

Page 144

Reading Comprehension: Bats

Bats are the only mammals that can fly. They have wings made of thin skin stretched between long fingers. Bats can fly amazing distances. Some small bats have been known to fly more than 25 miles in one night.

Most bats eat insects or fruit. But some eat only fish, others only blood and still others the nectar and pollen of flowers that bloom at night. Bats are active only at night. They sleep during the day in caves or other dark places. At rest, they always hang with their heads down.

You may have heard the expression "blind as a bat." But bats are not blind. They don't, however, use their eyes to guide their flight or to find the insects they eat. A bat makes a high-pitched squeak, then waits for the echo to return to it. This echo tells it how far away an object is. This is often called the bat's sonar system. Using this system, a bat can fly through a dark cave without bumping into anything. Hundreds of bats can fly about in the dark without ever running into each other. They do not get confused by the squeaks of the other bats. They always recognize their own echoes.

Directions: Answer these questions about bats.

1. Bats are the only mammals that
   □ eat insects. ☒ fly. □ live in caves.
2. Most bats eat
   □ plants. □ other animals. ☒ fruits and insects.
3. Bats always sleep
   ☒ with their heads down. □ lying down. □ during the night.
4. Bats are blind. True (False)
5. Bats use a built-in sonar system to guide them. (True) False
6. Bats are confused by the squeaks of other bats. True (False)

Page 145

Review: Venn Diagram

Directions: Make a Venn diagram comparing hummingbirds (see page 143) and bats (see page 77). Refer to the sample diagram on page 105 to help you. Write at least three characteristics for each section of the diagram.

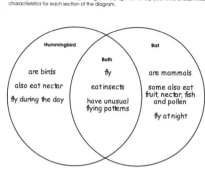

Hummingbird
- are birds
- also eat nectar
- fly during the day

Both
- fly
- eat insects
- have unusual flying patterns

Bat
- are mammals
- some also eat fruit, nectar, fish and pollen
- fly at night

Page 146

Recognizing Details: Giraffes

Directions: Read about giraffes. Then answer the questions.

Giraffes are tall, beautiful, graceful animals that live in Africa. When they are grown, male giraffes are about 18 feet tall. Adult females are about 14 feet tall.

Giraffes are not fat animals, but because they are so big, they weigh a lot. The average male weighs 2,800 pounds. Females weigh about 400 pounds less. Giraffes reach their full height when they are four years old. They continue to gain weight until they are about eight years old.

If you have ever seen giraffes, you know their necks and legs are very long. They are not awkward, though! Giraffes can move very quickly. They like to jump over fences and streams. They do this gracefully. They do not trip over their long legs.

If they are frightened, they can run 35 miles an hour. When giraffes gallop, all four feet are sometimes off the ground! Usually, young and old giraffes pace along at about 10 miles an hour.

Giraffes are strong. They can use their back legs as weapons. A lion can run faster than a giraffe, but a giraffe can kill a lion with one quick kick from its back legs.

Giraffes do not look scary. Their long eyelashes make them look gentle. They usually have a curious look on their faces. Many people think they are cute. Do you?

1. What is the weight of a full-grown male giraffe? __2,800 pounds__
2. What is the weight of an adult female? __2,400 pounds__
3. When does a giraffe run 35 miles an hour? __when it is frightened__
4. What do giraffes use as weapons? __their back legs__
5. For how long do giraffes continue to gain weight?
   __until they are 8 years old__
6. When do giraffes reach their full height?
   __when they are 4 years old__
7. Use a dictionary. What does **gallop** mean?
   __to run quickly; to run at full speed__

Page 147

Comprehension: More About Giraffes

Directions: Read more about giraffes. Then answer the questions.

Most people don't notice, but giraffes have different patterns of spots. Certain species of giraffes have small spots. Other species have large spots. Some species have spots that are very regular. You can tell where one spot ends and another begins. Other species have spots that are kind of blotchy. This means the spots are not set off from each other as clearly. There are many other kinds of spot patterns. The pattern of a giraffe's spots is called "markings." No two giraffes have exactly the same markings.

There is one very rare type of giraffe. It is totally black! Have you ever seen one? This kind of giraffe is called a melanistic (mel-an-iss-tick) giraffe. The name comes from the word "melanin," which is the substance in cells that gives them color. Giraffes' spots help them blend in with their surroundings. A black giraffe would not blend in well with tree trunks and leaves. Maybe that is why they are so rare.

Being able to blend with surroundings helps animals survive. If a lion can't see a giraffe, he certainly can't eat it. This is called "protective coloration." The animal's color helps protect it.

Another protection giraffes have is their keen eyesight. Their large eyes are on the sides of their heads. Giraffes see anything that moves. They can see another animal a mile away! It is very hard to sneak up on a giraffe. Those who try usually get a quick kick with a powerful back leg.

1. What are markings? __the pattern of an animal's spots__
2. How far away can a giraffe see another animal? __one mile__
3. Where are a giraffe's eyes? __on the sides of its head__
4. What is protective colorat __being able to blend into the surroundings__
5. What color is the very rare type of giraffe? __black__
6. How do giraffes protect themselves? __They kick with their back legs.__
7. How many kinds of spot patterns do giraffes have? □ two □ four ☑ many
8. Use a dictionary. What does **species** mean? __a group of animals closely related and capable of breeding with others in the same species__

Page 148

Following Directions: Puzzling Out Giraffes

Directions: Review what you read about giraffes. Read more about giraffes below. Then work the puzzle.

Have you noticed that giraffes have a curious look? That is because they are always paying attention. Their lives depend upon it! Giraffes cannot save themselves from a lion if they don't see it. Giraffes look around a lot. Even when they are chewing their food, they are checking to see if danger is near.

By nature, giraffes are gentle. They do not attack unless they are in danger. A giraffe will lower its head when it is angry. It will open its nostrils and its mouth. Then watch out!

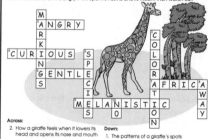

Across:
2. How a giraffe feels when it lowers its head and opens its nose and mouth
4. Giraffes look this way because they are always paying attention.
6. By nature, giraffes are _____.
7. The continent where giraffes live
9. Another name for a black giraffe is _____.

Down:
1. The patterns of a giraffe's spots
3. An animal's ability to blend with surroundings is called protective _____.
5. _____ means a certain kind of animal.
8. Giraffes' eyes are so keen they can see another animal a mile _____.
10. Are giraffes often mean?

Page 149

Recognizing Details: Giraffes

Directions: Review what you learned about giraffes. Then answer the questions.

1. How are a giraffe's spots helpful? __They help them blend in with their surroundings.__
2. Is it easy to sneak up on a giraffe? Why not? __No, because they are always paying attention and can see a long ways.__
3. What makes a giraffe look so gentle? __They have long eyelashes.__
4. How do you know when a giraffe is angry? __It will lower its head and open its nostrils and mouth.__
5. Do you think a giraffe in a zoo is as observant as a giraffe in the wilds of Africa? Why or why not?
   __Answers will vary.__
6. Do you think giraffes have any other enemies besides lions? __Yes__
   What animals might they be? __Answers may include: hyenas, cheetahs__
7. Why do you suppose giraffes grow so large? __Answers will vary.__
8. Use a dictionary. What does **habitat** mean? Describe the giraffe's natural habitat.
   __Habitat is a place where an animal lives in its natural state. Giraffes live on open grassy plains and sometimes near trees.__

Page 150

Comprehension: Wild Horses

Directions: Read about wild horses. Then answer the questions.

Have you ever heard of a car called a Mustang? It is named after a type of wild horse.

In the 1600s, the Spanish explorers who came to North America brought horses with them. Some of these horses escaped onto the prairies and plains. With no one to feed them or ride them, they became wild. Their numbers quickly grew, and they roamed in herds. They ran free and ate grass on the prairie.

Later, when the West was settled, people needed horses. They captured wild ones. This was not easy to do. Wild horses could run very fast. They did not want to be captured! Some men made their living by capturing wild horses, taming them and selling them. These men were called "mustangers." Can you guess why?

After cars were invented, people did not need as many horses. Not as many mustangers were needed to catch them. More and more wild horses roamed the western prairies. In 1925, about a million mustangs were running loose.

The government was worried that the herds would eat too much grass. Ranchers who owned big herds of cattle complained that their animals didn't have enough to eat because the mustangs ate all the grass. Permission was given to ranchers and others to kill many of the horses. Thousands were killed and sold to companies that made them into pet food.

Now, wild horses live in only 12 states. The largest herds are in California, New Mexico, Oregon, Wyoming and Nevada. Most people who live in these states never see wild horses. The herds live away from people in the distant plains and mountains. They are safer there.

1. What is one type of wild horse called? **a mustang**

2. What were men called who captured wild horses? **mustangers**

3. About how many wild horses were running free in the U.S. in 1925? **one million**

4. The wild mustangs were killed and turned into ☐ cars. ☑ pet food. ☐ lunch meat.

5. The largest herds of wild horses are now in

☑ Oregon. ☐ Ohio. ☑ New Mexico. ☑ Wyoming.
☑ California. ☑ Nevada. ☐ Kansas. ☐ Arkansas.

Page 151

Main Idea: More About Wild Horses

Directions: Read more about wild horses. Then answer the questions.

Have you noticed that in any large group, one person seems to be the leader? This is true for wild horses, too. The leader of a band of wild horses is a stallion. Stallions are adult male horses.

The stallion's job is important. He watches out for danger. If a bear or other animal comes close, he lets out a warning cry. This helps keep the other horses safe. Sometimes they all run away together. Other times, the stallion protects the other horses. He shows his teeth. He rears up on his back legs. Often, he scares the other animal away. Then the horses can safely continue eating grass.

Much of the grass on the prairies is gone now. Wild horses must move around a lot to find new grass. They spend about half their time eating and looking for food. If they cannot find prairie grass, wild horses will eat tree bark. They will eat flowers. If they can't find these either, wild horses will eat anything that grows!

Wild horses also need plenty of water. It is often hot in the places where they roam. At least twice a day, they find streams and take long, long drinks. Like people, wild horses lose water when they sweat. They run and sweat a lot in hot weather. To survive, they need as much water as they can get.

Wild horses also use water another way. When they find deep water, they wade into it. It feels good! It cools their skin.

1. What is the main idea? (Check one.)

____ Wild horses need plenty of water.

__✓__ Wild horses move in bands protected by a stallion.

____ Wild horses eat grass.

2. What are two reasons why wild horses need water? **to drink and to cool their skin**

3. Why do wild horses move around so much? **to find new grass**

4. What do wild horses most like to eat? **prairie grass**

5. What do wild horses spend half their time doing? **eating and looking for food**

Page 152

Recognizing Details: Wild Horses

Directions: Review what you read about wild horses. Then answer the questions.

1. How did horses come to North America and become wild? **Spanish explorers brought them. Some escaped and became wild.**

2. Why is it so difficult to capture, tame and train wild horses? **Wild horses can run very fast and do not want to be captured.**

3. Do you think it was right of the government to allow ___ing of wild horses? Explain your answer. **Answers will vary.**

4. Do you think the remaining ___ protected? Explain your answer. **Answers will vary.**

5. What is the role of the lead stallion in a wild horse herd? **to watch out for danger and protect the herd**

6. What are some things wild horses have in common with giraffes? **Answers will vary.**

7. What do you think will happen ___ prairie lands continue to disappear as a result of developm___ ___esses? **Answers will vary.**

Page 153

Reading Comprehension: Oceans

If you looked at Earth from up in space, you would see a planet that is mostly blue. This is because more than two-thirds of Earth is covered with water. You already know that this is what makes our planet different from the others, and what makes life on Earth possible. Most of this water is in the four great oceans: Pacific, Atlantic, Indian and Arctic. The Pacific is by far the largest and the deepest. It is more than twice as big as the Atlantic, the second largest ocean.

The water in the ocean is salty. This is because rivers are always pouring water into the oceans. Some of this water picks up salt from the rocks it flows over. It is not enough salt to make the rivers taste salty. But the salt in the oceans has been building up over millions of years. The oceans get more and more salty every century.

The ocean provides us with huge amounts of food, especially fish. There are many other things we get from the ocean, including sponges and pearls. The oceans are also great "highways" of the world. Ships are always crossing the oceans, transporting many goods from country to country.

The science of studying the ocean is called oceanography. Today, oceanographers have special equipment to help them learn about the oceans and seas. Electronic instruments can be sent deep below the surface to make measurements. The newest equipment uses sonar or echo-sounding systems that bounce sound waves off the sea bed and use the echoes to make pictures of the ocean floor.

Directions: Answer these questions about the oceans.

1. How much of the Earth is covered by water? **two-thirds**

2. Which is the largest and deepest ocean? **Pacific**

3. What is the science of studying the ocean? **oceanography**

4. What new equipment do oceanographers use? **sonar or echo sounding systems**

Page 154

Reading Comprehension: Whales

The biggest animal in the world is the whale. The blue whale is the largest animal that ever lived. It is even bigger than the great dinosaurs of long ago. Whales are close cousins to dolphins and porpoises, but these animals are fewer than 13 feet in length.

Whales spend their entire lives in water, usually in the ocean. Because of this, many people think that whales are fish. They are not. They are mammals. There are four things that prove that whales are mammals instead of fish: 1) Whales breathe with lungs instead of gills. A whale must come to the surface to breathe. It blows the old air from its lungs out of a hole in the top of its head. 2) They are warm-blooded. 3) They have hair—though not very much! 4) Baby whales are born alive and get milk from their mothers.

Because whales often live in cold water, they have a thick layer of fat under their skin to protect them. This fat is called blubber. For many centuries, people have hunted the whale for its blubber.

Whales are very sociable animals and "talk" with each other by making different noises, including clicks, whistles, squeaks, thumps and low moans. Because sound waves travel well in water, the "song" of some whales can be heard more than 100 miles away.

Directions: Answer these questions about whales.

1. Which whale is the biggest animal that has ever lived? **blue whale**

2. List four things proving that whales are mammals and not fish.

a. **They breathe air.**

b. **They are warm-blooded.**

c. **They have hair.**

d. **The babies are born alive and get milk from their mother.**

3. What are two "cousins" to the whale? **dolphins and porpoises**

4. What is the thick layer of fat under a whale's skin called? **blubber**

Page 155

Reading Comprehension: Dolphins and Porpoises

Dolphins and porpoises are members of the whale family. In fact, they are the most common whales. If they have pointed or "beaked" faces, they are dolphins. If they have short faces, they are porpoises. Sometimes large groups of more than 1,000 dolphins can be seen.

Dolphins and porpoises swim in a special way called "porpoising." They swim through the surface waters, diving down and then leaping up—sometimes into the air. As their heads come out of the water, they breathe in air. Dolphins are acrobatic swimmers, often spinning in the air as they leap.

Humans have always had a special relationship with dolphins. Stories dating back to the ancient Greeks talk about dolphins as friendly, helpful creatures. There have been reports over the years of people in trouble on the seas who have been rescued and helped by dolphins.

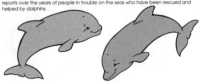

Directions: Answer these questions about dolphins and porpoises.

1. The small members of the whale family with the pointed faces are **dolphins**

2. Those members of the whale family with short faces are **porpoises**

3. What do you call the special way dolphins and porpoises swim? **porpoising**

4. Do dolphins breathe with lungs or gills? **lungs**

5. How did ancient Greeks describe dolphins? **friendly, helpful creatures**

6. Where have dolphins been reported to help people? **in trouble on the seas**

Page 156

Reading Comprehension: Sharks

Sharks are known as the hunters of the sea. They are fish who eat other fish and even other sharks. Most people are frightened of sharks, but only a few of the more than 300 types of sharks are dangerous to people. Sharks vary in size and shape. The whale shark can be up to 60 feet long, but it is harmless. Some kinds of dogfish sharks are only a few inches long!

Sharks usually live in warm water, although they can be found anywhere in the ocean. Because of their shape, they are great swimmers.

Sharks are different from most other fish in a few ways. One important way is that they don't have any bones. Instead, their bodies have tough material called cartilage. Another ways sharks are different is that their mouths are on the underside of the head. Most sharks have several rows of very sharp teeth. They never stop growing teeth. If a tooth wears out or is lost, a new one grows in its place.

Sharks spend most of their time eating and looking for food. They are excellent hunters. They can smell the smallest amount of blood from a long way off. Some kinds of sharks swim in packs, but the larger sharks hunt alone. Sharks usually approach their prey carefully, especially if it is big. Unless they are very hungry, they will swim around in a circle for some time before attacking. Experienced divers know how to swim with sharks and feed them. They can tell by the way a shark comes up to them if they should be afraid.

Directions: Answer these questions about sharks.

1. Sharks are the hunters of the sea. **(True)** False
2. There are thousands of kinds of sharks. True **(False)**
3. All sharks are dangerous to humans. True **(False)**
4. Sharks actually have very few teeth. True **(False)**
5. Sharks spend most of their time eating and looking for food. **(True)** False

Page 157

Reading Comprehension: Jacques Cousteau

Jacques Cousteau was one of the most famous undersea explorers in history. He revolutionized this study with his inventions. His inventions include the aqua-lung and the diving saucer.

Jacques-Yves Cousteau was born in France in 1910. His family traveled a lot when he was a boy. They often visited the Atlantic Ocean. Even then, he was developing what would become a lifelong love for the sea.

Because of all the moving his family did, Cousteau was a poor student in school. He was often in trouble. But there were some areas in which he did very well. He was a wonderful swimmer, and he loved to invent things. Even as a teenager, he invented things that amazed grown-ups. He also learned a lot about other languages. By the time he started college, he was one of the best students in school. Because of his good grades, he was able to go to the French Naval Academy.

During World War II, Cousteau served as an officer in the French Navy. Most of his life became centered around the sea. He dreamed of owning his own ship. Finally, in 1950, he bought the Calypso (ca-LIP-so) and turned it into a research ship. Cousteau and his sailors explored the oceans. They searched shipwrecks and made underwater movies. He eventually won three Academy Awards for his undersea films. He also wrote many books about sea life. He worked very hard to teach people about the sea and how to take care of it.

Directions: Complete these statements about Jacques Cousteau.

1. Jacques Cousteau was born in ___France___
2. As a boy, Cousteau liked to swim and to ___invent things___
3. Cousteau's ship was called ___Calypso___
4. Cousteau's undersea films won him ___three Academy Awards___

Page 158

Reading Comprehension: Deep-Sea Diving

One part of the world is still largely unexplored. It is the deep sea. Over the years, many people have explored the sea. But the first deep-sea divers wanted to find sunken treasure. They weren't really interested in studying the creatures or life there. Only recently have they begun to learn some of the mysteries of the sea.

It's not easy to explore the deep sea. A diver must have a way of breathing under water. He must be able to protect himself from the terrific pressure. The pressure of air is about 15 pounds on every square inch. But the pressure of water is about 1,300 pounds on every square inch!

The first diving suits were made of rubber. They had a helmet of brass with windows in it. The shoes were made of lead and weighed 20 pounds each! These suits let divers go down a few hundred feet, but they were no good for exploring very deep waters. With a metal diving suit, a diver could go down 700 feet. Metal suits were first used in the 1930s.

In 1937, a diver named William Beebe wanted to explore deeper than anyone had ever gone before. He was not interested in finding treasure. He wanted to study deep-sea creatures and plants. He invented a hollow metal ball called the bathysphere. It weighed more than 5,000 pounds, but in it Beebe went down 3,028 feet. He saw many things that had never been seen by humans before.

Directions: Answer these questions about early deep-sea diving.

1. What were the first deep-sea divers interested in? ___sunken treasure___
2. What are two problems that must be overcome in deep-sea diving?
   a. ___the terrific water pressure___
   b. ___breathing under water___
3. How deep could a diver go wearing a metal suit? ___700 feet___
4. Who was the deep-sea explorer who invented the bathysphere?
   ___William Beebe___

Page 159

Comprehension: Sea Lions

Directions: Read about sea lions. Then answer the questions.

Sea lions are friendly-looking animals. Their round faces and whiskers remind people of the faces of small dogs. The almond shape of their eyes gives them a look of intelligence. Whether it is true or not, sea lions often look as though they are thinking.

Sea lions behave like playful children. They push each other off rocks. They slide into the water. Sometimes they body surf! Like people, they often ride the crest of waves. They let the waves carry them near the shore. Then they swim back out to ride more waves.

Although sea lions do not have real toys, they like to play with seaweed. They toss it in the air. They catch it in their mouths. Yuck! They must not mind the taste!

If you have been to a marine park, you may have watched sea lions. Sea lions can be taught many tricks. They can balance balls on their noses. They can jump through hoops. Their trainers give them fish to reward them for doing tricks. Sea lions look very pleased with themselves when they perform. They love fish, and they grow to love applause.

1. What are three ways sea lions play? ___They push each other off rocks, slide into the water, body surf and play with seaweed.___

2. Why do sea lions look intelligent? ___They have almond-shaped eyes.___

3. What tricks can sea lions be taught to do? ___balance balls on their noses, jump through hoops___

4. As a reward, trainers give sea lions
   ☑ fish. ☐ hugs. ☐ applause.

Page 160

Recognizing Details: More About Sea Lions

Directions: Read more about sea lions. Then answer the questions.

Sea lions love water! That is a good thing, because they spend most of their lives in it. Usually, the water is very cold. People cannot stay in cold water very long. The coldness slows down a person's heartbeat. It can actually make a person's heart stop beating.

Sea lions do not feel the cold. Their bodies are covered with a special layer of fat called blubber. The blubber is like a thick coat. It keeps the sea lion's body heat in. It keeps the bone-chilling cold out.

Like people, sea lions are mammals. They have warm blood. They breathe air. Baby sea lions are born on land. The mother sea lions produce milk for their babies. Like human babies, sea lions snuggle up with their mothers when they nurse. The mother knows just what her baby smells like. This is how she tells which baby is hers. She will only nurse her own baby.

Baby sea lions are called pups. Female sea lions are called cows. Male sea lions are called bulls. When pups are a few days old, their mothers leave them for a while each day. They go into the ocean to hunt fish. The pups don't seem to mind. They gather together in small groups called pods. The pods are like a nursery school! But no teacher is in charge. As many as 200 pups may spend the day together playing, swimming and sleeping.

1. What are male, female and baby sea lions called? ___male — bulls, females — cows, babies — pups___
2. How do sea lions stay warm in cold water? ___Their bodies are covered with a layer of fat, called blubber.___
3. When do cows begin to leave their pups? ___when the pups are a few days old___
4. Where do the cows go? ___into the ocean to hunt fish___
5. What are small groups of pups called? ___pods___
6. How can a cow tell which pup is hers? ___by its smell___

Page 161

Main Idea: Pupping Time

Directions: Read about sea lion "pupping time." Then answer the questions.

When sea lion cows gather on the beach to give birth, it is called "pupping time." Pupping time is never a surprise. It always occurs in June. Thousands of sea lions may gather in one spot for pupping time. It is sort of like one big birthday party.

The cow stays with her pup for about a week after birth. During that time, she never leaves her baby. If she must go somewhere, she drags her pup along. She grabs the loose skin around her pup's neck with her teeth. To humans, it doesn't look comfortable, but it doesn't hurt the pup.

One place the mother must go is to the water. Because of her blubber, she gets hot on land. To cool off, she takes a dip in the ocean. When she comes out, she sniffs her pup to make sure she's got the right baby. Then she drags him back again to a spot she has staked out. After a week of being dragged around, do you think the pup is ready to play?

1. Why do thousands of sea lions gather together at a certain time? ___to give birth at pupping time___

2. Why isn't pupping time ever a surprise? ___It happens every June.___

3. How does a cow take her pup along when she goes for a cool dip?
First, grab ___the loose skin at the pup's neck with her teeth___
Then, ___drag it along___
After the swim, sniff ___the pup to be sure she's got the right pup___

4. What is the main idea? (Check one.)
   ✓ Thousands of cows gather at pupping time to give birth and afterwards stay with their pups for a week.
   ___ Thousands of sea lions take cools dips and usually drag their pups along.
   ___ Pups are born in June.

Page 162

Comprehension: Sea Lions

Directions: Review what you read about sea lions. Then answer the questions.

1. What makes sea lions so friendly looking? __their round faces and whiskers__

2. How are people like sea lions? __Answers may include: They both like to play in the water.__

3. Pretend you are a pup in a pod. What would your day be like? What would you do? What would you play?
__Answers will vary.__

4. Why do sea lions go into the water so much? __to cool off and to hunt for food__

5. How do you think sea lions protect themselves? _____

6. What is the sea lion's habitat like? _____

Answers will vary.

Page 163

Review

Directions: Follow the instructions. Write your answers.

1. Create a wild animal alphabet and illustrate it on drawing paper.

Example: A — ALLIGATOR
B — BEAR
C — CROCODILE

2. Select one of the wild animals you read about. Make a diorama of its habitat. A **diorama** is a three-dimensional model of a scene.

3. Compare the giraffe, wild horse and sea lion. Tell how the three animals are alike and the ways they are different.

	Giraffe		Seal Lions
Alike			
Different			

4. What physical characteristics of these animals help them survive. Which do you think is the best and why?

5. How do these animal stories differ from the animal legends and fables you read?
__These are nonfiction—facts about real animals. Legends and fables are fiction.__

Answers will vary.

Page 164

Recognizing Details: Orbiting Earth

Directions: Read about orbiting Earth. Then answer the questions.

John Glenn was the first American to circle Earth. When someone circles a planet, it is called "orbiting."

On February 20, 1962, John Glenn first went into space and started his trip around Earth. The name of his spaceship was _Friendship 7_.

Other American astronauts had already been into space. They knew what it was like to have no gravity. Their work helped John Glenn when he took his flight into space. John Glenn was the only astronaut on board _Friendship 7!_

John Glenn was not the first person to orbit Earth, though. The year before Glenn orbited Earth, a Russian man did it. Yuri Gagarin was the first person to travel around Earth.

1. Who was the first American to orbit Earth? __John Glenn__
2. What does **orbit** mean? __to circle a planet__
3. When did John Glenn orbit Earth? __February 20, 1962__
4. What was the name of John Glenn's spaceship? __Friendship 7__
5. Who orbited Earth before John Glenn? __Yuri Gagarin, a Russian man__
6. How long after the Russian orbited Earth did John Glenn make his journey? __1 year__
7. People who are the first to do something that has never been done before are called "pioneers." What could you do so that you would be considered to be a "pioneer"? Explain your choice.
__Answers will vary.__

Page 165

Main Idea: Chimpanzees Went First

Directions: Read about chimpanzees in space. Then answer the questions.

Chimpanzees went into space before astronauts! In the 1950s, scientists decided to try sending chimps into space because they are much like humans, except they are stronger.

The first two chimps to ride in a rocket were named Pat and Mike. Their ride was in 1953. Ham was the first chimpanzee to go into space. That was in 1961.

Before John Glenn orbited Earth, a chimpanzee had already done it. The chimp, named Enos, had circled Earth twice!

1. What is the main idea?
_____ Chimpanzees are better astronauts than people.
__✓__ Chimpanzees went into space before humans did.
_____ Only chimpanzees with names could become astronauts.

2. Who were the first two chimpanzees to ride in a rocket? __Pat and Mike__
3. Which chimpanzee orbited Earth before John Glenn? __Enos__
4. How many times did he circle Earth? __two times__

Directions: Circle the names of the four chimpanzees mentioned in the story.

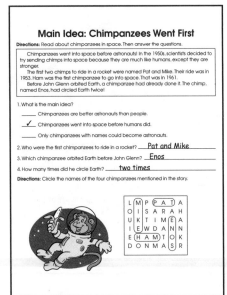

```
L M P A T A
O I S A R A H
U K T I M E A
I E W D A N N
E H A M T O K
D O N M A S R
```

Page 166

Space Pioneer

Neil Armstrong is one of the great pioneers of space. On July 20, 1969, Armstrong was commander of _Apollo 11_, the first manned American spacecraft to land on the Moon. He was the first person to walk on the Moon.

Armstrong was born in Ohio in 1930. He took his first airplane ride when he was 6 years old. As he grew older, he did jobs to earn money to learn to fly. On his 16th birthday, he received his student pilot's license.

Armstrong served as a Navy fighter pilot during the Korean War. He received three medals. Later, he was a test pilot. He was known as one of the best pilots in the world. He was also an engineer. He contributed much to the development of new methods of flying. In 1962, he was into an astronaut training program.

Armstrong had much experience when he was named to command the historic flight to the Moon. It took four days to fly to the Moon. As he climbed down the ladder to be the first person to step onto the Moon, he said these now famous words: "That's one small step for man, one giant leap for mankind."

Directions: Answer these questions about Neil Armstrong.

1. What did Neil Armstrong do before any other person in the world?
__He walked on the Moon.__

2. How old was Neil Armstrong when he got his student pilot's license?
__16 years old__

3. What did Armstrong do during the Korean War?
__served as a Navy fighter pilot__

4. On what date did a person first walk on the Moon?
__July 20, 1969__

Page 167

Recognizing Details: Sally Ride, First Woman in Space

Directions: Read about Sally Ride. Then answer the questions.

Sally Ride was the first American woman in space. She was only 31 years old when she went into space in 1982. Besides being the first American woman, she was also the youngest person ever to go into space!

Many people wanted to be astronauts. When Sally Ride was chosen, there were 8,000 people who wanted to be in the class. Only 35 were selected. Six of those people were women.

Sally Ride rode in the spaceship _Challenger_. She was called a mission specialist. Like an astronaut, Sally Ride had to study for several years before she went into space. She spent 6 days on her journey. She has even written a book for children about her adventure! It is called _To Space and Back_.

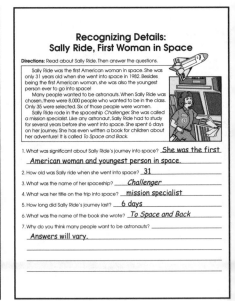

1. What was significant about Sally Ride's journey into space? __She was the first American woman and youngest person in space.__
2. How old was Sally Ride when she went into space? __31__
3. What was the name of her spaceship? __Challenger__
4. What was her title on the trip into space? __mission specialist__
5. How long did Sally Ride's journey last? __6 days__
6. What was the name of the book she wrote? __To Space and Back__
7. Why do you think many people want to be astronauts? _____
__Answers will vary.__

Page 168

Main Idea: Floating in Space

Directions: Read about life in space. Then answer the questions.

Life in space is very different from life on Earth. There is no gravity in space. Gravity is what holds us to the ground. In space, everything floats around.

Astronauts wear suction cups on their shoes to hold them to the floor of their spaceships. At night, they do not crawl into bed like you do. Instead, they climb into sleeping bags that hang on the wall and then they zip themselves in.

If an astronaut is thirsty, he or she cannot simply pour a glass of water. The water would form little balls that would float around the spaceship! Instead, water has to be squirted into the astronauts' mouths from bottles or containers.

When astronauts are in space, they do a lot of floating around outside their spaceship. Astronauts always have special jobs to do in space. One astronaut is the pilot of the spaceship. The other astronauts do experiments, make repairs and gather information about their trip.

1. What is the main idea?

   ✓ Life in space is much different than it is on Earth.

   ___ Without gravity, people on Earth would float around.

   ___ Gravity makes life on Earth much different than life in space.

2. What does gravity do? **Gravity holds us to the ground.**

3. How do astronauts sleep? **They climb into sleeping bags that hang on the wall and zip themselves in.**

4. What do astronauts do in space? **One astronaut is the pilot. Others do experiments, make repairs and gather information.**

5. How do astronauts drink water? **They squirt it into their mouths.**

6. Would you like to be an astronaut? Why or why not? **Answers will vary.**

Page 169

Review

Directions: Read about early ideas for space travel. Then answer the questions.

People have dreamed about going into space for thousands of years. There are legends that tell about inventors who wanted to get birds to fly to the Moon. In 1864, a French author named Jules Verne wrote a book called *From the Earth to the Moon*. In the book, he wrote about men being shot into space from a huge cannon.

During the 1920s, several scientists wrote about sending rockets into space. They decided that liquid fuel was needed. Since then, space exploration has come a long way!

A Russian named Yuri A. Gagarin was the first person in space. An American, Alan B. Shepard, Jr., went into space next. Both men did experiments that later helped other astronauts in their trips to outer space!

1. What is the main idea?

   ___ People have thought about going into space since 1920.

   ✓ People have thought about going into space for many years.

   ___ People like Jules Verne had many ideas about how to get to the Moon.

2. Who wrote a book called *From the Earth to the Moon*? **Jules Verne**

3. What did he write about? **men being shot into space from a huge cannon**

4. When was that book written? **1864**

5. In what country did Jules Verne live? **France**

6. What did scientists in the 1920s think we needed to go to space? **liquid fuel**

7. How did Yuri Gagarin and Alan Shepard help future astronauts? **They did experiments.**

Page 170

Reading Comprehension: Telescopes

A telescope is an instrument that makes distant objects, such as the stars and planets, seem closer and bigger. This allows us to get a better look at them and scientists to learn more about them. In 1990, a very special telescope was launched into the sky aboard the space shuttle *Discovery*. The Hubble Space Telescope (HST), which is named for the man who invented it, cost almost 2 billion dollars to make.

HST is a powerful eye in the sky that may help answer questions scientists have asked for a long time: How did the universe begin? How will it end? Is there other life in the universe?

Scientists need big telescopes to explore the universe. On Earth, there are two big problems that keep scientists from clearly seeing the heavens. The lights from the cities are so bright that they wash out the lights from the stars. A bigger problem is the blanket of air that covers Earth. It blurs the view. The HST will overcome these problems. In space there are no clouds and no bright city lights.

The HST is a huge telescope. It is 43 feet long and 14 feet across. It weighs 24,250 pounds. It is very powerful, too. Scientists say that if you put a dime on the top of the Washington Monument in Washington, D.C., you would be able to clearly read the date on it from New York City using the HST. That is 175 miles away!

Directions: Answer these questions about a special telescope.

1. What is a telescope? **an instrument that makes distant objects seem closer and bigger**

2. What is the name of the giant telescope that was launched into space in 1990? **The Hubble Space Telescope**

3. What are two problems for scientists trying to look at the stars and planets from Earth? **Lights from cities wash out stars, and the air blurs vision.**

4. How much does the HST weigh? **24,250 pounds**

Page 171

Comprehension: Clouds

Directions: Read about clouds. Then answer the questions.

Have you ever wondered where clouds come from? Clouds are made from billions and billions of tiny water droplets in the air. The water droplets form into clouds when warm, moist air rises and is cooled.

Have you ever seen your breath when you were outside on a very cold day? Your breath is warm and moist. When it hits the cold air, it is cooled. A kind of small cloud is formed by your breath!

Clouds come in many sizes and shapes. On some days, clouds blanket the whole sky. Other times, clouds look like wispy puffs of smoke. There are other types of clouds as well.

Weather experts have named clouds. Big, fluffy clouds that look flat on the bottom are called **cumulus** clouds. **Stratocumulus** is the name for rounded clouds that are packed very close together. You can still see patches of sky, but stratocumulus clouds are thicker than cumulus ones.

If you spot **cumulonimbus** clouds go inside. These clouds are wide at the bottom and have thin tops. The tops of these clouds are filled with ice crystals. On hot summer days, you may even have seen cumulonimbus clouds growing. They seem to boil and grow as though they are coming from a big pot. A violent thunderstorm usually occurs after you see these clouds. Often, there is hail.

Cumulus, stratocumulus and cumulonimbus are only three of many types of clouds. If you listen closely, you will hear television weather forecasters talk about these and other clouds. Why? Because clouds are good indicators of weather.

1. How are clouds formed? **Water droplets in the air form clouds when warm, moist air rises and cools.**

2. How can you make your own cloud? **by breathing outside on a cold day**

3. What should you do when you spot cumulonimbus clouds? **go inside**

4. What often happens after you see cumulonimbus clouds? **violent thunderstorms, sometimes hail**

5. What kind of big fluffy clouds look flat on the bottom? **cumulus**

Page 172

Recognizing Details: Clouds

Directions: Review what you learned about clouds. Then answer the questions.

1. How are clouds a good indicator of the weather? **Some types of clouds can bring rain, snow or hail.**

2. When you take something out of the freezer on a warm day, why do you think it looks like steam is rising from the object? **Answers will vary.**

3. What does this have to do with clouds? **Clouds are formed in the same way.**

Directions: Use cotton balls to make models of the three types of clouds.

Page 173

Following Directions: Rain

Directions: Read about rain. Then work the puzzle.

Rain develops from water vapor, dust and temperature inside clouds. From this combination, water droplets form and grow. When the droplets become too heavy for the cloud, they fall as rain. Weather experts say that when it storms, the raindrops are about 0.02 inches (0.5 millimeters) in size.

Sometimes the air below the rain cloud is very dry. The dry air dries out the wetness of the raindrop and turns it back into water vapor before it hits the ground. This is what happens in the summer when it looks as though it will rain but doesn't. The rain begins to fall, but it dries up before it falls all the way to the ground.

Across:
2. These form from water vapor, dust and the temperature inside clouds.
4. Falls when the water droplets become too heavy for the cloud.
5. Season when the air under the cloud sometimes dries the rain before it hits the ground.

Down:
1. When water droplets inside clouds get this way, rain falls.
2. Combines with water vapor and the temperature inside clouds.
3. Raindrops measure about 0.02 inches (0.5 mm) when it _____.

Page 174

Comprehension: Thunderstorms

Directions: Read about thunderstorms. Then answer the questions.

Thunderstorms can be scary! The sky darkens. The air feels heavy. Then the thunder begins. Sometimes the thunder sounds like a low rumble. Other times thunder is very loud. Loud thunder can be heard 15 miles away.

Thunderstorms begin inside big cumulonimbus clouds. Remember, cumulonimbus are the summer clouds that seem to boil and grow. It is as though there is a big pot under the clouds.

Thunder is heard after lightning flashes across the sky. The noise of thunder happens when lightning heats the air as it cuts through it. Some people call this quick, sharp sound a thunderclap. Sometimes thunder sounds "rumbly." This rumble is the thunder's sound wave bouncing off hills and mountains.

Weather experts say there is an easy way to figure out how far away a storm is. First, look at your watch. Count the number of seconds between the flash of lightning and the sound of thunder. To find how far away the storm is, divide the number of seconds by five. This will give the number of miles the storm is from you.

How far away is the storm if you count 20 seconds between the flash of lightning and the sound of thunder? Twenty divided by five is four miles. What if you count only five seconds? One mile! Get inside quickly. The air is charged with electricity. You could be struck by lightning. It is not safe to be outside in a thunderstorm.

1. Where do thunderstorms begin? __inside cumulonimbus clouds__

2. When is thunder heard? __after lightning flashes__

3. What causes thunder to sound rumbly? __the sound wave bounces off__ __hills and mountains__

4. To find out how far away a storm is, count the seconds between the thunder and lightning and divide by what number? __5__

5. If you count 40 seconds between the lightning and thunder, how far away is the storm? __8 miles__

6. What comes first, thunder or lightning? __lightning__

Page 175

Recognizing Details: Lightning Safety

Directions: Read about safety rules for lightning. Then answer the questions.

During a storm, lightning can be very dangerous. If you are outside when a thunderstorm begins, look for shelter in a building. If you are in the woods, look for a cave. If you are in an open field, lie down in a hole. If there is no hole, lie flat on the ground.

Standing in an open field, your body is like a lightning rod. Never look for shelter under a tree during a thunderstorm. Lightning is even more likely to strike there! You and the tree are two lightning rods standing together.

Water is also a good conductor of electricity. You must never go into the water when a storm is brewing. The air becomes charged. The charge attracts lightning. The lightning has to go somewhere, and it may go into the water. That is why lifeguards order everyone out of the pool even before a storm comes.

If a thunderstorm comes up when you are boating, get to shore fast. Do not hold fishing rods or other metal objects. They attract lightning.

A car is a good, safe place to be in a thunderstorm. The rubber tires "ground" the car's metal body and remove its charge. This means the electricity cannot go through the car. Lightning does not strike cars. You are safe inside a car.

1. What should you do if you are in a field when a thunderstorm begins? __lie down__ __in a hole or flat on the ground__

2. What is your body like if you are outside during a thunderstorm? __a lightning rod__

3. Why do lifeguards order people from the pool before a thunderstorm? __Water is a good conductor of electricity.__

4. Where is a good place to be during a thunderstorm? __in a car or a building__

5. Besides the human body, name two things that attract lightning. __Answers may__ __include: trees, water, metal objects__

Page 176

Review

Directions: Review what you learned about rain, thunder and lightning. Then answer the questions.

1. How are thunderstorms different from rain showers? __Thunderstorms include lightning, thunder, strong__ __winds and sometimes hail.__

2. Do you think thunderstorms are scary? Explain. __Answers will vary.__

3. What is thunder? __The noise made when lightning heats the__ __air as it cuts through it.__

4. Why do you think some thunder is louder or softer than other thunder? __because__ __it's closer (louder) or farther away (softer)__

5. Why shouldn't you be outside in a storm? __You could be struck by__ __lightning.__

6. Name ways you can seek shelter during a storm if you are:

   outside: __in a building__

   in the woods: __in a cave__

   in a field: __in a hole or ditch__

   in a field with no hole: __lie down flat on the ground__

7. What makes a car a safe place during a storm? __The rubber tires__ __"ground" the cars body and remove its charge.__

8. Would you have thought this to be true? Why or why not? __Answers will vary.__

Page 177

Comprehension: Hurricanes

Directions: Read about hurricanes. Then answer the questions.

Have you ever been in a hurricane? If you are lucky, you have not. Hurricanes are deadly! Thunderstorms are scary and can cause damage, but hurricanes are the most destructive storms on Earth.

There are three "ingredients" in a hurricane. They are turbulent oceans, fierce winds and lashing rains. Hurricane winds can blow as fast as 180 miles (290 kilometers) an hour. They can pull up trees, buildings, cars and people. Hurricanes can destroy anything in their paths.

There are other names for hurricanes. In some parts of the world, they are called cyclones. The people who live on the islands in the Pacific Ocean call them typhoons. In Australia, some people use a funny name to describe these terrible storms. They call them "willy-willies."

Although hurricanes can occur in most parts of the world, they all start in the same place. The place hurricanes are "born" is over the ocean near the equator.

Here is how a hurricane is born. At the equator, the sun is very, very hot. The scorching sun beats down on the ocean water. It heats the water and the air above the water. The heated air begins to spiral upward in tiny, hot circles. When the heated air combines with moist air, it is drawn farther up toward the sky.

The spiral of heated and moist air begins to twist. As it twists, it grows. As it grows, it spins faster and faster in a counterclockwise direction. (This means in the opposite direction from the way a clock's hands move.) Huge rain clouds form at the top of the spiral as the air at the top is cooled. The combination of rain, hot air and spiraling winds creates a hurricane.

1. What are other names for hurricanes? __cyclones,__ __typhoons, willy-willies__

2. Where do all hurricanes begin? __over the ocean__ __near the equator__

3. What direction does a hurricane's spiral move? __counterclockwise__

4. What three "ingredients" are needed to produce a hurricane? __turbulent__ __oceans, fierce winds and lashing rain__

Page 178

Recognizing Details: Hurricanes

Directions: Review what you learned about hurricanes. Then answer the questions.

1. What is the most destructive type of storm on Earth? __a hurricane__

2. What makes them so destructive? __The high winds can pull up trees,__ __buildings, people and cars.__

3. What makes hurricanes scarier than thunderstorms? __Hurricanes are more__ __destructive.__

4. How do hurricanes form? __The sun heats the ocean surface and the__ __air above it, the hot air rises in spirals, then the hot air__ __combines with moist air and begins to twist and grow.__

5. What parts of the United States are most likely to be struck by a hurricane? __areas in the southern United States along the coast of__ __the ocean__

6. Many people enjoy living or vacationing in beach areas. Do you think they would feel the same way if they were on the coast when a hurricane happened? Explain. __Answers will vary.__

7. What does counterclockwise mean? __in the opposite direction from__ __the way a clocks hands move__

Page 179

Main Idea: Tornadoes

Directions: Read about tornadoes. Then answer the questions.

Another type of dangerous weather condition is a tornado. While hurricanes form over water, tornadoes form over land. Tornadoes are more likely to form in some locations than in others. The areas where tornadoes frequently form are called "tornado belts." In the United States, a major tornado belt is the basin of land between Missouri and Mississippi.

Tornadoes are formed when masses of hot air meet masses of cold air. When these air masses slam together, bad thunderstorms begin. People in tornado belts are fearful when a severe storm threatens. They know a tornado may occur if the warm, moist air rushes upward and begins to spiral.

The tornado forms a funnel cloud. The funnel is narrow at the base and broad at the top. The tornado's funnel cloud can move very fast. The winds around the funnel can move 300 miles an hour. The winds inside the funnel are fast, too. The tornado acts like a giant vacuum cleaner. It sucks up everything in its path. People, animals, cars and houses are all in danger when a tornado strikes.

It is difficult to stay out of a tornado's path. The way it moves is unpredictable. It may move straight or in a zig-zag pattern. The winds of the tornado make a screaming noise like a huge train rushing by. People who have lived through a tornado usually say it was the most frightening experience of their lives.

1. What is the main idea? (Check one.)

   ____ Tornadoes form over land and hurricanes form over water.

   ____ Tornadoes sound like a rushing train.

   __✓__ Tornadoes, which form over land under certain weather conditions, are dangerous and frightening.

2. How fast can the winds around the funnel cloud move? __300 miles per hour__

3. Why is it hard to stay out of the path of a tornado? __The path is__ __unpredictable.__

4. What household appliance can a tornado be compared to? __vacuum__ __cleaner__

Page 180

Recognizing Details: Tornadoes

Directions: Review what you learned about tornadoes. Then answer the questions.

1. How do tornadoes form? __Tornadoes form when masses of warm air meet masses of cold air.__

2. What shape is a tornado? __a funnel__

3. What makes a tornado so dangerous? __high winds and an unpredictable path__

4. Which type of storm do you think is more dangerous, a tornado or a hurricane? Why? __Answers will vary.__

5. What types of weather conditions are not dangerous? __Answers may include: rain or snow showers.__

6. What types of winter storms are also dangerous? Why? __Answers may include: blizzards, ice storms__

Directions: Compare and contrast tornadoes and hurricanes in the Venn diagram.

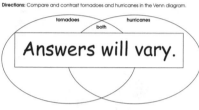

tornadoes   both   hurricanes

Answers will vary.

Page 181

Reading Comprehension: Your Five Senses

Your senses are very important to you. You depend on them every day. They tell you where you are and what is going on around you. Your senses are sight, hearing, touch, smell and taste.

Try to imagine for a minute that you were suddenly unable to use your senses. Imagine, for instance, that you are in a cave and your only source of light is a candle. Without warning, a gust of wind blows out the flame.

Your senses are always at work. Your eyes let you read this book. Your nose brings the scent of dinner cooking. Your tongue helps you taste dinner later. Your hand feels the softness as you stroke a puppy. Your ears tell you had a storm is approaching.

Your senses also help keep you from harm. They warn you if you touch something that will burn you. They keep you from looking at a light that is too bright, and they tell you if a car is coming up behind you. Each of your senses collects information and sends it as a message to your brain. The brain is like the control center for your body. It sorts out the messages sent by your senses and acts on them.

Directions: Answer these questions about the five senses.

1. Circle the main idea:

   Your senses keep you from harm.

   (Your senses are important to you in many ways.)

2. Name the five senses.

   a. __sight__

   b. __hearing__

   c. __touch__

   d. __smell__

   e. __taste__

3. Which part of your body acts as the "control center"? __your brain__

Page 182

Reading Comprehension: Touch

Unlike the other senses, which are located only in your head, your sense of touch is all over your body. Throughout your life, you receive an endless flow of information about the world and yourself from your sense of touch. It tells you if something is hot or cold, hard or soft. It sends messages of pain, such as a headache or sore throat, if there is a problem.

There are thousands of tiny sensors all over your body. They are all linked together. These sensors are also linked to your spinal cord and your brain to make up your central nervous system. Through this system, the various parts of your body can send messages to your brain. It is then the brain's job to decide what it is you are actually feeling. All this happens in just a split second.

Not all parts of your body have the same amount of feeling. Areas that have the most nerves, or sensors, have the greatest amount of feeling. For instance, the tips of your fingers have more feeling than parts of your arm.

Some sensors get used to the feeling of an object after a period of time. When you first put your shirt on in the morning, you can feel its pressure on your skin. However, some of the sensors stop responding during the day.

One feeling you cannot get used to is the feeling of pain. Pain is an important message, because it tells your brain that something harmful is happening to you. Your brain reacts by doing something right away to protect you.

Directions: Answer these questions about the sense of touch.

1. Circle the main idea:

   (The sense of touch is all over your body.)

   You cannot get used to the sense of pain.

2. The nerves, spinal cord and brain are linked together to make the __central nervous system__

3. One feeling you can never get used to is __pain__

4. All parts of your body have the same amount of feeling.   True   (False)

5. It is the brain's job to receive messages from the sensors on your body and decide what you are actually feeling.   (True)   False

Page 183

Reading Comprehension: Smell

Your nose is your sense organ for smelling. Smells are mixed into the air around you. They enter your nose when you breathe.

In the upper part of your nose, there are special smell sensors. They pick up smells and send messages to your brain. The brain then decides what it is you are smelling.

Smelling can be a pleasant sense. Sometimes smells can remind you of a person or place. Have you ever smelled a particular scent and then suddenly thought about your grandmother's house? Smell also can make you feel hungry. In fact, your sense of smell is linked very closely to your sense of taste. Without your sense of smell, you would not taste food as strongly.

Smelling also can be quite unpleasant. But this, too, is important. By smelling food you can tell if it is spoiled and not fit to eat. Your sense of smell also can sometimes warn you of danger, such as a fire.

The sense of smell tires out more quickly than your other senses. This is why you get used to some everyday smells and no longer notice them after a while.

Directions: Answer these questions about the sense of smell.

1. Smells are mixed in __the air around you__

2. The sense of smell is linked closely to the sense of __taste__

3. Give an example of why smelling bad smells can be important to you.

   __You can smell spoiled food or be warned of danger like a fire.__

Page 184

Reading Comprehension: Taste

The senses of taste and smell work very closely together. If you can't smell your food, it is difficult to recognize the taste. You may have noticed this when you've had a bad cold with a stuffed-up nose.

Tasting is the work of your tongue. All over your tongue are tiny taste sensors called taste buds. If you look at your tongue in a mirror, you can see small groups of taste buds. They are what give your tongue its rough appearance. Each taste bud has a small opening in it. Tiny pieces of food and drink enter this opening. There taste sensors gather information about the taste and send messages to your brain. Your brain decides what the taste is.

Taste buds located in different areas of your tongue recognize different tastes. There are only four tastes your tongue can recognize: sweet, sour, bitter and salty. All other flavors are a mixture of taste and smell.

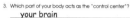

bitter
sour   sour
salty   salty
sweet   no taste

Directions: Answer these questions about the sense of taste.

1. It is difficult to taste your food if you can't __smell__

2. The tiny taste sensors on your tongue are called __taste buds__

3. The four tastes that your tongue can recognize are __sweet, sour, bitter and salty__

4. All other flavors are a mixture of __taste and smell__

Page 185

Reading Comprehension: Sight

You can see this page because of light. Without light, there would be no sight. In a dark room, you might see only a few large shapes. If it is pitch black, you can't see anything at all.

Light reflects or bounces off things and then travels to your eyes. The light enters your eye through the pupil. The pupil is the black circle in the middle of your eye. It gets bigger in low light to let in as much light as possible. In bright light, it shrinks so that too much light doesn't get in.

Light enters through the pupil and then passes through the lens. The lens bends the light so that it falls on the back of your eye on the retina. The retina has millions of tiny cells that are very sensitive to light. When an image is formed in the eye, it is upside down. This image is sent to your brain. The brain receives the message and turns the picture right side up again.

Some people are far-sighted. This means they can clearly see things that are far away, but things close by may be blurred. People who are near-sighted can clearly see things better if they are close by. Glasses or contact lenses can help correct these problems.

Some people can see only a little bit or perhaps not at all. This is called being blind. Blind people rely on their sense of touch to learn more about the world. They can even use their sense of touch to read. Some blind people read with a special printing system called Braille. The system is named for the man who invented it. Braille has small raised dots instead of letters on a page.

Directions: Answer these questions about the sense of sight.

1. Without __light__, there would be no sight.

2. Reflect means __to bounce off of__

3. The part of the eye that controls the amount of light entering your eye by getting bigger and smaller is called the __pupil__

4. To correct near-sightedness or far-sightedness, you can wear __glasses or contact lenses__

5. What is the name of the special printing system for blind people? __Braille__

Page 186

Reading Comprehension: Hearing

Every sound you hear is made by the movement of air. These movements, called vibrations, spread out in waves. Your outer ear collects these "sound waves" and sends them down a tube to the inner ear. The vibrations hit the eardrum, a flap of skin stretched across the inner end of the tube. As the eardrum vibrates, a tiny bone called the hammer moves back and forth. This helps the vibrations move to three small bones and then to the cochlea, where they are changed to nerve impulses. The impulses travel to the brain where they are recognized as sounds.

Some people have trouble hearing or cannot hear at all. This is called being deaf. Some deaf people can understand what you are saying by watching how your lips move. They use their eyes as their ears. Sometimes a hearing aid can help improve hearing. It is like a tiny radio that fits into the ear. Sounds enter the hearing aid and are made much louder.

Deaf people also have difficulty learning to speak because they cannot hear how to say words. Many deaf people "talk" by making pictures with their hands. This kind of talking is called sign language. Every letter of the alphabet has a sign. These signs are shown above.

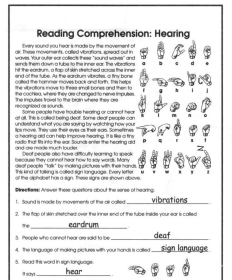

Directions: Answer these questions about the sense of hearing.

1. Sound is made by movements of the air called ___vibrations___

2. The flap of skin stretched over the inner end of the tube inside your ear is called the ___eardrum___.

3. People who cannot hear are said to be ___deaf___

4. The language of making pictures with your hands is called ___sign language___

5. Read this word in sign language.
   It says ___hear___

Page 187

Reading Comprehension: The Five Senses

Directions: Before each sentence, write the sense—hearing, sight, smell, taste or touch—that is being used. The first one is done for you.

___hearing___ 1. The rooster crows outside my window early each morning.

___touch___ 2. After playing in the snow, our fingers and toes were freezing.

___hearing___ 3. I could hear sirens in the distance.

___sight___ 4. I think this tree is taller than that one.

___taste___ 5. The delicious salad was filled with fresh, juicy fruits.

___smell___ 6. The odor of the bread baking in the oven was wonderful.

___sight___ 7. There was a rainbow in the sky today.

___touch___ 8. The kitten was soft and fluffy.

___smell___ 9. Her perfume filled the air when she walked by.

___sight___ 10. An airplane wrote a message in the sky.

___taste___ 11. The chocolate cake was yummy.

___hearing___ 12. The steamboat whistle frightened the baby.

___taste___ 13. The sour lemon made my lips pucker.

___hearing___ 14. Her gum-popping got on my nerves.

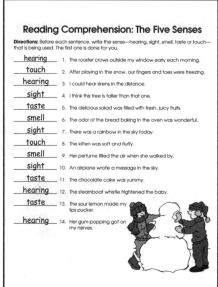

Page 188

Reading Comprehension: The Five Senses

Directions: Each word in the word box makes you think of hearing, sight, smell, taste or touch. Write each word under the sense that is used. One is done for you.

~~music~~	~~rainbow~~	~~talking~~	~~hot~~	~~sour~~
~~honking~~	~~moldy~~	~~butterfly~~	~~green~~	~~book~~
~~crying~~	~~silky~~	~~sweet~~	~~smoky~~	~~bitter~~
~~salty~~	~~skunk~~	~~cold~~	~~smooth~~	~~stinky~~

Touch	**Sight**	**Taste**
silky	rainbow	salty
cold	butterfly	sweet
hot	green	sour
smooth	book	bitter

Smell		**Hearing**
skunk		music
smoky		honking
stinky		talking
moldy		crying

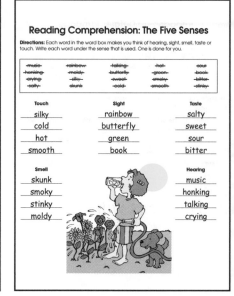

Page 189

Reading Comprehension: Helen Keller

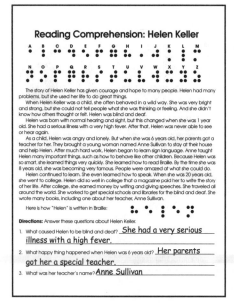

The story of Helen Keller has given courage and hope to many people. Helen had many problems, but she used her life to do great things.

When Helen Keller was a child, she often behaved in a wild way. She was very bright and strong, but she could not tell people what she was thinking or feeling. And she didn't know how others thought or felt. Helen was blind and deaf.

Helen was born with normal hearing and sight, but this changed when she was 1 year old. She had a serious illness with a very high fever. After that, Helen was never able to see or hear again.

As a child, Helen was angry and lonely. But when she was 6 years old, her parents got a teacher for her. They brought a young woman Anne Sullivan to stay at their house and help Helen. After much hard work, Helen began to learn sign language. Anne taught Helen many important things, such as how to behave like other children. Because Helen was so smart, she learned things very quickly. She learned how to read Braille. By the time she was 8 years old, she was becoming very famous. People were amazed at what she could do.

Helen continued to learn. She even learned how to speak. When she was 20 years old, she went to college. Helen did so well in college that a magazine paid her to write the story of her life. After college, she earned money by writing and giving speeches. She traveled all around the world. She worked to get special schools and libraries for the blind and deaf. She wrote many books, including one about her teacher, Anne Sullivan.

Here is how "Helen" is written in Braille:

Directions: Answer these questions about Helen Keller.

1. What caused Helen to be blind and deaf? ___She had a very serious illness with a high fever.___

2. What happy thing happened when Helen was 6 years old? ___Her parents got her a special teacher.___

3. What was her teacher's name? ___Anne Sullivan___

Page 190

Review

In this book, you have learned new ways to write and "talk." There are many other ways to express your thoughts to others. Here is another one.

For hundreds of years, Native Americans used their own system of sign language. These signs were understood by all tribes, even though their spoken languages were different.

The Plains tribes helped to develop and spread sign language. The Plains tribes liked to wander. They never camped in any one place for long. They used sign language so they could talk with other Native Americans wherever they went.

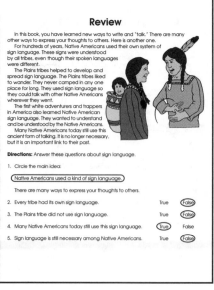

The first white adventurers and trappers in America also learned Native American sign language. They wanted to understand and be understood by the Native Americans.

Many Native Americans today still use this ancient form of talking. It is no longer necessary, but it is an important link to their past.

Directions: Answer these questions about sign language.

1. Circle the main idea:

   (Native Americans used a kind of sign language.)

   There are many ways to express your thoughts to others.

2. Every tribe had its own sign language.   True   (False)

3. The Plains tribe did not use sign language.   True   (False)

4. Many Native Americans today still use this sign language.   (True)   False

5. Sign language is still necessary among Native Americans.   True   (False)

Page 192

Writing: Sentences

A **sentence** is a group of words that expresses a complete thought.

Directions: Write **S** by each group of words that is a sentence and **NS** by those that are not a complete sentence.

Examples:

___NS___ A pinch of salt in the soup.

___S___ Grandmother was fond of her flower garden.

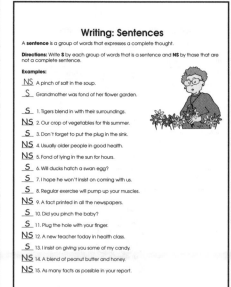

___S___ 1. Tigers blend in with their surroundings.

___NS___ 2. Our crop of vegetables for this summer.

___S___ 3. Don't forget to put the plug in the sink.

___NS___ 4. Usually older people in good health.

___NS___ 5. Fond of lying in the sun for hours.

___S___ 6. Will ducks hatch a swan egg?

___S___ 7. I hope he won't insist on coming with us.

___S___ 8. Regular exercise will pump up your muscles.

___NS___ 9. A fact printed in all the newspapers.

___S___ 10. Did you pinch the baby?

___S___ 11. Plug the hole with your finger.

___NS___ 12. A new teacher today in health class.

___S___ 13. I insist on giving you some of my candy.

___NS___ 14. A blend of peanut butter and honey.

___NS___ 15. As many facts as possible in your report.

Page 193

Kinds of Sentences: Statements and Questions

A **statement** tells some kind of information. It is followed by a period (.).

Examples: It is a rainy day. We are going to the beach next summer.

A **question** asks for a specific piece of information. It is followed by a question mark (?).

Examples: What is the weather like today? When are you going to the beach?

Directions: Write whether each sentence is a statement or question. The first one has been done for you.

1. Jamie went for a walk at the zoo.   statement
2. The leaves turn bright colors in the fall.   statement
3. When does the Easter Bunny arrive?   question
4. Madeleine went to the new art school.   statement
5. Is school over at 3:30?   question
6. Grandma and Grandpa are moving.   statement
7. Anthony went home.   statement
8. Did Mary go to Amy's house?   question
9. Who went to work late?   question
10. Ms. McDaniel is a good teacher.   statement

Directions: Write two statements and two questions below.

Statements:

Answers will vary.

Questions:

Page 194

Kinds of Sentences: Commands and Exclamations

A **command** tells someone to do something. It is followed by a period (.).

Examples: Get your math book. Do your homework.

An **exclamation** shows strong feeling or excitement. It is followed by an exclamation mark (!).

Examples: Watch out for that car! Oh, no! There's a snake!

Directions: Write whether each sentence is a command or exclamation. The first one has been done for you.

1. Please clean your room.   command
2. Wow! Those fireworks are beautiful!   exclamation
3. Come to dinner now.   command
4. Color the sky and water blue.   command
5. Trim the paper carefully.   command
6. Hurry, here comes the bus!   exclamation
7. Isn't that a lovely picture!   exclamation
8. Time to stop playing and clean up.   command
9. Brush your teeth before bedtime.   command
10. Wash your hands before you eat!   exclamation

Directions: Write two commands and two exclamations below.

Commands:

Exclamations: _Answers will vary._

Page 195

Writing: Four Kinds of Sentences

Directions: Write **S** for statement, **Q** for question, **C** for command or **E** for exclamation. End each sentence with a period, question mark or exclamation mark.

Example: **E** You better watch out!

S 1. My little brother insists on coming with us.
C 2. Tell him movies are bad for his health.
S 3. He says he's fond of movies.
Q 4. Does he know there are monsters in this movie?
S 5. He says he needs facts for his science report.
S 6. He's writing about something that hatched from an old egg.
Q 7. Couldn't he just go to the library?
Q 8. Could we dress him like us so he'll blend in?
E or Q 9. Are you kidding! or ?
Q 10. Would he sit by himself at the movie?
S or E 11. That would be too dangerous. or !
S 12. Mom said she'd give us money for candy if we took him with us.
Q 13. Why didn't you say that earlier?
C or E 14. Get your brother and let's go. or !

Page 196

Writing: Four Kinds of Sentences

Directions: For each pair of words, write two kinds of sentences (any combination of question, command, statement or exclamation). Use one or both words in each sentence. Name each kind of sentence you wrote.

Example: pump   crop

Question: What kind of crops did you plant?

Command: Pump the water as fast as you can.

1. pinch   health

2. fond   fact

3. insist   he

Answers will vary.

exclamation   command   statement   question

Page 197

Sentences: Subjects

The **subject** of a sentence tells you who or what the sentence is about. A subject is either a common noun, a proper noun or a pronoun.

Examples: Sue went to the store.
   Sue is the subject of the sentence.

   The tired boys and girls walked home slowly.
   The tired boys and girls is the subject of the sentence.

Directions: Underline the subject of each sentence. The first one has been done for you.

1. The birthday cake was pink and white.
2. Anthony celebrated his fourth birthday.
3. The tower of building blocks fell over.
4. On Saturday, our family will go to a movie.
5. The busy editor was writing sentences.
6. Seven children painted pictures.
7. Two happy dolphins played cheerfully on the surf.
8. A sand crab buried itself in the dunes.
9. Blue waves ran peacefully ashore.
10. Sleepily, she went to bed.

Directions: Write a subject for each sentence.

1. Chocolate-chip ice cream   was melting in the...
2. _____ ran do...
3. _____ ...
4. _____ ... me.
5. _____ ...er a beautiful dress.
6. _____ hopped, skipped and jumped all the way home.
7. _____ wrote a long letter.
8. _____ moved to Paris, France.

Answers will vary.

Page 198

Sentences: Predicates

The **predicate** of a sentence tells what the subject is doing. The predicate contains the action, linking and/or helping verb.

Examples: Sue went to the store.
   Went to the store is the predicate.

   The tired boys and girls walked home slowly.
   Walked home slowly is the predicate.

Hint: When identifying the predicate, look for the verb. The verb is usually the first word of the predicate.

Directions: Underline the predicate in each sentence with two lines. The first one has been done for you.

1. The choir sang joyfully.
2. Their song had both high and low notes.
3. Sal played the piano while they sang.
4. This Sunday the orchestra will have a concert in the park.
5. John is working hard on his homework.
6. He will write a report on electricity.
7. The report will tell about Ben Franklin's kite experiment.
8. Jackie, Mary and Amy played on the swings.
9. They also climbed the rope ladder.
10. Before the girls went home, they slid down the slide.

Directions: Write a predicate for each sentence.

1. Sam and Libby _____
2. At school, the children _____
3. The football team _____
4. Seven silly serpents _____
5. At the zoo, the animals _____

Answers will vary.

Page 199

Changing the Predicate

Directions: Circle the predicate in each sentence. Change the predicate to make a new sentence. The words you add must make sense with the rest of the sentence. The first one has been done for you.

1. Twelve students signed up for the student council elections.

Twelve students were absent from my class today!

2. Our whole family went to the science museum last week.

Sentences will vary.

3. The funny story made us laugh.

4. The brightly colored kites drifted lazily across the sky.

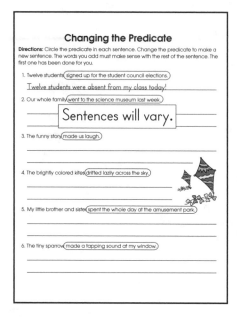

5. My little brother and sister spent the whole day at the amusement park.

6. The tiny sparrow made a tapping sound at my window.

Page 200

Subjects and Predicates

The **subject** tells who or what the sentence is about. The **predicate** tells what the subject does, did, is doing or will do. A complete sentence must have a subject and a predicate.

Examples:

Subject	Predicate
Sharon	writes to her grandmother every week.
The horse	ran around the track quickly.
My mom's car	is bright green.
Denise	will be here after lunch.

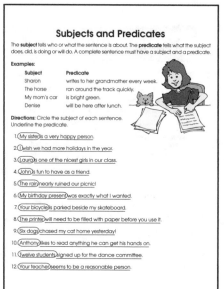

Directions: Circle the subject of each sentence. Underline the predicate.

1. My sister is a very happy person.
2. I wish we had more holidays in the year.
3. Laura is one of the nicest girls in our class.
4. John is fun to have as a friend.
5. The rain nearly ruined our picnic!
6. My birthday present was exactly what I wanted.
7. Your bicycle is parked beside my skateboard.
8. The printer will need to be filled with paper before you use it.
9. Six dogs chased my cat home yesterday!
10. Anthony likes to read anything he can get his hands on.
11. Twelve students signed up for the dance committee.
12. Your teacher seems to be a reasonable person.

Page 201

Subjects and Predicates

Directions: Write subjects to complete the following sentences.

1. _____ went to school last Wednesday.
2. _____ did not under_____ ke.
3. _____ Answers will vary. one could sleep a wink.
4. _____ felt unhappy when the ball game was rained out.
5. _____ wonder what happened at the end of the book.
6. _____ jumped for joy when she won the contest.

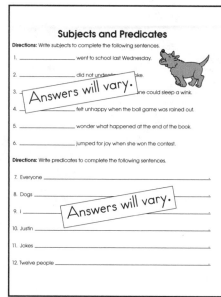

Directions: Write predicates to complete the following sentences.

7. Everyone _____
8. Dogs _____
9. I _____ Answers will vary.
10. Justin _____
11. Jokes _____
12. Twelve people _____

Page 202

Subjects and Predicates

A **sentence** is a group of words that expresses a complete thought. It must have at least one subject and one verb.

Examples:

Sentence: John felt tired and went to bed early.

Not a sentence: Went to bed early.

Directions: Write **S** if the group of words is a complete sentence. Write **NS** if the group of words is not a sentence.

NS 1. Which one of you?
S 2. We're happy for the family.
S 3. We enjoyed the program very much.
NS 4. Felt left out and lonely afterwards.
S 5. Everyone said it was the best party ever!
S 6. No one knows better than I what the problem is.
NS 7. Seventeen of us!
NS 8. Quickly before they.
S 9. Squirrels are lively animals.
S 10. Not many people believe it really happened.
S 11. Certainly, we enjoyed ourselves.
NS 12. Tuned her out.

SUBJECTS & PREDICATES

Page 203

Subjects and Predicates

Directions: On the previous page, some of the groups of words are not sentences. Rewrite them to make complete sentences.

1. _____

2. _____

3. _____ Answers will vary.

4. _____

5. _____

Page 204

Compound Subjects

A **compound subject** is a subject with two parts joined by the word **and** or another conjunction. Compound subjects share the same predicate.

Example:

Her shoes were covered with mud. Her ankles were covered with mud, too.

Compound subject: Her shoes and ankles were covered with mud.

The predicate in both sentences is **were covered with mud**.

Directions: Combine each pair of sentences into one sentence with a compound subject.

1. Bill sneezed. Kassie sneezed.

Bill and Kassie sneezed.

2. Kristin made cookies. Joey made cookies.

Kristin and Joey made cookies.

3. Fruit flies are insects. Ladybugs are insects.

Fruit flies and ladybugs are insects.

4. The girls are planning a dance. The boys are planning a dance.

The girls and boys are planning a dance.

5. Our dog ran after the ducks. Our cat ran after the ducks.

Our dog and cat ran after the ducks.

6. Joshua got lost in the parking lot. Daniel got lost in the parking lot.

Joshua and Daniel got lost in the parking lot.

Page 205

Compound Subjects

If sentences do not share the same predicate, they cannot be combined to write a sentence with a compound subject.

Example: Mary laughed at the story.
Tanya laughed at the television show.

Directions: Combine the pairs of sentences that share the same predicate. Write new sentences with compound subjects.

1. Pete loves swimming. Jake loves swimming.
   Pete and Jake love swimming.

2. A bee stung Elizabeth. A hornet stung Elizabeth.
   A bee and a hornet stung Elizabeth.

3. Sharon is smiling. Susan is frowning.

4. The boys have great suntans. The girls have great suntans.
   The boys and girls have great suntans.

5. Six squirrels chased the kitten. Ten dogs chased the kitten.
   Six squirrels and ten dogs chased the kitten.

6. The trees were covered with insects. The roads were covered with ice.

Page 206

Compound Predicates

A **compound predicate** is a predicate with two parts joined by the word **and** or another conjunction. Compound predicates share the same subject.

Example: The baby grabbed the ball. The baby threw the ball.
   Compound predicate: The baby grabbed the ball and threw it. The subject in both sentences is **the baby.**

Directions: Combine each pair of sentences into one sentence to make a compound predicate.

1. Leah jumped on her bike. Leah rode around the block.
   Leah jumped on her bike and rode around the block.

2. Father rolled out the pie crust. Father put the pie crust in the pan.
   Father rolled out the pie crust and put it in the pan.

3. Anthony slipped on the snow. Anthony nearly fell down.
   Anthony slipped on the snow and nearly fell down.

4. My friend lives in a green house. My friend rides a red bicycle.
   My friend lives in a green house and rides a red bicycle.

5. I opened the magazine. I began to read it quietly.
   I opened the magazine and began to read it quietly.

6. My father bought a new plaid shirt. My father wore his new red tie.
   My father bought a new plaid shirt and wore his new red tie.

Page 207

Compound Predicates

Directions: Combine the pairs of sentences that share the same subject. Write new sentences with compound predicates.

1. Jenny picked a bouquet of flowers. Jenny put the flowers in a vase.
   Jenny picked a bouquet of flowers and put them in a vase.

2. I really enjoy ice cream. She really enjoys ice cream.

3. Everyone had a great time at the pep rally. Then everyone went out for a pizza.
   Everyone had a a great time at the pep rally, then went out for pizza.

4. Cassandra built a model airplane. She painted the airplane bright yellow.
   Cassandra built a model airplane and painted it bright yellow.

5. Her brother was really a hard person to get to know. Her sister was very shy, too.

Page 208

Review

Directions: Circle the subjects.

1. (Everyone) felt the day had been a great success.
2. (Christina and Andrea) were both happy to take the day off.
3. (No one) really understood why he was crying.
4. (Mr. Winston, Ms. Fuller and Ms. Landers) took us on a field trip.

Directions: Underline the predicates.

5. Who can tell what will happen tomorrow?
6. Mark was a carpenter by trade and a talented painter, too.
7. The animals yelped and whined in their cages.
8. Airplane rides made her feel sick to her stomach.

Directions: Combine the sentences to make one sentence with a compound subject.

9. Elizabeth ate everything in sight. George ate everything in sight.
   Elizabeth and George ate everything in sight.

10. Wishing something will make it so. Dreaming something won't make it so.
    Wishing and dreaming something will make it so.

Directions: Combine the sentences to make one sentence with a compound predicate.

11. I jumped for joy. I hugged all my friends.
    I jumped for joy and hugged all my friends.

12. She ran around the track before the race. She warmed up before the race.
    She ran around the track and warmed up before the race.

Page 209

Writing: Nouns

A **noun** names a person, place or thing.

Examples: Persons — boy, girl, Mom, Dad
Places — park, pool, house, office
Things — bike, swing, desk, book

Directions: Read the following sentences. Underline the nouns. The first one has been done for you.

1. The girl went to school.
2. Grandma and Grandpa will visit us soon.
3. The bike is in the garage.
4. Dad went to his office.
5. Mom is at her desk in the den.
6. John's house is near the park.
7. Her brothers are at school.
8. We took the books to the library.

Words underlined in red can be used as both a noun and a verb.

Directions: Read the following words. Underline the nouns. Then categorize the nouns on another sheet of paper into groups of people, places and things.

tree	Mrs. Smith	Dad	cards	Grandma	skip	sell
house	car	truck	Mom	office	grass	sign
boy	run	Sam	stove	greet	grade	school
girl	camp	jump	weave	free	driver	room
salesperson	sad	teach	treat	stripe	paint	Jane
clay	man	leave	happy	play	desk	tape
watch	lives	painter	brother	rain	window	hop

Page 210

Nouns

Directions: Write nouns that name persons.

1. Could you please give this report to my _____?
2. The _____ works many long hours to plant crops.
3. I had to help my little _____ when he wrecked his bike yesterday.

Directions: Write nouns that name places.

4. I always keep my library books on top of the _____ so I can find them.
5. We enjoyed watching the kites fly.
6. Dad built a nice _____ to keep us warm.

Directions: Write nouns that name things.

7. The little _____ purred softly as I held it.
8. Wouldn't you think a _____ would get tired of carrying its house around all day?
9. The _____ scurried into its hole with the piece of cheese.
10. I can tell by the writing that this _____ is mine.
11. Look at the _____ I made in art.
12. His _____ blew away because of the strong wind.

Answers will vary.

Page 211

Writing: Common and Proper Nouns

Common nouns name general people, places and things.

Examples: boy, girl, cat, dog, park, city, building

Proper nouns name specific persons, places and things.

Examples: John, Mary, Fluffy, Rover, Central Park, Chicago, Empire State Building

Proper nouns begin with capital letters.

Directions: Read the following nouns. On the blanks, indicate whether the nouns are common or proper. The first two have been done for you.

1. New York City — proper
2. house — common
3. car — common
4. Ohio — proper
5. river — common
6. Rocky Mountains — proper
7. Mrs. Jones — proper
8. nurse — common
9. Dr. DiCarlo — proper
10. man — common
11. Rock River — proper
12. building — common
13. lawyer — common
14. Grand Canyon — proper
15. city — common
16. state — common

On another sheet of paper, write proper nouns for the above common nouns. **Answers will vary.**

Directions: Read the following sentences. Underline the common nouns. Circle the proper nouns.

1. (Mary)'s birthday is (Friday), (October) 7.
2. (She) likes having her birthday in a fall month.
3. Her friends will meet her at the (Video Arcade) for a party.
4. (Ms. McCarthy) and (Mr. Landry) will help with the birthday party games.
5. (Mary)'s friends will play video games all afternoon.
6. (Amy) and (John) will bring refreshments and games to the party.

Page 212

Proper Nouns: Capitalization

Proper nouns always begin with a capital letter.

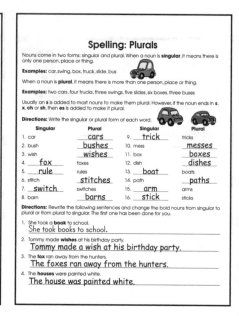

Examples:

Monday
Texas
Karen
Mr. Logan
Hamburger Avenue
Rover

Directions: Cross out the lower-case letters at the beginning of the proper nouns. Write capital letters above them. The first one has been done for you.

1. My teddy bear's name is Cocoa.
2. Ms. Bernhard does an excellent job at Crestview Elementary School.
3. Emily, Elizabeth and Megan live on Main Street.
4. I am sure our teacher said the book report is due on Monday.
5. I believe you can find Lake Street if you turn left at the next light.
6. Will your family be able join our family for dinner at Burger Barn?
7. The weather forecasters think the storm will hit the coast of Louisiana Friday afternoon.
8. My family went to Washington, DC, this summer.
9. Remember, we don't have school on Tuesday because of the teachers' meeting.
10. Who do you think will win the game, the Cougars or the Arrows?

Page 213

Spelling: Plurals

Nouns come in two forms: singular and plural. When a noun is **singular**, it means there is only one person, place or thing.

Examples: car, swing, box, truck, slide, bus

When a noun is **plural**, it means there is more than one person, place or thing.

Examples: two cars, four trucks, three swings, five slides, six boxes, three buses

Usually an **s** is added to most nouns to make them plural. However, if the noun ends in **s**, **x**, **ch** or **sh**, then **es** is added to make it plural.

Directions: Write the singular or plural form of each word.

Singular	Plural	Singular	Plural
1. car	cars	9. trick	tricks
2. bush	bushes	10. mess	messes
3. wish	wishes	11. box	boxes
4. fox	foxes	12. dish	dishes
5. rule	rules	13. boat	boats
6. stitch	stitches	14. path	paths
7. switch	switches	15. arm	arms
8. barn	barns	16. stick	sticks

Directions: Rewrite the following sentences and change the bold nouns from singular to plural or from plural to singular. The first one has been done for you.

1. She took a **book** to school.
   She took books to school.
2. Tommy made **wishes** at his birthday party.
   Tommy made a wish at his birthday party.
3. The **fox** ran away from the hunters.
   The foxes ran away from the hunters.
4. The **houses** were painted white.
   The house was painted white.

Page 214

Spelling: Plurals

When a word ends with a consonant before **y**, to make it plural, drop the **y** and add **ies**.

Examples:
party — parties
cherry — cherries
daisy — daisies

However, if the word ends with a vowel before **y**, just add **s**.

Examples:
boy — boys
toy — toys
monkey — monkeys

Directions: Write the singular or plural form of each word.

Singular	Plural	Singular	Plural
1. fly	flies	7. decoy	decoys
2. boy	boys	8. candy	candies
3. joy	joys	9. toy	toys
4. spy	spies	10. cry	cries
5. key	keys	11. monkey	monkeys
6. dry	dries	12. daisy	daisies

Directions: Write six sentences of your own using any of the plurals above.

Sentences will vary.

Page 215

Spelling: Plurals

Some words in the English language do not follow any of the plural rules discussed earlier. These words may not change at all from singular to plural, or they may completely change spellings.

No Change		Complete Change	
Singular	**Plural**	**Singular**	**Plural**
deer	deer	goose	geese
pants	pants	ox	oxen
scissors	scissors	man	men
moose	moose	child	children
sheep	sheep	leaf	leaves

Directions: Write the singular or plural form of each word. Use a dictionary to help if necessary.

Singular	Plural	Singular	Plural
1. moose	moose	6. leaf	leaves
2. woman	women	7. sheep	sheep
3. deer	deer	8. scissors	scissors
4. child	children	9. tooth	teeth
5. hoof	hooves	10. wharf	wharves or wharfs

Directions: Write four sentences of your own using two singular and two plural words from above.

Sentences will vary.

Page 216

Review

Review these rules for making singular words plural.

For most words, simply add **s**.
Examples: one book — two books   one house — four houses

For words ending with **s**, **ss**, **sh**, **ch** and **x**, add **es**.
Examples: one class — two classes   one church — three churches   one box — four boxes   one crash — five crashes

For words ending with a consonant before **y**, drop the **y** and add **ies**.
Examples: one daisy — three daisies   one cherry — two cherries

For words ending with a vowel before **y**, just add **s**.
Examples: one key — eight keys   one monkey — four monkeys

Directions: Write the singular or plural form of each word.

Singular	Plural	Singular	Plural
1. mattress	mattresses	10. candy	candies
2. bush	bushes	11. try	tries
3. sandwich	sandwiches	12. turkey	turkeys
4. fry	fries	13. copy	copies
5. cross	crosses	14. factory	factories
6. marsh	marshes	15. fox	foxes
7. supply	supplies	16. ax	axes
8. donkey	donkeys	17. berry	berries
9. stove	stoves	18. day	days

Page 217

Pronouns

A **pronoun** is a word that takes the place of a noun in a sentence.

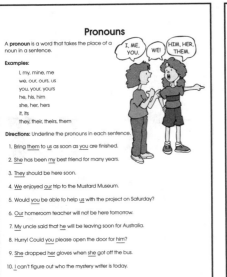

Examples:

I, my, mine, me
we, our, ours, us
you, your, yours
he, his, him
she, her, hers
it, its
they, their, theirs, them

Directions: Underline the pronouns in each sentence.

1. Bring them to us as soon as you are finished.
2. She has been my best friend for many years.
3. They should be here soon.
4. We enjoyed our trip to the Mustard Museum.
5. Would you be able to help us with the project on Saturday?
6. Our homeroom teacher will not be here tomorrow.
7. My uncle said that he will be leaving soon for Australia.
8. Hurry! Could you please open the door for him?
9. She dropped her gloves when she got off the bus.
10. I can't figure out who the mystery writer is today.

Page 218

Writing: Verbs

Verbs are the action words in a sentence. There are three kinds of verbs: action verbs, linking verbs and helping verbs.

An **action verb** tells the action of a sentence.

Examples: run, hop, skip, sleep, jump, talk, snore
Michael **ran** to the store. **Ran** is the action verb.

A **linking verb** joins the subject and predicate of a sentence.

Examples: am, is, are, was, were
Michael **was** at the store. **Was** is the linking verb.

A **helping verb** is used with an action verb to "help" the action of the sentence.

Examples: am, is, are, was, were
Matthew **was** helping Michael. **Was** helps the action verb **helping**.

action linking helping

Directions: Read the following sentences. Underline the verbs. Above each, write **A** for action verb, **L** for linking verb and **H** for helping verb. The first one has been done for you.

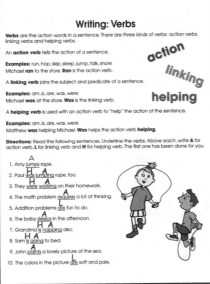

1. Amy jumps rope. (A)
2. Paul was jumping rope, too. (H A)
3. They were working on their homework. (H A)
4. The math problem requires a lot of thinking. (A)
5. Addition problems are fun to do. (L)
6. The baby sleeps in the afternoon. (A)
7. Grandma is napping also. (H A)
8. Sam is going to bed. (H A)
9. John paints a lovely picture of the sea. (A)
10. The colors in the picture are soft and pale. (L)

Page 219

Writing: Verb Tense

Not only do verbs tell the action of a sentence but they also tell when the action takes place. This is called the **verb tense**. There are three verb tenses: past, present and future tense.

Present-tense verbs tell what is happening now.

Example: Jane **spells** words with long vowel sounds.

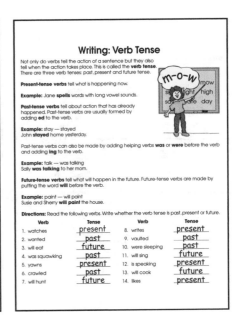

Past-tense verbs tell about action that has already happened. Past-tense verbs are usually formed by adding **ed** to the verb.

Example: stay — stayed
John **stayed** home yesterday.

Past-tense verbs can also be made by adding helping verbs **was** or **were** before the verb and adding **ing** to the verb.

Example: talk — was talking
Sally **was talking** to her mom.

Future-tense verbs tell what will happen in the future. Future-tense verbs are made by putting the word **will** before the verb.

Example: paint — will paint
Susie and Sherry **will paint** the house.

Directions: Read the following verbs. Write whether the verb tense is past, present or future.

Verb	Tense	Verb	Tense
1. watches	present	8. writes	present
2. wanted	past	9. vaulted	past
3. will eat	future	10. were sleeping	past
4. was squawking	past	11. will sing	future
5. yawns	present	12. is speaking	present
6. crawled	past	13. will cook	future
7. will hunt	future	14. likes	present

Page 220

Verbs: Present, Past and Future Tense

Directions: Read the following sentences. Write **PRES** if the sentence is in present tense. Write **PAST** if the sentence is in past tense. Write **FUT** if the sentence is in future tense. The first one has been done for you.

FUT 1. I will be thrilled to accept the award.
FUT 2. Will you go with me to the dentist?
PAST 3. I thought he looked familiar!
PAST 4. They ate every single slice of pizza.
PRES 5. I run myself ragged sometimes.
PRES 6. Do you think this project is worthwhile?
PAST 7. No one has been able to repair the broken plate.
PRES 8. Thoughtful gifts are always appreciated.
PAST 9. I liked the way she sang!
FUT 10. With a voice like that, he will go a long way.
PRES 11. It's my fondest hope that they visit soon.
PAST 12. I wanted that coat very much.
FUT 13. She'll be happy to take your place.
PRES 14. Everyone thinks the test is easy.
PRES 15. Collecting stamps is her favorite hobby.

Page 221

Writing: Using ing Verbs

Remember, use **is** and **are** when describing something happening right now. Use **was** and **were** when describing something that already happened.

Directions: Use the verb in bold to complete each sentence. Add **ing** to the verb and use **is**, **are**, **was** or **were**.

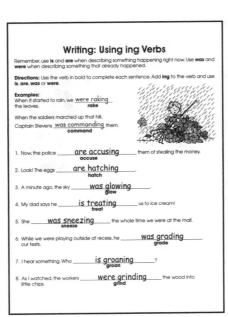

Examples:
When it started to rain, we were raking the leaves.
rake

When the soldiers marched up that hill, Captain Stevens was commanding them.
command

1. Now, the police are accusing them of stealing the money.
accuse
2. Look! The eggs are hatching.
hatch
3. A minute ago, the sky was glowing.
glow
4. My dad says he is treating us to ice cream!
treat
5. She was sneezing the whole time we were at the mall.
sneeze
6. While we were playing outside at recess, he was grading our tests.
grade
7. I hear something. Who is groaning?
groan
8. As I watched, the workers were grinding the wood into little chips.
grind

Page 222

Writing: Present-Tense Verbs

Directions: Write two sentences for each verb below. Tell about something that is happening now and write the verb as both simple present tense and present tense with a helping verb.

Example: run
Mia runs to the store. Mia is running to the store.

1. hatch
2. check
3. spell
4. blend
5. lick
6. cry
7. write
8. dream

Sentences will vary.

Grade 4 - Comprehensive Curriculum

Page 223

Writing: Verb Tense

Directions: Read the following sentences. Underline the verbs. Above each verb, write whether it is past, present or future tense.

past
1. The crowd was booing the referee.
future
2. Sally will compete on the balance beam.
present
3. Matt marches with the band.
present
4. Nick is marching, too.
past
5. The geese swooped down to the pond.
future
6. Dad will fly home tomorrow.
past
7. They were looking for a new book.
present
8. Presently, they are going to the garden.
future
9. The children will pick the ripe vegetables.
past
10. Grandmother canned the green beans.

Directions: Write six sentences of your own using the correct verb tense.

Past tense:
_____

Present tense:
_____

Future tense:

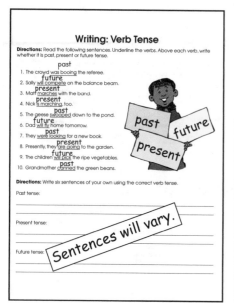

Sentences will vary.

Page 224

Adding "ed" to Make Verbs Past Tense

To make many verbs past tense, add **ed**.
Examples:
cook + ed = cooked   wish + ed = wished   play + ed = played
When a verb ends in a **silent e**, drop the **e** and add **ed**.
Examples:
hope + ed = hoped   hate + ed = hated
When a verb ends in **y** after a consonant, change the **y** to **i** and add **ed**.
Examples:
hurry + ed = hurried   marry + ed = married
When a verb ends in a single consonant after a single short vowel, double the final consonant before adding **ed**.
Examples:
stop + ed = stopped   hop + ed = hopped

Directions: Write the past tense of the verb correctly. The first one has been done for you.

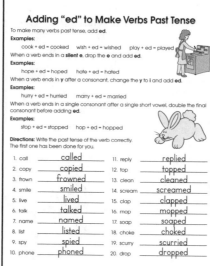

1. call	called	11. reply	replied
2. copy	copied	12. top	topped
3. frown	frowned	13. clean	cleaned
4. smile	smiled	14. scream	screamed
5. live	lived	15. clap	clapped
6. talk	talked	16. mop	mopped
7. name	named	17. soap	soaped
8. list	listed	18. choke	choked
9. spy	spied	19. scurry	scurried
10. phone	phoned	20. drop	dropped

Page 225

Writing: Past-Tense Verbs

To write about something that already happened, you can add **ed** to the verb.

Example: Yesterday, we **talked**.
You can also use **was** and **were** and add **ing** to the verb.

Example: Yesterday, we **were talking**.
When a verb ends with **e**, you usually drop the **e** before adding **ing**.

Examples: grade — was grading   weave — were weaving
tape — was taping   sneeze — were sneezing

Directions: Write two sentences for each verb below. Tell about something that has already happened and write the verb both ways. (Watch the spelling of the verbs that end with **e**.)

Example: stream

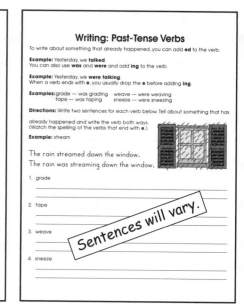

The rain streamed down the window.
The rain was streaming down the window.

1. grade
_____

2. tape
_____

3. weave
_____

4. sneeze
_____

Sentences will vary.

Page 226

Irregular Verbs: Past Tense

Irregular verbs change completely in the past tense. Unlike regular verbs, past-tense forms of irregular verbs are not formed by adding **ed**.
Example: The past tense of **go** is **went**.

Other verbs change some letters to form the past tense.
Example: The past tense of **break** is **broke**.

A **helping verb** helps to tell about the past. **Has**, **have** and **had** are helping verbs used with action verbs to show the action occurred in the past. The past-tense form of the irregular verb sometimes changes when a helping verb is added.

Present Tense Irregular Verb	Past Tense Irregular Verb	Past Tense Irregular Verb With Helper
go	went	have/has/had gone
see	saw	have/has/had seen
do	did	have/has/had done
bring	brought	have/has/had brought
sing	sang	have/has/had sung
drive	drove	have/has/had driven
swim	swam	have/has/had swum
sleep	slept	have/has/had slept

Directions: Choose four words from the chart. Write one sentence using the past-tense form of the verb without a helping verb. Write another sentence using the past-tense form with a helping verb.

1. _____
2. _____
3. _____
4. _____

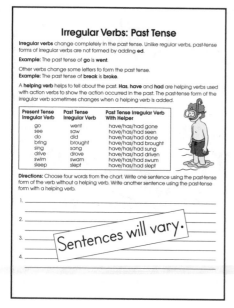

Sentences will vary.

Page 227

The Irregular Verb "Be"

Be is an irregular verb. The present-tense forms of **be** are **be**, **am**, **is** and **are**. The past-tense forms of **be** are **was** and **were**.

Directions: Write the correct form of **be** in the blanks. The first one has been done for you.

1. I **am** so happy for you!

2. Jared **was** unfriendly yesterday.

3. English can **be** a lot of fun to learn.

4. They **are** among the nicest people I know.

5. They **were** late yesterday.

6. She promises she **is** going to arrive on time.

7. I **am** nervous right now about the test.

8. If you **are** satisfied now, so am I.

9. He **was** as nice to me last week as I had hoped.

10. He can **be** very gracious.

11. Would you **be** offended if I moved your desk?

12. He **was** watching at the window for me yesterday.

Page 228

Verbs: "Was" and "Were"

Singular	Plural
I was	we were
you were	you were
he, she, it was	they were

I was over there when it happened

You were?

Directions: Write the correct form of the verb in the blanks. Circle the subject of each sentence. The first one has been done for you.

1. (He) was/were so happy that we all smiled, too. — **was**
2. Was/Were (you) at the party? — **Were**
3. (She) was/were going to the store. — **was**
4. (He) was/were always forgetting his hat. — **was**
5. Was/Were (she) there? — **Was**
6. Was/Were (you) sure of your answers? — **Were**
7. (She) was/were glad to help. — **was**
8. (They) was/were excited. — **were**
9. Exactly what was/were (you) planning to do? — **were**
10. (It) was/were wet outside. — **was**
11. (They) was/were scared by the noise. — **were**
12. Was/Were (they) expected before noon? — **Were**
13. (It) was/were too early to get up! — **was**
14. (She) was/were always early. — **was**
15. (You) were/was the first person I asked. — **were**

Page 229

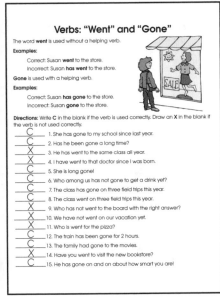

Verbs: "Went" and "Gone"

The word **went** is used without a helping verb.

Examples:

Correct: Susan **went** to the store.
Incorrect: Susan **has went** to the store.

Gone is used with a helping verb.

Examples:

Correct: Susan **has gone** to the store.
Incorrect: Susan **gone** to the store.

Directions: Write **C** in the blank if the verb is used correctly. Draw an **X** in the blank if the verb is not used correctly.

C 1. She has gone to my school since last year.
C 2. Has he been gone a long time?
X 3. He has went to the same class all year.
X 4. I have went to that doctor since I was born.
C 5. She is long gone!
C 6. Who among us has not gone to get a drink yet?
C 7. The class has gone on three field trips this year.
C 8. The class went on three field trips this year.
X 9. Who has not went to the board with the right answer?
X 10. We have not went on our vacation yet.
X 11. Who is went for the pizza?
C 12. The train has been gone for 2 hours.
C 13. The family had gone to the movies.
X 14. Have you went to visit the new bookstore?
C 15. He has gone on and on about how smart you are!

Page 230

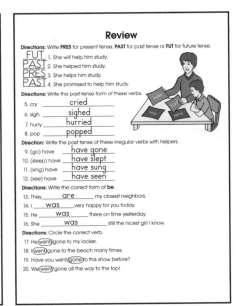

Review

Directions: Write **PRES** for present tense, **PAST** for past tense or **FUT** for future tense.

FUT 1. She will help him study.
PAST 2. She helped him study.
PRES 3. She helps him study.
PAST 4. She promised to help him study.

Directions: Write the past-tense form of these verbs.

5. cry ___cried___
6. sigh ___sighed___
7. hurry ___hurried___
8. pop ___popped___

Direction: Write the past tense of these irregular verbs with helpers.

9. (go) have ___have gone___
10. (sleep) have ___have slept___
11. (sing) have ___have sung___
12. (see) have ___have seen___

Directions: Write the correct form of **be**.

13. They ___are___ my closest neighbors.
14. I ___was___ very happy for you today.
15. He ___was___ there on time yesterday.
16. She ___was___ still the nicest girl I know.

Directions: Circle the correct verb.

17. He (went) gone to my locker.
18. I (went) gone to the beach many times.
19. Have you went (gone) to this show before?
20. We (went) gone all the way to the top!

Page 231

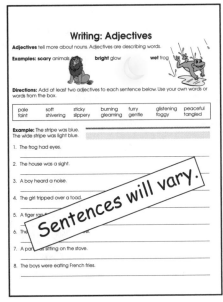

Writing: Adjectives

Adjectives tell more about nouns. Adjectives are describing words.

Examples: **scary** animals   **bright** glow   **wet** frog

Directions: Add at least two adjectives to each sentence below. Use your own words or words from the box.

| pale | soft | sticky | burning | furry | glistening | peaceful |
| faint | shivering | slippery | gleaming | gentle | foggy | tangled |

Example: The stripe was blue.
The wide stripe was light blue. _____

1. The frog had eyes.

2. The house was a sight.

3. A boy heard a noise.

4. The girl tripped over a toad.

5. A tiger ran

6.

7. A par... was sitting on the stove.

8. The boys were eating French fries.

Sentences will vary.

Page 232

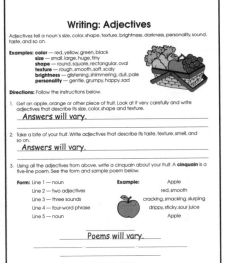

Writing: Adjectives

Adjectives tell a noun's size, color, shape, texture, brightness, darkness, personality, sound, taste, and so on.

Examples: color — red, yellow, green, black
size — small, large, huge, tiny
shape — round, square, rectangular, oval
texture — rough, smooth, soft, scaly
brightness — glistening, shimmering, dull, pale
personality — gentle, grumpy, happy, sad

Directions: Follow the instructions below.

1. Get an apple, orange or other piece of fruit. Look at it very carefully and write adjectives that describe its size, color, shape and texture.
   ___Answers will vary.___

2. Take a bite of your fruit. Write adjectives that describe its taste, texture, smell, and so on.
   ___Answers will vary.___

3. Using all the adjectives from above, write a cinquain about your fruit. A **cinquain** is a five-line poem. See the form and sample poem below.

Form: Line 1 — noun
Line 2 — two adjectives
Line 3 — three sounds
Line 4 — four-word phrase
Line 5 — noun

Example: Apple
red, smooth
cracking, smacking, slurping
drippy, sticky, sour juice
Apple

___Poems will vary.___

Page 233

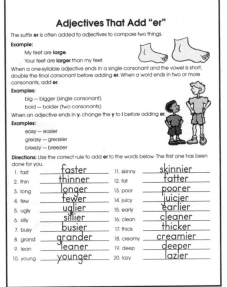

Adjectives That Add "er"

The suffix **er** is often added to adjectives to compare two things.

Example:

My feet are **large**.
Your feet are **larger** than my feet.

When a one-syllable adjective ends in a single consonant and the vowel is short, double the final consonant before adding **er**. When a word ends in two or more consonants, add **er**.

Examples:

big — bigger (single consonant)
bold — bolder (two consonants)

When an adjective ends in **y**, change the **y** to **i** before adding **er**.

Examples:

easy — easier
greasy — greasier
breezy — breezier

Directions: Use the correct rule to add **er** to the words below. The first one has been done for you.

1. fast ___faster___
2. thin ___thinner___
3. long ___longer___
4. few ___fewer___
5. ugly ___uglier___
6. silly ___sillier___
7. busy ___busier___
8. grand ___grander___
9. lean ___leaner___
10. young ___younger___
11. skinny ___skinnier___
12. fat ___fatter___
13. poor ___poorer___
14. juicy ___juicier___
15. early ___earlier___
16. clean ___cleaner___
17. thick ___thicker___
18. creamy ___creamier___
19. deep ___deeper___
20. lazy ___lazier___

Page 234

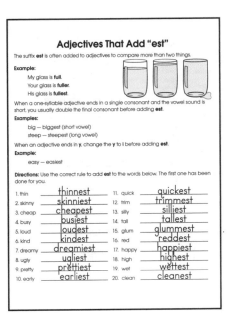

Adjectives That Add "est"

The suffix **est** is often added to adjectives to compare more than two things.

Example:

My glass is **full**.
Your glass is **fuller**.
His glass is **fullest**.

When a one-syllable adjective ends in a single consonant and the vowel sound is short, you usually double the final consonant before adding **est**.

Examples:

big — biggest (short vowel)
steep — steepest (long vowel)

When an adjective ends in **y**, change the **y** to **i** before adding **est**.

Example:

easy — easiest

Directions: Use the correct rule to add **est** to the words below. The first one has been done for you.

1. thin ___thinnest___
2. skinny ___skinniest___
3. cheap ___cheapest___
4. busy ___busiest___
5. loud ___loudest___
6. kind ___kindest___
7. dreamy ___dreamiest___
8. ugly ___ugliest___
9. pretty ___prettiest___
10. early ___earliest___
11. quick ___quickest___
12. trim ___trimmest___
13. silly ___silliest___
14. tall ___tallest___
15. glum ___glummest___
16. red ___reddest___
17. happy ___happiest___
18. high ___highest___
19. wet ___wettest___
20. clean ___cleanest___

Page 235

Adding "er" and "est" to Adjectives

Directions: Circle the correct adjective for each sentence. The first one has been done for you.

1. Of all the students in the gym, her voice was (louder, (loudest)).

2. "I can tell you are ((busier,) busiest) than I am," he said to the librarian.

3. If you and Carl stand back to back, I can see which one is ((taller,) tallest).

4. She is the (kinder, (kindest)) teacher in the whole building.

5. Wow! That is the (bigger, (biggest)) pumpkin I have ever seen!

6. I believe your flashlight is ((brighter,) brightest) than mine.

7. "This is the (cleaner, (cleanest)) your room has been in a long time," Mother said.

8. The leaves on that plant are ((prettier,) prettiest) than the ones on this plant.

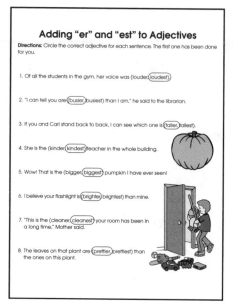

Page 236

Adjectives Preceded by "More"

Most adjectives of two or more syllables are preceded by the word **more** as a way to show comparison between two things.

Examples:
Correct: intelligent, more intelligent
Incorrect: intelligenter
Correct: famous, more famous
Incorrect: famouser

Directions: Write **more** before the adjectives that fit the rule. Draw an **X** in the blanks of the adjectives that do not fit the rule. To test yourself, say the words aloud using **more** and adding **er** to hear which way sounds correct. The first two have been done for you.

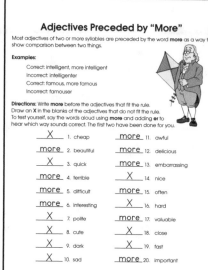

X	1. cheap	more	11. awful
more	2. beautiful	more	12. delicious
X	3. quick	more	13. embarrassing
more	4. terrible	X	14. nice
more	5. difficult	more	15. often
more	6. interesting	X	16. hard
X	7. polite	more	17. valuable
X	8. cute	X	18. close
X	9. dark	X	19. fast
X	10. sad	more	20. important

Page 237

Adjectives Using "er" or "More"

Directions: Add the word or words needed in each sentence. The first one has been done for you.

1. I thought the book was **more interesting** than the movie. (interesting)

2. Do you want to carry this box? It is **lighter** than the one you have now. (light)

3. I noticed you are moving **slower** this morning. Does your ankle still bother you? (slow)

4. Thomas Edison is probably **more famous** for his invention of the electric light bulb than of the phonograph. (famous)

5. She stuck out her lower lip and whined, "Your ice-cream cone is **bigger** than mine!" (big)

6. Mom said my room was **cleaner** than it has been in a long time. (clean)

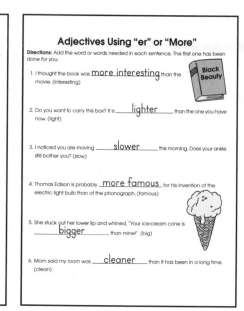

Page 238

Adjectives Preceded by "Most"

Most adjectives of two or more syllables are preceded by the word **most** as a way to show comparison between more than two things.

Examples:
Correct: intelligent, most intelligent
Incorrect: intelligentest
Correct: famous, most famous
Incorrect: famousest

Directions: Read the following groups of sentences. In the last sentence for each group, write the adjective preceded by **most**. The first one has been done for you.

1. My uncle is intelligent.
My aunt is more intelligent.
My cousin is the **most intelligent**.

2. I am thankful.
My brother is more thankful.
My parents are the **most thankful**.

3. Your sister is polite.
Your brother is more polite.
You are the **most polite**.

4. The blouse was expensive.
The sweater was more expensive.
The coat was the **most expensive**.

5. The class was fortunate.
The teacher was more fortunate.
The principal was the **most fortunate**.

6. The cookies were delicious.
The cake was even more delicious.
The brownies were the **most delicious**.

7. That painting is elaborate.
The sculpture is more elaborate.
The finger painting is the **most elaborate**.

Page 239

Adjectives Using "est" or "Most"

Directions: Add the word or words needed to complete each sentence. The first one has been done for you.

1. The star over there is the **brightest** of all (bright).

2. "I believe this is the **most delightful** time I have ever had," said Mackenzie. (delightful)

3. That game was the **most exciting** one of the whole year! (exciting)

4. I think this tree has the **greenest** leaves. (green)

5. We will need the **sharpest** knife you have to cut the face for the jack-o-lantern. (sharp)

6. Everyone agreed that your chocolate chip cookies were the **most delicious** of all. (delicious)

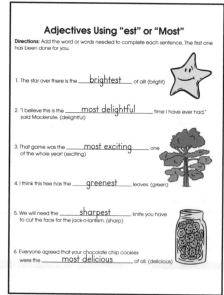

Page 240

Writing: Adverbs

Like adjectives, **adverbs** are describing words. They describe verbs. Adverbs tell how, when or where action takes place.

Examples: How	When	Where
slowly	yesterday	here
gracefully	today	there
swiftly	tomorrow	everywhere
quickly	soon	

Hint: To identify an adverb, locate the verb, then ask yourself if there are any words that tell how, when or where. The first one has been done for you.

Directions: Read the following sentences. Underline the adverbs, then write whether they tell how, when or where. The first one has been done for you.

1. At the end of the day, the children ran quickly home from school. — how
2. They will have a spelling test tomorrow. — when
3. Slowly, the children filed to their seats. — how
4. The teacher sat here at her desk. — where
5. She will pass the tests back later. — when
6. The students received their grades happily. — how

Directions: Write four sentences of your own using any of the adverbs above.

Sentences will vary.

Page 241

Adverbs

Adverbs are words that tell when, where or how.

Adverbs of time tell when.

Example:

The train left yesterday.

Yesterday is an adverb of time. It tells when the train left.

Adverbs of place tell where.

Example:

The girl walked away.

Away is an adverb of place. It tells where the girl walked.

Adverbs of manner tell how.

Example:

The boy walked quickly.

Quickly is an adverb of manner. It tells how the boy walked.

Directions: Write the adverb for each sentence in the first blank. In the second blank, write whether it is an adverb of time, place or manner. The first one has been done for you.

1. The family ate downstairs.	downstairs	place
2. The relatives laughed loudly.	loudly	manner
3. We will finish tomorrow.	tomorrow	time
4. The snowstorm will stop soon.	soon	time
5. She sings beautifully!	beautifully	manner
6. The baby slept soundly.	soundly	manner
7. The elevator stopped suddenly.	suddenly	manner
8. Does the plane leave today?	today	time
9. The phone call came yesterday.	yesterday	time
10. She ran outside.	outside	place

Page 242

Adverbs of Time

Directions: Choose a word or group of words from the box to complete each sentence. Make sure the adverb you choose makes sense with the rest of the sentence.

in 2 weeks	last winter
next week	at the end of the day
soon	right now
2 days ago	tonight

Sample answers:

1. We had a surprise birthday party for him ___2 days ago___

2. Our science projects are due ___in 2 weeks___

3. My best friend will be moving ___next week___

4. Justin and Ronnie need our help ___right now___!

5. We will find out who the winners are ___at the end of the day___

6. Can you take me to ball practice ___tonight___?

7. She said we will be getting a letter ___soon___

8. Diane made the quilt ___last winter___

Page 243

Adverbs of Place

Directions: Choose one word from the box to complete each sentence. Make sure the adverb you choose makes sense with the rest of the sentence.

inside	upstairs	below	everywhere
home	somewhere	outside	there

Sample answers:

1. Each child took a new library book ___home___

2. We looked ___everywhere___ for his jacket.

3. We will have recess ___inside___ because it is raining.

4. From the top of the mountain we could see the village far ___below___

5. My sister and I share a bedroom ___upstairs___

6. The teacher warned the children, "You must play with the ball ___outside___"

7. Mother said, "I know that recipe is ___somewhere___ in this file box!"

8. You can put the chair ___there___

Page 244

Adverbs of Manner

Directions: Choose a word from the box to complete each sentence. Make sure the adverb you choose makes sense with the rest of the sentence. One word will be used twice.

quickly	carefully	loudly	easily	carelessly	slowly

Sample answers:

1. The scouts crossed the old bridge ___carefully___

2. We watched the turtle move ___slowly___ across the yard.

3. Everyone completed the math test ___quickly___

4. The quarterback scampered ___easily___ down the sideline.

5. The mother ___carefully___ cleaned the child's sore knee.

6. The fire was caused by someone ___carelessly___ tossing a match.

7. The alarm rang ___loudly___ while we were eating.

Page 245

Adjectives and Adverbs

Directions: Write **ADJ** on the line if the bold word is an adjective. Write **ADV** if the bold word is an adverb. The first one has been done for you.

ADV	1. That road leads **nowhere**.
ADJ	2. The squirrel was **nearby**.
ADJ	3. Her **delicious** cookies were all eaten.
ADV	4. Everyone rushed **indoors**.
ADV	5. He **quickly** zipped his jacket.
ADJ	6. She hummed a **popular** tune.
ADJ	7. Her **sunny** smile warmed my heart.
ADV	8. I hung your coat **there**.
ADV	9. Bring that **here** this minute!
ADV	10. We all walked **back** to school.
ADJ	11. The **skinniest** boy ate the most food!
ADJ	12. She acts like a **famous** person.
ADJ	13. The **silliest** jokes always make me laugh.
ADV	14. She must have parked her car **somewhere**!
ADV	15. Did you take the test **today**?

Page 246

Adjectives and Adverbs

Directions: Read this story. Underline the adjectives. Circle the adverbs. Write the words in the correct column at the end of the story.

Surprise!

Emily and Elizabeth tiptoed *quietly* through the dark hallway. Even though none of the lights were lit, they knew the presents were there. Every year the two sisters had gone to Mom and Dad's bedroom to wake them on Christmas morning. This year would be different, they decided.

Last night after supper, they had secretly plotted to look early in the morning before Mom and Dad were awake. The girls knew that Emily's red-and-green stocking and Elizabeth's striped stocking hung by the brick fireplace. They knew the beautiful tree was in the corner by the rocking chair.

"Won't Mom and Dad be surprised to awaken on their own?" asked Elizabeth quietly. Emily whispered, "Click the overhead lights so we can see better."

"You don't have to whisper," said a voice.

There sat Mom and Dad as the Christmas-tree lights suddenly shone.

Dad said, "I guess the surprise is on you two!"

Answers may include:

Adverbs	Adjectives	
quietly	dark	striped
there	none	brick
secretly	every	beautiful
early	two	rocking
quietly	this	Christmas-tree
better	last	overhead
suddenly	different	
before	red-and-green	

ANSWER KEY

Page 247

Review

Directions: Write the correct words to complete the sentences. Use the words on the presents at the bottom of the page.

1. The suffix ___er___ and the word ___more___ are used when comparing two things.
2. One example of an adverb of time is ___tomorrow___.
3. When an adjective ends with ___y___, you change the y to i before adding er or est.
4. An ___adverb___ is a word that tells when, where or how.
5. An example of an adverb of place is ___there___.
6. The suffix ___est___ and the word ___most___ are used when comparing more than two things.
7. An ___adjective___ is a word that describes a noun.
8. An example of an adverb of manner is ___softly___.

adjective   est   softly   adverb
er   y
most   there   more   tomorrow

Page 248

Review

Directions: For the bold word in each sentence, write **N** for noun, **V** for verb, **ADJ** for adjective or **ADV** for adverb.

__ADJ__ 1. She is the **tallest** one outside.
__N__ 2. **She** is the tallest one outside.
__V__ 3. She **is** the tallest one outside.
__ADV__ 4. She is the tallest one **outside**.

Directions: For the bold word in each sentence, write **P** for adverb of place, **T** for adverb of time or **M** for adverb of manner.

__P__ 5. Your shoes are **downstairs**.
__M__ 6. His response was **speedy**.
__P__ 7. **Here** is my homework.
__T__ 8. The present will be mailed **tomorrow**.

Directions: Add er and est or more and most to the words below to show comparison.

9. fat __fatter__ __fattest__
10. grateful __more grateful__ __most grateful__
11. serious __more serious__ __most serious__
12. easy __easier__ __easiest__

Directions: For the bold word in each sentence, write **ADV** for adverb or **ADJ** for adjective.

__ADJ__ 13. **Grumpy** people are not pleasant.
__ADV__ 14. Put the package **there**, please.
__ADV__ 15. **Upstairs** is where I sleep.
__ADJ__ 16. **Warm** blankets feel toasty on cold nights.

Page 249

Writing: Using Conjunctions

Conjunctions are joining words that can be used to combine sentences. Words such as **and**, **but**, **or**, **when** and **after** are conjunctions.

Examples:
Sally went to the mall. She went to the movies.
Sally went to the mall, and she went to the movies.

We can have our vacation at home. We can vacation at the beach.
We can have our vacation at home, or we can vacation at the beach.

Mary fell on the playground. She did not hurt herself.
Mary fell on the playground, but she did not hurt herself.

Note: The conjunctions **after** or **when** are usually placed at the beginning of the sentence.

Example: Marge went to the store. She went to the gas station.
After Marge went to the store, she went to the gas station.

Directions: Combine the following sentences using a conjunction.
Sample answers:
1. Peter fell down the steps. He broke his foot. (and)
   Peter fell down the steps, and he broke his foot.
2. I visited New York. I would like to see Chicago. (but)
   I visited New York, but I would like to see Chicago.
3. Amy can edit books. She can write stories. (or)
   Amy can edit books, or she can write stories.
4. He played in the barn. John started to sneeze. (when)
   When John played in the barn, he started to sneeze.
5. The team won the playoffs. They went to the championships. (after)
   After the team won the playoffs, they went to the championships.
Directions: Write three sentences of your own using the conjunctions **and**, **but**, **or**, **when** or **after**.

Sentences will vary.

Page 250

"And," "But," "Or"

Directions: Write and, but or or to complete the sentences.

1. I thought we might try that new hamburger place, __but__ Mom wants to eat at the Spaghetti Shop.
2. We could stay home, __or__ would you rather go to the game?
3. She went right home after school, __but__ he stopped at the store.
4. Mother held the piece of paneling, __and__ Father nailed it in place.
5. She babysat last weekend, __and__ her big sister went with her.
6. She likes raisins in her oatmeal, __but__ I would rather have mine with brown sugar.
7. She was planning on coming over tomorrow, __but__ I asked her if she could wait until the weekend.
8. Tomato soup with crackers sounds good to me, __or__ would you rather have vegetable beef soup?

Page 251

"Because" and "So"

Directions: Write because or so to complete the sentences.

1. She cleaned the paint brushes __so__ they would be ready in the morning.
2. Father called home complaining of a sore throat __so__ Mom stopped by the pharmacy.
3. His bus will be running late __because__ it has a flat tire.
4. We all worked together __so__ we could get the job done sooner.
5. We took a variety of sandwiches on the picnic __because__ we knew not everyone liked cheese and olives with mayonnaise.
6. All the school children were sent home __because__ the electricity went off at school.
7. My brother wants us to meet his girlfriend __so__ she will be coming to dinner with us on Friday.
8. He forgot to take his umbrella along this morning __so__ now his clothes are very wet.

Page 252

"When" and "After"

Directions: Write when or after to complete the sentences.

Answers may vary.

1. I knew we were in trouble __when__ I heard the thunder in the distance.
2. We carried the baskets of cherries to the car __after__ we were finished picking them.
3. Mother took off her apron __after__ I reminded her that our dinner guests would be here any minute.
4. I wondered if we would have school tomorrow __after__ I noticed the snow begin to fall.
5. The boys and girls all clapped __when__ the magician pulled the colored scarves out of his sleeve.
6. I was started __when__ the phone rang so late last night.
7. You will need to get the film developed __after__ you have taken all the pictures.
8. The children began to run __when__ the snake started to move!

Page 253

Conjunctions

Directions: Choose the best conjunction from the box to combine the pairs of sentences. Then rewrite the sentences.

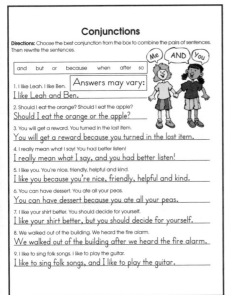

| and | but | or | because | when | after | so |

Answers may vary:

1. I like Leah. I like Ben.
I like Leah and Ben.

2. Should I eat the orange? Should I eat the apple?
Should I eat the orange or the apple?

3. You will get a reward. You turned in the lost item.
You will get a reward because you turned in the lost item.

4. I really mean what I say! You had better listen!
I really mean what I say, and you had better listen!

5. I like you. You're nice, friendly, helpful and kind.
I like you because you're nice, friendly, helpful and kind.

6. You can have dessert. You ate all your peas.
You can have dessert because you ate all your peas.

7. I like your shirt better. You should decide for yourself.
I like your shirt better, but you should decide for yourself.

8. We walked out of the building. We heard the fire alarm.
We walked out of the building after we heard the fire alarm.

9. I like to sing folk songs. I like to play the guitar.
I like to sing folk songs, and I like to play the guitar.

Page 254

Writing: Using Conjunctions

Directions: Combine each pair of sentences using the conjunctions **or**, **and**, **but**, **after** or **when**. You may need to change the word order in the sentences.

Example:
My stomach hurts.   I still want to go to the movies.
My stomach hurts, but I still want to go to the movies.

Sample answers:

1. He accused me of peeking.   I felt very angry.
When he accused me of peeking, I felt very angry.

2. The accident was over.   I started shaking.
After the accident was over, I started shaking.

3. Is that a freckle?   Is that dirt?
Is that a freckle or is that dirt?

4. I forgot my jacket.   I had to go back and get it.
I forgot my jacket, and I had to go back and get it.

5. I like Christmas.   I don't like waiting for it.
I like Christmas, but I dont like waiting for it.

6. Would you like to live in a castle?   Would you like to live on a houseboat?
Would you like to live in a castle, or would you like to live on a houseboat?

7. The general gave the command.   The army marched.
When the general gave the command, the army marched.

8. The trees dropped all their leaves.   We raked them up.
After the trees dropped all their leaves, we raked them up.

Page 255

"Good" and "Well"

Use the word **good** to describe a noun. Good is an adjective.

Example: She is a **good** teacher.

Use the word **well** to tell or ask how something is done or to describe someone's health. Well is an adverb. It describes a verb.

Example: She is not feeling **well**.

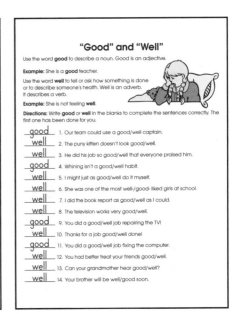

Directions: Write **good** or **well** in the blanks to complete the sentences correctly. The first one has been done for you.

good 1. Our team could use a good/well captain.
well 2. The puny kitten doesn't look good/well.
well 3. He did his job so good/well that everyone praised him.
good 4. Whining isn't a good/well habit.
well 5. I might just as good/well do it myself.
well 6. She was one of the most well-/good- liked girls at school.
well 7. I did the book report as good/well as I could.
well 8. The television works very good/well.
good 9. You did a good/well job repairing the TV!
well 10. Thanks for a job good/well done!
good 11. You did a good/well job fixing the computer.
well 12. You had better treat your friends good/well.
well 13. Can your grandmother hear good/well?
well 14. Your brother will be well/good soon.

Page 256

"Your" and "You're"

The word **your** shows possession.

Examples:
Is that **your** book?
I visited **your** class.

The word **you're** is a contraction for **you are**. A **contraction** is two words joined together as one. An apostrophe shows where letters have been left out.

Examples:
You're doing well on that painting.
If **you're** going to pass the test, you should study.

Directions: Write **your** or **you're** in the blanks to complete the sentences correctly. The first one has been done for you.

You're 1. Your/You're the best friend I have!
You're 2. Your/You're going to drop that!
Your 3. Your/You're brother came to see me.
your 4. Is that your/you're cat?
you're 5. If your/you're going, you'd better hurry!
your 6. Why are your/you're fingers so red?
your 7. It's none of your/you're business!
Your 8. Your/You're bike's front tire is low.
You're 9. Your/You're kidding!
your 10. Have it your/you're way.
your 11. I thought your/you're report was great!
you're 12. He thinks your/you're wonderful!
your 13. What is your/you're first choice?
your 14. What's your/you're opinion?
You're 15. If your/you're going, so am I!
You're 16. Your/You're welcome.

Page 257

"Good" and "Well"; "Your" and "You're"

Directions: Choose the correct word for each sentence: good, well, your or you're.

1. Are you sure you can see ____well____ enough to read with the lighting you have?

2. ____You're____ going to need a paint smock when you go to art class tomorrow afternoon.

3. I can see ____you're____ having some trouble. Can I help with that?

4. The music department needs to buy a speaker system that has ____good____ quality sound.

5. The principal asked, "Where is ____your____ hall pass?"

6. You must do the job ____well____ if you expect to keep it.

7. The traffic policeman said, "May I please see ____your____ driver's license?"

8. The story you wrote for English class was done quite ____well____.

9. That radio station you listen to is a ____good____ one.

10. Let us know if ____you're____ unable to attend the meeting on Saturday.

Page 258

"Its" and "It's"

The word **its** shows ownership.
Examples:
Its leaves have all turned red.
Its paw was injured.

The word **it's** is a contraction for **it is**.
Examples:
It's better to be early than late.
It's not fair!

Directions: Write **its** or **it's** to complete the sentences correctly. The first one has been done for you.

It's 1. Its/It's never too late for ice cream!
Its 2. Its/It's eyes are already open.
It's 3. Its/It's your turn to wash the dishes!
Its 4. Its/It's cage was left open.
Its 5. Its/It's engine is beyond repair.
Its 6. Its/It's teeth were long and pointed.
its 7. Did you see its/it's hind legs?
it's 8. Why do you think its/it's mine?
it's 9. Do you think its/it's the right color?
its 10. Don't pet its/it's fur too hard!
It's 11. Its/It's from my Uncle Harry.
it's 12. Can you tell its/it's a surprise?
its 13. Is its/it's stall always this clean?
It's 14. Its/It's not time to eat yet.
it's 15. She says its/it's working now.

Grade 4 - Comprehensive Curriculum

Page 259

"Can" and "May"

The word **can** means am able to or to be able to.

Examples:

I **can** do that for you.
Can you do that for me?

The word **may** means be allowed to or permitted to. May is used to ask or give permission. **May** can also mean **might** or **perhaps**.

Examples:

May I be excused?
You **may** sit here.

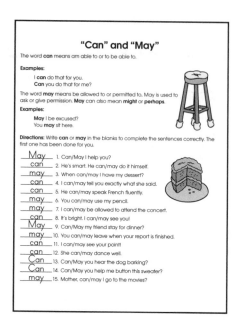

Directions: Write **can** or **may** in the blanks to complete the sentences correctly. The first one has been done for you.

- **May** 1. Can/May I help you?
- **can** 2. He's smart. He can/may do it himself.
- **may** 3. When can/may I have my dessert?
- **can** 4. I can/may tell you exactly what she said.
- **can** 5. He can/may speak French fluently.
- **may** 6. You can/may use my pencil.
- **may** 7. I can/may be allowed to attend the concert.
- **can** 8. It's bright. I can/may see you!
- **May** 9. Can/May my friend stay for dinner?
- **may** 10. You can/may leave when your report is finished.
- **can** 11. I can/may see your point!
- **can** 12. She can/may dance well.
- **Can** 13. Can/May you hear the dog barking?
- **Can** 14. Can/May you help me button this sweater?
- **may** 15. Mother, can/may I go to the movies?

Page 260

"Its" and "It's"; "Can" and "May"

Directions: Choose the correct word for each sentence: **its, it's, can** or **may**.

1. "It looks as though your arms are full, Diane. **May** I help you with some of those things?" asked Michele.

2. The squirrel **can** climb up the tree quickly with his mouth full of acorns.

3. She has had her school jacket so long that it is beginning to lose **its** color.

4. How many laps around the track **can** you do?

5. Sometimes you can tell what a story is going to be about by looking at **its** title.

6. Our house **may** need to be painted again in two or three years.

7. Mother asked, "Jon, **can** you open the door for your father?"

8. **It's** going to be a while until your birthday, but do you know what you want?

9. I can feel it in the air; **it's** going to snow soon.

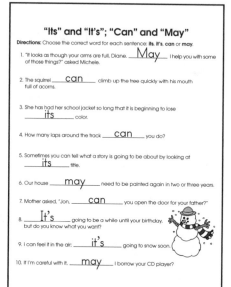

10. If I'm careful with it, **may** I borrow your CD player?

Page 261

"Sit" and "Set"

The word **sit** means to rest.

Examples:

Please **sit** here!
Will you **sit** by me?

The word **set** means to put or place something.

Examples:

Set your purse there.
Set the dishes on the table.

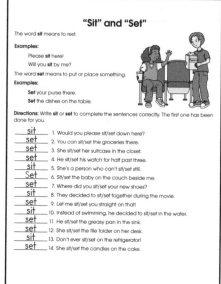

Directions: Write **sit** or **set** to complete the sentences correctly. The first one has been done for you.

- **sit** 1. Would you please sit/set down here?
- **set** 2. You can sit/set the groceries there.
- **set** 3. She sit/set her suitcase in the closet.
- **sit** 4. He sit/set his watch for half past three.
- **sit** 5. She's a person who can't sit/set still.
- **Set** 6. Sit/set the baby on the couch beside me.
- **set** 7. Where did you sit/set your new shoes?
- **sit** 8. They decided to sit/set together during the movie.
- **set** 9. Let me sit/set you straight on that!
- **sit** 10. Instead of swimming, he decided to sit/set in the water.
- **set** 11. He sit/set the greasy pan in the sink.
- **set** 12. She sit/set the file folder on her desk.
- **sit** 13. Don't ever sit/set on the refrigerator!
- **set** 14. She sit/set the candles on the cake.

Page 262

"They're," "Their," "There"

The word **they're** is a contraction for **they are**.

Examples:

They're our very best friends!
Ask them if **they're** coming over tomorrow.

The word **their** shows ownership.

Examples:

Their dog is friendly.
It's **their** bicycle.

The word **there** shows place or direction.

Examples:

Look over **there**.
There it is.

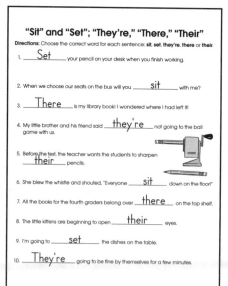

Directions: Write **they're**, **their** or **there** to complete the sentences correctly. The first one has been done for you.

- **There** 1. They're/Their/There is the sweater I want!
- **their** 2. Do you believe they're/their/there stories?
- **there** 3. Be they're/their/there by one o'clock.
- **there** 4. Were you they're/their/there last night?
- **they're** 5. I know they're/their/there going to attend.
- **their** 6. Have you met they're/their/there mother?
- **there** 7. I can go they're/their/there with you.
- **their** 8. Do you like they're/their/there new car?
- **They're** 9. They're/Their/There friendly to everyone.
- **they're** 10. Did she say they're/their/there ready to go?
- **their** 11. She said she'd walk by they're/their/there house.
- **there** 12. Is anyone they're/their/there?
- **there** 13. I put it right over they're/their/there!

Page 263

"Sit" and "Set"; "They're," "There," "Their"

Directions: Choose the correct word for each sentence: **sit, set, they're, there** or **their**.

1. **Set** your pencil on your desk when you finish working.

2. When we choose our seats on the bus will you **sit** with me?

3. **There** is my library book! I wondered where I had left it!

4. My little brother and his friend said **they're** not going to the ball game with us.

5. Before the test, the teacher wants the students to sharpen **their** pencils.

6. She blew the whistle and shouted, "Everyone **sit** down on the floor!"

7. All the books for the fourth graders belong over **there** on the top shelf.

8. The little kittens are beginning to open **their** eyes.

9. I'm going to **set** the dishes on the table.

10. **They're** going to be fine by themselves for a few minutes.

Page 264

"This" and "These"

The word **this** is an adjective that refers to things that are near. **This** always describes a singular noun. Singular means one.

Example:

I'll buy **this** coat.
(Coat is singular.)

The word **these** is also an adjective that refers to things that are near. **These** always describes a plural noun. A plural refers to more than one thing.

Example:

I will buy **these** flowers.
(Flowers is a plural noun.)

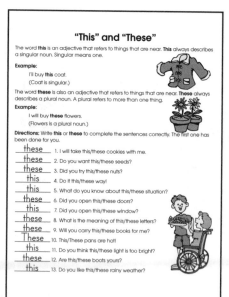

Directions: Write **this** or **these** to complete the sentences correctly. The first one has been done for you.

- **these** 1. I will take this/these cookies with me.
- **these** 2. Do you want this/these seeds?
- **these** 3. Did you try this/these nuts?
- **this** 4. Do it this/these way!
- **this** 5. What do you know about this/these situation?
- **these** 6. Did you open this/these doors?
- **this** 7. Did you open this/these window?
- **these** 8. What is the meaning of this/these letters?
- **these** 9. Will you carry this/these books for me?
- **These** 10. This/These pans are hot!
- **this** 11. Do you think this/these light is too bright?
- **these** 12. Are this/these boots yours?
- **this** 13. Do you like this/these rainy weather?

Page 265

Review

Directions: Complete the sentences by writing the correct words in the blanks.

good	1. You have a good/well attitude.
well	2. The teacher was not feeling good/well.
well	3. She sang extremely good/well.
good	4. Everyone said Josh was a good/well boy.
You're	5. Your/You're going to be sorry for that!
you're	6. Tell her your/you're serious.
Your	7. Your/You're report was wonderful!
You're	8. Your/You're the best person for the job.
it's	9. Do you think its/it's going to have babies?
Its	10. Its/It's back paw had a thorn in it.
It's	11. Its/It's fun to make new friends.
its	12. Is its/it's mother always nearby?
may	13. How can/may I help you?
may	14. You can/may come in now.
Can	15. Can/May you lift this for me?
can	16. She can/may sing soprano.
sit	17. I'll wait for you to sit/set down first.
set	18. We sit/set our dirty boots outside.
their	19. It's they're/their/there turn to choose.
There	20. They're/Their/There is your answer!
they're	21. They say they're/their/there coming.
this	22. I must have this/these one!
these	23. I saw this/these gloves at the store.
these	24. He said this/these were his.

Page 266

Review

Directions: Write the correct answers in the blanks using the words in the box.

good	well	your	you're	its
it's	can	may	sit	set
they're	there	their	this	these

1. __This__ is an adjective that refers to a particular thing.
2. Use __well__ to tell or ask how something is done or to describe someone's health.
3. __It's__ is a contraction for it is.
4. __These__ describes a plural noun and refers to particular things.
5. __Sit__ means to rest.
6. __Can__ means am able to or to be able to.
7. __They're__ is a contraction for they are.
8. __Your__, __its__ and __their__ show ownership or possession.
9. Use __may__ to ask politely to be permitted to do something.
10. __You're__ is a contraction for you are.
11. __Set__ means to place or put.
12. __Good__ describes a noun.
13. Use __there__ to show direction or placement.

Page 268

Capital Letters and Periods

The first letter of a person's first, last and middle name is always capitalized.

Example: Elizabeth Jane Marks is my best friend.

The first letter of a person's title is always capitalized. If the title is abbreviated, the title is followed by a period.

Examples: Her mother is **Dr.** Susan Jones Marks.
Ms. Jessica Joseph was a visitor.

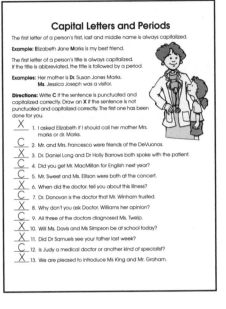

Directions: Write **C** if the sentence is punctuated and capitalized correctly. Draw an **X** if the sentence is not punctuated and capitalized correctly. The first one has been done for you.

- __X__ 1. I asked Elizabeth if I should call her mother Mrs. marks or dr. Marks.
- __C__ 2. Mr. and Mrs. Francesco were friends of the DeVuonos.
- __X__ 3. Dr. Daniel Long and Dr Holly Barrows both spoke with the patient.
- __C__ 4. Did you get Mr. MacMillan for English next year?
- __C__ 5. Mr. Sweet and Ms. Ellison were both at the concert.
- __X__ 6. When did the doctor. tell you about this illness?
- __C__ 7. Dr. Donovan is the doctor that Mr. Winham trusted.
- __X__ 8. Why don't you ask Doctor. Williams her opinion?
- __C__ 9. All three of the doctors diagnosed Ms. Twelp.
- __X__ 10. Will Ms. Davis and Ms Simpson be at school today?
- __X__ 11. Did Dr Samuels see your father last week?
- __C__ 12. Is Judy a medical doctor or another kind of specialist?
- __X__ 13. We are pleased to introduce Ms King and Mr. Graham.

Page 269

Punctuation: Commas

Use a comma to separate the number of the day of a month and the year. Do not use a comma to separate the month and year if no day is given.

Examples:

June 14, 1999
June 1999

Use a comma after **yes** or **no** when it is the first word in a sentence.

Examples:

Yes, I will do it right now.
No, I don't want any.

Directions: Write **C** if the sentence is punctuated correctly. Draw an **X** if the sentence is not punctuated correctly. The first one has been done for you.

- __C__ 1. No, I don't plan to attend.
- __C__ 2. I told them, oh yes, I would go.
- __C__ 3. Her birthday is March 13, 1995.
- __C__ 4. He was born in May, 1997.
- __C__ 5. Yes, of course I like you!
- __X__ 6. No I will not be there.
- __X__ 7. They left for vacation on February. 14.
- __C__ 8. No, today is Monday.
- __C__ 9. The program was first shown on August 12, 1991.
- __X__ 10. In September, 2007 how old will you be?
- __X__ 11. He turned 12 years old on November, 13.
- __X__ 12. I said no, I will not come no matter what!
- __C__ 13. Yes, she is a friend of mine.
- __C__ 14. His birthday is June 12, 1992, and mine is June 12, 1993.
- __X__ 15. No I would not like more dessert.

Page 270

Punctuation: Commas

Use a comma to separate words in a series. A comma is used after each word in a series but is not needed before the last word. Both ways are correct. In your own writing, be consistent about which style you use.

Examples:

We ate apples, oranges, and pears.
We ate apples, oranges and pears.

Always use a comma between the name of a city and a state.

Example:

She lives in Fresno, California.
He lives in Wilmington, Delaware.

Directions: Write **C** if the sentence is punctuated correctly. Draw an **X** if the sentence is not punctuated correctly. The first one has been done for you.

- __X__ 1. She ordered shoes, dresses and shirts to be sent to her home in Oakland California.
- __C__ 2. No one knew her pets' names were Fido, Spot and Tiger.
- __X__ 3. He likes green beans lima beans, and corn on the cob.
- __C__ 4. Typing paper, pens and pencils are all needed for school.
- __C__ 5. Send your letters to her in College Park, Maryland.
- __X__ 6. Orlando Florida is the home of Disney World.
- __C__ 7. Mickey, Minnie, Goofy and Daisy are all favorites of mine.
- __C__ 8. Send your letter to her in Reno, Nevada.
- __X__ 9. Before he lived in New York, City he lived in San Diego, California.
- __X__ 10. She mailed postcards, and letters to him in Lexington, Kentucky.
- __C__ 11. Teacups, saucers, napkins, and silverware were piled high.
- __C__ 12. Can someone give me a ride to Indianapolis, Indiana?
- __X__ 13. He took a train car, then a boat to visit his old friend.
- __X__ 14. Why can't I go to Disney World to see Mickey, and Minnie?

Page 271

Book Titles

All words in the title of a book are underlined. Underlined words also mean italics.

Examples:

The Hunt for Red October was a best-seller!
(The Hunt for Red October)

Have you read Lost in Space? (Lost in Space)

Directions: Underline the book titles in these sentences. The first one has been done for you.

1. The Dinosaur Poster Book is for eight year olds.
2. Have you read Lion Dancer by Kate Waters?
3. Baby Dinosaurs and Giant Dinosaurs were both written by Peter Dodson.
4. Have you heard of the book That's What Friends Are For by Carol Adorjan?
5. J.B. Stamper wrote a book called The Totally Terrific Valentine Party Book.
6. The teacher read Almost Ten and a Half aloud to our class.
7. Marrying Off Mom is about a girl who tries to get her widowed mother to start dating.
8. The Snow and The Fire are the second and third books by author Caroline Cooney.
9. The title sounds silly, but Goofbang Value Daze really is the name of a book!
10. A book about space exploration is The Day We Walked on the Moon by George Sullivan.
11. Alice and the Birthday Giant tells about a giant who came to a girl's birthday party.
12. A book about a girl who is sad about her father's death is called Rachel and the Upside Down Heart by Eileen Douglas.
13. Two books about baseball are Baseball Bloopers and Oddball Baseball.
14. Katharine Ross wrote Teenage Mutant Ninja Turtles: The Movie Storybook.

Page 272

Book Titles

Capitalize the first and last word of book titles. Capitalize all other words of book titles except short prepositions, such as **of**, **at** and **in**; conjunctions, such as **and**, **or** and **but**; and articles, such as **a**, **an** and **the**.

Examples:

Have you read *War and Peace*?

Pippi Longstocking in Moscow is her favorite book.

Directions: Underline the book titles. Circle the words that should be capitalized. The first one has been done for you.

1. (murder) in the (blue room) by Elliot Roosevelt
2. (growing up) in a (divided society) by Sandra Burnham
3. (the corn king) and the (spring queen) by Naomi Mitchison
4. (new kids) on the (block) by Grace Catalano
5. (best friends don't tell lies) by Linda Barr
6. (turn your kid into) a (computer genius) by Carole Gerber
7. (50 simple things you can do) to (save) the (earth) by Earth Works Press
8. (garfield goes) to (waist) by Jim Davis
9. (the hunt) for (red october) by Tom Clancy
10. (fall into darkness) by Christopher Pike
11. (oh) (the) (places you'll go) by Dr. Seuss
12. (amy) the (dancing bear) by Carly Simon
13. (the great waldo search) by Martin Handford
14. (the time) and (space) of (uncle albert) by Russel Stannard
15. (true stories about abraham lincoln) by Ruth Gross

Page 273

Punctuation: Quotation Marks

Use quotation marks (" ") before and after the exact words of a speaker.

Examples:

I asked Aunt Martha, "How do you feel?"

"I feel awful," Aunt Martha replied.

Do not put quotation marks around words that report what the speaker said.

Examples:

Aunt Martha said she felt awful.

I asked Aunt Martha how she felt.

Directions: Write **C** if the sentence is punctuated correctly. Draw an **X** if the sentence is not punctuated correctly. The first one has been done for you.

C 1. "I want it right now!" she demanded angrily.
X 2. "Do you want it now? I asked.
X 3. She said "she felt better" now.
C 4. Her exact words were, "I feel much better now!"
C 5. "I am so thrilled to be here!" he shouted.
C 6. "Yes, I will attend," she replied.
X 7. Elizabeth said "she was unhappy."
X 8. "I'm unhappy," Elizabeth reported.
C 9. "Did you know her mother?" I asked.
X 10. I asked "whether you knew her mother."
C 11. I wondered, "What will dessert be?"
C 12. "Which will it be, salt or pepper?" the waiter asked.
C 13. "No, I don't know the answer!" he snapped.
X 14. He said "yes he'd take her on the trip.
X 15. Be patient, he said. "It will soon be over."

Page 274

Punctuation: Quotation Marks

Use quotation marks around the titles of songs and poems.

Examples:

Have you heard "Still Cruising" by the Beach Boys?

"Ode To a Nightingale" is a famous poem.

Directions: Write **C** if the sentence is punctuated correctly. Draw an **X** if the sentence is not punctuated correctly. The first one has been done for you.

C 1. Do you know "My Bonnie Lies Over the Ocean"?
X 2. We sang The Stars and Stripes Forever" at school.
C 3. Her favorite song is "The Eensy Weensy Spider."
X 4. Turn the music up when "A Hard Day's Night comes on!
C 5. "Yesterday" was one of Paul McCartney's most famous songs.
C 6. "Mary Had a Little Lamb" is a very silly poem!
C 7. A song everyone knows is "Happy Birthday."
C 8. "Swing Low, Sweet Chariot" was first sung by slaves.
X 9. Do you know the words to Home on the "Range"?
C 10. "Hiawatha" is a poem many older people had to memorize.
X 11. "Happy Days Are Here Again! is an upbeat tune.
C 12. Frankie Valli and the Four Seasons sang "Sherry."
X 13. The words to "Rain, Rain" Go Away are easy to learn.
C 14. A slow song I know is called "Summertime."
C 15. Little children like to hear "The Night Before Christmas."

Page 275

Review

Directions: The following sentences have errors in punctuation, capitalization or both. The number in parentheses ( ) at the end of each sentence tells you how many errors it contains. Correct the errors by rewriting each sentence.

1. I saw mr. Johnson reading War And Peace to his class. (3)

I saw Mr. Johnson reading War and Peace to his class.

2. Do you like to sing "Take me Out to The Ballgame"? (2)

Do you like to sing "Take Me Out to the Ballgame"?

3. He recited Hiawatha to Miss Simpson's class. (2)

He recited Hiawatha to Miss Simpson's class.

4. Bananas, and oranges are among Dr smith's favorite fruits. (3)

Bananas and oranges are among Dr. Smith's favorite fruits.

5. "Daisy, daisy is a song about a bicycle built for two. (2)

"Daisy, Daisy" is a song about a bicycle built for two.

6. Good Morning, Granny Rose is about a woman and her dog. (1)

"Good Morning, Granny Rose" is about a woman and her dog.

7. Garfield goes to waist is a very funny book! (3)

Garfield Goes to Waist is a very funny book!

8. Peanut butter, jelly, and bread are Miss. Lee's favorite treats. (1)

Peanut butter, jelly and bread are Miss Lee's favorite treats.

Page 276

Proofreading

Proofreading means searching for and correcting errors by carefully reading and rereading what has been written. Use the proofreading marks below when correcting your writing or someone else's.

To insert a word or a punctuation mark that has been left out, use this mark ∧. It is called a caret.

Example: We∧to the dance together.
　　　　　　 went

To show that a letter should be capitalized, put three lines under it.

Example: Mrs. jones drove us to school.

To show that a capital letter should be small or lowercase, draw a diagonal line through it.

Example: Mrs. Jones Drove us to school.

To show that a word is spelled incorrectly, draw a horizontal line through it and write the correct spelling above it.

Example: The wolros is an amazing animal.
　　　　　　　　 walrus

Directions: Proofread the two paragraphs using the proofreading marks you lear The author's last name, Towne, is spelled correctly.

The Modern ark

My book report is on the modern ark by Cecilia Fitzsimmons. The book tells abut 80 of worlds endangered animals. The book also an are and animals inside for kids put together.

Their House

there house is a great book! The arthur's name is Mary Towne. they're house tells about a girl name Molly. Molly's Family buys an old house from some people named warren. Then these big problems begin!

Page 277

Proofreading

Directions: Proofread the sentences. Write **C** if the sentence has no errors. Draw an **X** if the sentence contains missing words or other errors. The first one has been done for you.

C 1. The new Ship Wreck Museum in Key West is exciting!
X 2. Another thing I liked was the litehouse.
C 3. Do you remember Hemingway's address in Key West?
X 4. The Key West sematery is on 21 acres of ground.
X 5. Ponce de eon discovered Key West.
C 6. The cemetery in Key West is on Francis Street.
X 7. My favorete tombstone was the sailor's.
C 8. His wife wrote the words on it. Remember?
X 9. The words said, "at least I know where to find him now!"
C 10. That sailor must have been away at sea all the time.
X 11. The troley ride around Key West is very interesting.
X 12. Do you why it is called Key West?
C 13. Can you imagine a lighthouse in the middle of your town?
X 14. It's interesting to no that Key West is our southernmost city.
C 15. Besides Harry Truman and Hemingway, did other famous people live there?

Page 278

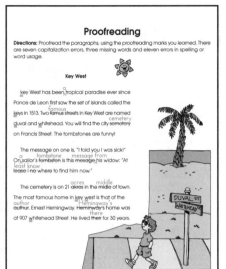

Proofreading

Directions: Proofread the paragraphs, using the proofreading marks you learned. There are seven capitalization errors, three missing words and eleven errors in spelling or word usage.

Key West

key West has been a tropical paradise ever since Ponce de Leon first saw the set of islands called the keys in 1513. Two famus streets in Key West are named duval and whitehead. You will find the city cemetery on Francis Street. The tombstones are funny!

The message on one is, "I told you I was sick!" On sailor's tombstone is this message his widow: "At least I ne where to find him now."

The cemetery is on 21 akres in the midle of town.

The most famous home in key west is that of the auther, Ernest Hemingway. Heminway's home was at 907 whitehead Street. He lived their for 30 years.

Page 279

Proofreading

Directions: Read more about Key West. Proofread and correct the errors. There are eight errors in capitalization, seven misspelled words and three missing words.

More About Key West

a good way to lern more about key West is to ride the trolley. Key West has a great trolley system. The trolley will take on a tour of the salt ponds. You can also three red brick forts. The trolley tour goes by a 110-foot high lighthouse. It is rite in the middle of the city. Key west is the only city with a Lighthouse in the midle of it! It is also the southernmost city in the United States.

If you have time, the new Ship Wreck Museum. Key west was also the hom of former president Harry truman. During his presidency, Trueman spent many vacations on key west.

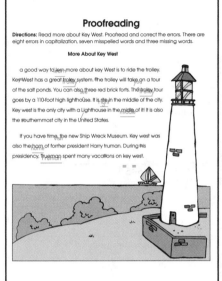

Page 280

Run-On Sentences

A **run-on sentence** occurs when two or more sentences are joined together without punctuation.

Examples:

Run-on sentence: I lost my way once did you?
Two sentences with correct punctuation: I lost my way once. Did you?
Run-on sentence: I found the recipe it was not hard to follow.
Two sentences with correct punctuation: I found the recipe. It was not hard to follow.

Directions: Rewrite the run-on sentences correctly with periods, exclamation points and question marks. The first one has been done for you.

1. Did you take my umbrella I can't find it anywhere!
Did you take my umbrella? I can't find it anywhere!

2. How can you stand that noise I can't!
How can you stand that noise? I can't!

3. The cookies are gone I see only crumbs.
The cookies are gone. I see only crumbs.

4. The dogs were barking they were hungry.
The dogs were barking. They were hungry.

5. She is quite ill please call a doctor immediately!
She is quite ill. Please call a doctor immediately!

6. The clouds came up we knew the storm would hit soon.
The clouds came up. We knew the storm would hit soon.

7. You weren't home he stopped by this morning.
You weren't home. He stopped by this morning.

Page 281

Writing: Punctuation

Directions: In the paragraphs below, use periods, question marks or exclamation marks to show where one sentence ends and the next begins. Circle the first letter of each new sentence to show the capital.

Example: My sister accused me of not helping her rake the leaves, that's silly! I helped at least a hundred times.

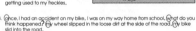

1. I always tie on my fishing line. When it moves up and down, I know a fish is there. After waiting a minute or two, I pull up the fish. It's fun!

2. I tried putting lemon juice on my freckles to make them go away. Did you ever do that? It didn't work. My skin just got sticky! Now, I'm slowly getting used to my freckles.

3. Once, I had an accident on my bike. I was on my way home from school. What do you think happened? My wheel slipped in the loose dirt at the side of the road. My bike slid into the road.

4. One night, I dreamed I lived in a castle. In my dream, I was the king or maybe the queen. Everyone listened to my commands. Then Mom woke me up for school. I tried commanding her to let me sleep. It didn't work!

5. What's your favorite holiday? Christmas is mine. For months before Christmas, I save my money, so I can give a present to everyone in my family. Last year, I gave my big sister earrings. They cost me five dollars!

6. My dad does exercises every night to make his stomach flat. He says he doesn't want to grow old. I think it's too late. Don't tell him I said that!

Page 282

Writing: Putting Ideas Together

Directions: Make each pair of sentences into one sentence. (You may have to change the verbs for some sentences—from **is** to **are**, for example.)

Example: Our house was flooded. Our car was flooded.
Our house and car were flooded.

1. Kenny sees a glow. / Carrie sees a glow.
Kenny and Carrie see a glow.

2. Our new stove came today. / Our new refrigerator came today.
Our new stove and refrigerator came today.

3. The pond is full of toads. / The field is full of toads.
The pond and field are full of toads.

4. Stripes are on the flag. / Stars are on the flag.
Stripes and stars are on the flag.

5. The ducks took flight. / The geese took flight.
The ducks and geese took flight.

6. Joe reads stories. / Dana reads stories.
Joe and Dana read stories.

7. French fries will make you fat. / Milkshakes will make you fat.
French fries and milkshakes will make you fat.

8. Justine heard someone groan. / Kevin heard someone groan.
Justine and Kevin heard someone groan.

Page 283

Writing: Putting Ideas Together

Directions: Write each pair of sentences as one sentence.

Example: Jim will deal the cards one at a time. Jim will give four cards to everyone.
Jim will deal the cards one at a time and give four cards to everyone.

1. Amy won the contest. / Amy claimed the prize.
Amy won the contest and claimed the prize.

2. We need to find the scissors. / We need to buy some tape.
We need to find the scissors and buy some tape.

3. The stream runs through the woods. / The stream empties into the East River.
The stream runs through the woods and empties into the East River.

4. Katie tripped on the steps. / Katie has a pain in her left foot.
Katie tripped on the steps and has a pain in her left foot.

5. Grandpa took me to the store. / Grandpa bought me a treat.
Grandpa took me to the store and bought me a treat.

6. Charity ran 2 miles. / She walked 1 mile to cool down afterwards.
Charity ran 2 miles and walked 1 mile to cool down afterwards.

Page 284

Writing: Using Fewer Words

Writing can be more interesting when fewer words are used. Combining sentences is easy when the subjects are the same. Notice how the comma is used.

Example: Sally woke up. Sally ate breakfast. Sally brushed her teeth.

Sally woke up, ate breakfast and brushed her teeth.

Combining sentences with more than one subject is a little more complicated. Notice how commas are used to "set off" information.

Examples: Jane went to the store. Jane is Sally's sister.

Jane went to the store with Sally, her sister.

Eddie likes to play with cars. Eddie is my younger brother.

Eddie, my younger brother, likes to play with cars.

Directions: Write each pair of sentences as one sentence.

1. Jerry played soccer after school. He played with his best friend, Tom.
   Jerry played soccer after school with his best friend, Tom.

2. Spot likes to chase cats. Spot is my dog.
   Spot, my dog, likes to chase cats.

3. Lori and Janice both love ice cream. Janice is Lori's cousin.
   Lori and Janice, Lori's cousin, both like ice cream.

4. Jayna is my cousin. Jayna helped me move into my new apartment.
   Jayna, my cousin, helped me move into my new apartment.

5. Romeo is a big tomcat. Romeo loves to hunt mice.
   Romeo, a big tomcat, loves to hunt mice.

Page 285

Combining Sentences

Some simple sentences can be easily combined into one sentence.

Examples:

Simple sentences: The bird sang. The bird was tiny. The bird was in the tree.
Combined sentence: The tiny bird sang in the tree.

Directions: Combine each set of simple sentences into one sentence. The first one has been done for you.

1. The big girls laughed. They were friendly. They helped the little girls.
   The big, friendly girls laughed as they helped the little girls.

2. The dog was hungry. The dog whimpered. The dog looked at its bowl.

3. Be quiet now. I want you to listen. You listen to my joke!

4. I lost my p

Answers may vary.

5. I see my mother. My mother is walking. My mother is walking down the street.

6. Do you like ice cream? Do you like hot dogs? Do you like mustard?

7. Tell me you'll do it! Tell me you will! Tell me right now!

Page 286

Combining Sentences in Paragraph Form

A **paragraph** is a group of sentences that share the same idea.

Directions: Rewrite the paragraph by combining the simple sentences into larger sentences.

Jason awoke early. He threw off his covers. He ran to his window. He looked outside. He saw snow. It was white and fluffy. Jason thought of something. He thought of his sled. His sled was in the garage. He quickly ate breakfast. He dressed warmly. He got his sled. He went outside. He went to play in the snow.

Jason awoke early and threw off his covers. He ran to his window and looked outside. He saw white and fluffy snow. Jason thought of his sled in the garage. He quickly ate breakfast and dressed warmly. He got his sled and went outside to play in the snow.

Answer may vary.

Page 287

Nouns and Pronouns

To make a story or report more interesting, pronouns can be substituted for "overused" nouns.

Example:

Mother made the beds. Then Mother started the laundry.

The noun **Mother** is used in both sentences. The pronoun **she** could be used in place of **Mother** the second time to make the second sentence more interesting.

Directions: Cross out nouns when they appear a second and/or third time. Write a pronoun that could be used instead. The first one has been done for you.

we 1. My friends and I like to go ice skating in the winter. ~~My friends and I~~ usually fall down a lot, but ~~my friends and I~~ have fun!

they 2. All the children in the fourth-grade class next to us must have been having a party. ~~All the children~~ were very loud. ~~All the children~~ were happy it was Friday.

he 3. I try to help my father with work around the house on the weekends. ~~My father~~ works many hours during the week and would not be able to get everything done.

they 4. Can I share my birthday treat with the secretary and the principal? The ~~secretary and the principal~~ could probably use a snack right now!

him 5. I know Mr. Jones needs a copy of this history report. Please take it to ~~Mr. Jones~~ when you finish.

Page 288

Nouns and Pronouns

Directions: Cross out nouns when they appear a second and/or third time. Write a pronoun that could be used instead.

it 1. The merry-go-round is one of my favorite rides at the county fair. I ride the ~~merry-go-round~~ so many times that I sometimes get sick.

we 2. My parents and I are planning a 2-week vacation next year. ~~My parents and I~~ will be driving across the country to see the Grand Canyon. ~~My parents and I~~ hope to have a great time.

he/she 3. The new art teacher brought many ideas from the city school where ~~the art teacher~~ worked before.

them 4. Green beans, corn and potatoes are my favorite vegetables. I could eat ~~green beans, corn and potatoes~~ for every meal. I especially like ~~green beans, corn and potatoes~~ in stew.

it 5. I think I left my pen in the library when I was looking up reference materials earlier today. Did you find ~~my pen~~ when you cleaned?

she 6. My grandmother makes very good apple pie. ~~My grandmother~~ said I could learn how to make one the next time we visit.

us 7. My brothers and I could take care of your pets while you are away if you show ~~my brothers and me~~ what you want done.

Page 289

Pronoun Referents

A **pronoun referent** is the noun or nouns a pronoun refers to.

Example:

Green beans, corn and potatoes are my favorite vegetables. I could eat them for every meal.

The pronoun **them** refers to the nouns green beans, corn and potatoes.

Directions: Find the pronoun in each sentence, and write it in the blank below. Underline the word or words the pronoun refers to. The first one has been done for you.

1. The fruit trees look so beautiful in the spring when they are covered with blossoms.
   they

2. Tori is a high school cheerleader. She spends many hours at practice.
   she

3. The football must have been slippery because of the rain. The quarterback could not hold on to it.
   it

4. Aunt Donna needs a babysitter for her three year old tonight.
   her

5. The art projects are on the table. Could you please put them on the top shelf along the wall?
   them

Page 290

Pronoun Referents

Directions: Find the pronoun in each sentence, and write it in the blank below. Underline the word or words the pronoun refers to.

1. Did Aaron see the movie _Titanic_? Jay thought it was a very good movie.
   ___it___

2. Maysie can help you with the spelling words now, <u>Tasha</u>.
   ___you___

3. The new tennis <u>coach</u> said to call him after 6:00 tonight.
   ___him___

4. <u>Jim, John and Jason</u> called to say they would be later than planned.
   ___they___

5. <u>Mrs. Burns</u> enjoyed the cake her class had for the surprise party.
   ___her___

6. The <u>children</u> are waiting outside. Ask Josh to take the pinwheels out to them.
   ___them___

7. <u>Mrs. Taylor</u> said to go on ahead because she will be late.
   ___she___

8. The whole <u>team</u> must sit on the bus until the driver gives us permission to get off.
   ___us___

9. <u>Dad</u> said the umbrella did a poor job of keeping the rain off him.
   ___him___

10. The <u>umbrella</u> was blowing around too much. That's probably why it didn't do a good job.
    ___it___

Page 291

Writing: Topic Sentences

A **paragraph** is a group of sentences that tells about one main idea. A **topic sentence** tells the main idea of a paragraph.

Many topic sentences come first in the paragraph. The topic sentence in the paragraph below is underlined. Do you see how it tells the reader what the whole paragraph is about?

<u>Friendships can make you happy or make you sad.</u> You feel happy to do things and go places with your friends. You get to know each other so well that you can almost read each others' minds. But friendships can be sad when your friend moves away—or decides to be best friends with someone else.

Directions: Underline the topic sentence in the paragraph below.

<u>We have two rules about using the phone at our house.</u> Our whole family agreed on them. The first rule is not to talk longer than 10 minutes. The second rule is to take good messages if you answer the phone for someone else.

Directions: After you read the paragraph below, write a topic sentence for it.

There are many ways you can
earn money.

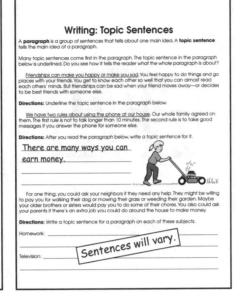

For one thing, you could ask your neighbors if they need any help. They might be willing to pay you for walking their dog or mowing their grass or weeding their garden. Maybe your older brothers or sisters would pay you to do some of their chores. You also could ask your parents if there's an extra job you could do around the house to make money.

Directions: Write a topic sentence for a paragraph on each of these subjects.

Homework: _____

Television: _____

Sentences will vary.

Page 292

Writing: Supporting Sentences

Supporting sentences provide details about the topic sentence of a paragraph.

Directions: In the paragraph below, underline the topic sentence. Then cross out the supporting sentence that does not belong in the paragraph.

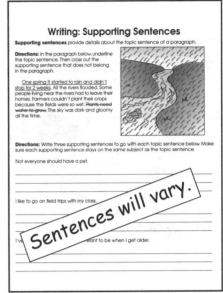

<u>One spring it started to rain and didn't stop for 2 weeks.</u> All the rivers flooded. Some people living near the rivers had to leave their homes. Farmers couldn't plant their crops because the fields were so wet. ~~Plants need water to grow.~~ The sky was dark and gloomy all the time.

Directions: Write three supporting sentences to go with each topic sentence below. Make sure each supporting sentence stays on the same subject as the topic sentence.

Not everyone should have a pet.

_____

I like to go on field trips with my class.

Sentences will vary.

I've _____ want to be when I get older.

_____

Page 293

Writing: Topic Sentences and Supporting Details

Directions: For each topic below, write a topic sentence and four supporting details.

Example:
Playing with friends: (topic sentence) Playing with my friends can be lots of fun.
(details)
1. We like to ride our bikes together.
2. We play fun games like "dress up" and "animal hospital."
3. Sometimes, we swing on the swings or slide down the slides on our swingsets.
4. We like to pretend we are having tea with our stuffed animals.

Recess at school: _____

_____

Summer vacation: _____

Answers will vary.

Brothers or _____

Page 294

Writing: Topic Sentences and Supporting Details

Directions: Select a topic from page 293. Arrange the topic sentence and detail sentences in paragraph form.

Example: Playing With Friends
Playing with my friends can be lots of fun. We play fun games like "animal hospital" and "dress up." We like to pretend we are having tea with our stuffed animals. Sometimes, we swing on the swings or slide down the slides on our swingsets. We also like to ride our bikes together.

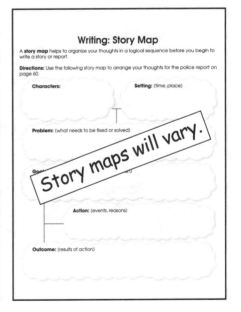

Note: Notice how the first line of the paragraph is indented. Also note how the order of the sentences changed to make the paragraph easier to read.

Directions: Choose a topic. Write a five-sentence paragraph about it. Don't forget the topic sentence, supporting details and to indent your paragraph. Make sure the detail sentences stick to the topic.

_____

Paragraphs will vary.

Page 295

Writing: Story Map

A **story map** helps to organize your thoughts in a logical sequence before you begin to write a story or report.

Directions: Use the following story map to arrange your thoughts for the police report on page 60.

Characters: _____   **Setting:** (time, place)

Problem: (what needs to be fixed or solved)

Story maps will vary.

Goal:

Action: (events, reasons)

Outcome: (results of action)

Page 296

Review

Directions: Write a police report about an event in which someone your age was a hero or heroine. Follow these steps:

1. Write all your ideas in any order on another sheet of paper. What happened? Who saw it? Who or what do you think caused it? Why were the police called?

2. Choose the ideas you want to use and organize them with the story map on page 59.

3. Now, write in complete sentences to tell what happened. Combine some short sentences using **and, but, or, after** or **when**. Make sure all your sentences end with a period or question mark.

4. Read your sentences aloud. Did you leave out any important facts? Will your "commanding officer" know what happened?

5. Make any necessary changes and write your report below.

6. Read your report to someone.

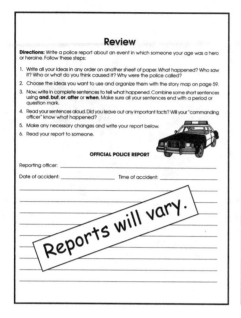

OFFICIAL POLICE REPORT

Reporting officer: _____

Date of accident: _____   Time of accident: _____

Reports will vary.

Page 297

Review

Directions: On another sheet of paper, write three paragraphs that tell a story about the picture below. Tell who lives in the house, what happened and why it happened. Begin each paragraph with a topic sentence that tells the main idea. Read your paragraphs aloud, make any necessary changes and copy them below.

Who lives there:

What happened:

Why it happened:

Paragraphs will vary.

Page 298

Writing: Paragraphs

Each paragraph should have one main idea. If you have a lot of ideas, you need to write several paragraphs.

Directions: Read the ideas below and number them:
1. If the idea tells about Jill herself.
2. If the idea tells what she did.
3. If the idea tells why she did it.

_2_ found a bird caught in a kite string

_2 or 1_ plays outside a lot

_1_ in grade four at Center School

_3_ knew the bird was wild

_2_ untangled the bird

_1_ likes pets

_3_ wouldn't want to live in a cage

_2_ gave the bird its freedom

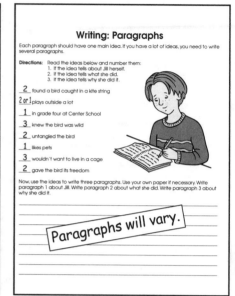

Now, use the ideas to write three paragraphs. Use your own paper if necessary. Write paragraph 1 about Jill. Write paragraph 2 about what she did. Write paragraph 3 about why she did it.

Paragraphs will vary.

Page 299

Writing: Paragraphs

When you have many good ideas about a subject, you need to organize your writing into more than one paragraph. It is easy to organize your thoughts about a topic if you use a "cluster of ideas" chart.

Example:

Details — Details — Details — Main Topic — Details — Details — Details

The main topic of your story is stated in the middle circle. Details about the main topic are listed in the outer circles.

Study the following "cluster of ideas" and note how the thoughts are organized in paragraph form on the following page.

1. **Introduction:** working in yard, autumn—cool weather

2. **Pants:** blue jeans, old, cotton, good for yard work, comfortable

3. **Shirt:** yellow, short-sleeved, matches slacks and sweater, not too hot

4. **Sweater:** red with yellow and blue designs, white buttons, warmth for cold day, cotton, long sleeves

5. **Shoes:** white sneakers, comfortable, good for walking and standing

6. **Closing:** busy, but ready

Clothes for Saturday

Page 300

Writing: Paragraphs

Once your ideas are "clustered," go back and decide which ideas should be the first, second, third, and so on. These numbers will be the order of the paragraph in the finished story.

Directions: Read the story paragraphs below.

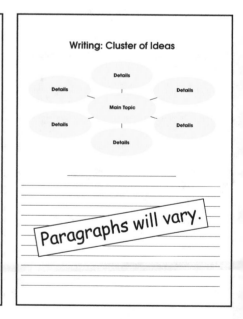

Clothes for Saturday

This Saturday, my family and I will be working in the yard. We will be mowing grass, raking leaves and pulling weeds. When I get up that day, I know I will need to wear clothes that will keep me warm in the autumn air. My clothes will also need to be ones that will not be ruined if they get muddy or dirty.

The best choice of pants for our busy day will be my jeans. They are nicely faded and well worn, which means they are quite comfortable. They will be good for yard work since mud and grass stains wash out of them easily.

My shirt will be my yellow golf shirt. It will match the blue of my jeans. Also, its short sleeves will be fine if the weather is warm.

For warmth on Saturday, if the day is cool, will be my yellow and red sweater. It is made from cotton and has long sleeves and high buttons to keep out frosty air.

Yard work means lots of walking, so I will need comfortable shoes. The best choice will be my white sneakers. They aren't too tight or too loose and keep my feet strong.

Saturday will be a busy day, but I'll be ready!

When "Clothes for Saturday" was written, the author added both an introductory and concluding paragraph. This helps the reader with the flow of the story.

Directions: Now, it's your turn. Select a topic from the list below or choose one of your own. Complete the "cluster of ideas" chart on page 73 and write a brief story. (You may or may not use all the clusters.)

Topics:

| chores | holidays | all about me | sports |
| homework | family | pets | vacation |

Page 301

Writing: Cluster of Ideas

Details — Details — Details — Main Topic — Details — Details — Details

Paragraphs will vary.

Page 302

Taking Notes

Taking notes effectively can help you in many ways with schoolwork. It will help you better understand and remember what you read and hear. It will also help you keep track of important facts needed for reports, essays and tests.

Each person develops his/her own way of taking notes. While developing your style, keep in mind the following:

▶ Write notes in short phrases instead of whole sentences.
▶ Abbreviate words to save time.
  Examples: pres for president or **&** for and
▶ If you use the same name often in your notes, use initials.
  Examples: GW for George Washington **AL** for Abraham Lincoln.
▶ Be brief, but make sure you understand what you write.
▶ Number your notes, so you can understand where each note starts and stops.
▶ When taking notes from a long article or book, write down one or two important points per paragraph or chapter.

Directions: Reread the article "Floating in Space" on page 168. As you read the first three paragraphs, fill in the note-taking format below with your notes.

Title of Article or Story _____ Floating in Space _____

Notes may include: Important Points

Paragraph 1 __life different in space & on Earth:__
__no gravity in space__

Paragraph 2 __astros have suction cup shoes:__
__astros zip themselves into sleeping bags on the wall__

Paragraph 3 __astros have to squirt to drink bottles &__
__containers of water__

Page 303

Taking Notes

Directions: Use this guide for taking notes on the articles in the next two pages. Set up your own paper in a similar way, or make several photocopies, for note-taking on future pages.

Penguins Are Unusual Birds
(Title)

Paragraph or
Chapter numbers   Important Points

1 _____
2 _____
3 _____

Notes will vary.

From Grapes to Raisins
(Title)

Paragraph or
Chapter numbers   Important Points

1 _____
2 _____
3 _____

Notes will vary.

Page 304

Taking Notes: Penguins Are Unusual Birds

Directions: Use a sheet of paper to cover up the story about penguins. Then read the questions.

1. Why are penguins unusual?
2. Do penguins swim?
3. Where do penguins live?
4. Do penguins lay eggs like other birds?

Directions: Read about penguins. While reading, make notes on the note-taking sheet on the previous page.

Penguins may be the most unusual birds. They cannot fly, but they can swim very fast through ice-cold water. They can dive deep into the water, and they can jump high out of it. Sometimes they make their nests out of rocks instead of twigs and grass. Some penguins live in very cold parts of the world. Others live in warmer climates. All penguins live south of the equator.

Unlike other birds, penguins lay only one egg at a time. Right after a mother penguin lays her egg, she waddles back to the ocean. The father penguin holds the egg on his feet, covering it with part of his stomach to keep it warm. When the egg is ready to hatch, the mother penguin returns. Then the father penguin takes a turn looking for food.

When a penguin swims, its white belly and dark back help it hide from enemies. From under the water, predators cannot see it. From on top of the water, large birds cannot see it either. This is how the penguin stays safe!

Directions: Use your notes to complete these sentences.

1. Penguins cannot fly, but __they can swim fast__ .
2. Penguins can dive deep and __jump high out of the water__ .
3. Penguins lay only __one egg at a time__ .
4. Father penguins keep the egg __warm__ .
5. Mother penguins return when the egg __is ready to hatch__ .

Page 305

Taking Notes: From Grapes to Raisins

Directions: Use a piece of paper to cover up the story about how grapes become raisins. Then read the questions.

1. How do grapes become raisins?
2. What happens after the grapes become raisins?
3. Why are raisins brown?
4. In what countries do grapes grow?

Directions: Read about how grapes become raisins. While reading, make notes on the note-taking sheet on page 25.

Grapes grow well in places that have lots of sun. In the United States, California is a big producer of grapes and raisins. When grapes are plump and round, they can be picked from their vines to be made into raisins. After the grapes are picked, they are put on big wooden or paper trays. They sit in the sun for many days.

Slowly, the grapes begin to dry and turn into wrinkled raisins. The sun causes them to change colors. Grapes turn brown as they become raisins. Machines take off the stems. Then the raisins are washed. After being dried again, they are put into boxes.

Some places use machines to make raisins dry faster. The grapes are put into ovens that have hot air blowing around inside. These ovens make the grapes shrivel and dry.

Raisins are made in many countries that grow grapes. Besides the United States, countries such as Greece, Turkey, Iran, Spain and Australia produce a lot of raisins.

Directions: Use your notes to answer the four questions at the top of the page. Write your answers on the lines below.

1. __After the grapes are picked, they are put on wooden or__
   __paper trays to dry in the sun for many days.__
2. __When the grapes become raisins, machines take off the__
   __stems. The raisins are washed and dried. Then they are__
   __put into boxes.__
3. __As the sun dries the raisins, they turn brown.__
4. __United States, Greece, Turkey, Iran, Spain, Australia__

Page 306

Taking Notes: Graham Crackers

Directions: Use a piece of paper to cover up the story about Graham crackers. Then read the questions.

1. Where did Graham crackers come from?
2. Who invented Graham crackers?
3. What are Graham crackers made of?
4. Why were Graham crackers made?

Directions: Read about Graham crackers. While reading, make notes on another sheet of paper.

Graham crackers were invented around 1830. A minister named Sylvester Graham wanted people to eat healthier foods. He did not think that people should eat meat or white bread. He wanted people to eat more fruits and vegetables and wheat breads that were brown instead of white.

Graham crackers were named after Sylvester Graham. He liked them because they were made of whole-wheat flour. There are many other kinds of crackers, but not all of them are as good for you as Graham crackers. Graham crackers are still considered a healthy snack!

Directions: Use your notes to answer the four questions at the top of the page. Write your answers on the lines below.

1. __Graham crackers were invented by Sylvester Graham__
   __around 1830.__
2. __Sylvester Graham, a minister__
3. __They are made of whole-wheat flour.__
4. __Sylvester Graham wanted people to eat healthier foods.__

Page 307

Compare and Contrast

To **compare** means to look for ways two items are alike. To **contrast** means to look for ways two items are different.

Directions: Use the Venn diagram to compare and contrast penguins (page 304) with most birds you see where you live.

Penguins
only — cannot fly, swim fast, nests of rocks, 1 egg at a time

Penguins / Other Birds (both) — make nests, lay eggs, parents get food for the babies, parents sit on egg

Other Birds
only — fly, don't swim, nest of twigs & grass, several eggs at a time

Venn diagram

Penguins   Other birds

Sample answers:

To write a comparison paragraph, begin with a topic sentence which states your main idea. Write sentences that provide supporting details. End your paragraph with a conclusion sentence. A conclusion sentence often restates the topic sentence.

Directions: Use the information from your Venn diagram to write a short comparison paragraph.

__Although they are birds, penguins are different from the birds__
__in my neighborhood. Penguins don't fly—but they do swim.__
__These unusual birds make their nests out of rocks, and only__
__have one egg at a time. Penguins, however, are the same as__
__other birds in some ways. They do sit on their eggs and get__
__food for their babies like other birds do. Penguins are certainly__
__a different kind of bird!__

Page 308

Outlining

Outlines are plans that help you organize your thoughts. If you are writing an essay, an outline helps you decide what to write. An outline should look similar to this:

I. First main idea
  A. A smaller idea
    1. An example
    2. An example
II. Second main idea
  A. A smaller idea
  B. Another smaller idea
III. Third main idea
  A. A smaller idea
  B. Another smaller idea
    1. An example

I. Planting a garden
  A. Choosing seeds
    1. Tomatoes
    2. Lettuce
II. Taking care of the garden
  A. Pulling the weeds
  B. Watering the garden
III. Harvesting
  A. Are they ripe?
  B. How to pick them
    1. Pick only the tomato off the vine

Directions: Use the outline for planting a garden to answer the questions.

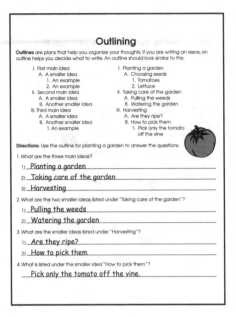

1. What are the three main ideas?
1) __Planting a garden__
2) __Taking care of the garden__
3) __Harvesting__

2. What are the two smaller ideas listed under "Taking care of the garden"?
1) __Pulling the weeds__
2) __Watering the garden__

3. What are the smaller ideas listed under "Harvesting"?
1) __Are they ripe?__
2) __How to pick them__

4. What is listed under the smaller idea "How to pick them"?
__Pick only the tomato off the vine.__

Page 309

Outlining: Building a Tree House

Directions: Study the sample outline for building a house. Then use words and phrases from the box to fill in the missing parts of the outline on how to build a tree house.

I. Find land
  A. On a hill
  B. By a lake
  C. In the city
II. Gather materials
  A. Buy wood
  B. Buy nails
  C. Buy tools
    1. Hammer
    2. Screwdriver
    3. Drill
    4. Saw
III. Build the house
  A. Who will use the tools?
  B. Who will carry the wood?

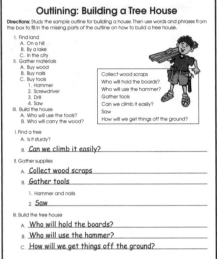

Collect wood scraps
Who will hold the boards?
Who will use the hammer?
Gather tools
Can we climb it easily?
Saw
How will we get things off the ground?

I. Find a tree
  A. Is it sturdy?
  B. __Can we climb it easily?__

II. Gather supplies
  A. __Collect wood scraps__
  B. __Gather tools__
    1. Hammer and nails
    2. __Saw__

III. Build the tree house
  A. __Who will hold the boards?__
  B. __Who will use the hammer?__
  C. __How will we get things off the ground?__

Page 310

Outlining: Finishing the Tree House

Directions: Use words and phrases from the box to fill in the missing parts of the outline of what to do once your tree house is built.

Sisters and brothers	When can they visit?
Parents	Spray paint
Tables	Choose a kind of paint
Chairs	Who can visit?

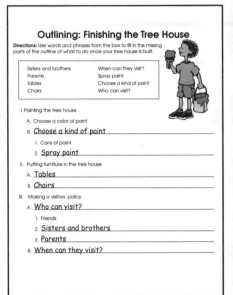

I. Painting the tree house
  A. Choose a color of paint
  B. __Choose a kind of paint__
    1. Cans of paint
    2. __Spray paint__

II. Putting furniture in the tree house
  A. __Tables__
  B. __Chairs__

III. Making a visitors' policy
  A. __Who can visit?__
    1. Friends
    2. __Sisters and brothers__
    3. __Parents__
  B. __When can they visit?__

Page 311

Outlining: The *Mayflower*'s Voyage

Directions: Read about the *Mayflower*. Then complete the outline for an essay.

The *Mayflower* left England in 1620. It carried 101 passengers. Some of those passengers were called Pilgrims. Pilgrims were people who had wandered from country to country looking for a place to make their home.

It took 66 days to cross the Atlantic Ocean. The ship was crowded. There were some accidents on board. The *Mayflower* landed at the tip of Cape Cod in Massachusetts. Several men searched the area to find the best place to start a colony. They finally settled on Plymouth.

The Pilgrims lived on the *Mayflower* through the winter. The *Mayflower* returned to England in April 1621. None of the Pilgrims went back with it.

Sample answers:

I. The Mayflower leaves England
  A. __101 passengers__
  B. __Some people were Pilgrims__

II. The journey
  A. __Took 66 days__
  B. __Crowded__
  C. __Some accidents__

III. Landing in America
  A. __Landed at Cape Cod, MA__
  B. __Pilgrims settled in Plymouth__

Page 312

Outlining: The First Thanksgiving

Directions: Read about the first Thanksgiving. Then complete the outline.

The Pilgrims arrived at Plymouth Rock just as winter set in. Many people died that winter from cold and hunger. The following spring, the Pilgrims started planting vegetable gardens. A Native American named Squanto helped them. They planted peas, wheat, beans, corn and pumpkins.

When fall came, the Pilgrims were so glad to have enough food that they invited the Native Americans to share their first Thanksgiving. In addition to food from their garden, they also shared wild geese that they had killed and other food like sweet potatoes and fresh berries.

Sample answers:

I. The first winter
  A. __Came right away__
  B. __Many people died__

II. Spring
  A. __Befriended Squanto__
  B. __Squanto helped them plant gardens__

III. Fall
  A. __Had enough food from their gardens__
  B. __Had a Thanksgiving dinner__
    1. __Invited Native Americans__
    2. __Ate harvest from garden__
    3. __Ate wild geese__

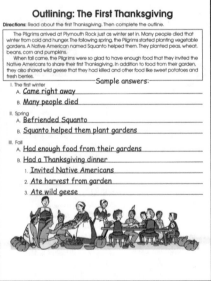

Page 313

Using an Outline to Write an Essay

Outlines help you organize information and notes into a manageable form. Outlines also help you prepare to write reports and essays by keeping your thoughts in a logical order or sequence. Once you have a good outline, converting it to paragraph form is easy.

To convert an outline to an essay, add your own words to expand the words and phrases in the outline into sentence form. Information from the first main topic becomes the first paragraph.

I. Painting the tree house
  A. Choose a color of paint
  B. Choose a kind of paint
    1. Cans of paint
    2. Spray paint

Information from the second and third main topics become the second and third paragraphs of the essay.

II. Putting furniture in the tree house
  A. Tables
  B. Chairs
III. Making a visitors' policy
  A. Who can visit?
    1. Friends
    2. Sisters and brothers
    3. Parents
  B. When can they visit?

To write an essay, remember to indent each paragraph, begin each paragraph with a topic sentence and include supporting details.

Directions: Read the beginning of the essay. Then finish it on another sheet of paper using your own words and information from the outline.

Finishing Touches

Finishing a tree house takes a lot of thought and planning. First, it needs to be painted. The paint will help protect the wood from rain and snow. The best kind of paint for finishing the wood would be in cans. It would brush on easily, smoothly and quickly. Green would be a great color for the tree house because it would blend in with the green leaves of the trees.

__Essays will vary.__

Page 314

Using an Outline to Write a Book Review

Directions: Prepare to write a book review by organizing your thoughts in the outline form provided.

Sample   Your Book Review

I. Book Information   I. _____

  A. Title   A. _____

  B. Author   B. _____

  C. Illustrator   C. _____

  D. Publisher and publishing date   D. _____

II. Fun facts of book   II. _____

  A. Setting   A. _____

  B. Characters   B. _____

  C. Plot   C. _____

III. Good points   III. _____

  A. What I liked best about book   A. _____

   1. Why?

IV. Not so good points   IV. _____

  A. What I didn't like about book   A. _____

   1. Why?

V. Should others read book?   V. _____

  A. Why or why not?   A. _____

Outlines will vary.

Directions: Write a book review essay on another sheet of paper, using notes from your outline.

Page 315

Summarizing: Writing an Autobiography

When you **summarize** an article, book or speech, you are simply writing a shorter article that contains only the main points. This shorter article of main points is called a **summary**.

To prepare for writing a summary of your life, you would begin with an outline. Since a summary is a brief account of main points, you will not be able to include every detail of your life. Your summary should include only basic facts.

I. Yourself
  A. Name
  B. Age and grade in school
   1. Subjects you like in school
   2. Subjects you do not like in school
  C. Looks
   1. Eye color
   2. Hair color
   3. Other features
II. Your family
  A. Parents
  B. Brothers/sisters
  C. Pets
III. Hobbies and interests
  A. Sports
  B. Clubs

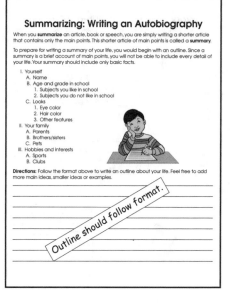

Directions: Follow the format above to write an outline about your life. Feel free to add more main ideas, smaller ideas or examples.

Outline should follow format.

Page 316

Summarizing: Writing an Autobiography

A summary of your life would include when you were born, who your parents are, other members of your family, your age and your grade in school. Details like your favorite joke, today's weather or how much homework you had yesterday would not be included in a summary.

Directions: Use the information from your outline to write a summary of your life.

Summaries will vary.

Page 317

Summarizing: The North Pole

Directions: Read about the North Pole. Then use the main points of the article to write a paragraph summarizing conditions at the North Pole.

At the North Pole, the sun does not shine for half of the year. It stays dark outside for six months, but for the other six months of the year, the sun does not set. It is light through the night.

The North Pole is as far north as you can go. If you traveled north to the North Pole and kept going, you would start going south. You could call the North Pole the top of the Earth.

The average temperature at the North Pole is –9 degrees Fahrenheit. That is not any colder than many places in the United States get in the winter. In fact, some places get much colder than that, but at the North Pole, it stays very cold for a very long time.

The cold winds that blow off the Arctic Ocean make the North Pole a very cold place most of the time. In the summer when the sun is shining all day and all night, the temperature can rise to 38 degrees Fahrenheit in places that are sheltered from the wind. But that is still very cold.

The Arctic Ocean is at the North Pole. The area surrounding the North Pole is called the Arctic Region. Some of Canada, Alaska, Greenland, Russia and Scandinavia are in the Arctic Region. These places get very cold in the long, dark winters, too!

The main points of this article are:

1. At the North Pole, the sun is never out in the winter. It is always out in the summer.
2. The North Pole is very cold all year.
3. Winds from the Arctic Ocean make the North Pole stay very cold. The Arctic Ocean surrounds the North Pole.
4. There is some land in the Arctic Region.

Paragraph should include main points listed.

Page 318

Summarizing: Settler Children

Directions: Read about settler children. Then complete the list of main points at the end of the article.

In the 1700s and 1800s, many children from other countries came with their parents to America. In the beginning, they had no time to go to school. They had to help their families work in the fields, care for the animals and clean the house. They also helped care for their younger brothers and sisters.

Sometimes settler children helped build houses and schools. Usually, these early school buildings were just one room. There was only one teacher for all the children. Settler children were very happy when they could attend school.

Because settler children worked so much, they had little time to play. There were not many things settler children could do just for fun. One pastime was gardening. Weeding their gardens taught them how to be orderly. Children sometimes made gifts out of the things they grew.

The settlers also encouraged their children to sing. Each one was expected to play at least one musical instrument. Parents wanted their children to walk, ride horses, visit friends and relatives and read nonfiction books.

Most settler children did not have many toys. The toys they owned were made by their parents and grandparents. They were usually made of cloth or carved from wood. The children made up games with string, like "cat's cradle." They also made things out of wood, such as seesaws. Settler children did not have all the toys we have today, but they managed to have fun anyway!

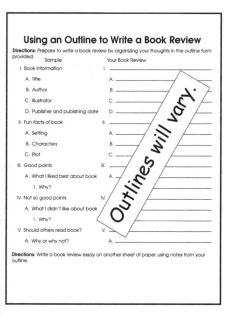

The main points of this article are:

1. Settler children worked hard.
2. Settler children had many jobs.
3. <u>Settler children liked school.</u>
4. <u>Settler children had little time to play.</u>
5. <u>Settler children had few toys.</u>

Directions: Use the main points to write a summary of this article on a separate sheet of paper.

Page 319

Summarizing: On Your Own

Directions: Read a story or a short book from your library. Write the title and author, then list the main points.

Title: _____

Author: _____

The main points are:

1. _____
2. _____
3. _____
4. _____
5. _____

Directions: Use the format you lear_____ ___ ___ book.

Answers will vary.

Directions: Use the main points you listed and your outline to write a summary of this book or story on another sheet of paper.

Page 320

Library Skills: Using the Library Catalog

Every book in a library is listed in the library's catalog. Videos, CD's, and other materials may also be included. Some library catalogs are drawers filled with file cards; some are computerized. Here is an example of a card from a card catalog:

```
970.2
G84a    Indians
        Gridley, Marion E.
        American Indian Women
        Hawthorn Books, Inc., 1974
```

The catalog helps you find books and other materials. Library catalogs list items by titles, authors and subjects. All three of these listings are in alphabetical order.

To find a book titled *Great Explorer: Christopher Columbus*, you would look under G in the card catalog. To find other books about Columbus, you would look under C. If you knew the name of an author who had written a book about Columbus, you could look in the card catalog under the author's last name.

Many libraries use computer catalogs instead of card catalogs. The computer catalog is also organized by titles, authors and subjects. To find a book, type in the title, subject or author's name.

Directions: Answer the questions about using a library catalog.

1. To find the book *American Indian Women*, would you look under the author, title or subject? **title**

2. To find a book about the Cherokee people, would you look under the author, title or subject? **subject**

3. To find a book called *Animals of Long Ago*, would you look under the author, title or subject? **title**

4. Marion E. Gridley has written books about Native Americans. To find one of her books, would you look under the author, title or subject? **author (or subject)**

5. To find books about the Moon, would you look under the author, title or subject? **subject**

6. To find the book *Easy Microwave Cooking for Kids*, would you look under the author, title or subject? **title**

7. Diana Reische has written a book about the Pilgrims. Would you look under the author, title or subject to find it? **author or subject**

Page 321

Library Skills: Using the Library Catalog

Authors are alphabetized by their last names first. In a library catalog, Blume, Judy would come before Voirst, Judith. Books are alphabetized by title. If a title begins with **The**, **A** or **An** ignore it, and use the second word of the title.

Directions: Look at the list of authors, subjects and titles. Write **A** for author, **S** for subject or **T** for title in the blanks. Then write each on the card where it belongs in alphabetical order. Some have been done for you.

Author
Dicerto, Joseph J.
Gallant, Roy A.
Herbst, Judith
Sandak, Cass R.

- **A** Gallant, Roy A.
- **S** Native Americans
- **T** Animals of Long Ago
- **S** gardens
- **T** The White House
- **A** Sandak, Cass R.
- **T** The Pony Express
- **A** Herbst, Judith
- **S** Pilgrims
- **T** The Hobbit
- **A** Dicerto, Joseph J.
- **S** planets

Title
Animals of Long Ago
The Hobbit
The Pony Express
The White House

Subject
gardens
Native Americans
Pilgrims
planets

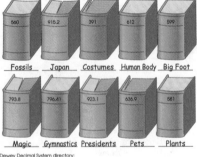

Page 322

Library Skills: Call Numbers

The **call number** of a book tells where it can be found among nonfiction books.

Information is presented differently on the title, subject and author card for the same book. A computer listing for this book would look quite similar.

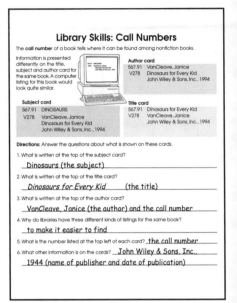

Subject card
```
567.91   DINOSAURS
V278     VanCleave, Janice
         Dinosaurs for Every Kid
         John Wiley & Sons, Inc., 1994
```

Author card
```
567.91   VanCleave, Janice
V278     Dinosaurs for Every Kid
         John Wiley & Sons, Inc., 1994
```

Title card
```
567.91   Dinosaurs for Every Kid
V278     VanCleave, Janice
         John Wiley & Sons, Inc., 1994
```

Directions: Answer the questions about what is shown on these cards.

1. What is written at the top of the subject card? **Dinosaurs (the subject)**

2. What is written at the top of the title card? **Dinosaurs for Every Kid (the title)**

3. What is written at the top of the author card? **VanCleave, Janice (the author) and the call number**

4. Why do libraries have three different kinds of listings for the same book? **to make it easier to find**

5. What is the number listed at the top left of each card? **the call number**

6. What other information is on the cards? **John Wiley & Sons, Inc., 1944 (name of publisher and date of publication)**

Page 323

Library Skills: The Dewey Decimal System

Using a library catalog helps you find the books you want. All nonfiction books—except biographies and autobiographies—are filed according to their call number. **Nonfiction books** are books based on facts. **Biographies** are true books that tell about people's lives. **Autobiographies** are books that people write about their own lives.

The call numbers are part of the **Dewey Decimal System**. Each listing in a library catalog will include a book's call number.

Example:
```
918.8    Bringle, Mary
B85e     Eskimos
         F. Watts, 1973
```

All libraries using the **Dewey Decimal System** follow the same system for filing books. The system divides all nonfiction books into 10 main groups, each represented by numbers.

0–099	General works (libraries, computers, etc.)
100–199	Philosophy
200–299	Religion
300–399	Social Sciences
400–499	Language
500–599	Pure Science (math, astronomy, chemistry, etc.)
600–699	Applied Science (medicine, engineering, etc.)
700–799	Arts and Recreation
800–899	Literature
900–999	History

Each book is given a specific call number. A book about ghosts could be 133.1.

This is where some subjects fall in the Dewey Decimal System.

Pets	630	Maps	910	Cathedrals	236	Dinosaurs	560
Baseball	796	Monsters	791	Trees	580	Presidents	920
Butterflies	595	Mummies	390	Space	620	Cooking	640

Directions: Write the Dewey Decimal number for the following books.

- **560** *Animals of Long Ago*
- **580** *City Leaves, City Trees*
- **640** *Easy Microwave Cooking for Kids*
- **620** *To Space and Back*
- **796** *Amazing Baseball Teams*
- **920** *Our American Presidents*
- **390** *Mummies Made in Egypt*
- **791** *Real-Life Monsters*
- **236** *Great Churches in Europe*
- **910** *The Children s Atlas*

Page 324

Library Skills: The Dewey Decimal System

All libraries that use the Dewey Decimal System follow the same order. All books between 500 and 599 are related to science. All books between 900 and 999 are history.

Each library divides its system even further. For example, one library may have kites at 796.15, while another library may have kites at 791.13.

Directions: Look at the number on each book. Then use the Dewey Decimal System directory at the bottom of the page to find out what the book is about. Write the subject on the line.

560	915.2	391	612	599
Fossils	Japan	Costumes	Human Body	Big Foot

793.8	796.41	923.1	636.9	581
Magic	Gymnastics	Presidents	Pets	Plants

Dewey Decimal System directory:

390–399 Costumes	590–599 Big Foot	790–795 Magic	920–929 Presidents
560–569 Fossils	610–619 Human Body	796–799 Gymnastics	
580–589 Plants	630–639 Pets	910–919 Japan	

Page 325

Library Skills

Some books in a library are not filed by the Dewey Decimal System. Those books include biographies, autobiographies and fiction. Biographies and autobiographies may be filed together in the 920s or be assigned a call number by subject.

Fiction books are stories that someone has made up. They are filed in alphabetical order by the author's last name in the fiction section of the library.

Directions: For each title, write **B** if it is a biography, **A** if it is an autobiography or **F** if it is fiction. Then circle the titles that would not be filed by the Dewey Decimal System.

- **F** (Tales of a Fourth Grade Nothing)
- **B** The Real Tom Thumb
- **F** (Ramona the Pest)
- **A** Bill Peet: An Autobiography
- **B** Abraham Lincoln
- **F** (Charlotte's Web)
- **A** The King and I
- **A** My Life With Chimpanzees
- **F** (Sara Plain and Tall)
- **B** Michael Jordan, Basketball's Soaring Star
- **B** The First Book of Presidents
- **B** The Helen Keller Story

Page 326

Putting Library Skills to Use

You can improve your library skills by using them at your local library.

Directions: While at the library, follow the instructions and answer the questions.

1. Use the library catalog to find a book about dinosaurs. What is its title?

Answers will vary.

2. What is the call number for that book? _Answers will vary._

3. Who is the author of that book? _Answers will vary._

4. Go to the shelf and look for the book. Did you find it? _Answers will vary._

5. Use the library catalog to find the author of the book, *Mummies Made in Egypt*. Who wrote it?

Aliki

6. Use the library catalog to find other books by that author. What are the names of four other books by that author? **Answers may include:**

My Hands

Feelings

Jack and Jake

Dinosaur Bones

7. Use the library catalog to find a book written by Judy Blume with the word "fudge" in the title. What is its title?

Superfudge or **Fudgemania**

8. What is the library's most recent book by Ezra Jack Keats?

Answers will vary based on selection available.

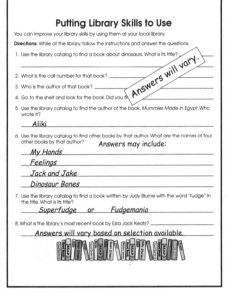

Page 327

Review

Directions: Write **A** for author, **S** for subject or **T** for title to show how you would look for each item in the library catalog.

1. **S** dinosaurs
2. **S** Russia
3. **A** Scarry, Richard
4. **A** Christopher, Matt
5. **A** Milne, A.A.
6. **T** *The Arctic and the Antarctic*
7. **T** *The Figure in the Shadows*
8. **S** Eskimos

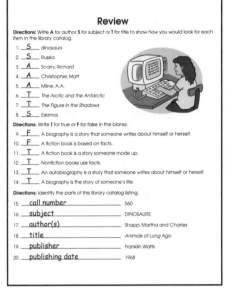

Directions: Write **T** for true or **F** for false in the blanks.

9. **F** A biography is a story that someone writes about himself or herself.
10. **F** A fiction book is based on facts.
11. **T** A fiction book is a story someone made up.
12. **T** Nonfiction books use facts.
13. **T** An autobiography is a story that someone writes about himself or herself.
14. **T** A biography is the story of someone's life.

Directions: Identify the parts of this library catalog listing.

15. **call number** 560
16. **subject** DINOSAURS
17. **author(s)** Shapp, Martha and Charles
18. **title** *Animals of Long Ago*
19. **publisher** Franklin Watts
20. **publishing date** 1968

Page 328

Encyclopedia Skills

Encyclopedias are sets of books that provide information about different subjects. If you want to know when cars were first made or who invented the phonograph, you could find the information in an encyclopedia.

Encyclopedias come in sets of books and on computer CD's. They contain many facts, illustrations, maps, graphs and tables. Encyclopedias are **reference books** found in the reference section of the library.

Each subject listed in an encyclopedia is called an **entry**. Entries are organized alphabetically.

Some good encyclopedias for students are *World Book Encyclopedia, Compton's Encyclopedia* and *Children's Britannica*.

Specialty encyclopedias, like the *McGraw-Hill Encyclopedia of Science and Technology,* contain information on one particular subject.

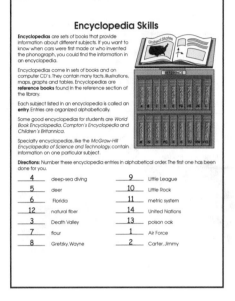

Directions: Number these encyclopedia entries in alphabetical order. The first one has been done for you.

4	deep-sea diving	**9**	Little League
5	deer	**10**	Little Rock
6	Florida	**11**	metric system
12	natural fiber	**14**	United Nations
3	Death Valley	**13**	poison oak
7	flour	**1**	Air Force
8	Gretzky, Wayne	**2**	Carter, Jimmy

Page 329

Encyclopedia Skills: Using the Index

The **index** of an encyclopedia contains an alphabetical listing of all entries. To find information about a subject, decide on the best word to describe the subject. If you want to know about ducks, look up the word "duck" in the index. If you're really interested in learning about mallard ducks, then look under "mallard ducks." The index shows the page number and volume where the information is located.

Look at the index entry below about Neil Armstrong. Most index entries also tell you when a person lived and died and give a short description of the person.

> ARMSTRONG, NEIL   United States astronaut. b. 1930
>   Commander of *Gemini 8*, 1966; first man to walk on the Moon, July 1969
>   References in
>   Astronaut: Illus. 2:56
>   Space travel 17:214

Neil Armstrong is listed under "Astronaut" and "Space travel." You can find information about him in both articles. The first entry shows there is an illustration (illus.) of Neil Armstrong in volume 2 on page 56 (2:56).

If Neil Armstrong were listed in a separate article in the encyclopedia, the index would look something like this:

> main article Armstrong, Neil
> 2:48

Directions: Answer these questions about using an encyclopedia index.

1. According to the index listing for Neil Armstrong, when was he born? **1930**

2. According to the index listing, who was Neil Armstrong? **commander of** **Gemini 8** and first man to walk on the Moon

3. When did he walk on the Moon? **July 1969**

4. What are the titles of the two articles containing information about Neil Armstrong?

Astronaut **Space travel**

5. Where would you find the article on Space travel?

Volume number **17**, page number **214**.

Page 330

Encyclopedia Skills

Directions: Answer each question about using the encyclopedia.

1. To find information about Tyrannosaurus Rex, where would you look first?

in the encyclopedia index

2. If there is no listing in the index for Tyrannosaurus, what other subject(s) could you look under? **dinosaurs,** **prehistoric animals, extinct animals**

3. To find information about President George Bush, under which index entry would you look? **Bush, George**

4. If there is no separate entry for George Bush, where else could you look?

under presidents

5. Why should you use the encyclopedia index first? **It tells exactly where** **to find information.**

6. If the encyclopedia says that Tyrannosaurus is in 17:97, what does that mean?

The article is in volume 17 on page 97.

7. If the encyclopedia says "references in." does that refer you to a main article about the subject? **no**

8. Is there always only one place to find a subject in the encyclopedia? Why or why not?

No, a topic can be found in many articles.

9. Will an encyclopedia index tell you when a person was born? **yes**

10. To find information about the *Discovery* space shuttle, where would you look?

in the index under *Discovery*, under space shuttle, **under space program**

Page 331

Encyclopedia Skills

Each book in a set of encyclopedias has a volume number and lists the range of subjects included. Volume 10 shown below includes all articles that would fall alphabetically between insect and leaf. Note that Volume 30 in this set is the index.

Directions: Answer the questions.

12 1. In which volume would you look to find an article on lungs?

10 2. Which volume would contain an article on ladybugs?

23 3. In which volume would an article on Saturn be found?

26 4. Which volume would contain an article on swimming?

22 5. In which volume would you check for an article on John D. Rockefeller?

25 6. An article on soccer would be in which volume?

13 7. Which volume would contain an article on magic?

15 8. In which volume would you look to find an article on melons?

Page 332

Putting Encyclopedia Skills to Use

Directions: Read the questions below about blue jays. Use the index to find **blue jay** in the encyclopedia. Read the article about blue jays and take notes. Then answer the questions.

1. What does a blue jay look like? _____

2. What are two other kinds of jays? _____

3. What do blue jays eat? _____

4. Are blue jays friendly to other types _____

5. How do blue jays sound? _____

6. What do you think blue_____ o eat from a bird feeder where other birds are eating? _____

7. Are all jays _____

8. Can blue jays b_____ed? _____

9. How would you tame a blue jay? _____

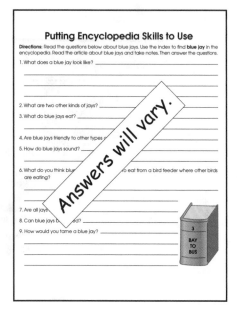

Answers will vary.

Page 333

Putting Encyclopedia Skills to Use

Directions: Read the questions about comets. Use the index to find **comet** in the encyclopedia. Read the article about comets and take notes. Then answer the questions.

1. What did the Greeks call comets? _____

2. What does "comet" mean in Greek? _____

3. Were comets recently discovered? _____

4. What do you have to use sometimes to see comets? _____

5. Can you ever see comets with your eyes only? _____

6. Name the comet that came close to Earth in 198_____

7. Who discovered that comet? _____

8. Name the comet that came close to E_____

9. Who discovered that comet? _____

10. What did Sir Isaac Newton dis_____

11. Are comets lighter or _____

12. Did your encyclo_____ er articles that include mo_____ed to comets? _____

13. To what other article_____ ur encyclopedia refer? _____

Answers will vary.

Page 334

Review

Directions: Write T for true or F for false.

1. **F** Every subject you look up in an encyclopedia will have a whole article written about it.

2. **T** You should always use the index to find a subject in the encyclopedia.

3. **T** An index may refer you to more than one article about a subject.

4. **F** Entries in an encyclopedia are in order according to when they happened.

5. **T** The index will give you some information about your subject.

Directions: Write the answers.

6. Name two subjects you could look under in an index to find **Jupiter** in an encyclopedia.
   1) _Answers may include: Jupiter, planets, solar system,_
   2) _mythology_

7. Name two possible entries for **George Washington** in an encyclopedia.
   1) _Washington, George_
   2) _presidents_

8. Which entry would include information about ants, flies, bees and gnats?
   insects

Directions: Number these encyclopedia entries in alphabetical order.

4 Bush, George		**7** meteor
8 planets		**2** Brazil
3 bush		**10** William I
9 whole wheat flour		**6** Lincoln, Abraham
1 Bell, Alexander Graham		**5** Japan

Page 335

Using Reference Sources: Out of This World

The history of the American space program is a very fascinating topic. The articles presented earlier in this book (pages 164–170) provided many interesting facts about some of the astronauts, what their jobs were and what space travel was like.

Besides books and encyclopedias, magazine articles and the Internet are other good reference sources you can use to learn more about a topic.

Directions: Neil Armstrong was the first man to walk on the Moon in July 1969. Use reference sources to answer these questions.

1. What two other astronauts were with him? _Edwin Aldrin and Michael Collins_

2. What was the name of the Apollo mission that went to the Moon? _Apollo 11_

3. What was the exact date of the first Moon landing? _July 20, 1969_

4. Why was the U.S. racing Russia to the Moon? _Answers will vary._

Directions: John Glenn first orbited Earth in 1962. Use reference sources to answer these questions.

5. How old was he then? _41_

6. When did John Glenn return to space? _1998_

7. How old was he on this second trip? _77_

8. Why did he return to space? _to assist in the study of the effects of no gravity on aging_

Directions: Compare and contrast Glenn's two trips.

9. _Answers will vary._

Page 336

Using Reference Sources: Out of This World

Directions: Use reference sources to answer these questions.

1. What caused the "Space Race" in the 1950s? _Answers may include: the launching of Sputnik I by Russia in 1957_

2. In testing rockets, why were chimps used instead of other animals? _They are physically much like humans._

3. What is the astronaut training program like? _____

4. Why do you think the training is so difficult? _____

Directions: Use what you lear_____ questions.

5. Do you think being an a_____ or you? Explain. _____

6. What do_____ like on a space station or in a space colony? _____

For fun, look up i_____ mation on "Space Camp" at one of NASA's training centers in Alabama.

Answers will vary.

Page 337

Putting It All Together

You have learned many new skills. Now it's time to use those skills to write a report about a planet.

Directions: Choose a planet in our solar system other than Earth. Then answer the following questions about the report you will write.

1. What planet will you write about? _____

2. Decide on questions you want to answer about your planet. W_____

3. Where will you find information ab_____

4. What should you do_____ e planet?

5. After y_____ out your planet, what should you do next?

Answers will vary.

Page 338

Putting It All Together

It's time to begin your research. You can use reference books as well as information from the Internet.

Directions: Fill in the information below to help you continue preparing to write a report about a planet.

1. Begin gathering information about your planet by looking for books with the planet's name in the title. What other subjects could you look under that might include information about your planet?

   <u>solar system, planets, astronomy</u>

2. Use the library catalog to find the names of four books that contain information about your planet. List their titles, authors and call numbers.

   TITLE   AUTHOR   CALL NUMBER
   1)
   2)
   3)
   4)

3. Name at least two sources ~~for~~ ~~your report~~.
   1)
   2)

4. Read the book~~s~~ ~~notes should cover the main points. Use separate~~ sheets of pa~~per~~.

Answers will vary.

Page 339

Putting It All Together

Now it's time to move on and gather information from encyclopedias for your report. There are many good encyclopedias available on CD's.

Directions: Fill in the information below to help you continue preparing to write a report about a planet.

1. When you use an encyclopedia to get information, what should you do first?

2. Where does the index say to look for information abou~~t~~

3. Read the article or articles. Then write n~~otes~~

Answers will vary.

Page 340

Putting It All Together

Once you have gathered information and made notes, it's time to make an outline of your report.

Directions: Complete the outline using the information you found in books, encyclopedias and other sources.

I. The location of the planet
   A.
      1.
      2.
   B.
II. What does the planet look like?
   A.
   B.
III. What is the surface of
   A.
   B.
   C.
IV. Could we ~~live there~~ ~~or~~ why not?
   A.
   B.
   C.

Now, you are ready to write!

Answers will vary.

Page 341

Putting It All Together

Directions: Use your outline and notes to write a report about your planet. Use your own paper to finish this writing project. Add illustrations to make your report more interesting.

Reports will vary.

Page 342

Writing Haiku

Haiku is a form of unrhymed Japanese poetry. A haiku poem has only three lines. Each line has a specific number of syllables.

Haiku poems usually describe a season or something in nature. Sometimes haiku are written about feelings.

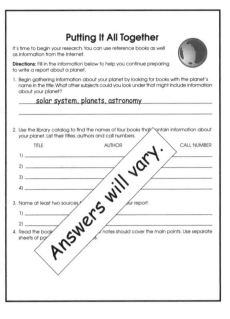

The Haiku pattern:
Line 1 — 5 syllables
Line 2 — 7 syllables
Line 3 — 5 syllables

Example haiku:
Winter snow slides from
The eave. Drops—plop—on my head,
As I walk under.
— D.S. Underwood

When writing haiku you do not count words per line. Count only the number of syllables.

Directions: To prepare for writing your poem, think of words about a snowy day. Write them on the lines. After each word, write the number of syllables in the word.

<u>frosty</u> (2)   <u>white</u> (1)   <u>snowflakes</u> (2)

Answers will vary.

When writing any type of poetry, it is a good idea to start on scrap paper so you can write, erase, cross out and rewrite.

Directions: Write a haiku poem about a snowy day on scrap paper. When you are satisfied with your poem, rewrite it below. At the end of each line, write the number of syllables in the line.

5
7
5

Poems will vary.

Directions: Select one of the topics in the box. Prewrite your poem on scrap paper. Write it on good paper when you are satisfied with it.

| rainy day | summer | spring | fall |
| a sparrow | joy | sadness | friendship |

Page 343

Tankas

Haiku poems are given to friends as gifts. A **tanka** is a poem written in response to haiku. If a person receives a haiku, he or she is supposed to send a tanka in reply! A tanka is much like a haiku but has two more lines.

The tanka pattern:
Line 1 — 5 syllables
Line 2 — 7 syllables
Line 3 — 5 syllables
Line 4 — 7 syllables
Line 5 — 7 syllables

Example tanka:
The snow on your head
It did plop—slop and slide down
Your neck to your socks.
The winter wind blew, gave you
A chill, now you sneeze—Ah choo!
— D.S. Underwood

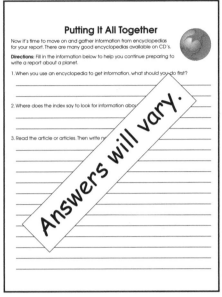

Remember to count syllables per line.

Directions: Write a tanka in response to one of the two haiku poems you wrote. Prewrite it below. At the end of each line, write the number of syllables in the line.

5
7
5
7
7

Poems will vary.

Directions: Trade your haik~~u~~ ~~with a partner. Write~~ a tanka in response to your partner's haiku.

Page 344

Cinquains

Another form of unrhymed poetry that can express many ideas in only a few words is the **cinquain**. A cinquain is a simple five-line verse.

In a cinquain, the number of syllables does not matter. What is important is the number of words in each line and the specific type of words used.

Cinquain pattern:
Line 1 — A noun
Line 2 — 2 adjectives describing the noun in line 1
Line 3 — 3 ing verbs describing the noun in line 1
Line 4 — A 4-word phrase
Line 5 — A noun that is a synonym for the word in line 1

Example cinquains:
Apple	Mary
Shiny, smooth	Young, active
Crunching, munching, slurping	Trying, discovering, learning
Healthy snack to eat	Anxious to grow up
Fruit	Daughter

Directions: Think of someone you know well. Write a cinquain about that person. Prewrite words and phrases to get started. Write your final draft on the lines.

Directions: Select your fav... ...rite a cinquain about it.

Poems will vary.

Page 345

Shape Poems

A **shape poem** or **pattern poem** uses its shape or pattern of words to tell what the poem is about.

Example:

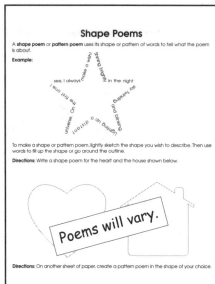

To make a shape or pattern poem, lightly sketch the shape you wish to describe. Then use words to fill up the shape or go around the outline.

Directions: Write a shape poem for the heart and the house shown below.

Poems will vary.

Directions: On another sheet of paper, create a pattern poem in the shape of your choice.

Page 346

Limericks

A **limerick** is a short, silly poem. Limericks are five lines long and follow a specific pattern.

Limerick pattern:
Lines 1,2 and 5 rhyme and have 8, 9 or 10 syllables per line.
Lines 3 and 4 rhyme and have 5,6 or 7 syllables per line.

Example limerick:
There once was a lion at the zoo
Who in his mane got sticky goo.
The situation looked grim,
So they gave him a trim
And turned his one mane into two.

Directions: Write two limericks. Prewrite on scrap paper. Write your final drafts below. Add a short title to your limericks.

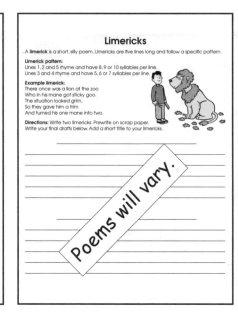

Poems will vary.

Page 348

Place Value

Place value is the value of a digit, or numeral, shown by where it is in the number. For example, in 1,234, 1 has the place value of thousands, 2 is hundreds, 3 is tens and 4 is ones.

Directions: Write the numbers in the correct boxes to find how far the car has traveled.

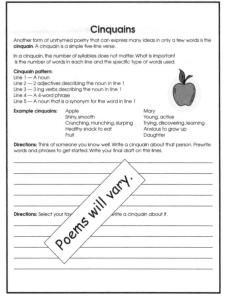

one thousand
six hundreds
eight ones
nine ten thousands
four tens
two millions
five hundred thousands

millions	hundred thousands	ten thousands	thousands	hundreds	tens	ones
2	5	9	1	6	4	8

How many miles has the car traveled? __2,591,648 miles__

Directions: In the number . . .

2,386	__6__	is in the ones place.
4,957	__9__	is in the hundreds place.
102,432	__0__	is in the ten thousands place.
489,753	__9__	is in the thousands place.
1,743,998	__1__	is in the millions place.
9,301,671	__3__	is in the hundred thousands place.
7,521,834	__3__	is in the tens place.

Page 349

Place Value: Standard Form

For this activity, you will need a number spinner or number cube.

Directions: Roll the cube or spin the spinner the same number of times as there are spaces in each place value box. The first number rolled or spun goes in the ones place, the second number in the tens place, and so on.

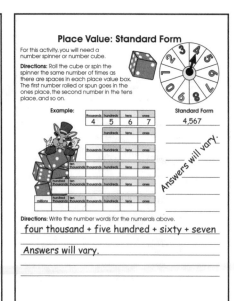

Example:

thousands	hundreds	tens	ones
4	5	6	7

Standard Form
4,567

Answers will vary.

Directions: Write the number words for the numerals above.

__four thousand + five hundred + sixty + seven__

__Answers will vary.__

Page 350

Place Value: Expanded Notation and Standard Form

Directions: Use the number cube or spinner to create numbers for the place value boxes below. Then write the number in expanded notation and standard form.

Example:

thousands	hundreds	tens	ones
8	6	2	4

Standard Form __8,624__
Expanded Notation __8,000 + 600 + 20 + 4__

thousands	hundreds	tens	ones

Standard Form _____
Expanded Notation _____

ten thousands	thousands	hundreds	tens	ones

Standard Form _____
Expanded Notation _____

hundred thousands	ten thousands	thousands	hundreds	tens	ones

Standard Form _____
Expanded Notation _____

Answers will vary.

Directions: Write the value of the 4 in each number below.

742,521	__4 ten thousands (40,000)__
456	__4 hundreds (400)__
1,234,567	__4 thousands (4,000)__
65,504	__4 ones (4)__
937,641	__4 tens (40)__

Page 351

Add 'Em Up!

Addition is "putting together" or adding two or more numbers to find the sum.

Directions: Add the following problems as quickly and as accurately as you can.

3 +2 = **5**	6 +4 = **10**	5 +4 = **9**	2 +9 = **11**
6 +2 = **8**	4 +1 = **5**	9 +6 = **15**	7 +6 = **13**	8 +7 = **15**	8 +9 = **17**
9 +4 = **13**	1 +8 = **9**	4 +7 = **11**	7 +9 = **16**	5 +6 = **11**	5 +3 = **8**
6 +6 = **12**	8 +8 = **16**	7 +7 = **14**	4 +4 = **8**
2 +8 = **10**	5 +2 = **7**	3 +6 = **9**	5 +8 = **13**

How quickly did you complete this page? **Answers will vary.**

Page 352

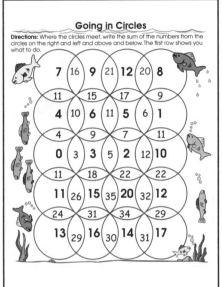

Going in Circles

Directions: Where the circles meet, write the sum of the numbers from the circles on the right and left and above and below. The first row shows you what to do.

Row 1: 7 16 9 21 12 20 8
Row 2: 11 15 17 9
Row 3: 4 10 6 11 5 6 1
Row 4: 4 9 11
Row 5: 0 3 3 5 2 12 10
Row 6: 11 18 22 22
Row 7: 11 26 15 35 20 32 12
Row 8: 24 31 34 29
Row 9: 13 29 16 30 14 31 17

Page 354

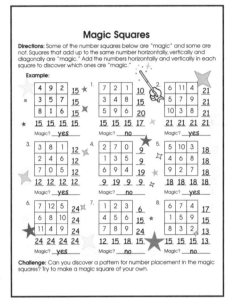

Magic Squares

Directions: Some of the number squares below are "magic" and some are not. Squares that add up to the same number horizontally, vertically and diagonally are "magic." Add the numbers horizontally and vertically in each square to discover which ones are "magic."

Example:

4	9	2	15 ★
3	5	7	15
8	1	6	15
15	**15**	**15**	**15**

★ Magic? **yes**

7	2	1	10
3	4	8	15
5	9	6	20
15	**15**	**15**	**17**

Magic? **no**

2.
6	11	4	21
5	7	9	21
10	3	8	21
21	**21**	**21**	**21**

Magic? **yes**

3.
3	8	1	12
2	4	6	12
7	0	5	12
12	**12**	**12**	**12**

Magic? **yes**

4.
2	7	0	9
1	3	5	9
6	9	4	19
9	**19**	**9**	**9**

Magic? **no**

5.
5	10	3	18
4	6	8	18
9	2	7	18
18	**18**	**18**	**18**

Magic? **yes**

6.
7	12	5	24
6	8	10	24
11	4	9	24
24	**24**	**24**	**24**

Magic? **yes**

7.
1	2	3	6
4	5	6	15
7	8	9	24
12	**15**	**18**	**15**

Magic? **no**

8.
6	7	4	17
1	5	9	15
8	3	2	13
15	**15**	**15**	**13**

Magic? **no**

Challenge: Can you discover a pattern for number placement in the magic squares? Try to make a magic square of your own.

Page 355

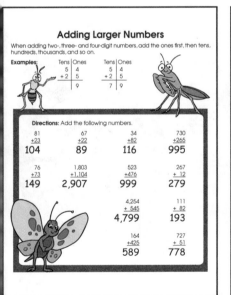

Adding Larger Numbers

When adding two-, three- and four-digit numbers, add the ones first, then tens, hundreds, thousands, and so on.

Examples:

Tens	Ones		Tens	Ones
5	4		5	4
+2	5		+2	5
	9		7	9

Directions: Add the following numbers.

81 +23 = **104**	67 +22 = **89**	34 +82 = **116**	730 +265 = **995**
76 +73 = **149**	1,803 +1,104 = **2,907**	523 +476 = **999**	267 + 12 = **279**
		4,254 + 545 = **4,799**	111 + 82 = **193**
		164 +425 = **589**	727 + 51 = **778**

Page 356

Addition: Regrouping

Regrouping uses 10 ones to form one 10, 10 tens to form one hundred, one 10 and 5 ones to form 15, and so on.

Directions: Add using regrouping. Color in all the boxes with a 5 in the answer to help the dog find its way home.

63 + 22 = **85**	5,268 4,910 + 1,683 = **11,861**	248 + 463 = **711**	291 + 543 = **834**	2,934 + 112 = **3,046**
1,736 + 5,367 = **7,103**	2,946 + 7,384 = **10,330**	3,245 1,239 + 981 = **5,465**	738 + 692 = **1,430**	896 + 728 = **1,624**	594 + 738 = **1,332**
2,603 + 5,004 = **7,607**	4,507 + 289 = **4,796**	1,483 + 6,753 = **8,236**	1,258 + 6,301 = **7,559**	27 469 + 6,002 = **6,498**	4,637 + 7,531 = **12,168**
782 + 65 = **847**	485 + 276 = **761**	3,421 + 8,064 = **11,485**			
48 93 + 26 = **167**	90 263 + 864 = **1,217**	362 453 + 800 = **1,615**			

Page 357

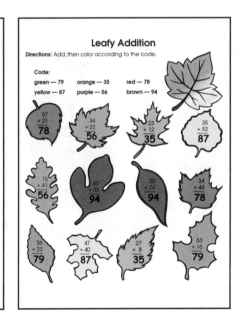

Leafy Addition

Directions: Add, then color according to the code.

Code:

green — 79   orange — 35   red — 78
yellow — 87   purple — 56   brown — 94

57 +21 = **78**	34 +22 = **56**	23 +12 = **35**	35 +52 = **87**
15 +41 = **56**	62 +32 = **94**	20 +74 = **94**	34 +44 = **78**
56 +23 = **79**	47 +40 = **87**	27 + 8 = **35**	63 +16 = **79**

Page 358

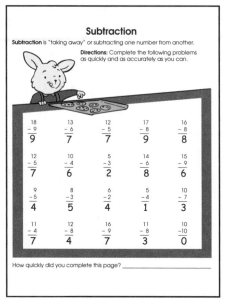

Subtraction

Subtraction is "taking away" or subtracting one number from another.

Directions: Complete the following problems as quickly and as accurately as you can.

18 − 9 = **9**	13 − 6 = **7**	12 − 5 = **7**	17 − 8 = **9**	16 − 8 = **8**
12 − 5 = **7**	10 − 4 = **6**	5 − 3 = **2**	14 − 6 = **8**	15 − 9 = **6**
9 − 4 = **4**	8 − 3 = **5**	6 − 2 = **4**	5 − 4 = **1**	10 − 7 = **3**
11 − 4 = **7**	12 − 8 = **4**	16 − 9 = **7**	11 − 8 = **3**	10 − 10 = **0**

How quickly did you complete this page? _____

Page 359

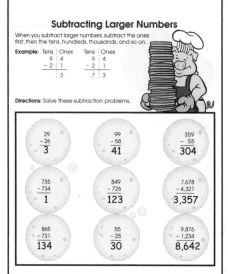

Subtracting Larger Numbers

When you subtract larger numbers, subtract the ones first, then the tens, hundreds, thousands, and so on.

Example:

Tens	Ones		Tens	Ones
9	4		9	4
− 2	1		− 2	1
	3		7	3

Directions: Solve these subtraction problems.

29 − 26 = **3**	99 − 58 = **41**	359 − 55 = **304**
735 − 734 = **1**	849 − 726 = **123**	7,678 − 4,321 = **3,357**
865 − 731 = **134**	55 − 25 = **30**	9,876 − 1,234 = **8,642**

Page 360

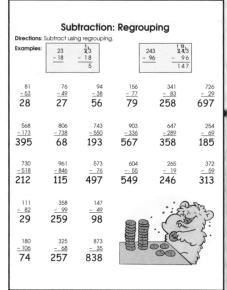

Subtraction: Regrouping

Directions: Subtract using regrouping.

Examples:

23 − 18	1 / ₂3 − 18 = 5		243 − 96	1 13 / ₂4̸3 − 96 = 147

81 − 53 = **28**	76 − 49 = **27**	94 − 38 = **56**	156 − 77 = **79**	341 − 83 = **258**	726 − 29 = **697**
568 − 173 = **395**	806 − 738 = **68**	743 − 550 = **193**	903 − 336 = **567**	647 − 289 = **358**	254 − 69 = **185**
730 − 518 = **212**	961 − 846 = **115**	573 − 76 = **497**	604 − 55 = **549**	265 − 19 = **246**	372 − 59 = **313**
111 − 82 = **29**	358 − 99 = **259**	147 − 49 = **98**			
180 − 106 = **74**	325 − 68 = **257**	873 − 35 = **838**			

Page 361

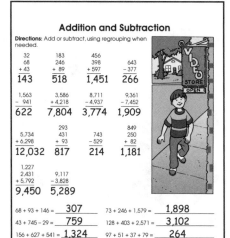

Addition and Subtraction

Directions: Add or subtract, using regrouping when needed.

32 + 68 + 43 = **143**	183 + 246 + 89 = **518**	456 + 398 + 597 = **1,451**	643 − 377 = **266**
1,563 − 941 = **622**	3,586 + 4,218 = **7,804**	8,711 − 4,937 = **3,774**	9,361 − 7,452 = **1,909**
5,734 + 6,298 = **12,032**	293 + 431 + 93 = **817**	743 − 529 = **214**	849 + 250 + 82 = **1,181**
1,227 + 2,431 + 5,792 = **9,450**	9,117 − 3,828 = **5,289**		

68 + 93 + 146 = **307**

73 + 246 + 1,579 = **1,898**

43 + 745 − 29 = **759**

128 + 403 + 2,571 = **3,102**

156 + 627 + 541 = **1,324**

97 + 51 + 37 + 79 = **264**

Tom walks 389 steps from his house to the video store. It is 149 steps to Elm Street. It is 52 steps from Maple Street to the video store. How many steps is it from Elm Street to Maple Street? **188 steps**

Page 362

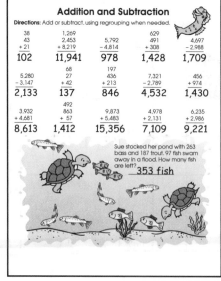

Addition and Subtraction

Directions: Add or subtract, using regrouping when needed.

38 + 43 + 21 = **102**	1,269 + 2,453 + 8,219 = **11,941**	5,792 − 4,814 = **978**	629 + 491 + 308 = **1,428**	4,697 − 2,988 = **1,709**
5,280 − 3,147 = **2,133**	68 + 27 + 42 = **137**	197 + 436 + 213 = **846**	7,321 − 2,789 = **4,532**	456 + 974 = **1,430**
3,932 + 4,681 = **8,613**	492 + 863 + 57 = **1,412**	9,873 + 5,483 = **15,356**	4,978 + 2,131 = **7,109**	6,235 + 2,986 = **9,221**

Sue stocked her pond with 263 bass and 187 trout. 97 fish swam away in a flood. How many fish are left? **353 fish**

Page 363

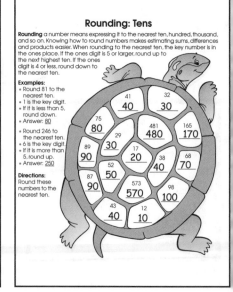

Rounding: Tens

Rounding a number means expressing it to the nearest ten, hundred, thousand, and so on. Knowing how to round numbers makes estimating sums, differences and products easier. When rounding to the nearest ten, the key number is in the ones place. If the ones digit is 5 or larger, round up to the next highest ten. If the ones digit is 4 or less, round down to the nearest ten.

Examples:
- Round 81 to the nearest ten.
- 1 is the key digit.
- If it is less than 5, round down.
- Answer: 80

- Round 246 to the nearest ten.
- 6 is the key digit.
- If it is more than 5, round up.
- Answer: 250

Directions: Round these numbers to the nearest ten.

41 = **40** 32 = **30**
75 = **80** 481 = **480** 165 = **170**
29 = **30**
89 = **90** 17 = **20** 38 = **40** 68 = **70**
87 = **90** 52 = **50** 573 = **570** 98 = **100**
43 = **40** 12 = **10**

Page 364

Rounding: Hundreds and Thousands

When rounding to the nearest hundred, the key number is in the tens place. If the tens digit is 5 or larger, round up to nearest hundred. If the tens digit is 4 or less, round down to the nearest hundred.

Examples:
Round 871 to the nearest hundred.
7 is the key digit.
If it is more than 5, round up.
Answer: <u>900</u>

Round 421 to the nearest hundred.
2 is the key digit.
If it is less than 4, round down.
Answer: <u>400</u>

Directions: Round these numbers to the nearest hundred.

255 <u>300</u>   368 <u>400</u>   443 <u>400</u>   578 <u>600</u>
562 <u>600</u>   698 <u>700</u>   99 <u>100</u>   775 <u>800</u>
812 <u>800</u>   592 <u>600</u>   124 <u>100</u>   10,235 <u>10,200</u>

When rounding to the nearest thousand, the key number is in the hundreds place. If the hundreds digit is 5 or larger, round up to the nearest thousand. If the hundreds digit is 4 or less, round down to the nearest thousand.

Examples:
Round 7,932 to the nearest thousand.
9 is the key digit.
If it is more than 5, round up.
Answer: <u>8,000</u>

Round 1,368 to the nearest thousand.
3 is the key digit.
If it is less than 4, round down.
Answer: <u>1,000</u>

Directions: Round these numbers to the nearest thousand.

8,631 <u>9,000</u>   1,248 <u>1,000</u>   798 <u>1,000</u>
999 <u>1,000</u>   6,229 <u>6,000</u>   8,461 <u>8,000</u>
9,654 <u>10,000</u>   4,963 <u>5,000</u>   99,923 <u>100,000</u>

Page 365

Rounding

Directions: Round these numbers to the nearest ten.

18 <u>20</u>   33 <u>30</u>   82 <u>80</u>   56 <u>60</u>
24 <u>20</u>   49 <u>50</u>   91 <u>90</u>   67 <u>70</u>

Directions: Round these numbers to the nearest hundred.

243 <u>200</u>   689 <u>700</u>   263 <u>300</u>   162 <u>200</u>
389 <u>400</u>   720 <u>700</u>   351 <u>400</u>   490 <u>500</u>
463 <u>500</u>   846 <u>800</u>   928 <u>900</u>   733 <u>700</u>

Directions: Round these numbers to the nearest thousand.

2,638 <u>3,000</u>   3,940 <u>4,000</u>   8,653 <u>9,000</u>
6,238 <u>6,000</u>   1,429 <u>1,000</u>   5,061 <u>5,000</u>
7,289 <u>7,000</u>   2,742 <u>3,000</u>   9,460 <u>9,000</u>
3,109 <u>3,000</u>   4,697 <u>5,000</u>   8,302 <u>8,000</u>

Directions: Round these numbers to the nearest ten thousand.

11,368 <u>10,000</u>   38,421 <u>40,000</u>
75,302 <u>80,000</u>   67,932 <u>70,000</u>
14,569 <u>10,000</u>   49,926 <u>50,000</u>
93,694 <u>90,000</u>   81,648 <u>80,000</u>
26,784 <u>30,000</u>   87,065 <u>90,000</u>
57,843 <u>60,000</u>   29,399 <u>30,000</u>

Page 366

Estimating

Estimating is used for certain mathematical calculations. For example, to figure the cost of several items, round their prices to the nearest dollar, then add up the approximate cost. A store clerk, on the other hand, needs to know the exact prices in order to charge the correct amount. To estimate to the nearest hundred, round up numbers over 50. Round down numbers less than 50. **Example:** 251 is rounded up to 300. Round down numbers less than 50. **Example:** 128 is rounded down to 100.

Directions: In the following situations, write whether an exact or estimated answer should be used.

Example:
You make a deposit in your bank account. Do you want an estimated total or an exact total?   <u>Exact</u>

1. Your family just ate dinner at a restaurant. Your parents are trying to calculate the tip for your server. Should they estimate by rounding or use exact numbers?   <u>Estimate</u>

2. You are at the store buying candy, and you want to know if you have enough money to pay for it. Should you estimate or use exact numbers?   <u>Estimate</u>

3. Some friends are planning a trip from New York City to Washington, D.C. They need to know about how far they will travel in miles. Should they estimate or use exact numbers?   <u>Estimate</u>

4. You plan a trip to the zoo. Beforehand, you call the zoo for the price of admission. Should the person at the zoo tell you an estimated or exact price?   <u>Exact</u>

5. The teacher is grading your papers. Should your scores be exact or estimated?   <u>Exact</u>

Page 367

Estimating

To **estimate** means to give an approximate, rather than an exact, answer. To find an estimated sum or difference, round the numbers of the problem, then add or subtract. If the number has 5 ones or more, round up to the nearest ten. If the number has 4 ones or less, round down to the nearest ten.

Directions: Round the numbers to the nearest ten, hundred or thousand. Then add or subtract.

Examples:

Ten	Hundred	Thousand
74 → 70 + 39 → + 40 110	352 → 400 − 164 → − 200 200	7,681 → 8,000 + 4,321 → + 4,000 12,000
64 → 60 − 25 → − 30 30		

Round these numbers to the nearest ten.

18 → 20   49 → 50   67 → 70
+ 24 → + 20   − 33 → − 30   − 56 → − 60
40   20   10

Round these numbers to the nearest hundred.

255 → 300   526 → 500   102 → 100
− 99 → − 100   + 145 → + 100 − 75 → − 100
200   600   0

Round these numbers to the nearest thousand.

8,361 → 8,000   9,926 → 10,000
+ 889 → + 1,000   + 3,645 → + 4,000
9,000   14,000

Page 368

Estimating

Directions: Round the numbers to the nearest hundred. Then solve the problems.

Example:
Jack and Alex were playing a computer game. Jack scored 428 points. Alex scored 132. About how many more points did Jack score than Alex?

Round Jack's 428 points down to the nearest hundred, 400.

Round Alex's 132 points down to 100. Subtract.

400
− 100
estimate   300

258 → 300 + 117 → + 100 375 400	493 → 500 + 114 → + 100 600	837 → 800 − 252 → − 300 500
928 → 900 − 437 → − 400 500	700 → 700 − 491 → − 500 200	319 → 300 + 630 → + 600 900
332 → 300 + 567 → + 600 900	493 → 500 − 162 → − 200 300	1,356 → 1,400 + 2,941 → + 2,900 4,300

Page 369

Skip Counting

Skip counting is a quick way to count by skipping numbers. For example, when you skip count by 2's, you count 2, 4, 6, 8, and so on. You can skip count by many different numbers such as 2's, 4's, 5's, 10's and 100's.

The illustration below shows skip counting by 2's to 14.

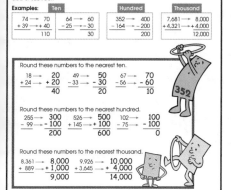

0 1 2 3 4 5 6 7 8 9 10 11 12 13 14 15 16 17 18 19 20

Directions: Use the number line to help you skip count by 2's from 0 to 20.
0, <u>2</u>, <u>4</u>, <u>6</u>, 8, <u>10</u>, <u>12</u>, 14, <u>16</u>, <u>18</u>, <u>20</u>

Directions: Skip count by 3's by filling in the rocks across the pond.

3 <u>6</u> 9 <u>12</u> <u>15</u> 18 <u>21</u>

Page 370

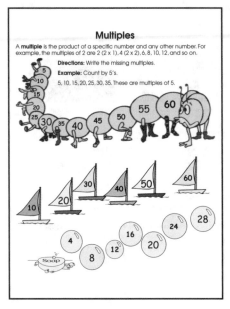

Multiples

A **multiple** is the product of a specific number and any other number. For example, the multiples of 2 are 2 (2 x 1), 4 (2 x 2), 6, 8, 10, 12, and so on.

Directions: Write the missing multiples.

Example: Count by 5's.

5, 10, 15, 20, 25, 30, 35. These are multiples of 5.

Page 371

Review

Directions: Add or subtract using regrouping.

67		732		8,453
93	5,029	801	2,467	
+ 48	− 3,068	+ 18	+ 3,184	− 6,087
208	1,961	1,551	5,651	2,366

5,792	7,489	463	3,567	6,342
− 3,889	+ 5,938	− 209	− 2,394	+ 959
1,903	13,427	254	1,173	7,301

Directions: Write the numbers in the boxes. In the blanks, write the numbers in standard form.

millions	hundred thousands	ten thousands	thousands	hundreds	tens	ones
8	4	0	0	9	5	2

8,400,952

eight millions, four hundred thousands, zero ten thousands, zero thousands, nine hundreds, five tens, two ones

hundred thousands	ten thousands	thousands	hundreds	tens	ones
5	3	5	0	4	1

535,041

five hundred thousands, three ten thousands, five thousands, zero hundreds, four tens, one one

Directions: Write the missing multiples in the blanks.

6, 12, 18, _24_, 30, _36_   3, _6_, _9_, 12, 15

4, _8_, 12, 16, _20_, 24   _5_, 10, 15, _20_, _25_

Page 372

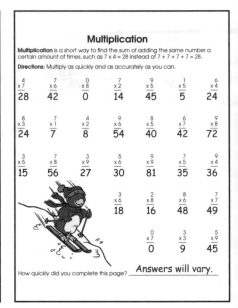

Multiplication

Multiplication is a short way to find the sum of adding the same number a certain amount of times, such as 7 x 4 = 28 instead of 7 + 7 + 7 + 7 = 28.

Directions: Multiply as quickly and as accurately as you can.

4 x 7 = 28	7 x 6 = 42	0 x 8 = 0	7 x 2 = 14	9 x 5 = 45	1 x 5 = 5	6 x 4 = 24
8 x 3 = 24	7 x 1 = 7	9 x 2 = 8	9 x 6 = 54	8 x 5 = 40	6 x 7 = 42	9 x 8 = 72
3 x 5 = 15	7 x 8 = 56	3 x 9 = 27	5 x 6 = 30	9 x 9 = 81	7 x 5 = 35	9 x 4 = 36
			3 x 6 = 18	2 x 8 = 16	8 x 6 = 48	7 x 7 = 49
			0 x 7 = 0	3 x 3 = 9	5 x 9 = 45	

How quickly did you complete this page? _____ Answers will vary.

Page 373

Fact Factory

Factors are the numbers multiplied together in a multiplication problem. The **product** is the answer.

Directions: Write the missing factors or products.

X	5
1	5
5	25
4	20
6	30
3	15
2	10
7	35
9	45

X	9
8	72
3	27
4	36
9	81
6	54
7	63
2	18
1	9

X	7
2	14
5	35
6	42
8	56
7	49
4	28
3	21
0	0

X	3
7	21
4	12
6	18
3	9
2	6
5	15
8	24

X	1
1	1
12	12
10	10
3	3
5	5
7	7
6	6
4	4

X	8
9	72
8	64
4	32
5	40
6	48
7	56
3	24
2	16

X	2
12	24
1	2
11	22
2	4
10	20
3	6
9	18
4	8

X	4
2	8
9	36
6	24
8	32
1	4
3	12
5	20
7	28

X	6
7	42
6	36
5	30
4	24
3	18
2	12
1	6
0	0

X	10
2	20
3	30
4	40
5	50
6	60
7	70
8	80
9	90

X	11
4	44
7	77
9	99
10	110
3	33
5	55
6	66
8	88

X	12
1	12
2	24
3	36
4	48
5	60
6	72
7	84
8	96

Page 374

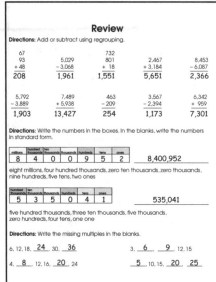

Multiplication: Tens, Hundreds, Thousands

When multiplying a number by 10, the answer is the number with a 0. It is like counting by tens.

Examples:

10 x 1 = 10	10 x 2 = 20	10 x 3 = 30	10 x 4 = 40	10 x 5 = 50	10 x 6 = 60

When multiplying a number by 100, the answer is the number with two 0's. When multiplying by 1,000, the answer is the number with three 0's.

Examples:

100 x 1 = 100	100 x 2 = 200	100 x 3 = 300	1,000 x 1 = 1,000	1,000 x 2 = 2,000	1,000 x 3 = 3,000
4 x 2 = 8	400 x 2 = 800	8 x 3 = 24	800 x 3 = 2,400	7 x 5 = 35	700 x 5 = 3,500

Directions: Multiply.

10 x 3 = 30   60 x 5 = 300   400 x 5 = 2,000   700 x 8 = 5,600   50 x 7 = 350

80 x 9 = 720   4,000 x 2 = 8,000   6,000 x 4 = 24,000   300 x 9 = 2,700   700 x 6 = 4,200

Page 375

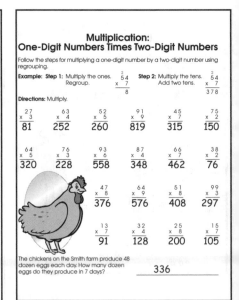

Multiplication: One-Digit Numbers Times Two-Digit Numbers

Follow the steps for multiplying a one-digit number by a two-digit number using regrouping.

Example: Step 1: Multiply the ones. Regroup.

54 x 7 = 8 (with 2 regrouped)

Step 2: Multiply the tens. Add two tens.

54 x 7 = 378

Directions: Multiply.

27 x 3 = 81	63 x 4 = 252	52 x 5 = 260	91 x 9 = 819	45 x 7 = 315	75 x 2 = 150
64 x 5 = 320	76 x 3 = 228	93 x 6 = 558	87 x 4 = 348	66 x 7 = 462	38 x 2 = 76
	47 x 8 = 376	64 x 9 = 576	51 x 8 = 408	99 x 3 = 297	
	13 x 7 = 91	32 x 4 = 128	25 x 8 = 200	15 x 7 = 105	

The chickens on the Smith farm produce 48 dozen eggs each day. How many dozen eggs do they produce in 7 days?   336

Page 376

Multiplication:
Two-Digit Numbers Times Two-Digit Numbers

Follow the steps for multiplying a two-digit number by a two-digit number using regrouping.

Example:

Step 1: Multiply the ones. Regroup.

$$63 \times 68$$
$$504$$

Step 2: Multiply the tens. Regroup. Add.

$$\begin{array}{r} 63 \\ \times 68 \\ \hline 504 \\ 3,780 \\ \hline 4,284 \end{array}$$

Directions: Multiply.

12 × 55 = 660	27 × 15 = 405	65 × 27 = 1,755	19 × 39 = 741	99 × 13 = 1,287	35 × 14 = 490
43 × 26 = 1,118	38 × 17 = 646	53 × 86 = 4,558	47 × 72 = 3,384	57 × 62 = 3,534	48 × 33 = 1,584
27 × 54 = 1,458	93 × 45 = 4,185	64 × 16 = 1,024	53 × 23 = 1,219		

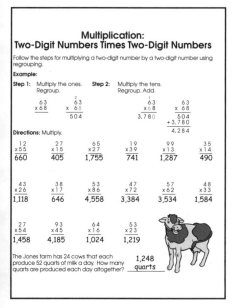

The Jones farm has 24 cows that each produce 52 quarts of milk a day. How many quarts are produced each day altogether? **1,248 quarts**

Page 377

Multiplication:
Two-Digit Numbers Times Three-Digit Numbers

Follow the steps for multiplying a two-digit number by a three-digit number using regrouping.

Example: Step 1: Multiply the ones. Regroup.

$$\begin{array}{r} 287 \\ \times 43 \\ \hline 861 \end{array}$$

Step 2: Multiply the tens. Regroup. Add.

$$\begin{array}{r} 287 \\ \times 43 \\ \hline 861 \\ 11,480 \\ \hline 12,341 \end{array}$$

Directions: Multiply.

- 261 × 36 = 9,396
- 434 × 48 = 20,832
- 357 × 75 = 26,775
- 231 × 46 = 10,626
- 754 × 65 = 49,010
- 614 × 59 = 36,226
- 549 × 89 = 48,861
- 372 × 94 = 34,968
- 458 × 85 = 38,930
- 368 × 98 = 36,064

At the Douglas berry farm, workers pick 378 baskets of peaches each day. Each basket holds 65 peaches. How many peaches are picked each day? **24,570**

Page 378

Multiplication: Two-Digit Numbers
Times Two- and Three-Digit Numbers

Directions: Multiply.

25 × 72 = 1,800	70 × 66 = 4,620	844 × 24 = 20,256	124 × 15 = 1,860
45 × 41 = 1,845	76 × 78 = 5,928	74 × 69 = 5,106	261 × 88 = 22,968
48 × 36 = 1,728	263 × 57 = 14,991	37 × 64 = 2,368	52 × 43 = 2,236
321 × 78 = 25,038	544 × 58 = 31,552	797 × 24 = 19,128	998 × 37 = 36,926
249 × 33 = 8,217	24 × 19 = 456	48 × 20 = 960	817 × 59 = 48,203

Page 379

Multiplication:
Three-Digit Numbers Times Three-Digit Numbers

Directions: Multiply. Regroup when needed.

Example:

$$\begin{array}{r} 563 \\ \times 248 \\ \hline 4,504 \\ 22,520 \\ 112,600 \\ \hline 139,624 \end{array}$$

Hint: When multiplying by the tens, start writing the number in the tens place. When multiplying by the hundreds, start in the hundreds place.

842 × 167 = 140,614	932 × 272 = 253,504	759 × 468 = 355,212	531 × 556 = 295,236
383 × 476 = 182,308	523 × 349 = 182,527	229 × 189 = 43,281	738 × 513 = 378,594

James grows pumpkins on his farm. He has 362 rows of pumpkins. There are 593 pumpkins in each row. How many pumpkins does James grow? **214,666 pumpkins**

Page 380

Multiplication Drill

Directions: Multiply.

134 × 22 = 2,948	48 × 66 = 3,168	876 × 13 = 11,388	432 × 64 = 27,648
68 × 11 = 748	5,478 × 8 = 43,824	248 × 61 = 15,128	6,897 × 6 = 41,382
82 × 4 = 328	6,798 × 5 = 33,990	79 × 86 = 6,794	694 × 38 = 26,372

Directions: Color the picture by matching each number with its paintbrush.

43,824
11,388
748
27,648
2,948
328
26,372
3,168
33,990
6,794
41,382
15,128

Page 381

Division

Division is a way to find out how many times one number is contained in another number. For example, 28 ÷ 7 = 4 means that there are 4 groups of 7 in 28.

Division problems can be written two ways: $36 \div 6 = 6$ or $6\overline{)36}$

These are the parts of a division problem:

dividend → $36 \div 6 = 6$ ← quotient
divisor ↑

divisor → $6\overline{)36}$ ← quotient, dividend

Directions: Divide.

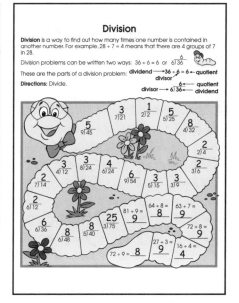

$7\overline{)21} = 3$
$2\overline{)12} = 6$
$5\overline{)25} = 5$
$4\overline{)32} = 8$
$4\overline{)12} = 3$
$8\overline{)24} = 3$
$6\overline{)24} = 4$
$2\overline{)4} = 2$
$7\overline{)14} = 2$
$9\overline{)54} = 6$
$5\overline{)15} = 3$
$3\overline{)9} = 3$
$6\overline{)12} = 2$
$6\overline{)36} = 6$
$8\overline{)48} = 6$
$5\overline{)40} = 8$
$3\overline{)75} = 25$
$81 \div 9 = 9$
$64 \div 8 = 8$
$63 \div 7 = 9$
$72 \div 8 = 9$
$72 \div 9 = 8$
$27 \div 3 = 9$
$16 \div 4 = 4$

Page 382

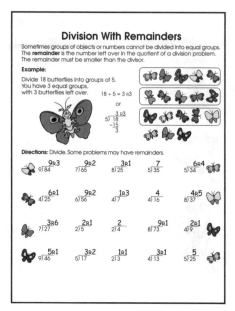

Division With Remainders

Sometimes groups of objects or numbers cannot be divided into equal groups. The **remainder** is the number left over in the quotient of a division problem. The remainder must be smaller than the divisor.

Example:

Divide 18 butterflies into groups of 5. You have 3 equal groups, with 3 butterflies left over.

$18 \div 5 = 3 \text{ R} 3$

or

$3 \text{ R}3$
$5\overline{)18}$
$\underline{-15}$
3

Directions: Divide. Some problems may have remainders.

$9\text{R}3$ $9\text{R}2$ $3\text{R}1$ 7 $6\text{R}4$
$9\overline{)84}$ $7\overline{)65}$ $8\overline{)25}$ $7\overline{)35}$ $5\overline{)34}$

$6\text{R}1$ $9\text{R}2$ $1\text{R}3$ 4 $4\text{R}5$
$4\overline{)25}$ $6\overline{)56}$ $4\overline{)7}$ $4\overline{)16}$ $8\overline{)37}$

$3\text{R}6$ $2\text{R}1$ 2 $9\text{R}1$ $2\text{R}1$
$7\overline{)27}$ $2\overline{)5}$ $2\overline{)4}$ $8\overline{)73}$ $4\overline{)9}$

$5\text{R}1$ $3\text{R}2$ $1\text{R}1$ $3\text{R}1$ 5
$9\overline{)46}$ $5\overline{)17}$ $2\overline{)3}$ $4\overline{)13}$ $5\overline{)25}$

Page 383

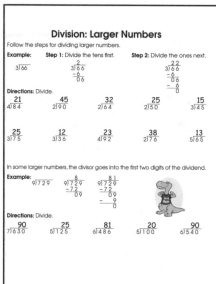

Division: Larger Numbers

Follow the steps for dividing larger numbers.

Example: **Step 1:** Divide the tens first. **Step 2:** Divide the ones next.

$3\overline{)66}$

$\begin{array}{r} 2 \\ 3\overline{)66} \\ -6 \\ \hline 06 \end{array}$

$\begin{array}{r} 22 \\ 3\overline{)66} \\ -6 \\ \hline 06 \\ -6 \\ \hline 0 \end{array}$

Directions: Divide.

21 45 32 25 15
$4\overline{)84}$ $2\overline{)90}$ $2\overline{)64}$ $2\overline{)50}$ $3\overline{)45}$

25 12 23 38 13
$3\overline{)75}$ $3\overline{)36}$ $4\overline{)92}$ $2\overline{)76}$ $5\overline{)65}$

In some larger numbers, the divisor goes into the first two digits of the dividend.

Example:
$9\overline{)729}$

$\begin{array}{r} 8 \\ 9\overline{)729} \\ -72 \\ \hline 09 \end{array}$

$\begin{array}{r} 81 \\ 9\overline{)729} \\ -72 \\ \hline 09 \\ -9 \\ \hline 0 \end{array}$

Directions: Divide.

90 25 81 20 90
$7\overline{)630}$ $5\overline{)125}$ $6\overline{)486}$ $5\overline{)100}$ $6\overline{)540}$

Page 384

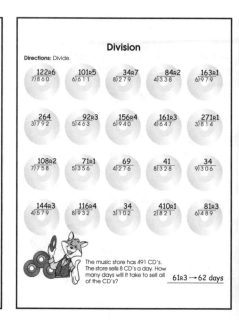

Division

Directions: Divide.

$122\text{R}6$ $101\text{R}5$ $34\text{R}7$ $84\text{R}2$ $163\text{R}1$
$7\overline{)860}$ $6\overline{)611}$ $8\overline{)279}$ $4\overline{)338}$ $6\overline{)979}$

264 $92\text{R}3$ $156\text{R}4$ $161\text{R}3$ $271\text{R}1$
$3\overline{)792}$ $5\overline{)463}$ $6\overline{)940}$ $4\overline{)647}$ $3\overline{)814}$

$108\text{R}2$ $71\text{R}1$ 69 41 34
$7\overline{)758}$ $5\overline{)356}$ $4\overline{)276}$ $8\overline{)328}$ $9\overline{)306}$

$144\text{R}3$ $116\text{R}4$ 34 $410\text{R}1$ $81\text{R}3$
$4\overline{)579}$ $8\overline{)932}$ $3\overline{)102}$ $2\overline{)821}$ $6\overline{)489}$

The music store has 491 CD's. The store sells 8 CD's a day. How many days will it take to sell all of the CD's?

$61\text{R}3 \rightarrow 62 \text{ days}$

Page 385

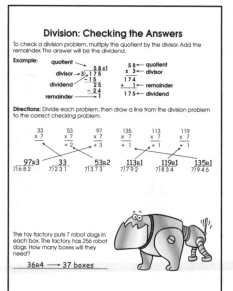

Division: Checking the Answers

To check a division problem, multiply the quotient by the divisor. Add the remainder. The answer will be the dividend.

Example:

quotient $\longrightarrow$ $58\text{ R}1$
divisor $\longrightarrow 3\overline{)175}$
$\qquad \underline{-15}$
dividend $\longrightarrow \quad 25$
$\qquad \underline{-24}$
remainder $\longrightarrow \quad 1$

$58 \longleftarrow$ quotient
$\times 3 \longleftarrow$ divisor
$\overline{174}$
$\underline{+ 1} \longleftarrow$ remainder
$175 \longleftarrow$ dividend

Directions: Divide each problem, then draw a line from the division problem to the correct checking problem.

33 53 97 135 113 119
$\times 7$ $\times 7$ $\times 7$ $\times 7$ $\times 7$ $\times 7$
$\underline{+ 2}$ $\underline{+ 3}$ $\underline{+ 1}$ $\underline{+ 1}$ $\underline{+ 1}$ $\underline{+ 1}$

$97\text{R}3$ 33 $53\text{R}2$ $113\text{R}1$ $119\text{R}1$ $135\text{R}1$
$7\overline{)682}$ $7\overline{)231}$ $7\overline{)373}$ $7\overline{)792}$ $7\overline{)834}$ $7\overline{)946}$

The toy factory puts 7 robot dogs in each box. The factory has 256 robot dogs. How many boxes will they need?

$36\text{R}4 \longrightarrow 37 \text{ boxes}$

Page 386

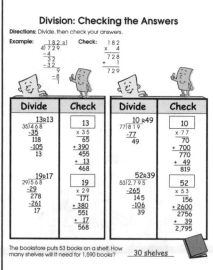

Division: Checking the Answers

Directions: Divide, then check your answers.

Example:

$\begin{array}{r} 182 \text{ R}1 \\ 4\overline{)729} \\ \underline{-4} \\ 32 \\ \underline{-32} \\ 9 \\ \underline{-8} \\ 1 \end{array}$

Check: $\begin{array}{r} 182 \\ \times 4 \\ \hline 728 \\ \underline{+ 1} \\ 729 \end{array}$

Divide	Check	Divide	Check
$13\text{R}13$ $35\overline{)468}$ $\underline{-35}$ 118 $\underline{-105}$ 13	13 $\times 35$ $\overline{65}$ $\underline{+ 390}$ 455 $\underline{+ 13}$ 468	$10 \text{ R}49$ $77\overline{)819}$ $\underline{-77}$ 49	10 $\times 77$ $\overline{70}$ $\underline{+ 700}$ 770 $\underline{+ 49}$ 819
$19\text{R}17$ $29\overline{)568}$ $\underline{-29}$ 278 $\underline{-261}$ 17	19 $\times 29$ $\overline{171}$ $\underline{+ 380}$ 551 $\underline{+ 17}$ 568	$52\text{R}39$ $53\overline{)2,795}$ $\underline{-265}$ 145 $\underline{-106}$ 39	52 $\times 53$ $\overline{156}$ $\underline{+ 2600}$ 2756 $\underline{+ 39}$ $2,795$

The bookstore puts 53 books on a shelf. How many shelves will it need for 1,590 books? 30 shelves

Page 387

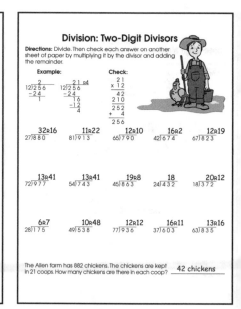

Division: Two-Digit Divisors

Directions: Divide. Then check each answer on another sheet of paper by multiplying it by the divisor and adding the remainder.

Example:

$\begin{array}{r} 2 \\ 12\overline{)256} \\ \underline{-24} \end{array}$ $\begin{array}{r} 21 \text{ R}4 \\ 12\overline{)256} \\ \underline{-24} \\ 16 \\ \underline{-12} \\ 4 \end{array}$

Check: $\begin{array}{r} 21 \\ \times 12 \\ \hline 42 \\ 210 \\ \overline{252} \\ \underline{+ 4} \\ 256 \end{array}$

$32\text{R}16$ $11\text{R}22$ $12\text{R}10$ $16\text{R}2$ $12\text{R}19$
$27\overline{)880}$ $81\overline{)913}$ $65\overline{)790}$ $42\overline{)674}$ $67\overline{)823}$

$13\text{R}41$ $13\text{R}41$ $19\text{R}8$ 18 $20\text{R}12$
$72\overline{)977}$ $54\overline{)743}$ $45\overline{)863}$ $24\overline{)432}$ $18\overline{)372}$

$6\text{R}7$ $10\text{R}48$ $12\text{R}12$ $16\text{R}11$ $13\text{R}16$
$28\overline{)175}$ $49\overline{)538}$ $77\overline{)936}$ $37\overline{)603}$ $63\overline{)835}$

The Allen farm has 882 chickens. The chickens are kept in 21 coops. How many chickens are there in each coop? 42 chickens

Page 388

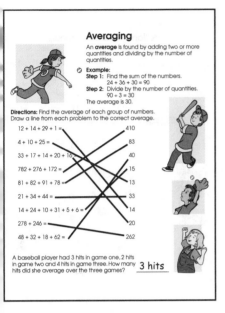

Averaging

An **average** is found by adding two or more quantities and dividing by the number of quantities.

Example:
Step 1: Find the sum of the numbers.
24 + 36 + 30 = 90
Step 2: Divide by the number of quantities.
90 ÷ 3 = 30
The average is 30.

Directions: Find the average of each group of numbers. Draw a line from each problem to the correct average.

12 + 14 + 29 + 1 =   410
4 + 10 + 25 =   83
33 + 17 + 14 + 20 + 16 =   40
782 + 276 + 172 =   15
81 + 82 + 91 + 78 =   13
21 + 34 + 44 =   33
14 + 24 + 10 + 31 + 5 + 6 =   14
278 + 246 =   20
48 + 32 + 18 + 62 =   262

A baseball player had 3 hits in game one, 2 hits in game two and 4 hits in game three. How many hits did she average over the three games? **3 hits**

Page 389

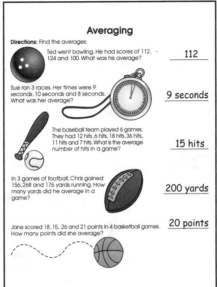

Averaging

Directions: Find the averages.

Ted went bowling. He had scores of 112, 124 and 100. What was his average? **112**

Sue ran 3 races. Her times were 9 seconds, 10 seconds and 8 seconds. What was her average? **9 seconds**

The baseball team played 6 games. They had 12 hits, 6 hits, 18 hits, 36 hits, 11 hits and 7 hits. What is the average number of hits in a game? **15 hits**

In 3 games of football, Chris gained 156, 268 and 176 yards running. How many yards did he average in a game? **200 yards**

Jane scored 18, 15, 26 and 21 points in 4 basketball games. How many points did she average? **20 points**

Page 390

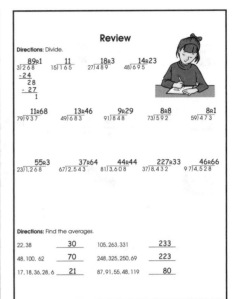

Review

Directions: Divide.

89R1
3)268
-24
28
-27
1

11
15)165

18R3
27)489

14R23
48)695

11R68
79)937

13R46
49)683

9R29
91)848

8R8
73)592

8R1
59)473

55R3
23)1,268

37R64
67)2,543

44R44
81)3,608

227R33
37)8,432

46R66
97)4,528

Directions: Find the averages.

22, 38   **30**   105, 263, 331   **233**

48, 100, 62   **70**   248, 325, 250, 69   **223**

17, 18, 36, 28, 6   **21**   87, 91, 55, 48, 119   **80**

Page 392

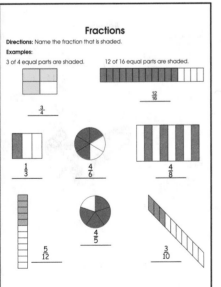

Fractions

Directions: Name the fraction that is shaded.

Examples:

3 of 4 equal parts are shaded.   12 of 16 equal parts are shaded.

$\frac{3}{4}$ $\frac{12}{16}$

$\frac{1}{3}$ $\frac{4}{6}$ $\frac{4}{8}$

$\frac{5}{12}$ $\frac{4}{5}$ $\frac{3}{10}$

Page 397

Fractions: Addition

When adding fractions with the same denominator, the denominator stays the same. Add only the numerators.

Example: numerator $\frac{1}{8}$ + $\frac{2}{8}$ = $\frac{3}{8}$ denominator

Directions: Add the fractions on the flowers. Begin in the center of each flower and add each petal. The first one is done for you.

Page 398

Fractions: Subtraction

When subtracting fractions with the same denominator, the denominator stays the same. Subtract only the numerators.

Directions: Solve the problems, working from left to right. As you find each answer, copy the letter from the key into the numbered blanks. The answer is the name of a famous American. The first one is done for you.

1. $\frac{3}{8} - \frac{2}{8} = \frac{1}{8}$ 9. $\frac{11}{12} - \frac{7}{12} = \frac{4}{12}$

2. $\frac{2}{4} - \frac{1}{4} = \frac{1}{4}$ 10. $\frac{7}{8} - \frac{3}{8} = \frac{4}{8}$

3. $\frac{5}{9} - \frac{3}{9} = \frac{2}{9}$ 11. $\frac{4}{7} - \frac{2}{7} = \frac{2}{7}$

4. $\frac{2}{3} - \frac{1}{3} = \frac{1}{3}$ 12. $\frac{14}{16} - \frac{7}{16} = \frac{7}{16}$

5. $\frac{8}{12} - \frac{7}{12} = \frac{1}{12}$ 13. $\frac{18}{20} - \frac{13}{20} = \frac{5}{20}$

6. $\frac{4}{5} - \frac{1}{5} = \frac{3}{5}$ 14. $\frac{13}{15} - \frac{2}{15} = \frac{11}{15}$

7. $\frac{6}{12} - \frac{3}{12} = \frac{3}{12}$ 15. $\frac{5}{8} - \frac{3}{8} = \frac{2}{8}$

8. $\frac{4}{9} - \frac{1}{9} = \frac{3}{9}$

T $\frac{1}{8}$	P $\frac{5}{24}$	H $\frac{1}{4}$
F $\frac{4}{12}$	E $\frac{2}{7}$	J $\frac{3}{12}$
E $\frac{3}{9}$	O $\frac{2}{9}$	F $\frac{4}{8}$
R $\frac{7}{16}$	O $\frac{3}{8}$	Y $\frac{8}{20}$
Q $\frac{1}{32}$	M $\frac{1}{3}$	S $\frac{5}{20}$
A $\frac{1}{12}$	R $\frac{12}{15}$	S $\frac{3}{5}$
N $\frac{2}{6}$	O $\frac{11}{15}$	

Who helped write the Declaration of Independence?

T H O M A S   J E F F E R S O N

Page 399

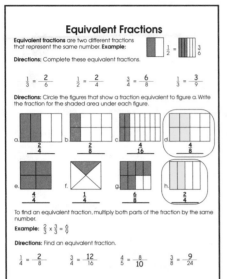

Equivalent Fractions

Equivalent fractions are two different fractions that represent the same number. **Example:** $\frac{1}{2} = \frac{3}{6}$

Directions: Complete these equivalent fractions.

$\frac{1}{3} = \frac{2}{6}$ $\frac{1}{2} = \frac{2}{4}$ $\frac{3}{4} = \frac{6}{8}$ $\frac{1}{3} = \frac{3}{9}$

Directions: Circle the figures that show a fraction equivalent to figure a. Write the fraction for the shaded area under each figure.

a. $\frac{2}{4}$ b. $\frac{2}{8}$ c. $\frac{4}{8}$ d. $\frac{4}{8}$

e. $\frac{4}{4}$ f. $\frac{1}{4}$ g. $\frac{6}{8}$ h. $\frac{2}{4}$

To find an equivalent fraction, multiply both parts of the fraction by the same number.

Example: $\frac{2}{3} \times \frac{3}{3} = \frac{6}{9}$

Directions: Find an equivalent fraction.

$\frac{1}{4} = \frac{2}{8}$ $\frac{3}{4} = \frac{12}{16}$ $\frac{4}{5} = \frac{8}{10}$ $\frac{3}{8} = \frac{9}{24}$

Page 400

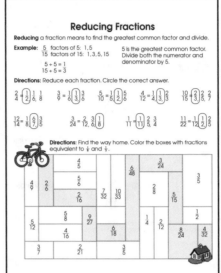

Reducing Fractions

Reducing a fraction means to find the greatest common factor and divide.

Example: 5 factors of 5: 1, 5
15 factors of 15: 1, 3, 5, 15

$5 \div 5 = 1$
$15 \div 5 = 3$

5 is the greatest common factor. Divide both the numerator and denominator by 5.

Directions: Reduce each fraction. Circle the correct answer.

$\frac{2}{4} = 1\frac{1}{2}, \circ\frac{1}{2}, \frac{1}{8}$ $\frac{3}{9} = \frac{1}{9}, \circ\frac{1}{3}, \frac{2}{3}$ $\frac{5}{10} = \frac{1}{5}, \circ\frac{1}{2}, \frac{2}{10}$ $\frac{4}{12} = 1\circ\frac{1}{3}, \frac{2}{3}$ $\frac{10}{15} = \frac{2}{3}, \frac{2}{5}, \frac{6}{7}$

$\frac{12}{14} = 1\circ\frac{6}{7}, \frac{3}{8}$ $\frac{3}{24} = \frac{2}{12}, \circ\frac{1}{8}$ $\frac{1}{11} = 1\circ\frac{1}{11}, \frac{3}{4}$ $\frac{11}{22} = 1\circ\frac{1}{2}, \frac{2}{2}, \frac{6}{7}$

Directions: Find the way home. Color the boxes with fractions equivalent to $\frac{1}{4}$ and $\frac{1}{3}$.

Page 401

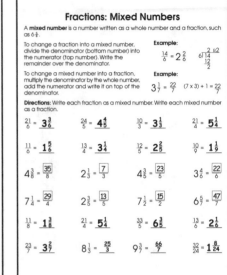

Fractions: Mixed Numbers

A **mixed number** is a number written as a whole number and a fraction, such as $6\frac{1}{2}$.

To change a fraction into a mixed number, divide the denominator (bottom number) into the numerator (top number). Write the remainder over the denominator.

Example: $\frac{14}{6} = 2\frac{2}{6}$

To change a mixed number into a fraction, multiply the denominator by the whole number, add the numerator and write it on top of the denominator.

Example: $3\frac{1}{7} = \frac{22}{7}$ $(7 \times 3) + 1 = \frac{22}{7}$

Directions: Write each fraction as a mixed number. Write each mixed number as a fraction.

$\frac{21}{6} = 3\frac{3}{6}$ $\frac{24}{5} = 4\frac{4}{5}$ $\frac{10}{3} = 3\frac{1}{3}$ $\frac{21}{4} = 5\frac{1}{4}$

$\frac{11}{6} = 1\frac{5}{6}$ $\frac{13}{4} = 3\frac{1}{4}$ $\frac{12}{5} = 2\frac{2}{5}$ $\frac{10}{9} = 1\frac{1}{9}$

$4\frac{3}{8} = \frac{35}{8}$ $2\frac{1}{3} = \frac{7}{3}$ $4\frac{3}{5} = \frac{23}{5}$ $3\frac{4}{6} = \frac{22}{6}$

$7\frac{1}{4} = \frac{29}{4}$ $2\frac{3}{5} = \frac{13}{5}$ $7\frac{1}{2} = \frac{15}{2}$ $6\frac{5}{7} = \frac{47}{7}$

$\frac{11}{8} = 1\frac{3}{8}$ $\frac{21}{4} = 5\frac{1}{4}$ $\frac{33}{5} = 6\frac{3}{5}$ $\frac{13}{6} = 2\frac{1}{6}$

$\frac{23}{7} = 3\frac{2}{7}$ $8\frac{1}{3} = \frac{25}{3}$ $9\frac{3}{7} = \frac{66}{7}$ $\frac{32}{24} = 1\frac{8}{24}$

Page 402

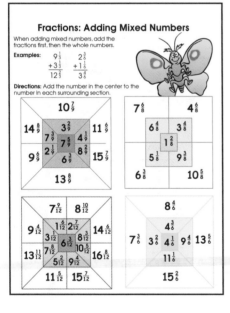

Fractions: Adding Mixed Numbers

When adding mixed numbers, add the fractions first, then the whole numbers.

Examples: $9\frac{1}{3} + 3\frac{1}{3} = 12\frac{2}{3}$ $2\frac{1}{6} + 1\frac{1}{6} = 3\frac{2}{6}$

Directions: Add the number in the center to the number in each surrounding section.

$10\frac{7}{9}$ $14\frac{8}{9}$ $3\frac{2}{9}$ $11\frac{6}{9}$ $7\frac{5}{9}$ $7\frac{7}{9}$ $4\frac{1}{9}$ $9\frac{6}{9}$ $6\frac{3}{9}$ $8\frac{8}{9}$ $15\frac{7}{9}$ $13\frac{8}{9}$

$7\frac{6}{8}$ $4\frac{6}{8}$ $6\frac{4}{8}$ $3\frac{4}{8}$ $1\frac{2}{8}$ $5\frac{1}{8}$ $9\frac{3}{8}$ $6\frac{3}{8}$ $10\frac{5}{8}$

$7\frac{9}{12}$ $8\frac{10}{12}$ $9\frac{4}{12}$ $1\frac{6}{12}$ $2\frac{1}{12}$ $14\frac{6}{12}$ $3\frac{1}{12}$ $6\frac{3}{12}$ $8\frac{3}{12}$ $13\frac{11}{12}$ $7\frac{7}{12}$ $10\frac{5}{12}$ $16\frac{8}{12}$ $5\frac{1}{12}$ $9\frac{2}{12}$ $11\frac{5}{12}$ $15\frac{7}{12}$

$8\frac{4}{6}$ $4\frac{3}{6}$ $7\frac{3}{6}$ $3\frac{2}{6}$ $4\frac{1}{6}$ $9\frac{4}{6}$ $13\frac{5}{6}$ $11\frac{1}{6}$ $15\frac{2}{6}$

Page 403

Fractions: Subtracting Mixed Numbers

When subtracting mixed numbers, subtract the fractions first, then the whole numbers.

Directions: Subtract the mixed numbers. The first one is done for you.

$7\frac{3}{6} - 4\frac{2}{6} = 3\frac{1}{6}$ $4\frac{5}{6} - 3\frac{1}{6} = 1\frac{4}{6}$ $4\frac{1}{2} - 3 = 1\frac{1}{2}$ $7\frac{3}{8} - 6\frac{1}{8} = 1\frac{2}{8}$ $6\frac{6}{9} - 1\frac{1}{9} = 5\frac{5}{9}$ $5\frac{3}{4} - 1\frac{1}{4} = 4\frac{2}{4}$

$5\frac{4}{6} - 3\frac{3}{6} = 2\frac{1}{6}$ $4\frac{6}{10} - 3\frac{1}{10} = 1\frac{5}{10}$ $9\frac{8}{9} - 4\frac{3}{9} = 5\frac{5}{9}$ $7\frac{5}{6} - 6\frac{3}{6} = 1\frac{1}{3}$ $7\frac{2}{3} - 5 = 2\frac{2}{3}$ $9\frac{8}{10} - 6\frac{3}{10} = 3\frac{5}{10}$

$4\frac{6}{6} - 2 = 2\frac{7}{9}$ $6\frac{7}{8} - 3\frac{4}{8} = 1\frac{4}{8}$ $6\frac{4}{6} - 3\frac{1}{6} = 3\frac{2}{4}$ $5\frac{7}{9} - 3\frac{2}{9} = 2\frac{5}{9}$ $7\frac{9}{7} - 2\frac{2}{7} = 5\frac{2}{7}$

Sally needs $1\frac{1}{8}$ yards of cloth to make a dress. She has $4\frac{3}{8}$ yards. How much cloth will be left over? $3\frac{2}{8}$

Page 404

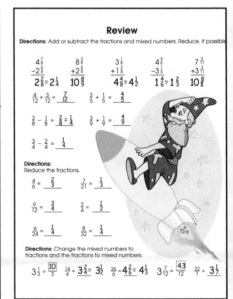

Review

Directions: Add or subtract the fractions and mixed numbers. Reduce, if possible.

$4\frac{7}{8} - 2\frac{3}{8} = 2\frac{4}{8} = 2\frac{1}{4}$ $8\frac{5}{9} + 2\frac{4}{9} = 10\frac{9}{9}$ $3\frac{1}{8} + 1\frac{3}{8} = 4\frac{4}{8} = 4\frac{1}{2}$ $4\frac{2}{5} - 3\frac{1}{5} = 1\frac{1}{5} = 1\frac{3}{5}$ $7\frac{11}{11} + 3\frac{1}{11} = 10\frac{1}{11}$

$\frac{4}{12} + \frac{3}{12} = \frac{7}{12}$ $\frac{3}{5} + \frac{1}{5} = \frac{4}{5}$

$\frac{3}{8} - \frac{1}{8} = \frac{2}{8} = \frac{1}{4}$ $\frac{3}{9} + \frac{1}{9} = \frac{4}{9}$

$\frac{3}{4} - \frac{2}{4} = \frac{1}{4}$

Directions: Reduce the fractions.

$\frac{4}{6} = \frac{2}{3}$ $\frac{7}{21} = \frac{1}{3}$

$\frac{9}{12} = \frac{3}{4}$ $\frac{2}{4} = \frac{1}{2}$

$\frac{6}{24} = \frac{1}{4}$ $\frac{8}{32} = \frac{1}{4}$

Directions: Change the mixed numbers to fractions and the fractions to mixed numbers.

$3\frac{1}{3} = \frac{10}{3}$ $\frac{14}{4} = 3\frac{2}{4} = 3\frac{1}{2}$ $\frac{26}{6} = 4\frac{2}{6} = 4\frac{1}{3}$ $3\frac{7}{12} = \frac{43}{12}$ $\frac{22}{7} = 3\frac{1}{7}$

ANSWER KEY

Page 405

Fractions to Decimals

When a figure is divided into 10 equal parts, the parts are called tenths. Tenths can be written two ways—as a fraction or a decimal. A **decimal** is a number with one or more places to the right of a decimal point, such as 6.5 or 2.25. A **decimal point** is the dot between the ones place and the tenths place.

Examples:

ones	tenths
0	3

$\frac{3}{10}$ or 0.3 of the square is shaded.

Directions: Write the decimal and fraction for the shaded parts of the following figures. The first one is done for you.

$\frac{6}{10}$ 0.6

$\frac{3}{10}$ 0.3 $\frac{9}{10}$ 0.9 $1\frac{5}{10}$ 1.5

$1\frac{8}{10}$ 1.8 $\frac{4}{10}$ 0.4 $\frac{8}{10}$ 0.8

Page 406

Decimals

Directions: Add or subtract. Remember to include the decimal point in your answers.

Example:
$1\frac{3}{10} = 1.3$
$$\begin{array}{r} 1.3 \\ + 1.6 \\ \hline 2.9 \end{array}$$
$1\frac{6}{10} = 1.6$

| 8.1 +1.7 = 9.8 | 4.1 +6.2 = 10.3 | 0.5 +1.6 = 2.1 | 7.6 −6.5 = 1.1 | 7.2 −2.6 = 4.6 | 1.2 +5.0 = 6.2 | 8.7 −3.9 = 4.8 | 6.8 −3.7 = 3.1 |

| 7.8 −6.8 = 1.0 | 16.5 −7.3 = 9.2 | 6.4 +5.3 = 11.7 | 10.0 +3.5 = 13.5 |

| 0.42 +0.35 = 0.77 | 0.98 −0.87 = 0.11 | 0.78 −0.13 = 0.65 | 0.83 +0.12 = 0.95 |

| 0.95 −0.14 = 0.81 | 3.23 +2.48 = 5.71 | 4.68 −2.65 = 2.03 | 5.86 −2.73 = 3.13 |

| 6.98 +1.40 = 8.38 | 3.27 +1.82 = 5.09 | 4.65 −1.32 = 3.33 | 5.97 +2.77 = 8.74 |

Mr. Martin went on a car trip with his family. Mr. Martin purchased gas 3 times. He bought 6.7 gallons, 7.3 gallons, then 5.8 gallons of gas. How much gas did he purchase in all? **19.8 gallons**

Page 407

Decimals: Hundredths

The next smallest decimal unit after a tenth is called a hundredth. One hundredth is one unit of a figure divided into 100 units. Written as a decimal, it is one digit to the right of the tenths place.

Example:
One square divided into hundredths, 34 hundredths are shaded. Write: 0.34.

ones	tenths	hundredths
0	3	4

0.34

Directions: Write the decimal for the shaded parts of the following figures.

0.24   0.50   0.53   0.05

1.48   1.10

Page 408

Fractions and Decimals

Directions: Compare the fraction to the decimal in each box. Circle the larger number.

Example: $\frac{1}{4}$ ⟷ 0.1

$\frac{2}{4}$ 0.2	$\frac{3}{4}$ 0.3	$\frac{1}{2}$ (0.6)	$\frac{1}{4}$ (0.4)	$\frac{1}{3}$ 0.1
$\frac{1}{4}$ (0.7)	$\frac{2}{4}$ (0.8)	$\frac{3}{4}$ (0.9)	$\frac{5}{9}$ 0.5	$\frac{2}{5}$ (0.6)
$\frac{3}{12}$ (0.9)	$\frac{1}{6}$ (0.2)	$\frac{2}{3}$ (0.8)	$\frac{1}{9}$ (0.3)	$\frac{2}{3}$ (0.7)
$\frac{3}{10}$ (0.5)	$\frac{1}{9}$ (0.4)	$\frac{4}{5}$ 0.7	$\frac{1}{3}$ (0.7)	$\frac{6}{12}$ 0.1

Page 409

Adding and Subtracting Decimals

Directions: Add or subtract the problems. Then fill in the circle next to the correct answer.

Example: 2.4 +1.7 = ●4.1

2.8 +3.4 = ●6.2	5.7 −3.8 = ●1.9	7.6 +8.9 = ●16.5
16.3 +9.8 = ●26.1	28.6 +43.9 = ●72.5	43.9 +56.5 = ●100.4
12.87 −3.45 = ●9.42	47.56 −33.95 = ●13.61	93.6 −79.8 = ●13.8
11.57 +10.64 = ●22.21	27.83 −14.94 = ●12.89	106.935 −95.824 = ●11.111

The high-speed train traveled 87.90 miles on day one, 127.86 miles on day two and 113.41 miles on day three. How many miles did it travel in all? **329.17 miles**

Page 410

Measurement: Inches

An **inch** is a unit of length in the standard system equal to $\frac{1}{12}$ of a foot. A ruler is used to measure inches.

This illustration shows a ruler measuring a 4-inch pencil, which can be written as 4" or 4 in.

Directions: Use a ruler to measure each object to the nearest inch.

1. The length of your foot
2. The width of your hand
3. The length of this page
4. The width of this page
5. The length of a large paper clip
6. The length of your toothbrush
7. The length of a comb
8. The height of a juice glass
9. The length of your shoe
10. The length of a fork

Answers will vary.

Page 411

Measurement: Inches

Directions: Use a ruler to measure the width of each foot to the nearest inch.

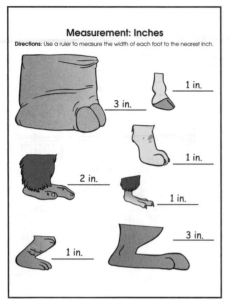

3 in.

1 in.

1 in.

2 in.

1 in.

1 in.

3 in.

Page 412

Measurement: Fractions of an Inch

An inch is divided into smaller units, or fractions of an inch.

Example: This stick of gum is $2\frac{1}{4}$ inches long.

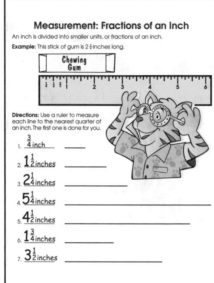

Directions: Use a ruler to measure each line to the nearest quarter of an inch. The first one is done for you.

1. $\frac{3}{4}$ inch _____
2. $1\frac{1}{2}$ inches _____
3. $2\frac{1}{4}$ inches _____
4. $5\frac{1}{4}$ inches _____
5. $4\frac{1}{2}$ inches _____
6. $1\frac{3}{4}$ inches _____
7. $3\frac{1}{2}$ inches _____

Page 413

Measurement: Fractions of an Inch

Directions: Use a ruler to measure to the nearest quarter of an inch.

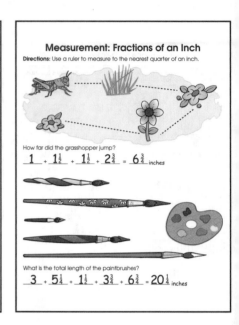

How far did the grasshopper jump?

$1 + 1\frac{1}{2} + 1\frac{1}{2} + 2\frac{3}{4} = 6\frac{3}{4}$ inches

What is the total length of the paintbrushes?

$3 + 5\frac{1}{4} + 1\frac{1}{2} + 3\frac{3}{4} + 6\frac{3}{4} = 20\frac{1}{4}$ inches

Page 414

Measurement: Foot, Yard, Mile

Directions: Choose the measure of distance you would use for each object.

1 foot = 12 inches
1 yard = 3 feet
1 mile = 1,760 yards or 5,280 feet

inches

yards

miles

yards

inches

yards

miles

Page 415

Metric Measurement: Centimeter, Meter, Kilometer

In the metric system, there are three units of linear measurement: centimeter (cm), meter (m) and kilometer (km).

Centimeters (cm) are used to measure the lengths of small to medium-sized objects. **Meters (m)** measure the lengths of longer objects, such as the width of a swimming pool or height of a tree (100 cm = 1 meter). **Kilometers (km)** measure long distances, such as the distance from Cleveland to Cincinnati or the width of the Atlantic Ocean (1,000 m = 1 km).

Directions: Write whether you would use cm, m or km to measure each object.

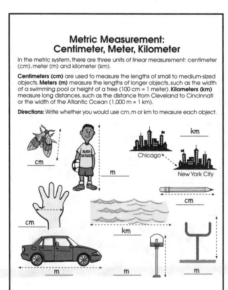

cm

m

km

Chicago

New York City

cm

cm

km

cm

m

m

m

Page 416

Metric Measurement: Centimeter

Directions: Use a centimeter ruler to measure the width of each foot to the nearest centimeter.

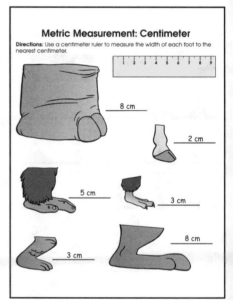

8 cm

2 cm

5 cm

3 cm

3 cm

8 cm

Page 417

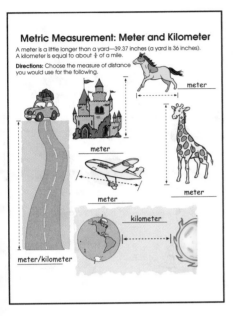

Metric Measurement: Meter and Kilometer

A meter is a little longer than a yard—39.37 inches (a yard is 36 inches). A kilometer is equal to about ⅝ of a mile.

Directions: Choose the measure of distance you would use for the following.

meter

meter

meter

meter

meter

kilometer

meter/kilometer

Page 418

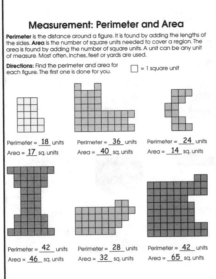

Measurement: Perimeter and Area

Perimeter is the distance around a figure. It is found by adding the lengths of the sides. **Area** is the number of square units needed to cover a region. The area is found by adding the number of square units. A unit can be any unit of measure. Most often, inches, feet or yards are used.

Directions: Find the perimeter and area for each figure. The first one is done for you.

☐ = 1 square unit

Perimeter = __18__ units
Area = __17__ sq. units

Perimeter = __36__ units
Area = __40__ sq. units

Perimeter = __24__ units
Area = __14__ sq. units

Perimeter = __42__ units
Area = __46__ sq. units

Perimeter = __28__ units
Area = __32__ sq. units

Perimeter = __42__ units
Area = __65__ sq. units

Page 419

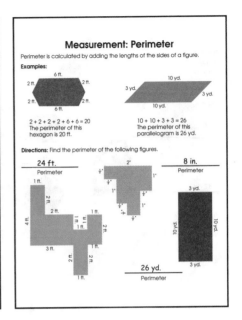

Measurement: Perimeter

Perimeter is calculated by adding the lengths of the sides of a figure.

Examples:

6 ft.
2 ft.   2 ft.
2 ft.   2 ft.
6 ft.

$2 + 2 + 2 + 2 + 6 + 6 = 20$
The perimeter of this hexagon is 20 ft.

10 yd.
3 yd.   3 yd.
10 yd.

$10 + 10 + 3 + 3 = 26$
The perimeter of this parallelogram is 26 yd.

Directions: Find the perimeter of the following figures.

__24 ft.__
Perimeter

__8 in.__
Perimeter

__26 yd.__
Perimeter

Page 420

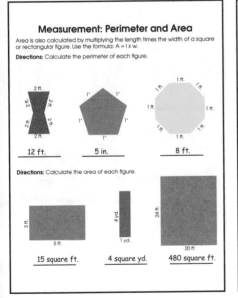

Measurement: Perimeter and Area

Area is also calculated by multiplying the length times the width of a square or rectangular figure. Use the formula: A = l x w.

Directions: Calculate the perimeter of each figure.

12 ft.

5 in.

8 ft.

Directions: Calculate the area of each figure.

15 square ft.

4 square yd.

480 square ft.

Page 421

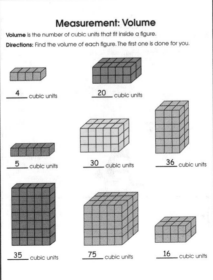

Measurement: Volume

Volume is the number of cubic units that fit inside a figure.

Directions: Find the volume of each figure. The first one is done for you.

4 cubic units

20 cubic units

5 cubic units

30 cubic units

36 cubic units

35 cubic units

75 cubic units

16 cubic units

Page 422

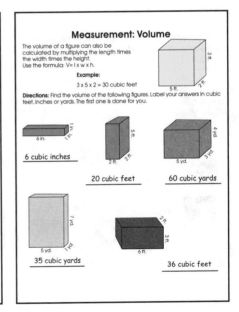

Measurement: Volume

The volume of a figure can also be calculated by multiplying the length times the width times the height. Use the formula: V= l x w x h.

Example:

$3 x 5 x 2 = 30$ cubic feet

Directions: Find the volume of the following figures. Label your answers in cubic feet, inches or yards. The first one is done for you.

6 cubic inches

20 cubic feet

60 cubic yards

35 cubic yards

36 cubic feet

Page 423

Metric Measurement: Perimeter

Directions: Calculate the perimeter of each figure.

Example:

$4 + 5 + 4 + 1 + 2 + 3 + 2 = 21$ meters

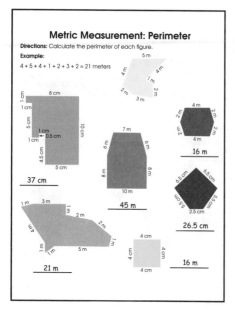

Page 424

Metric Measurement: Area and Volume

Directions: Calculate the area of each figure. Use the formula: A = l x w.

4 sq. m   15 sq. cm

18 sq. m   480 sq. cm   24 sq. m

Directions: Calculate the volume of each figure. Use the formula: V = l x w x h.

5 cu. m   30 cu. cm   30 cu. m

35 cu. m   45 cu. m   24 cu. m

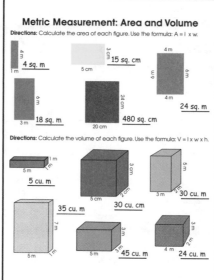

Page 425

Measurement: Ounce, Pound, Ton

The **ounce**, **pound** and **ton** are units in the standard system for measuring weight.

Directions: Choose the measure of weight you would use for each object.

16 ounces = 1 pound
2,000 pounds = 1 ton

ounce   pound   ton

Example: ounces

tons/pounds

pounds

ounces

ounces/pounds

tons

tons

ounces/pounds

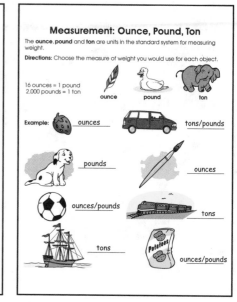

Page 426

Metric Measurement: Gram and Kilogram

Grams and **kilograms** are measurements of weight in the metric system. A gram (g) weighs about 1/28 of an ounce. A grape or paper clip weighs about one gram. There are 1,000 grams in a kilogram. A kilogram (kg) weighs about 2.2 pounds. A brick weighs about 1 kilogram.

Directions: Choose grams or kilograms to measure the following.

Example: grams

grams   kilograms

grams   kilograms

grams   grams

kilograms   kilograms

kilograms   grams

Page 427

Measurement: Liquid

The **cup**, **pint**, **quart** and **gallon** are units in the standard system for measuring liquids.

Directions: Gather the following materials: 2 dish tubs, one filled with water, sand or rice; measuring cups; pint container; quart container; gallon container. Then answer the questions and complete the chart.

1. Use the cup measure to pour water, sand or rice into the pint container. How many cups did it take?

___2___ cups = 1 pint

2. Use the cup measure to find out how many cups are in a quart and a gallon.

___4___ cups = 1 quart
___16___ cups = 1 gallon

3. Use the pint container to pour water, sand or rice into the quart container. How many pints are in a quart?

___2___ pints = 1 quart

4. How many pints does it take to fill a gallon?

___8___ pints = 1 gallon

5. Use the quart measure to find out how many quarts are in a gallon.

___4___ quarts = 1 gallon

Measurement Chart		
_2_ cups = 1 pint		_2_ pints = 1 quart
_4_ cups = 1 quart		_8_ pints = 1 gallon
_16_ cups = 1 gallon		_4_ quarts = 1 gallon

Page 428

Measurement: Cup, Pint, Quart, Gallon

Directions: Circle the number of objects to the right that equal the objects on the left. The first one is done for you.

2 cups = 1 pint
2 pints = 1 quart
4 quarts = 1 gallon

= 1 cup   = 1 pint   = 1 quart   = 1 gallon

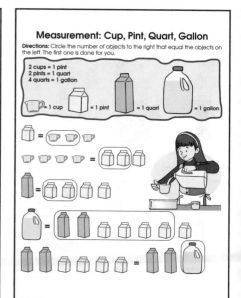

Page 429

Metric Measurement: Milliliter and Liter

Liters and **milliliters** are measurements of liquid in the metric system. A milliliter (mL) equals 0.001 liter or 0.03 fluid ounces. A drop of water equals about 1 milliliter. Liters (L) measure large amounts of liquid. There are 1,000 milliliters in a liter. One liter measures 1.06 quarts. Soft drinks are often sold in 2-liter bottles.

Directions: Choose milliliters or liters to measure these liquids.

Example: __milliliters__

__milliliters__

__liters__

__milliliters__

__milliliters__

__liters__

__liters__

__liters__

Page 430

Metric Measurement: Weight and Liquid

Directions: Choose grams (g) or kilograms (kg) to weigh the following objects. The first one is done for you.

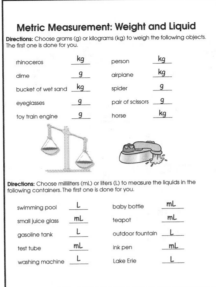

rhinoceros	**kg**	person	**kg**
dime	**g**	airplane	**kg**
bucket of wet sand	**kg**	spider	**g**
eyeglasses	**g**	pair of scissors	**g**
toy train engine	**g**	horse	**kg**

Directions: Choose milliliters (mL) or liters (L) to measure the liquids in the following containers. The first one is done for you.

swimming pool	**L**	baby bottle	**mL**
small juice glass	**mL**	teapot	**mL**
gasoline tank	**L**	outdoor fountain	**L**
test tube	**mL**	ink pen	**mL**
washing machine	**L**	Lake Erie	**L**

Page 431

Temperature: Fahrenheit

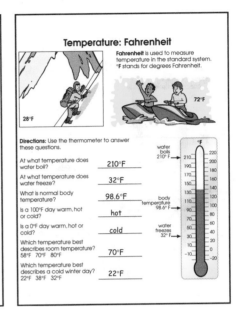

Fahrenheit is used to measure temperature in the standard system. °F stands for degrees Fahrenheit.

28°F   72°F

Directions: Use the thermometer to answer these questions.

At what temperature does water boil?	**210°F**
At what temperature does water freeze?	**32°F**
What is normal body temperature?	**98.6°F**
Is a 100°F day warm, hot or cold?	**hot**
Is a 0°F day warm, hot or cold?	**cold**
Which temperature best describes room temperature? 58°F 70°F 80°F	**70°F**
Which temperature best describes a cold winter day? 22°F 38°F 32°F	**22°F**

Page 432

Temperature: Celsius

Celsius is used to measure temperature in the metric system. °C stands for degrees Celsius.

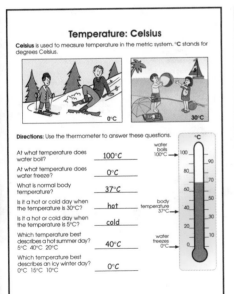

0°C   30°C

Directions: Use the thermometer to answer these questions.

At what temperature does water boil?	**100°C**
At what temperature does water freeze?	**0°C**
What is normal body temperature?	**37°C**
Is it a hot or cold day when the temperature is 30°C?	**hot**
Is it a hot or cold day when the temperature is 5°C?	**cold**
Which temperature best describes a hot summer day? 5°C 40°C 20°C	**40°C**
Which temperature best describes an icy winter day? 0°C 15°C 10°C	**0°C**

Page 433

Review

Directions: Find the perimeter and area of each figure.

□ = 1 square unit

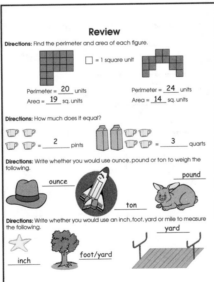

Perimeter = **20** units
Area = **19** sq. units

Perimeter = **24** units
Area = **14** sq. units

Directions: How much does it equal?

= **2** pints

= **3** quarts

Directions: Write whether you would use ounce, pound or ton to weigh the following.

ounce   **pound**   **ton**

Directions: Write whether you would use an inch, foot, yard or mile to measure the following.

inch   **foot/yard**   **yard**

Page 434

Review

Directions: Choose centimeters, meters or kilometers to measure the following.

meters height of a tree	**centimeters** length of a shoe
kilometers distance around Earth	**meters** height of a building
meters length of your yard	**kilometers** distance a plane flies

Directions: Choose grams or kilograms to measure the following.

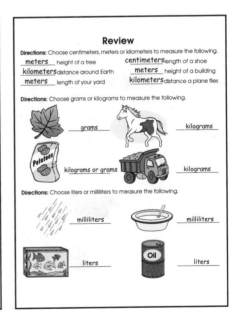

grams   **kilograms**

kilograms or grams   **kilograms**

Directions: Choose liters or milliliters to measure the following.

milliliters   **milliliters**

liters   **liters**

Page 435

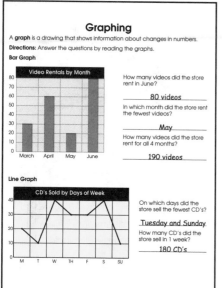

Graphing

A **graph** is a drawing that shows information about changes in numbers.

Directions: Answer the questions by reading the graphs.

Bar Graph

Video Rentals by Month

How many videos did the store rent in June?

80 videos

In which month did the store rent the fewest videos?

May

How many videos did the store rent for all 4 months?

190 videos

Line Graph

CD's Sold by Days of Week

On which days did the store sell the fewest CD's?

Tuesday and Sunday

How many CD's did the store sell in 1 week?

180 CD's

Page 436

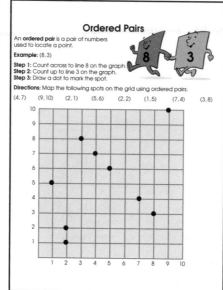

Ordered Pairs

An **ordered pair** is a pair of numbers used to locate a point.

Example: (8, 3)

Step 1: Count across to line 8 on the graph.
Step 2: Count up to line 3 on the graph.
Step 3: Draw a dot to mark the spot.

Directions: Map the following spots on the grid using ordered pairs.

(4, 7)　(9, 10)　(2, 1)　(5, 6)　(2, 2)　(1, 5)　(7, 4)　(3, 8)

Page 437

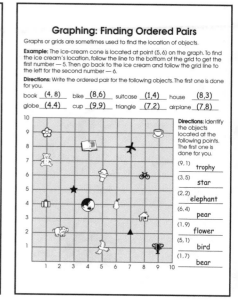

Graphing: Finding Ordered Pairs

Graphs or grids are sometimes used to find the location of objects.

Example: The ice-cream cone is located at point (5, 6) on the graph. To find the ice cream's location, follow the line to the bottom of the grid to get the first number — 5. Then go back to the ice cream and follow the grid line to the left for the second number — 6.

Directions: Write the ordered pair for the following objects. The first one is done for you.

book __(4, 8)__　bike __(8, 6)__　suitcase __(1, 4)__　house __(8, 3)__
globe __(4, 4)__　cup __(9, 9)__　triangle __(7, 2)__　airplane __(7, 8)__

Directions: Identify the objects located at the following points. The first one is done for you.

(9, 1) __trophy__
(3, 5) __star__
(2, 2) __elephant__
(6, 4) __pear__
(1, 9) __flower__
(5, 1) __bird__
(1, 7) __bear__

Page 438

Geometry: Polygons

A **polygon** is a closed figure with three or more sides.

Examples:

| triangle 3 sides | square 4 equal sides | rectangle 4 sides | pentagon 5 sides | hexagon 6 sides | octagon 8 sides |

Directions: Identify the polygons.

octagon　　rectangle

square　　hexagon

pentagon　　triangle

Page 439

Geometry: Line, Ray, Segment

A **line segment** has two end points.

A ———— B　　Write: __AB__

A **line** has no end points and goes on in both directions.

C ———— D　　Write: __CD__

A **ray** is part of a line and goes on in one direction. It has one end point.

E ———— F　　Write: __EF__

Directions: Identify each of the following as a line, line segment or ray.

A B __line segment__
C D __ray__
E F __line__
X Y __ray__
M N __line__
O P __line__

Page 440

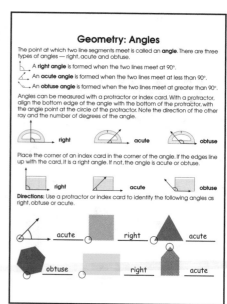

Geometry: Angles

The point at which two line segments meet is called an **angle**. There are three types of angles — right, acute and obtuse.

A **right angle** is formed when the two lines meet at 90°.

An **acute angle** is formed when the two lines meet at less than 90°.

An **obtuse angle** is formed when the two lines meet at greater than 90°.

Angles can be measured with a protractor or index card. With a protractor, align the bottom edge of the angle with the bottom of the protractor, with the angle point at the circle of the protractor. Note the direction of the other ray and the number of degrees of the angle.

right　　acute　　obtuse

Place the corner of an index card in the corner of the angle. If the edges line up with the card, it is a right angle. If not, the angle is acute or obtuse.

right　　acute　　obtuse

Directions: Use a protractor or index card to identify the following angles as right, obtuse or acute.

acute　　right　　acute

obtuse　　right　　acute

Page 441

Geometry: Circles

A **circle** is a round figure. It is named by its center. A **radius** is a line segment from the center of a circle to any point on the circle. A **diameter** is a line segment with both end points on the circle. The diameter always passes through the center of the circle.

Directions: Name the radius, diameter and circle.

Example:

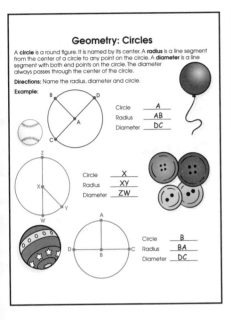

Circle	A
Radius	AB
Diameter	DC

Circle	X
Radius	XY
Diameter	ZW

Circle	B
Radius	BA
Diameter	DC

Page 442

Review

Directions: Complete the line graph using the information in the box.

Team	Games Played
Red	10
Blue	20
Green	15
Yellow	25

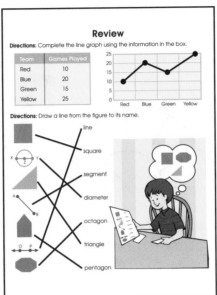

Directions: Draw a line from the figure to its name.

line
square
segment
diameter
octagon
triangle
pentagon

Page 443

Number Patterns

Figuring out the secret to a number pattern or code can send you into "thinking overtime."

Directions: Discover the pattern for each set of numbers. Then write the missing numbers.

a) 20, 21, 19, 20, 18, 19, 17, __18__, 16, 17, 15, __16__, __14__, __15__, __13__, __14__.

b) 1, 6, 16, 31, 51, __76__, __106__, 141, __181__, 226.

c) 3, 5, 9, 15, __23__, __33__, 45, __59__, 75.

d) 55, 52, 50, 49, 46, __44__, __43__, __40__, __38__, __37__, 34.

e) 1, 3, 6, 10, 15, 21, __28__, __36__, __45__, 55, 66, 78.

f) 10, 16, 13, 19, 16, __22__, 19, __25__, __22__, 28, __25__.

g) 3, 4, 7, 12, __19__, __28__, 39, __52__, 67, __84__.

h) 100, 90, 95, 85, 90, 80, 85, __75__, __80__, __70__, 75.

Directions: Make up a number pattern of your own. Have a parent, brother or sister figure it out!

Patterns will vary.

Directions: Follow the instructions to solve the number puzzler.

Use only these numbers: 2, 4, 5, 7, 8, 11, 13, 14, 16.

Each number may only be used once.

Write even numbers in the squares.

Write odd numbers in the circles.

Each row must add up to 26.

Hint: Work the puzzle in pencil, so you can erase and retry numbers if needed.

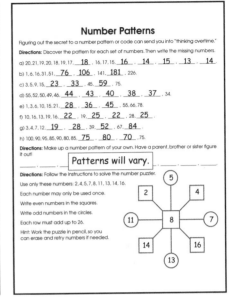

Page 444

Finding Common Attributes

The things that items have in common are called **common attributes**.

Example:

These are Pee-Wees.	These are not Pee-Wees.	Circle the Pee-Wees.
A E I O U	B C M W Z	S O T U R E

When you look at the Pee-Wees, you see what they have in common. They are all vowels. That is their common attribute. The items in the middle box are not Pee-Wees because they are all consonants. In the last box, only the vowels are circled.

Directions: Find the common attributes of the Wobbles, Whimzees, Dwibbles and Zanies. Circle the correct answers.

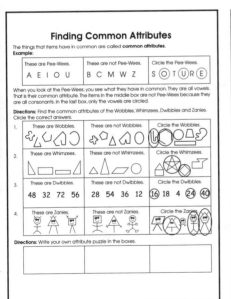

1. These are Wobbles. / These are not Wobbles. / Circle the Wobbles.

2. These are Whimzees. / These are not Whimzees. / Circle the Whimzees.

3. These are Dwibbles. / These are not Dwibbles. / Circle the Dwibbles.
   48 32 72 56 / 28 54 36 12 / 16 18 4 24 40

4. These are Zanies. / These are not Zanies. / Circle the Zanies.

Directions: Write your own attribute puzzle in the boxes.

Page 445

Probability

Another thinking skill to get your brain in gear is figuring probability. **Probability** is the likelihood or chance that something will happen. Probability is expressed and written as a ratio.

The probability of tossing heads or tails on a coin is one in two (1:2).

The probability of rolling any number on a die is one in six (1:6).

The probability of getting a red on this spinner is two in four (2:4).

The probability of drawing an ace from a deck of cards is four in fifty-two (4:52).

Directions: Write the probability ratios to answer these questions.

1. There are 26 letters in the alphabet. What is the probability of drawing any letter from a set of alphabet cards? 1:26

2. Five of the 26 alphabet letters are vowels. What is the probability of drawing a vowel from the alphabet cards? 5:26

3. Matt takes 10 shots at the basketball hoop. Six of his shots are baskets. What is the probability of Matt's next shot being a basket? 6:10

4. A box contains 10 marbles: 2 white, 3 green, 1 red, 2 orange and 2 blue. What is the probability of pulling a green marble from the box? 3:10
   A red marble? 1:10

5. What is the probability of pulling a marble that is not blue? 8:10

Page 446

Probability

Directions: Write the probability ratios to answer these questions.

1. Using the spinner shown, what is the probability of spinning a 4? 1:8

2. Using the spinner show, what is the chance of not spinning a 2? 7:8

3. Using the spinner shown, what is the probability of getting a 6 in three spins? 3:8

4. What is the probability of getting heads or tails when you toss a coin? 1:2

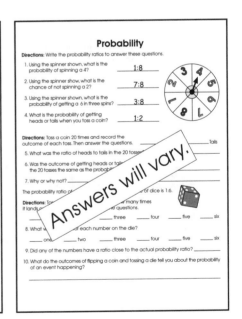

Directions: Toss a coin 20 times and record the outcome of each toss. Then answer the questions.

Heads ____ Tails ____

5. What was the ratio of heads to tails in the 20 tosses?

6. Was the outcome of getting heads or tails in the 20 tosses the same as the probability?

7. Why or why not?

The probability ratio of ___ number ___ dice is 1:6.

Directions: To ___ how many times it lands ___ questions.

one ___ three ___ four ___ five ___ six

8. What ___ of each number on the die?
   one ___ two ___ three ___ four ___ five ___ six

9. Did any of the numbers have a ratio close to the actual probability ratio? ____

10. What do the outcomes of flipping a coin and tossing a die tell you about the probability of an event happening?

Answers will vary.

Page 447

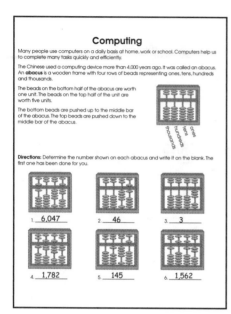

Computing

Many people use computers on a daily basis at home, work or school. Computers help us to complete many tasks quickly and efficiently.

The Chinese used a computing device more than 4,000 years ago. It was called an abacus. An **abacus** is a wooden frame with four rows of beads representing ones, tens, hundreds and thousands.

The beads on the bottom half of the abacus are worth one unit. The beads on the top half of the unit are worth five units.

The bottom beads are pushed up to the middle bar of the abacus. The top beads are pushed down to the middle bar of the abacus.

Directions: Determine the number shown on each abacus and write it on the blank. The first one has been done for you.

1. 6,047
2. 46
3. 3
4. 1,782
5. 145
6. 1,562

Page 448

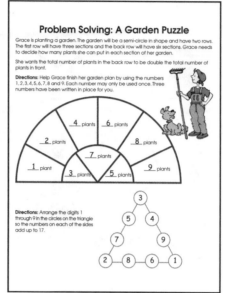

Problem Solving: A Garden Puzzle

Grace is planting a garden. The garden will be a semi-circle in shape and have two rows. The first row will have three sections and the back row will have six sections. Grace needs to decide how many plants she can put in each section of her garden.

She wants the total number of plants in the back row to be double the total number of plants in front.

Directions: Help Grace finish her garden plan by using the numbers 1, 2, 3, 4, 5, 6, 7, 8 and 9. Each number may only be used once. Three numbers have been written in place for you.

4 plants   6 plants
2 plants   8 plants
7 plants
1 plant   3 plants   5 plants   9 plants

Directions: Arrange the digits 1 through 9 in the circles on the triangle so the numbers on each of the sides add up to 17.

3
5 4
7 9
2 8 6 1

Page 449

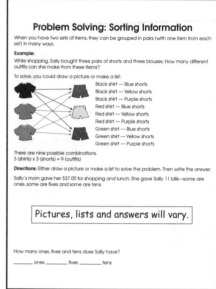

Problem Solving: Sorting Information

When you have two sets of items, they can be grouped in pairs (with one item from each set) in many ways.

Example:
While shopping, Sally bought three pairs of shorts and three blouses. How many different outfits can she make from these items?

To solve, you could draw a picture or make a list:

Black shirt — Blue shorts
Black shirt — Yellow shorts
Black shirt — Purple shorts
Red shirt — Blue shorts
Red shirt — Yellow shorts
Red shirt — Purple shorts
Green shirt — Blue shorts
Green shirt — Yellow shorts
Green shirt — Purple shorts

There are nine possible combinations.
3 (shirts) x 3 (shorts) = 9 (outfits)

Directions: Either draw a picture or make a list to solve the problem. Then write the answer.

Sally's mom gave her $37.00 for shopping and lunch. She gave Sally 11 bills—some are ones, some are fives and some are tens.

Pictures, lists and answers will vary.

How many ones, fives and tens does Sally have?
_____ ones _____ fives _____ tens

Page 450

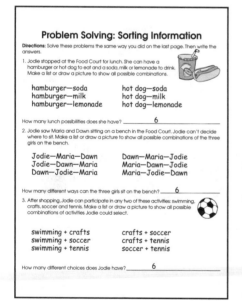

Problem Solving: Sorting Information

Directions: Solve these problems the same way you did on the last page. Then write the answers.

1. Jodie stopped at the Food Court for lunch. She can have a hamburger or hot dog to eat and a soda, milk or lemonade to drink. Make a list or draw a picture to show all possible combinations.

   hamburger—soda   hot dog—soda
   hamburger—milk   hot dog—milk
   hamburger—lemonade   hot dog—lemonade

   How many lunch possibilities does she have? _____ 6

2. Jodie saw Maria and Dawn sitting on a bench in the Food Court. Jodie can't decide where to sit. Make a list or draw a picture to show all possible combinations of the three girls on the bench.

   Jodie—Maria—Dawn   Dawn—Maria—Jodie
   Jodie—Dawn—Maria   Maria—Dawn—Jodie
   Dawn—Jodie—Maria   Maria—Jodie—Dawn

   How many different ways can the three girls sit on the bench? _____ 6

3. After shopping, Jodie can participate in any two of these activities: swimming, crafts, soccer and tennis. Make a list or draw a picture to show all possible combinations of activities Jodie could select.

   swimming + crafts   crafts + soccer
   swimming + soccer   crafts + tennis
   swimming + tennis   soccer + tennis

   How many different choices does Jodie have? _____ 6

ADDITION AND SUBTRACTION

Help your child practice basic facts with flash cards.

Play addition and subtraction games at the grocery store by adding and subtracting prices. Tally the total number of items to be purchased.

When adding or subtracting larger numbers, provide your child with counting sticks or another type of manipulative. When your child "carries" or "borrows" with concrete materials, he/she will better understand the operations involved.

ADJECTIVES AND NOUNS

Remind your child that a noun names a person, place or thing. Have him/her write nouns on plain white index cards. Remind your child that an adjective describes a noun. Have him/her write adjectives on colored index cards. Since adjectives are describing words, this can visually help your child connect adjectives with ways to make sentences more colorful. He/she could match the cards to show nouns and adjectives that would go together.

Practice recognizing adjectives and nouns when you and your child are in the car on a trip or waiting at a traffic light. Point out an object or a building. Ask your child to name adjectives to describe it. Challenge your child to come up with 10 describing words in a specified length of time.

ADVERBS

Adverbs tell place, time or manner. Have your child label three containers with those words. One container could be decorated to represent a building (place), one to represent a clock (time) and one with a big smiley face (manner). Give your child adverb word cards and have him/her put them in the correct container. He/she could select an adverb and write a sentence using that word.

AVERAGING

Brainstorm daily situations with your child in which you use averaging: the cost of groceries for a month, the cost of lunches for a week, the amount of gas used in a car for a month, and so on.

CAPITALIZATION

Help your child write a letter to a relative or friend. Remind him or her that proper nouns begin with capital letters. Check the return address and the mailing address to make sure capital letters are used where needed. You may want your child to practice addressing an envelope on a sheet of paper before writing on an envelope.

Help your child develop listening skills while playing a capitalization game. Have your child listen as you say a sentence. Have him/her say which word or words need to be capitalized and why those words should begin with a capital letter.

Your child can list the days of the week or months of the year, write down names of family members, stores in your community or names of the streets in your neighborhood. This will provide good practice in writing proper nouns with capital letters.

CLASSIFYING

Play a game with your child to help him/her understand classifying. Tell your child three or four related words (oak, pine, elm, maple). Then ask him/her to tell you the group in which they belong (trees). If your child has trouble doing this mental activity, write the words on strips of paper and have your child place them under the headings you have provided.

Invite your child to give you groups of objects to place under the headings. If your child can name several things that belong together, then he/she probably understands the concept. Your child may find that it is harder to come up with the words than it is to place them in the correct group, so use this as a challenge activity.

COMPREHENSION

Enhance your child's understanding of a story by encouraging him/her to "picture in his/her head" what the characters look like or how a scene looks as the author describes it.

Comprehension involves understanding what is seen, heard or read. To help your child with this skill, talk about a book, movie or television program you've enjoyed together. Discuss the details of the story and ask questions to guide your child to understand something important that happened in the beginning, middle and end of the story. Many stories have a problem that needs to be solved or a situation that needs to be addressed. Discuss these details with your child to broaden his/her understanding. If your child comprehends what he/she has seen or read, he/she should be able to recount the main events in sequential order and retell the story in his/her own words. By listening to what he/she says, you can tell whether the book, movie, etc. was understood. If your child does not fully understand part of it, discuss that section further. Reread the book or watch the program again, if possible.

Ask your child questions about a story before he/she begins to read it. For example: "What do you think the people in this picture are doing?" "What do you think the title means?" "Do you think this will be a true story or a made-up story?" Then as your child reads, he/she will already be thinking about the answers to these questions.

Your child can make an advertising poster for a book or movie. Have him/her include the important events, most exciting parts, favorite part and reasons why someone else should read or view it.

Creating a book jacket for a book he/she has read is another way for your child to show he/she has understood what was read. The jacket should include a picture depicting a main event in the story and a brief summary on the back. If the book belongs to your child, he/she could use the cover on the book.

DECIMALS

Using the sports section of the newspaper, help your child locate "times" from swim meets, track meets, auto races, and so on. Point out that the times are in tenths and hundredths of seconds. Have your child practice by adding and subtracting the times of sporting events.

DETAILS

It is important for your child to be able to recognize and remember details of what he/she has read and seen. After reading a book or watching a movie together, ask your child questions about details, like what the main character wore, when and where the story took place, names of minor characters, etc.

Play a game to help strengthen your child's attention to detail. Gather 20 to 25 common everyday objects and set them out on a table (button, dice, pen, scissors, cup, spoon, small toys, book, paper clip, straw, spool of thread, disk, etc.). Ask your child to study the objects and see how many he/she can remember. Then cover the objects with a towel and ask him/her to name as many as possible. Do this several times with the same items, then with a different set of items.

Encourage your child to be observant about details in everyday life. After walking or driving past a building or billboard, ask your child to recall as many details as possible.

DIVISION

Practice division facts in tandem with multiplication facts. Show your child how multiplication and division facts can be grouped into "fact families."

Examples: $7 \times 9 = 63$ $9 \times 7 = 63$ $63 \div 7 = 9$ $63 \div 9 = 7$
$6 \times 5 = 30$ $5 \times 6 = 30$ $30 \div 6 = 5$ $30 \div 5 = 6$

Give your child three numbers such as 7, 8 and 56, and ask him/her to name the fact family. Have your child practice with other number groups.

Drill division facts with flash cards and oral quizzes. Point out division applications in real-life situations. If mastery of facts is still a problem, have your child use counting sticks to divide large groups into smaller groups of equal size. This activity is also helpful when introducing division with remainders: $73 \div 8 = 9\ R1$. Do not go on to more difficult division problems until your child has mastered the basics.

ESTIMATING

Use the following situations to reinforce estimating with your child:

a. Round the price of several grocery items and estimate the total cost.

b. Round the total cost at a restaurant and calculate the tip.

c. Estimate the number of miles between home and school or other destinations.

d. Use a pizza carry-out menu to estimate the costs of pizzas with various toppings.

FABLES AND LEGENDS

Read fables and legends from many cultures with your child. Check your library or favorite bookstore for titles. After reading several together, make up your own. Brainstorm some ideas and write them down in the form of a question: Why is the sky blue? Why do birds fly? How did a giraffe get such a long neck? Why are hummingbirds so small? Select one and make up your story together. You can write it or tape it, then read or play it back. Encourage your child to draw an illustration for your legend or fable.

FOLLOWING DIRECTIONS

By fourth grade, your child should be able to listen carefully and follow directions. Before your child begins an activity, remind him/her to read carefully and make sure he/she understands the directions.

Building models and making craft projects are other ways for your child to learn to follow directions. Reading the instructions and learning to play a new board game or video game helps your child practice this skill.

Let your child help with the cooking and baking. Not only does this give your child good experience in reading and following directions, he/she also uses many math skills to measure ingredients. Have your child look for recipes in newspapers and magazines, as well as cookbooks. Most libraries have a large selection of cookbooks. It's a fun way to learn, and the results can be delicious.

Cooking is one of many daily activities that involves following directions. Whether it is heating a can of vegetables, cooking a frozen pizza or making pudding, all involve following directions. Read the package directions with your child and have him/her help you. Explain to your child why ingredients must be mixed in a certain order and why some steps must be done before others.

Ask your child to take a turn preparing a meal for the family once a week. Write out the directions and be very specific. Remember, until he/she has had experience cooking, what seems obvious to you may not be obvious to your child. For example, if you tell your child to add a can of vegetables to make a casserole and don't mention that the vegetables should be drained first, you might end up with a very juicy casserole.

When you have a bicycle, toy or other item to assemble, allow your child to help. Point to each step in the directions. Read each step together. Then follow the steps in order. Like following package directions or a recipe, assembling an item enables your child to see that following directions is a skill used in everyday situations.

FRACTIONS

Use foods such as pizza, cake, pie and brownies to help your child identify halves, fourths, thirds, and so on. Review identification of numerators denominators. With the foods listed above, practice adding and subtracting like fractions. Example: If Sally takes $\frac{1}{6}$ of the pie and Jane takes $\frac{2}{6}$ of the pie, how much of the pie is gone? How much of the pie is left over?

GEOMETRY

Look for shapes in everyday objects. Point out the differences in the number of angles and sides of several figures: triangles, squares, rectangles, pentagons, and so on.

Have fun using a compass and protractor to draw circles and designs. Show your child that you set the compass measure for one-half of the size of the desired circle. The compass needs to be set at the radius measure.

GRAMMAR

On index cards or poster board pieces, write the following words: good, well, your, you're, its, it's, can, may, sit, set, they're, their, there, this and these. On additional pieces, write sentences that have one of the above words missing. After shuffling the word cards and the sentences cards, place them facedown on two separate areas. Have the first player turn over a word card and a sentence card and see if they match. If they do, the player keeps the match and takes another turn. If there is no match, turn the cards facedown and the next player selects two cards. Play continues until all the cards have been matched.

GRAPHING

Show your child that graphing has many practical applications in daily life. Use the business section of the newspaper to practice reading graphs. Have your child identify whether the graph is a line graph, bar graph or pictograph. Help your child graph: weather for a month; food eaten for a week; number of books read over a specific period of time; favorite colors, music, sports, games; and so on.

IDENTIFYING PARTS OF SPEECH

Help your child learn or review parts of a sentence using a dictionary. Explain that a dictionary entry is a reference that will help identify parts of speech. Examine several dictionary entries together. When your child has difficulty recognizing what part of speech a word is, the dictionary can be a ready source.

LANGUAGE ARTS CHALLENGES

Write sentences that need correcting. Your child's challenge is to correct the grammar, punctuation, spelling, capitalization, etc.

Introduce new words. Challenge your child to look up the definitions and pronunciations. Encourage him/her to use the new words in conversation and writing and to learn the spelling of the new words.

Write book titles. Have your child find the author's name, locate the book in the library and read it. Further the challenge by asking your child to tell you the main ideas of the book or to outline it.

List book character names. Challenge your child to find in what stories the characters are found. Include characters from unfamiliar books.

MAIN IDEA

Newspapers are one of the most convenient and versatile learning tools you have around your home. Encourage your child to read parts of the newspaper every day. You might notice a headline that looks interesting and ask your child to read the article and tell you what it is about. This helps him/her find the main idea of an article.

Look for articles of interest to your child—ones about neighborhood events, people you know, items relating to school and special hobbies or sports of interest to your child.

Sometimes it helps to cut out articles and let your child read one article a day. It can be less intimidating to start by reading one short article than to try to read an entire newspaper. Leave your newspaper folded in such a way that an interesting photo or headline is showing. That may help catch your child's attention and encourage him/her to read that article and others.

Encourage your child to read editorials and write an editorial to the paper expressing his/her views.

When an interesting story is developing in your local newspaper, encourage your child to follow it for several days to learn the latest developments. Have him/her select the main idea of the story and write it down each day. After several days, he/she will have a sequential report of the story.

MATH CHALLENGES

Write story problems with too much information. Before solving, have your child decide which information is not needed to solve the problem.

Write out number patterns like those in this book. Challenge your child to discover the pattern and write in the missing numbers.

Write story problems for your child to solve. Make sure the problems include an assortment of operations—addition, subtraction, multiplication and division. Use the names of your child, his/her friends, relatives, pets, etc. to personalize the problems.

MEASUREMENT

Help your child see that you measurement on a daily basis. You measure ingredients for recipes, mileage to and from work and school, and so on. Allow your child to help measure whenever possible. Have him/her find the area and/or volume of his/her room. Send your child on a "measuring safari" equipped with a ruler and a list of objects to measure. Have him/her assist in cooking by measuring ingredients. Note: Do not make comparisons of standard and metric measures. This will only confuse your child. Standard/metric conversions can be learned at a later time.

MULTIPLICATION

The key to success in multiplication is the mastery of single-digit multiplication facts from 0 to 12. Help your child practice these facts with multiplication flash cards, bingo games, homemade activity sheets and timed tests. Play multiplication games with number cubes, dice or spinners. Have your child roll the number cubes and multiply the two numbers rolled or spun.

Make up multiplication story problems. Example: You make 9 cupcakes. On each cupcake you want to place 5 pieces of candy. How many pieces of candy will you need in all?

PLACE VALUE

To enhance your child's understanding of place value, have him/her practice counting and grouping craft sticks or toothpicks into bundles of tens, hundreds and thousands. Have your child manipulate these groupings on a place value chart to make various numbers. After making numbers with manipulatives, your child can write the numbers on the chart.

POETRY

Read poems you enjoyed as a child together with your own child. Ask your child to share his/her favorite poems with you. Libraries carry many good anthologies of poetry, from nursery rhymes to long, narrative poems. Sample many different kinds including both rhymed and unrhymed verse. Limericks are always fun to read and write. If your child says he/she doesn't like poetry, try authors like Ogden Nash, Shel Silverstein and Edward Lear.

PREDICATES AND SUBJECTS

Have your child dictate five to ten sentences to you. Write them on strips of paper. Cut the strips between the subject and the predicate. Mix up the subject sections and place them in a pile. Place the predicate sections in another pile. Have your child put the sentences back together so they make sense. Example: He / caught the ball and ran for a touchdown.

Make "silly sentences" with your child by combining a subject and a predicate that usually don't belong together. Have your child glue the silly sentence to a sheet of drawing paper and illustrate it.
Example: The cuddly kitten / caught the ball and ran for a touchdown.

Your child can use these sentence strips and make new subjects for the predicates and new predicates for the subjects.
Example: The running back / caught the ball and ran for a touchdown.

PROOFREADING

As your child writes sentences and stories, he/she needs to be able to express his/her thoughts without concern for correct spelling and punctuation. The first draft of a story should be one in which the writer doesn't worry about mechanics. He/she needs to get his/her thoughts down. When the story is completed, you can guide your child in proofreading before making a final copy.

Proofreading should consist of looking for grammatical errors, overuse of words (synonyms could be used instead), misspellings, punctuation mistakes and capitalization errors. Work with your child without being critical to enable him/her to see the types of mistakes he/she made. Make the corrections together until you see that your child is able to handle proofreading on his/her own.

You could do some practice sentences, providing written work with obvious mistakes and have your child correct them. The mistakes, at first, could be names of family members or pets. Help your child rewrite them with the corrections made. You may want to write sentences with blank spaces and have your child write the missing proper nouns. Progress to other types of errors such as commas, quotation marks, question marks and misspelled words.

ROUNDING

Give your child several numbers to round to the nearest ten, hundred or thousand. Have him/her determine where the numbers would fall on the respective number lines. Then he/she can round the number by deciding to which ten, hundred or thousand it comes closest.

To help build your child's understanding of rounding numbers, make several number lines on adding machine tape. Number each as follows:

a. from 0 to 100, counting by tens (for rounding to the nearest ten).

b. from 0 to 1,000, counting by hundreds (for rounding to the nearest hundred).

c. from 0 to 10,000, counting by thousands (for rounding to the nearest thousand).

SEQUENCING

Sequencing can be done in several ways. Words can be arranged in alphabetical order. Events can be arranged in chronological order. Steps to complete a task can be arranged in logical order. Items can be arranged by size or shape from largest to smallest.

Remind your child that letters have to be in a certain order to make words, words have to be in a certain order to make sentences that make sense and paragraphs and story events have to be in a certain order.

As you are traveling, tell a story together. Begin the story. After a few sentences, have your child continue the story. Take turns until you arrive at your destination or get to the end of the story.

Present a math word problem for your child to solve. Have him/her explain and write in sequence how to solve the problem.

Find a comic strip that has three or four sections and read it with your child. Cut the sections apart and have your child put them back together.

Encourage your child to tell you about events that have occurred at school or other places where you were not present. As he/she recalls what happened, encourage him/her to recall the events in order and add details.

Have your child keep a journal. This not only helps with sequencing but is also a good way to record what is happening in his/her life for the future. Each night in the journal, have your child write in order four things that he/she did during the day. When the journal is full, put it away in a safe place and save it for your child to reread when he/she is a few years older.

SKIP COUNTING

To help your child practice skip counting, make a large number line on several sheets of construction paper, using one sheet per number. Number the sheets from 0 to 100. As your child practices skip counting, he/she can literally "skip" from one number to the next. The physical movement of skip counting will enhance your child's understanding of this concept.

VOCABULARY BUILDING

Encourage your child to learn a new word each week. He/she should learn its meaning and use it when applicable throughout the week. You may select the word from those your child brings home from his/her science, math, reading, spelling or social studies school work.

Be aware of words your child may overuse in his/her language and writing. Decide together on synonyms that can be used in place of the overused words. Buy a thesaurus and help your child use it when he/she is doing homework. This handy reference can also be used to decide on new "words of the week."

Play a matching game with your child. Write new vocabulary words on tagboard cut into playing-card size pieces. For each word card, make a definition card (synonym, antonym, and so on). Place the cards facedown on a table. Turn over two cards at a time to see if they match. If they don't match, the next player tries to locate a match.

INDEX

Abacus 447

Action Verbs 218

Addition 351–357, 361, 362, 371

Adjectives 231–239, 245–248

Adverbs 240–244, 245–248

Advertisements 54–56

Analogies 43–45

Angles 440

Antonyms 27–29

Area 418, 420, 424, 433

Articles 272

Autobiography 323, 325

Averaging 388–390

Biography 323, 325

Book Titles 271, 272, 275

Can/May 259, 260, 265, 266

Capital Letters 212, 268, 272, 275

Cause and Effect 91, 95

Circle 441

Classifying 38–42, 45

Cluster of Ideas 299–301

Combining Sentences 204–208,
282–286

Commands 194–196

Commas 269, 270, 275

Common Attributes 444

Common Nouns 211, 212

Compare and Contrast 88, 97, 105,
124, 142, 145,
163, 180, 307

Compound Predicates 206, 207, 209

Compound Subjects 204, 205, 208

Comprehension 75, 76, 79, 80,
84–89, 91, 93, 96, 100,
102–104, 110, 112, 114,
115, 118, 119, 126, 128,
130, 135, 138, 143, 144,
147, 150, 153–159, 162, 166,
170, 171, 174, 177, 181–190

Conjunctions 249–254

Context Clues 59–63

Contractions . . 256–258, 262, 263, 265, 266

Creative Writing 113, 125

Decimals 405–409

Details 73, 74, 78, 82, 107,
108, 117, 120, 136,
137, 139, 146, 149,
152, 160, 164, 167,
169, 172, 175, 178, 180

Diameter 441, 442

Division 381–387, 390

Divisor 381, 385

Encyclopedia Skills 328–336

Estimating 366–368

Exclamations 194–196

Fables 90–105

Facts and Opinions 57, 58

Fairy Tales 84–89

Following Directions 46–49, 94, 111,
127, 134, 140,
141, 148, 173

Fractions 391–405, 408

Geometry 438–442

Good/Well 255, 257, 265, 266

Graphing 435–437, 442

Helping Verbs 218

Homophones 31–33

Irregular Verbs 227, 229

Its/It's 258, 260, 265, 266

Labels 52, 53

Legends 106–124

Length 410–417, 433, 434

Library Skills 320–327, 335, 336

Line 439, 442

Line Segment 439, 442

Linking Verbs 218

Liquid Measurement . . . 427–430, 433, 434

Long Vowels 9–15

Main Idea 68–72, 116,
121, 131, 151, 161,
165, 168, 169, 179

Measurement 410–434

Mixed Numbers 401–404

Multiples 370, 371

Multiplication 372–380

Nouns 209–216, 287–290

Number Patterns 443

Ordered Pairs 436, 437

Outlining 308–316

Palindromes 30

Paragraphs 298–301

Perimeter 418–420, 423

Periods 268, 275

Place Value 348–350, 371

Plural Nouns 213–216

Poetry 120, 125–133, 342–346

Polygons 438, 442

Predicates 198–203, 206–208

Predicting 93, 109

Prefixes 34, 35

Probability 445, 446

Problem Solving 448–450

Pronouns 217, 287–290

Pronoun Referents 289, 290

Proofreading 276–279

Proper Nouns 211, 212

Punctuation 268–275, 281

Questions 193, 195, 196

Quotation Marks 273–275

Radius 441

Ray 439, 442

Rounding 363–365

Run-On Sentences 280

Schedules 50, 51

Sentences 192–208

Sequencing 64–67, 77, 81, 92,
97, 98, 106, 122,
125, 129, 132

Short Vowels 6–8

Sit/Set 261, 263, 265, 266

INDEX

Skip Counting 369

Statements 193, 195, 196

Story Map 295, 296

Subjects 197, 200–205, 208

Subtraction 358–362, 371

Suffixes 36, 37

Summarizing 315–319

Supporting Details 292–294

Syllables 23, 24

Synonyms 25, 26, 29

Taking Notes 302–306

Temperature 431, 432

The f sound 18–20

The k sound 16, 17

The s sound 21, 22

They're/Their/There 262, 263, 265, 266

This/These 264–266

Topic Sentences 291, 293, 294, 297

Underlined Words 271, 272, 275

Using an Outline 313–316

Venn Diagram . 97, 105, 142, 145, 180, 307

Verbs 218–230

Verb Tense 219–227, 230

Volume 421, 422, 424

Weight 425, 426, 430, 433, 434

Writing 89, 105, 123, 268–346

Writing Poetry 342–346

Writing a Report 337–341

Your/Yours 256, 257, 265, 266